What People Are Saying About...

Spelling Power

"*Spelling words and rules are attacked with a variety of auditory and kinesthetic tools, then applied to the writing process, all in about 15 minutes a day. Dictation and proofreading help your child cement spelling words, not as isolated lists, but as part of the bigger goal of making him a better communicator. Constant testing and review and simple-to-prepare learning games round out the program. Spelling Power offers your child the academic equivalent of a daily trip to the gym: a well-balanced workout that pumps up those spelling muscles.*" (♥♥♥♥)

Mary Pride
Practical Homeschooling

"*You can successfully use this one book to teach all of your children through their school years.*"

Cathy Duffy
Christian Home Educator's Curriculum Manual

"*Picks up where phonics leaves off. Comprehensive, easy to use, and truly designed for home schoolers.*"

Sarah Rose, KONOS Representative

"*Spelling Power is a manual allowing you to teach both structural and phonetic word patterns to every member of your family. An extensive series of diagnostic tests allows each individual to find their comfort level quickly and efficiently. The research proven test-study-test format, along with immediate self-correction, allows you to master word lists which are organized by both phonetic and structural principles. This could be the last spelling book you'll ever have to buy.*"

Inland Empire Home School News

"It's like Saxon for Spelling!"
1994 WHO Convention Delegate

"Adams-Gordon's seven years of home schooling and home school consulting, as well as her educational background, are evident throughout the work. She never assumes the reader is familiar with technical terms or techniques, yet does not talk down to the more experienced teacher. This is a rare and refreshing approach in educational texts."
Family Booknotes

"It's true ... with just 15 minutes each evening I have been able to help my son pass his weekly spelling test while bringing him up to grade level."
C.B., parent of child attending school

"If I could use only one word, it would have to be ***thorough****."*
Tena Spears
Portland State University

"It is excellent, and may answer your particular need. ... The author recommends a systematic learning program, grouping words according to spelling rules. Habits of dictionary use, applying generalizations (spelling rules and phonetic principles), and proofreading are to be taught. The book guides you in this and provides lists that go through 5,000 of the more commonly used words. In all, the work is a great contribution to spelling methodology."
Ted Wade
The Home School Manual

"The resources included in Spelling Power alone are well worth the cost of the book."
B.A., Seattle Classroom Teacher

"The game section is particularly impressive. (Ms. Adams-Gordon calls them 'discovery activities' but they look like games to me.) This section begins with a list of 134 games and reproducible materials for them (when needed) are included. Commercial games and computer software are listed also... Independent homeschoolers will appreciate the self-correction that is integral to the program."
Mary Ehrmin, The Drinking Gourd Magazine

"The most comprehensive spelling program ever developed."
Bernadine Rogstad
Fourth Corner Books

"Spelling is now my favorite subject."
nine-year-old boy who has always hated spelling
Son of Kelly Hoelzen, Maple Valley, Washington

Spelling Power

Complete with
Quick-Start Introduction

A List of the 5,000 Most Frequently Used Words Organized by Phonetic Principles and Spelling Rules

Diagnostic Spelling Scales

An Alphabetical Listing of the 12,000 Most Frequently Used Words

Over 134 Games and Activities That Make Spelling Lessons Fun

Third Edition
by Beverly L. Adams-Gordon

Castlemoyle Books
Pomeroy, Washington

Castlemoyle Books
The Hotel Revere Building
Post Office Box 520
Pomeroy WA 99347-0520
Telephone: 509-843-5009
Fax: 509-843-3183
Toll Free Orders: 1-888-773-5586
www.castlemoyle.com

User Help Line — 509-843-6098
Monday through Thursday, 2:30 p.m. to 5:30 p.m. (Pacific Time)
For more information, see page vi

You may also direct questions to
spellhelp@castlemoyle.com

Answers to frequently asked questions are found
at our web site at www.castlemoyle.com.

ISBN: 1-888827-19-X

Library of Congress Cataloging in Publication Data

Adams-Gordon, Beverly Lynn, 1955-
Spelling Power
p. cm.
Includes bibliographies and index.
1. Basic education - United States - Curricula - Language Arts - Spelling.
2. Educational tests and measurements.
3. Reference: Word frequency lists
4. Bibliography: p.
I.
II. Title.
LCCN: 96-085073

Published August 2001

Printed in the United States of America

In loving memory of
my grandfather
Ole Lillehei
who told me I could
do anything I set out to do.

and

For my daughter
Angelina,
who kept trying and
continued to believe
I would find the best way
to help her learn to spell.

Disclaimers and Other Important Notices

Trademarks

The following trademarks are used throughout this manual. Whenever you come across them, please remember that they are the trademarks or registered trademarks of the companies listed below.

Spelling Power Teaching Manual, Spelling Power Student Record Books, Spelling Power Activity Task Cards, Spelling Power Quick Start Videos, Spelling Power Skill Builder CDRom, Writing Power, Writing Power Student Journals, Writing Power Prescriptive Grammar CDRom, and Writing Power Activity Task Cards are trademarks of Beverly L. Adams-Gordon and Castlemoyle Books.

Rummy Roots and More Roots are trademarks of Eternal Hearts.

All other names are trademarks or registered trademarks of their respective owners.

Limited Warranty

This book is designed to provide information in regard to the subject matter covered. It is sold with the understanding that the publisher and author are not engaged in rendering legal, financial, or academic counseling. If legal or other assistance is required, the services of a qualified professional should be sought.

The purpose of this book is to educate and entertain. The author and Castlemoyle Books shall have neither liability nor responsibility to any person or entity with respect to loss or damage caused, or alleged to be caused, directly or indirectly by the information contained in this book.

Any person not wishing to be bound by the above may return this book to the retail at which it was purchased. The publisher will refund the retail outlet for books which are returned pursuant to this limited warranty.

Help Line

Castlemoyle Books wants you to be comfortable with using your program, so we offer a no-charge Help Line. When you call our Help Line, you will talk with Beverly L. Adams-Gordon, the author of the *Spelling Power* program. The Help Line phone is 509-843-6098.

The scheduled time for the Help Line is 2:30 to 5:30 p.m. Pacific Time (12:30 to 3:30 Hawaiian Time, 1:30 to 4:30 Alaskan Time, 3:30 to 6:30 Mountain Time, 4:30 to 7:30 Central Time, 5:30 to 8:30 Eastern Time, 6 p.m. to 9 p.m. in Newfoundland) Monday through Thursday.

While we try to keep the line available to you during the posted time, because Beverly travels doing seminars, the Help Line is only answered when Beverly is in the office and able to answer it. The Help Line number also serves as our company's fax line, so if you get a fax tone, it most likely means we are out of the office and are traveling. If you get a busy signal, that means Beverly is in the office and helping another user. Please try your call again after a reasonable interval. As a guide, the average call takes ten minutes.

Because of time constraints, we are unable to return calls. If you call on our normal business line requesting a return call to help you with the program, we will not be able to call you back. You may also direct questions to spellhelp@castlemoyle.com or visit the *Frequently Asked Question* section at www.castlemoyle.com.

"God wove a web of loveliness,
Of clouds and stars and birds,
But made not anything at all
So beautiful as words."

Anna Hempstead Branch

Important Notes

Throughout this book *teacher* will be referred to with the pronoun *she* and *student* with the pronoun *he*. The author has chosen not to use "he or she" because it is cumbersome and disturbs the natural flow of reading.

Western Dialect Used

Regional variations in pronunciation or speech patterns may affect spelling instruction. Linguists who have studied regional variations in pronunciation say there are three or four great geographical speech regions in the United States. These are (1) *Eastern American* (New England and New York City), (2) *Southern American* (the old Confederacy and Kentucky, with west and central Texas excluded), and (3) *General American* (the remaining states). General American is often referred to as the "Western" dialect.

The Flow-Word-List groups which emphasize a particular phonetic principle or particular phoneme-grapheme relationship are based on the speech sounds used in what is considered the *General American* or the "Western" dialect. There are several reasons why the speech sounds in "Western" dialect have been accepted for the standard list of spelling generalizations found in this book. First, as most linguists agree, "GA [General American] comes closest to the common currency of speech in this country. It is accepted anywhere and is spoken far more widely in the United States than are either EA or SA" [Carrell & Tiffany 1960, p. 7]. Second, changes in pronunciation habits in the United States will probably continue to be in the direction of "Western" dialect because the population shifts in the country are generally in this direction. The westward tilt of the nation's population will result in ever-increasing numbers of speakers of the "Western" dialect. Third, among the most important influences on uniform American speech are television, radio, and movies. These mass media tend to use *General American* dialect. Fourth, with few exceptions, dictionaries use *General American* dialect in their phonemic spelling of words. For all these reasons it seems appropriate for us to use this dialect as our guide for the phonemes needed to explain how phonics may be used to teach spelling principles.

The teacher of children who speak a different dialect will have to make adjustments for these differences. We do not assume that teachers should teach the phonetic aspects of this program in any other dialect than that considered standard for their speech region. To do otherwise would be impractical, if not impossible. In the United States we do not have a standard form of pronunciation that is used by educated people in all geographical regions. The *General American* dialect presented in *Spelling Power*, therefore, is neither better nor worse than any other regional dialect.

Use of Symbols

Throughout this text phonemes (speech sounds) are represented between two slashes (e.g. /a/). The first slash can be read "the," and the final slash "sound." The letter or letters within the slashes should be read as the actual sound heard. Example: /a/ is read "the 'a' sound." Short vowel sounds are written with lowercase letters. Long vowel sounds are written as /ā/ or /ī/. Other vowel sounds are marked using standard symbols.

Letter(s) which appear underlined represent the graphemes (letters) used to spell the phoneme (sound). The letter or letters underlined should be read as "the letter" using the alphabetical name(s).

Acknowledgments

First, I must acknowledge those responsible for the person that I am: my Heavenly Father and my earthly parents Elsie and Bruce Adams. I also must recognize the great thinkers whose work and writings have been instrumental in the development of my educational philosophy: Dr. Maria Montessori, Mortimer J. Adler, Donald H. Parker, Helen Parkhurst, Carleton W. Washburne, Dorothy L. Sayers, and Madeline Justus.

Next, for their patient indulgence with and enthusiastic participation in my various educational experimentations, I must thank my daughters, Amelia J. Sylvester and Angelina J. Cavanaugh, and all of the students I have worked with over the years. But especially for Angelina, who kept trying and continued to believe I would find the best way to help her learn to spell.

There are no words to adequately express my gratitude to John, my best friend and loving husband. Without his support this book would not be in your hands. He supported my original efforts to develop an effective spelling curriculum and has not withdrawn that support in the past nine years. He doesn't complain when a few chores are left undone as I work on various aspects of "the book" and listens patiently as I quote the latest "spelling facts" I have uncovered. Most importantly, he has, for the most part, been able to keep my computer and me on "speaking terms." Finally, he assisted in calculating the grade placement survey of spelling words — a task that would have been unbelievably boring to most folks, but to a "data nerd" such as he it was merely a challenge he took on enthusiastically.

There are too many professionals to whom I owe a debt of gratitude for their unselfish advice and suggestions to list them all, but I would be remiss not to mention:

Chris Saunders, M.Ed., for her suggestion that I include information on "standard" grade placement of the spelling words and that I offer Diagnostic Spelling Scales with both *Spelling Power* and "standard grade placement" levels.

Tena Spears, of Portland State University, for her help and encouragement throughout this project, but especially for her assistance in coordinating the *Italic Handwriting Series* and general information regarding the publication of this manuscript.

Ruth Beechick with Education Services (Golden, Colorado), Jane Hoffman, Backyard Scientist (Irvine, California), and Merna McCullock, Riggs Institute (Beaverton, Oregon) for their words of encouragement and excellent advice on writing, publishing, and marketing this book.

Finally, I would like to express my appreciation to the many teachers and home educators who have attended my workshops, completed surveys, and written letters containing suggestions, criticisms, and praise. This supportive encouragement and valuable feedback has been my motivation and inspiration for the third edition of *Spelling Power.*

How to Get the most out of the *Spelling Power* program

First, read the entire Teacher's Guide section of this book (pages 1-97). Begin with the Quick Start Introduction.

> Highlight and take notes as you read -- we've left wide margins for this very purpose.
>
> Keep a list of your own questions as you read on a separate sheet of paper. Usually further reading will provide many of the answers.
>
> Quietly read aloud -- this often helps retention and understanding. It takes an average reader 12 uninterrupted hours to read the complete Teacher's Guide section.

Second, re-read the Quick Start Introduction on pages 1-14. Try to do this in one uninterrupted sitting. It takes an average reader under an hour of uninterrupted reading to do this.

Third, Go back and apply each step, step-by-step.

> Steps 1 through 4 are placement steps. Each takes one or more days once a year.
>
> Steps 5 through 8 and 12 are completed each day.
>
> Steps 9, 10, and 11 are completed as your student progresses through the list.

Finally, a week after you begin using the program, you should plan to review the Quick Start Introduction. Research shows we tend to forget most of what we read within a week. This review will increase your effectiveness. Regular reviews of the Quick Steps are advised.

Remember, spelling is one of the most important subjects you will teach your child. An investment of two or three days of your time in order to teach your child most effectively will pay off many times over his lifetime.

Preface to First Edition

This book began five years ago when I left my teaching position at a private school to teach my two daughters Angelina (Angie) and Amelia at home. I soon discovered my younger daughter, then in sixth grade, could spell only on a second grade level. Always having been a hopeless speller, I did not want my daughter to suffer the embarrassment and difficulties related to writing that I had. I set out to find a means to help her, as it was obvious that the programs used in the schools had not proven effective. This led me to the extensive research and experimentation of which this book is a result.

My first impulse was to give my daughter "intensive phonics instruction." I had received such training in graduate school when I took a series of courses on teaching using the Montessori Method of Education. It had helped me immensely with my own spelling difficulties and I was confident it would help Angie. While my daughter was insulted by what she called the "babyish" approach to the materials, she submitted willingly to the work. She loved to write and she really wanted others to be able to read what she had written.

After a complete course in intensive phonics, Angie's spelling ability had increased by only one grade level. Of course, her reading ability soared four grade levels and she could read almost anything she picked up. I began to suspect that phonics instruction alone, especially when geared to reading, was not enough to make a competent speller.

That summer I attended a seminar on teaching spelling. The speaker confirmed my suspicions that phonics was not sufficient in itself to teach spelling competency. In fact, she said phonics as a means of teaching spelling was useless and she backed up her point of view with many facts, explaining that spelling is primarily visual and that the only way for students to learn to spell is through configuration exercises. Inspired by this "expert" I went out and found the latest spelling program — one with an emphasis on configuration exercises. I convinced my daughter this would work — an expert had advised it as the only way to go — so we set down to work, again.

By Christmas, both my daughter and I were convinced that this method was not producing results either. According to Angie, the only thing she had gained was the knowledge that there is only one accepted way to spell a word. This was something she had not concluded from previous instruction. She was now consistently misspelling words; that is, she misspelled them the same way every time!

At this point, I began my serious research (see bibliography) and created a list of the essential aspects of an effective spelling curriculum. As I discovered these proven methods, I incorporated as many of them as possible into the spelling program with which we began the school year. By the end of the school year, my daughter, now having completed grade seven work, was spelling at the level of an average fourth grader.

Over the summer, armed with my knowledge of what constitutes proven, effective spelling instruction, I continued my search for a spelling program that would solve Angie's problem. During my search, I came to the realization that most commercial spelling programs do not take advantage of the "facts" of effective spelling instruction even though they are well established. I was disturbed that the introductions in the teacher's editions of many programs would quote the same facts I had found in my research and then would proceed to ignore them in the actual processes prescribed in their texts.

So I went looking in another direction. Now my goal was to find a reliable, high-frequency word list to use as a basis for "Angie's Spelling Program." I soon discovered that most word frequency lists available were created between 1915 (Ayer's) and 1945 (Rinsland's). Realizing that language usage has changed somewhat in the last 45 years I kept searching until I found more recent information. I found only two such studies: one conducted in Canada in 1979 using a relatively small sampling of Canadian students and one conducted in 1971, which was an extensive study of words used in written material, geared more toward reading than spelling. I also found a number of lists of frequently misspelled words geared to different age groups; that is, words frequently misspelled by elementary students (by grade), by high school students, by college students, and by secretaries and business people. These lists were used to select words for each level in the program.

These sources were compared and combined, a few archaic words were taken out, and new words were added (many computer related) to provide the most reliable and useful list possible. This list was then divided into levels based on frequency of use, and each level was then divided into groups to present spelling rules and phonetical principles. (Since deciding to publish Angie's program, the basic lists which she used have been compared to those used in five standard textbook series, to provide parents with an idea of the normal grade placement level of each word.)

Armed with this list, I added the elements of the self-corrected test methods and the review of the student's pronunciation. I also taught Angie the ten research-proven steps for word study that I had discovered in my research. Within months we were seeing dramatic improvements in Angie's spelling abilities.

Unfortunately, as time passed, the growth in Angie's spelling progress markedly slowed. I analyzed what we were doing and discovered Angie had stopped using all of the study steps she had been taught. At this point I created a special study sheet for her which would remind her of each study step. The special study-sheets, combined with a demonstration of their value, got her "back on track." Again spelling growth became rapid and noticeable. By the end of her eighth grade year Angie was spelling on a seventh grade level "according to achievement testing." She had progressed three grade levels in one school year!

While Angie's test results were extremely encouraging, when we examined her writing, the spelling errors, while less frequent, were still very obvious. She would still be judged a poor speller by any reasonable standard. In an attempt to find the root of this problem, I carefully analyzed her writing and the lists of the "high-frequency" words. In this process I made two discoveries. First, the "high-frequency" words, especially on the lower levels, tend to be non-meaning bearing words, such as articles, prepositions, and so on. Misspelling of words which carry the unique meaning of a sentence stand out more than other misspelled words. Second, Angie was not always spelling the words correctly in her written work that she had spelled correctly in her spelling lessons. These discoveries led to the creation of the remaining aspects of the program: the Review, Delayed Recall and End-of-Level test series; the integration with daily writing; the Discovery Activities; and the Dictionary Skills programs.

While Angie, now 16 and in tenth grade, is still not a perfect speller, as few who write English are, she now has an adequate knowledge of both those universally frequently used words and those she personally uses on a regular basis. What's more, Angie now has the skills to deal with words she does not know how to spell and a specific method she can use to proofread all her writing meant for others to read.

I decided to share "Angie's Spelling Program," and the research it was based on, about one year ago when other teachers and parents began asking me how I had achieved such remarkable progress with my daughter's spelling. It is my hope that Angie's program, which she named *Spelling Power*, will provide other teachers and parents an effective way to help their students to achieve Spelling Power, too.

Beverly L. Adams-Gordon
Seattle, Washington
June 1993

Preface to the Third Edition

As I sit down to write the preface to the revised third edition of *Spelling Power*, I marvel at the mysterious ways God works in our lives. Almost nine years have passed since I first began research on how to effectively teach my daughters to spell. Now they are young wives and mothers. My younger daughter, Angie, for whom the program was developed, was married in November 1996, to a handsome sailor named Sam, but I still dedicate major portions of each day to "spelling" — answering questions, conducting workshops and seminars, and reading the latest research. It is this work that has led to this major revision. While the third edition maintains the same procedures and research-proven approaches, this edition, I believe, presents the "How-to" in a clearer manner.

The valuable feedback I have received from users of the program has shown me points that need to be made clearer, areas that need to be expanded, and even areas which were not applicable to the majority of teachers. There are three main changes to this edition:

New Content — This edition begins with the new Quick-Start Introduction. Being an analytical type by nature, in the previous two editions I jumped right into the nitty-gritty of teaching spelling, not realizing the importance of an overview to the more global learner. Thus I have written this section in a casual, user-friendly style. For many busy teachers, this section will be all they need to read to begin using the program effectively. In addition, I have added several new features including an index, a glossary, British spellings [in brackets alongside the American spellings], and an entirely new approach to the Discovery Activities index.

New Arrangement — I have rewritten and moved around some of the material to make it easier for you to use. The main change in this area affects Chapter Four which deals with individualizing skills instruction. Chapter Four is now mainly a description of how to teach skills and how to deal with specific skills evaluations and remediation. The resources needed to accomplish these goals are found in the Discovery Activities section. Easier-to-use indices (featuring skills, learning styles, and number of participants) mean that you can choose games and activities that will benefit your student quickly.

New Look — In addition to new, crisper page designs, the book's format has changed. This change reflects the way many users are actually using the book. At seminars and workshops I discovered that teachers had cut off the spiral binding, three-hole punched the book at the local quick print shop, and inserted it into a binder. The new page design makes this approach more feasible. We upgraded the paper (heavier, acid free) so the book will stand up to the wear and tear it is sure to get.

It is my sincere hope that these changes will make the book of even greater benefit to you as you help your children acquire Spelling Power.

Beverly L. Adams-Gordon
Lynnwood, WA
December 1997

Table of Contents

Quick-Start Introduction

Program Overview

Spelling Power is a multi-sensory, multi-level, individualized spelling program designed to help your student master spelling skills in just 15 minutes per day. This 15 minutes requires approximately five minutes of your time (per student) and little or no lesson planning. Your student will typically use this 15 minute spelling session to complete three basic activities:

5 + 5 + 5
test study act.

You will spend the first five minutes of each session retesting or pretesting words from *Spelling Power*'s Flow-Word-Lists containing the 5,000 words most frequently used and misspelled by children and adults. These words are organized into 11 levels of frequency. Each of these 11 levels is further divided into word groups based on phonetic principles and spelling rules. Your student will master these words because a series of six reviews is built into each level. While it is possible to use peer-testing, best results are achieved when you conduct this portion of the daily sessions using *Spelling Power*'s research-proven, special teaching-test procedures.

Read Chapter One, beginning on page 15, for a detailed description of the instructional philosophy and program rationale.

Following the teaching-test session, your student will study (on his own) those words that the pretest or his daily writing have shown he needs to learn. He will usually complete this activity in under five minutes, using *Spelling Power*'s ten special multi-sensory study steps to master each of his personal spelling words. This process is completed on forms which guide your student through the steps proven most effective for learning how to spell words.

Your student will spend the remaining five or so minutes of the daily spelling session involved in activities and playing games designed to teach, reinforce, and drill spelling words and skills. The "Games and Activities" section of the *Spelling Power* manual provides over 134 directions and ideas for hands-on games and activities to be used during this portion of the spelling session. All of these teaching activities are indexed to quickly and easily locate games which will benefit your student.

Information on selecting the proper line size for your student's writing is found on the back of the Order Form in the Miscellaneous Section.

Spelling Power's individualized, self-paced approach allows you to easily integrate the spelling program with the rest of your curriculum and especially with your English or Composition program. Chapter Three of *Spelling Power* explains just how easy this integration can be. A particular teaching model for Grammar and Composition instruction is described in this section: Integrated Functional Writing. You can take the basic approach described and use it with whatever program you are currently using.

Spelling Power gives you everything you need to provide your students (from eight years of age to college level) a comprehensive spelling program. You will also find helpful information for working with those students still learning their basic phonics and handwriting (generally students under eight). While pre-printed student record books and other convenience items are available, masters for every form described and directions for every game are provided in the book. It truly is the last spelling book you will ever need to own.

Spelling Power has been written to be user-friendly. Even if you are new to teaching, you will find that *Spelling Power*'s easy-to-understand, detailed, step-by-step directions show you exactly how to administer the program and how to adapt it to your student's specific needs. You will find these "Quick-Start Steps," and the in-depth material to which those steps direct you, will make using the *Spelling Power* program easy and hassle-free, but, most importantly, effective!

Quick-Start Steps

When you follow the guidelines outlined in these "Quick-Start Steps" you will need to do little or no lesson planning, because the basic steps you will follow are the same from day to day. Each of the first four "Quick Steps" outlined in this section can be thought of as a day's lesson plan. These steps are used to place your student within the 11 levels of the *Spelling Power* program. You should plan on completing these steps at the beginning of each school year.

These Quick-Start Steps do not replace reading the manual, but provide an overview of procedures and a plan for implementing the program in bite-size chunks.

Quick Steps 5 through 8 are repeated daily (during the 15 minute sessions) until you come to a Delayed Recall Test or an End-of-Level Test. You will then follow the steps described in Quick-Start Steps 9 and 10. Once you have completed Quick Step 10, you will then return to repeating Steps 5 through 8 each day.

Quick Step 11 is used to integrate *Spelling Power* with the rest of your student's school work and is incorporated into the daily procedures (Quick Steps 5 through 8). You may begin this integration with *Spelling Power* when your student is familiar with the basic procedures and is above Level D in the Flow-Word-List.

Quick Step 12 is a record keeping step which you should complete as you go through the other steps.

Chapter Two is a Key chapter of Spelling Power. *You should read the entire chapter before beginning the program. It's only 20 pages.*

These Quick Steps do not replace reading the manual. They are presented as a guide to help you get a Quick Start — by breaking up the study process into "bite-size chunks" and highlighting keynotes. Do not make adjustments, skip, or in any way alter these procedures without a thorough reading of the text pages referred to in the margins. If, after reading the entire manual, you still think you should deviate from the outlined procedures, please call the author. You may contact her for a free *Spelling Power* consultation Monday through Thursday between 3:30 p.m. and 5:30 p.m. (PST) by calling the Help-Line number at the top of copyright page. Calls are taken on a first-come, first-served order. If you reach a voice mail machine or a busy signal, she is on another line. Please attempt your call again, as no calls can be returned. You may leave a detailed message or write (fax) your questions for a written reply. Be sure to include your address so we may send you a written reply.

While the *Spelling Power* manual has material on teaching spelling skills to students ages five through college level, the core of the program is designed for students above age eight. Since students develop at widely varying rates (even an individual child varies in his readiness for different subjects), it is necessary for you to determine if your student is academically and developmentally prepared for daily pretesting and spelling study of the Flow-Word-Lists before beginning the *Spelling Power* program.

Quick Step 1: Determine Readiness

If your student exhibits the following traits, he should be able to be placed appropriately on one of the 11 levels of Flow-Word-Lists and succeed using the basic approaches described in the *Spelling Power* program:

Your student

- ☑ is able to write each separate letter of the alphabet from dictation and can write some words without having to copy them;
- ☑ speaks and is able to read on at least a second grade level;
- ☐ can speak clearly and accurately pronounce most English words;
- ☑ has a basic understanding of phonetic principles (sound-to-spelling correspondences);
- ☑ is able to stay "on task" (totally concentrate on the task at hand) for periods of approximately five minutes; and
- ☑ asks about words and how they are spelled.

Read pages 29 through 32 of Chapter Two for a more detailed explanation of each of the items on the readiness check list.

If your student does not exhibit all the above characteristics, you should follow the suggestions outlined on pages 29 through page 32 to help prepare him for the standard *Spelling Power* procedures. You may also wish to adapt the program for him by following the procedures outlined on pages 93-94. Additional suggestions you can use with your student, while he is developing the needed readiness, are found in Chapters Three and Five.

One of the key and outstanding aspects of the *Spelling Power* program is that each student begins exactly where he needs to begin academically. Then he proceeds at his own optimal pace to develop spelling skills and master the 5,000 most frequently used and misspelled words. A three-step process is used in the *Spelling Power* program to ensure that each student, who shows readiness, is placed exactly where he needs to begin. The first of these steps is to "survey" your student's ability using the Survey Test.

Quick Step 2: Survey Student Ability

*Survey Tests can be found on pages 102 and 103 of the **Placement Test** section.*

The Survey Test consists of 50 words which represent a sampling of all 11 levels of the *Spelling Power* program (Levels A - K). The words are arranged in sequential order — from the easiest, most frequently used words to the hardest, least frequently used words. It is designed to give you an idea of where your student should begin Placement Testing. There are two forms of the test: A and B. You will give only one form of the test each year. These test forms can be used interchangeably, as they are of equal difficulty.

Before beginning the test, it is helpful to briefly introduce the *Spelling Power* program to the student. You may want to show him the manual and give him an idea of what he will be doing during his daily spelling lessons, as well as explain the research basis of the program. You may find that the program overview at the beginning of this section and the material presented on pages 32-33 contain helpful information for this step. Make it clear to your student that in this program he will "begin where he is at" and work "at his own pace."

You can now show him the necessity of the series of placement tests: since in this program he must begin at his own level, you must conduct a test of his skills. Encourage him to make his best effort and to spell the words the best way that he knows how. Assure your student that he will not be graded on the results, the information will be used only to determine where he will begin in the *Spelling Power* program.

*Masters, in four sizes of lines, for every form used in Spelling Power are included in the **Teaching Aids and Masters** section. Pre-printed form books, called Student Record Books, are available in four styles through your Spelling Power dealer.*

To conduct the Survey Test, provide your student with a copy of the Survey Test Form. The date, test form used, and your student's name should be recorded on the test sheet. Conduct the test in the "traditional" spelling test manner by saying the word, using it in a sentence, and repeating the word. Before beginning the test, explain these procedures to your student and impress upon him the importance of not writing the word until you have finished the sentence. This will prevent him from making unnecessary errors in spelling homonyms.

Your student will most likely not need to complete the entire Survey Test. You should stop the testing session when he has misspelled three words in a row or a total of six words within a word or two of each other. To determine this point, you must observe his spelling as you test the words. Do not comment on whether his spelling is incorrect or correct. Simply observe, and stop testing as directed above.

*Information on selecting the proper line size for your student's writing is found on the back of the Order Form in the **Miscellaneous Section**.*

While it is best to test each child separately, you may want to test several students together. In this case you should watch each student's spelling and quietly excuse students as they come to the point where they have missed three to five words.

After the testing session (when your student is not present), you should score the test by counting the total number of words he has spelled **correctly**.

The "number correct" score is used to determine which Placement Test should be given in the next step. You will need to use the chart provided on page 104 (titled Scoring Placement Tests) in the Tests Section (starts on page 101) to determine this. Directions for using this chart are provided on the same page as the chart.

Quick Step 3: Conduct Placement Test

Because the Survey Test has such a small sampling of words from each level, it is usually necessary for you to make a more detailed assessment of your student's ability. This is done by conducting a Placement Test. There is a Placement Test for each level of the *Spelling Power* program. Each Placement Test is a sampling of a particular level. It gives a much broader sampling of words from that level than is possible in the Survey Test. There is only one form of each Placement Test.

*Placement Tests begin on page 105. Masters for the Placement Test forms are found in the **Teaching Aids and Masters** section.*

Give your student the Placement Test which was indicated in the previous step (Quick Step 2). You will administer it in basically the same way as you conducted the Survey Test above. The only differences in these steps are that you will be giving the entire test and that it is completed on a Placement Test form. Since your students will take the entire test, you may easily group together those who need to take the same Placement Test.

Upon completion of the Placement Test, you will score the test, this time counting the number of words **misspelled**. The chart at the bottom of each Placement Test will tell you exactly what to do. Based on the number of errors the student made, you will be instructed to proceed in one of three ways. You will either conduct Placement Testing at a higher level or study words at the Placement Test level or at one level lower. The chart at the bottom of each Placement Test also tells you exactly on which page of the Flow-Word-Lists you should begin working with your student.

Quick Step 4: Fine-Tune Placement

Because some students do not test well and others do better on spelling tests than they do in their daily writing, it may be advisable to "fine-tune" your student's placement using a sampling of his writing. This is a relatively simple procedure.

Begin by collecting a sample of your student's writing. To collect this writing sample you may wish to use an entire day's spelling period (15 minutes) to have your student write on a topic of his choice. He should be told to try and write continuously during this session (even if it is on a variety of topics) and that he should do his best without using a dictionary or other writing aid (it can be typed on the computer, but he should not use the spell checker.) You should require at least a full page of writing from your student during this period.

Take the writing sample your student has provided and proofread it for misspelled words. Circle each misspelled word. Now look up each misspelled word in the Alphabetical Word List (see fourth section).

The Alphabetical Word List gives in alphabetical order the 12,000 most frequently used and misspelled words. Following each word is a series of codes. These codes — using the letter of the level and the group number following a hyphen (i.e. G-11) — first list the level and group number of each of the 5,258 words that appear in the *Spelling Power* program. Other codes such as the word's position on two different word frequency programs and the average grade at which it is generally taught are also provided. For complete explanations of these codes, read the introduction to the Alphabetical Word List on page 221.

Chapter Two is a key chapter of Spelling Power. *You should read the entire chapter before beginning the program. It's only 20 pages.*

Now record, above or beside each word, the *Spelling Power* level at which each misspelled word is taught. Compare the level at which these errors occur in your student's writing in relation to his Placement Test score. If many of the words are from lower *Spelling Power* levels, it is suggested you give a lower level Placement Test or begin studying at the lower level. Likewise, if your student has misspelled only words at a higher level, it may be wise to give him the higher level Placement Test.

A Note About Testing: Some students, especially older students, are more difficult to place in the *Spelling Power* program because they may have gaps in their word knowledge, making it likely that their placement results will not fit normal patterns. The natural tendency for the teacher is to place the student on a much lower than necessary level — thinking if nothing else the student will get a good review. This, however, may not be the best approach when using the *Spelling Power* program. It is important to keep in mind that a fine balance of challenge and opportunity to succeed are necessary to maintain student motivation. Remember *Spelling Power* already has six levels of built-in review. Words are repeatedly reviewed at higher levels, especially those words which are frequently misspelled. You will also choose from those words that your student misspells in his other writing to cycle them back into your student's personal list.

Quick Step 5: Begin Daily Teaching Tests

When you conduct the first pretesting or "teaching test" of Flow-Word-Lists groups, you should begin with Group 1of the level on which your student was placed. You will present each of these words using the special testing procedures described below. Your student will record his answers to the pretest on the special testing sheets called Daily Test Sheets. Masters for Daily Test Sheets are found in the Teaching Aids and Masters section or you can use the optional Student Record Book which contains the preprinted forms.

Masters for the Daily Test forms are found in the ***Teaching Aids and Masters*** *section.*

In addition to providing spaces for the "test," the form has places for your student to record the group-level number on which he is working and the date. If you are using individual copies of the form, you should also have the student record his name on the form.

Testing is conducted for five minutes or until the end of the list, whichever comes first. **Testing sessions should never exceed five minutes** except as described on page 36 of Chapter Two. Subsequent testing sessions will begin with a retest of previously misspelled and studied words and then you'll pick up at the point where you left off at the previous session. In this way, for example, if it takes two minutes to retest previously misspelled words, you will spend only three minutes adding new pretest words.

Please see the note on Use of Symbols (found at the beginning of the book on page viii and at the beginning of the Flow-Word-Lists, page 122) for diacritical markings.

Before new words are tested (and after the retesting of words) the group's spelling rule (which is listed right below the group number) is stated or "announced" and your student will write the rule in the space provided for it at the top of the Daily Test Sheet. In the case of Group 1 the rule is "/a/ is usually spelled a as in cat." (The phonograms presented between slashes are read "the sound of" and underlined letter(s) are read "the letter a.")

Some of the group rules can be quite long for younger students to write out. These students can abbreviate the rule by writing the sound symbol and example words as was done in the example below:

/a/

cat plan tramp.

Daily Testing sessions include multi-sensory procedures which include immediate self-correction and checks of your student's pronunciation. Each of the elements of the teaching test have been included because research has overwhelmingly found them beneficial to the majority of students. Do not skip or alter the steps without careful consideration of all the material presented in the teaching manual! The four daily test steps follow.

5 min test

1. Say the word, use it in a sentence, then repeat the word. Do not exaggerate the pronunciation. Say the word clearly, but naturally.

Note: If the word is a homonym, a brief definition follows the word in parentheses. If the word has an alternative British spelling, the British spelling is provided in brackets. Words followed by (R) are words reviewed from lower levels. Do not read these notations to your student during the testing process.

2. Your student should then pronounce the word so that you can check and correct (if necessary) his pronunciation. Helping your student with his pronunciation can improve his spelling. Research has shown that approximately 33 percent of all spelling errors occur because of poor pronunciation.

3. Your student will then write the word the best way he knows how. You should encourage him to double-check (proofread) his response. When he is satisfied with his spelling, he will repeat the word to you to indicate he is ready to go on.

Do not skip or alter the test steps! Each element has been included because research overwhelmingly supports it as important to student success.

4. You will then spell the word, letter by letter, as your student checks his spelling. If he has correctly spelled it, you can go on to the next word. If incorrect, he crosses out the misspelled word and you will help him record the correct spelling in the column marked "Words to Learn."

This step, called immediate self-correction, is extremely important. It gives your student immediate feedback. With 44 sounds in the English language and approximately 250 ways to write those sounds, it is often the case that your student is trying to remember the correct combination between two possibilities such as ent and ant. This step provides your student the answer to any element of a word of which he is unsure immediately after he wonders about it. If he spells it correctly, his choice is reinforced. If he has chosen the incorrect spelling, he is helped to correct it. Much learning is forfeited in the traditional approaches that delay providing this important feedback!

You continue test sessions in this manner for the remainder of the five minutes or until you come to the end of the group list, whichever comes first. All words that are misspelled during this session will be studied using the procedures described in the next Quick Step and then retested at the beginning of the next testing session.

5 min. Study

Quick Step 6: Study Misspelled Words

Masters for the 10-Step-Study Sheets are found in the ***Teaching Aids and Masters*** *sections of your manual.*

Information on selecting the proper line size for your student's writing is found on the back of the Order Form in the ***Miscellaneous Section****.*

Please read the more detailed description of each study step found on pages 40 through 44 before beginning the program with your student.

One of the things that students love best about *Spelling Power* is that they only have to study those words which they need to learn. This gives them credit for what they know, which can be very motivating. Another motivating aspect of the *Spelling Power* program is that your students are given a specific, effective way to study using the 10-Step-Study Sheets.

After your student has transferred the words in the "Words to Learn" column of the Daily Test Sheet to the "Words to Learn" column of the 10-Step-Study Sheet, he proceeds through the steps to study each word. (You may want to check your student's copying before he begins the ten study steps which are summarized below.) The words in the left-hand column are the "key words" that are found on the top of the columns of the 10-Step-Study Sheet. The study sheet provides a space to either complete the step or make a check mark after the step is complete.

1. Say Say the word, pronouncing it quietly, aloud.

This step is designed to allow your student to practice the proper pronunciation of the word. Remind your student to pay particular attention to this step for words with which he may have had difficulty during the testing session.

2. Look Look carefully at each part of the word.

Teach your student to ask himself questions such as are listed on page 41 or the inside back cover of the Student Record Book. You must teach your student which things to look for to help him remember its spelling. Do not expect him to automatically know how to look at a word to his best advantage. Introduce a variety of different things for your student to "look for," one at a time, over a period of time.

3. Say Say the word and then spell it out, letter-by-letter, in order while looking at the model.

4. Close Eyes Your student should close his eyes and try to see the word as he spells it out letter-by-letter.

5. Check Your student will check (or compare to the model) to see if he has spelled the word accurately. This step is subjective since there is no written record.

6. Trace & Say Each letter should be traced (with his fingers) on a solid surface or in a tray of sand as each letter is pronounced. The tracing should be large and involve the movement of the entire arm, not just the fingers or hand. **Do Not Skip This Step!** It is an important step for students of all ages and learning styles.

It is possible to guide several students through the 10-Step-Study process by being generic in your instructions, e.g. "Pronounce your first word quietly aloud. Make sure you pronounce it accurately. Now look at it carefully, are there any double consonants, are all the vowels spelled the way they sound?" and so on without actually saying a particular word.

7. Check Student checks to see if he traced the word correctly. If not done in a tray of sand the step is subjective.

8. Write Now your student will write the word, in the space provided, without looking at the model. The student should cover the model with the hand with which he is not writing.

9. Check Student checks to see if he spelled the word correctly. This should be done in a letter-by-letter approach, not a quick glance.

10. Repeat Repeat steps one through eight if the study word was misspelled in step eight.

Sentence Your student should write the word in a sentence of his own creation.

This 10-Step-Study process is done immediately following the daily teaching test. Usually your student will do this work independently, once he is familiar with the steps. Use of the special 10-Step-Study Sheets facilitates this independent work because it forces your student to remember each step of the study process. However, you may want to go over the study steps with at least one study word each day until you are sure your student understands the steps.

Once your student is familiar with these basic ten steps, he can be reminded or taught things to look for (See Step Two) with short messages written in the "Spelling Study Tips" space on the study form. This space can also be used to provide penmanship tips or ideas for different surfaces on which he can trace the words. In addition, it serves as a space for directing your student to specific activities for the next Quick Step: Reinforcing Spelling Rules and Skills.

Quick-Start Steps 5 through 8 are repeated daily. They represent the basic format for your daily spelling lessons.

Occasionally it happens that your student will not misspell any words during his testing session (especially during a review test.) On such occasions you have two options: you can have him study words which you have selected from his daily writing (see Quick Step 11) or you can have him do more in-depth lessons, such as those suggested in the next step (Quick Step 7). This is an excellent time to incorporate some of the dictionary skill activities detailed in Chapter Five.

Quick Step 7: Reinforcing Spelling Skills

Following the study of the misspelled words, your student should participate in activities designed to teach or reinforce spelling words and skills. In the *Spelling Power* program, this activity is referred to as Individually Prescribed Instruction and/or Discovery Activities. The activities and exercises used during this portion of the spelling period are designed to replace the more traditional worksheet

5 min. Act.

pages. This aspect of the program can be the most time consuming and is the only portion of the program where teacher planning may be required.

Chapter Four of the teaching manual gives you detailed information on how to make decisions regarding the most beneficial lessons for each of your students. These lessons can come from a variety of sources, but you'll find your *Spelling Power* manual has provided everything you need for Individually Prescribed Instruction.

The Games and Activities section (fifth section) of the *Spelling Power* manual provides you with suggestions and directions for more than 134 different "Discovery Activities." These activities are designed specifically to fit the time frame (for most students) of this portion of the spelling period each day. Many of the activity directions are written in language appropriate for students. The Discovery Activities are indexed, to make it easy for you to select the most appropriate activity. You can select activities based on learning style (modality), number of participants, skill, or purpose.

Whether your source of lesson materials and activities comes strictly from Spelling Power *or you draw from additional resources, it is important that you select the activities for their educational value, not just as busy work!*

Most of the activities are multi-sensory and many use the inductive or discovery teaching method. All have educational value for your spelling curriculum. You can use many of the Discovery Activities with any group list — these are excellent activities to assign when you do not have time to plan a direct lesson as described in Chapter Four. Other activity suggestions are geared to teaching specific skills.

Other sources for activities that you can use during this portion of the spelling period are also provided in the teaching manual. Chapter Four describes how to provide teacher directed-instruction. Dictionary lessons and games (Chapter Five), proofreading exercises (page 53 in Chapter Three), and dictation activities are also described in the manual. Some of these activities take more than five minutes and occasionally you may want to spend an entire spelling period on them.

Additional "lessons" can also be found outside of the *Spelling Power* program. Your student may find an occasional worksheet a fun change of pace. Worksheets included in grammar or phonics programs can often be used with profit (depending on the group list being studied) during the lesson portion of your spelling time. If you prefer strictly "game type" or inductive lessons you will find the *Spelling Power* Activity Task Cards an excellent resource. These cards were designed specifically to make the Individually Prescribed Instruction aspects of the program easy for busy teachers. Additional information regarding the Activity Task Cards is available from your *Spelling Power* dealer.

Quick Step 8: Retest Misspelled Words

Quick-Start Steps 5 through 8 are repeated daily. They represent the basic format for your daily spelling lessons.

One of the most dynamic aspects of the *Spelling Power* program is that every word is studied until it is spelled correctly at least once. This differs dramatically from the old "weekly" approach where the student may fail the test on Friday and then is given a new list on Monday, regardless of whether he has learned the words or not.

Spelling Power's approach also ensures that every word is put in long term memory. Scientist have determined that you will forget a large percentage of new information within 24 hours of it being presented to you. *Spelling Power*'s retesting of misspelled words at the beginning of every session tests retention and gives your student another opportunity to study the word.

Quick Steps 5 through 8 are repeated daily. They represent the basic format for your daily spelling lesson plan.

Since all words studied since the last testing session are recorded on the 10-Step-Study Sheet (during the process described in Quick Step 7), it serves as a record of words to retest. You should retest the words on the most recently used study sheet at the beginning of each testing session, before announcing the group's rule. These words are retested in the same manner as described in Quick Step 5.

After presenting the retest words, you will again announce the group's rule and then pick up where you left off the day before. (If you forget what the last word you gave was, simply look at the last entry on the last Daily Test Sheet used.) Depending on your student, you may or may not have the student copy the rule on the additional days spent on a list. But you will always announce or state the rule before words are added. The rule is not announced until after the retest words, because often you will have retest words and words from other writing that do not fit the rule. You want all words that follow announcing the rule to be examples of that rule.

Remember, **the total testing time should not exceed five minutes** except as explained on page 36 of Chapter Two. For example, if it takes three minutes to retest words, you only add two minutes of new words. This time-control element is an important aspect of the program, since it not only controls the time needed to operate the program, it controls the number of words your student must deal with at any particular time. Limiting the number of words to be studied allows the student to focus on that rule or the words themselves.

Quick Step 9: Check Retention of Spelling Words

The *Spelling Power* Flow-Word-Lists have six levels of built-in review. These spaced-repeated-reviews assure you that your students will master every spelling word. The first level of built-in review is that every word is studied until it is spelled correctly at least once, as described in Quick Step 8. Additional review is conducted by the spaced Review Tests, Delayed Recall Tests, and End-of-Level Tests. Selected words are also automatically reviewed at higher levels. Recycling words, which are misspelled in your student's daily writing, back into the program is the sixth level of built-in review and is discussed in Quick Step 11.

The sequence-of-review tests are built into each level of the program. This means you do not have to turn to another section to find them or keep track of when to give them. You will know exactly when it is time to give a test because it will be the next "group" in the Flow-Word-List. The type of test will dictate how you proceed with the testing.

The sequence-of-review tests are built into each level of the program. This means you do not have to turn to another section to find them or keep track of when to give them.

The Review Tests (which are the second level of built-in review) occur approximately every five groups. These tests are handled exactly as any other Daily Teaching Test. The only difference is that there is no group rule. Any misspelled words should be studied and retested as described in Quick Steps 5 through 8.

The Delayed Recall Tests occur approximately halfway through each level and at the end of each level. Each test reviews the previous half of a *Spelling Power* level. There are two forms of each of these tests (Form A and Form B). Initially only one form of each test (generally Form A) is given.

Since there are no "study words" following Delayed Recall or End-of-Level tests, you may have more time for the games and activities.

Delayed Recall and End-of-Level tests should be given after your student has successfully spelled each previously tested word correctly at least once. The entire Delayed Recall Test is given to your student in one setting, even if it takes more than five minutes. The immediate self-correction step is not completed in this session. You will score the test at another time. Testing procedures include:

Teacher: Says the word, uses it in a sentence, and repeats the word. (Do not read the numeral which follows it, you will use this information later in Quick Step 10.)

Student: Pronounces the word.

Teacher: Checks and corrects any faulty pronunciation.

Student: Writes the word.

The End-of-Level test is a review of an entire level and is handled in exactly the same manner as prescribed above for the Delayed Recall Test.

Quick Step 10: Reteach For Mastery

Chapter Four gives you detailed instruction and ideas on how you can effectively teach spelling skills.

Following each word on the Delayed Recall and End-of-Level Tests you will notice a numeral. This numeral tells you from which group a word was selected. If your student misspelled any words on a Delayed Recall Test or End-of-Level Test, this generally indicates that there may be some confusion on his part regarding the rule or phonetic principle which the word represents. This information can be used to make decisions regarding the reteaching of rules or other useful instructions.

In most cases you will review the phonetic principle or other spelling rule. You should try to provide instruction via a different approach than used previously for the group of each of the misspelled words. Following the reteaching session (usually on another day), it is suggested that the student retest the entire group list for each misspelled word. When the student has restudied the rule and Group List for each word he misspelled, he is ready to take the second form (generally Form B) of the Delayed Recall Test or End-of-Level Test.

Quick Step 11: Integrate with Your Curriculum

While 15 minutes per day are devoted to the sole pursuit of spelling skills, in reality spelling must be an all day, every day subject. To reach this goal, it is necessary for you to establish a link or "integration" between the spelling program and the rest of your curriculum. Most often this link is made through the Grammar and Composition curriculum. This integration facilitates the sixth level of built-in review.

The sixth level of built-in review is selecting those words your student misspells in his daily writing. By daily writing it is meant any writing he does. This step can be completed using whatever Grammar and/or Composition program (if any) you are currently using. The material in Chapter Three includes a description of just one possible approach to writing instruction and how the *Spelling Power* program can be integrated.

The Alphabetical Word List which begins on page 221 is designed to help you select words from your student's own writing.

Selecting words to add to the spelling study is simply a matter of proofreading (and teaching your student to proofread) his writing for spelling errors and having the student correct the errors as he discovers them. If your student has made only a few errors, he can study the correct spelling of those words on any remaining lines of his last 10-Step-Study Sheet. The words your students studies on the 10-Step-Study Sheet automatically become a part of the *Spelling Power* program.

If your student has misspelled a large number of words, over five or so, it may be necessary to make judgments or prioritize which words will be most profitable to have him study at this time. Selecting and prioritizing words is a fairly simple process. It requires that you look up each of the words in the Alphabetical Word List found in the fourth section. This list includes the 12,000 most frequently used and misspelled words (7,000 words beyond those which your student will master through the Flow-Word-List work.) Behind each of the words on this alphabetical list is a series of codes designed to help you prioritize them.

The first code to look for is the code that tells you in which level and group of the *Spelling Power* program the word is introduced. This code is a letter for the level, followed by a number designating the group number (e.g. G-21). If there is no combination with an hyphen, then it means the word is not taught in the *Spelling Power* program. Since words taught in the program are the most frequently used words, usually you will want to add words which are included in the *Spelling Power* program before you add words which do not appear in the program. You generally will want to select words below the level and group on which your student is currently working. In this way he will review the words he should have already mastered.

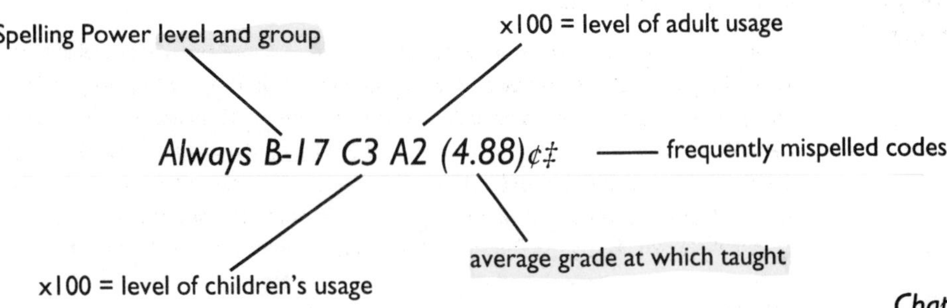

The other codes which follow words included on the Alphabetical Word List are designed to help you prioritize words used less frequently. A more detailed description of these codes is found immediately preceding the word lists on page 221. Words not found on the Alphabetical Word List are usually too rarely used to commit to memory. These words should be considered dictionary words. (To teach dictionary skills, please see Chapter Five.)

Chapter Three provides detailed explanations on how to train your students to proofread effectively.

Your student should take an active part in the proofreading and selection process, and this participation should expand as he matures, until he is proofreading independently and studying words of his own choice. He may add words he personally wants to learn, such as words from a hobby or interest area. He may also add words that he knows are difficult for him. It is also especially important that you ask him to select words which are important to your family and/or community, such as the name of your city or last names of relatives. It is unlikely that these words will appear on any high-frequency word list.

After you and your student have determined which words you want to study (three to five is plenty), you can create a list of them. Usually the student will study these words, on the 10-Step-Study Sheet, following the next test session. The words will then automatically become a part of the *Spelling Power* program.

Quick Step 12: Record Student Progress

Providing your student with a method of tracking his progress and seeing his results is one of the ten key ways to motivate student learning in any subject. In the *Spelling Power* program, two easy-to-maintain charts can be used to provide this motivating information: the Teacher's Record Sheet and the Student Progress Chart. Establishing a portfolio of samples of your student's writing is also recommended. Step-by-step instructions for maintaining these charts and creating a portfolio are provided in Chapter Two on pages 46 and 47. Masters for both charts are found in the Teaching Aids and Masters section of the manual.

A step-by-step guide to recording student progress is found on pages 46 and 47.

Both charts can be maintained — one by the student and one by the teacher — or only one. At a minimum, the student should maintain the Student Progress Chart as he progresses through the program. This chart is designed to keep the student aware of his progress. It is the most motivating if it is maintained by the student. When maintained according to the instructions, the chart can also serve to let the student and teacher know what should be the next course of action. A copy of the Student Progress Chart is also printed on the back of each Student Record Book.

The Teacher's Record Sheet provides space for tracking the progress of up to 30 students. It should be copied onto an 11"x17" sheet of paper and posted on a classroom wall. The main purpose of this chart is to help the teacher quickly determine which students are on or near the same "Group Number." Because the group rules are consistent from level to level (**however, not every level has every group**), this information can be used to organize students for direct group instruction and activities. If you are using this chart with only a few students, leaving blank lines below each name will allow you to maintain the same chart over several levels of the program.

Important Note

We want you to succeed, and we want your students to succeed. If after following these steps and reading the manual you find you are having difficulty with any procedure or you have unusual circumstances, please consult the author. For information on the free *Spelling Power* program consulting she offers, please see page vi of this book.

Chapter One
What Research Says About Teaching Spelling

> *But what is this tool called spelling? Originally the word* spell, *derived from the ancient word* spellian, *meant to tell or convey meaning. Today, spelling is considered a device for recording the sounds that are uttered when words are spoken. It refers to hearing, saying, or writing the letters of a word in the generally accepted order.*[1]

Accurate spelling is standard equipment for functioning in daily life. In order to communicate effectively, a person needs to develop the ability to spell quickly and accurately the words he uses in his everyday writing. Those who fail to develop spelling skills are often judged negatively by their peers, business associates, employers, and often even by themselves. While few cases are as blatant as the teenage girl who wrote a flowery love letter to her boyfriend only to have him return it with the errors marked with red pen, embarrassing situations persist for all poor spellers. Fortunately, only a very few are destined to be poor spellers. And by the same token, only a very few will be considered "natural spellers" (those who can see a word only once and spell it correctly from then on). Most people need to be taught how to spell.

To ensure that proper techniques are being utilized in the classroom, the teacher must be aware of the research evidence.[4]

The most effective approach to spelling instruction has been persistently debated since before the introduction of Webster's "Blue-Backed Speller" (*The American Spelling Book*) in 1783. In fact, Hodges[2], in his *Short History of Spelling Reform* in the United States, noted that dissatisfaction with spelling and its instruction has existed at least since 1300. These debates have led to a proliferation of research designed to "settle the matter once and for all," making spelling instruction one of the most researched school subjects.

Today, it appears that the greatest concern of educators is the apparent lack of application of the research evidence. In 1982, Stetson, Taylor, and Boutin stressed the need for developers of spelling curriculums to adopt teaching strategies that follow confirmed research in the learning and transferring of spelling skills into everyday writing.[3]

Ves Thomas also expressed concern regarding the lack of research-based spelling curriculum, but was especially concerned by the classroom teacher's lack of knowledge regarding the proven teaching strategies.

In this chapter, the research basis for effective spelling instruction and how it is incorporated into the *Spelling Power* program will be explained so that you will be able to understand the importance and relevance of each of the aspects of the program as described in the rest of the book.

Establishing a Spelling Curriculum

Before any fruitful discussion of "how to teach spelling" can be had, we must be in agreement of what we hope to accomplish. What are the desired outcomes or learning objectives? Ernest Horn, one of the twentieth century's prominent educational researchers, has stated that "the most commonly accepted single objective for the teaching of spelling is to enable pupils to spell the words they need to write now and in the future."[5] Horn's statement may seem simplistic, but in truth it is the overall goal of any spelling program.

Now that we have a general idea of what we are trying to accomplish, we can look at what skills and habits must be provided to assure that students succeed at being able to spell well. Below are listed the seven main spelling objectives which students will need to master to be considered proficient spellers.

Common Spelling Instructional Objectives

☐ The student will understand the importance of accurate spelling as an aid to his reader's understanding of what he has written. He will appreciate accurate spelling as a common courtesy to his reader.

☐ The student will be able to accurately spell the 5,000 most frequently used English words.

☐ The student will be able to accurately spell additional words he personally uses on a regular basis.

☐ The student will learn the most effective way to study a word, so that he can continue to build his spelling vocabulary throughout his lifetime.

☐ The student will understand and apply phonetic principles, spelling rules, and other linguistic principles when attempting to spell unfamiliar words.

☐ The student will establish the habit of effectively using spelling resources, such as dictionaries.

☐ The student will establish the habit of using effective proofreading skills on all writing he intends others to read.

Establishing an Approach to Spelling Instruction

The way to accomplish the above goals has become an emotional and divisive issue in American education. There are a variety of positions taken. Some believe if we teach reading by the phonics method there will be no need to teach spelling as a separate course. Others believe that spelling should be taught formally by memorizing words presented in organized lists. Still others believe that we should not teach spelling at all, but that students should learn as they use writing through a "functional" or "experiential" method.

The truth of the matter is that in spelling, as in other curriculum areas, there is seldom one complete approach that is significantly superior to all others. Instead, the answer often lies in a well-selected and blended combination of the best elements from various approaches. It does not appear to be a matter of deciding whether to use a purely traditional approach or a totally linguistic approach. In fact, the real danger may be in utilizing one approach to the exclusion of others.

Experiential Programs Are Not Enough

Recently enthusiasts for modern methods in education have asked, "Why not teach spelling wholly in connection with curriculum units, with actual writing assignments?" Some of these educators have even gone so far as to encourage made-up or "invented spellings." They reason that ignoring spelling and other conventions encourages "spontaneity, content, and style." They believe that they are freeing the student to be creative. Unfortunately, one of the chief failings of this approach is that creativity actually suffers.

It is quite possible and even more desirable to achieve creativity through mastery of skills rather than by ignoring them. A student who has at his command many high-frequency words is truly free to concentrate on the more creative aspects of his compositions. Students **want** to spell correctly. Research has shown that poor spellers will frequently choose words which they know how to spell over more precise and effective words which are part of his spoken vocabulary, but which he does not know how to spell.

> *Too typical is the boy who hurls himself at the building of a birdhouse and gets disgusted when his poorly sawed boards don't match and his nails split the wood. Creativity for him was a bust. Along with the general loss of self-confidence, his next act of creativity may have been pushed days, weeks, or months away, at least where hammers and saws are concerned. Here is where a little training in the skills of sawing and nailing might have saved the day and encouraged rather than discouraged further creative adventures.*[6]

Another reason this approach is not effective is that the poor speller tends to be less motivated to write because writing is such a chore for him. His compositions also tend to be less organized because his thought flow is disturbed every time he comes to a word he cannot spell. To be able to spell with confidence eases the task of putting thoughts on paper. This confidence frees the writer to concentrate more fully on organizing his ideas, thus increasing his capacity for self-expression.

To be able to spell with confidence eases the task of putting thoughts on paper. This confidence frees the writer to concentrate more fully on organizing his ideas, thus increasing his capacity for self-expression.

The fact that skills are best learned in a systematic way, however, does not negate the value of the use of such skills in functional situations. It is well known by both parents and educators that transfer of spelling words into daily writing is not automatic. In fact, the chief complaint of the strictly "word list" programs has been that students often misspell words in their daily writing that they have studied in their weekly tests.

Teachers must plan for and encourage children to utilize newly acquired spelling skills. Children should spell correctly and independently when writing stories, reports, and other assignments. In the real world, unfortunately, children do not always automatically practice accurate spelling.[7]

According to Vergason, students need to be helped to make this transfer.[8] They have to be given opportunities to write and motivation to write. They must also be shown how spelling relates to the rest of their school work. The only way to help them do this is if spelling becomes an all day, every day aspect of the curriculum.

Phonics Instruction Is Not Enough

With the renewed emphasis on the teaching of intensive and/or analytical phonics in the primary grades has come the attitude that spelling, as a separate subject of the curriculum, need not be taught. A number of points should be considered in this regard.

First, the skills involved in using phonics to spell a word are very different from—and more complex than—those needed to read a word. In reading, the emphasis is upon letter-to-sound relationships. The student has the visual clue of the phonogram to help him decode the word. He is also aided by other factors, such as story or sentence context, pictures on the page, and the configuration of the word. Trying to encode or spell is the reverse process and is much more difficult. Often the student is faced with choosing only one of several reasonable alternatives. For example, the word *since* can be read in only one way, whereas the sound **/sins/** could be spelled *cince, sinse, cynce, synce, since,* or *sence.* Which alternative is correct must be established by memory, after many repetitions, unless the student has an almost photographic visual recall.

There are about 250 spellings for the 44 basic English sounds which makes using phonics for spelling a much more complicated task than using it for reading.

Additionally, though linguists do not always agree on the exact number of variable sounds which exist for each letter, it is estimated that there are at least 250 spellings for the 44 basic English sounds. Research done by Hanna, Hanna, and Hodges[9] has proven that one or more such phonetic principles and spelling rules can be applied to approximately 85 percent of those words used frequently by children and adults, which means that as many as 15 percent of the words frequently used by children and adults do not fit any regular spelling patterns.

When you consider other factors of our language, you see additional problems for spellers. It is estimated that two-thirds of the words in a dictionary contain silent letters. Consider all the silent letters in such words as *could, light, tongue, foreign, through, night, trouble.* Some of these silent letters were formerly pronounced and the words have retained the letter so that the root of the word is clear. The word *debt* is such a word. The b is silent in *debt*, but not *debit*. Inclusion of these letters, when spelling, must simply be memorized.

While Hanna's research has proven that the English language is not as illogical as it once was considered to be, the complexities and the inconsistencies of the English language still contribute to the problem of learning to spell.

Homonyms can add to the trouble as well. Homonyms fall into two categories: homophones (words which sound the same but may be spelled differently) and homographs (words which are spelled the same but may be pronounced differently). The words in both categories usually have different meanings. Homophones generally cause the most difficulty in spelling; however, homographs must also be considered. The way a word is used in a sentence is another source of confusion for spellers. For example, when faced with writing the sentence, "I read the book *The Little House on the Prairie*," the student who has been taught by strictly phonetic methods will assume he should write "I red the book *The Little House on the Prairie*."

While Hanna's research has proven that English is not as illogical as it once was considered to be, the complexities and the inconsistencies of the English language still contribute to the problem of learning to spell. Such inconsistencies make the importance of instruction in morphology (meaningful units) and etymology (word origins) in addition to phonics, as well as the isolation of at least some words for special drill, a necessity for most students. A program which includes all of these elements is generally referred to as a "linguistic approach."

The value of linguistics and/or phonics has been promoted successfully for many years, not only in spelling but in all areas of the language arts. The linguistic approach is readily integrated with functional spelling instruction, as well as systematic study of word lists when the words are grouped by phonetic principles, spelling rules, and other linguistic principles. Furthermore, spelling instruction should not only be integrated as a meaningful component of the language arts curriculum, but must be integrated with every phase of a student's written work, as was stated earlier.

Memorizing Word Lists Is Not Enough

> *There is evidence that the high frequency vocabulary in the writing of children and adults is very similar. Over and above the security segment of the spelling curriculum, pupils should be encouraged to pursue their own writing needs and interests.*[10]

Studies of the writing of children and adults have determined that the average person uses a core vocabulary of about 10,000 words. From these, researchers have been able to determine with considerable accuracy what will be the most common 4,000 to 5,000. These investigations have determined that a basic core of approximately 4,000 words account for about 98 percent of the spelling requirements of the average person.

Frequency of Word Use		
Number of Words	Percent of Use	% Gain in use per thousand words
10	25%	
100	60%	
500	82%	
1000	89%	89%
2000	95%	6%
3000	97%	2%
4000	99%	1%

The table on this page illustrates the frequency of word use by both children and adults including the percentage gains for each thousand words used. This table shows that if a student learns to spell only a limited number of words, he gains a larger percentage increase from learning the first thousand words than from learning any other thousand words. Such statistics indicate the value of frequency-based word lists over contrived grade level lists. By beginning with the most frequently used words and progressing to less frequently used words, dramatic results can be achieved quickly. This can be an important factor, especially in remedial situations.

While the most dramatic improvement will be seen with the learning of the first one thousand frequently used words, the student will gain more in terms of communication by learning the next two to five thousand frequently used words. This is because the first thousand words consist primarily of prepositions, articles, pronouns, etc., integral to the English language. While the gain in usage of the second thousand, third thousand, etc., appears to be small, the words in these groupings begin to include the many nouns, verbs, and modifiers that enhance the student's use of English. Thus, learning the correct spelling of at least the first 4,000 to 5,000 most frequently used words is vitally important to a student's continued use of language throughout his life.

While the most dramatic improvement will be seen with the learning of the first 1,000 frequently used words, the student will gain more in terms of communication by learning the next 2,000 to 5,000 most frequently used words.

As students mature, their spelling needs begin to vary and become more and more individualized. The words they personally use frequently, beyond the core list, will be determined by their hobbies, interests, and vocational choices. Considering this inevitable individualization, it is difficult to establish a larger word list equally serviceable to all students. Therefore, the basic word lists must be supplemented according to local and personal needs. Such supplementation ideally would come from the errors found in the student's own daily writing. Such inclusion necessitates providing the student an effective and efficient method of proofreading his own writing.

There are approximately 600,000 words in the English language. That means, if the average person uses 10,000 words on a regular basis, there are about 590,000 words which he uses infrequently. Even though they are used infrequently, they need to be spelled accurately when used. These words, and any word the student does not know how to spell, require facility with use of the dictionary. Knowing how and when to use a dictionary is not automatic; it is a learned skill and should be included in a well-planned spelling curriculum.

An Integrated Approach to Spelling Instruction is Needed

No method, however efficient it may be by scientific measures, remains effective if it becomes stereotyped, loses variety, does not call forth interest and zest on the part of children.[11]

The evidence quoted above makes it clear that establishing an effective spelling curriculum is not a matter of teaching spelling through a direct approach as opposed to the use of a functional approach. Nor is it simply a matter of combining one of these two approaches with a linguistic approach. Each approach has a valuable role to play in the overall acquisition and application of spelling skills.

Spelling power is achieved through a systematic method of spelling study based on word usage. An individualized, functional method of spelling study should be incorporated into this study to discover those words the student frequently uses and needs to learn. Finally, the student must be provided with specific skills he can use to discover his own spelling needs (proofreading skills) and a method by which he can find the correct spelling of any word he needs to write (dictionary skills).

Establishing Effective Teaching Strategies

In the last section, the three basic approaches to spelling instruction were discussed. Why each has an important role to play in the spelling curriculum was also explained. In addition to the basic approaches to spelling instruction, there are key elements and teaching strategies which contribute to the effectiveness of the spelling curriculum. Research conducted over the last century has given us clear guidelines as to which teaching strategies are most effective. Many of these strategies are applicable to all areas of the curriculum, while others are specific to teaching spelling. In this section, these key strategies will be explored.

Multi-level Instructional Materials

> *The pupils differ in the time at which they need to study particular words, in the types of mistakes they make, in the amount of repetition they need to learn a given word, and the vocabulary requirements of the spelling they need to do in writing. There is a saving of time when each pupil works only with words he needs to learn. Each pupil, ideally, should start at his own level and proceed at the rate at which he makes most progress. Each child should work on his own difficulties and no others.*[12]

While individual differences in all aspects of student growth come forcibly to the attention of those who work with students, research and experience have shown spelling to be one of the areas of the curriculum in which wide differences create instructional problems. Research by Hildreth has consistently shown that within same-age grouped classrooms there is a wide span of spelling abilities and that the span increases with each year of schooling. By the fourth grade, the variation in spelling ability in any typical group will range over five or six grade levels, and it is not unusual to find a range in spelling ability equal to ten school years among students in most sixth grade classrooms.

This variability in spelling is well illustrated by the performances of students in one school on the Morrison-McCall Spelling Scale (which includes words ranging in difficulty from the first to the eighth grade or higher). Form Three of this test was given to all students at the middle of the term in grades three through six. The results showed that the students' scores in grade three ranged from the first through the fourth grade level. In grade four, the range was from the middle of the second grade to the ninth grade. In grade five, the scores varied from the middle of the third grade to the tenth grade in difficulty. And in grade six, the students ranged from just below the fourth grade to the senior high school level.

The data for this school are fairly typical of results found in schools all over the country, no matter what kinds of students are enrolled, what grades they are in, or what methods have been used in teaching them. It points to the importance of providing each teacher with a program which allows her to provide each student the appropriate instructional materials at the appropriate time. Such materials are found only in multi-level programs such as the *Spelling Power* program.

Individualized Lists

> *Curtis and Dolch hold that typical grade lists are not good guides to the spelling words children need to study. Completely prescribed lists for the year make it impossible for children to receive drill on words they most need to practice.*[13]

Assigning a weekly word list has definite disadvantages, if the teacher's goal is that each student master the word list. Formerly, it was assumed that when a word had been taught once, it was "finished." Now it is known that the first teaching of a word may be only the introduction to a long sequence of systematic presentations and reviews. Although some words seem to be universally troublesome, most words vary in difficulty depending on a student's ability and experience.

In 1975, C. A. McGuigan[14] introduced the concept of the "Flow-Word-List" to address this aspect of learner variability. In his approach, as each word is mastered by the student it is dropped from the list and new words are added. Automatic retention checks of frequently misspelled words are built into the word lists. In addition, a series of review tests are included to assure long-term retention of the spelling words.

McGuigan experimented with this approach at the Experimental Education Unit of the University of Washington with over 30 students ages seven to 13 and in many public school classrooms, including adult re-education programs. Data from this investigation indicate that the students learn words more quickly with add-a-word lists and have similar or even superior retention than with fixed word lists.

Effects of the Test-Study-Test Approach

If the purpose of the pretest is clearly understood and the errors made are immediately and carefully corrected by the student, and if children understand that alert, conscientious correction of the test contributes greatly to the elimination of errors, the corrected test is by far the most efficient learning procedure.[15]

Research (first conducted by Kingsley in 1923) has repeatedly shown that the test-study-test plan is the most effective for the study of spelling. Research has produced about twice as many investigations favoring the test-study-test versus the study-test plan. The test-study-test plan involves the use of the following procedures: a pretest of a list of words is given the student, the student then studies the words missed on the pretest, and a final test is given to verify that he has learned the words.

This approach enables the student to get full recognition for words the spelling of which he has already learned in another context, and thus enables him to concentrate upon those difficulties that have been identified by the pretest. Limiting a student's study to his identified needs is more efficient; and it generally produces a more favorable attitude toward his instructional program.

The debate regarding the test-study-test plan vs. the study-test plan has often been centered not on its effectiveness but on at what grade levels it should be used. In 1931, Gates[16] concluded that the test-study-test plan was most effective with students beyond grade three only. While investigation summarized by Ernest Horn in 1960[17] concluded that the test-study-test method is superior with all classes and at all grade levels. However, many educators (including this writer) express concern that students in the lower grades (kindergarten through grade two) will benefit more from the study-test method, because of their limited writing vocabulary. Students who are likely to misspell every word on the pretest will profit more emotionally from a method which allows them to study the words prior to any testing.

Immediate Self-Correction

In 1947, Thomas Horn concluded through scientific investigation that adding the simple immediate-self-correction step to the test-study-test plan produced significant gains in spelling achievement.[18] His findings have been consistently reaffirmed by a number of studies, most recently in 1980 by Fitzsimmons and Loomer.[19] Horn's immediate-self-correction step requires the teacher to provide the student with the correct spelling immediately after he has attempted spelling the word.

> *Research has shown that the self-corrected test is the most efficient single learning procedure in spelling instruction and study. On the basis of such findings, it is difficult to justify having students exchange spelling papers or to have the teacher correct them.*[20]

One of the reasons that the immediate self-correction step is so effective is that with 44 sounds in the English language and approximately 250 ways to write them, often the student is puzzling over which is the appropriate spelling for the sound he hears. The immediate self-correction gives him the answer right after he has puzzled over it. With the self-correction process, everyone learns from his mistakes; some learn to avoid them, others to repeat them.

Additional Notes Regarding the Immediate Correction Process: Many teachers may be concerned that the self-correction process forces the student to concentrate on his errors. Their natural reaction is to feel that it is best to keep the student from seeing his error to prevent him retaining a faulty visual impression of the word. To refute this philosophy, Gillingham and Stillman make two very good points: "First, a poor speller is usually a poor speller because he does not retain clear visual images of words, so he will not likely remember the appearance of the wrong spelling. Second, people do not go through life with a patient mentor always at hand to obliterate the wrong and substitute the right."[21] They add that the self-correction process "will be a greater boon to train them into more and more knowledge and skill in detecting their own mistakes."

The value of the immediate self-correction, when combined with the other procedures in the Spelling Power *program, should not be underestimated.*

The value of the immediate self-correction, when combined with the other procedures in the *Spelling Power* program, should not be underestimated. According to research done by Thomas Horn and others, the effect of the immediate self-corrected test is the single most important factor contributing to success in spelling study. It alone will contribute 90 to 95 percent of the achievement resulting from the combined effects of the pronunciation exercises, corrected test, and study sheet work.[22]

> *The success of self-correction as a learning tactic may be related to three factors. First, students may feel more personally involved with their own learning when they correct their own work. Second, the immediacy of feedback during the self-correction may influence learning. . . Finally, the discrimination involved in correcting one's own spelling may result in closer attention to misspellings.*[23]

"Reinforcement" is the term used by psychologists, and other specialists in the learning process, to explain the *extra-strength* learning which occurs when students find out immediately whether they are right or wrong. When a student finds out immediately, while the elements of the problem are fresh in his mind, his knowledge is "reinforced": if he finds he is right, he becomes positive; if he finds he is wrong and checks at once to find out why he was wrong, he can sort out the points of the words that puzzled him and becomes sure of them.

For example, suppose you ask him to spell "buoyant." He starts to write but hesitates; "Is it b-u-o or b-o-u?" After deciding about that, he puzzles further; "And is it e-n-t or a-n-t?" Having then written the word one way or another, he wonders whether he has spelled the word correctly. By confirming the correct spelling immediately, while he remembers what parts of the word troubled him, his knowledge of the spelling of "buoyant" and words like it will be much surer.

"Hard Spot" Identification Is Not Advised

It is important not to confuse the effectiveness of the self-discovery of errors made possible through the immediate self-correction procedures with the concept of pre-marking "hard spots." Several studies have been made of the value of using diacritical marks, pre-marking hard spots with colored pencil, writing words in separate syllable form, or calling attention to incorrect forms. The first such study was conducted in 1927. After studying 4,000 pupils and over 500,000 words, Tireman[24] concluded that pre-marking "hard spots" actually lowered spelling scores. In a later study by Gates[25], it was shown that prior identification of hard spots in words was impractical because different students experience different "hard spots."

Horn's work with self-corrected tests has suggested that one of the reasons the self-corrected test seems so beneficial is that the student discovers his own "hard spots."

Schonell's[26] recommendations that the student discover his own common errors by underlining them with a colored pencil seems to confirm this philosophy.

Multi-Sensory Study Approach Required

Research by Hildreth and others has shown that there is a direct correlation between learning style or modality and spelling ability. Spelling is primarily a sensory-motor habit. The correct spelling of a word is both learned and recalled by repeated motor reactions to certain sensory stimuli. Most successful spellers depend upon one of their senses to tell whether the word is right or not.

Most good spellers can tell you whether the word "looks" right or wrong. Their memory is predominantly visual. They have become successful spellers because traditional instructional approaches have been limited to visual approaches. (Most evaluations of spelling ability also favors the visual learner.)

It is important to remember when discussing application of learning style theory that while each person has a predominant learning style, we all learn through all of our senses.

Poor spellers tend to have poor visual recall. They learn best through other sensory input. Some learn best through auditory impressions. They depend on remembering the sounds of the letters being recited in order. Still others learn well by recalling physical or tactile impressions. Individuals in this last group would recall the spellings in terms of lip and throat movements (by saying the letters) and the movements of the hand in writing the word. Tactile learners are aided in learning the spelling of words by the stronger sensation of "feeling" or touching the shapes of the words.

Armed with this information, it would be easy to assume that one should determine the student's learning style and then teach in an appropriate manner. This would be a mistake. First, it would be impractical to create a separate spelling curriculum for each student. Furthermore, it is important to remember when discussing application of learning style theory that while each person has a predominant learning style, we all learn through all of our senses. Additionally, it should be remembered that dominant modality also has developmental factors. For example, Piaget and others found that very young children learn through auditory avenues; early elementary ages tend to be kinesthetic and concrete; while older students tend to rely on their abstract reasoning or analytical powers along with visual recall.

Finally, using an exclusive learning style could possibly result in the neglect of other important skills. For instance, proofreading is primarily a visual task. To develop this skill, a strong emphasis should be placed upon visual discrimination in the presentation of words for study. This emphasis should be both on building visual discrimination skills and utilizing such skills. In this regard, presenting words in columnar form is more efficient than presenting them in context. A child should be taught to observe the whole word in isolation, to observe the word syllable by syllable, and to note the peculiar combinations of letters. Developing auditory discrimination, needed for accurate pronunciation and application of phonetic principles, is also very important.

Because each person's optimum learning style varies, as we have seen, spelling study must include procedures which help all learners succeed. The following multi-sensory steps are those accepted as being the most effective for the systematic study of spelling words:

1. Say the word.
2. Look at the word and its parts carefully.
3. Say the word and pronounce each letter, as they are pointed to.
4. Close eyes and try to visualize word and spell it letter-by-letter.
5. Check to see if it was correctly spelled in step four.
6. Trace each letter on desk top as it is spelled.
7. Check to see if the word was correctly spelled in step six.
8. Cover model and write the word.
9. Check attempted spelling; if wrong, repeat steps one through eight.
10. Write a sentence using the word.

These multi-sensory steps are the most effective for the systematic study of spelling words.

Spelling Rules Should Be Taught

Knowing phonetic principles and spelling rules can help the student to develop the ability to spell an unstudied word and probably spell it right because the pattern has been learned.

Earlier in this chapter, the work of Hanna, Hanna and Hodges[27] was discussed. Their gigantic "computer-based study" at Stanford University, which involved the analysis of 17,000 words, proved the value of teaching students phonetic principles. This research was not limited to phonetic principles; it also included linguistic principles which affect the proper spelling of words, for instance, the rules for adding suffixes to words. This research showed that phonetic generalizations and linguistic principles cover one or more elements of 85 percent of the words analyzed.

Not only did this landmark study show that rules apply to at least some part of many words, they showed that the exceptions to these rules were less frequent than had been previously thought. Another of the valuable outcomes of this research was learning that there are 46 rules and linguistic principles which have few or no exceptions and apply to the largest number of high frequency words. (Some of the rules used in the study, while stable, affect so few words that it would not be economical in terms of instructional time to teach them.)

Their research also suggested that word selection and organization according to these key linguistic principles can be an aid to spelling study. Knowing these principles and rules can help the student to develop the ability to spell an unstudied word and probably spell it right because the pattern has been learned.

Linguistically oriented spelling material lends itself well to various teaching strategies not peculiar to linguistics: for example, the inductive approach, arriving at patterns or generalizations from observing words in word lists, not just mechanically memorizing them, and a "spiral curriculum," teaching the same principles over and over but with ever-increasing ramifications.[28]

Skill Building Activities Are Important

Among the spelling activities they look for are high-interest, game-type exercises, such as puzzles, anagrams, and code solving to practice the words.

An effective spelling program must include skill building activities that appeal to the students. Some students are self-motivated. They enjoy academic work and, therefore, naturally enjoy the spelling studies and exercises of a well-planned workbook. Other students, however, require additional motivation. Among the spelling activities they look for are high-interest, game-type exercises, such as puzzles, anagrams, and code solving to practice the words. These exercises often focus on the letter arrangement of the spelling words, rather than on word meanings or context.

Many exercises can also be used to teach and reinforce spelling rules and other related skills. Since generalizations (spelling rules which are generally true) should be taught inductively (through understanding) and not as memorized statements, games and puzzles offer the student a valuable and interesting "discovery" method.

McSweeney has demonstrated the need for inclusion of activities that transfer words to writing in order to maintain spelling vocabulary. To demand arbitrarily that a word be written "50 times to stamp it on your mind" may not accomplish the intended purpose. In fact, as various investigators, such as Peterson and Dunlap, have shown quite conclusively, learning may progress in direct opposition to the factor of frequency of repetition or drill. Drill appears to be an effective aid to learning, chiefly when it is but a part of a larger configuration involving student interest, understanding, desire, and purpose.

Wagner[29] and others concluded that games and puzzle-type activities and exercises should be part of the formal spelling program. Therefore, "Discovery Activities" should not be used as a reward, they should be considered a basic part of the spelling program.

Plan to Study Spelling Every Day

In addition to checking spelling accuracy in written work, time should be set aside every day of the week for all students (above second grade) for specific and systematic spelling study. This daily period should include a short period for the initial study or review of troublesome words as well as specific instruction in related spelling skills. One or two periods a week are not frequent enough for economical learning and retention.

According to Ernest Horn's summary of spelling research in the 1960 edition of the *Encyclopedia of Educational Research*[30], there appears to be general agreement that this daily spelling period should not consume more than 15 minutes. More than 15 minutes does not result in comparable increases in spelling achievement. In fact, there is some evidence that extending the length of time spent can often have a negative effect on the results and especially upon the attitudes of students.

Research by Horn and others has provided evidence that spirited, expeditious work in the spelling period has the most favorable influence on learning. Making students study words which they already know how to spell, or having them do meaningless exercises in relation to the weekly list, is not only time wasted but is often detrimental in terms of student achievement and attitude. Therefore, the spelling period should be limited to active, meaningful work that enables each student to focus upon his own problem words and special needs for 15 minutes each day.

The spelling period should be limited to active, meaningful work that enables each student to focus upon his own problem words and special needs for 15 minutes each day.

In addition to a consistent schedule for spelling study, a consistent approach or lesson format is also a factor in instructional effectiveness. According to research, when the students' study follows a consistent format, they can then focus on the words and/or skills being taught, not the ever-changing lesson format. This does not mean there should be no variety in activity, but only that there is a definite, predictable format to the lessons.

Positive Attitudes and a Spelling Conscience

The development of a spelling conscience—a real desire to spell correctly—is a major goal in all spelling instruction.[31]

The greatest force which impedes the learning of spelling is a lack of interest or the presence of undesirable attitudes toward spelling instruction. Encouraging a positive attitude towards spelling study and toward becoming a competent speller is crucial to the effectiveness of the program. To accomplish this, Bruner stresses the need for teachers to appeal to curiosity, to the need for competence, to the need for identification with a nurturing adult, and to the need for responding to others and working cooperatively with them toward an objective.[32] These motives are as applicable to spelling as they are to other learning activities. Assuming that these categories provide an adequate basis for facilitating maximum learning, how then can they be used in today's spelling program?

1. Developing interest in words: Interest in improving spelling often can be increased by talking about words, their derivations and their peculiarities, by bringing in rare and amusing words, by having fun and playing with words, by talking about classes of words and related words, synonyms and antonyms, simplified spelling, disputed spellings, through pronunciation and syllabication practice, and dictation in context. Knowledge of the roots of words, the evolution of language, the derivation of words are also of some help in spelling irregular and unusual words.

Encouraging a positive attitude towards spelling study and toward becoming a competent speller is crucial to the effectiveness of the program.

2. Showing the student that the words taught are those most likely to be needed by him now and in the future: Students sometimes get the wrong notion that textbook writers and teachers accumulate all the difficult words and assign these for study. This creates a negative attitude among students who feel that the teacher is trying to assign words that are most likely to produce errors. It is usually therefore helpful to discuss with the student the basis for the spelling curriculum.

3. Limiting the student's study to those words which tests have shown him to be unable to spell: Most students want to be treated as individuals and this includes receiving credit when credit is due. A more positive attitude can be expected when students know they will be given credit for words they already know how to spell.

This approach also enables the student to see for himself that any word that he is required to study is a word that he is unable to spell. The pretest before study can be used effectively to show the student which words he has already learned and which ones he must study.

4. Opportunity for success: Motivation is key to spelling success and to the transfer of spelling words into daily writing. An effective spelling program includes opportunities for the student to experience success. More simply stated, *success breeds success* in spelling.

Proper placement within the spelling program is essential to this source of motivation. A student who misses most of the words on the pretest becomes overwhelmed and discouraged. Conversely, a high degree of success on the pretest means that 100 percent success on the retest is a reasonable and attainable goal.

5. Providing the student with a definite and efficient method of learning: Some students do not know how to study on their own. If such students are poor achievers, their attitudes toward spelling can often be improved when they realize that the teacher is actually interested in helping them to study and learn.

6. Knowledge of results: The student's knowledge of progress or success is another important source of interest and other desirable attitudes. According to Skinner, "positive reinforcement" of correct responses or immediate feedback is crucial to continued progress.

> *On the human level, praise, gifts, money and privileges of various kinds can serve as reinforcers. The most easily applicable reinforcer is simply knowledge of results. When a human learner emits a response, and this response is then shown to be correct, this knowledge of results is found to reinforce with sufficient potency to obviate any other "rewards."*[33]

7. Emphasizing individual progress: Most teachers use a variety of techniques for keeping students informed of their progress. The important aspect here is not the record keeping itself but the appropriate utilization of such information. The major emphasis of these records is to keep each child informed of his current progress in relation to his past performances.

8. Teacher attitudes: The teacher's own attitude toward spelling is an important factor in determining her students' attitudes and consequently how well they learn to spell. Enthusiastic, sympathetic teachers often get good results even though they do not otherwise make use of the most efficient learning procedures. Conversely, teachers who use efficient procedures, but in a mechanical way without enthusiasm or sympathetic understanding of the needs of individual students, get poor results. There is no reason why enthusiasm, sympathy, and efficiency should not be combined.

Closely related to the above teacher-student relationship is the portrayal of the teacher as a role model. The interaction of children with warm, nurturing adults usually results in at least a modicum of identification. If these adults are highly motivated toward competence, the students then tend to assume the same attitudes. If the teacher can be such an individual, she increases the level of motivation of her students. By providing a day-to-day working model with whom students can interact, she becomes someone whose standards they respect. The teacher who recognizes her potential influence will strive to establish the quality of relationship which will facilitate identification and also manifest the enthusiasm and learning habits which merit adoption by the student.

9. Peer interaction and socialization: Peer interaction also offers numerous possibilities for use in facilitating learning. Teachers should create spelling activities that permit students to work in pairs or small groups. These groups may work together to discover spelling rules and patterns or to gather information about words which will assist them in learning more readily. They may play games or apply practice techniques that will make the spelling of words more automatic. Tutoring and testing can be carried on efficiently; and when care is exercised in setting up pairs and groups, high levels of motivation can be maintained.

Spelling Power Is Research Based

The teaching strategies and techniques described in this section are in no way intended to be an exhaustive list of the key ingredients of an effective curriculum, nor do they represent the only factors included in the *Spelling Power* program. They do, however, represent those factors which have been universally proven, yet frequently ignored, in the creation of other spelling programs. I have highlighted them in this section to bring them to the attention of the users of the program so they will understand their relevance to the program's effectiveness.

The *Spelling Power* program has been designed to meet the requirements of effective spelling instruction (as established by reliable, proven research) some of which has been summarized in this chapter. It constitutes a complete spelling curriculum, for kindergarten through college level. Using this program, any student (within a class or family) may start where he is and move ahead as fast and as far as his learning rate and capacity will let him to reach the program's objectives.

The *Spelling Power* program helps students reach these objectives by providing the student with an integration of the three basic approaches to spelling instruction. All the skills, techniques, and principles which research has overwhelmingly and consistently shown to help students to become efficient spellers are contained in the program. Finally, elements of student motivation were considered throughout creation of the program.

Detailed procedures for using the *Spelling Power* program are outlined in the remaining chapters of this manual. Chapter Two is the most important. After reading it, you may begin using the program with your student. Then, as you have time, continue reading the remaining chapters incorporating the additional aspects of the program as appropriate for your students.

References For Chapter One

1 Gertrude A. Boyd and E. Gene Talbert, *Spelling in the Elementary School* (Arizona State University) (Columbus, OH: Charles E. Merrill Publishing Co., 1971).

2 Paul R. Hanna and R. E. Hodges Jr., "Spelling and Communications Theory: A Model and an Annotated Bibliography," *Elementary English*, 40: 483-505ff.; May 1963.

3 Eldon Stetson and others, "Eight Years of Theory and Practice in Spelling and Those Who Wrote the Programs Forgot to Read the Literature," (Clearwater, FL: National Reading Conference, 1982).

4 Ves Thomas, *Teaching Spelling: Canadian Word Lists and Instructional Techniques* (Calgary, Alberta, Canada: Gage Educational Publishing Limited, 1974).

5 Ernest Horn, "Teaching Spelling," Department of Classroom Teachers, American Education Research Association of the National Education Association, (p. 16), NEA, January 1954.

6 Donald H. Parker, *Schooling for Individual Excellence* (New York: Thomas Nelson & Sons, 1963).

7 Norris G. Haring and others, *The Fourth R: Research in the Classroom* (Columbus, OH: Charles E. Merrill, 1978).

8 G. A. Vergason, "Facilitation Of Memory In The Retardate," *Exceptional Children*, 1968, 34, (8), 589-594.

9 Paul R. Hanna and others, *Phoneme-Grapheme Correspondences as Cues to Spelling Improvement* (Washington, D.C.: Government Printing Office, U.S. Office of Education, 1966).

10 Gertrude A. Boyd and E. Gene Talbert, *Spelling in the Elementary School* (Arizona State University), (Columbus, OH: Charles E. Merrill Publishing Co., 1971).

11 Carleton W. Washburne and Sidney Marland Jr., *Winnetka: The History and Significance of an Educational Experiment* (Englewood Cliffs, NJ: Prentice-Hall, Inc., 1963).

12 Gertrude Hildreth, *Teaching Spelling: A Guide to Basic Principles and Practices* (New York: Henry Holt & Co., 1955).

13 Gertrude Hildreth, *Learning the 3 R's*, Minneapolis, Cumberland Education Series, Educational Publishers, Inc., 1947.

14 C. A. McGuigan, "The Effects of a Flowing Word List and the Implementation of Procedures in the Add-a-word Spelling Program," *Working Paper No. 52*, Experimental Education Unit, University of Washington (Seattle, 1975).

15 Thomas Horn, "Spelling," in *Encyclopedia of Educational Research*, 4th ed, edited by R.C. Ebel (London: Macmillan Co., 1969), pp. 1285-1299.

16 Arthur Gates, "An Experimental Comparison in the Study-Test and the Test-Study Method in Spelling," *Journal of Educational Psychology*, Vol. 22, Jan. 1931, pp. 1-19.

17 Ernest Horn, "Spelling," in *Encyclopedia of Educational Research* (New York: Macmillan and Company, 1960), p. 1346.

18 Thomas Horn, "The Effect of the Corrected Test on Learning to Spell," *Elementary School Journal*, 47, pp. 277-285, 1947.

19 Robert J. Fitzsimmons and Bradley M. Loomer, *Spelling: The Research Basis* (Iowa City: University of Iowa, 1980).

20 Thomas Horn, "The Effect of the Corrected Test on Learning to Spell," *Elementary School Journal*, 47, pp 277-285, 1947.

21 Anna Gillingham and Bessie W. Stillman, *Remedial Training for Children with Specific Disability in Reading, Spelling, and Penmanship*, 5th ed. (Cambridge, MA: Educators Publishing Service, Inc., 1964).

22 Thomas D. Horn, "The Effect of the Corrected Test on Learning to Spell", *Elementary School Journal 47*, pp. 277-285, 1947.

23 Norris G. Haring and others, *The Fourth R: Research in the Classroom* (Columbus, OH: Charles E. Merrill Publishing Company, 1978).

24 L. S. Tireman, "The Value of Marking Hard Spots in Spelling," (Master's Thesis, University of Iowa, Iowa City, 1927).

25 Arthur Gates, *A List of Spelling Difficulties in 3,876 Words* (New York: Bureau of Publication, Teachers College, Columbia University, 1937).

26 Fred J. Schonell, *The Essential Spelling List: 3200 Everyday Words Selected, Graded and Grouped According to Common Difficulty* (London: Macmillan Co., Ltd. 1932).

27 Paul R. Hanna and others, *Phoneme-Grapheme Correspondences as Cues to Spelling Improvement* (Washington, D.C.: Government Printing Office, U.S. Office of Education, 1966).

28 Ralph M. Williams, "The Teaching of Spelling" in *The Encyclopedia of Education*, Crowell-Collier Educational Corporation (The Macmillan Co., 1971), Vol. 8, pp. 387-391.

29 Wagner and others, *Language Games* (Darien, CT: Teacher's Publishing Corporation, 1963).

30 Ernest Horn, "Spelling," in *Encyclopedia of Educational Research* (New York: Macmillan and Company, 1960), p. 1346.

31 Gertrude A. Boyd and E. Gene Talbert, *Spelling in the Elementary School* (Arizona State University), (Columbus, OH: Charles E. Merrill Publishing Co., 1971).

32 Jerome S. Bruner, *Toward a Theory of Instruction* (Cambridge: Harvard University Press, 1966). (1st: pp. 113-138 and 2nd p. 114)

33 B. R. Bugelski, *The Psychology of Learning Applied to Teaching*, Second Edition (Indianapolis, IN: The Bobbs-Merrill Company, Inc., 1964).

Chapter Two
Teaching the High Frequency Words

The core of the *Spelling Power* program is working with the high-frequency, Flow-Word-Lists. All of the elements required for effective learning of essential spelling skills discussed in the last chapter are incorporated into the basic 15-minute-a-day *Spelling Power* sessions. During this daily regime, you will begin by pretesting (or retesting) the high frequency words, which have been organized into levels of frequency and divided into groups based on phonetic principles and spelling rules. Your student will then spend approximately five minutes on his own studying any words misspelled during the pretest or in his other school work. During the final five minutes of the daily work, your student will work on skill building activities.

In this chapter, you will be given detailed instructions on how to begin working with the program; how to conduct the basic daily work with the Flow-Word-Lists; and how to record your student's progress.

Determining Readiness

> *We speak of starting with a child "where he is," which is in one sense not to assert an educational desideratum but an inescapable fact: there is no other place the child can start from. There are only other places the teacher can start from.*[1]

Virtually all experts concerned with spelling instruction agree that the ages between eight and twelve are the best years to intensify spelling study. This age group coincides with what Montessori and Piaget refer to as the "period when the child loves facts and figures and increases in reasoning power." This is the age which is typified by a passion for collecting just about anything: baseball cards, rocks, and so forth. This age group also finds great pleasure in knowing and sharing many facts, solving puzzles, and inventing secret codes. It is the perfect age to introduce your children to the joy of collecting and manipulating words and their spellings.

The ages between eight and twelve are the best years to intensify spelling study.

While the ages between eight and twelve are the ideal ages to provide your student with intensive spelling study, it should not be implied that spelling instruction and drill should not begin before age eight or that it should be discontinued after the age of twelve. For the majority of students under age eight, spelling instruction should be closely associated with reading and phonics instruction. Students need a variety of experiences with written expression before they are ready for demanding systematic study. However, some of these younger students may profit from an adaptation to the methods outlined in this chapter by using the study-test-study method rather than the test-study-test (described in detail on page 93).

With the ever increasing demands of the content subjects during the junior high school and high school years, there has been a growing tendency not to teach spelling as a formal subject beyond the sixth grade. To assume that, by this point, all students have acquired all the skills and motivations necessary to continue learning to spell new words is absurd. Teachers of older students have as great an obligation to further develop their students' spelling mastery as do the teachers of younger students.

The responsibility for teaching spelling to older students lies in three directions: first, "mastery" of those high-frequency words not yet mastered; second, "upkeep" practice for commonly misspelled words; and third, practice in spelling the new technical vocabulary that each subject area requires. Here, as with younger students, frequency of use still serves as a guide for the selection of words.

Of course, the age of your student is not the only requirement for determining readiness for spelling study. Your student must also have acquired a number of specific skills before advancing to this stage of spelling instruction. The following general guidelines should prove helpful in determining your student's readiness for the program.

Your student must also have acquired a number of specific skills before advancing to this stage of spelling instruction.

Does your student demonstrate facility in handwriting? Prior to beginning systematic spelling study, your student should have the ability to write each letter of the alphabet correctly from dictation (without a model), be able to associate the letter name with the letter form, be able to write his own name without copying, and be able to copy words correctly.

Facility in handwriting is a major factor in determining readiness for any spelling study which requires any testing of words. Young children and some students with specific language disabilities, who are so immature or retarded in eye-hand coordination that it is very difficult for them to write words correctly, will need much guidance and patience in helping them to learn to write before they are ready for spelling lessons.

If your student has serious handwriting difficulties, he should be given remediation in these skills before initiating the *Spelling Power* program. However, some students with mild cases may proceed with the program while receiving handwriting instruction. We recommend *The Italic Handwriting Series*, published by Portland State University, for both beginning writers and those who have been unsuccessful in acquiring abilities in handwriting by other methods. Older students who need to improve handwriting may find *Write Now!*, also published by Portland State University, a more suitable means for learning the Italic Handwriting system.

This handwriting program teaches the student a legible handwriting style and is one of the easiest methods to learn. It has been widely recommended for a number of reasons. The main advantage is this style requires learning the least number of letter forms of any style available. After learning the letter forms, the student is taught a series of joins to form the cursive style.

According to Dr. Samuel Orton, "Irreparable harm is done (for remedial students) by some schools which start with manuscript and change to cursive in the second or third grades."

> *Dr. Orton repeatedly asserted that impressions made on nerve tissues are never wholly eradicated. They are only white-washed over. They linger on, confusing later impressions. This change of penmanship system may often be traced in papers of high school students, where manuscript form asserts itself in the middle of words begun in cursive form.*[2]

Before your student is expected to write and spell a word, he should have already acquired it as a meaningful part of his listening, speaking, and reading vocabularies.

Does your student have an oral and reading vocabulary of at least the second-grade level? There is a high correlation between spelling and reading in the primary grades. The words students are learning to read at this stage are the same words they must learn. From grade three (about eight) this is no longer true. Beyond this age, the student's listening, speaking, and reading vocabulary is increasing at such a fast rate it is impossible to expect him to be able to write every word he can read. However, before a student should be expected to write and spell a word, he should have already acquired it as a meaningful part of his listening, speaking, and reading vocabularies.

The easiest way to determine if your student is reading above a second grade level is to have him read from a basal reader designed for that grade. First, have your student read orally a small section (one or two paragraphs). You should choose a selection from near the end of the book. As he reads, make a note of the errors he makes in reading.

Follow this with a informal assessment of his comprehension of the piece. Also, select some of the more advanced words from the piece to make sure he understands their meaning.

If your student had some difficulty reading the piece orally, you may want to repeat this process with a silent reading of another similarly sized piece. Some students read silently better than they read orally. Have him read the piece to himself and then ask him comprehension and vocabulary questions.

Spelling Power is not a vocabulary program. Vocabulary skills are best improved in conjunction with your student's work in reading and other subject areas.

Students who are not reading on this level will need to spend more time with basic reading and phonics instruction. You may find beginning work with the adapted approach to the Flow-Word-Lists described on page 93 is helpful for your student. Learning to spell these high frequency words can often help your student learn to read them. Many of *Spelling Power*'s multi-sensory study steps are as beneficial for reading as they are to spelling.

Can your student enunciate words clearly? Shortcomings in speech, such as mispronunciations and articulatory defects, have been found to be related to disabilities in spelling. The student who has obvious speech impediments or mispronounces a large number of words in his normal conversation should be helped to overcome these handicaps before beginning spelling study. The removal of these shortcomings will result in greater success in the spelling program, since research has shown that approximately one third of all spelling errors are pronunciation errors.

It is not intended here to imply that the student who occasionally mispronounces words or who mispronounces commonly mispronounced words (such as *denist* for *dentist*, etc.), should be subjected to specific remediation. These students will be helped to eliminate the 'tendency towards slovenly speech' as part of *Spelling Power*'s testing and study steps. They, therefore, should not be prevented from beginning the program. Likewise, those early grade students who are missing teeth should not necessarily be given remediation, since their condition is one only time can cure.

If your student has a more serious problem with enunciation, an excellent resource for providing remediation is *Sound and Articulation Activities for Children with Speech Problems.*[3] This program allows you to work with one speech sound at a time (and thereby also builds additional phonics practice), so you can pick and choose the materials suited to your student. The multi-sensory, cross-curricula activities of this speech program are geared to preschool through third grade.

Most students grade four and above would find the lessons in *Sound and Articulation Activities for Children with Speech Problems* "babyish," which indeed, they are. A creative teacher could take the lessons and easily adapt them for her older students. However, one note of concern: an older student that is still having trouble with clear enunciation should in most cases be evaluated by a speech specialist.

Does your student have a beginning sense of phonetic principles? It is assumed students using this program have had some beginning phonics instruction. However, if this is not true for your student, knowledge of the regular consonant sounds and their graphic representation should be considered a minimum requirement for beginning *Spelling Power.*

It is assumed students using this program have had some beginning phonics instruction.

For those lacking basic phonics skills, beginning phonics can be effectively taught using a number of methods and commercially available materials. No specific material is recommended here since the age of the students and their learning styles, to a large part, will determine the materials most appropriate.

Does your student demonstrate sufficient maturity? Until a certain stage in auditory and visual perception has been reached, your student will not be ready to make the fine visual and sound discriminations that correct spelling requires. Furthermore, your student must possess the ability to formulate and apply rules. The attempt to present spelling as a *thought subject* cannot succeed with most students under eight or those students who have extremely low I.Q.s. Both categories of students lack the ability to handle abstract thought and need more concrete instructions to achieve spelling success.

The ability to concentrate on the task at hand is still another consideration in determining if the student possesses sufficient maturity for Systematic Spelling Study. *Spelling Power* is designed around focused, expeditious work in three five-minute segments. Most of your students over six have sufficient attention span to complete these requirements. If you are working with an ADD or ADHD student, you will find additional information on how you can help them in the detailed descriptions of each step.

See Chapter Three for specific ideas on getting your students to write.

Does he demonstrate a desire and interest in learning to spell? Another way your student will show his readiness for spelling study is through his own incidental learning and through showing an interest in words, word meanings, and their use in functional writing. This includes asking for help with words when he is in doubt, being able to write a few simple words from memory, and being able to express at least a few thoughts in writing.

Many classic word games, rhymes, and word puzzles can help pique your student's interest in words. Many of the Discovery Activities (found in the fifth section of the book), as well as ideas in Chapter Four, may be used with profit to motivate your student. Work and encouragement in developing writing skills is another natural motivator for most students.

Help Students to Acquire Readiness

If your student does not exhibit the above skills, he should generally not begin work with the Flow-Word-Lists. While only time and nature can affect a number of the areas of readiness, younger children and students retarded by specific language disabilities can and should be helped to acquire it. Participation in the Integrated Functional Writing aspects of this program, described in Chapter Three and *Writing Power* (available in the Fall of 1998), is advised for all of your students. However, the formal instruction in beginning spelling skills should not be neglected. It may be desirable for some students who exhibit partial readiness to participate in an adapted approach using the study-test-study approach as described on page 93 in Chapter Six (Planning, Organizing, and Adjusting Instruction) under the section "Using the Study-Test-Study Approach."

Introducing the Program

If your student has made poor progress in spelling up to this point, you may wish to point out that being a poor speller does not mean he lacks intelligence. Assure him he can and will learn how to spell, you and this program are going to help him learn.

> *In the early training stages, the teacher's assistance and attitude are all-important. She shows the children how to find the words they need to study, how to study words,... She sets standards for the children and gives individual aid where it is needed. She creates a study situation in which the children are free from distraction, prepares study materials, and makes frequent checks of accomplishments.*[4]

Once you have determined that your student possesses the necessary skills to begin the *Spelling Power* program, he should be introduced to the program. It is vital that you take the time to fully explain the program. Your student should be shown what is involved and why it will help him to learn to be a better speller. All students need to understand how and why this program works. This introduction is especially important if your student has studied spelling in the past with less-than-satisfactory results. A positive Hawthorne Effect often results from this type of detailed introduction. (See sidebar.) The Quick-Start Introduction and Chapter One contain excellent information in this regard. Some teachers have found reading the Preface to the First Edition to their older students encouraging and motivating.

The following points should be made to your student:

1. The program he will be using is a proven, research-based program designed to make him a better speller. The steps he will take and methods he will use have worked for many people of varying abilities and ages, and it will work for him as well.

2. Explain to him that he will spend about 15 minutes a day on spelling. About one half of this time will be used to study lists of words he needs to learn. The other half will be spent completing assigned lessons, participating in activities, and playing games selected to help him learn important spelling skills.

3. Your student should understand at the onset and be reminded throughout the year that this program is individualized. He only studies the words that a pretest of Flow-Word-Lists or his own writing shows he needs to learn. Furthermore, this program is designed so he is free to progress (or learn) at the pace best for him.

4. Show your student the Flow-Word-Lists. It should be explained to him that the words on the Flow-Word-Lists are those words researchers have determined (by examining millions of samples of children's and adults' writing) are the most frequently used and most useful words for every person to learn. It is also helpful if the teacher points out how the Levels of the Flow-Word-Lists are based on the frequency with which the words are used in writing and are not necessarily related to traditional school grade levels. Explain to him that he will learn how to add words to the word lists he has misspelled in his other school work or that he wants to learn to spell.

The Hawthorne Effect

The term comes from studies made by R.J. Roethlisberger and W.J. Dickson (1939) at Western Electric's plant in Hawthorne, NJ, where girl (sic) employees were studied under different work conditions. The girls were given to understand that their employment was quite secure and that nothing was going to happen that in any way would jeopardize their status. They were further given to understand that they were partners in a scientific effort and that their cooperation was being sought as individuals, not as mere employees. It appeared that the girls began to feel themselves to be important and unique. Their morale and motivation were high. When the experimenters began to make changes in the working environment, the work productivity of the girls began to rise. It soon became evident that the actual environmental changes had nothing to do with the productivity because the direction of the changes did not appear to matter. If the work areas were better lighted, production rose; if the areas were darkened, production rose. With every change the girls worked harder and more effectively than before. Simply knowing that something new was being tried (and with themselves as the centers of attention) appeared to have strong effect on the girls' attitudes and motivation. E.L. Solomon (1949) showed that a similar effect could occur in a teaching situation. In connection with the introduction of a new method of spelling, he found that simply giving a preliminary test prior to introducing the new procedure had an effect on the subsequent spelling learning.[5]

These are important points to make, because often students are under the mistaken notion that textbook and program writers and teachers accumulate all the difficult words they can find and assign these for study. This idea can create a negative attitude.

5. Every learning activity you assign him will be selected especially to help him learn the skills he needs to learn, when he needs to learn them. These assignments are called prescriptions, because like prescriptions for medicine, a doctor only prescribes the right amount and only when the patient needs it.

Surveying Student Ability

To take the doctor analogy a little further, you can explain that before the doctor prescribes any treatment, he must examine the patient. This is also the first step in prescribing spelling study in the *Spelling Power* program. Before you can begin helping him learn to spell, you must know what words he is likely to know and what spelling skills he already possesses. This will be determined by taking a series of special tests: a Survey Test, one or more Placement Tests, and a functional test.

The first test you will give your student is called the Survey Test, designed to help determine at what level placement testing should begin. It should only be administered to those students who demonstrate readiness for spelling study as previously described.

Two forms of the Survey Test are located in the "Placement Tests" section of this book. Both tests are of equal difficulty. The Survey Test was created by taking a sampling of words from each level of the Flow-Word-Lists. The test allows you to get a general idea of where Placement Testing should begin. A Placement Test includes a sampling of words from a particular Flow-Word-List level.

"Form A" of the Survey Test should be administered at the beginning of instruction and "Form B" should be given at the end of the year. If your school is using a year-round schedule you need to administer only one test per year on a designated date. In this way, the Survey Test can provide definite reference points, which can be used to measure growth in spelling ability gained during the year.

*The blackline masters provided in the **Teaching Aids and Masters** section provide generic test form masters for each line size.*

Before administering the Survey Test, you should provide your student with his own copy of the Student Record Book. This book is designed to coordinate with the *Italic Handwriting Series*, published by Portland State University, and uses the same style of lines as this program. Blackline masters of all the forms provided in the Student Record Book are provided in the Teaching Aids and Masters section of this manual. If you are using blackline masters, you should provide the student with a copy of the Survey Test form.

Administering the Survey Test

*Information on selecting the proper line size for your student's writing is found on the back of the Order Form in the **Miscellaneous Section**.*

To administer the Survey Test, you should first copy the blackline master found in this manual (or help your student find the page in his Student Record Book designated for the Survey Test) and make sure he has two sharpened pencils. (The blackline masters provided in the "Teaching Aids and Masters" section provide generic test form masters for each line size.) Your student should be instructed to record the appropriate date in the place provided for it. Before beginning, it may be helpful to remind him this test is only to determine where he is to begin spelling instruction and his performance will not be graded.

The test should be given in the usual school setting with the environment as free from distractions as is possible. Only the Student Record Book or test sheet and pencils should be on your student's desk. The testing process should be explained fully before beginning the test.

Survey Test

Name: ______ Date: ______ Form: ______

1		19	
2		20	
3		21	
4		22	
5		23	
6		24	
7		25	
8		26	
9		27	
10		28	
11		29	
12		30	
13		31	
14		32	
15		33	
16		34	
17		35	
18		36	

Explain to your student that you will say a word, use it in a sentence, and say the word again. Your student is not to begin writing until the word has been repeated. He should be told to write the word in the best way he knows how. There should be no interruptions while the test is in progress.

When your student understands the purpose and procedures for the Survey Test, the test may be begun. The Survey Test should always begin with the first word of the test form being used and dictation of words should continue until your student has made three errors in close succession or a total of six words. While administering this test, it is necessary for you to sit next to your student and observe his answers as he proceeds. The purpose of this observation is only to determine where the Survey Test should end. Do not expect your student to spell words far beyond his ability; this would be very demotivating.

Many older students will misspell words randomly. In this case, you should discontinue the test when he has misspelled a total of six words. It is important to end the test at this point. To do otherwise will skew the results. If your student insists he wants to try all the words, and you allow this, remember when you evaluate the Survey Test to ignore those words tested or attempted after testing would normally have ended.

After testing the last word, tell your student he will take a more detailed Placement Test tomorrow. The chart which follows Form B of Survey Test will help you determine where placement testing should begin. A detailed description of how to score the

Survey Test and how to use the chart is provided on this page as well.

Giving the Placement Test

There is one Placement Test form for each level of the *Spelling Power* Flow-Word-Lists. (Tests are located in the "Placement Tests" section.) These tests were created by taking a random sampling of words from that level.

Before beginning the Placement Test, you should help your student locate the first Placement Test sheet in his Student Record Book or provide him with a copy of the Placement Test form. The student should be shown where he is to record the date and level of this test. Remind him that this test is only to determine the best level for him to begin spelling instruction, and that he will not be graded in the traditional sense.

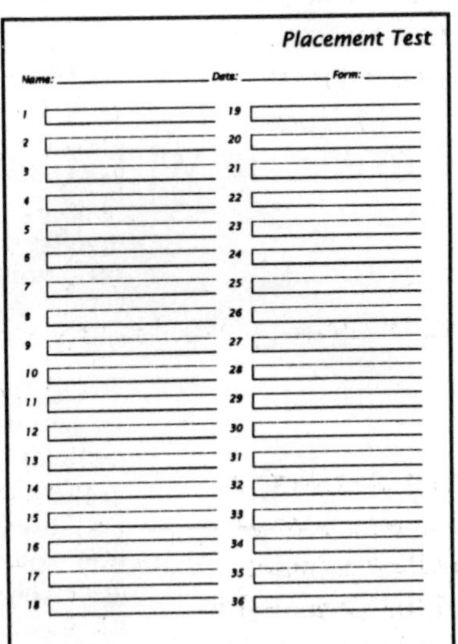

Placement Test

Name: ______ Date: ______ Form: ______

1		19	
2		20	
3		21	
4		22	
5		23	
6		24	
7		25	
8		26	
9		27	
10		28	
11		29	
12		30	
13		31	
14		32	
15		33	
16		34	
17		35	
18		36	

Placement Tests are administered in almost the same manner as the Survey Test. Again, the testing process should be explained fully to your student before beginning the test. For this test, it is not necessary to sit next to him or to check spelling as the test progresses. The entire Placement Test list should be dictated to your student.

Placement Tests should be scored and analyzed at a later time, without your student present. They should be corrected by you or some other reliable person. As you analyze the Placement Tests, you should not rely solely on your own spelling ability, but should refer as needed to the list while verifying the spelling of each word. The chart at the bottom of each Placement Test will help you determine what your student is to be instructed to do next. He will either study on the level of the Placement Test given or he will be given another Placement Test on a higher or lower level than the one he has just taken.

Fine-Tuning Placement Level

Some students are adept at taking tests, yet when you examine their written work you discover numerous spelling errors. Conversely, some students are "test phobic" and their spelling ability is not well reflected by testing. It cannot be too strongly emphasized that teacher observation, judgment, and evaluation are most important and that you must consider the results of the Survey and Placement Tests in light of your student's overall spelling correctness in written work.

To evaluate your student's "actual writing," you will need a recent sample of his writing. You may select this from some other school work or you may wish to have him write continuously for 15 minutes (one day's spelling session). With the writing sample in hand, locate each spelling error. After you have located the errors, you may use the Alphabetical Word List to determine the level of each misspelled word. Above each word your student has misspelled (or on a separate list), you may write the letter which indicates the level at which the word is taught. Compare whether misspelled words are from levels below or above those designated by his Placement Test. If many of the words are above the placement level, you may want to move him up to a higher Flow-Word-List level. Conversely, if many words are below the level indicated by the Placement Test, you may want him to begin working at a lower level on the Flow-Word-Lists.

Using a sampling of an older student's writing is very important. Placement within the program is sometimes more difficult with older students since you will often see erratic results. A number of factors contribute to this, but the main factor is learning gaps. It is important to not place these students at too low of a level, which can be demotivating. Remember, *Spelling Power* has six levels of built-in review. Those gaps will be filled in as you follow all of *Spelling Power*'s procedures.

When examining a sampling of student writing, also compare the student's writing ability to his oral use of language. If you see he is not using the same level of vocabulary he does when speaking, it may indicate he is avoiding many words he regularly uses, but is unable to spell.

The Survey Test and Placement Tests are not patterns to be used in teaching nor are the words the pupil misses in the Placement Test necessarily the ones to be practiced in subsequent spelling lessons. Teaching from these diagnostic tests would invalidate their future use. However, you should note the kinds of errors made by your student on the Placement Test. (A detailed description of methods for analyzing errors and using them for prescribing specific formal instruction is described in detail in Chapter Four.)

Pretesting with Flow-Word-Lists

After determining where your student should begin working with the Flow-Word-List, you are ready to begin establishing a daily routine for him. Remind your student he will spend 15 minutes a day on formal spelling study: five minutes testing, five minutes studying the words he misspells, and five minutes involved in skill building activities.

Usually the test of a Flow-Word-List group is given before your student has the opportunity to study the words. After taking the test, he studies only those words which he has misspelled, using the special 10-Step-Study Sheets as guides. There are two exceptions to this rule. Words added from the Integrated Functional Writing aspects of the program (see Chapter Three) are added directly to the 10-Step-Study Sheets and then tested with the retest words. The other exception has to do with special cases of very young students (under eight years old) and other students whose writing vocabulary is so limited it would be unproductive to test them to determine which words need to be studied. These students will study the words, using the special 10-Step-Study Sheets, prior to any testing using the study-test-study method explained in Chapter Six (pages 93-94) under the section "Using the Study-Test-Study Approach."

Each student's testing session should average five minutes. This time limit is an integral aspect of the program. Sessions of longer duration tend to have a negative effect because your student will tire of the systematic process and his attention will wane. The five-minute session also controls the number of words your student will have to study, which optimally will not exceed five words.

*In some situations the number of words to be **studied** should be considered as well as the amount of time allowed for testing.*

In some situations the number of words to be **studied** should be considered as well as the amount of time allowed for testing. Because each Flow-Word-List (beyond level A) includes a number of easier and review words, your student should be able to correctly spell 50 percent or more of the words presented during each session. Occasionally, your student will miss almost every word on the pretest. In such a case, you need to be aware of the number of words your student can effectively study in one session and may wish to discontinue testing for the day before the allotted time has expired.

Of course the number of words that can be effectively studied at one time varies with each individual and only the teacher's experience with the individual will tell her what is right for her student. In general, your student should not be expected to learn (study) more than ten words in one sitting and five study words is the optimum.

If your student regularly misses most of the words presented during the testing session, you may need to re-evaluate his placement level. Students working at the beginning levels, who are missing large numbers of words during the testing session, should be re-evaluated for readiness for formal spelling instruction. It may be possible that the study-test-study method will be most appropriate for students making large numbers of errors on each testing session.

How to Conduct Test Sessions

The testing procedures should be explained in detail the first time used. After that, your student should be reminded of the fine points of the testing process at the beginning of each test session until you are sure he knows them and knows how to proceed effectively.

You should begin each test session by reminding your student that this test is only to determine which words he needs to study. You should explain to him that the procedures will allow him to study the words he does not know how to spell and to work at his own pace. He does not have to wait for others or try to keep up with them.

You will follow the procedures outlined below for each Flow-Word-List Pretest (teaching) session:

Record Basic Information on Test Sheet — After helping your student find a blank Daily Test Sheet in his Student Record Book (or providing him with a copy of the Test Sheet found in the "Teaching Aids and Masters" section), you should tell him the date and the Level and Group number he should record in the spaces provided at the top of the Test Sheet.

Daily Test

Date: ________ Level: ________

Test Words | Words to Learn

State the Group Rule — The Flow-Word-List test should always begin with the "announcement" (or reading) of the spelling rule under consideration for that group of words. The Group Rule is provided at the top of each word list for your convenience. A space is furnished at the top of each Daily Test Sheet for your student to write the generalization. You may wish to write this on the blackboard or to provide your student with a copy of the Group Rule to make it easier for him to write the rule. In rare cases it may be necessary for the teacher to write the generalization for the student. It may not be necessary or desirable for the student to copy the Group Rule every day that a particular group is studied. However, it should always be written the first time the group is studied at each level and it should be announced before adding additional words from any group on subsequent days.

Some of the Group Rules are quite long and younger students should not be expected to copy the whole rule. You may find an abbreviation or summary of the rule more effective; for example, if you are working with a list featuring a phonetic principle, you may wish to write the sound symbol (e.g., /a/) and have your student volunteer words which contain that sound. Together you can record the words he volunteered below the sound symbol.

/A/

cake rain play weigh veil

Note: After the first testing session, the spelling generalization is always announced **after** you have retested any words from the student's last 10-Step-Study Sheet. This is an important point. Some of these retest words will be from lists tested previously or from the student's daily writing and are therefore not related to the Group Rule.

Dictate the Word — You begin the testing of each word by saying the word clearly and naturally. Pronunciation of the word should never be exaggerated. Then use the word in a meaningful sentence. If the word is a homonym, a brief note (in parentheses) often follows the word on the Flow-Word-List so that the meaning is not mistaken (e.g. piece [of cake]). The word is again pronounced clearly. Have your student look at you as you pronounce the word and use it in a sentence.

Note: If the word is a homonym, a brief definition follows the word in parentheses. If the test word has an alternative British spelling, the British spelling is provided in brackets. Words followed by (R) are words reviewed from lower levels. Do not read these notations to your students during the testing process.

Student Repeats the Word — Before your student begins to write the word, he should repeat the word out loud. This gives you the opportunity to check his pronunciation of the word. If he is having a problem pronouncing it properly, help him to correct it now or it will be harder for him to learn to spell the word correctly. This is an important step! Poor pronunciation causes nearly one-third of all spelling errors according to a study conducted by Ves Thomas.[6]

A student who mispronounces words like *dentist* will often write denist. It is not enough for you to pronounce the word correctly, because the student using phonetic clues to spell a word will still pronounce it at least subvocally the way he normally does and spell it the way he hears it in his head. Ideally, this is the best time to teach proper pronunciation as it is less threatening to the student and he can see the immediate value of learning to pronounce the word correctly as an aid to his spelling.

This is an important step! Poor pronunciation causes nearly one-third of all spelling errors.

Furthermore, saying the word aloud helps the student slow down and think about the word which he is about to write. This is what Romalda Spalding eloquently referred to as allowing it to percolate, like water through a coffeepot. "The idea pleases them, and they get the point of thinking first, before acting."[7]

It is advisable to remind your student of the "percolation principle" at the beginning of each testing session. He should also be reminded to think about the phonetic principle or spelling rule featured in the group, to think about the sounds he hears in the word, and to try and visualize the word before he attempts to write it.

Student Writes the Word — After your student has correctly pronounced the word, you will again dictate the word. This time your student will record its spelling under the *Test Words* column of the Daily Test Sheet.

You should remind your student before the testing session begins to use his best penmanship, as words that are not clearly written will be counted as incorrect. This policy eliminates the tendency of some students to write letters such as e and *i* in such a way as to cover up their lack of knowledge. In general, the student should use the style of penmanship with which he is most comfortable. For this reason, it is advisable for the student just learning cursive formations to use manuscript form during testing sessions. This will allow him to concentrate on the spelling of the word instead of the formation.

Student Checks the Spelling — After your student has written the word he should be taught to look at what he has written. This gives him a few seconds to proofread his spelling and to correct any poorly formed letters, before beginning the immediate self-correction process. This procedure helps to build the habit of proofreading his own work.

Immediate Self-correction Test — Immediate self-correction requires you to repeat the word and then spell it letter-by-letter as your student points to each letter with the tip of his pencil. You should observe carefully as your student checks his spelling to discover whether he has carefully checked the word. Extra care should be taken with word groups which deal with proper nouns, abbreviations, hyphens, and apostrophes. Words that should be capitalized, but are not; words that should have apostrophes or other punctuation, but do not; and words without dotted i's and crossed t's should be counted as wrong—because they are.

Spelling the word letter-by-letter should be done with every word, even if it is obvious the word is spelled correctly. Establishing this habit prevents students from trying to make "quick fixes" when you begin to respell the word.

If your student seems to have difficulty in checking his own work, you may find it helpful to write the correct spelling on the chalkboard or chart paper. Then he can use it to visually check the word, as you point to and say each letter.

The self-correction step is an excellent time for you to analyze your student's penmanship. If any word, or part of a word, is written illegibly, it should be counted as misspelled. The study of the word then would concentrate on its proper formation.

The actual correction of any penmanship problems should not be conducted during the testing process or study session, but should be dealt with during a separate session devoted to penmanship. Simply make a note to yourself of any letter forms, joins, or other penmanship skills with which your student needs specific practice. You can use this information to prescribe specific exercises or work with your student to improve on the skill involved.

Cross Out Any Misspelled Words — If your student has misspelled the word, he should be directed to draw a line through it or cross it out. Now you can help him record the correct spelling in the column to the right of the new words column. This column is labeled *Words to Learn*. In this step, you will say the word and then respell it, letter-by-letter, as your student rewrites it. Again, your student may benefit by having a model from which he can work as he writes the word and you dictate.

Repeat the Steps Until the End of the Session — If the word is spelled correctly (or after you record the correct spelling of any misspelled word), you go on to the next word on the Flow-Word-List. Some students are positively motivated by entering a large "C" in the *Words to Learn* column. Students who have had a history of difficulty in learning to spell seem to benefit most from this type of motivation. Whether your student should be directed to do this is left to you to suggest. It is **not** described in the directions at the beginning of the Student Record Book.

The testing session is ended when daily testing-time (generally five minutes) has expired or at the end of a group of words (a new group of words should never be started mid-session). Do not worry if you do not complete an entire word list. You will pick up tomorrow where you left off today, after retesting any words misspelled during this testing session.

Studying Words Using Multisensory Study Methods

> *The best spellers are those who can retain an accurate impression of a word, associate the sound of the word with its visual image, and call up a clear visual, auditory, or kinesthetic image of the word when it is to be written.*[8]

Time should be allowed to study the misspelled words immediately after the testing session. Your student should copy the correct spelling of each word he misspelled during the pretest to the *Words to Learn* column of the 10-Step-Study Sheet (usually this will be the next left-hand page). In addition to transferring misspelled words, he should be encouraged to add to his Study Sheet any word given during the test which he was not really sure of, but spelled correctly.

Most students can do this step independently. However, younger students may need to use a model, especially when transferring to the next page of the book. After all the words have been copied to the 10-Step-Study Sheet and before your student completes the ten study steps, you should check to be certain the words were copied correctly. This is an important step for all students, as the Study Sheet exercises will be of little value if your student studies the incorrect spelling of the word.

The 10-Step-Study Sheets are designed to help your student use the most effective multi-sensory techniques for learning to spell a word. A multi-sensory approach, which incorporates visual, auditory, structural, touch, and movement aspects, is extremely important. The interaction of the multi-sensory impressions helps to reinforce learning. The steps prescribed by the Study Sheets ensure your student has the opportunity to learn using the spelling techniques which have proven to be most effective with all learning styles.

Poorer spellers are likely to need special help and encouragement in using all the steps, but they will use them when they discover that the steps really help them learn to spell. The steps which provide for attempts to recall the correct spelling of a word should be strongly emphasized, since they make learning a more active process.[9]

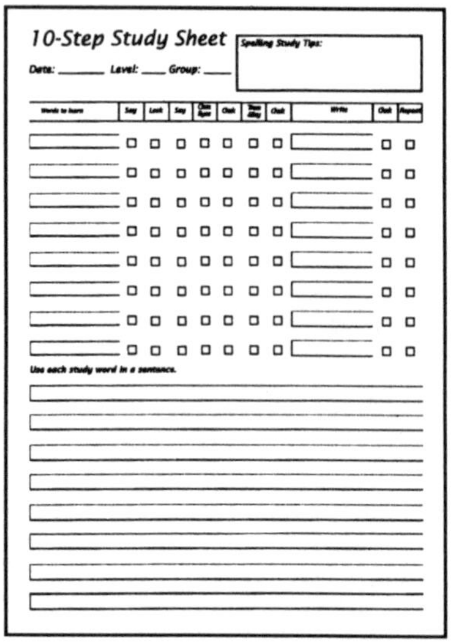

Very few students are able to fix the spelling of a word at a glance; most need to study words according to a planned sequence of steps. It has been found that many students who are told simply to "study the words" do not know how to do so effectively. Poor spellers habitually attack words by trial and error rather than by a specific, methodical study of words. When your student is taught how to study, his retest results are greatly improved. However, it has been also been found that without continued emphasis on the learning steps, he will tend to forget some of the steps of the study procedure. This can cause your student's progress to suffer. The 10-Step-Study Sheets were designed to eliminate this possibility.

When your student fully understands the procedure, the key words at the top of each column of the Study Sheets serve as a reminder of each of the steps. If the step does not require a written response, you should direct your student to place a check mark or X in the column after he has completed the step. The Study Sheet may also serve as a record of study for each word.

It has proven most effective to give a detailed explanation of each step of the study procedure when first introducing the program and, thereafter, at the beginning of each year. It is also advisable to work through the study process step-by-step with each word after the first testing session. In addition, it is helpful to work through the study process step-by-step on the first word of each session until you are certain that your student can work through the steps independently. Moreover, you should occasionally ask your student questions about how he uses the study steps or observe him while he completes the steps to be certain that he continues to use all of the steps to his advantage.

Introducing and Using the 10-Step Study Sheet

At the top of each 10-Step-Study Sheet is a section labeled "Spelling Study Tips." This section is available for you to write a short note to your student on ways he can make his spelling study more effective. Notes might include "Try doing your tracing on the flash card model today," "Remember to watch the way you form your ie and ei joins," and so forth. It is not necessary to use this section every day, but your student should be told to look at this section each day and watch for messages. Speaking of messages, some days it may be nice to simply say "Keep up the good work!"

1. Say the Word — In this step, your student should practice saying the word correctly and carefully. That does not mean that he should draw it out in an exaggerated pronunciation, but that he should try to say it at normal speaking speed in the proper way. This is especially important with words which have received special attention focused on their pronunciation during the testing session. Your student should always say the words quietly aloud, so he can hear himself as he says them.

2. Look at the Parts — You should not expect your student to automatically know how to look at the words to his best advantage. Most students need to be taught how to do this. This is evidenced by the fact that most spelling mistakes are made in the middle of words, which tend to be overlooked during the reading process. Experts note that the reader usually becomes conscious first of the letters at beginning and ends of words, and often may never need to note the letters in the middle.

Gates[10] suggests that a student be taught to ask himself the following questions when studying spelling words:

Can I write the word the way it sounds?
How many syllables are there?
What is the vowel in each syllable?
Are there any double letters?
Are the double letters vowels?
How many letters does the word contain?
To what class of words does this word belong? (noun, verb, etc.)
Are there any odd syllables?
Are there any word parts which are spelled unlike their sound?
Are there any silent letters?
Is there any special peculiarity of the whole word?
Are there any difficult letter combinations?
Are there any smaller words within the word?

By teaching your student what to look for when concentrating on a word he wishes to learn, you can help him to form a strong visual image of the word. Clear visual image of words is necessary for all students if they are to become effective proofreaders of their own writing. It may take many practice sessions (with you asking your student questions about the words) for your student to develop the habit of looking at and asking questions about words on his own.

If you feel your student is particularly weak in visualization skills, you may wish to prescribe a number of the formal exercises over a period of time to help your student with this step. Many helpful exercises and suggestions are described under Discovery Activities Section. Two helpful techniques which you can use during the study sessions are Masking and Boxing.

Masking requires you to cut a small window (the size of one line on the study sheet) into a sheet of lightweight cardboard. The student can then center this over the word under consideration, thereby only exposing the individual word. This will allow the student to completely isolate the word. He can also use it to cover and uncover the word, each time trying to imagine it is still there. The length of time the word is covered should gradually be increased.

Boxing is a configuration exercise. The student draws a box around the word, outlining its configuration. This will help him to recall the general shape of the word and whether his attempts to spell it look right. Another form of this exercise requires your student to outline the individual letters of the word. This procedure forces the student to really focus on each individual letter. (A sample configuration exercise "Configuration Words" is shown on page 275.)

3. Say the Letters — In this step, your student should pronounce the word and say the letters while looking at the word carefully. This should be done quietly but orally, for it is not an "auditory" exercise if your student cannot hear himself say the word.

4. Close Eyes and Spell — With eyes closed, your student should try to visualize and spell the word. Visualizing words, with eyes closed, does not come naturally for many students. Some may never acquire the skill. Others may be helped to learn to visualize the word by quickly covering and uncovering the word as described in the Masking procedure above. Other visualization exercises are found in Chapter Four and the Discovery Activities section of this manual.

5. Check — Immediately after step four, your student should check the original in the *Words To Learn* column to see if he has spelled or visualized the word correctly. This step is subjective since the student has not actually written the word. The idea is that it requires him to look at the correct spelling of the word again. Remember, really looking at a word and how it is spelled will not only help the student learn its spelling, but it will also help him become a better proofreader.

6. Trace and Say — While the tracing exercises have proven to be effective with normal students of all ages and all learning styles, they are especially valuable for the tactile and kinesthetic learner. Moreover, for many students with spelling or specific language disabilities, tracing exercises are essential. When used with handwriting models, they have also proven to be a great aid to those who have handwriting difficulties.

The tracing procedure requires your student to first say the word, then the letter names as he traces each letter using his index and middle finger in contact with a surface. Your student should always say and spell the words quietly aloud (so he can hear himself) as he completes the tracing exercise. It is essential that this tracing be done with large movements so as to make a definite kinesthetic image of the word as it is traced. Simply writing the word is not enough, since the handwriting of most writers tends to involve only the hand. Likewise, tracing should never be done in the air as some methods prescribe. To be most effective, the tracing fingers should be in contact with a solid surface.

The more texture to the surface (e.g., sand, sandpaper, etc.) your student works with, the better. In this way, a vivid tactile impression is added to the kinesthetic impression, which creates an even stronger neural impression. You may wish to give your student a box filled with about an inch of sand, cornmeal, rice, or baby cereal in which to complete the tracing exercises. The advantage of using the "sand box" is that your student will get the added advantage of a visual image of the word in the "sand." This visual image also makes it possible to check his work.

If your students are older or you have a whole classroom of students with which to work, you may want a more convenient surface. There are several excellent choices. First, the top of the desk is probably the most convenient. If you want to add a little more texture, a piece of fabric can make an interesting, yet convenient, surface. Select a fabric such as velvet, satin, corduroy, or burlap, that appeals to your student. (Classroom teachers may want to have several options available.) A one-third yard strip of fabric is perfect (12"x45-54"). If you have time and feel it is beneficial for your student, you may wish to stitch penmanship lines in the fabric. These strips can be easily rolled up for storage.

Another excellent tracing surface can be made using a strip of stair-step tread (available at hardware stores) and a large strip of tag or mat board. Stair-step tread is a bumpy, sometimes luminous, material used to keep people from slipping on stairs. It comes in several textures; smooth bumps and gritty like sandpaper. Usually it is available for just a few cents per yard. One yard should be ample for one "stair step" board.

If your student needs to work on his penmanship skills, you may wish to make him a flash card board. To make this board, you will need a piece of tagboard, several report cover sliders, and large "flash card" letters. You will need several copies of each consonant, and about twice as many of each vowel. It is also a good idea to have a set of capital letters. You want these letters to be large; remember you want your student to use his whole arm in tracing. The *Portland State University Italic Handwriting* Wall Charts are the ideal size. To assemble the board, glue the report cover sliders just far enough apart to accommodate the flash card letters. The open ends of the sliders should be facing one another. (See illustration on page 43). This board and letter set will allow your student to insert each letter (in order) of his study words, then trace the outline of the letters.

Another way to provide a model for students who need penmanship improvement is for you to write the word very large on a blackboard or white board. The student then can erase the letters with his fingers as he traces over it. If you purchase a large 4'x8' sheet of melamine board and have the hardware store cut it into one-foot by 31-inch sections, you will have 12 small white boards. Having a number of these will allow you to make models for each of your student's study words. You are then free to pursue other activities while the student studies the word(s).

If the student is using a flash card model, he should first trace the model and then try it without the model on the desk surface or in the sand tray. Some students may need to trace the word several times.

In many cases, the student will receive a stronger impression by looking away while tracing the word on the desk surface. The teacher may wish to guide his hand as he traces the model with his head averted. These techniques help him to focus attention upon feeling the form of the letters as he follows them with his hand.

Once you have selected your tactile surface, stick to it. While you will want to provide your student with an interesting and enjoyable surface on which to work, during the study sessions you should keep experimenting to a minimum. You want to follow a pretty static system and keep the focus on the words, not every changing procedure.

If your student particularly enjoys or benefits from this tactile and kinesthetic work, he will enjoy many of the Drill Activities in the Activity Task Card sets and Discovery Activities in this manual. Some of these include wild and messy activities such as tracing the words in shaving cream and finger paint. These can be completed during the Skill Building portion of the daily sessions.

Note: Some educators have advocated having students contort their body into "the shape of the letters" as they spell the word. This practice, while fun for young children, is of little value for spelling. The purpose of the kinesthetic exercises is for the student to get a mental "feel" of the way the word is written.

7. Check — Immediately after this tracing step, your student should check to see if he traced it accurately. As before, this step will be subjective unless he completed the work in a "sand box." Nonetheless, it is important that your student always go back to the model in the *Words To Learn* Column. An additional auditory step can be added by having your student say each letter aloud as he checks his spelling.

8. Write the Word — You should direct your student to wait to attempt this step until he is sure of every part of the word. He should cover the model and write it in the space provided. Furthermore, he should be encouraged to use his best handwriting, as this will build the habit of forming each part of the word legibly.

Schonell stresses the large part that the grapho-motor act plays in learning to spell and in spelling correctly. Writing out the words aids visualization, helps to control attention, and serves to bridge the gap between visual and auditory impressions of words. By writing the word, the pupil gets accustomed to feeling the correct spelling.[11]

9. Check — Immediately after writing the word it should be checked letter-by-letter against the model in the *Words To Learn* column.

10. Repeat — If the word is misspelled in step eight, the student should repeat steps one through nine on an unused line of the Study Sheet. The entire procedure should be repeated until a word has been spelled correctly during the writing step.

For some students, even when a word has been spelled correctly during the first try, it may be desirable to repeat the procedure immediately to reinforce learning. If you feel your student would benefit from going through the steps twice in every study session, you should instruct him to skip a line between each word when he is copying them from the *Words To Learn* column of the Test Sheet. This will give two lines on which to study each word.

Write a Sentence Using Study Word

Spaces are provided in the section at the lower half of the Study Sheet for this step. The purpose of the sentence writing step is to aid transfer of the spelling word to your student's daily writing. Therefore, it is to the greatest advantage to have your student compose his own sentence. As a further aid to transfer, the student should be encouraged to try writing the word from memory in a sentence sometime later in the day.

According to a number of experts, the student who completes this step or other meaningful writing exercise (such as found in the Discovery Activities), which requires him to use the words in a meaningful sentence, transfers up to five times as many spelling words into his daily writing than students who do not do such writing activities. Since moving words into daily writing is one of the main goals of *Spelling Power*, all students should complete this step to assure maximum transfer.

You may find your student benefits from doing the first nine steps for all his study words, then completing step ten. This approach has a number of advantages. First, if you have a student who consistently dawdles, it will allow you to have him use the tenth step as "homework." This threat preserves the integrity of the five minutes and works remarkably well at promoting expeditious work. Second, many older students really enjoy the challenge of trying to write one sentence that uses all of their study words. This is fine - the important thing is that the sentences are the student's own creation. (If sent home as homework it will be important to inform the parent of this fact.)

Another reason you may want to have your student complete step ten with all his words together is if you need to help write his sentences. Students who have limited spelling vocabulary should be helped to record their sentences. The process used to help him is called Intermediate Double Dictation. In this procedure the student will dictate the sentence and you will write it down. He will then copy "his sentence" to the study sheet. This will allow him to write sentences at his vocabulary level, but prevents him from misspelling any words during the process.

Skill Building Activities

Your student should spend the final five minutes of the daily spelling session participating in a skill-building activity. These can take many forms. You may select activities from the optional Activity Task Card box, the discovery activities described in this manual, or from outside the program. In Chapter Four and the Discovery Activities section you are provided with all the details you need to prescribe appropriate activities for your student.

Checking Retention of Spelling Words

All of the words which your student has studied since the last testing session (on the Study Sheet) should be retested at the beginning of your next test session. Your student should not study or look over these words just before the retest! The purpose of this retest is to determine if he has remembered how to spell the word. Studying immediately before the retest would hide any lack of retention.

Retesting procedures are exactly the same as those used during regular Flow-Word-List pretests (see above). The retest should be written on the Daily Test Sheet opposite the 10-Step-Study Sheet. Sitting next to your student, you can insert a blank sheet of paper between the Test Sheet and the Study Sheet (see illustration) to obscure his view of the words.

This saves you from having to keep a separate list of words to retest. The Study Sheet serves as the record for you.

If your student misspells a retest word, he will be required to study it again on the 10-Step-Study sheet. In this way, every word will be retested until it is spelled correctly at least once. You should make a quick mental note of how many words your student will be required to restudy as a result of the retesting. It may affect the number of new words you will want to pretest as was explained earlier. If you determine that your student is ready to add more Flow-Word-List words, you may begin pretesting where you left off yesterday (after the last word tested). How many new words you will pretest is generally determined by the available time. For example, if retesting requires three minutes, after the spelling rule is announced, only two minutes of new words are added.

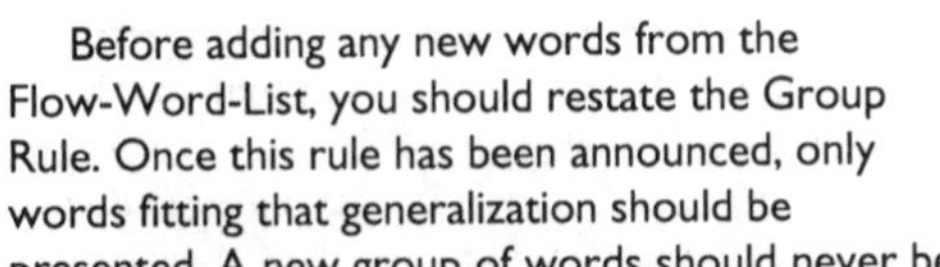

Before adding any new words from the Flow-Word-List, you should restate the Group Rule. Once this rule has been announced, only words fitting that generalization should be presented. A new group of words should never be begun mid-session.

Daily pretesting and/or retesting, 10-Step-Study, and skill-building sessions proceed in this manner until your student has completed all the groups and Review Tests up to the next Delayed Recall Test or End-of-Level Test. (Review tests are handled just like a daily test, except that they have no Group Rule associated with them.)

Evaluating Long-term Retention

Delayed recall has long been recognized and employed as an effective method of measuring learning retention. The *Spelling Power* program utilizes this "spiral" curriculum technique to determine the extent of retention and to recycle students through the groups of words where a lack of retention is evident. (This procedure also discourages any student who might be tempted to rush through a level without thoroughly learning all the words. It takes only one experience of going back over groups for the student to learn that "haste makes waste.")

There are a total of six levels of built-in review in the *Spelling Power* program. The first level is the retesting of every word until it is spelled correctly at least once. This is followed by Review Tests (approximately every five groups), two Delayed Recall Tests, and one End-of-Level Test. Frequently misspelled words are also reviewed at higher levels. Finally, the sixth level of review pulls misspelled words from the student's daily writing back into the program.

The Review Tests are conducted in the same manner as a regular Flow-Word-List Test. The Review Tests words are taken from a sampling of words from the **five** groups preceding it. The two Delayed Recall Tests retest selected words from groups presented in either the first half or the last half of the Level. The End-of-Level Test retests selected words from the entire level.

Delayed Recall and End-of-Level Tests are administered in a slightly different fashion than standard Group Tests.

The student should have spelled correctly each word on the last retest session before taking a Delayed Recall or End-of-Level Test. Special test pages have been provided in the back of the Student Record Book for the Delayed Recall and End-of-Level Tests. (Review Tests are taken on the regular test pages.) There are two forms of the Delayed Recall and End-of-Level Tests (Form A and Form B). The forms are of equal difficulty. Initially only one form of each test is given, generally Form A. These tests are given in almost the same manner as regular Flow-Word-List tests. The only difference is that the self-correction process is eliminated and the entire test is administered in one session. These tests are always scored by the teacher. Each word presented in the test is followed by a numeral, which indicates the group number in which the word appeared at this level. These numbers should not be read to your student during the test session. You will use them later when you are evaluating your student's progress.

To "pass," the student should score 100 percent on each of these tests. If the student misspells any word on one of these tests, the teacher will instruct him to restudy the rule in which it was first presented at this level (as indicated by the numeral following the word). This study should ideally be more direct and concentrated. You will find many useful tips for devising these lessons in Chapter Four.

Sometimes the student's retention problems are caused because he does not use the study steps effectively. You will learn much by observing the student using the Study Sheet to see if this is the cause of the problem. If this is the case, help him correct any errors he makes during the procedure. In some cases, he simply requires more work with each word. You may wish to instruct him to study each word twice as described in the "study procedures" and/or to reduce the number of words he studies each day.

Once your student has restudied the spelling principle involved, he should be retested on the entire word list. After the student has restudied each of the groups he was assigned, he should take the alternate form of the Delayed Recall or End-of-Level test, generally Form B.

If your student again misspells a word, you must decide whether he should proceed to the next group or level. When doing this, it is important to take into consideration both the student's need for mastery and his need for motivation.

How to determine if he should go to the next level

When your student has scored 100 percent on the End-of-Level Test, he may proceed to the first group of words on the next level, if it is not the end of the school year. Because the word groups are not related to traditional grade levels and because the program is designed to allow your student to progress as fast and far as he is able, if he completes a level he should not assume that no additional spelling is needed for the remainder of the school year. Your student should study spelling every day of the school year.

Likewise, not completing the level by the end of the school year should not be seen as poor progress. The goal of the program is mastery of every word studied! It is also important to remember that the Flow-Word-Lists are not the only source of words learned and that many additional words will have been learned through incidental and Integrated Functional Writing activities.

Recording Spelling Study Progress

The most important sources of interest and other desirable attitudes is the child's awareness of progress or success.[12]

You may use a variety of techniques to keep you and your student informed of his progress. The important aspect here is not the record keeping itself but the appropriate use of such information. The model record keeping presented here is intended to serve as just one method which you may find helpful. The major emphasis of any record keeping system should be to keep your student informed of his current progress in relationship to his past performance and to help you plan future instruction.

You should begin each year with the *Spelling Power* Survey Test and the Placement Test process, as your student will have learned many words and skills during the year through the Integrated Functional Spelling Study, the prescribed lessons and activities, and incidentally through his reading, composition, and content area instruction. What's more, students sometimes lose many skills over the traditional summer vacation months. Administration of these tests at the beginning of each year provides an opportunity to recycle your student over materials he has failed to retain from the previous year and gives a beginning benchmark for progress evaluation.

Once your student's placement level has been established, it should be recorded in the appropriate column, next to his name, on the Teacher's Record Sheet. A master for this form is found in the "Teaching Aids and Masters" section. As each student progresses through each group, Review Test, Delayed Recall Test, or End-of-Level Test and onto higher levels, you are able to track his progress and his assigned level. Such information is useful in planning group instruction as well.

When your student has completed the whole group of words, and after he has studied and been retested on each misspelled word for that group, he should place a dot in the center of the appropriate box on his Student Progress Chart.

When taking a Delayed Recall Test, have your student write the date in the box for the appropriate form taken. After scoring the Delayed Recall Test, you should place a slash diagonally across each box that does not need to be retested. Any remaining boxes which he needs to restudy will then be easily visible to both of you.

Group 5	●										
Group 6	●										
Group 7											
Group 8											
Group 12											

When each group has been restudied, your student will take the alternate form of the Delayed Recall Test. After this test, you can place a slash in the boxes which were retested and that do not need to be restudied. If a group must be retested a third time, the slash is placed in the box after the group has been successfully retested.

Recording the progress on End-of-Level Tests is done in similar fashion to the Delayed Recall Test, only a slash is drawn in the opposite direction. This will create an X in each group's box that does not need to be restudied or after the group has been restudied.

Delayed Recall 1 Form A	[illegible]	[illegible]									
Delayed Recall 1 Form B		Feb 13									
Group 14											
Group 15											
Group 16	●										
Group 17	●										
Group 18											

When both the Teacher's Record and the Student's Progress Chart are thus maintained, they provide you with an instant view of where each student is in the *Spelling Power* Program.

Summary of Systematic Spelling Study

> *In almost all learning researches, a second learning session goes better than the first, and the third still better. This is owed to the "practice effect." The practice effect may also contain or hide a "warm-up effect" that will help out the later learning assignment. People do become better and better at learning successive assignments if these assignments are of more or less the same form. And if the content does not contain interfering material.*[13]

You may be concerned by the apparent rigid style of these procedures; however, while they are set and systematic, they are in no way rigid. A number of suggestions have been made for possible adjustments to meet individual needs for many of the procedures in this chapter. Having set procedures for each step of Flow-Word-List testing and study sessions simplifies the process. What you and your student say and do remains the same for each list and from day to day. Once the basic format is learned, handling subsequent lists is relatively easy and requires little or no preparation time. The set procedures also help your student concentrate and focus on the words being presented, as the words themselves are the only variant. The result is not a routine performance but a vigorous, aggressive attack by each pupil in learning the words he needs to learn.

References for Chapter Two

1 Fred C. Ayer, "An Evaluation of High School Spelling," *School Review* 59, April 1951, p. 236.

2 Anna Gillingham and Bessie W. Stillman, *Remedial Training for Children with Specific Disability in Reading, Spelling, and Penmanship*, 5th ed. (Cambridge, MA: Educators Publishing Service, Inc., 1964).

3 Elizabeth Krepelin, 1996 Prentice Hall, New York, The Center For Applied Research in Education.

4 Gertrude Hildreth, *Learning the 3 R's* (Minneapolis, MN: Cumberland Education Series, Educational Publishers, Inc., 1947).

5 B. R. Bugelski, *The Psychology of Learning Applied to Teaching*, 2nd ed., (Indianapolis, IN: The Bobbs-Merrill Company, Inc., 1964).

6 Ves Thomas, "A Spelling Errors Analysis and an Appraisal of Its Usefulness in Improving the Spelling of Selected Alberta Students" (unpublished doctoral dissertation, University of Oregon), 1966.

7 Romalda Bishop Spalding and Walter T. Spalding, *The Writing Road to Reading* (New York: Quill/William Morrow, 1957).

8 Gertrude Hildreth, *Learning the 3 R's.*

9 Richard E. Hodges and E. Hugh Rudof, *Searching Linguistics for Cues for the Teaching of Spelling.*

10 Arthur I. Gates and D. H. Russell, *Diagnostic and Remedial Spelling Manual* (New York: Bureau of Publications, Teacher's College, Columbia University, 1940).

11 Fred J. Schonell, *The Essential Spelling List: 3200 Everyday Words Selected, Graded and Grouped According to Common Difficulty* (London: Macmillan & Co., 1932).

12 Mary Ann Nelson, *Spelling Guide for Grades 1 to 6* (Tacoma, WA: Tacoma Public Schools, 1964).

13 B. R. Bugelski, *The Psychology of Learning Applied to Teaching*, page 256.

Chapter Three
Integrated Functional Writing

> *Skills cannot be acquired in a vacuum. They must be practiced in the very study of the three basic areas of subject matter, as well as in the process of acquiring linguistic competence, competence in communication, competence in the handling of symbolic devices, and competence in critical thinking.*[1]

The research reported in Chapter One makes two things very obvious: while learning a "basic core" of frequently used words is a good beginning, to become a competent speller a person must know how to discover the words (beyond the core) he needs to know, and he needs to know what to do when faced with a word he does not know how to spell. These two essential skills are the most often neglected in the traditional approaches to spelling instruction. *Spelling Power* utilizes a system of Integrated Functional Writing to teach the important skills of proofreading to students. (How to teach dictionary skills is covered in Chapter Five.)

Integrated Functional Writing is the process used to integrate your spelling instruction with the rest of your curriculum, especially your Grammar and Composition program. In a nutshell, it means you will teach your student an efficient method of proofreading his written work. In this proofreading process he will undoubtedly find at least a few spelling errors. Grammar and punctuation errors and other weaknesses with written expression will also be uncovered. You will help your student to find and correct these errors using an approach referred to as "coaching."

The integration with the *Spelling Power* program occurs when you select a few of his misspelled words to study. The Alphabetical Word List, found in the fourth section of the manual, will help you choose these words. Your student will study these words on a 10-Step-Study Sheet, automatically recycling the words into the *Spelling Power* program. This method of pulling words back into the program from daily writing comprises the sixth level of built-in review of the *Spelling Power* program and will be described in detail in this chapter.

Integrated Functional Writing incorporates many skills beyond the scope of the traditional spelling program. Its main component is writing, using words to communicate, and learning effective proofreading, revising, and editing skills. These skills are best taught in conjunction with real situations such as the writing of material for publication and display, letter writing, and other uses in or beyond the classroom. Experts agree you need to provide your student with many opportunities to write for a variety of purposes, if he is to become a competent writer. Studies have proven, over and over again, that the more your student writes, the more he will learn. Writing, in schooling, is more than just a communication skill; it is a "thinking tool." Purposeful writing unlocks your student's thinking about spelling, grammar, language mechanics, and content subject matter by engaging him in the process of writing.

What's more, the positive motivational value of writing to the spelling curriculum is immense. When spelling is taught as an isolated subject—as just one in a series of subjects—the student often does not make the connection of why he is being asked to learn the words presented.

The goal of the Integrated Functional Writing aspects of the program is for your student to develop an attitude of self-evaluation. You will give him a careful, individualized course in self-correction or proofreading. He is not forced to patiently wait for you to indicate his errors; rather, he is being trained in what he most needs, namely to detect them for himself. The independence achieved by acquiring these skills is a boost to your student's self-esteem.

To facilitate the learning that takes place in the Integrated Functional Writing program, the teaching method which Mortimer J. Adler refers to (in *The Paideia Program*) as "coaching" is used. In these sessions your role is something akin to the coach of an athletic team.

> *A coach does not teach simply by telling or giving the learner a rule book to follow. A coach trains by helping the learner to do, to go through the right motions, and to organize a sequence of acts in a correct fashion. He corrects faulty performance again and again and insists on repetition of the performance until it achieves a measure of perfection.*[2]

In essence, it is a kind of spontaneous individual tutoring, a lively conversation about your student's skills. Using an artful blend of information ("Remember to use . . ."), challenge ("Why is this . . ."), drill ("Here's another one . . ."), and encouragement ("Right! . . ."), you help your student to master skills under consideration and to develop the habit of using the right steps and procedures involved in the operations.

The concept of coaching, as a vital method of instruction, is introduced here only in the briefest way. Coaching by nature is a complicated set of skills and attitudes. Some teachers come to it more naturally than others. While the attitudes must come from within, all can be taught the necessary skills. If you would like more information on effective coaching techniques than is presented in this manual, *The Paideia Program* is an excellent resource.

Applying Coaching to Integrated Functional Writing

> *The best coaching, whoever does it—teachers, parents, grandparents, siblings, other students—is done by people who are more concerned with helping a child understand what he reads and hears, to say what he wants to say, and to write what he wants to write, than with correcting every error.*[3]

Coaching is used to help your student analyze his own writing for spelling, mechanical, grammatical, and syntactical errors. To be effective, it cannot be limited to a specific time of the day. Coaching should be used whenever the opportunity arises. It takes advantage of those serendipitous "teachable moments." With this background, it is important to note that time for coaching must also be planned and allowed for in the schedule. A one-on-one, language arts coaching session should be scheduled on a regular basis (at least once each week) for each of your students. These sessions are designed to establish thinking as part of the writing process and revision as a normal sequence in writing.

Through coaching, your student is taught the "Check, C.A.T.C.H. and Correct" system, a systematic method of proofreading, revising, and editing, and establishes the habit of using it.

Check, C.A.T.C.H. and Correct is a mnemonic device that has proven helpful in reminding the student of the most effective ways to attack the proofreading and revising process. Each letter in the mnemonic "C.A.T.C.H" stands for one of the five aspects of proofreading a composition, letter, or report: "C" refers to **content**, and asks the student "Does it say everything that I need or want to say?" "A" reminds the student to **analyze** the structure and style of his sentences, paragraphs, etc. "T" indicates the student should check for the **technicalities** of mechanics and punctuation. "C" asks the student to check for **correct** spelling. And "H" encourages the student to evaluate the quality of his **handwriting** and to make sure he has used the proper **headings** or format for his paper.

The goal of the Check, C.A.T.C.H. and Correct system is to help your student learn to be his own proofreader. To facilitate this, you generally should never mark, correct, or write anything on his paper. Your job as coach is to help your student, not to do his work. You can help best by asking "probing questions" so that your student discovers the error(s) for himself. Over a period of time, he will develop the habit of asking himself the same type of questions. It is no favor to your student to allow him to become dependent on someone else to find his errors. He learns far more by simply being "helped to do it himself."4

Writing Power, a sequel to Spelling Power, expands on this concept and also provides information on composition projects, scope and sequence, and information on evaluating student writing.

The Check, C.A.T.C.H. and Correct system will be explained in more detail as each step of the implementation is explained. However, those steps not directly related to the spelling program will be discussed only in a brief way. It is not the function of this manual to provide detailed descriptions of grammar and composition skills. You will be given just enough information needed to adapt the coaching concept to his regular curriculum.

Introducing Integrated Functional Writing

Before implementing Integrated Functional Writing and coaching sessions with your student, you should briefly explain the program. At this point, you can explain that you believe you have found the best method for helping him to improve his writing. You should explain that research (as well as common sense) has proven that the best way to become a better writer (and a better speller) is to write.

Students will understand this concept more fully when you compare writing to a favorite sport or hobby. "If you want to become an expert tennis player, you practice and play lots of tennis. You may even take lessons or hire a tennis coach." You can then go on to explain that this is also true of writing, and that you will be his "writing coach" by working with him on a regular basis (indicate a specific schedule if one is planned) to improve actual samples of his writing. Explain to him that during these sessions he will learn how to check, catch, and correct his own mistakes. He should be further assured that, in addition to these regular sessions, you will work with him on writing anytime he wishes or feels the need for it.

Ask your student to bring his own sample writing to each of the coaching sessions. He can work on any writing he chooses; it doesn't have to be written for the session or even his regular school work. However, it does have to be writing that he sincerely wants to improve. There is a distinct advantage to having the writing analyzed in the coaching session be for a real purpose or writing that your student cares about and wants to share. Writing which is intended primarily to satisfy you, the teacher, seldom generates the interest necessary to produce the kind of thoughtful, careful writing that coaching sessions are intended to encourage. The writing of letters to be mailed, bulletins to be posted, and other forms of creative writing to be published, constitute important motives for learning to communicate effectively which, of course, includes spelling accurately.

The insecure writer should be told to write the best he knows how. The idea is to keep his ideas flowing. He may need to be frequently reassured that he is not expected to produce a perfect example of writing on his first try (or draft). It may even be pointed out to him that, in fact, if he were expected to produce perfect writing, there would be no reason to schedule coaching sessions. You should also remind him that he will be helped to put his writing into shape during each session. Let him know that normal writing requires many drafts or "rewrites" before it is perfect or sometimes even acceptable.

Many students are under the mistaken impression that a writer just sits down and writes his book or article—from the beginning to the end—without an error or revision of any kind. This illusion, frequently portrayed in the mass media, makes writing an overwhelming and frightening proposition to the inexperienced writer. It may be helpful for your student to interview an author or have one visit as a guest speaker. When an outside "expert" explains the importance of proofreading, editing, and revising work, students tend to find new respect for the processes they are learning.

The idea of working directly with you on his writing or the simple thought of writing can be very intimidating to some students. An insecure student may need extra reassurance that you will be guiding him step-by-step, coaching him in the art of writing. Similarly, he should be assured that the goal of the program is to establish the habit of checking and correcting his own work. Your student should also understand how work done related to Integrated Functional Writing exercises will be graded, if it is to be graded at all. Later in this chapter is a discussion and description of various grading options that you should review and make decisions about before beginning the program.

Students with a Limited Spelling Vocabulary

The student with a limited spelling vocabulary often feels intimidated or discouraged in writing by his lack of spelling ability. He often feels that he must stop his work to look up a word or ask for its spelling, which interrupts his thought processes and makes writing a chore. Such a student can be encouraged to try to think of all the words he may use in writing this piece/story/report and look them up or dictate them for the teacher to write out in list form. He can then have the list ready to copy as he writes.

The student can also be encouraged to underline words which he is unsure of the spelling or to write only the beginning of the word (as a clue) followed by a line. This is a signal that help is needed in spelling that word: either by consulting a dictionary, thesaurus, or word bank or by asking the teacher. The amount of direct assistance given should depend on the difficulty of the word and the expectations for the individual student.

Conducting a C.A.T.C.H. Coaching Session

> *We have little information about children's judgments of their own spellings. How many misspellings are let stand because a child gives up on them rather than because he believes they are correct? How many are let stand because he knows the teacher will correct them? If children were not in effect relieved of correcting responsibilities by their teacher's red pencils, we might better distinguish errors committed in ignorance from those committed inattentively, and thus focus instruction appropriately.*[5]

When your student arrives at the first coaching session with paper in hand, you should remind him that he was promised he would be shown a system designed to help him "Check, Catch, and Correct" his writing mistakes. The Check, C.A.T.C.H. and Correct chart, included in the "Teaching Aids and Masters" section, is helpful in introducing the C.A.T.C.H. mnemonic. (See illustration on next page.) Briefly explain each of the steps in language the child can understand. The Check, C.A.T.C.H. and Correct chart may be copied from this book and posted on the wall, in a visible place, for later reference by your student. Furthermore, you should explain that together you will work through each of these steps with each composition until he is comfortable working through them on his own.

At this time, you may also want to show your student the "Symbols for Proofreading" chart. This chart, also included in the Teaching Aids and Masters section, illustrates each of the standard proofreading symbols. All students at sixth grade (about age 12) and above should be taught to use these or equivalent symbols. When working with younger students, you will want to gradually introduce the symbols. It is important to only teach the proofreading symbols as they are needed. There is very little value in teaching them in an artificial setting.

Coaching for Clear Content

The first step to the Check, C.A.T.C.H. and Correct method is judging if the content is clearly stated. This begins with and should be aided by your student reading aloud (in a quiet but audible voice) what he has written. Mistakes and weak spots that pass unnoticed in silent reading will strike—and shock—his ear. Many glaring errors are caught just by his reading his writing aloud. He should be instructed to add any missing words or correct any obvious errors to his paper as he discovers them.

Check

C.A.T.C.H.

C. = Does it clearly communicate?

A. = Have I analyzed the structure?

T. = Have I checked all the technicalities?

C. = Are all the words correctly spelled?

H. = Have I used my best handwriting and used the proper headings?

and

Correct

You should begin each coaching session with a positive comment. At this point, comments should all be content related—his message is what is important. There is always something positive you can comment on. It is important to note, however, that your comments must be sincere. Students, both young and old, have a strong sense for insincere comments. They tend to lose respect for those who give them. "If you sincerely cannot think of anything positive to say—don't say anything" is good advice in such situations.

Now the actual coaching begins by your asking your student probing questions about the content of his writing. Ask questions such as, "Does it sound right to you?" "Does it say what you intended to say?" and "Does it tell everything the reader needs to know?"

Other coaching questions that invite your student to clarify what he is saying should be asked. With less mature writers, these "questions" will often be in an effort to get them to provide more detail. With more mature writers, it is often the case that you must get him to simplify his message. It is not unusual for a student to use complex terminology or phrases inappropriately in an effort to impress his readers. When this occurs, the student should be reminded that his goal is to clearly communicate his message.

By being encouraged to put himself in his reader's place your student will see why more detail must be added to his composition. Your student may need to be reminded that the reader, in many cases, does not know unless he is told. Demonstrate the difference his "audience" makes. Discuss with him how many more details he would need to explain if he were writing to a new pen pal about a family event than if he were writing to his grandmother about the same event. Another example that older students seem to understand and enjoy is the doctor writing about heart surgery; what he says and how he says it to other doctors will be much different than what he says to one of his patients.

A copy of the Check, C.A.T.C.H. and Correct Chart and the Proofreading Symbols chart is included with each Student Record Book

Usually, revision for content requires your student to completely rewrite the paper (draft). Some students, especially younger ones, enjoy knowing that professional journalists and writers call this a "rewrite." Encourage your student to ask himself the same types of questions you have asked him during the coaching session—to "coach himself" in a sense—whenever he writes. Rewriting should be done immediately following the coaching session, while the ideas and suggestions are fresh in his head.

Sometimes it may be necessary for this step to be repeated many times before moving on to the next step. The number of "rewrites" for content that are needed or advised will vary with the type or importance of the composition (i.e. a term paper vs. a personal letter) or, in some cases, the disposition of the student. As your student matures and as you feel he can handle it, this process may be repeated again and again before you ever get to the actual writing mechanics and spelling.

Analyze the Papers for Effective Structure

When the student is happy with the content, he is ready for the next step of the Check, C.A.T.C.H. and Correct process: Analyze Structure. He should read his paper again—not necessarily aloud. Together you will look for structural errors. Among the areas of concern are the general organization of the composition as a whole and paragraph unity and development, clearness and effectiveness of each sentence and grammatical correctness. Analyzing the composition's structure is very similar to analyzing the content; the difference is in the level of detail.

Teach your student to identify sentence fragments and run-on sentences ("What is the verb in this sentence?" "Can you think of a way this long sentence can be made more concise?" and so on). You also show him efficient ways to keep participial phrases, prepositional phrases, and dependent clauses clearly attached to the words they modify. Additionally, this is the time your student should be **helped to discover** any lack of subject/verb agreement and any unnecessary shifts in pronouns.

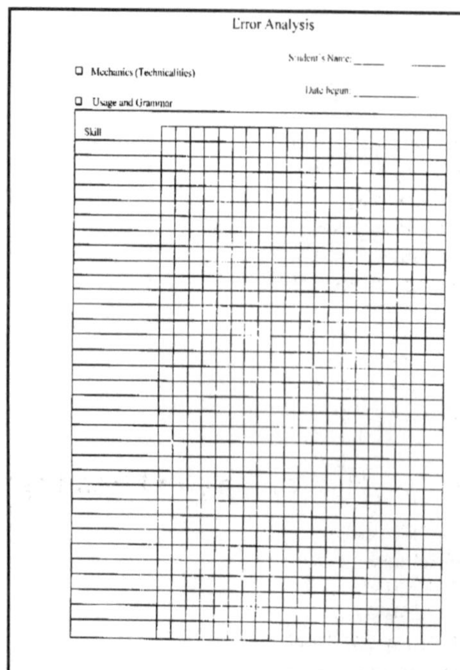
Error Analysis

Student's Name: ______

☐ Mechanics (Technicalities)

Date begun: ______

☐ Usage and Grammar

Skill

In this step, of particular significance to the spelling curriculum is the use of descriptive words, repetition, and so on. These items afford you an excellent opportunity to coach on the efficient use of a thesaurus. ("The word <u>said</u> seems to be used frequently in this story. Let's look up <u>said</u> in the thesaurus to see if we can find other ways to say the same thing.") It is also an excellent time for you to point out the morphographic changes that words undergo when the tense is changed or when the parts of speech are altered: slow/slowly.

The extent these items should be analyzed will depend on the background of your student. However, there should be an increasing emphasis and demand for quality as the student progresses.

Tracking Down Technicalities

Examining the paper for mechanical details is the next step of the Check, C.A.T.C.H. and Correct process. Capitalization and punctuation (commas, end marks, quotation marks, etc.) are the major technicalities that should be checked.

Instruct your student to look at each sentence to make sure that it begins with a capital letter and ends with a proper end mark. ("Is 'Are you coming to my party' a statement or a question?")

The student should be held accountable for any skill that he has been taught in his regular grammar course. A check list of technicalities the student should look for may be helpful. Such a list can easily be made in two ways. First, you can create a list using the scope and sequence chart from the teacher's edition of a grammar text. Or you can have your student make a summary of each skill/rule as he encounters it in his lessons.

This skills check list can also be designed with boxes following each item (see illustration). When you or your student analyze his written work, you can record the number of each type of error he makes or corrects. A quick scan of this chart will quickly show you where a lesson may be needed.

Checking for Correct Spelling

Throughout the coaching session(s) the emphasis has been to help your student "make his meaning clear and easy for the reader to understand." When correct spelling is also presented from this standpoint, its importance has greater meaning for your student. You may have to explain that "people accustomed to reading rapidly get annoyed trying to read our writing when it contains incorrect spellings." This empathy for his reader is what is meant by a spelling conscience.

Encourage your student to try to discover and correct as many spelling errors as he can before coming to each session ("I want you to look at the paper again . . . see if you can find any words that do not look right to you.") He should challenge every word. One trick, which really helps you see each word, is to read the paper backwards. Starting with the last word, read each word to the beginning of the composition. Because most writing will make little sense when read this way, it focuses attention on the word and its spelling.

As he finds questionable words, your student should underline them. He can then refer to a dictionary or to other word resources to determine the correct spelling. This is the most natural and productive time to offer coaching in dictionary skills. It should never be assumed your student will know how to look up words in a dictionary. Each student should be provided with comprehensive instruction in dictionary skills as part of their spelling curriculum. Even older students can and should be taught how to use the dictionary more effectively. A complete description of the dictionary skills that all students should know and sequential suggestions for teaching them are provided in Chapter Five.

In addition to the basic spelling errors, proper use of the apostrophe, the hyphen (especially related to numbers), and syllabication (when a word must be continued on the next line) can be reinforced and taught during these sessions more effectively than at any other time. Additionally, the capitalization of proper nouns and proper use of abbreviations should be considered as spelling problems. Even in the elementary grades, your student should be taught to avoid the use of contractions and to always write out numbers in essays and reports. This is generally the accepted standard for formal writing done in high school, college, and business. It is far easier to develop this good habit in the earlier grades than to break bad habits later.

All words misspelled on the paper(s) should be corrected. Words for Systematic Spelling Study will be selected from these misspelled words. A complete description on how words should be selected for study is offered beginning on page 58 (Selecting Words to be Studied).

Handwriting and Headings

Analysis of handwriting quality should also be a part of every coaching session. Teach your student to ask himself these questions about his own handwriting: "Is it my best?" "Is it readable?" "Is my spacing between letters and between words correct?" and "Is the shape, size, and slope of each letter consistent and properly formed?" You may wish to take the time to remind him of some of the finer points of handwriting ("Look at the third line of your paper. It seems a little hard to read to me . . . When the space between the words is the size of an 'n,' it is much easier to read."). An excellent list of questions which the student should ask himself, listed by grade level, is found in the *Italic Handwriting* Teacher's Manual published by Portland State University.

As stated earlier, penmanship **must** be associated with spelling. If letters are improperly made or if spacing between letters and words is incorrect, it becomes quite impossible to distinguish poor handwriting from poor spelling. In fact, a student may consciously make his letters indistinct in the hopes that his reader will give him the benefit of the doubt and accept the misspelled words.

The policy that any confusion will be counted as a misspelled word should be stated early. While not necessarily considered as a word for study in the spelling program, **it should be pointed out and corrected.** You may want to make a note of instruction in handwriting skills from which your students would benefit.

The second part of this step is **Headings**. Headings, as indicated here, refers to the method the student uses to record his name and date on each paper, as well as the format when applied to business and personal letters, reports and term papers, and other specialty papers. All students should be taught a specific way to label or format their papers and should check that they follow the form.

While coaching handwriting is a part of every session, it may not be desirable or necessary to have your student recopy every paper. It may be possible, depending in part on the type of writing involved, to simply erase and correct serious flaws. Only those papers which are intended for publication need to be perfect.

Putting It All Together

Students should become so completely accustomed to the apt and suggestive process of questioning what they have written that they form the habit of doing it by themselves to themselves the rest of their lives.[6]

In this section, each aspect of the Check, C.A.T.C.H. and Correct process has been discussed as a separate unit. While your student will generally proofread his paper step-by-step using the C.A.T.C.H. mnemonic, teacher and student sessions will seldom be so straightforward. Nor should they necessarily be. Sometimes it may be necessary to work on the same piece of writing during several sessions. It isn't necessary to identify all of the student's mistakes at once, especially with larger pieces of writing or writing done by younger students.

Only you can determine how much detail to push for with your student during each session. You must decide what is improved writing or what is an acceptable standard for him. The depth of this analysis, of course, depends on the skills you have taught your student to date. He should not be expected to work on every paper to perfection, but he should be held accountable for anything that he has been taught in his grammar and composition lessons. Remember, all errors will not disappear in one fell swoop. The goal is the formation of the good habits of revision and thinking through the writing process.

Note: It is important that your student "own" the results of the work sessions. Your role is to lead him to discover how to improve his own paper. Any corrections to the paper itself, or details added to the paper, should be done by your student. Except when working with beginning writers, you should avoid writing on your student's paper. If you need to illustrate a principle, use a separate sheet of paper.

Teaching the Student to be His Own Editor

Children must be guided to recognize the importance of "proof-reading." They must be given time and all the supervision they need to learn to proofread effectively. This habit of proofreading all written work must be firmly established.7

Through the one-on-one coaching sessions described above, your student has been introduced to the concept of revising and editing as a normal sequence of the writing process. Obviously it is unrealistic to coach your student through every school assignment or writing project. It not only is impractical, it is not advisable. He cannot just sit and expect you to tell him or help him to discover all his errors. Your student must learn to take the skills he has learned and apply them on his own. He must take more and more responsibility for "catching and correcting" his own errors.

Graves' observations of Scottish schools[8] show that children, given the responsibility for correcting errors in their own writing, can do so. The student should be given this responsibility and should gradually be taught to grade his own paper before he turns it in to you for grading or before he arrives at a coaching session with it.

You must train your student to proofread his papers to the point that he feels positively guilty if he fails to do it. Just looking back over a paper is not enough. Many mature students would submit much better productions if they had formed this habit.

Repeatedly, we find them handing in manuscripts either without rereading them at all or after a perfunctory glance which failed to reveal even glaring errors. The C.A.T.C.H. mnemonic provides your student with an orderly set of purposes for which he is to reread his papers. Remind him to reread each of his papers a number of times, each time with a different purpose in mind. Proofreaders who are looking for just any error often overlook more than they see.

Whenever possible, papers—especially creative writing papers and major compositions of all sorts—should be set aside for a day or so before they are proofread. Most students tire of their papers as soon as they have finished writing them. Generally, after a day away from his paper, your student will feel more objective about what he has written.

You can quite easily make finding misspelled words and other errors a fun challenge. One way is give points for the number of errors your student "catches" himself and take away points for those you find. For instance, your student could keep a tally of the number of words he has found for himself. When he turns the paper in (or when he joins you for his coaching session) you try to "catch" any that he missed and take away points from him for each you find. One teacher, using this system, gave her students tickets for each point they ended up with. The students could use these tickets to purchase special privileges (extra recess, arts and craft time, etc.) and school supplies (wild pencils, erasers, and such). When schemes such as this are used, it can help your student develop the proofreading "habit" in a positive way.

Establishing "Proxy" Coaching Sessions

You can help your student develop an attitude of self-evaluation using a paper grading scheme that reinforces the Check, C.A.T.C.H. and Correct aspects of revising and editing. This scheme serves as a "proxy-coaching session." Using "proxy-coaching," you let your marks on the paper do the coaching for you.

In the earliest stages of proxy-coaching, as with actual coaching, you may write the correct spelling of a word above the misspelled word and insert missing punctuation for the student to correct. When analyzing content, you may ask specific questions of your student, such as might be asked in a coaching session, on an attached sheet of paper.

You may find it more acceptable to record misspelled words on a separate sheet of paper rather than to write on your student's paper. Your student must then locate them on his paper and correct them. This requires greater skill in visual discrimination; therefore, it is generally the next step in training your student to proofread his own work.

Training should proceed so that very soon the fact that there is an error is merely indicated by the appropriate proofreading symbol placed above it (see proofreading symbol chart). When an error is thus indicated, your student must think out or look up the correct form, a step in advance of being told. Even this is but preliminary to genuine discovery of error. If your student writes <u>percieve</u> rather than <u>perceive</u> and the misspelling is labeled <u>sp</u>, he merely writes the other form with a minimum of thought or looks up the word in the dictionary.

Your student must be helped to establish the habit of challenging each word and deciding whether it is right. As a means to this end, you can indicate, by use of the appropriate symbol placed in the margin, that an error has been found on that line. Your student is then required to question every word and punctuation mark on the line to find it.

Symbols for Proofreading

Instruction	Margin Mark	Mark in Text	Corrected Version
Insert	black	the ∧ purse	the black purse
Delete		the black purse	the purse
Let it Stand	stet	the black purse	the black purse
Capitalize	Cap	the purse	the Purse
Make lower case	lc	the Purse	the purse
close space		the pur se	the purse
transpose	tr	the pruse	the purse
spell out	sp	40 purses	forty purses
Insert space	#	thepurse	the purse
Insert period	⊙	Carry the purse ∧	Carry the purse.
Insert Comma	∧	purses ∧ belts, and wallets	purses, belts, and wallets
Start new paragraph	¶	Mary bought a new purse. She went to a gala ball.	Mary bought a new purse. She went to a gala ball.
Run in	runin	Mary bought a new purse. She went to a gala ball.	Mary bought a new purse. She went to a gala ball.

Still more responsibility is placed upon your student if you do not indicate the character and place of the mistakes, but merely put X marks in the margin, each of which represents an error. After your pupil has done his best to identify these mistakes, he may be shown the errors (or given the model or correction sheet in some cases). In this way he can see how successful he was in discovering the meaning of the X marks.

Prescribing Future Assignments

When your attitude toward grading allows you to take on the role of editor and proofreader, rather than that of judge and jury, you can find many positive results. Each example of your student's written work can be a guide to what to teach him next. When you take your colored pencil, you should use it with special consideration for the particular student. Errors for which your student is not responsible, involving facts not yet introduced, are indicated in some special way, e.g. with a different color, or are not marked at all, being merely noted for future instruction. Likewise, you should keep in mind the importance of positive remarks and the motivation which can be achieved by pointing out to your student what progress he is making.

What wonderful words to hear from a teacher, "Jim, you're improving! Your sentences are so much better. Now, we will work on a better vocabulary!"

What a wonderful thing, too, to be able to say to a girl, "Mary, you're slipping a little. Let's talk it over together so that I can help you."

Saying a thing is good if it's bad doesn't help a child to grow. But seeing only the bad also does more harm than good.

As you read your student's paper, you should list one or two skills he needs to develop or areas in need of improvement: sentences and possessives, for example. You can then use this information to prescribe future assignments and lessons. It is the next paper you hope will show improvement, not this old one. This paper has already served its purpose; it has shown both you and your student where he is in need of help. Furthermore, looking over your student's papers has provided both you and your student with a list of words he needs to learn how to spell. Some of these words may be selected for Systematic Spelling Study.

Selecting Words to be Studied

During the coaching sessions or proxy-coaching process, a number of misspelled words are discovered—some by your student and others you will *help* him discover. Working with you, the correct spelling of each word is found and the document is corrected. If this is all that you do, it would lead to many words and skills being learned. But, additional spelling power can be achieved by going one step further. He should study at least some of these misspelled words using the systematic spelling strategies used with Flow-Word-List study. Studying words from these sources is referred to as "Functional Spelling Study."

Generally, the student will concentrate more on Flow-Word-Lists work until he has advanced beyond Level D.

"You did a great job of finding and fixing spelling mistakes in your story. Let's pick a couple words which you have corrected to include in your Flow-Word-List study."

The words your student should learn to spell fall into three categories: first, words that should be learned universally by all students; second, words of interest only to a specific group or of only local or regional interest; and finally, words and special terms that are important for the individual student to learn. The Flow-Word-Lists are composed of those universally used high-frequency words. The other two categories of words must come from the Integrated Functional Writing aspects of the spelling program.

Before selecting any words for Systematic Spelling Study, you should decide how many words are appropriate for your student to study in a session. As a general rule, no more than five words should be identified for study on any one paper! As with the Flow-Word-List work, some students do better with a smaller number of words on which to concentrate. However, as your student progresses through the Flow-Word-Lists, greater and greater emphasis is placed on the learning of words from the Integrated Functional Writing study. For a high school student, who has mastered the standard Flow-Word-Lists, virtually all of his spelling words will come from this work. For the younger student, who is not yet engaged in Systematic Spelling Study, virtually all of his study words will come from Functional Spelling Study as well.

When deciding which words to add to your student's "functional list," you must consider its frequency of use; how likely it is he will learn it simply from repeated use; how much trouble he has had learning it; and his own needs.

The Alphabetical List of High Frequency Words, found in the "Alphabetical Word List" section, contains all the words on the Flow-Word-Lists, plus an additional 7,500 frequently used words. Following each word is the Level and Group number where the word is first introduced, the word frequency data, and standard grade level. Frequently misspelled words are followed by one or more special characters (¢, ¡, ¿, £) showing the level at which writers have problems spelling the words. (See the key in the Alphabetical List section for more details.) It is designed to aid you and your student in determining the most appropriate words for study.

By referring to the Alphabetical List, you and/or your student can make decisions regarding which words would be most profitable to study now and which should (at least for now) be left for reference in the dictionary. Words found on this Alphabetical List should be given priority over other words. Below are a few of the considerations you should take into account when selecting words for functional study.

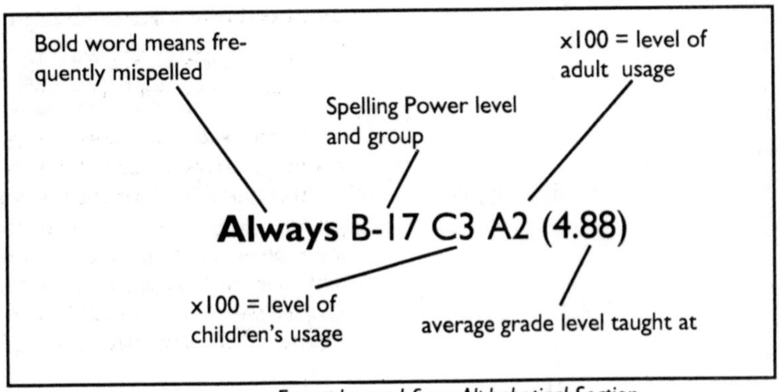

Bold word means frequently mispelled

x100 = level of adult usage

Spelling Power level and group

Always B-17 C3 A2 (4.88)

x100 = level of children's usage

average grade level taught at

Example word from Alphabetical Section

Words that have been studied at a previous level (or on a lower group on the level at which the student is currently working) should be considered for spelling study over all other words. In this way, the functional study serves as the sixth level of built-in review for your student. On the other hand, words not yet taught—but that are included in an upcoming group or level—should not be studied formally at this time. Research shows that spelling skills are most effectively and efficiently learned when words are grouped by common phonetic principles and spelling rules. It is, therefore, advantageous to study words as they are presented in the Flow-Word-List whenever possible.

Words of local interest (state names, city, etc.) cannot practically be included in a list such as provided in this text; however, you can, with a little time and effort, add such words to the Flow-Word-Lists under the generalization and at a level you deem appropriate. You can add words of local, regional, or common activities (e.g. religious) that you feel should be considered high-frequency words for your students at the end of each letter in the Alphabetical Section.

The next category of words to be included in the Functional Spelling Study are words your student is likely to use frequently. Addresses, family names, or the terminology related to hobbies or non-academic interest should be memorized to facilitate his writing. For example, if your student is involved in 4-H activities, he may have a very real need to learn to spell holstein, even though this word will not show up on any high-use word frequency chart.

Sometimes your student may want to learn a word just because he likes the way it sounds or because it is expressive. A student should never be discouraged from adding such words to his functional spelling lists. One of the goals all spelling teachers should have is to create a love of words in her students. This is also an important factor in motivating spelling (accuracy) success. This again points out one of the great values of the *Spelling Power* program—it allows not only for the individualization of level and pace but for the very words studied.

Another category to consider are words that you believe are needed in current writing. The Functional Spelling Study provides an opportunity for you to integrate other aspects of the curriculum, such as current events, unit studies, and outside reading, into the spelling program. However, caution must be taken when adding words from content areas. Too often the words that come from the content areas are not those words most necessary for students to know how to spell; they are used too seldom for them to be part of the basic list. You should consult the Alphabetical Word List to determine if a word from this category is likely to be needed beyond the unit currently being studied. If the word is high-frequency, you can then compare the level and group in which it appears with the level and group your student is working on as described above.

Many of the words in this category, which are not used frequently enough to be considered for Systematic Spelling Study, will be learned incidentally (simply by repeated use). You can do much to facilitate the writing needs and incidental learning of your students by creating "Unit Words" charts, so your student does not have to look up these words every time he wishes to use them.

Adding to the 10-Step-Study Sheet

After selecting words for Systematic Spelling Study, they should be studied as soon as is convenient. Your student begins by adding the words to his most recent 10-Step-Study Sheet. In this way, each word will be retested along with the Flow-Word-List words during the next testing session. All the Study Sheet steps should be followed. No pretest is needed as it has already been determined that it would be beneficial for the student to study the word.

Measuring Recall of Functional Spelling Words

The desired goal in spelling is for your student to remember how to spell words once instruction is discontinued. Frequent maintenance checks on retention of spelling words is automatically built into the Flow-Word-Lists. Because of the individual nature of the Functional Word Lists, it would be very time consuming for you to create similar review lists of words which your student has studied as part of this functional work. Don't worry, in most cases such systematic review of functional words isn't really necessary. You will catch them again, if he misspells them again. You can simply keep adding them back onto a study sheet until they are mastered.

Some students benefit from creating, in a separate notebook or on a computer file, an alphabetical list of all the words misspelled in his written work. If you choose to have your student do this, instruct him to place a star next to any word which was chosen for Flow-List-Word Study. The list can be used to check if the word has been studied in the past, as well as to check for the frequency of misspelling of the word. This information is helpful when deciding which words to add to his Functional Spelling Program.

Recording Integrated Functional Writing Progress

Measuring progress is more difficult with the Integrated Functional Writing and Functional Spelling Study than it is with the Flow-Word-List. The most visual tactic is to have your student keep a record of his individual writings. A folder or binder used to store his best composition of the week (student chooses the samples) is a stimulus for steady improvement. By reviewing it occasionally, your child will see the improvement in his writing, spelling and penmanship as the year progresses.

An Error Analysis Chart, as described earlier, also can be maintained by you or your student. It should list the Grammar and Composition skills and the number of errors of each type or the type of spelling errors (see Chapter Four). This chart could then be used to determine what instruction will most benefit your student.

Grading and Reporting Progress

Some may see these approaches as "soft grading" or letting the student off easily. In reality, however, grades mean very little in the whole scheme of education. When the teacher concentrates more on giving a grade than giving a skill, we must question her tactics. The grading of papers in the traditional sense does not improve writing or mathematics or any other skill for that matter. It merely ranks the skills of a student against other students and in some cases against himself.

Additionally, students can lose track of the purpose of education when too much emphasis is placed on grades. Many a student has been known to simply look at his "D" or even his "A" and never think again about how he might continue to improve. Quite the opposite happens when he is helped to discover his errors and is required to correct them. Furthermore, most students do not see it as "getting off easy." Few would agree that being required to correct their errors is easier than filing a paper away and never thinking about it again.

References For Chapter Three

1 Mortimer J. Adler, *The Paideia Proposal: An Educational Manifesto* (New York: Macmillan Publishing Co., 1982).

2 Mortimer J. Adler, *The Paideia Program: An Educational Syllabus (Essays by the Paideia Group)* (New York: Macmillan Publishing Co., 1984).

3 Charles Van Doren in *The Paideia Program*

4 Maria Montessori, *The Secret of Childhood* (Bombay: Orient Longmans, 1936).

5 Glenda L. Bissex, *GNYS At Work: A Child Learns to Write and Read* (Cambridge: Harvard University Press, 1980).

6 Adler, *The Paideia Program*.

7 Harriett Carmody, *Let's All Teach Spelling* (Tacoma WA: Tacoma Public Schools, 1952).

8 Donald H. Graves, *Balance the Basics: Let Them Write* (New York: Ford Foundation, 1978).

Chapter Four
Teaching Spelling Skills

If children's learning of spelling is largely systematic, as is our orthography, then we would learn more instructionally from observing what a child knows about the system - what principles he can apply and what strategies he uses in his writings (as reflected in his concept of the spelling system) than we would learn from asking what and how many words he knows.[1]

The typical spelling textbook provides your student with three to five days of prepared exercises as a means of teaching the "unit words" and related spelling skills. Even though some of these exercises have been carefully designed and have relevance for some students, they often become nothing more than "busy work" when indiscriminately assigned to your student. Requiring your student to study words and skills he has already mastered or which are above his achievement level is an inefficient approach to instruction.

There is no reason such learning and teaching conditions should exist. It is possible and desirable to provide specific spelling instruction and "drill" in a more interesting and efficient manner through an individualized approach. This individualization is accomplished in *Spelling Power* through "Individually Prescribed Instruction," "Discovery Activities," and "Activity Task Cards."

One of the key advantages to such individualized instruction is the ability to select activities that match your student's academic needs, developmental needs, and learning style. This has particular importance when working with both remedial and gifted students. Often a remedial student is working several "grades" below level, yet developmentally he is at grade level. If you are working with a sixth grader who is spelling on a second grade level, it would be inappropriate for you to give him a second grade spelling book. While the words may be those your student needs to study, the activities would not be developmentally appropriate for him. Likewise, if you have a second grader spelling on a sixth grade level, he may not be developmentally ready for the abstract approach most sixth grade texts would take. In the *Spelling Power* program, the Individually Prescribed Instruction allows you to completely tailor instruction for each student. Not only are you able to select the words he academically needs to learn, you are able to select activities that are developmentally appropriate.

In this chapter, you will be given information on how to select specific learning activities, make decisions regarding the most beneficial lessons for your student, and conduct teacher-directed lessons. Directions for specific activities are found in the "Discovery Activities" Section of this manual. Other learning activities such as proofreading exercises and dictionary skills are handled in separate chapters.

Discovery Activities Make Spelling Fun

The prescribed learning activities, exercises, and games presented in the fifth section of your *Spelling Power* manual are designed to replace the "workbook-type" activities found in most basal textbooks. These games and activities feature application of spelling principles, expand vocabulary and usage, and increase knowledge and writing skill. A rich variety of games, puzzles, projects, and activities can provide valuable, effective motivation for practice. Repetition and drills are fun when they take the form of a game. Additionally, such activities can teach and reinforce spelling rules and skills. Many of the games and activities are designed to inductively teach spelling rules. Well-devised games stimulate your student to think, reason, and concentrate. The activities discussed in this section fall into six broad categories: Activity Task Cards, Word Card Games, Teacher-Made Games, Worksheet-type Activities, Teacher-Directed Activities, Commercial Games and Computer Software.

Activity Task Cards provide your student with specific tasks to complete. There are five basic types of activities presented on Activity Task Cards: creative drill activities, skill building assignments, mini-worksheets, writing prompters, and game directions. You can easily make your own activity task cards. Simply copy the examples presented in the Discovery Activity section onto index cards and store them in a 4"x6" recipe box. You can create additional activities using the basic ideas presented in the program as well. You can also purchase a ready-made Activity Task Card box. Very few of the ideas or activities in the pre-prepared Activity Task Cards duplicate those presented in the Discovery Activity section.

Word Card Games are games and activities that encourage students to manipulate and organize words written on small cards into various linguistic patterns. Many of the games are also used for drills similar to flash card type activities.

Teacher-Made Games are board-type games (usually made on the inside of a file folder for ease in storage) that may be played with word cards or other word lists.

Worksheet-type Activities provide the teacher with ideas for creating her own worksheets. The ideas are general and may be applied to most word lists and groups. Worksheets can be created as full size sheets or on activity task cards. In addition to teacher-made worksheets, you may find that your grammar program has lessons or worksheets which have application to your spelling curriculum. This is particularly true when working on groups 30-41. Phonics workbooks can also make a contribution when working on groups one through 29. Crossword and other word-type puzzles fall under the worksheet category. You can make these or collect appropriate activities from other sources. In the Teaching Aids and Masters section you will find forms that will make it easy for you to create some of these for your student.

Teacher-Directed Activities are frequently adaptations of "spelling bee" type games which are played with several children. Most are considered "impromptu," requiring little or no preparation or materials. They can be played anywhere at anytime.

Commercial Games and Computer Software are also listed in this section to help you evaluate materials in which it may be profitable to invest. Many of these games add a fun change of pace to the five minute skill building session of each spelling period.

Selecting Appropriate Activities

Discovery Activities are often prescribed, contracted, or assigned. However, you can also make many of them available to your students for additional use outside of the spelling program (once they have been introduced). Your task is to select activities that combine enjoyment with learning. In doing this, certain criteria for the selection and use of activities should be carefully observed.

1. All activities must be carefully selected for specific purposes. Games should be simple and designed to concentrate on individual spelling skills. While drill-type activities can be used at any time to reinforce the proper spelling of words, they are especially valuable when working with Review Group lists. Drill Activities are also very helpful with those words in groups that do not follow phonetic patterns or specific principles: 35, 36, 37, 38, 39, 41, and 47. Other activities can be selected by using the Group Rule Index or Modality Index found in the Discovery Activity section or in the teacher's guide

to the Activity Task Cards box. To use the group rule index, you simply look up the Group Number your student is working on and select from the listed cards or activities. The Modality Index lists cards or activities that appeal to or build skills which emphasize a particular Modality, e.g., tactile, visual, auditory, kinesthetic. (The information in the last half of this chapter will help you evaluate more specifically each of your student's spelling needs.)

2. They should provide immediate feedback and be self-correcting whenever possible.

3. When the purpose of spelling games and activities is for your student to practice the correct spelling of words, care must be taken to make sure that your student has a model of the correct spelling; practicing the incorrect spelling should be carefully avoided. Until your student is prepared to spell a word accurately, provision should be made for immediate correction of any possible error.

4. Competitive activities and games should only be used for small groups or pairs which are on the same level. There must be a reasonable chance for each pupil to win. Competition is aroused only when such conditions exist. You cannot expect your student to be interested and motivated when failure is viewed as inevitable.

5. The specific spelling needs of your student should be diagnosed and activities and/or games should be selected which focus attention on the spelling process. It is easy for insignificant features of an activity to assume such importance that the spelling process is obscured. Maximum benefit can probably be best obtained if the activities contribute significantly to the current spelling tasks being mastered.

6. Activities and games should be selected which maximize the involvement of each student in a meaningful experience. This criterion suggests the need to avoid activities which reduce your student to a passive observer such as is the case in many often-used classroom games. More than 90 percent of your student's spelling practice time may be wasted when he passively waits in line for 29 other students to spell words.

7. Games must not become rewards and privileges that are attainable by only a select group of superior spellers. It is often the poorest speller who most needs this type of activity and it must be available to him at his level of ability.

8. Do not overuse any one activity or overplay any one game.

Writing Power, a sequel to Spelling Power, expands on this concept and also provides information on composition projects, scope and sequence, and information on evaluating student writing.

Presenting Discovery Activities to Students

After you have selected which activity will be most profitable for your student to complete, you must find a convenient way to communicate that which you wish him to do. Activities may be presented to student as "prescription slips," "contracts," "Activity Task Cards," or as a worksheet assignment. Most teachers will use a combination of these.

The easiest, most direct assignment method is to record the activity you wish the student to complete in the space labeled "Spelling Study Tips" on his 10-Step-Study Sheet (i.e., "Please complete Activity Task Card 127 today."). You can also simply provide him with a copy of the worksheet or Activity Task Card you would like him to complete.

Sometimes you will want to write a more detailed assignment in the Spelling Study Tips space or have a cumulative assignment. If you have several students with which you work, this can be done over the weekend so the week is completely laid out for each of your students. For instance, on Saturday you look over your student's Progress Chart and see that next week he will begin Group 6. You decide he would benefit from some inductive work which requires him to analyze the possible phoneme-grapheme relationships of the long A sound. You break up this task, suggested in the "linguists" word card activity section, into a week-long project. On Monday's study sheet you write: "Select an article from a magazine to read. As you read, record on word cards each word that contains the long A sound. See how many long A words you can find in five minutes." On Tuesday's 10-Step-Study Sheet your assignment reads: "Sort the Long A word cards you collected yesterday by the phonographs used to make the sound. Which long A phonograph is used the most?" On Wednesday you continue the work by writing: "Look at the long A word cards you collected on Monday. Which long A sound is most likely to occur at the end of a syllable?" On Thursday you may have your student analyze which phonogram is used for the long A sound in different positions within words. Your final assignment, on Friday, may ask your student to write his "discovery" or summarize his research about how the long A sound actually functions in words and syllables.

Weekly assignments or cumulative assignments such as described above can also be prescribed on "Prescription Slips." After evaluating your student's specific lesson needs, assignments (for the week) are prescribed for your student on special prescription sheets that resemble those given out by a doctor. A master form for prescriptions slips is provided in the "Teaching Aids and Masters" section.

The only difference between a prescription and a contract is that a contracted lesson is determined by you and your student working together. In this situation, after discussing what areas your student needs to develop skills in, he agrees to complete certain assignments and/or meet certain learning objectives by a specific date. The agreement is written up in a formal way and both you and he sign it. Once a contract is created, most of the responsibility for completing the assignment or meeting the objectives is placed on your student. Usually contracts are used for longer periods of time, e.g., a week, month, term or even an entire school year with older students.

Teacher-Directed Instruction

While most of the lessons you give your students will be through such devices as Activity Task Cards, Discovery Activities, and other assignments as described above, sometimes you must provide direct instruction. Teacher-Directed Instruction refers to lessons or lectures you present verbally to your student or small groups of your students. It is most frequently used to introduce syllabication, practice dictionary skills, and teach spelling rules inductively. Direct instruction can and should also occur informally during your weekly coaching sessions.

In relation to the value of the direct teaching of spelling rules or generalizations, Horn states that "the only spelling generalizations that should be taught as rules are those that apply to a large number of words and have few exceptions." The following generalizations, in addition to the basic phoneme-grapheme relationships (especially vowel sounds), are those that most linguistic experts agree are profitable for your student to learn.

1. When spelling words of one syllable ending in a single consonant, preceded by a single vowel, double the final consonant before a suffix beginning with a vowel. (*lag, lagging; plan, planned*) (See Group Rule 34.)

2. When spelling words of more than one syllable ending in a single consonant, preceded by a single vowel, double the final consonant before adding a suffix if: 1) the syllable preceding the suffix is accented, 2) the last syllable ends in a consonant with one vowel before it, and 3) the suffix or ending begins with a vowel. (*occur, occurred; prefer, preferring, preference; repel, repellent; travel, traveled, traveling; but admit, admittance*) (See Group Rule 32, 33, and 34.)

3. Final y, preceded by a consonant, changes to ie before adding an s. (*army, armies; fly, flies* but *turkey, turkeys; attorney, attorneys* because a vowel precedes the y) (See Group Rule 32.)

4. In adding a suffix to a word ending in silent e, retain the e if the suffix begins with a consonant, but drop the e if the suffix begins with a vowel. (See Group Rule 26, 27, 32, and 34.)

5. Add s to words to form plurals or to change the tense of verbs, but

es must be added to words ending with the hissing sounds (x, s, sh, ch). (*glass, glasses; watch, watches, check, checks*) (See Group Rule 30, 31, and 32.)

6. When s is added to words ending in a single f, the f is changed to v and es is added. (*half, halves; shelf, shelves*) (See Group Rule 31)

7. In the ei, ie combinations (pronounced e as in *feel*) i comes before e except after c. (*believe, receive*) The most common exceptions to this generalization are contained in this sentence: "*Neither leisurely financier seized either weird species.*" (This rule is not specifically taught as a group rule, but is associated with Group 7.)

8. Use a hyphen in compound numbers from *twenty-one* to *ninety-nine*, and in specific fractions: twenty-five dollar bills ($25), twenty five dollar bills ($100) (the hyphen prevents confusion) three-fourths, four and two-thirds, thirty-hundredths, thirty-one hundredths). The hyphen should also be used in compound nouns such as *son-in-law*. (See Group Rules 36, 38, and 39.)

9. The letter q is always followed by u in common English words. (*queen, quite*) (See Group Rule 21.)

10. No English words end in v. (*glove, love*) (See Group Rule 23.)

11. Proper nouns and most adjectives formed from proper nouns should begin with a capital letter. (*America, American*) (See Group Rule 35.)

12. Most abbreviations end with a period. (*etc., Nov.*) (See Group Rule 41.)

13. The apostrophe is used to show the omission of letters in contractions. (*he's, don't, it's*) (See Group Rule 37.)

14. The apostrophe is used to indicate the possessive form of nouns but not pronouns. (*boy's, dog's, its, theirs*) (See Group Rule 40.)

There are some exceptions to these generalizations (that is why we usually call them generalizations and not rules), but they are sufficiently universal to aid spelling instruction. The *Spelling Power* program provides for instruction and review of the phoneme-grapheme relationships of vowel sounds in groups 1 to 20, 25, and 29 and spelling generalizations in groups 21-24, 26-28, 30 to 46 of the Flow-Word-Lists. However, you should provide more direct instruction on each spelling generalization to your student before he encounters it the first time in a Flow-Word-List.

Foran[2] makes the following conclusions regarding such instruction:

1. Only one rule or skill should be introduced at a time.

2. A generalization should only be taught when there is a need for it.

3. The teaching of rules should be integrated whenever possible with the arrangement or grouping of the words in the lists.

4. Once the generalization has been introduced, it should be systematically reviewed and applied. Both in original teaching and in reviews, emphasis should be upon the use of the rule rather than upon the mere memorization of the verbal statement.

5. Spelling generalizations should be taught inductively rather than deductively whenever possible.

Teaching Spelling Rules Inductively

Better to never teach a rule at all than to leave it a memorized statement without an established habit of use. A rule may be memorized in a lesson, but the fixing of a habit to ensure its functioning requires weeks, perhaps months, during which the pupil encounters numerous unexpected situations where it must be applied. Providing varied encounters by means of ingeniously planned exercises is the essential element of this type of thoroughness.

Prior to the first presentation of a Flow-Word-List Group, which provides a list of words which illustrates a particular phonetic principle or spelling rule, the rule should be taught inductively. Inductive teaching strategies are designed to help your student to achieve an understanding of the principles behind the use of a generalization, the *why* and *how* of it, not just a memorization of the verbal statement. Such understanding can be achieved by allowing your student to "discover" its purpose through manipulation of the words or through questioning. The following is an excellent example of an inductive lesson:

Inductive Rule Teaching

The teacher writes *hate*, *name*, *arrange*, *fate*, and *like*. She asks the student what all of these words have in common and gets the answer that each ends in a silent e. Then she asks him to spell *hateful*, *namely*, *arrangement*, *fateful*, and *likeness*, and she writes these words in a column opposite the first list, underlining the suffixes as she writes. "What would happen if we didn't keep the e in *hateful?*" she inquires. The student explains that the e prevents confusion between *hateful* and *hatful* and between *fateful* and *fatful*, and that one would tend to mispronounce *arrangement* if the e were not there. The teacher questions the student as to whether the suffixes have anything in common, and is told that each begins with a consonant. She then asks him to provide other words ending in silent e; the student finds suffixes to add to words like *state*, *late*, *white*, etc., but he notices that many words, such as *dice*, *while*, and *please* do not take suffixes beginning with consonants.

At this point, the teacher may pause to have the student formulate a rule which says that "when a suffix beginning with a consonant is added to a word ending in silent e, the e is retained." She may, however, first go back to the original list and ask the student to spell *hating*, *naming*, *arranging*, *fatal*, and *likable*, which she writes in a third column. Here is something new, since the e has been dropped. A little judicious questioning reveals that the distinction between these words and the ones in the second column exists because here the suffix begins with a vowel. The teacher points out that there is a good reasons for dropping the e, for if one saw such a word as *fateal* he might have trouble pronouncing it. More illustrations, and then on to the formulation of a rule something like this: "In adding a suffix to a word ending in silent e, retain the e if the suffix begins with a consonant, but drop the e if the suffix begins with a vowel."

One more step remains—mentioning the most important exceptions. On the board the teacher writes *singe* and tells the student that this word is an exception. She writes *singeing*, and lets the student see that the e is retained here before a vowel. "Why?" she asks. Immediately the student sees that singing would be confusing. The teacher refers to *shoeing* and *hoeing*, commenting perhaps that *shoing* and *hoing* would look like names of Chinese provinces if the e were dropped. She may mention a few other exceptions, such as *dyeing*, *courageous*, and *noticeable*. Later Flow-Word-List work involves the restating of the generalization which reinforces the learning from this inductive session. In addition, at subsequent sessions, you will give your student the opportunity to practice applying the rules. Without such practice and reinforcement, the rule will have little value.

Inductive teaching can also be used to help your student to establish phoneme-grapheme relationships, as was shown in the cumulative assignment example earlier in this chapter. Organizing and conducting this type of miniature research (into the relative frequencies of graphemes which represent a given phoneme in common written material and searching for clues which will guide the selection of an appropriate grapheme), provides your student the opportunity to experience the satisfaction of breaking the code of our spelling system for himself. Many of the activities described in the "Discovery Activities" section are designed to help students make these discoveries for themselves.

Recording Individually Prescribed Instruction Efforts

Progress achieved through Individually Prescribed Instruction is easily recorded by use of a Prescription Record (see "Teaching Aids and Masters" section.) The Prescription Record allows you and/or your student to record specific spelling skills, activities, and lessons he has been assigned or chosen during the course of the year. A separate folder may also be maintained of worksheets or written activities completed during the term.

Many teachers find it beneficial to create a checklist of spelling skills based on the scope and sequence lists at the end of Chapter Six. This checklist could then be used to record the student's progression through the traditional spelling curriculum.

Evaluating Instructional Needs

The Discovery Activities and Direct Instruction described so far in this chapter and provided in the Discovery Activities section of the manual will satisfy most of your assignment needs. Occasionally, however, more detailed evaluation is needed. Most often, such remediation is needed when your student is not progressing as you would expect or with a student who is repeatedly failing Delayed Recall and End-of-Level Tests.

The first step to remediating such problems is to evaluate or analyze the possible causes for your student's problems. Unlike the student evaluations which have been discussed in earlier chapters of this book, this evaluation goes beyond the counting of incorrectly spelled words to include an analysis of the type of errors your student has made in his spelling. Hanna, Hodges, and Hanna[3] have argued for error analysis. It provides you with data regarding which spelling skills your student needs to develop, and thus provides direction for developing more meaningful, individualized instruction.

Analyzing Error Types

Errors can be classified into five basic types: 1) confusion of the phoneme-grapheme relationship; 2) misapplication of generalizations; 3) misuse of homonyms; 4) confusions due to incorrect pronunciation; and 5) difficulties resulting from poor penmanship (those words which are unreadable).

Confusion of the phoneme-grapheme relationship can be caused both by inadequate phonics instruction and poor auditory skills and habits. Words are organized in the Flow-Word-Lists (in Groups 1 to 20, 25, and 29) by phoneme relationships to help the student associate the sound with all the possible graphemes for that sound. A large number of the Discovery Activities are designed to teach and reinforce the phoneme-grapheme relationships.

Misapplication of the generalizations generally results in such errors as transpositions, inappropriate doubling of letters and letter substitutions, omissions, and insertions. Often when your student has merely memorized the spelling rules, he will apply them sporadically to his spelling. For your student to consistently apply spelling principles, he must understand their purpose. This can be facilitated by inductively introducing the spelling rule prior to working with a particular group of words applying to a generalization and allowing your student to manipulate words to which the generalization applies in a variety of ways. A model of teaching of a spelling rule inductively was given earlier. Ideally, you will present an inductive lesson prior to introducing any Flow-Word-List group work.

Misuse of homonyms is generally caused by your student not associating the correct meaning of the word with its spelling. However, lack of emphasis upon the meaning of the word during the initial presentation of its spelling can cause errors of this type to persist. The most effective procedure to correct such errors is the presentation of the words in such a way that the context is clear and initiating activities that require the use of such words in their proper setting. A list of homonyms, found in the "Miscellaneous" section of this manual, may be helpful to you in preparing activities that will help your student learn their spelling. Generally these activities take the form of worksheets which require the student to insert the correct homonym form. An entire section of the optional Activity Task Cards box focuses on this area of instruction.

Confusions due to incorrect pronunciation has at its root one of four common causes: Failure to get an accurate auditory impression, careless or inaccurate pronunciation, failure to distinguish between informal speech and formal speech that serves as a basis for spelling, and careless listening habits. The Flow-Word-List testing methods does much to eliminate errors of this type. Additional remediation can be provided by using activities designed to improve these skills. Sound and Articulation Activities for children with Speech-Language Problems is an excellent resource for younger students with difficulty in this area. Older students with severe difficulties in this area will be best served if you have them evaluated by a specialist.

While **difficulties caused by poor penmanship** are not the purpose of this program, those areas of difficulty related to spelling should be noted and addressed during the time devoted to handwriting study.

Conducting an Informal Evaluation

In the *Spelling Power* program, the written work used for error analysis often is the same composition you have discussed with your student in his weekly "coaching" session. Other compositions may also be used. To conduct an informal evaluation, you analyze the types of spelling errors your student makes in his free-flow writing and record the number of errors of each basic type. For the purpose here, it is not necessary for you to record the specific words misspelled. However, you may wish to determine and to record if your student consistently has trouble with a particular phoneme-grapheme relationship, spelling generalization, commonly mispronounced words (see list in the Miscellaneous section) or syllable, or frequently misuses a specific set of homonyms.

You may also find the Prescriptive Tests (found in the "Placement Test" section) a helpful evaluation tool. These are especially useful at the beginning of the school year or when you are having a difficult time pinpointing the student's instructional needs. Such difficulties occur more frequently with older students who have instructional gaps. The Prescriptive Test helps you identify the gap quickly. Prescriptive Tests and directions for their use begin on page 116.

Using the resulting data, you can determine what skill(s) and/or spelling generalizations will be most beneficial for your student to work on at this time. Usually this will be in the category in which he has made the greatest number of errors. However, you must also consider the Level and Group number at which the student is working with the Flow-Word-Lists, as this will often affect the student's individual instructional plans. For example, if your student will soon begin work with a new "group rule" you will want to introduce it in a formal way prior to introducing that group of words.

Once you have analyzed your student's errors and considered current instructional needs, you can then arrange specific instruction which will help him to achieve the objective you have determined for him. This instruction can be provided to the student via lessons conducted by the teacher directly, as well as through Discovery Activities.

Spelling Disabilities

Why, it's a looking-glass book, of course! And if I hold it up to a glass the words will all go the right way again.

Alice: Through the Looking Glass
Lewis Carroll

One error type briefly mentioned in this chapter is reversals and transpositions. It can apply to reversals of individual letters or static reversals (d-b; p-b), reversal of an entire word called kinetic reversals (was-saw), or to the position of individual letters within a word referred to as transpositional reversals (ie-ei). Almost everyone makes errors of these types from time to time, but for some of your students they may present a larger problem than for others.

It is especially common for very-early-grade school children to have the tendency to reverse letters and words. This usually will correct itself with time and continued instruction using multi-sensory techniques. If your student continues to have persistent difficulties with reversals beyond age eight or so, specific remediation may be needed.

One in seven students will be seen to have the tendency to reversals to some degree or another beyond age eight. Your male students will have this tendency three times as often as your female students. If you have a student who shows these tendencies, you should have him evaluated by a specialist. The following discussion of language disabilities is intended to help you make intelligent decisions about remediation options.

The tendency to excessive errors of this type is referred to by many labels, among them dyslexia, strephosymbolism, and specific language disabilities. Strephosymbolism is the term Samuel T. Orton, one of the pioneer researchers in this area, used to describe the phenomena. It is the most descriptive term for those students whose difficulties are manifest in spelling difficulties. Literally, this word means "twisted symbols" and refers to the types of errors mentioned above. While the term dyslexia has a much broader meaning (literally "dys," which comes from the Greek, meaning "lack of" or "inadequate" and *lexia,* also from the Greek, meaning "verbal language"), it is often used universally to describe students with learning disabilities related to reading, writing, and spelling. The term "specific language disability" is becoming the favored term, because it emphasizes the fact that the student has a specific disability dealing with some aspect of language (vs. general retardation).

Whatever you call the disability, it is important to note that the condition is in no way related to intelligence. Many people of great achievement and in high position have been know to have varying levels of dyslexia, among them Leonardo de Vinci, Thomas Edison, General George S. Patton, Woodrow Wilson, Hans Christian Anderson, and Albert Einstein.

Many theories have been promoted on what causes reversals and reading and spelling failure. At one point, the cause was thought to be emotional blocks. In fact, this concept is what led to Orton's initial work in this area. He summarized that the emotional difficulties of those he examined were more likely to have been caused by their disability than vice versa.

Orton's research led him to develop and promote the concept of cerebral dominance or lack of cerebral dominance as the cause of "dyslexia." He and Anne Gillingham developed specific multi-sensory exercises which were designed to help these students. Many aspects of their approach have been incorporated into the development of *Spelling Power*. The Slingerland reading method is based on parts of the work by Orton and Gillingham as well.

Others have proposed that dyslexia is caused by minor brain damage or retarded development in certain portions of the brain. Persons who prescribe to this theory generally promote perceptual development therapy. These approaches range from exercises and activities (such as daily crawling) to develop eye-hand coordination to special glasses designed to improve eye-coordination. The work of Glenn Dolman (*How to Help Your Brain Injured Child* and the Institutes for Human Potential) has this theory as its basis.

Because learning problems such as dyslexia are often associated with A.D.D. and A.D.H.D., other researchers have summarized that they are related to the lack of sufficient neurotransmitters. These practitioners promote everything from nutritional therapy to drug therapy as an aid to students. Among the most important books in this group is *Is This Your Child?* by Dr. Doris Rapp.

It may be that all of these "experts" are right. It may be that literacy problems occur when one or more combinations of these factors exist. This may account for the extreme variances in disability. (Unlike pregnancy, you **can** be just a little bit dyslexic.) This author has experimented and investigated various applications of the theories described above and found many have important elements to offer students in need of remediation.

Unfortunately, parents of afflicted students are easy targets for "scam" cures. I highly recommend that any parent with a child showing severe reversal tendencies and other learning disabilities do extensive research and investigate anyone they consult regarding an evaluation. An excellent book to begin with is *Dyslexia: Understanding Reading Problems* by John F. Savage. You may also wish to consult the Orton Dyslexia Society at 724 York Road, Baltimore, MD 21204 or the Association for Children and Adults with Learning Disabilities.

Chapter Summary

In this chapter you have been given guidelines for assigning activities for the daily skill-building sessions, as well as how to conduct effective lessons directly with your student. With the materials provided in this chapter, the Discovery Activities section, and the proofreading and coaching lessons described in Chapter Three, you will be able to provide your student with excellent spelling skills. The next chapter, The Writer's Right Hand, will describe how you can provide your student with comprehensive dictionary skills which will round out your spelling curriculum.

References For Chapter Four

1 Glenda L. Bissex, *GNYS At Work: A Child Learns to Write and Read* (Cambridge, MA: Harvard University Press, 1980).
2 Thomas G. Foran, *The Psychology and Teaching of Spelling* (Washington, D.C.: The Catholic Education Press, 1934).
3 Paul R. Hanna and others, *Spelling: Structure and Strategies* (Boston, MA: Houghton Mifflin Co., 1971).

Chapter Five
The Writer's Right Hand: The Dictionary

Fortunately for the average reader, the vast majority of the million or more words in an unabridged English dictionary can stay there because so many of them are special terms that most people will never meet them in reading.[1]

The dictionary is a complicated reference tool that is often not used to its full advantage. It might be described as a "half-used book." Much of its value is lost due to inadequate instruction. Training in dictionary use cannot be left to chance. You must so train your student that he acquires a definite *modus operandi* or approach to using it as a spelling and vocabulary tool.

It is also important to make using the dictionary a habit for your student. Beginning in the early grades, your child must constantly be guided to understand that the dictionary is an essential reference book which should be consulted whenever a question about spelling, pronunciation or meaning arises. Through continued instruction in and modeling of its use for vocabulary and spelling purpose, the dictionary can become a "more-used book."

Pleasure and not boredom should be associated with the use of the dictionary, so your student will come to see it as his "best friend and writing companion." This type of motivation enhances the likelihood of your student learning to make optimum use of his dictionary.

Games and game-like activities make learning fun. You will find many game-type dictionary lessons, presented in sequential order, in this chapter. These activities comprise the full-range of dictionary skills from alphabetizing skills to using etymological information.

Planning for Instruction

Dictionary skills and habits cannot be established by conducting an occasional two-week dictionary unit, but must be an ongoing part of your spelling curriculum. Your lesson plans should include a regular schedule for teaching dictionary skills. You may choose to set aside one spelling period per week for Dictionary Day and use this time to give your students a sequential presentation of dictionary skills. Setting aside a Dictionary Day allows you to work with all of your students simultaneously and facilitates group and small group game-type activities which are very motivating.

You may also have your students work on dictionary and dictionary-related skills during the 10-Step-Study and skill-building time. Days on which they have no words to study or following a review test work best for this type of activity since they tend to be more time consuming. The optional Activity Task Card box provides an entire section, titled Dictionary Skills, which presents dictionary activities in a sequential order. Many of the activities described in the Discovery Activities section of this manual also focus on dictionary skills.

At the end of Chapter Six, you will find a complete Scope and Sequence for teaching dictionary skills. The following is a list of key fundamentals which are presented through game-type activities in this chapter:

1. Knowledge of alphabetical sequence;
2. Ability to locate relative position of letters;
3. Knowledge of possible phoneme-grapheme correspondence;
4. Ability to represent graphically the sounds heard in words;
5. Skill in quickly locating words once a possible spelling is selected;
6. Ability to use the dictionary for spelling words for which the main entry is only the base word; and
7. Ability to use meaning as a clue for selecting the appropriate spelling.

Systematic Teaching of Dictionary Skills

Alphabetical Sequence

By the time most children reach eight years of age, they can say the letters of the alphabet in their proper sequence. However, this ability does not assure a complete working knowledge of alphabetical sequence. How often have you heard an older student or adult subvocally reciting the alphabet, to think through which letter comes next? When your student "really knows" his alphabetical sequence, he will be able to start with any letter and go forward and backwards with ease. In colonial days, this ability was automatically acquired through the drill associated with the "horn book." Today, we must provide this skill through other methods.

Being able to recite the alphabet does not necessarily mean your student will transfer the knowledge to use of his dictionary. It is obvious students are not born knowing how dictionaries are organized, but it seems to surprise many teachers when their students do not make the discovery for themselves. The fact is that a considerable number, even some high school students, do not know that the alphabetical arrangement applies beyond the initial letter of words. Your student will need considerable experience manipulating letters and words to establish competent skills in alphabetizing whole words.

Alphabet Sequence — After your student has learned the alphabet song and can recognize the graphic symbol for each letter, provide him with a set of large alphabet cards (5"x7") or Letter Tiles which have been shuffled or mixed up and have him practice putting them in alphabetical sequence. Provide him with an alphabetical chart so he can check his accuracy when he is finished.

Dot-To-Dot Letters — Another way to provide students practice with alphabetizing is to make up or purchase dot-to-dot worksheets which emphasize alphabetizing skills. At the earliest stages, these worksheets should focus on alphabetizing letters. More advanced levels can include whole word dot-to-dot activities (see Alphabetizing Words below for sequence to follow).

Dot-to-dot worksheets can easily be made using simple drawings found in coloring books, especially those intended for young children. An extension activity could include having your students create their own dot-to-dots. These can be used to challenge their classmates.

Alphabetizing Words — You do not need to wait (and you probably shouldn't) until your student is totally proficient in alphabetizing letters before advancing to the next step: arranging or locating words in alphabetical order. New elements must constantly be introduced to maintain interest. As a beginning activity, allow your student to arrange word cards into alphabetical order. (Arranging cards is easier than recopying lists.) Copy sets of words like those listed below onto word cards (or onto the backs of old business cards), each on a separate card. Shuffle them and then give the cards to your student to arrange alphabetically.

Have your students arrange the words in different directions, on different occasions.

This gives him familiarity with looking at lists arranged both horizontally and vertically. Familiarity with both directions is necessary to efficient dictionary use. The four sample sets become progressively more difficult:

Set 1: Only initial letters need be considered in the first group:

tub	**a**nt	**s**ail	**m**an
boy	**w**ind	**g**ate	**f**ence
rain	**q**ueen	**v**iolin	**o**range

Set 2: When your student is fairly quick at getting initial letter words in order, you can move him up a level of difficulty. In the next group, the first two letters must be considered:

atlas	**ad**mit	**ab**out	**an**gry
acorn	**ar**ch	**am**ber	**aw**ake
apart	**al**most	**ax**is	**as**ter

Set 3: Your student will find even more challenge in alphabetizing to the third letter.

belong	**bes**ide	**bea**ch	**beg**in
become	**ben**t	**ber**g	**beh**ave
bevel	**bef**all	**bet**ray	**bed**eck

Set 4: When your student is proficient at alphabetizing Group Four he will have mastered the concept.

consult	**cong**ress	**conc**eal	**cont**ent
condense	**conv**erse	**conq**uer	**coni**fer
connect	**conj**ugate		

Additional groups of this type can easily be made by consulting the dictionary. By the time several exercises like this have been completed, most students realize that alphabetical arrangement continues beyond the first letters in the dictionary.

Another level of difficulty can be added to this work by teaching your student how to add words to an already organized list. After your student can arrange the words speedily, give him another word to insert in the line or column between the two words where it belongs alphabetically.

If your student is above fourth grade and has had some experience arranging the cards, he can be given the same type of words to alphabetize on lists instead of on individual cards. He should be taught to check the words one by one as selected. A master list in correct alphabetical order should be provided so that he can check his own work. The student can also be assigned to alphabetize his study words or the entire group list. Months of the year, holidays, states, and so on can also make interesting words for practicing alphabetizing.

Skill in alphabetizing is useful in many kinds of work: alphabetizing and filing letters, organizing club lists, etc. Whenever possible, students who have been learning these skills should be involved in such "real life applications." Your student may enjoy working with kits, designed for business education classes, which contain miniature letters and file folders for students to learn filing. Younger students enjoy "playing office" with these, while older students realize the full value of the skills through the use of these kits.

Locating the Relative Position of a Letter

Drill in the relative position of the letters in the alphabet goes one step beyond typical alphabetizing skills. When a student has a firm concept of what letters come before and after each letter or its relative alphabetical position, it helps him locate a word in the dictionary and other directories faster and easier. This is important. Being able to find things quickly and easily will motivate your student to use these resources. A number of stimulating activities (presented in the approximate order they should normally be introduced) can provide this type of drill. The following are a few suggestions for developing these skills.

Alphabet Position Drill — Have your student spread out a set of Alphabet Cards or Letter Tiles in proper sequence on a large table or on the floor. Show him how the middle of the alphabet falls between m and n. Have him look over the letters carefully with particular attention to what letters come before m and which come after n. Now have your student stand directly in front of the m and n and close his eyes. Then ask him to point in the direction in which p would be located, then c, f, r, w, etc.

This activity can be given a bit of variety by making it into a group game. Two students or two teams of students can play this as a game of "baseball." One student or team "pitches" the letter to the other. If the letter position is correctly pointed to, the team at bat scores a point and a new batter is "up" (or takes his turn). If the position of the letter is named incorrectly, it is counted as an out and a new batter is selected. Three outs and the other student or team is up to bat.

After your student has gained some proficiency with locating in which half of the alphabet a letter can be found, the activity can be made even more challenging by dividing the alphabet into thirds (A-H, I-P, and Q-Z) or quarters (A-G, H-M, N-S, and T-Z.) In this case you would have him indicate in which portion this letter is found by holding up one finger to indicate the first section, two fingers for the second section, and so on. This should be done while pointing in the general direction of the section.

Alphabet Scramble — Another excellent activity for helping your student locate the relative position of letters in the alphabet places the focus on starting from each vowel. In this activity the single vowels cards or tiles are laid down first. (You may need to teach or remind the student the vowel jingle to help him place these letters.) Then help your student distribute the consonants. "What should we put between a and e?" "Now what should we put between e and i?" and so on.

What's Missing

Name: ______________________ Date: ______________

Part 1. Fill in the missing letters. Time yourself how quickly you can solve the puzzle in Part 2.

1. A _ C	2. c d _	3. m n _ p q
4. e _ g h	5. _ i j k l	6. _ B C
7. N O _	8. O _ Q	9. X _ Z
10. f g _ i	11. _ f g	12. _ B C
13. P Q _	14. S _ U V	

Part 2.

Solve the puzzle by inserting each of the letters from above.

_ _   _ _   _ _ _ _ _   _ _ _ _ _
1 2   3 4   5 6 7 8 9   10 11 12 13 14

At first your student may need to begin with a and recite the letters straight through to the second vowel of the pair in question. The goal is for your student to be able to recite and place the letters by beginning at any vowel. You want your student to become so proficient in alphabetizing that he can take a deck of shuffled alphabet cards (or mixed-up letter tiles) and put them in their proper position without reciting all the letters. Timing this activity adds a fun dimension. Students are often eager to beat their own record from day to day.

What's Missing? — After all the alphabet cards or letter tiles have been laid down in proper sequence, have your student close his eyes and while his eyes are closed remove a letter. When he reopens his eyes, ask him to tell you what letter belongs in the vacant space. The goal is to be able to do this without saying the entire alphabet. To add variety, this game can also be played using felt letters on a flannelboard.

This activity can also be adapted to worksheet assignments by having your student insert the missing letters (on blank lines) in a series of letters or to tell which letter comes next. A good impromptu activity can be developed by asking him to tell, without looking at the alphabet cards, what follows or precedes a named letter.

Opening the Dictionary to a Given Letter

Your student also needs to develop skill in opening the dictionary to a given letter. You want your student to refine this skill to the point where he can open a dictionary to the exact page. Begin by having your student determine which letters are in the middle of his dictionary. Dictionaries do vary, depending on the amount of extra material included in the beginning, but for most the middle is usually around m. After determining the division of the dictionary, challenge him to see how near he can open the dictionary to a particular letter.

"See how close you can come to opening the dictionary to the letter p. In which half of the alphabet is p ?"

"In the back half."

"That's right! Now, open your dictionary and see if you can open it to the p on your first attempt." (Pause while he opens it.) "What letter have you opened it to?"

"r"

"Which way must you turn for p?"

"Toward the back of the book."

"Say the letters beginning with n again."

"n, o, p, q, r, oh, toward the front of the book."

Below are several extensions and variations of this activity which can be used to keep up interest while building competency with this skill.

1. Proceed with the same type of activity using smaller sections of the dictionary. Your student should eventually be able to determine just which letters fall in the first quarter of his dictionary, the second quarter, the third quarter, and the last quarter.

2. Have partners or a group of students "race" to see who can open the dictionary nearest a given letter. "Who can hit the bull's eye?"

3. Have one student open the dictionary to any page and have the other students guess to which letter the dictionary is opened. If this is being done with a group, the one who comes closest to the letter will be the next one to stand and open the dictionary. If working as partners, the students simply take turns.

4. Telephone directories, encyclopedias, or other alphabetically arranged reference books may be used for this activity.

5. After the student has been introduced to alphabetizing words, these same activities can be used with whole words.

Looking Up Words in a Dictionary

Your student should now be able to open the dictionary relatively close to the letter with which the word begins. He will also know how to find a word, using alphabetizing principles in a list. However, to become really efficient at dictionary use, he must be taught how to use guide words as clues rather than starting at the beginning of a letter and going down every word until he comes to the word for which he is looking. This technique must be firmly established if dictionary use is not to be seen as a chore.

All page numbers referred to here are from Merriam-Webster's dictionary.

A lesson on the use of guide words might be conducted as follows:

"*Maze* is an interesting word. Let's try to find it. Listen to the beginning sound of the word. What sound do you hear? What letter makes that sound? Yes, it does begins with *m*. See how close to *m* you can open your dictionary. Remember that *m* will be found near the center of the dictionary. I've found it on page 463. At the top right corner of the page you will find two words, *maw* and *mean*. These are guide words. *Maw* is repeated at the top of the first column, and *mean* at the bottom of the second column. They are the first and last words you will find on this page. There are guide words at the top of every page of the dictionary and it is important to always use them. I know that *maze* must be on this page, because *maz* comes after *maw* and before *mea* (mean). See, here it is."

Several example words should be attempted with the teacher giving less and less help locating each word with each additional example.

After this introduction to dictionary guide words, activities using a "skeleton dictionary" will establish the habit of using them. The skeleton dictionary only contains the key information and thereby forces the student to have recourse to the guide words.

It is easy to prepare your own skeleton dictionaries. Begin by folding four sheets of blank paper and stapling them together to make a booklet of eight pages about the size of a dictionary page. Copy the actual page numbers, guide words, and last word in each column, as found on eight consecutive pages of the dictionary used in your classroom, onto each "page" of the booklet. (See figure for a sample page.)

One of these booklets is made for each of perhaps a dozen letters—for example *b* (pages 36 to 48), *d* (pages 145 to 157), *t* (pages 510 to 522). [All page number and dictionary references made in this section are based on *Merriam-Webster's Intermediate Dictionary.*]

A sample lesson you could follow when introducing and using the skeleton dictionary activities might proceed as follows:

Show your student the "skeleton dictionary" open at page 39 and explain that this page might be called a skeleton of page 39 in his real dictionary. Let him compare the two.

Write the word *barge* on the blackboard or provide him with the word card or small slip of paper with the word written on it.

"The word barge belongs on this page. Can you tell me how I know this?"

If your student does not mention the guide words, you may need to remind him that the guide words are clues that show the first and last words between which all the words on that page are alphabetically arranged. In this case, the guide words are *bare* and *barreling.*

Now help him to consider the word *barge* again. Barg would come after bare and before barr of *barreling.*

"The word must be somewhere on that page. Look in your dictionary. See, there it is."

After this, the dictionary is set aside for a time, while the student practices locating words in the skeleton dictionary.

With the booklet open at page 47, let the student explain independently how he can know that *bevel* is on that page between the guide words *bet* and *bicycling.*

After your student has a dozen or so experiences looking up words in the skeleton dictionary, you can expand his skills. Help him to decide in which column to look for a word. As an example: *bevel* was found to be on page 47. The last word of the first column is *beware*, therefore *bevel* must be in that column, because the bev in *bevel* comes before bew of *beware. Bible* belongs in the second column because bib comes after bew of *beware.*

The final step is for your student to find for himself the page and column on which a word belongs. Here is how he might proceed: given a booklet including pages 340 to 348 and a paper on which is written the word *okra,* he decides that the word cannot be on page 340 between the guide words *ocean* and *off*, or on page 341 between *off* and *oil*, but must be on page 342, between *oil* and *on*, and in the first column because ok comes after oi of *oil*, the first word in the first column, but before *old* of *old-timer*, the last word in the first column. If he now turns to his dictionary, he will find that he is correct.

You must not assume that only a few lessons will be necessary. Repeat these exercises over an extended period to ensure competency. Drill lists should be carefully constructed to provide practice in locating all the letters so that the pupil may come to have a basic feeling as to approximately where to turn for each letter.

Working With An Older Student

Often an older student will try to convince you he knows how to look up words in the dictionary. If yours makes this claim, give him an opportunity to prove his skills. Generally he will demonstrate faulty techniques, fumbling with alphabetical order, ignoring guide words, searching over the pages at random, or starting at the first page of the initial letter and looking down each column.

For such older students, practice with the skeleton dictionary seems at times almost indispensable if correct habits are to be established. He may really try to use the guide words, but old habits die hard. Instead of using them, he will often end up scanning the words up and down the printed page until he happens upon the right one, thus unintentionally evading acquisition of the new technique. The beauty of the skeleton dictionary is you can help him break his bad habits, since such scanning is impossible. He will be forced repeatedly to use the guide words correctly since there are no words in the columns.

Word	*Dictionary Page*	*Column*
________	________	________
________	________	________
________	________	________
________	________	________

You may want to conduct speed exercises with the skeleton dictionary (for example, see how many words can be located in five minutes). Another extension is to create a worksheet-type activity. Provide your student with a paper divided into three columns. In the first row, provide a list of words for your student to look up. He will then try to determine on which page and column the word is found. See sample above.

This same type of exercise can be followed as review work and extension activities by creating skeleton dictionary worksheet pages, as illustrated in figure below.

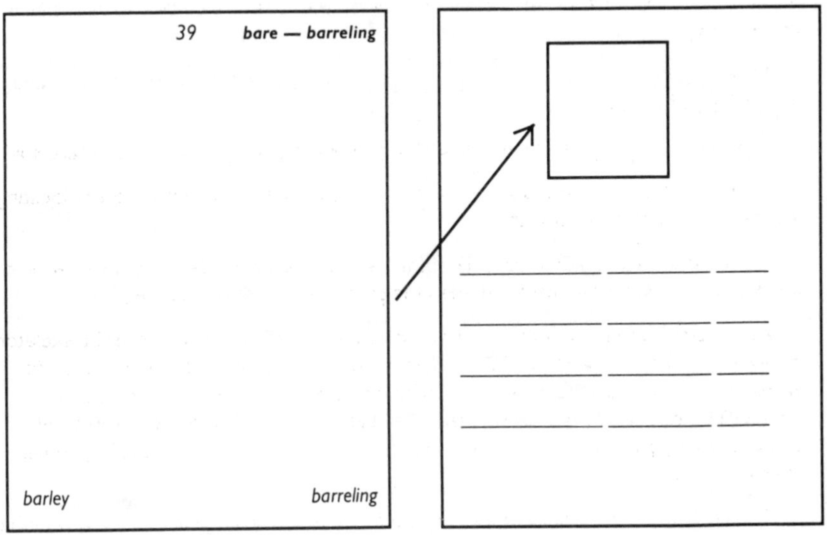

39 ***bare — barreling***

barley *barreling*

A variety of worksheet pages can be made which are simpler or more advanced, with directions such as the following:

"Look at this list of words. For each word, put a Y (for yes) after it if it would be found on this dictionary page, put a N (for no) if the word would not be found on this page."

"Look at the words below. For each word, decide if it would appear in column one or column two of this dictionary page. Write the column number after each word."

Any of these exercises can be made more difficult by adding more words or more "skeleton" pages.

"Look at the two dictionary skeleton pages. Now look at the list of words below. After each word, write the page number the word would be found on."

Group or partner games can be played by conducting races to see who can locate the guide words for a given word first.

Individual "List Activities" can be created, using worksheet forms, skeleton dictionaries, or the real dictionary, to have the student record the guide words, page number and column for each of his study words as well.

"Which of your spelling words would be found on this skeleton dictionary page?"

Practice with skeleton dictionaries and related worksheets must be repeated until a swift glance at the guide words becomes so much of an habit that it continues when the real dictionary is used. You should make occasional observations of your student's use of the dictionary to assure that use of the skills are being maintained. A series of review activities may be all that is needed to re-establish the habit.

How to Look up a Word When the Spelling is Unknown

How often, when told to look up a troublesome word, has the inadequately prepared student been heard to mumble, "How can I look up a word in the dictionary if I can't spell it?" Even adults can be heard to make this complaint. Using the dictionary as a spelling tool is a skill which does not come automatically. Your student must be shown how to look up a word in the dictionary even if he doesn't know how to spell it.

First, you must teach him how to encode or sound out the possible spelling by asking him questions about the way he "thinks" the word might be spelled. He should be helped to figure out the first sound or syllable and then the next sound and so on. You may also need to model for him the application of spelling rules as he tries to "figure out how to spell a word." With many words, there may be more than one possible way to spell a particular syllable or phoneme so he may come up with more than one possible spelling. Once your student has come up with one or more possible spelling(s), he can be shown how to use the dictionary to check his "educated guesses."

Phoneme-Grapheme Correspondences

The ability to come up with "possible spellings" for a word demands a firm grasp of possible phoneme-grapheme correspondences. Knowledge of the relative frequencies of graphemes for a given phoneme in particular positions can greatly reduce the errors made in locating a word when checking its spelling. There are a number of activities which can help your student to discover these principles for himself. These concepts will also facilitate accurate spelling.

One such activity that has proven helpful puts your student in the role of a "linguist" to unlock the rules which govern phoneme-grapheme relationships. Provide your student with a set of Word Cards or a list of words containing a common phoneme, such as f. Many of the Flow-Word-Lists Groups, especially Groups 6 to 25, will apply and may be used as a list source for Word Cards. These Word Cards are then manipulated into groups or recorded on lists according to the grapheme that represents the phoneme to be explored.

List of Words Containing /f/:
fish, phone, laugh, graph, calf
rough, shuffle, café, raffle, gruff

Grouped Listing (f, ph, ff, gh)
fish, phone, shuffle, laugh
calf, graph, gruff, rough

Written material at your student's reading level, such as textbook excerpts, magazine passages, or newspaper articles, can also be used for a variation of this work. The advantage of such material is that your student will see or discover (inductively) the relative frequency with which each phoneme is represented and its relative grapheme correspondences in a natural setting.

Your student can be given a list of tasks for this activity to complete, which also applies to Word Card sorting, such as the following:

1. List all the graphemes you can find for /ā/ and record the number of times each is used.

2. Arrange the graphemes for /ā/ in order of frequency.

3. List the graphemes for /ā/ which you find used at the beginning of a syllable and record the number of times each is used. Arrange these in order of frequency.

4. List the graphemes for /ā/ which you find used at the end of a syllable and record the number of times each is used. Arrange these in order of frequency.

5. List the graphemes for /ā/ which you find used in the middle of a syllable and record the number of times each is used. Arrange these in order of frequency.

6. List the graphemes for /ā/ which you find used in only one position.

Ideally you will give your student the opportunity to conduct one or more of the above "investigations" with each of the separate sounds, of which there are approximately 44.

You can also directly teach your student the following seven keys for finding words in the dictionary. (This is from *How to Spell It Right*, Dell Publishing.) As they conduct the linguistic investigations above, help them formulate these keys for themselves, rather than just having them memorize them.

If a word begins /s/, but you cannot find it, try ps (psalm) or c (cellar).

If a word begins with /f/, but you cannot find it, try under ph (phrase).

If a word begins with /r/, but you cannot find it, look for it under wr (write).

If a word begins with /n/, but you cannot find it, look for it under kn (know) or pn (pneumonia) or gn (gnarl) or en (energy).

If a word begins with /k/, but you cannot find it, look for it under c (cat).

If a word begins with /j/, but you cannot find it, try g (gentle).

If a word begins with /o/, but you cannot find it, try en as encore.

Secret Codes are Great Fun

Another activity which emphasizes phoneme-grapheme relationships requires your student to code the sounds in a word as it is heard. For example, you may pronounce the word telephone. Your student then codes the sounds heard as he might find these represented in his dictionary respelling /tel' a fō n/. Using his knowledge of phoneme-grapheme correspondences, he derives possible spellings and then checks their accuracy in his dictionary and selects the correct spelling.

Most dictionaries provide, at the bottom of the pages, a key to the diacritical marks. This does not, however, serve as a guide in the case of consonants with two sounds: c (k) or (s) or for digraphs such as wh (hw). Moreover, there is much additional information in the pronunciation guide found in the front of most dictionaries. You must familiarize yourself thoroughly with this information so you can answer any questions as they come up. How much of this information should be used with your student will depend upon his maturity and other individual factors.

The material "translated" should be challenging, intrinsically interesting, and brief enough so that the number of words to be checked in the dictionary is not overwhelming. In addition to your dictated words, material for translating can also be provided on worksheets in the form of secret code (2-mar-o) or rebus drawings.

Using Meaning to Select the Correct Spelling

To recognize a word in print is always easier than to recall from memory how the word is spelled. However, your student must be taught not to rely solely on his visual memory. A good dictionary supplies many additional aids for him to determine if he has found the correct spelling of the word.

First you must teach the student to read the definition to be sure he has found the correct word. The concentrated, elliptical style in which definitions are often written makes them difficult to understand and calls for direct instruction in how to read and interpret them.

Moreover, there are frequently different shades of meaning: *plant, n* 1, 2, 3, 4, - *vb* 1, 2, 3, 4, 5. Your pupil must learn to select the definition that throws light on the word as used in a particular instance. Is *plant* a noun or a verb? Is it used in connection with vegetation (1) or with manufacturing (2).

Locating Homonyms and Homophones

In other cases, there are separate entries for words of the same spelling and pronunciation, but entirely different meaning, such as in the word *font*. One boy, reading about printing, located font explained as a receptacle used in baptism and exclaimed, "It doesn't make sense." Just above it was *font*, defined as a printer understands it. The student must be on the lookout for such possibilities when a definition does not seem to fit.

Other homonyms or homophones, e.g., *to, two, too*, are also valuable in teaching the necessity of reading the definition. They also present special problems in spelling. Not only must your student master a variety of possible graphemes for the same phonemes, but he must also learn to associate a particular meaning with each of the different spellings. Certainty, with respect to the spelling of a word which sounds identical to other words, can be presented only when the word is presented in a context which reveals its meaning. Such words, pronounced in isolation, are ambiguous in both spelling and meaning. Knowledge of the meaning of a homophone, therefore, provides an essential clue for its spelling. Once your student recognizes this important relationship, the dictionary can assist him in selecting the appropriate spelling to convey his meaning.

Initial introduction to the spelling of homophones may be made via the dictionary. Using a set of homophones such as *so, sew*, and *sow*, students may be asked to determine how the words are alike and how they are different. After concluding that they are pronounced alike but differ in spelling and meaning, interesting material which uses the words in appropriate contexts may be provided for use in verifying their conclusions. Exercises may then follow which require your pupil to supply the appropriate spelling for the word when it is omitted in a given context. For example, use the correct spelling for /tû/ in each of the following blanks:

Do you ________ girls want ________ go ________ the movie ________?

You can create a large variety of such exercises in worksheet format using the homonym list found in the Miscellaneous section (last section of the book). The optional Activity Task Card box also has an entire section devoted to lessons on the use of homonyms, antonyms, and synonyms. These activities are presented in the same sequence that the homonyms appear in the *Spelling Power* Flow-Word-Lists.

The most frequent need for using the dictionary with respect to the spelling of homophones occurs when the meaning is clear but it cannot be associated with a particular spelling. All of the different spellings for the homophones may be known. Each spelling is then checked in the dictionary to identify the one whose meaning is consistent with that intended. Exercises which force the student to choose between homophones on the basis of context clues, and to verify the choice by using the dictionary, will emphasize the value of the dictionary for this purpose.

Dealing with Baffling Spellings

Silent letters and erratic combinations of letters present a much more difficult situation for your student. Even though you have taught him to decode or read some of these in his reading and phonics instruction and he has learned to spell a few of them, he may not think to look under the silent letter in his search for a new word in the dictionary.

When he learns to translate pronunciations, silent letters at the end of a word or within a syllable will not cause him a great deal of trouble. Thumb, comb, diaphragm, column, and hymn may be found because they begin sensibly and can then be recognized as the desired object of search since the pronunciation and definition are satisfactory. When the initial letter is silent, it is a different story. Your student will not be able to locate the word unless he has memorized the common silent letter combinations which may begin a word: kn /n/ as in *knee*; gn as in *gnash*. It will also be helpful for him to learn that a silent h often appears after g and r, as in *ghost* and *rhinoceros*.

The idea of silent letters can be made interesting and their use in some words may be remembered if you establish a link with its origin: column [L. columna], hymn [L. hymnus], Wednesday [A.S. Woden's daeg, i.e., Woden's day]. Often greater tolerance is felt for words with silent letters when they are viewed as a leftover from an older pronunciation: "Silent letters are the ghosts of departed sounds."

More baffling than silent letters are combinations which, translated phonetically, do not produce the sound usually attributed to them. In some cases a student may be helped to find such a word by the indicated pronunciation, e.g., there are only two words in which the letter o follows furl, furlong (fûr löng) and furlough (fûr' lō); only two begin with the combination porp, porphyry (pôr' fi ri) and porpoise (pôr' pus). Again the pronunciation decides for your pupil.

But consider the word *iron*. Your student will expect to it to be spelled *iern* or *iurn*. *Iern* would be on page 371, if there were such a word; iurn on page 403. Iron is on page 400! Nothing in his training has prepared him for such a spelling. He will come to you complaining he cannot find anything like it in his dictionary. There is nothing you can do but to write it out for him and to say, "Spell it i-r-o-n. You are not able to find it because it is not spelled the way it sounds at all. It is one of those pesky exceptions." You might also explain that in a few cases we are faced with such difficulties because we have borrowed words from other languages so they do not fit our normal spelling patterns.

But such situations are not common. By and large, the dictionary is a writer's "best friend," especially when he has learned how to approach it systematically.

Finding Words When the Main Entry Is Only a Base Word

While many words containing inflectional and derivational affixes are found intact in some dictionaries—especially those intended for younger students—the spelling of many others must be determined through locating the base word entry and using information associated with its listing. Therefore, you must teach your student to identify the base word and the meaning of the common suffixes and prefixes. You also must help your student develop skill in using the dictionary entry form to determine the appropriate spelling.

Root words, inflections, and derivatives of selected words may be taught. These words may be studied in the dictionary with attention focused on how the inflections and derivatives are indicated, which ones are included as separate entries, and which are not. You might also include several carefully selected lists of words, each of which has a common root. Three types of lists are suggested:

1. Those which include only separate entries;

2. Those having most of the information in a single entry showing all the needed spellings; and

3. Those which include words having highly regular forms for which the student must apply a rule accepted by the dictionary as sufficiently applicable to warrant omission of the inflected form.

Your student may then work with these lists and the dictionary to discover the patterns used to determine the spelling of inflected and derived forms.

Understanding Run-On Entries

The relationship of words with different functions derived from a common source is not always illustrated in dictionaries by separate entries complete with spelling, pronunciation, etc., but sometimes by words given at the end of the entry, with part of speech indicated but without definitions:

Main Entries	**Run-On Entries**	
arti' ist, n.	ar tis' tic, adj. art' is try, n.	ar tis' ti cal ly, adv.
art' less, adj.	art' less ly, adv.	art' less ness, n.

The definitions of these *run-on*entries can often be supplied by one who knows the meaning of the *suffixes* When the derivative cannot be explained easily, has several meanings, or a figurative significance, the word is given as a main entry: finalist, barbarism, bookish.

The makers of the dictionary presuppose a working knowledge of certain suffixes, e.g., -ly and -ness, and words in which these occur are seldom defined. To a lesser extent this is true of -er, -al, -ment and a few others. However, almost any suffix may appear in a run-on entry, e.g., -able, in *consumable*, -ish in *girlish* -ism in *sectionalism*, -ity in *jocularity*

Prefixes:

ab	means *away* or *from*
ad	means *to*
be	means by
com	means with
de	means from or down
dis	means from. away, apart
en	means in
ex	means out, beyond, or from
in	means into
pre	means not
pro	means before
re	means back or again
sub	means under
un	means not

Derivatives made by prefixes are usually given separate entries, though there are exceptions, e.g., some words made with out-, over-, ultra-, un-.

It is clear that familiarity with affixes (both prefixes and suffixes) is extremely important for your student to be able to use his dictionary skillfully. During the junior and senior high school years, your student should develop an understanding of the meaning of the most common prefixes and suffixes. He should realize that they are listed alphabetically in the dictionary, but are not always connected to the root word.

A full 24 percent of English words have prefixes. Fifteen prefixes account for 82 percent of the total number of prefixes. The boxes on this and the following pages contain a list of the most frequently used affixes and their meaning.

Several fun "games" can be made to help your student memorize the meaning of affixes. Two require providing your student with pairs of Word Cards. On one card the affix is written, while its mate has the affix's meaning. Use the list above as a beginning, since these are the most frequently used affixes. The back-side of these cards should all be exactly the same, either blank or with a common design (like playing cards). An "Affix Dictionary" (listing prefixes and suffixes) similar to those on these two pages should be made available to your student so that he may check his answers.

The first game is based on the classic concentration game. Your student shuffles the cards and distributes them face down in even rows on the table top or floor. For each turn, your student is allowed to turn over two cards, one at a time, and tries to make matches by remembering where its mate is located. If two students are playing, they take turns trying to make matches. If they are successful making a match they are allowed another turn. The winner is the player with the most sets at the end of the game.

Suffixes:	
al	means having to do with
ance	means act, process, or fact of
ence	means act, process, or fact of
d/ed	shows action in the past
er	means one who has to do with or shows comparison
est	shows comparison
ful	means full of or able to
ing	means the act of
ish	means in the nature of or belonging to
less	means without or unable to
ly	means *like* or *in a specified manner* (adverb form)
ness	condition of being
or	means state or quality of
ous	means full of
tion	denotes act of
sion	denotes act of
ion	denotes act of

The other game is based on the card game "Go Fish." First you must make a deck of cards which includes 24 sets of affixes and their definitions (48 cards total). The cards are shuffled and each player is given five cards (minimum of two players). The remaining cards are placed in the stack in the center of the table. The player on the left of the "dealer" plays first. He looks over the cards in his hand to see if he has any "matches" (he may consult the "Affix Dictionary"). If he has any matches, he lays them down in front of him. He then asks the player to the left for either the affix or the definition to an affix which matches one in his hand. If no match is made, he must take a card from the stack. If a match is made, he lays it down and continues his turn until he can no longer make a match.

The game continues in this manner until one player has no cards in his hand. If the center stack is gone before one of the players has "won," draws can then be made from any other player's hand. The winner is the player with the most matches at the end of the game.

Another activity which will help your student to memorize the suffixes or prefixes is "wrap-ups." You can purchase these or easily make your own. To make them, write the suffixes or prefixes in a row down the left side of a 3"x8" strip of cardboard or matte board. On the other side, in mixed up order, write the definitions. Cut very small notches near each of the affixes and definitions. Attach a string to the card. To solve the puzzle, the student must wrap the string so it connects the prefix (or suffix) with its definition. You may draw lines on the back, as guides, so your student can check his work. If the string matches the line he is correct.

Teaching Other Supplementary Information

Once interested in his dictionary, your student may at times inquire as to the meaning of other symbols following a word. The lower case letters n, adj. , vb., etc., denoting parts of speech, are often useful in identification, but have slight significance for the student who has not studied grammar. It is possible that they may interest him in grammatical terms. For the older student, they are indispensable. They often determine pronunciation and definition: *con vict'* vb, *con' vict* n.; *re bel'* vb., *reb' el* n.

Students will often ask about the brackets containing capital letters, [L.], [A.S.], etc., followed by foreign words in italics. These derivations are not of immediate assistance in looking up a word, but they often furnish a student with his first opportunity to increase his knowledge of language history for himself. He discovers that he can investigate the origin of any word he wishes.

His first inquiry about the brackets should be met with especially picturesque illustrations. Consider, for example, the word nasturtium. It has an amusing derivation. It comes from two Latin words, *nasus*, "nose" and *tortum*, "twisted." The name was given because of the pungent biting tastes of the juice.

Other words suggested because of their interesting histories are escape, salary, sandwich, boycott, forsythia, algebra, cloud, ukulele, khaki, calico, curfew, hippopotamus.

The *Merriam-Webster Dictionary* series also provide the student with "Word Histories" following selected entries. Some other elementary dictionaries do not include derivations, but the young student can have his interest in this topic kept active by having his teacher tell him some of the word histories from her dictionary or by reading books on the history of language or the history of words. Several excellent selections are listed below. The games Rummy Roots and More Roots are excellent for piquing interest in word origins.

Arthur Alexander, *The Magic of Words*, Prentice-Hall, Inc., Englewood Cliffs, NJ, 1962.

Maureen Applegate, *The First Book of Language and How to Use It*, Franklin Watts, Inc., New York, 1962.

Sam and Beryl Epstein, *The First Book of Words: Their Family History*, Franklin Watts, Inc., New York, 1954.

Roy A. Gallant, *Man Must Speak: The Story of Language and How We Use It*, Random House, New York, 1969.

Picturesque Word Origins: From *Webster's New International Dictionary*, G. & C. Merriam Co., Springfield, MA. 1933.

Specialized Sections

The student should be introduced to the information contained in the sections of the many dictionaries: Explanatory Notes, Abbreviations, Signs and Symbols, Proper Names, and so on. It is not enough to point to one section after another. If your own background with this information is limited, pre-digest the introductory information for a given section and discuss some of the features which will help your student at the moment he needs it or the "teachable moments." In many elementary dictionaries, all terms, including abbreviations and proper names, are listed as vocabulary entries.

A Word about Selecting Dictionaries

Formal dictionary skills have traditionally been introduced beginning in the third or fourth grade. With the introduction of the formal skills, it is recommended that each of your students be provided with his own dictionary so that he may have easy access to one whenever he needs it. Selecting the proper dictionary is very important. "Not all dictionaries are created equal." There are several factors to consider: number of entries, diacritical marking systems, reputation of publisher, and the copyright date.

First, you must consider the number of entries a dictionary contains. Your selection must keep in mind the intended user. Insisting that your eight-year-old use a complete unabridged Oxford dictionary as his spelling resource would be inappropriate. Selecting an elementary dictionary with fewer entries, but entries within the student's vocabulary range, will be more beneficial to your student. Elementary dictionaries generally have larger type which is easier for beginning readers. They also do not assume that your student has been taught suffixes and prefixes, so each variation of the word is listed. The major publishers of dictionaries generally offer dictionaries at the following levels: picture dictionary (for pre-readers through second grade); elementary dictionary (for grades 2 to 4); Intermediate dictionary (for grades 5 through 8), school dictionary (for grades 9 through 12) and collegiate (for college students and adults). Each dictionary level has significantly greater numbers of entries and more and more sophisticated information.

Next, you must consider the diacritical marking system which the dictionary you select uses. There is more than one system. It is important once you begin teaching your students one system, you provide dictionaries that are consistent. One way to prevent problems is to always use the same brand of dictionaries. Merriam-Webster is one publisher that offers a full range of dictionaries with consistent diacritical marking systems.

The diacritical marking system a dictionary uses can also be affected by the dialect used by the publisher. For instance, some publishers of religious textbooks have produced their own dictionaries. Their main motivation is to control exposure to "inappropriate language." Unfortunately, many of these publishers are located in the south and therefore use a diacritical marking system which presents a southern dialect. (For more information on dialectic effects on language see the "Important Notes" page at the beginning of this book.)

Note of Caution: Many of the inexpensive paperback pocket or notebook dictionaries available at back-to-school time are poor choices for students. They have few words and limited definitions.

Closely associated with the diacritical marking system is the reputation of the publishers. In recent years, almost all the major publishing houses have come out with their own dictionary because dictionaries are consistent sellers. Creation of a dictionary requires a skilled lexicographer and isn't a part-time business. Choose a dictionary created by a company that specializes in dictionary and reference materials.

When looking at the name brand of the dictionary, you should also note that there is no restrictions on the term "Webster's." That term is now in the public domain. Any company can use this name. The company that produced Webster's original dictionary is still around though. It is called Merriam-Webster.

Finally, you must look at the dictionary's copyright date. The English language is not static, it is constantly changing. It is important that your dictionary is contemporary enough to reflect general usage, but not so contemporary that it includes every passing slang word.

The release of Noah Webster's 1828 Dictionary has caused some concern for this author. It is important to understand the value of this resource is for reading historical documents, not as a spelling resource. This dictionary, while excellent for high schoolers studying history, is a poor choice for students as a spelling resource.

I highly recommend the Merriam-Webster series of dictionaries as they meet all of the requirements outlined above. They are produced in quality hardback form and are available in a wide range of age levels: elementary, intermediate, school, and collegiate. Most bookstores stock the school and collegiate editions. You may have to special order the elementary and intermediate from an educational supplier.

Chapter Summary

No teacher must suppose that the use of the dictionary can be taught and finished on a particular date. As other types of work proceed, there must be occasional practice in looking up a few words. Often these will be words required in correcting papers, as well as the lessons accompanying the study of a particular sound in the Flow-Word-List generalizations; for example, words containing /ô/, or on another day /oi/, may constitute one practice lesson. A word may have other ambiguities, but the designated sound will be the one to be especially watched for. Other times these will be short discussions regarding use of the dictionary at an opportune "teachable moment."

In this chapter, a brief explanation of many of the essential dictionary skills has been introduced, along with concrete suggestions for fun ways you can teach and reinforce these skills. The skills have been presented in as sequential an order as possible, but you must remember, as in teaching any subject, that a certain amount of backtracking is always necessary. You also must not suppose that you will be done once and for all with teaching dictionary skills. Time must be devoted to continual monitoring and modeling its appropriate use.

References For Chapter Five

1 Gertrude Hildreth, *Teaching Reading: A Guide to Basic Principles and Modern Practices* (New York: Henry Holt & Co., 1958, page 121).

Chapter Six
anning, Organizing, and Adjusting Instruction

Having read to this point, you may feel a little overwhelmed and wondering whatever happened to the "15 minutes a day" that we started with. In fact, you may feel a little like the fourth-grader who arrived home late from school one day. "I'm sorry to be late," she apologized as she came in, "but we've been making a display for science and I had to stay and finish the universe."

In this chapter, all of the various segments of the *Spelling Power* program, which have been individually described in detail, will be brought together into a cohesive, manageable lesson plan. You will be shown several approaches to the basic daily spelling schedule, each modified slightly for various situations. Adapting these procedures for younger and/or remedial students, multi-age groups, and classroom environments, as well as evaluating and reporting a student's progress, will be discussed. The chapter ends with a complete Scope and Sequence of Spelling and Dictionary skills.

Important Elements of Scheduling Spelling Instruction

Time must be set aside every day of the week for spelling study. One or two periods a week are not frequent enough for economical learning and retention. These periods require approximately 15 minutes per day. It is important that you resist allowing other activities to encroach on your daily spelling period.

In the ideal approach to this program, as described in the Quick-Start Introduction and Chapter Four, about one-third of the spelling period will be used for testing and/or retesting Flow-Word-List words, one-third to studying misspelled words using the 10-Step-Study sheets, and one-third of the scheduled time will be used for skill building activities presented in the Discovery Activities section, the optional Activity Task Card box, Skill-Builder CDRom, computer games, or directly by you as described in Chapter Four.

Coaching Sessions, discussed in Chapter Three, are not generally considered specifically "spelling study" since they deal with the total Language Arts curriculum. However, those words your student needs to study which are discovered during the Coaching Sessions should be studied and retested during the "formal spelling period."

Monday	*Tuesday*	*Wednesday*	*Thursday*	*Friday*
5 minutes pre-test	5 minutes pre-test	5 minutes pre-test	5 minutes pre-test	5 minutes pre-test
5 minutes study	5 minutes study	5 minutes study	5 minutes study	5 minutes study
5 minutes skill building	5 minutes skill building	5 minutes skill building	5 minutes skill building	5 minutes skill building
Coaching Sessons as a scheduled part of the English Grammar and Composition				

Figure 1: Basic Daily Lesson Plan

As pointed out at various points in this manual, you may also want to set aside some time on a regular basis for teaching dictionary skills, proofreading skills (both as part of coaching sessions and as formal exercises), and dictation exercises. Each of these activities has valuable contributions to make towards the spelling curriculum. If it is not possible to set aside separate weekly blocks for each of these activities (which would be ideal since these activities are not strictly a matter of spelling), you may elect to set aside one spelling session each week for such activities. The weekly "Activity Day" can be used for any of these items or other whole-group lessons which require more time than allowed for during the five minute daily skill-building sessions. (See Lesson Plan Chart 1 & 2)

Adjusting Instruction for Classroom Use

The *Spelling Power* program is designed as an individualized program. It is the philosophy of the author that maximum effectiveness will be seen with a teacher working with the program on a one-to-one basis with each of her students. A teacher, working with five or fewer students at a time, will not find it difficult to operate such an intensive individualized program. She simply schedules the spelling study work with each pupil in such a way that while one student is being tested, the remaining students are working on studying the words they need to learn or are doing the prescribed learning tasks presented through Discovery Activities.

Monday	*Tuesday*	*Wednesday*	*Thursday*	*Friday*
5 minutes pre-test	5 minutes pre-test	Activity Day used	5 minutes pre-test	5 minutes pre-test
5 minutes study	5 minutes study	for Dictionary Skills,	5 minutes study	5 minutes study
5 minutes skill building	5 minutes skill building	proofreading, etc.	5 minutes skill building	5 minutes skill building

Coaching Sessons as a scheduled part of the English Grammar and Composition

Figure 2: Basic Daily Lesson Plan

Unfortunately, in the traditional classroom of 30 or more students, this procedure would be impossible and some adjustments may be necessary for effective classroom management. Such adjustments fall into three basic categories: General Time Savers, Peer Testing, and Multi-level and Small Group Instruction.

General Time Savers

Developing systems and procedures which save time should be the teacher's first choice when she is trying to individualize instruction. These systems and procedures should include shortcuts and time savers that ensure students are working at their own level and at their own pace. Such items might include giving whole class orientation to the program, whole class survey testing, and conducting placement testing in small groups at the appropriate level.

The next area of teacher timesaving might be found in the use of pre-taped Delayed Recall and End-of-Level Tests so your students may administer these tests themselves when they are ready for them. Both forms of the test should be taped, one on each side of a separate audio cassette. Each tape should be clearly labeled so your students can access them easily.

You may find taping the daily tests a time saver as well. You will then only be required to test each student on the words he misspelled in the prior test. You may also choose to have your student take a daily test, study the misspelled words and take the entire test the next day. However, this is not the best use of your student's time and there is significant loss of instructional economy. It is far better to try to get an assistant in the classroom than to go to whole list retesting.

A parent volunteer or teacher's aide may be employed to help conduct the daily testing. The addition of such a helper is most effective when the assistant understands the program thoroughly; therefore, the aide should be required to read at least the Quick-Start Introduction before working in the classroom. Also it is most effective when the assistant is involved from the beginning of the year and has been involved in the student orientation and initial testing.

In very large classrooms, with only one teacher and an aide, it may be necessary to divide the class in half, which would allow each student to receive individual testing every other day. The opposite day he would be involved in Discovery Activities or other individual studies (e.g. general study hall).

Peer Testing

Peer Testing is another option that is often effective for large classes. Peer Testing requires pairs of students, assigned as partners, to take turns giving each other the daily Flow-Word-List and Review Tests. (Such an arrangement requires the teacher or school to purchase classroom sets of the *Spelling Power* Flow-Word-List folders.)

When selecting partners, it is important that the partners be on or about the same level (no more than three levels apart). Usually the students alternate which student tests first each day.

While the students test one another, your role is one of overseer and program guide. You will circulate among your students during the spelling period and be available to give Delayed Recall and End-of-Level Tests, if you have not provided for them through taped tests. A student whose partner is taking a Delayed Recall or End-of-Level test (or is absent) may be tested by another student whose partner is testing, by you, or by the teacher's aide. When you become the "temporary partner," you have the opportunity to see how your student functions during the testing process. You may find it necessary to change partners every month or so.

Monday	*Tuesday*	*Wednesday*	*Thursday*	*Friday*
10 minutes for peer testing, partners take turns testing each other. 5 minutes word study	15 minutes of Individually Prescribed Instruction Actitities or Small Group Teacher-led lessons.	Whole Class Activity Day used for dictionary skills, proofreading, etc.	15 minutes of Individually Prescribed Instruction Actitities or Small Group Teacher-led lessons.	10 minutes for peer testing, partners take turns testing each other. 5 minutes word study

Coaching Sessons as a scheduled part of the English Grammar and Composition

Figure 3: Peer Testing Lesson Plan

Peer Testing has both negative and positive points. On the positive side, the student who is testing his peer is exposed to the peer's list in columnar format (considered ideal for visualization) and says the word and spells it orally at least once (excellent for auditory learning). While the excellent exposure that the student is receiving may not be the list the student is currently working on, it remains excellent exposure.

On the negative side is the loss of the quality of pronunciation checks which a teacher or an adult aide may conduct more reliably. This negative can be partially remedied by establishing the policy that a student who has misspelled a word twice on the daily tests needs to be tested by the teacher before going on. This allows the teacher to determine if pronunciation is the cause of his spelling difficulty.

Even when modifying instruction for peer teaching, your students should still complete all the testing steps. Saying the word aloud, even if there is no actual pronunciation check, is still recommended as it helps him slow down and think about the word which he is about to write.

For peer teaching to be successful, it is vital to carefully and thoroughly teach your students how to administer the daily tests and review tests, how to use the 10-Step-Study Sheets, and how to record their progress. It is especially important that direct instruction on how the Group Rules should be read is given. Generally these items must also be reviewed on a periodic basis, say daily, until well understood and then reviewed monthly. You may wish to remind your class of the finer points of the daily testing and word study procedures at the beginning of each testing session. Furthermore, you must still allow time in your schedule for teaching spelling skills and rules whether it is to small groups of students working on the same group number (even if on different levels) or a group of students having difficulty with particular skills or to the whole class. Likewise, you are encouraged to work with students individually during coaching sessions for the Integrated Functional Writing segment of the program.

Multi-level and Small Group Instruction

Individualizing spelling instruction does not mean that every child necessarily should be taught every aspect of the program separately from every other child in the class. It may be quite possible to set up the classroom with several small groups of students working at the same level as in the "reading group" concept. This would allow you to give instruction on specific spelling generalizations to groups of your students as they are ready for them. You can also conduct group testing of Flow-Word-Lists, at least the first day the students begin a new list. Such grouping and regrouping requires you to keep very accurate records of where each child is in the program. If you wish to use this teaching option, you will find the information in the section of Chapter Two, titled "Evaluating and Recording Progress," especially helpful.

Whole Group Instruction

Since the Flow-Word-Lists use consistent spelling rules from level to level, it is often possible to have all students working on the same group number, but at different levels. This allows you to introduce the spelling skill or concept to the entire group. In this model, you would introduce the concept on Monday. Tuesday, individual students or small groups of students working at the same level would be tested on Flow-Word-Lists using the self-correcting procedures. Wednesday, all students would study the words each needs to learn, using the 10-Step-Study Sheet, and be prepared to be retested on the whole Flow-Word-List on Thursday, again using the self-correcting procedures. Friday is used to summarize the concept and for group activities which focus on the spelling skill (such as the Teacher-Directed Games described in the "Discovery Activities" section). Fridays can also be used to retest students who made errors on Thursday's spelling test.

This scenario is slightly different from the Study-Test-Study plan described below, which can also be used for small group instruction within a larger classroom.

While this approach does take a bit away from the efficiency of each student studying at his own level and pace, it has a possible edge in that your students quickly learn that it is to their advantage to not only study the words they misspelled but also those of which they were not really sure. Thus, if a student guessed correctly at the spelling of a word, such as receive, he may decide to spend some additional time studying that word in preparation for the final test. The major drawback is dealing with students who still misspell words following Friday's retest day.

Monday	***Tuesday***	***Wednesday***	***Thursday***	***Friday***
Small group or whole group pre-testing of entire flow-word group, followed by 10-Step Study of misspelled words.	Small group or whole group instruction focusing on the specific study skills followed by group or individual activities.	Individual prescription of activities which re-inforce specific skills and/or practice spelling of words.	Small group or whole group retesting of entire flow-word group, followed by 10-Step Study of misspelled words.	Retest for students who missed words yesterday and/or group dictation exer-cises & dictionary skills.

Coaching Sessons as a scheduled part of the English Grammar and Composition program

Figure 4: Group Lesson Plan

The least effective and efficient instructional method would be having the entire class study the same group, the same level, and the same words. Such a program should be avoided if at all possible as it is contrary to the findings of spelling research.

Using the Study-Test-Study Approach

If your student has extremely limited experiences in spelling and writing, he should not participate in the regular *Spelling Power* program. To subject him to the pretesting of words he is unlikely to know would be contrary to what research has found conducive to motivation. Therefore, another approach which allows your student to study the words prior to testing is necessary. Such an approach is referred to as the Study-Test-Study approach.

The Study-Test-Study approach should be considered for all students age eight and below. It should also be considered for those students whose placement testing placed them on Level A or B. Both categories of students should have completed a basic phonics program, as these suggestions are not intended to replace the general readiness as described in Chapter Two. The Study-Test-Study plan as presented here requires focusing on one word group or review group per week. Using this list, each day of the week a different activity is completed as described below:

Monday: The phonetic principle or spelling rule featured in the group list being studied is presented using an inductive or discovery approach as described on page 68-69 in Chapter Four. Following the formulation of this principle or rule, your student will copy the rule to the Daily Test Sheet. He then copies each word, under the appropriate letter in his Spelling Dictionary.

Tuesday: The rule is reviewed and each word is copied to a 10-Step-Study Sheet. After each word has been copied and you have checked them for accurate copying, steps one through ten are completed with particular emphasis on the *Trace and Say* step. Your student will not be writing the words in a sentence until tomorrow.

Wednesday: After restating and reviewing the spelling principle which is the focus of this week's list, your student should write a sentence of his own for each word. A separate form is provided for this step in the Red Student Record Book. Other levels of the Student Record Books provide space for this step on the bottom of the 10-Step-Study sheet.

For some students, it may be necessary to use Intermediate Double Dictation for this step. This procedure provides your student with a model to copy and prevents him from misspelling the other words in his sentence. Intermediate Double Dictation requires your student to dictate a sentence of his own composition for you to write out. Using your copy of his sentence as a model, he can then copy it to his paper.

Thursday: After reviewing the rule once again, you should test your student in the fashion prescribed in the regular approach to Systematic Spelling Study. Following this pretest, your student will study any words he has misspelled and participate in a skill-building activity. (See Quick Step 5 through Quick Step 7 on pages 6-9.)

Friday: Restate the spelling principle which is the focus of the week's word list. After going over the principle, the entire word list should be retested using the regular teaching test approach. Any words misspelled during this session should be recorded on blank word cards by your student. A word bank can be created for each student by storing these cards in individual business card file boxes. These word cards can then be used for many of the activities described in the Games and Activities section. One activity which is of particular interest, especially for the remedial student, is found in the Word Card Activities section (#7 Word Card Testing).

How to make a Spelling Dictionary

You should provide each student with at least 26 copies of the "Spelling Dictionary" page found in the Teaching Aids and Masters section. (Since this form uses the rather large 8mm lines, you may wish to use notebook paper if you are working with an older student.) These pages should be printed on one side of a sheet only. A different letter of the alphabet should be written in the space provided for it on each page. The pages should then be placed in alphabetical order in a small three-ring binder. Your student may wish to decorate the cover of his spelling binder. Have your student record each word on the appropriate page each Tuesday. Upon filling any letter's page, your student should be shown how to remove the page from his notebook and cut the page so that each word is a separate slip of paper. He arranges the word slips in alphabetical order. After you have checked his work, he will copy the words in alphabetical order to a replacement "Dictionary Page." The dictionary can thus be added to and maintained throughout the year, giving the student and his parent a visible picture of his progress.

In this approach, Review Group lists are handled just like any weekly word list. Because it is not necessary to formulate or "discover" the spelling principle for a review list, Mondays of these weeks can be used to study word cards in the student's word bank. Also since the student will already have recorded these words in his dictionary, this step can be replaced by alphabetizing dictionary pages.

Monday	*Tuesday*	*Wednesday*	*Thursday*	*Friday*
Presentation of Group Rule through inductive lessons. Student copies rule to his Daily Test Sheet. Words are copied to spelling dictionary.	Rule is reviewed and student completes 10-Step Study Sheet steps for each word.	Rule is reviewed and student writes each word in a sentence of his own.	After reviewing rule, words are tested in the regular *Spelling Power* testing approach.	Retest for students who missed words yesterday and/or group dictation exercises & dictionary skills.

Coaching Sessons as a scheduled part of the English Grammar and Composition

Figure 5: Study-Test-Study Lesson Plan

When the week's list would be a Delayed Recall Test or End-of-Level Test, a very different approach is needed. For these weeks it is suggested that your student be given the first form of the test on Monday.

Students using the Study-Test-Study approach, studying on level D or below, and those students participating in an intensive phonics program prior to formal spelling study should participate in all appropriate aspects of the Integrated Functional Writing program except the selection of words for Systematic Spelling Study.

If your student achieves 100 percent, he can use his spelling time during the rest of the week to review his word bank cards using his choice of activities. He may also participate in dictionary activities or other skill building exercises. At the end of the week, his word bank cards should be put in storage.

If your student has scored less than 100 percent, he should study the spelling principles and representative word lists from which each misspelled word came (see numeral following each word on Delayed Recall Test.) This review may be conducted using any activity you feel is appropriate. On Friday your student will be given the second form of the test.

While, ideally, your student should achieve 100 percent on at least one of the two forms of the test, this does not always happen. If you are working with individual students in a tutorial situation, you may elect to continue working on review before going on. However, if you are using this approach as a whole class or small group activity, you will have to decide how to proceed with the individual student who has not achieved 100 percent on the final test.

It is important to remember that usually a student using this approach is at lower levels of the Flow-Word-Lists or is younger and that he will have many additional opportunities to review these words when involved in the regular approach to Systematic Spelling Study and Integrated Functional Writing. Most students who use this approach with levels A and B, along with the Integrated Functional Writing activities, will be well prepared for the normal presentation of Systematic Spelling Study upon completion of level B, regardless of their age or whether they have totally mastered all of these lists. However, since levels A and B include the 488 most frequently used words and account for approximately 82 percent of the words children and adults use on a regular basis, it is definitely worth the effort to help your student master these words early in his schooling.

What If a Student Cheats

At this point it may be valuable to make a few remarks about cheating (not counting a misspelled word wrong and/or changing the spelling after the testing process). Cheating rarely happens in the process of the immediate self-correction, if the testing session procedures and the self-correction procedures have been explained clearly to the student. When your student understands that the purpose of the test is to determine the words he needs to study and that he will not be graded on the results, he seldom feels the need to cheat. The student soon learns that it is to his advantage to know which words he needs to study, as he will face them again in the Review, Delayed Recall and End-of-Level Tests. He knows also that many of the words will reappear in the next level as well.

If peer-testing, taped-testing, or small-group testing is being used in the program, you may wish to circulate around the room during the testing process to make sure procedures are being followed. You may also wish to occasionally check each Student's Record Book to check procedures. If a student is not recording misspelled words, you should not assume that he is cheating. Most often, not counting a misspelled word as wrong during the self-correction process is due to carelessness or lack of the skills necessary for the task. If taped-testing or small-group-testing is being used, the problem may be that the pace of the testing is too rapid for this particular student.

If you feel that actual "cheating" has occurred, then you should be aware that cheating is not specifically a spelling problem, it is a problem that has broader implications. A student who is afraid of having his peers see him make an error (or many errors) or has a strong desire to look good (or please) may resort to the undesirable practice of cheating when he is put in a situation in which he cannot succeed. It may be necessary to reevaluate the level at which the student is working or the choice of peer-testing partners.

Organizing Individually Prescribed Instruction

Probably the easiest way to organize your prescribed learning activities is to create a "Language Arts Activity Center." In this area, you can organize spelling resources (e.g., dictionaries, games, writing and art materials, and so on) necessary to complete prescribed activities. This does not have to be an elaborate setup. The key is that all the materials are easily accessible, so students do not have to waste time looking for them. Space on a bookshelf or near a desk area where all the materials can be gathered is sufficient. Sharon Edwards and Robert Maloy (*Kids Have All the Write Stuff*) suggest creating "Writing Boxes" using clear plastic sweater boxes or old briefcases as storage places for writing materials. Some students use their desk or backpacks as their writing boxes.

The items which should be provided to your students in the Language Arts Center or Writing Boxes fall into six categories: editing/publishing, creative materials, writing tools, writing surfaces, word sources, and miscellaneous games and materials. Depending upon the age or learning styles of the students, some of the materials which may be included in the Language Arts Center and Writing Boxes are:

Editing/publishing

paste/glue
tape
scissors
erasers
staplers
rulers
editor's visor
paper clips
hole punch
metal rings
correction fluid or tape

Creative Materials

glitter
string
yarn
toothpicks
stencils
clay
rubber stamps & ink pad
stickers
brass fasteners
felt markers

Writing tools

crayons
pencils
pens
chalk
soap
letter beads
finger paints
paint & brushes
typewriter
computer
alphabet stamps
colored pencils
label maker

Writing Surfaces	**Word Sources**	**Misc. Material:**
chalkboard	dictionaries	bulletin board
graph paper	thesaurus	telephone
cake pan of sand	rhyming dictionary	tape recorder
blank word cards	grammar handbook	sharpener
all kinds of paper	newspapers	letter cards
magic slate	alphabetical word list	letter tiles
envelopes	magazines	xylophone
blank flash cards	graded word list	resonator bells
postcards	prepared flash cards	Activity Task Cards
notebooks	style handbook	homemade games
tablets	prepared word cards	computer games
clipboards	word & phrase origin dictionary	other games
notepads	book of Latin & Greek roots	
blank books		
lap desk		
address labels		

Edwards and Maloy also suggest that students be given many supplies of their own. "When the children own them, they have the freedom to create without worrying about *wasting* something." In classroom situations, the materials can be brought from home at the beginning of the year, or—if funds are available—supplied by the school. In home situations, these items can be purchased on a "shopping spree" at the beginning of the program to build anticipation. Not all the materials need to be or should be provided at once; by continually adding to the Language Arts Center or the student's own Writing Box, interest may be maintained.

Evaluating Student Progress

Spelling, like any other curriculum area, should be evaluated in terms of objectives. The terminal objectives (desired outcome upon completion of schooling) for the *Spelling Power* program are:

1. The student will be able to accurately spell the 5,000 most frequently used English words.

2. The student will be able to accurately spell the words he uses on a regular basis.

3. The student will learn the most effective way to study a word, so that he can continue to build his spelling vocabulary throughout his lifetime.

4. The student will understand and apply the "spelling generalizations" to spell unfamiliar words with considerable accuracy.

5. The student will establish the habit of effectively using spelling resources, such as the dictionary.

6. The student will understand the importance of accurate spelling as an aid to his reader's understanding of what he has written. He will appreciate accurate spelling as a common courtesy to his reader.

7. The student will establish the habit of using effective proofreading skills and habits on all writing he intends others to read.

More specific annual objectives, which lead in the general direction of these goals, should be outlined at the beginning of each school year for each student. These objectives should include mastery to a realistic predetermined level of the Flow-Word-List and the learning and general application of specific spelling skills. It is often advantageous to include the student in setting his specific annual objectives. In any case, the objectives should be clearly outlined for each of your students and evaluation should be consistent with predetermined objectives.

The introduction to the Flow-Word-Lists has information regarding the general grade levels of each level of the *Spelling Power* program. Likewise, the scope and sequence presented at the end of this chapter provides the teacher with the normal sequence in which specific spelling skills are taught. This information may serve as useful a tool in determining objectives for each student.

Reporting Progress and Communicating with Parents

It is strongly recommended that students using the *Spelling Power* program not receive traditional letter grades. Rather it is more productive to give an evaluation of student's progress (e.g., satisfactory, excellent, etc.) It is especially important that your student not be given grades based on his placement level. Students who have been placed at lower levels should be working at those levels. A grading system that punishes your student for starting at his proper instructional level will only lead to cheating and poor student attitudes.

It is recognized your student will want to be given some specific appraisal of his progress. In addition to the knowledge that he is progressing through levels, the student often is motivated by knowing what percentage of high frequency words he has mastered. (These data are available at the beginning of the Flow-Word-Lists.)

In addition to the student's need for progress reports, parents expect and deserve meaningful information from teachers. It is recommended that you inform them about:

1. The program and the major operations of the program
2. The level on which their child is working.
3. The quality of their child's work
4. Ways in which they can assist their child.

Scope and Sequence for Spelling Skills

- I. Auditory recognition of phonemes
  - A. Consonant sounds
    - 1. The eighteen primary consonant sounds: b, d, f, g, h, j, k, l, m, n, p, r, s, t, v, w, y, z
    - 2. The sh, ch, wh, and ng sounds.
- II. Graphemic representation of phonemes
  - A. Consonant sounds
    - 1. The regular consonant sounds
    - 2. sh, ch, ng, wh, and th sounds
    - 3. nk spellings of the ngk sounds
    - 4. c, k, ch, and ck spellings of the k sound
    - 5. s spelling of the s and z sounds
    - 6. gh and ph spellings of the f sounds
    - 7. wh spelling of the hw sound
    - 8. x spelling of the ks sounds
    - 9. g spelling of the g and j sounds
    - 10. Consonant sounds spelled with double letters
    - 11. Silent consonants
  - B. Vowel sounds
    - 1. Short vowel sound regularly spelled in initial or medial position
    - 2. Long vowel spelled by
      - a. Single vowel at the end of a short word in open syllables
      - b. Two vowels together
      - c. Vowel-consonant-silent e
      - d. ow spelling of long o sound
      - e. ay spelling of long a sound
      - f. Final y spelling of long e sound
      - g. Final y spelling of long i sound
    - 3. Additional vowel sounds and spellings
      - a. oo spelling of ie and ii sounds
      - b. ow and ou spellings of the ou sound
      - c. oy spelling of the oi sound
      - d. Vowel sounds before r
    - 4. Unexpected spellings
      - a. Single vowel spellings (e.g., kind, cost)
      - b. Vowel-consonant-silent e (e.g., give, done)
      - c. Two vowels together (e.g., been, said)
      - d. Miscellaneous (e.g., they, eye, could, aunt, etc.,)
    - 5. The le spelling of the el sound
- III. Using morphemes to make structural changes
  - A. s or es plural
  - B. Changing y to i before es
  - C. ing ending
    - 1. With double consonants
    - 2. With dropped silent e
  - D. Adding er and est endings
  - E. er noun agent ending
  - F. Adding d or ed ending
  - G. Using final s to show possession
  - H. s or es for third person singular
  - I. Irregular plural noun changes
  - J. Using the number suffixes
  - K. Using suffixes to change the parts of speech
  - L. Using prefixes to change meanings
- IV. Devices to aid spelling recall
  - A. Syllabication

B. Recognizing compounds
C. Recognizing rhyming words, homonyms, and antonyms
D. Alphabetizing

V. Miscellaneous
- A. Vowel-consonant/consonant-vowel syllabication
- B. Vowel/consonant-vowel syllabication
- C. Remembering irregular spellings
- D. Spelling compounds by parts
- E. Spelling contractions and possessives
- F. Spelling abbreviations
- G. Capitalization of proper nouns
- H. Spelling by analogy

VI. Ability to use spelling resources
- A. Dictionary skills (see separate scope and sequence at end of Chapter Six.)
- B. Proofreading skills
  1. ability to understand and use proofreading marks
  2. ability to detect the majority of his own errors

Scope & Sequence for Dictionary Skills

I. Locating Words in the Dictionary
- A. Alphabetical Sequence
  1. Recognition of letters of the alphabet
  2. Ability to arrange letters sequentially
     - a. determine which letter comes before and after each letter
     - b. into three groups, A-G, H-Q, and R-Z
  3. Ability to open the dictionary to a particular section
  4. Ability to arrange words written on lists or cards according to
     - a. the first letter
     - b. second letter
     - c. third letter
     - d. fourth letter
     - e. fifth letter and so on
- B. Entry words are listed alphabetically.
  1. Usually printed in dark type (4)
  2. Separate numbered entries for words spelled the same but with completely different meanings and uses (4)
  3. Root words, but not inflected forms, listed (4)
  4. Common abbreviations given (4)
  5. Special phrases listed (5)
- C. Guide words show the first and last word on each page.

II. Pronunciation of Words
- A. The dictionary shows pronunciation by spelling words as they sound.
  1. Silent letters omitted (4)
  2. Consonant sounds represented by a single consonant (4)
  3. Two-letter consonant sounds (sh, ch, ng, th, wh) (4)
  4. One s spelling (says) shown as z (4)
  5. The hard c (can) shown as K (4)
  6. The soft c (cent) shown as s (4)
  7. The ck spelling (tack) shown as k (4)
  8. The soft g spelling (giant) shown as j (4)
  9. The x spelling (box) shown as ks (4)
  10. The qu spelling (quick) shown as kw (4)
  11. The nk spelling (ink) shown as ngk (4)
  12. The ch spelling (choir) shown as k (6)
  13. The ph spelling (elephant) shown as f (4)
  14. Short vowel sounds (a, e, i, o, u) (4)

15. Long vowel sounds (a, e, i, o, u) (4)
16. The sound (moon, tune) (4)
17. The sound (foot, should) (4)
18. The sound (her, turn, bird) (4)
19. The sound (haul, saw, all) (4)
20. The oi sound (oil, boy) (4)
21. The sound (arm, artist) (4)
22. The a sound of ay (may) (4)
23. The i sound of y (busy) (4)

B. The dictionary uses devices to show the pronunciation of multi-syllabic words.
   1. Syllable division (4)
   2. Primary and secondary accent marks (4)
   3. The schwa sound () in certain unaccented syllables (4)

III. Definitions and Word Forms
   A. Various devices are used to define a word.
      1. Separately numbered definitions (4)
      2. Illustrative sentences (4)
      3. Illustrations (4)
      4. Illustrations with fraction representing size of the object (5)
      5. Synonyms (6)
   B. Some irregular word forms are given
      1. Irregular plurals (5)
      2. Irregular comparative and superlative forms for adjectives (5)
      3. Irregular verb forms (5)

IV. Miscellaneous
   A. Other spelling and pronunciation helps are shown
      1. Capitalization (4)
      2. Abbreviations (4)
      3. Alternate spellings (4)
      4. Alternate pronunciations (4)
      5. Preferred spellings (5)
      6. Key words for pronunciation symbols (4)
   B. Additional language helps are given.
      1. Parts of speech (5)
      2. Word usage (4)
      3. Word origin (4)

Spelling Power Tests
Adams-Gordon Spelling Scales

The following two standardized 50 word spelling tests constitute the *Spelling Power* Diagnostic Survey Tests. They are adapted from the Adams-Gordon Spelling Scales for use with the *Spelling Power* program. The tests are of equal difficulty. Words included in the list were selected from each level of the *Spelling Power* program which also corresponded to data regarding average grade level at which the words are normally taught. (This information was acquired by comparing spelling programs published by five different publishers.) Each test is graduated in difficulty from Grade 1.0 (beginning of first grade) through grade 12 (12.0).

These tests are for diagnosing student placement and evaluating student progress, not for teaching spelling words. If used properly the tests may be used repeatedly by rotating the tests given. Following the directions for administration of the Survey Test is imperative. **Read the directions and advice on determining placement provided in Chapter Two carefully before proceeding.** The validity of the evaluation depends on the accuracy of administration.

The Survey Test should always begin with the first word of the test form being used and dictation of words should continue until the student has made three to five errors in succession. These Survey Tests were designed to be given by the teacher reading the word, using it in a sentence and repeating the word. The student should then write the word. There is no self-correction operation during these tests. The student should be encouraged to attempt to spell every word. If he cannot he should skip the line. At the beginning of the test students should be advised that capital letters should only be used for words that are proper nouns.

Form A

1. going	Are you *going* to the store?	going
2. did	She *did* well on her test.	did
3. get	I will *get* a new coat today.	get
4. nut	Susan found a *nut* in her yard.	nut
5. when	John will call *when* he gets in.	when
6. will	Where there's a *will*, there's a way.	will
7. fish	Dad caught a big *fish*.	fish
8. six	My little brother is *six* years old.	six
9. lost	He got *lost* on the way home.	lost
10. cold	He was very *cold* when he got home.	cold
11. help	Next time please call for *help*.	help
12. picked	Mother *picked* berries for dessert.	picked
13. paths	These *paths* are easy to follow.	paths
14. apple	An *apple* a day keeps the doctor away.	apple
15. dollar	A *dollar* saved is a dollar earned.	dollar
16. threw	Bill *threw* the ball.	threw
17. street	Cindy lives up the *street*.	street
18. since	I have not been there *since* yesterday.	since
19. felt	I *felt* like I was ill.	felt
20. shoot	Danny likes to *shoot* baskets.	shoot
21. nothing	Nothing ventured, *nothing* gained.	nothing
22. planet	The earth is a *planet*.	planet
23. eighty	This puzzle has *eighty* pieces.	eighty
24. become	I hope to *become* a doctor someday.	become
25. visit	We had a pleasant *visit* with them.	visit
26. quarter	Our team was ahead in the second *quarter*.	quarter
27. covered	I *covered* all the bases.	covered
28. knowledge	The *knowledge* that I was right was enough.	knowledge
29. arithmetic	I enjoy *arithmetic* class.	arithmetic
30. dentist	I really dislike going to the *dentist*.	dentist
31. courtesy	Please show us some *courtesy*.	courtesy
32. butcher	My uncle is a *butcher*.	butcher
33. prairie	The *prairie* is hot in the summertime.	prairie
34. region	The *region* we live in is prosperous.	region
35. annoyance	Little sisters can be an *annoyance*.	annoyance
36. character	He is of good *character*.	character
37. memorize	You must *memorize* the multiplication facts.	memorize
38. attraction	It was quite an *attraction*.	attraction
39. familiar	He seemed so *familiar*.	familiar
40. dissolve	We watched the plans *dissolve*.	dissolve
41. discipline	You must submit to *discipline*.	discipline
42. thrive	These plants *thrive* in the shade.	thrive
43. attentive	Everyone was *attentive* throughout the show.	attentive
44. manicure	A *manicure* costs $2.50 this week.	manicure
45. available	No one is *available* to help us.	available
46. delinquent	This bill is *delinquent*.	delinquent
47. tendency	He has a *tendency* to postpone things.	tendency
48. occasionally	I only go *occasionally*.	occasionally
49. apparatus	I find such *apparatus* interesting.	apparatus
50. catastrophe	It was a terrible *catastrophe*.	catastrophe.

Form B

1. went	He *went* to the store.	went
2. not	This is *not* my coat.	not
3. us	She went with *us*.	us
4. five	My sister is *five* years old.	five
5. from	It is *from* China.	from
6. what	Tell me *what* you would like.	what
7. black	I have a *black* cat.	black
8. dark	I am afraid of the *dark*.	dark
9. want	What do you *want* now?	want
10. book	I have read that *book* also.	book
11. great	That hat looks *great* on you.	great
12. write	Please *write* in ink.	write
13. sock	He wore one red *sock* and one blue sock.	sock
14. scream	We heard the loud *scream*.	scream
15. babies	The *babies* were fast asleep.	babies
16. dinner	I had a baked potato with my *dinner*.	dinner
17. guess	She never did *guess* my name.	guess
18. learn	I hope you *learn* a lesson from this.	learn
19. busy	I was *busy* all day long.	busy
20. building	He went in that *building*.	building
21. corner	Cindy hid in the *corner* all day.	corner
22. against	Jim was *against* every proposal.	against
23. lovely	You look *lovely* today.	lovely
24. medal	She won a *medal* at the Olympic Games.	medal
25. carnival	Danny took us all to the *carnival*.	carnival
26. ache	I had a tooth *ache* last week.	ache
27. Arkansas	President Clinton was born in *Arkansas*.	Arkansas
28. tiniest	It was only the *tiniest* of spots.	tiniest
29. according	Put it together *according* to directions.	according
30. squad	He was on my volleyball *squad*.	squad
31. stupid	It was a *stupid* mistake to make.	stupid
32. angriest	That was the *angriest* I have ever been.	angriest
33. community	The local *community* is actively involved.	community
34. magnify	This will only *magnify* the problem.	magnify
35. conservation	We studied soil *conservation* in biology.	conservation
36. dutiful	He did his chores in a *dutiful* way.	dutiful
37. gymnasium	We played in the *gymnasium*.	gymnasium
38. attraction	It was quite an *attraction*.	attraction
39. exhibition	We saw that at the *exhibition*.	exhibition
40. actually	I didn't *actually* do it myself.	actually
41. nuisance	My brother was a *nuisance*.	nuisance
42. tremendous	It took a *tremendous* effort by us all.	tremendous
43. alcohol	Wipe the wound with rubbing *alcohol*.	alcohol
44. professional	He was a *professional* race car driver.	professional
45. privilege	It was a *privilege* to serve you.	privilege
46. accumulate	We all have a tendency to *accumulate* junk.	accumulate
47. thermometer	This is a *thermometer* for babies.	thermometer
48. ligament	He tore a *ligament* in his knee.	ligament
49. souvenir	This is my most treasured *souvenir*.	souvenir
50. expectation	The product didn't live up to *expectation*.	expectation

Scoring Survey Tests

The Diagnostic Survey Test should be corrected by you out of the presence of your student. Each word must be absolutely correct. They must be counted as either right or wrong, there is no partial credit given. Words which do not have all their t's crossed or their i's dotted are considered wrong. Likewise, only proper nouns should be capitalized. (The teacher should not use test words at the beginning of a sentence to avoid any question regarding the appropriateness of capitalization.)

The Placement Testing Level Chart which follows should be used to determine at what level placement testing should begin. To determine your student's level of spelling mastery, you simply determine the word number at which the student begins making numerous errors in succession (say 3-5) on the Survey Test. Determine the total number of words tested. (If you have given the entire test to your student, do not count any words tested beyond the sixth misspelled word.) Subtract from this number the number of words your student misspelled. You will then have his total number correct score. The letter adjacent to it (in the left column, under Placement Testing Level) determines the level at which Placement Testing should begin. If your student started missing numerous words at number fifteen, for example, you would subtract his total number of misspelled words from fifteen (not 50). If he missed five words, his total correct score would be ten and his placement testing would begin at Level B.

To determine approximate grade level equivalency, count the total number of words spelled correctly on the Survey Test. Then, locate that number on the chart and look to the right for grade level equivalent. The Grade Level Equivalency data is provided only as an aid to determining your student's approximate grade level equivalence. Our sample student above would have a grade level equivalency of 2.7 (seventh month of second grade or close to third grade). The teacher is cautioned to keep in mind that *Spelling Power*'s Flow-Word-Lists are not strictly divided by "normal grade level taught" but are based on the frequency of word usage. Therefore there may be many words introduced at each level above or below the equivalent grade level scale normally used in other programs. (See chart on page 123.)

If the number correct is	the grade level is	and you should begin Placement Testing at this level (on page #).
0	1.0	A (105)
1	1.3	A (105)
2	1.5	A (105)
3	1.6	A (105)
4	1.7	A (105)
5	1.8	A (105)
6	2.0	B (106)
7	2.2	B (106)
8	2.4	B (106)
9	2.5	B (106)
10	2.7	B (106)
11	3.0	B (106)
12	3.2	C (107)
13	3.3	C (107)
14	3.5	C (107)
15	3.7	C (107)
16	3.8	C (107)
17	4.0	C (107)
18	4.2	D (108)
19	4.5	D (108)
20	4.7	D (108)
21	4.8	D (108)
22	5.0	D (108)
23	5.2	E (109)
24	5.3	E (109)
25	5.5	E (109)
26	5.7	E (109)
27	6.0	E (109)
28	6.1	F (110)
29	6.2	F (110)
30	6.3	F (110)
31	6.5	F (110)
32	6.7	F (110)
33	7.0	F (110)
34	7.2	G (111)
35	7.4	G (111)
36	7.6	G (111)
37	7.7	G (111)
38	7.8	G (111)
39	8.0	G (111)
40	8.2	H (112)
41	8.5	H (112)
42	8.7	H (112)
43	9.0	H (112)
44	9.4	I (113)
45	9.8	I (113)
46	10.3	I (113)
47	10.7	J (114)
48	11.0	J (114)
49	11.7	K (115)
50	12.0	K (115)

Tommy
(912) 381-5716

Zak

~~measuring~~
~~San Francisco~~
X ~~junior high school~~
~~parts of speech~~
~~New Year's Day~~
~~Chicken Pox~~
~~peanut butter~~
~~inner tube~~
~~Wed.~~
~~Thurs.~~
~~Tues.~~
X ~~Mrs.~~
~~Ms.~~
~~Dr.~~
~~ft.~~
~~yd.~~
~~friend~~
X ~~weather~~
X ~~trouble~~
X ~~busy~~
~~laugh~~
X build
~~guy~~
X ~~against~~
~~skier~~
X ~~toward~~

~~truly~~
X ~~young~~
X ~~tough~~
~~skiing~~
~~rough~~
~~Arctic~~
~~there's~~
~~United States~~
~~Thurs.~~
~~laughing~~

12
24
36
48
60
72
84
96
108
120
132
144

12
12
120
132

Emily

science
bye
excited
crying
surprised
nineteen
goes
rope
though
throw
ocean
below
gopher
loyal
voice
poison
disappointed
choice
avoid
Moisture
annoy
from
done
honey
probably
months

Stomach
government
governor
colored
quarter
quiz
squirm
turquoise
mosquito
squirrels
quarter
questions
squirrel
equipment
square
lion
roast
moisture
probably
answer
tomb
signs
honor
wrench
folk
psalm

wrestle
wriggle
guess
recess
hutt
treasure
measure
assure
mature
temperature
pleasure
suddenly
finally
usually
lonely
hearty
accidentally
lightly
quietly
deeply
safety
directly
[illegible]
beautiful
colorful
graceful

healthful
forgetful
dreadful
delightful
tomb
wrestle
recess
picture
feature
delight

Placement Tests

These placement tests are designed to be given by reading the word, using it in a sentence, and repeating the word. Your student should then write the word. There is no self-correction operation during these tests. The entire test for the level which was indicated by the results of the Survey Tests should be given.

The test should be scored and analyzed (at a time when your student is not present) by you or some other reliable person. You should not rely solely on your own spelling ability when checking the Placement Test, but should refer often to the list while verifying the spelling of each word. If your student has capitalized a word which is not a proper noun but was used to begin the sentence he should not be penalized for capitalizing it. Otherwise only proper nouns should be capitalized.

The chart at the bottom of each Placement Test will instruct you as to how you are to proceed based on the results of the test. However, your should make adjustments in student placement when sufficient evidence exists to indicate that you student could be working more efficiently at a level other than the one on which he was placed as a result of placement testing. See page five and 35 for more details on teacher adjustments to placement level.

Placement Test A

1. at	Meet me *at* the library.	at
2. that	Is *that* the book you wish to get?	that
3. get	You'll have to *get* a library card.	get
4. his	This is *his* new computer.	his
5. it	Where did you find *it*?	it
6. after	I gave up looking *after* three days.	after
7. from	Did someone hide it *from* me?	from
8. just	That would be *just* like them.	just
9. home	Welcome to our *home*.	home
10. be	We will *be* right back.	be
11. see	I came by to *see* you yesterday.	see
12. go	I hope you do not *go* too soon.	go
13. our	This is *our* new home.	our
14. about	What shall we talk *about*?	about
15. you	I am glad *you* came.	you
16. do	Please *do* come again.	do
17. come	Bring Cindy next time you *come*.	come
18. what	I don't know *what* to do next.	what
19. the	This is the *end*.	the
20. they	Will *they* come to see us again?	they

Number of Words Misspelled	Placement Level	Go To Page
13-20	Do not begin formal spelling study at this time.	N/A
3-12	Study Level A	Flow Word List Page 125
0-2	Test on Level B	Page 106

Placement Test B

1. happy — I was *happy* to see you. — happy
2. men — There were three *men* in a tub. — men
3. every — I like *every* type of vegetable. — every
4. long — Have you been waiting *long?* — long
5. think — What do you *think* of this one? — think
6. much — Thank you very *much.* — much
7. toy — Is this your *toy?* — toy
8. white — I'd like a *white* bicycle. — white
9. sleep — Be sure to get enough *sleep.* — sleep
10. tree — This *tree* is very old. — tree
11. only — If I were *only* sure of it. — only
12. snow — I love the *snow.* — snow
13. hood — My new coat has a *hood.* — hood
14. moving — We are *moving* to Ireland. — moving
15. are — Which way *are* you going? — are
16. April — I hope to go there in *April.* — April
17. today — I cannot play *today.* — today
18. police — The *police* are community helpers. — police
19. should — You *should* call them for help. — should
20. won't — They *won't* leave you stranded. — won't

Number of Words Misspelled	Placement Level	Go To Page
13-20	Study Level A	Flow Word List Page 125
3-12	Study Level B	Flow Word List Page 128
0-2	Test on Level C	Page 107

Placement Test C

1. hand	Please take my *hand.*	hand
2. ten	I have *ten* fingers.	ten
3. sing	I love to *sing* around the campfire.	sing
4. clock	The *clock* struck ten.	clock
5. lunch	It was still two hours to *lunch.*	lunch
6. taste	I can already *taste* the cake.	taste
7. street	Bonnie lives up the *street* from me.	street
8. almost	I *almost* forgot to thank you.	almost
9. science	His favorite subject is *science.*	science
10. music	She loves beautiful *music.*	music
11. dollar	I spent my last *dollar* yesterday.	dollar
12. round	The table is *round.*	round
13. watched	We *watched* the game on television.	watched
14. earth	The *earth* is a planet.	earth
15. stars	I enjoy the *stars* on a clear night.	stars
16. month	My birthday is this *month.*	month
17. write	Be sure to *write* me a letter.	write
18. babies	The *babies* are twins.	babies
19. stepped	He *stepped* down from the train.	stepped
20. tripped	He *tripped* on the wet floor.	tripped

Number of Words Misspelled	Placement Level	Go to Page
13-20	Study Level B	Flow Word List Page 128
3-12	Study Level C	Flow Word List Page 133
0-2	Test on Level D	Page 108

Placement Test D

1. land	Did Columbus discover this *land*?	land
2. fence	I hope the new *fence* is attractive.	fence
3. swim	I can *swim* ten laps.	swim
4. pond	The *pond* is home to many frogs.	pond
5. jump	They *jump* and croak all night long.	jump
6. tail	The puppy wagged its *tail*.	tail
7. reach	I hope we *reach* home soon.	reach
8. flying	Jim is *flying* in today from Chicago.	flying
9. phone	He will *phone* us from the airport.	phone
10. soup	My mother makes chicken noodle *soup*.	soup
11. garage	Father has two cars in the *garage*.	garage
12. thirty	It is more than a *thirty* block walk.	thirty
13. color	Cindy's favorite *color* is red.	color
14. push	Please do not *push* when in line.	push
15. answer	I could not *answer* the phone in time.	answer
16. bakeries	Mary's father delivers food to *bakeries*.	bakeries
17. halves	He divided the cakes in *halves*.	halves
18. there's	When this is gone, *there's* more.	there's
19. home school	Do you like *home school* better?	home school
20. Easter	Is *Easter* next Sunday?	Easter

Note: the term *home school* is relatively new and there are different opinions regarding its spelling. We have chosen the two word compound because it is consistent with other similar compound words, i.e. high school, grade school, private school, etc.

Number of Words Misspelled	Placement Level	Go To Page
13-20	Study Level C	Flow Word List Page 133
3-12	Study Level D	Flow Word List Page 139
0-2	Test on Level E	Page 109

Placement Test E

1. smash	Be careful not to *smash* it.	smash
2. tent	We slept in a *tent* outdoors.	tent
3. million	A *million* dollars is a lot of money.	million
4. straight	Go *straight* down this road one mile.	straight
5. screamed	She *screamed*, "Get out of my way!"	screamed
6. surprised	He was *surprised* by the party.	surprised
7. gopher	The *gopher* tore up our lawn.	gopher
8. disappointed	I hope you are not *disappointed*.	disappointed
9. government	Next year we will study *government*.	government
10. turquoise	I love the color *turquoise*.	turquoise
11. wrench	Use a *wrench* to tighten it.	wrench
12. temperature	What is the *temperature* today?	temperature
13. accidentally	Did he do it *accidentally*?	accidentally
14. wonderful	You look *wonderful* today.	wonderful
15. passenger	He was *passenger* number 57.	passenger
16. sprinkle	Please *sprinkle* this lightly.	sprinkle
17. monsters	There are no such things as *monsters*.	monsters
18. activities	We participated in many *activities*.	activities
19. Connecticut	She came from *Connecticut*.	Connecticut
20. grandmother	My *grandmother* is ninety-nine.	grandmother
21. shouldn't	I really *shouldn't* eat this.	shouldn't
22. restaurant	This is my favorite *restaurant*.	restaurant
23. first aid	We learned *first aid* in health.	first aid
24. Sept.	Please write the abbreviation for September	Sept.
25. up-to-date	She was always *up-to-date*.	up-to-date

Number of Words Misspelled	Placement Level	Go To Page
16-25	Study Level D	Flow Word List Page 139
4-15	Study Level E	Flow Word List Page 145
0-3	Test on Level F	Page 110

Placement Test F

1. drank	He *drank* coffee every day.	drank
2. medicine	This is helpful *medicine*.	medicine
3. village	He lives in the next *village*.	village
4. cottage	She owns the brown *cottage* on the right.	cottage
5. buffalo	The *buffalo* are almost extinct.	buffalo
6. greatest	Elizabeth I was the *greatest* queen.	greatest
7. cleaned	We *cleaned* all day Saturday.	cleaned
8. higher	We looked for a *higher* road.	higher
9. blowing	He was *blowing* his horn.	blowing
10. church	Our *church* was built in 1863.	church
11. porridge	Goldilocks ate the *porridge*.	porridge
12. carrots	I truly dislike *carrots*.	carrots
13. hearing	He was always in *hearing* range.	hearing
14. sour	Some cherries have a *sour* taste.	sour
15. quarters	Grandpa gave me *quarters* and dimes.	quarters
16. unknown	He wasn't an *unknown* man.	unknown
17. geese	We have geese in the yard.	geese
18. crazier	Jerry was even *crazier* than he thought.	crazier
19. preparing	She is *preparing* for Confirmation.	preparing
20. America	I live in *America*.	America
21. they'll	Soon *they'll* arrive from California.	they'll
22. baby-sitter	Mary was often my *baby-sitter*.	baby-sitter
23. dictionary	The *dictionary* is a useful tool.	dictionary
24. trouble	He had *trouble* learning to spell.	trouble
25. position	It was a difficult *position*.	position

Number of Words Misspelled	Placement Level	Go To Page
16-25	Study Level E	Flow Word List Page 145
4-15	Study Level F	Flow Word List Page 152
0-3	Test on Level G	Page 111

Placement Test G

1. package	I am expecting a *package* any day now.	package
2. smelling	She was *smelling* the cake for hours.	smelling
3. wished	Joseph *wished* he could go too.	wished
4. subjects	The normal number of *subjects* is six.	subjects
5. changed	Eileen *changed* at least five times.	changed
6. breathe	He could *breathe* freely in the country.	breathe
7. invited	She was never *invited* to parties.	invited
8. located	It's *located* at the fork in the road.	located
9. pollute	Please do not *pollute* our river.	pollute
10. particular	Dad was *particular* about that.	particular
11. remembered	Jane always *remembered* our birthdays.	remembered
12. ordinary	Mom often made *ordinary* days holidays.	ordinary
13. northern	We live in the *northern* part of town.	northern
14. smaller	Cindy was always *smaller* than I.	smaller
15. pointing	He had a way of *pointing* things out.	pointing
16. discovered	Vancouver *discovered* the Puget Sound.	discovered
17. swerve	We watched the car *swerve* wildly.	swerve
18. embarrass	The situation would *embarrass* anyone.	embarrass
19. temperatures	The *temperatures* soared this week.	temperatures
20. invisible	It's like an *invisible* wall before us.	invisible
21. sisters	Barbara has two *sisters*.	sisters
22. cloudiness	The *cloudiness* of February is dreary.	cloudiness
23. Scotland	My ancestors come from *Scotland*.	Scotland
24. long-distance	It was a *long-distance* call.	long-distance.
25. dead end	We live on a *dead end* road.	dead end
26. teacher's	This is the *teacher's* pen.	teacher's
27. TX	Please write the postal abbreviation for Texas	TX
28. punctuation	Be careful of your *punctuation*.	punctuation
29. decorator	She hopes to become an interior *decorator*.	decorator
30. shoulder	Always lend a *shoulder* to cry on.	shoulder

Number of Words Misspelled	Placement Level	Go To Page
15-30	Study Level F	Flow Word List Page 152
4-14	Study Level G	Flow Word List Page 160
0-3	Test on Level H	Page 112

Test Section

Placement Test H

1. language	He speaks our *language* well.	language
2. necessary	It is *necessary* to speak well.	necessary
3. chickens	How many *chickens* do you have?	chickens
4. property	We have six on this *property*.	property
5. greater	That is a *greater* obstacle.	greater.
6. speech	His *speech* was flawless.	speech
7. smiled	Mother *smiled* at him from across the room.	smiled
8. clothing	We gave our old *clothing* to the poor.	clothing
9. schools	There are ten *schools* in our area.	schools
10. peculiar	It is a *peculiar* institution.	peculiar
11. learning	She is *learning* many things.	learning
12. forests	There are bears living in the *forests*.	forests
13. correct	You have given the *correct* answer.	correct
14. engineers	I used to work with *engineers*.	engineers
15. surrounding	He is *surrounding* me with love.	surrounding
16. exhaust	The *exhaust* was recirculated.	exhaust
17. succumb	You must never *succumb* to fear.	succumb
18. instinctive	For a cat it's *instinctive*.	instinctive
19. progress	We look forward to *progress*.	progress
20. immediately	Don't expect it *immediately*.	immediately
21. kindergarten	I learned that in *kindergarten*.	kindergarten
22. alcohol	Using *alcohol* can be dangerous.	alcohol
23. machines	He has many *machines* for that.	machines
24. larva	The butterfly *larva* has hatched.	larva
25. throughout	We watched *throughout* the process.	throughout
26. Apt.	Please write the abbreviation for apartment.	Apt.
27. communication	Keeping *communication* open is crucial.	communication
28. mischievous	Tad has a *mischievous* nature.	mischievous
29. performance	We had tickets to the *performance*.	performance
30. remainder	This is the *remainder* of the glue.	remainder

Number of Words Misspelled	Placement Level	Go To Page
15-30	Study Level G	Flow Word List Page 160
4-14	Study Level H	Flow Word List Page 173
0-3	Test on Level I	Page 113

Placement Test I

1. gasoline	We ran out of *gasoline*.	gasoline
2. baskets	I picked seven *baskets* full.	baskets
3. welcome	You are *welcome* to my share.	welcome
4. privilege	It is a *privilege* to serve you.	privilege
5. considered	You are *considered* more important.	considered
6. promise	I *promise* to obey my parents.	promise
7. bucket	The *bucket* of water spilled.	bucket
8. ascertain	I came to *ascertain* your needs.	ascertain
9a. neighborhood	I live in your *neighborhood*.	neighborhood
9b. neighbourhood	I live in your *neighbourhood*.	neighbourhood
10. disease	She had an incurable *disease*.	disease
11. breathing	John had trouble *breathing*.	breathing
12. recognize	I could not *recognize* her painting.	recognize
13. automobiles	Father has five *automobiles*.	automobiles
14. improve	She tried hard to *improve* her spelling.	improve
15. molecules	These *molecules* are made of atoms.	molecules
16. determined	Mother was *determined* to win.	determined
17. orchestra	He played in the *orchestra*.	orchestra
18. paralyzed	Richard was *paralyzed* by fear.	paralyzed
19. irresponsible	It's a very *irresponsible* thing to do.	irresponsible
20. conqueror	Balboa was a *conqueror*.	conqueror
21. connected	I do not feel *connected*.	connected
22. manicure	I wish to have a *manicure* on Tuesday.	manicure
23. constantly	I think of you *constantly*.	constantly
24. deceitful	Julie did a *deceitful* thing to me.	deceitful
25. excellent	His reputation was *excellent*.	excellent
26. noticeable	Her limp was hardly *noticeable*.	noticeable
27. oceans	The world has seven major *oceans*.	oceans
28. multiplied	Any number *multiplied* by zero is zero.	multiplied
29. Philadelphia	My grandmother lived in *Philadelphia*.	Philadelphia
30. nevertheless	It is *nevertheless* an important point.	nevertheless
31. pronunciation	Your *pronunciation* says a lot about you.	pronunciation
32. mountainous	Father came from *mountainous* country.	mountainous
33. independence	Angie wants her *independence*.	independence
34. accomplishment	This is quite an *accomplishment*.	accomplishment
35. composition	It's the largest *composition* written.	composition

Number of Words Misspelled	Placement Level	Go To Page
22-35	Study Level H	Flow Word List Page 173
5-21	Study Level I	Flow Word List Page 186
0-4	Test on Level J	Page 114

Placement Test J

1. appropriate	This behavior is not *appropriate.*	appropriate
2. associated	He is no longer *associated* with them.	associated
3. developing	Dan is *developing* good spelling techniques.	developing
4. pedestrian	The *pedestrian* fell on the sidewalk.	pedestrian
5. admitted	She was *admitted* to the early game.	admitted
6. introduced	I *introduced* them just weeks before.	introduced
7. complicated	The directions were *complicated.*	complicated
8. remaining	Her *remaining* students passed today.	remaining
9. succeeded	Gary seems to have *succeeded.*	succeeded
10. franchise	He hoped someday to own a *franchise.*	franchise
11. approached	Jack *approached* his work cautiously.	approached
12. microscope	Venus has her own *microscope.*	microscope
13. manufacturing	It was founded on *manufacturing.*	manufacturing
14. thermometer	The *thermometer* is inaccurate.	thermometer
15. corresponding	Jasmine is *corresponding* with her.	corresponding
16. appointment	He was unable to keep his *appointment.*	appointment
17. inflammable	This liquid is *inflammable.*	inflammable
18. comparatively	It is *comparatively* minor in scope.	comparatively
19. undoubtedly	You are *undoubtedly* hungry.	approximately
20. parentheses	Review words are in *parentheses.*	parentheses
21. mechanical	John is not very *mechanical.*	mechanical
22. principles	You must always live by *principles.*	principles
23. Switzerland	The watch is made in *Switzerland.*	Switzerland
24. must've	She *must've* known her before.	must've
25. recommendation	He made a sound *recommendation.*	recommendation
26. abbreviation	Use the *abbreviation* carefully.	abbreviation
27. contagious	Chicken pox is a very *contagious* disease.	contagious
28. precedence	Age has *precedence* over beauty.	precedence
29. documentary	He is known for his *documentary* films.	documentary
30. expedition	The boys began their *expedition.*	expedition
31. cylinder	Jennifer held the *cylinder* upright.	cylinder
32. primitive	The country was very *primitive.*	primitive
33. incredulous	He had an *incredulous* grin.	incredulous
34. parliamentary	The meetings follow *parliamentary* rules.	parliamentary

Number of Words Misspelled	Placement Level	Go To Page
22-35	Study Level I	Flow Word List Page 186
5-21	Study Level J	Flow Word List Page 200
0-4	Test on Level K	Page 115

Placement Test K

1. catastrophe	It was a major *catastrophe*.	catastrophe
2. pageant	She was in a local *pageant*.	pageant
3. ecstasy	It was a feeling of *ecstasy*.	ecstasy
4. accessible	It is only *accessible* to some.	accessible
5. diphtheria	The natives died of *diphtheria*.	diphtheria
6. inhabitant	He was the original *inhabitant*.	inhabitant
7. justifiable	Mary's anger was *justifiable*.	justifiable
8. auditorium	We waited in the *auditorium*.	auditorium
9. campaign	It was a fair *campaign*.	campaign
10. frames	I bought several *frames*.	frames
11. feasible	Dad did not think it *feasible*.	feasible
12. preceding	She is *preceding* the others.	preceding
13. controversy	I did not wish a *controversy*.	controversy
14. inaugurate	The Chief Justice was to *inaugurate* him.	inaugurate
15. preferable	It is *preferable* to all others.	preferable
16. corrugated	Sally looked for a *corrugated* box.	corrugated
17. orchard	Someday I would like an *orchard*.	orchard
18. consecutively	They were numbered *consecutively*.	consecutively
19. melancholy	Old movies always make me *melancholy*.	melancholy
20. superintendent	He was *superintendent* of schools.	superintendent
22. souvenir	This is the best *souvenir* yet.	souvenir
23. psychology	I did not enjoy *psychology* class.	psychology
24. symmetrical	Please arrange them in a *symmetrical* way.	symmetrical
25. emptiness	I have a feeling of *emptiness*.	emptiness
26. controlled	Tom *controlled* the money well.	controlled
27. submitting	She was *submitting* to authority.	submitting
28. moreover	You can use the word *moreover*.	moreover
29. teammates	He congratulated his *teammates*.	teammates
30. celebration	It was a grand *celebration*.	celebration
31. cooperation	It took everyone's *cooperation*.	cooperation
32. acquaintance	She was only an *acquaintance*.	acquaintance
33. circumference	What's the *circumference* of the circle?	circumference
34. incompatible	They found themselves *incompatible*.	incompatible
35. idiosyncrasy	It was his *idiosyncrasy*.	idiosyncrasy

Number of Words Misspelled	**Placement Level**	**Go To Page**
22-35	Study Level J	Flow Word List Page 200
5-21	Study Level K	Flow Word List Page 212
0-4	This student's high proficiency in spelling indicates he has mastered approximately 97 percent of all the words children and adults use in their writing. He will benefit more from study in another field than he will from formal spelling study at this time.	

Prescriptive Tests

The following three Prescriptive Spelling Tests have been created to help you determine specific spelling skills instruction from which your student will profit. The tests should be administered in the usual manner: each word should be pronounced individually, used in a sentence, and then pronounced again.

After the entire test is administered, you should examine the misspelled words and compare them to the "elements tested" chart at the bottom of the test. While each word was selected for a specific element, you should examine each error and determine its root cause. From such an evaluation you will be able to create a list of skills you will use to begin Individually Prescribed Instruction. Later lessons and skills sessions may be determined from evaluation of your student's errors in daily work.

Prescriptive Test 1

For students whose placement is below *Spelling Power* Level D.

1. man	Father is a tall *man.*	man
2. get	Can I *get* you anything?	get
3. sit	Please *sit* down, now!	sit
4. not	He is *not* here.	not
5. but	Mary is here, *but* Joe is not.	but
6. much	I feel *much* better.	much
7. say	I really did not know what to *say.*	say
8. train	Tom has a new toy *train.*	train
9. like	We *like* ice cream.	like
10. boat	We sailed our *boat* on the pond	boat
11. those	This is one of *those* new trucks.	those
12. show	He will *show* us the way.	show
13. soon	Our grandmother will be here *soon.*	soon
14. garden	This is my favorite *garden.*	garden
15. first	He was the *first* to know.	first
16. after	We play *after* our chores are done.	after
17. sister	My *sister* is older than I.	sister
18. horse	She always wanted a *horse.*	horse
19. very	We are *very* glad you came.	very
20. dear	He was a *dear* friend.	dear
21. flower	The iris is my favorite *flower.*	flower
22. pounds	I'd like to lose ten *pounds.*	pounds
23. thought	The *thought* of it frightens me.	thought
24. toy	I'd like a new *toy* train.	toy
25. boil	Bring the mixture to a *boil.*	boil
26. would	I *would* like to go along with you.	would
27. good	She is a *good* girl.	good
28. come	Please *come* to our party.	come
29. one	I have only *one* book.	one
30. know	He does not *know* anyone here.	know
31. will	Who *will* help us?	will
32. doll	Make a dress for the *doll.*	doll

33. smells	He *smells* funny.	smells
34. little	Tom Thumb was a *little* man.	little
35. animal	My cat is my favorite *animal.*	animal
36. nickel	A candy bar costs a *nickel.*	nickel
37. evil	It was an *evil* thing to do.	evil
38. pretty	She is a *pretty* woman.	pretty
39. been	I have *been* to the castle.	been
40. eyes	He has blue *eyes.*	eyes

Elements Tested in List I

short vowel sounds	words 1-6	Groups 1-5
long vowel sounds	words 7-13	Groups 6-10
R influenced vowels	words 14-21	Groups 11-15
/ou/ spelled ou & ow	words 21-22	Group 16
/o/ spellings	word 23	Group 17
/oi/ spellings	words 24 & 25	Group 18
/u/ spellings	word 27	Group 19
unusual sounds of o	words 28 & 29	Group 20
silent letters	word 30	Group 22
final letters doubled	words 31-33	Group 24
simple plural	word 33	Group 30
/al/ spellings	words 34-37	Group 29
non-phonetic spellings	words 38-40	Group 47

Prescriptive Test 2

For students whose placement is above *Spelling Power* Level D but below level F.

1. splash	He made a big *splash.*	splash
2. president	He was the sixth *president.*	president
3. problems	Mother had many *problems* with her.	problems
4. night	Last *night* I went to the movies.	night
5. each	Give *each* of them three cookies.	each
6. shoot	He told them not to *shoot.*	shoot
7. third	It was the *third* time we saw him.	third
8. hear	I cannot *hear* well.	hear
9. flower	The iris is my favorite *flower.*	flower
10. mouth	Your *mouth* should be closed.	mouth
11. because	He left *because* he was angry.	because
12. brought	We *brought* a sack lunch with us.	brought
13. noises	We heard *noises* in the night.	noises
14. furniture	He is good at moving *furniture.*	furniture
15. measured	I was *measured* for new clothes.	measured
16. apple	An *apple* fell on Newton's head.	apple
17. control	He lost *control* of the vehicle.	control
18. jump	We like to *jump* rope.	jump
19. jumps	Mary *jumps* rope well.	jumps
20. jumped	We *jumped* rope together.	jumped
21. jumping	The girls are *jumping* rope now.	jumping

22. hit	Jason *hit* the ball.	hit
23. hitting	John has trouble *hitting* the ball.	hitting
24. bite	Our dog does not *bite.*	bite
25. biting	The dog is *biting* on the bone.	biting
26. study	She did not *study* for the test.	study
27. studies	He *studies* every day after school.	studies
28. Canadians	He visited the *Canadians.*	Canadians
29. afternoon	I will see you tomorrow *afternoon.*	afternoon
30. grandmother	My *grandmother* is out of town.	grandmother
31. can't	Tracy *can't* go to the store.	can't
32. doesn't	Cindy *doesn't* have a coat.	doesn't
33. one-way	It was a *one-way* street.	one-way
34. grown-ups	Always respect *grown-ups.*	grown-ups
35. Dr.	The abbreviation for *doctor* is ...	Dr.
36. Rev.	The abbreviation for *reverend* is...	Rev.
37. bureau	He worked for the crime *bureau.*	bureau
38. again	I hope to see you *again.*	again
39. laugh	Cindy has a cute *laugh.*	laugh
40. through	He ran *through* the store.	through

Elements Tested in List 2

short vowel sounds	Words 1-3	Groups 1-5
long vowel sounds	Words 4-6	Groups 6-10
R influenced vowels	Words 7-9	Groups 11-15
ow-ou spellings	Words 9-10	Group 16
/o/ (au) spellings	Words 11-12	Group 17
/oi/ spellings	Word 13,	Group 18
/yur/ spellings	Words 14-15	Group 25
/al/ spellings	Words 16-17	Group 29
addition of suffixes	Words 18-27	Groups 30-34
capitalization	Word 28	Group 35
compound words	Words 29-30	Group 36
contractions	Words 31-32	Group 37
hyphenated words	Words 33-34	Group 38
abbreviations	Words 35-36	Group 41
non-phonetic spellings	Words 37-40	Group 47

Prescriptive Test 3

For Students whose placement level is above *Spelling Power* Level F.

1. advantage	He has an *advantage* over us.	advantage
2. medication	The doctor prescribed *medication.*	medication
3. proceed	Mother said we should *proceed.*	proceed
4. safety	Please watch over her *safety.*	safety
5. slavery	Carver was born into *slavery.*	slavery
6. notoriety	Even so, he gained much *notoriety.*	notoriety
7. counting	Marybeth is *counting* the sheep.	counting
8. watering	Sandy was *watering* the lawn.	watering
9. annoyance	He was a real *annoyance.*	annoyance
10. smother	I like to *smother* it with cheese.	smother
11. acquainted	Are you *acquainted* with her yet?	acquainted
12. written	It is *written* in stone.	written
13. climb	Do not *climb* on this tree.	climb
14. proudly	Mary walked *proudly* to the stage.	proudly
15. differently	From then on he acted *differently.*	differently
16. industrial	This is an *industrial* area.	industrial
17. principle	The main *principle* is to keep calm.	principle
18. win	He will surely *win.*	win
19. winner	He was the *winner* of the race.	winner
20. winning	For him, *winning* was easy.	winning
21. wittiest	She is the *wittiest* girl I know.	wittiest
22. untidiness	Your habit of *untidiness* is bothersome.	untidiness
23. Romans	The *Romans* fought many wars.	Romans
24. Apollo	The first men on the moon came on *Apollo* XI.	Apollo
25. heartrending	It was a *heartrending* story.	heartrending
26. exploration	This *exploration* was done recently.	exploration
27. explosion	It was a big *explosion.*	explosion
28. physician	He was my favorite *physician.*	physician
29. declaration	She made a firm *declaration.*	declaration
30. convenience	It is here for your *convenience.*	convenience
31. maintenance	Proper *maintenance* is crucial.	maintenance
32. resemblance	You have quite a *resemblance* to her.	resemblance
33. allotment	We all got our fair *allotment.*	allotment
34. amendment	He added an *amendment* to the by-laws.	amendment
35. sentiment	It was a sweet *sentiment.*	sentiment
36. disappear	He made the rabbit *disappear.*	disappear
37. explanatory	She added an *explanatory* note.	explanatory
38. uneducated	It was obvious he was *uneducated.*	uneducated
39. rheumatism	Many people suffer from *rheumatism.*	rheumatism
40. symmetry	The *symmetry* was pleasing to look at.	symmetry

Elements Tested in List 3

short vowel sounds	Words 1-2	Groups 1-5
long vowel sounds	Words 2-4	Groups 6-10
R influenced vowels	Words 5-6	Groups 11-15
ow-ou spellings	Word 7	Group 16
/o/ (au) spellings	Word 8	Group 17
/oi/ spelling	Word 9	Group 18
unusual sound of o	Word 10	Group 20
Q followed by u	Word 11	Group 21
silent letters	Words 12 & 13	Group 19
ly endings	Word 14 & 15	Group 26
/al/ endings	Word 16 & 17	Group 29
adding suffixes	Words 18-22	Groups 30-34
capitalization	Words 23 & 24	Group 35
compound words	Word 25	Group 36
/shun/ spellings	Words 26-29	Group 42
/ance/ spellings	Words 30-32	Group 44
/ment/ spellings	Words 33-35	Group 45
adding of prefixes	Words 35-37	Group 46
non-phonetic	Words 38-40	Group 47

Spelling Power Flow-Word-Lists

Development of the Spelling Power Word Lists

In line with the spelling research already described in this text, high-frequency words are presented in list form. The *Spelling Power* Flow-Word-Lists were created by creating a base list of 12,711 words compiled by using a number of word frequency studies. These studies include: 2,000 words from a 1979 study of children's word usage, a listing of the 10,000 words most frequently used by adults and children (1971), 3,970 words from Rinsland's *A Basic Vocabulary of Elementary School Children* (1945), and first 4,000 words from Horn's *A Basic Writing Vocabulary* (1926). The author modified this basic list with the addition of words which have recently come into use (mainly computer related) and the deletion of a few archaic words.

The resulting list was compared to lists used in five grade-based spelling programs to help determine the average grade level at which these words are taught. This information was valuable in creating reliable Diagnostic Spelling Surveys.

The most frequently used and taught 5,000 words were selected from this basic list for Systematic Spelling Instruction. An additional 258 words which are frequently misspelled by high school students, college students, and business people, but not found on the high frequency list, were added to the words selected for instruction. The resulting list consists of 5,258 words that are believed everyone should be able to spell. The entire base list is presented in alphabetical format in the "Alphabetical Word List" section to facilitate Integrated Functional Writing.

Placement in Achievement Levels

One factor that contributes to word difficulty is the pupil's familiarity or lack of familiarity with the meaning of the word. Assigning words within the different levels according to frequency of use means that students assigned to a particular level are

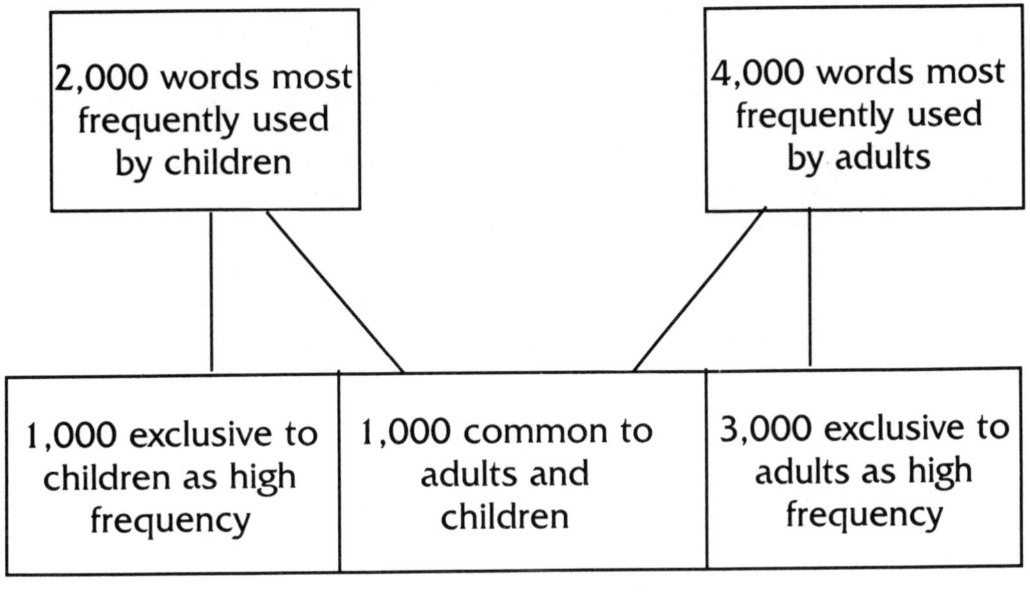

studying words they can ordinarily understand and read, and which they use in writing but may not be able to spell.

The list of the most frequently used 5,000 words was divided into 11 levels of frequency and instruction. Two criteria were used in determining the level of placement for each word: a) frequency of use and b) contribution of specific words to teaching generalizations and spelling principles.

Once the student learns all of the words in the first six levels (completes Level E) of the *Spelling Power* program, he will know 95 percent of all the words children (under sixth grade) use in writing. If he masters the words in all 11 levels, he will know 98 percent of all the words both children and adults use in ordinary daily writing, as well as those words which are frequently misspelled.

While the *Spelling Power* program is designed to allow the student to begin where he is at and advance as far and as fast as he is able, a few restrictions should be placed on his progress. Generally speaking, students should be in third grade or above before beginning the *Spelling Power* program and the Test-Study-Test method. Furthermore, because of the high level of adult and business vocabulary presented beyond level H, it is not advised that students below sixth grade study at this level. It will prove to be more beneficial to such advanced students to study lists of frequently misspelled words and words generated from their own daily writing.

Grouping Within Levels

Each level was further divided into groups based on phonetic and structural principles, or spelling rule. Through the study of general principles of English spelling, made possible by grouping words with common elements, students are able to help themselves to the spelling of a wide array of words not specifically taught in a particular group.

On the lower levels, emphasis is on working with phonetic principles (mainly vowel sounds). At the middle level and upper levels, the focus gradually shifts to structural and morphographic rules. Group numbers consistently represent the same phonetic principles or spelling rules from level to level to allow for multi-level lessons. However, each Group is not necessarily studied at every level resulting in "skipped groups." An example is in Level E which jumps from Group 9 to Group 18.

Use of Symbols

Throughout this text, phonemes (speech sounds) are represented between two slashes (e.g. /a/). The first slash can be read "the" and the final slash "sound." The letter or letters within the slashes should be read as the actual sound heard. Example: /a/ is read the 'a' sound. Short vowel sounds are represented as lowercase letters and have no diacritical markings. Long vowel sounds are written as /ā/ or /ī/. Other vowel sounds are marked using standard symbols.

A letter or letters which appear underlined represent the graphemes (letters) used to spell the phoneme (sound). The letter or letters underlined should be read as "the letter" using the alphabetical name(s).

Selection of Review Words

Most students do not learn a word by meeting it once; permanent learning results only when commonly used words are repeated and practiced at regular intervals. Students need varying amounts of practice and review depending on aptitude, study effort, and retentiveness. The amount of review required for particular words varies also with word difficulty and irregularity. A word such as brick or sidewalk is easy to retain, but calendar or oxygen requires more study and review for permanent retention. Since the *Spelling Power* program is designed to achieve mastery of spelling, cumulative and systematic review with these factors in mind have been built into the program. There are six levels of review built in to the word study process. This review is accomplished in four ways, as follows:

1. A word is studied until it is spelled correctly at least once. Each testing session begins with words which were misspelled during the last testing session.

2. Words most frequently missed within a level are reviewed in Review Groups, Delayed-Recall Tests, and End-of-Level Tests. These review words were determined by compiling a number of different lists of frequently misspelled words based on levels as follows:

by elementary students by grade (A-F)

by high school students (E-J)

by college students (I-L)

by business persons (I-L)

3. Spelling principles and common phonetic and structural elements are reviewed from level to level.

4. The words in the Flow-Word-Lists include new words from the basic list of the level on which the student is working, and also review words that show a high frequency of error from the previous levels. When a difficult word from one level is reviewed in a later level, the word is placed in the corresponding group of the succeeding levels. If a derivative of a word is more frequently used by children than is the root word, the derivative is taught first.

5. Words misspelled in daily writing are recycled into the program using the 10-Step-Study process.

Level	Total # of words this level	Words Intro-duced	Review Words from Previous Level	% Words exclusive to Spelling Power	1	2	3	4	5	6	7	8	Running Total of new Words	Percen-tage of Use
A	199	199	0	3%	25	38	34						199	
B	362	289	73	7%		27	37	24					488	82%
C	467	329	138	13%		17	39	25	10				817	
D	484	335	149	22%			20	33	21				1152	89%
E	606	483	123	19%			11	29	29	16			1635	
F	709	519	190	33%				19	20	25	12		2154	95%
G	827	622	205	28%				19	24	18	15		2776	
H	881	688	193	29%				19	22	21	17		3464	97%*
I	1041	767	274	33%					17	24	22	17	4231	98%
J	879	605	274	41%					18	19	25	16	4836	#
K	704	422	282	27%					16	20	32	21	5258	#

* 97% at 3,000 words
# 98% plus frequently misspelled college and business words.

Level A

Group 1

Usually /a/ is spelled a as in *cat*.

an
and
as
at
back
had
has
man
that
can

Group 2

Usually /e/ is spelled e as in *nest*.

get
went
when
then
hen
sled
beg
desks
tenth
seventh

Group 3

Usually /i/ is spelled i as in *big*.

did
him
his
big
this
if
in
is
it
will

Group 4

Usually /o/ is spelled o as in *not*.

dog
got
not
off
on
hop
chop
rob

Group 5

Usually /u/ is spelled u as in *run*.

but
just
up
us
nut
rug
tub
bun
rub
hut

Review Test 1

The following words have been previously tested. (Student need not record this statement.)

an
had
then
seventh
this
will
off
just
us

Group 6

/ā/ can be written ay, ai, ey, ei, eigh, ea, or a followed by a consonant and silent e.

day
they
play
came
rage
rake
grape
sprain
skate
trade

Group 7

/ē/ can be spelled ea, ee, y, ie, ei, ey, or e followed by a consonant and silent e.

see
be
he
she
me
we
eat
each
freeze
cheek

Group 8

/ī/ can be spelled ie, igh, y, or i followed by two consonants as in *wild* or as i followed by a consonant and silent e as in *kite*.

by (close to)
my
I
time
like
nice
kite
slice
fright
wipe

Group 9

/ō/ can be spelled oe, ow, oa, or o followed by two consonants as in *told* or as o followed by a consonant and silent e as in *home*.

goes
so
no
go
going
home
toe
bowling
slowed
snowed

Group 10

/ū/ can be spelled ew as in *few*, ue as in *blue*, ui as in *suit*, o as in *to*, or as u followed by a consonant and silent e as in *mule*.

to
too (also)
do
you
cube
stool
boot
broom
school
room

Review Test 2

The following words have been previously tested. (Student need not record this statement.)

they
came
each
eat
like
nice
goes
home
to
too (also)

Level A

Delayed Recall Test I

Form A

Before administering this test, read pgs 45-46.

an 1
then 2
him 3
off 4
but 5
play 6
eat 7
nice 8
goes 9
too 10

Form B

that 1
went 2
this 3
off 4
just 5
skate 6
each 7
time 8
going 9
school 10

Group 12

/ûr/ can be spelled ir as in *bird*, er as in *her*, ur as in *survey*, er as in *eternity*, ear as in *pearl*, our as in *journal*, or or after w as in *work*.

her
were
after
over
girl
first
water
better
teacher
giraffe

Group 13

/or/ can be spelled or as in *corn*, oar as in *boar*, oor as in *door*, our as *your*, and ar as *dwarf*.

or
for
your
more
four (numeral)
glory
door
morning
story
before

Group 14

/âr/ can be spelled are as *care*, air as in *hair*, ere as in *there*, ear as in *bear*, and eir as in *their*.

their (possessive pronoun)
there (location)
very
cared
fairies
stair
scared
where
bear (animal)
air (for breathing)

Group 16

Usually /ou/ is spelled ou before most consonants as in *cloud*. Sometimes /ou/ is spelled ow before final l or n as in *howl* or *clown* or at the end of a word or syllable as in *how* or *tower*.

now
down
about
around
our
out
house
how
found
town

Group 17

/ô/ can be spelled a, o, and au before most consonants as in *already*, *cost*, and *sauce* and *caught* or as aw before final k, l, n as *hawk*, *crawl*, and *lawn* or at the end of a word or stressed syllable as in *awful* or *law*.

because
saw
all
wants
straw
ball
call
small
watch
father

Review Test 3

The following words have been previously tested. (Student need not record this statement.)

were
first
your
story
there (location)
their (possessive pronoun)
about
around
because
wants

Group 20

Sometimes the letter o represents unexpected sounds as in *come*, *mother* and *one*.

come
some
one (numeral)
once
from
mother
brother
other
love

Group 23

No English words end with the letter v.

gave
cave
have
give
live
five
drove
twelve
leave
drive

Group 24

Consonant letters are often doubled after a short vowel in short vowel words such as *egg*, *fluff*, *sniffle*, and *mess*.

well
grass
fell
smell
tell
bill
still
kill
hill
full

Group 35

Proper nouns must begin with a capital letter because they refer to a specific name or title of a person, place, time, thing, or idea such as Monday.

Monday
Tuesday
Wednesday
Thursday
Friday
Saturday
Sunday
John
God
Tom

Group 47

These words are unusual words and are exceptions to the most common generalizations.

said
a
the
two (numeral)
was
what
friend
head
of
dead
many

Review Test 4

The following words have been previously tested. (Student need not record this statement.)

mother
once
twelve
leave
still
grass
Tuesday
Wednesday
said
friend

Delayed Recall Test 2 Form A

Before administering this test, read pgs 45-46.

were 12
your 13
their 14 (possessive pronoun)
house 16
because 17
mother 20
twelve 23
smell 24
Tuesday 35
friend 47

Delayed Recall Test 2 Form B

first 12
before 13
there 14 (location)
around 16
because 17
once 20
twelve 23
still 24
Wednesday 35
said 47

End-of-Level A Test Form A

Before administering this test, read pgs 45-46.

back 1
then 2
this 3
got 4
just 5
they 6
each 7
by 8
goes 9
too 10 (also)
were 12
your 13
their 14 (possessive pronoun)
about 16
once 20
twelve 23
tell 24
Saturday 35
two 47 (numeral)

End-of-Level A Test Form B

that 1
seventh 2
did 3
not 4
just 5
trade 6
each 7
slice 8
toe 9 (body part)
school 10
first 12
four 13 (numeral)
very 14
found 16
straw 17
love 20
twelve 23
hill 24
Thursday 35
many 47

Important Notes

- The "jump" in Group Numbers is intentional. See Page 122, "Grouping within Levels" for an explanation.
- Words followed by an (R) are Review words. Do not say the (R) when dictating them.
- Words in [brackets] are the British spelling. When correcting the test, use the proper spelling for your country.

Level B

Group 1

Usually /a/ is spelled a as in *cat*.

an (R)
had (R)
back (R)
that (R)
cat
am
last
ran
black
asked
happy
bad
family
clap
slam

Group 2

Usually /e/ is spelled e as in *nest*.

then (R)
seventh (R)
tenth (R)
when (R)
men
best
red (color)
next
bed
left
help
let
every
pet
yes

Group 3

Usually /i/ is spelled i as in *big*.

this (R)
will (R)
his (R)
him (R)
think
fish
spring
thing
which
hit
king
lived
with
six
wish

Group 4

Usually /o/ is spelled o as in *not*.

got (R)
not (R)
off (R)
long
mom
lot
hot
stop
box
lost
top
shot
song
rock

Group 5

Usually /u/ is spelled u as in *run*.

just (R)
but (R)
us (R)
up (R)
much
fun
run
cut
gun
sun (our star)
must
bus
hundred
under

Review Test 1

The following words have been previously tested. (Student need not record this statement.)

am
family
black
happy
every
next
help
think
which
spring
song
hundred
under
much
must

Group 6

/ā/ can be written ay, ai, ey, ei, eigh, ea, or a followed by a consonant and silent e.

they (R)
play (R)
came (R)
day (R)
sprain (R)
away
way
baby
made (of clay)
make
great (large, good)
rain
grade
same
wait (stay)

Group 7

/ē/ can be spelled ea, ee, y, ie, ei, ey, or e followed by a consonant and silent e.

eat (R)
cheek (R)
freeze (R)
each (R)
three
tree
green
sleep
feet
even
read (a book)
week (day of)
keep

Group 8

/ī/ can be spelled ie, igh, y, or i followed by two consonants as in *wild* or as i followed by a consonant and silent e as in *kite*.

like (R)
I (R)
nice (R)
fright (R)
time (R)
why
right (direction)
night (time)
ride
white
find
might
while
bike
nine

Group 9

/ō/ can be spelled oe, ow, oa, or o followed by two consonants as in *told* or as o followed by a consonant and silent e as in *home*.

goes (R)
toe (R) (body part)
home (R)
going (R)
so (R)
oh
told
only
old
also
most
boat
gold
snow
cold

Group 10

/ū/ can be spelled ew as in *few*, ue as in *blue*, ui as in *suit*, o as in *to*, or as u followed by a consonant and silent e as in *mule*.

to (R)
too (also) (R)
school (R)
room (R)
who
through (finished)
new
blue (color)
soon
food
few
used
moon
together
tomorrow

Review Test 2

The following words have been previously tested. (Student need not record this statement.)

away
baby
grade
three
green
week (day of)
right (direction)
night (time)
while
only
also
most
together
through (finished)
blue (color)

Group 11

/àr/ is usually spelled ar as in *jar*.

are
car
farm
started
hard
dark
large
garden
far
park
part
start
barn
party
yard

Group 12

/ûr/ can be spelled ir as in *bird*, er as in *her*, ur as in *survey*, er as in *eternity*, ear as in *pearl*, our as in *journal*, or or after w as in *work*.

after (R)
teacher (R)
were (R)
girl (R)
first (R)
heard
world
never
ever
sister
work
turned
summer
supper
later

Group 13

/or/ can be spelled or as in *corn*, oar as in *boar*, oor as in *door*, our as *your*, and ar as *dwarf*.

your (R)
more (R)
four (R)
morning (R)
before (R)
horse
store
fourth
floor
course
favorite [favourite]
orange
poor
war
fort

Group 14

/âr/ can be spelled are as *care*, air as in *hair*, ere as in *there*, ear as in *bear*, and eir as in *their*.

their (possessive pronoun) (R)
there (location) (R)
where (R)
scared (R)
air (R)
hair
stair (R)
bears (animal)
pear (fruit)
wear
care
chair
cherry
stare
scare

Level B

Group 15

/îr/ can be spelled ear as in *hear*, eer as in *deer*, ere as in *here*, ier as in *pier*, er as in *period*, or eir as in *weird*.

cheer
hear
here
dear
near
tear
fear
ear
clear
year

Review Test 3

The following words have been previously tested. (Student need not record this statement.)

are
farm
started
heard
sister
world
orange
horse
fourth
hair
cherry
stare
cheer
dear
year

Delayed Recall Test 1 Form A

Before administering this test, read pgs 45-46.

am 1
every 2
think 3
which 3
rock 4
hundred 5
great 6
three 7
why 8
only 9
used 10
large 11
turned 12
fourth 13
chair 14
tear 15

Delayed Recall Test 1 Form B

am 1
best 2
think 3
which 3
stop 4
under 5
grade 6
sleep 7
while 8
only 9
through 10
garden 11
summer 12
favorite [favourite] 13
stair 14
clear 15

Group 17

/ô/ can be spelled a, o, and au before most consonants as in already, cost, and sauce or as augh or ough before t as in sought and caught or as aw before final k, l, n as hawk, crawl, and lawn or at the end of a word or stressed syllable as in awful or law.

wants (R)
because (R)
father (R)
ball (R)
watch (R)
caught
thought
called
wanted
want
brought
always
bought
fall
tall

Group 18

/oi/ can be spelled oy as in *toy* or oi as *boil*.

boy
boys
noise
toy
voice
spoil
foil
boil
oil
toys
loyal
joint
poison
join
joy

Group 19

/u/ can be spelled u as in *put*, ou as in *would* or as oo as in *took*.

would
could
put
good
took
look
looked
should
pull
book
wood
foot
cook
hood
woods
looking

Important Notes

- The "jump" in Group Numbers is intentional. See Page 122, "Grouping within Levels" for an explanation.
- Words followed by an (R) are Review words. Do not say the (R) when dictating them.
- Words in [brackets] are the British spelling. When correcting the test, use the proper spelling for your country.

Group 30

Words are normally made plural by adding s.

things
birds
friends
cars
days
years
trees
horses
animals
flowers
lots
wheels
holidays
cats
minutes

Group 33

When adding a suffix that begins with a vowel, the final e is usually dropped, as in *chase* to *chasing*.

coming
sliding
writing
riding
liking
loving
having
living
taking
making
skating
moving
giving
racing
leaving

Review Test 4

The following words have been previously tested. (Student need not record this statement.)

caught
thought
brought
poison
boy
noise
would
should
looking
friends
coming
writing
liking
loving
taking

Group 34

In short vowel words, the final consonant is usually doubled before adding a suffix, such as when changing in stop to stopped.

getting
swimming
stopped
running
stopping
sitting
dropped
grabbed
bigger
putting
spotted
biggest

Group 35

Proper nouns must begin with a capital letter because they refer to a specific name or title of a person, place, time, thing, or idea such as Monday.

Tuesday (R)
Wednesday (R)
Thursday (R)
January
February
March
April
May
June
July
August
September
October
November
December

Group 36

New words are often made by putting two short words together into one word as in cowboy.

into
sometimes
something
birthday
outside
upon
nobody
without
today
baseball

Group 37

An apostrophe is used to take the place of a letter when two words are joined. These words are called contractions.

didn't
don't
I'll
I'm
it's
couldn't
that's
can't
wasn't
he's
o'clock
let's
won't
I'd

Group 47

These words are unusual words and are exceptions to the most common generalizations.

two (R)
said (R)
friend (R)
many (R)
head (R)
dead (R)
of (R)
again
pretty
been
any
police
eyes
ready
sorry
ninth
gone

Level B

Review Test 5

The following words have been previously tested. (Student need not record this statement.)

getting
happened
sitting
January
February
September
something
birthday
without
didn't
couldn't
that's
pretty
sorry
ninth

Delayed Recall Test 2 Form A

Before administering this test, read pgs 45-46.

horse 13 (animal)
scare 14
here 15
thought 17
voice 18
should 19
animals 30
coming 33
taking 33
sitting 34
September 35
November 35
birthday 36
o'clock 37
sorry 47

Delayed Recall Test 2 Form B

fourth 13
bears 14
ear 15
caught 17
loyal 18
would 19
holidays 30
making 33
writing 33
swimming 34
February 35
December 35
something 36
couldn't 37
ready 47

End of Level B Test Form A

Before administering this test, read pgs 45-46.

am 1
next 2
which 3
long 4
much 5
make 6
sleep 7
ride 8
snow 9
through 10
part 11
never 12
war 13
chair 14
tear 15
caught 17
poison 18
would 19
wheels 30
writing 33
swimming 34
August 35
ninth 47

End of Level B Test Form B

am 1
every 2
think 3
lost 4
hundred 5
baby 6
feet 7
white 8
told 9
tomorrow 10
party 11
supper 12
poor 13
wear 14
clear 15
always 17
poison 18
would 19
coming 33
putting 34
October 35
ninth 47

Level C

Group 1

Usually /a/ is spelled a as in *cat*.

am (R)
happy (R)
family (R)
asked (R)
black (R)
paths
grab
math
than
rabbit
camp
mad
fast
hand
sat
hat
half
catch
apple
landed

Group 2

Usually /e/ is spelled e as in *nest*.

then (R)
every (R)
when (R)
next (R)
them
end
ten
second
letter
seven
except
met
rest
jelly
self

Group 3

Usually /i/ is spelled i as in *big*.

which (R)
wish (R)
six (R)
thing (R)
fishing
killed
trip
city
its (own)
milk
wind
pick
picked
finished
grip
bit
pig
sit
sing
chip

Group 4

Usually /o/ is spelled o as in *not*.

lot (R)
long (R)
off (R)
rock (R)
song (R)
rocket
hockey
robin
hog
clock
job
fox
drop
spot
sock
frog
pop
soft
cost

Group 5

Usually /u/ is spelled u as in *run*.

fun (R)
must (R)
under (R)
hundred (R)
bus (R)
jumped
truck
bug
mud
cup
skunk
such
lunch
duck
ugly
hungry
lucky
dug
gum

Review Test 1

The following words have been previously tested. (Student need not record this statement.)

than
its (own)
math
half
catch
milk
sing
finished
second
except
seven
jelly
clock
soft
sock
rocket
lunch
such
hungry
lucky

Important Notes

- The "jump" in Group Numbers is intentional. See Page 122, "Grouping within Levels" for an explanation.
- Words followed by an (R) are Review words. Do not say the (R) when dictating them.
- Words in [brackets] are the British spelling. When correcting the test, use the proper spelling for your country.

Level C

Group 6

/ā/ can be written ay, ai, ey, ei, eigh, ea, or a followed by a consonant and silent e.

great (R)
rain (R)
grade (R)
same (R)
wait (stay) (R)
played
may
plane (fly a)
space
okay
taste
face
skate (R)
eight (numeral)
neighbor [neighbour]
hate
name
change
stay
snail

Group 7

/ē/ can be spelled ea, ee, y, ie, ei, ey, or e followed by a consonant and silent e.

eat (R)
each (R)
three (R)
read (a book) (R)
green (R)
seen
sea
feel
street
real
decided
these
mean
field
scream
beach
please
feed
began

Group 8

/ī/ can be spelled ie, igh, y, or i followed by two consonants as in *wild* or as i followed by a consonant and silent e as in *kite*.

right (direction) (R)
nine (R)
white (R)
while (R)
why (R)
high
fly
life
kind
fine
sky
fight
light
wild
liked
side
fire
science
bright
nice (R)

Group 9

/ō/ can be spelled oe, ow, oa, or o followed by two consonants as in *told* or as o followed by a consonant and silent e as in *home*.

snow (R)
cold (R)
most (R)
only (R)
goes (R)
clothes
road (travel on)
almost
hope
woke
pony
opened
broke
hole
yellow
window
cone
grow
those
ago

Group 10

/ū/ can be spelled ew as in *few*, ue as in *blue*, ui as in *suit*, o as in *to*, or as u followed by a consonant and silent e as in *mule*.

to (R)
through (finished) (R)
too (also) (R)
moon (R)
few (R)
used (R)
together (R)
tomorrow (R)
doing
zoo
pool
true
threw (a ball)
music
move
whose
shoots
huge
cute
blew (past tense: blow)
use

Review Test 2

The following words have been previously tested. (Student need not record this statement.)

those
almost
yellow
window
music
whose
threw (a ball)
true
neighbor [neighbour]
eight (numeral)
taste
okay
street
please
scream
field
science
life
liked
high

Important Notes

- The "jump" in Group Numbers is intentional. See Page 122, "Grouping within Levels" for an explanation.
- Words followed by an (R) are Review words. Do not say the (R) when dictating them.
- Words in [brackets] are the British spelling. When correcting the test, use the proper spelling for your country.

Group 11

/àr/ is usually spelled ar as in *jar*.

started (R)
farm (R)
large (R)
party (R)
yard (R)
smart
arms
bar
hardly
mark
stars
grammar
dollar
bark
sharp
arm
art
farther
starting
jar

Group 12

/ûr/ can be spelled ir as in *bird*, er as in *her*, ur as in *survey*, er as in *eternity*, ear as in *pearl*, our as in *journal*, or or after w as in *work*.

summer (R)
first (R)
were (R)
heard (R)
girl (R)
sister (R)
heard (R)
teacher (R)
bird
hurt
turn
sure
river
different
monster
earth
dinner
person
winter
remember

Group 16

Usually /ou/ is spelled ou before most consonants as in *cloud*. Sometimes /ou/ is spelled ow before final l or n as in *howl* or *clown* or at the end of a word or syllable as in *how* or *tower*.

around (R)
about (R)
our (R)
town (R)
found (R)
cow
brown
ground
houses
mountain
flower
mouse
round
sound
thousand
clown
loud
mouth
sounds
shout

Group 17

/ô/ can be spelled a, o, and au before most consonants as in already, cost, and sauce or as augh or ough before t as in sought and caught or as aw before final k, l, n as hawk, crawl, and lawn or at the end of a word or stressed syllable as in awful or law.

always (R)
thought (R)
caught (R)
because (R)
brought (R)
tall (R)
straw (R)
wants (R)
already
wall
haunted
calling
daughter
washed
watched
naughty
wash
calm
awful

Group 20

Sometimes the letter o represents unexpected sounds as in *come*, *mother* and *one*.

another (R)
other (R)
from (R)
brother (R)
once (R)
won
does
comes
money
front
blood
month
ones
done
honey
son
none
dozen
above
wonder

Review Test 3

The following words have been previously tested. (Student need not record this statement.)

grammar
dollar
starting
farther
different
dinner
remember
person
mountain
thousand
houses
flower
daughter
naughty
haunted
already
blood
month
honey
dozen

Level C

Delayed Recall I Form A

Before administering this test, read pgs 45-46.

than 1
second 2
except 2
finished 3
city 3
cost 4
ugly 5
lunch 5
taste 6
neighbor 6 [neighbour] 6
street 7
scream 7
science 8
almost 9
music 10
whose 10
hardly 11
dollar 11
different 12
mountain 16
already 17
naughty 17
month 20
dozen 20

Delayed Recall I Form B

rabbit 1
seven 2
letter 2
grip 3
picked 3
frog 4
truck 5
skunk 5
change 6
played 6
field 7
decided 7
bright 8
opened 9
shoots 10
true 10
sharp 11
grammar 11
winter 12
remember 12
thousand 16
daughter 17
front 20

Group 22

Some words have silent letters such as with the k in *knew*, the w in *write*, and the l in *talk*.

walked
walk
ghost
know
lamb
comb
knit
knew
whole
write (with a pen)
hours
hour
knot
talking
wrecked
wrinkle
numb
knife
dumb

Group 24

Consonant letters are often doubled after a short vowel in short vowel words such as *egg*, *fluff*, *sniffle*, and *mess*.

kill (R)
hill (R)
full (R)
smell (R)
grass (R)
well (R)
guess
across
egg
miss
bull
dress
boss
bell
class
kiss
doll

Group 30

Words are normally made plural by adding s.

wheels (R)
holidays (R)
cats (R)
minutes (R)
animals (R)
horses (R)
years (R)
friends (R)
gets
smells
kids
rocks
dogs
dollars
makes
grades
weeks
likes
miles
girls

Group 32

When adding a suffix to a word ending in y, change the y to i, unless a vowel proceeds the y, as in try to *tried* and baby to *babies*.

libraries
prettier
daisies
tried
playing
cries
babies
sleepier
cried
easiest
hobbies
cookies
cities
stories
puppies
prettiest
happiness
families
ladies
tries

Important Notes

- The "jump" in Group Numbers is intentional. See Page 122, "Grouping within Levels" for an explanation.
- Words followed by an (R) are Review words. Do not say the (R) when dictating them.
- Words in [brackets] are the British spelling. When correcting the test, use the proper spelling for your country.

Group 33

When adding a suffix that begins with a vowel, the final e is usually dropped, as in *chase* to *chasing*.

coming (R)
writing (R)
liking (R)
loving (R)
taking (R)
giving (R)
having (R)
exploring
scary
shining
juicy
diving
driving
biting
mining
gravy
officer
using
trading
hiding

Review Test 4

The following words have been previously tested. (Student need not record this statement.)

stories
ladies
tries
easiest
write (with a pen)
whole
dumb
wrinkle
across
guess
sleepier
libraries
grades
miles
girls
smells
shining
driving
trading
officer

Group 34

In short vowel words, the final consonant is usually doubled before adding a suffix, such as when changing in stop to stopped.

swimming (R)
getting (R)
stopped (R)
grabbed (R)
biggest (R)
shopping
slipper
planned
slammed
stepped
tripped
trotting
wrapped
cutting
dragged
hitting
ripped
sitting (R)
zipper

Group 35

Proper nouns must begin with a capital letter because they refer to a specific name or title of a person, place, time, thing, or idea such as Monday.

February (R)
December (R)
September (R)
Tuesday (R)
Wednesday (R)
Saturday (R)
Calgary *
Christmas
Montreal *
Judy
Jim
Joe
Sally
Sam
Jack
Boston *
Edmonton *
Halloween
Mars
Canada

* May be substituted for major cities in your locality.

Group 36

New words are often made by putting two short words together into one word as in cowboy.

upon (R)
nobody (R)
without (R)
today (R)
baseball (R)
outside (R)
everything
someone
everyone
everybody
afternoon
anything
beside
himself
maybe
breakfast
football
grandma
myself
weekend

Group 47

These words are unusual words and are exceptions to the most common generalizations.

said (R)
friend (R)
again (R)
many (R)
sorry (R)
ninth (R)
dead (R)
ready (R)
what (R)
was (R)
police (R)
been (R)
any (R)
aunt
enough
country
cousin
trouble
instead
weather

Review Test 5

The following words have been previously tested. (Student need not record this statement.)

ninth
instead
weather
cousin
aunt
country
anything
someone
breakfast
everyone
everybody
Christmas
Canada
Tuesday
February
Wednesday
sitting
zipper
shopping
planned

Delayed Recall Test 2 Form A

Before administering this test, read pgs 45-46.

thousand 16
mouth 16
daughter 17
haunted 17
money 20
front 20
knew 22
write 22
across 24
dollars 30
babies 32
tries 32
driving 33
wrapped 34
Christmas 35
anything 36
breakfast 36
aunt 47
country 47

Delayed Recall Test 2 Form B

flower 16
mountain 16
haunted 17
already 17
honey 20
month 20
whole 22
knife 22
guess 24
girls 30
ladies 32
cities 32
officer 33
cutting 34
Halloween 35
afternoon 36
myself 36
cousin 47
enough 47

End of Level C Test Form A

Before administering this test, read pgs 45-46.

math 1
second 2
killed 3
soft 4
lunch 5
taste 6
street 7
fight 8
broke 9
pool 10
farther 11
different 12
houses 16
washed 17
does 20
comb 22
across 24
likes 30
libraries 32
exploring 33
stepped 34
Canada 35
himself 36
trouble 47

End of Level C Test Form B

rabbit 1
except 2
picked 3
spot 4
ugly 5
change 6
beach 7
wild 8
cone 9
huge 10
sharp 11
dinner 12
brown 16
awful 17
front 20
hours 22
guess 24
girls 30
prettier 32
trading 33
sitting 34
Judy 35
football 36
weather 47

Level D

Group 1

Usually /a/ is spelled a as in *cat*.

an (R)
had (R)
catch (R)
apple (R)
half (R)
sack
rack
bat
fat
glad
land
rang
planet
sad
ask
bag
gas
magic
sandy
candy

Group 2

Usually /e/ is spelled e as in *nest*.

then (R)
except (R)
tenth (R)
self (R)
elephant
felt
fence
kept
set
yelled
else
gem
lend
jerk
velvet
neglect
dent
invent
sketch

Group 3

Usually /i/ is spelled i as in *big*.

think (R)
which (R)
with (R)
this (R)
spring (R)
bring
ship
since
swim
witch
prince
pink
sick
win
inch
fist
spill
sting
skip

Group 4

Usually /o/ is spelled o as in *not*.

hockey (R)
off (R)
clock (R)
song (R)
cost (R)
lot (R)
monkey
nothing
hospital
holiday
bottom
dock
chocolate
problem
soccer
office
block
contest
pond

Group 5

Usually /u/ is spelled u as in *run*.

cup (R)
skunk (R)
such (R)
ugly (R)
hungry (R)
lunch (R)
duck (R)
lucky (R)
hunting
stuck
jump
puck
struck
runs
ducks
sunny
pups
dust
bunch
puppy

Review Test 1

The following words have been previously tested. (Student need not record this statement.)

since
planet
magic
candy
rack
elephant
felt
yelled
invent
witch
prince
bring
chocolate
hospital
nothing
problem
struck
bunch
hunting
puppy

Important Notes

- The "jump" in Group Numbers is intentional. See Page 122, "Grouping within Levels" for an explanation.
- Words followed by an (R) are Review words. Do not say the (R) when dictating them.
- Words in [brackets] are the British spelling. When correcting the test, use the proper spelling for your country.

Level D

Group 6

/ā/ can be written ay, ai, ey, ei, eigh, ea, or a followed by a consonant and silent e.

wait (stay) (R)
eight (numeral) (R)
neighbor [neighbour] (R)
name (R)
stay (R)
change (R)
race
stayed
tail
cake
hate (R)
hay (food for cattle)
late
snake
hey (you)
plane (fly a) (R)
take
named
lake
say
game
ate (have eaten)

Group 7

/ē/ can be spelled ea, ee, y, ie, ei, ey, or e followed by a consonant and silent e.

street (R)
decided (R)
week (day of) (R)
feed (R)
please (R)
beach (R)
began (R)
behind
clean
creek
reached
sleeping
reach
season
dream
free
team
chief
received

Group 8

/ī/ can be spelled ie, igh, y, or i followed by two consonants as in *wild* or as i followed by a consonant and silent e as in *kite*.

like (R)
nice (R)
fight (R)
fly (R)
life (R)
time (R)
bye (leaving)
giant
ice
flying
buy (some bread)
died (not living)
hi
line
tired (sleepy)
try
trying
mine
tiny
wife

Group 9

/ō/ can be spelled oe, ow, oa, or o followed by two consonants as in *told* or as o followed by a consonant and silent e as in *home*.

told (R)
clothes (R)
almost (R)
grow (R)
those (R)
ago (R)
both
coat
nose
own
rode (a horse)
show
phone
throw
though
goal
coach
soap
follow
rope

Group 10

/ū/ can be spelled ew as in *few*, ue as in *blue*, ui as in *suit*, o as in *to*, or as u followed by a consonant and silent e as in *mule*.

through (finished) (R)
to (R)
too (also) (R)
together (R)
whose (R)
threw (a ball) (R)
true (R)
huge (R)
cute (R)
smooth
moved
snoopy
use (R)
shoot
shooting
grew
soup
flew (an airplane)
roof
tooth
crew

Review Test 2

The following words have been previously tested. (Student need not record this statement.)

stayed
snake
named
game
behind
dream
received
season
giant
tired
ice
bye (leaving)
coat
phone
though
coach
smooth
shooting
flew (an airplane)
tooth

Important Notes

- The "jump" in Group Numbers is intentional. See Page 122, "Grouping within Levels" for an explanation.
- Words followed by an (R) are Review words. Do not say the (R) when dictating them.
- Words in [brackets] are the British spelling. When correcting the test, use the proper spelling for your country.

Group 11

/àr/ is usually spelled ar as in *jar*.

grammar (R)
hardly (R)
dollar (R)
garden (R)
farm (R)
part (R)
apart
heart
farms
garbage
card
farmer
startled
garage
starts
bars
parts

Group 12

/ûr/ can be spelled ir as in *bird*, er as in *her*, ur as in *survey*, er as in *eternity*, ear as in *pearl*, our as in *journal*, or or after w as in *work*.

first (R)
heard (R)
different (R)
sure (R)
remember (R)
were (R)
later (R)
world (R)
upper (R)
rather (R)
yesterday
stubborn
silver
third
sir
thirty
learn
turkey
working
dirt
paper
closer

Group 13

/or/ can be spelled or as in *corn*, oar as in *boar*, oor as in *door*, our as *your*, and ar as *dwarf*.

morning (R)
before (R)
your (R)
favorite [favourite] (R)
fourth (R)
course (R)
floor (R)
orange (R)
horse (R)
swarm
wars
forest
warm
doctor
short
horror
born
color [colour]
storm
shore
corner

Group 19

/u/ can be spelled u as in *put*, ou as in *would* or as oo as in *took*.

book (R)
would (R)
took (R)
good (R)
looks
foot (R)
stood
wood (R)
pushed
cook (R)
hook
bush
books
crooked
pulling
sugar
brook
shook
hood (R)
crooks
push
puts
pushing
cooking

Group 22

Some words have silent letters such as with the k in *knew*, the w in *write*, and the l in *talk*.

know (R)
ghost (R)
whole (R)
knew (R)
knife (R)
dumb (R)
numb (R)
hours (R)
write (with a pen) (R)
knitting
hymn
often
answer
talk

Review Test 3

The following words have been previously tested. (Student need not record this statement.)

garbage
startled
heart
apart
yesterday
thirty
third
paper
doctor
color [colour]
sugar
crooked
puts
stubborn
stood
forest
pushed
hymn
often
answer
talk

Level D

Delayed Recall Test I Form A

Before administering this test, read pgs 45-46.

glad 1
velvet 2
neglect 2
since 3
bring 3
hospital 4
contest 4
struck 5
named 6
reached 7
sleeping 7
mine 8
though 9
moved 10
soup 10
apart 11
thirty 12
closer 12
horror 13
forest 13
pulling 19
knitting 22
answer 22

Delayed Recall Test I Form B

magic 1
fence 2
elephant 2
prince 3
witch 3
holiday 4
chocolate 4
bunch 5
stayed 6
chief 7
wife 8
own 9
grew 10
tooth 10
heart 11
paper 12
corner 13
doctor 13
cooking 19
often 22
hymn 22

Group 30

Words are normally made plural by adding s.

flowers (R)
dollars (R)
weeks (R)
girls (R)
elephants
takes
apples
hands
legs
tastes
bikes
kinds
lights
times
shoes
scores
words
miles (R)

Group 31

Plurals of some nouns are formed irregularly. Some nouns ending in f or fe change those terminations to ve in the plural form as in *leaf* to *leaves*.

lives
leaves
wolves
calves
shelves
elves
selves
knives
thieves
halves
potatoes
witches
themselves
wives
wharves
scarves
grieves

Group 32

When adding a suffix to a word ending in y, change the y to i, unless a vowel proceeds the y, as in try to *tried* and baby to *babies*.

libraries (R)
babies (R)
prettier (R)
cried (R)
tried (R)
playing (R)
Gypsies
cavities
memories
armies
diaries
bakeries
groceries
easier
bodies
flies
easily
dried

Group 33

When adding a suffix that begins with a vowel, the final e is usually dropped, as in *chase* to *chasing*.

coming (R)
writing (R)
using (R)
hiding (R)
giving (R)
driving (R)
raising
changing
hoping
becoming
promised
rising
smiling
simplest
facing
measuring
dividing
finest
compared
dying

Important Notes

- The "jump" in Group Numbers is intentional. See Page 122, "Grouping within Levels" for an explanation.
- Words followed by an (R) are Review words. Do not say the (R) when dictating them.
- Words in [brackets] are the British spelling. When correcting the test, use the proper spelling for your country.

Group 34

In short vowel words, the final consonant is usually doubled before adding a suffix, such as when changing in stop to stopped.

swimming (R)
tripped (R)
ripped (R)
slammed (R)
bigger (R)
sunny (R)
trotting (R)
trapped
winning
hopped
slipped
popped
planning
whizzed
upper
nodded
digging
dotted
fitted
rubbed

Review Test 4

The following words have been previously tested. (Student need not record this statement.)

becoming
dying
digging
upper
whizzed
hopped
potatoes
themselves
scarves
wives
memories
cavities
groceries
bodies
smiling
rising
bikes
shoes
scores
times

Group 35

Proper nouns must begin with a capital letter because they refer to a specific name or title of a person, place, time, thing, or idea such as Monday.

Christmas (R)
Wednesday (R)
September (R)
February (R)
Tuesday (R)
Easter
Indians
Smith
Bible
Arctic
Chicago
England
Disneyland
Mommy
Mexico
Thanksgiving
Japan
Jesus
British
Germans

Group 37

An apostrophe is used to take the place of a letter when two words are joined. These words are called contractions.

that's (R)
it's (R)
don't (R)
o'clock (R)
I've (R)
won't (R)
I'd (R)
let's (R)
we're
wouldn't
there's
they're (they are)
you're

Group 39

Sometimes two words are used together but are spelled separately, such as home school.

all right
ice cream
New York
United States
dining room
San Francisco
New York City
junior high school
high school
home school
parts of speech
New Year's Day
chicken pox
inner tube
a lot
peanut butter
blue jay
string beans
sleeping bag
tape recorder

Group 41

A period is used after most abbreviations such as in Sun. for Sunday. Initials are also abbreviations and should be followed with a period. Two letter state and provincial postal are exceptions.

Fri.
Sun.
Wed.
Mon.
Thurs.
Sat.
Tues.
Mr.
Mrs.
Ms.
T.V.
p.m. (afternoon)
a.m. (morning)
E. (east)
N. (north)
S. (south)
W. (west)
ft. (foot)
in. (inch)
yd. (yard)

Level D

Group 47

These words are unusual words and are exceptions to the most common generalizations.

again (R)
friend (R)
two (R)
weather (R)
trouble (R)
busy
laugh
build
laughing
guy
laughed
against
skier
building
toward
truly
young
touch
skiing
rough

Review Test 5

The following words have been previously tested. (Student need not record this statement.)

Arctic
Germans
dining room
British
we're
peanut butter
they're (they are)
you're
there's
Bible
junior high school
rough
toward
United States
Thurs. (Thursday)
laughing
ft. (foot)
against
yd. (yard)

Delayed Recall 2 Form A

Before administering this test, read pgs 45-46.

push 19
hymn 22
knitting 22
apples 30
takes 30
leaves 31
halves 31
promised 33
finest 33
nodded 34
whizzed 34
Chicago 35
Indians 35
you're 37
all right 39
Thurs. (Thursday) 41
T.V. (television) 41
laugh 47
skier 47
busy 47

Delayed Recall 2 Form B

sugar 19
often 22
answer 22
shoes 30
scores 30
knives 31
potatoes 31
diaries 32
measuring 33
dividing 33
trapped 34
winning 34
Jesus 35
Easter 35
they're 37
tape recorder 39
ft. (foot) 41
in. (inch) 41
laugh 47
truly 47

Important Notes

- The "jump" in Group Numbers is intentional. See Page 122, "Grouping within Levels" for an explanation.
- Words followed by an (R) are Review words. Do not say the (R) when dictating them.
- Words in [brackets] are the British spelling. When correcting the test, use the proper spelling for your country.

End of Level D Form A

Before administering this test, read pgs 45-46.

planet 1
felt 2
fist 3
nothing 4
puppy 5
tail 6
clean 7
flying 8
though 9
flew 10
heart 11
born 13
sugar 19
hymn 22
takes 30
shelves 31
memories 32
promised 33
planning 34
Thanksgiving 35
wouldn't 37
all right 39
Tues. 41
building 47

End of Level D Form B

candy 1
kept 2
sting 3
bottom 4
hunting 5
game 6
received 7
giant 8
follow 9
soup 10
startled 11
yesterday 12
shore 13
crooks 19
scores 30
calves 31
bakeries 32
measuring 33
dotted 34
England 35
let's 37
string beans 39
Mrs. 41
touch 47

Level E

Group 1

Usually /a/ is spelled a as in *cat*.

than (R)
family (R)
apple (R)
planet (R)
magic (R)
half (R)
smash
wrap
plank
ramp
bank
camping
daddy
stand
cabin
passed
standing
past
path
blanket
rabbits
plants

Group 2

Usually /e/ is spelled e as in *nest*.

then (R)
except (R)
self (R)
when (R)
else (R)
elephant (R)
leg
tent
wet
yet
fresh
present
sent
twenty
hello
helped
neck
test
yelling
slept
lets
elect
educate
penalty
dessert

Group 3

Usually /i/ is spelled i as in *big*.

its (own) (R)
since (R)
which (R)
city (R)
bring (R)
lived (R)
rich
visit
drink
pigs
singing
million
killing
bridge
minute
gives
tickets
tricks
dig
ring
stick
chill
riddle
ditch
twist
skin

Group 6

/ā/ can be written ay, ai, ey, ei, eigh, ea, or a followed by a consonant and silent e.

they (R)
plane (fly a) (R)
hey (you) (R)
hay (food for cattle) (R)
great (R)
grade (R)
gate (close the)
saying
waiting
break (apart)
lay
main (principal)
straight
strange
train
pay
safe
tasted
cage
grey
plays
races
tray
eighty
sway

Group 7

/ē/ can be spelled ea, ee, y, ie, ei, ey, or e followed by a consonant and silent e.

received (R)
chief (R)
dream (R)
team (R)
reach (R)
season (R)
free (R)
piece (of pie)
meat (a piece of)
need
screamed
sweet
asleep
meet (a friend)
seat
seemed (to me)
means
cream
deep
reason
teeth
beat
fifteen
between
reading

Review Test 1

The following words have been previously tested. (Student need not record this statement.)

passed
daddy
cabin
blanket
plants
slept
educate
dessert
test
fresh
visit
million
minute
riddle
twist
waiting
strange
plays
eighty
break (apart)
fifteen
between
meet (a friend)
meat (a piece of)
asleep

Level E

Group 8

/ī / can be spelled ie, igh, y, or i followed by two consonants as in *wild* or as i followed by a consonant and silent e as in *kite*.

science (R)
bright (R)
bye (leaving) (R)
giant (R)
high (tall) (R)
hi (greeting) (R)
right (direction) (R)
fighting
tied
driver
excited
mile
sight
eye (his eye)
crying
hike
size
surprised
tiger
nineteen
pie
alive
lion
mind
die (not alive)

Group 9

/ō/ can be spelled oe, ow, oa, or o followed by two consonants as in *told* or as o followed by a consonant and silent e as in *home*.

goes (R)
clothes (R)
goal (R)
phone (R)
rope (R)
though (R)
throw (R)
blow
goals
hold
phoned
showed
followed
low
poem
ocean
sold
below
rolled
roast
window (R)
moment
grows
gopher
hose

Group 18

/oi/ can be spelled oy as in *toy* or oi as *boil*.

joy (R)
loyal (R)
noise (R)
toy (R)
boy (R)
voice (R)
poison (R)
join (R)
joined
point
pointed
coin
noises
enjoyed
disappointed
choice
points
enjoy
avoid
soil
voices
moisture
coil
annoy

Group 20

Sometimes the letter o represents unexpected sounds as in *come*, *mother* and *one*.

another (R)
from (R)
once (R)
done (R)
honey (R)
above (R)
son (R)
none (R)
others
probably
months
mothers
become
loved
wonder (R)
wondered
stomach
covered
undone
government
governor
among
cover
colored [coloured]

Group 21

Q is always followed by u in English words such as in *quite*.

quite
quickly
quart
squeeze
quiz
squirm
squirt
queen
quiet
quest
turquoise
squeezed
mosquito
squirrels
quit
quarter
questions
squirrel
equipment
square
liquid

Review Test 2

The following words have been previously tested. (Student need not record this statement.)

size
nineteen
alive
lion
eye
phoned
poem
roast
gopher
hose
point
enjoy
choice
avoid
moisture
others
probably
loved
stomach
government
quite
squirm
quiet
quarter
quit

Group 22

Some words have silent letters such as with the k in *knew*, the w in *write*, and the l in *talk*.

whole (R)
answer (R)
knife (R)
dumb (R)
knocked
tomb
climb
island
signs
knowing
honor [honour]
wrench
folk
psalm
wrestle
wriggle
thumb
written
ghosts
bomb
knows

Group 24

Consonant letters are often doubled after a short vowel in short vowel words such as egg, *fluff*, *sniffle*, and *mess*.

across (R)
guess (R)
boss (R)
bell (R)
class (R)
dress (R)
smell (R)
kiss (R)
doll (R)
recess
pass
pulled
till
cliff
stuff
hull
pull
mess
hall

Group 25

Sometimes /yûr/ can be spelled ure as in *pure*.

figure
picture
adventure
pictures
treasure
pure
nature
measure
assure
lecture
mature
gesture
feature
mixture
texture
cure
future
temperature
pressure
pleasure

Group 26

When adding the suffixes ness and ly to words not ending in y the spelling of the base word stays the same, as in *slowly*.

suddenly
finally
really
slowly
usually
friendly
lonely
lovely
safely
nearly
shortly
accidentally
slightly
quietly
surely
directly
likely
badly
deeply
lightly

Group 27

When added to another syllable or used as a suffix, till and full are spelled with only one l as in *until* and *beautiful*.

until
beautiful
thankful
hopeful
handful
wonderful
playful
painful
joyful
truthful
cheerful
colorful [colourful]
harmful
graceful
healthful
forgetful
dreadful
watchful
delightful
untruthful

Important Notes

- The "jump" in Group Numbers is intentional. See Page 122, "Grouping within Levels" for an explanation.
- Words followed by an (R) are Review words. Do not say the (R) when dictating them.
- Words in [brackets] are the British spelling. When correcting the test, use the proper spelling for your country.

Level E

Review Test 3

knows
folk
tomb
knowing
wrestle
recess
pull
cliff
mess
hall
adventure
pictures
measure
temperature
feature
accidentally
friendly
directly
safely
really
beautiful
until
truthful
delightful
wonderful

Delayed Recall Test I Form A

Before administering this test, read pgs 45-46.

blanket 1
camping 1
fresh 2
elect 2
million 3
gives 3
waiting 4
grey 4
fifteen 7
reading 7
excited 8
nineteen 8
moment 9
poem 9
noises 18
probably 20
governor 20
squeezed 21
equipment 21
knocked 22
ghosts 22
mess 24
measure 25
temperature 25
accidentally 26
friendly 26
wonderful 27
watchful 27

Delayed Recall Test I Form B

standing 1
plank 1
hello 2
present 2
tricks 3
ditch 3
main 6
eighty 6
between 7
free 7
surprised 8
alive 8
grows 9
sold 9
avoid 18
annoy 18
months 20
government 20
questions 21
mosquito 21
signs 21
psalm 22
recess 24
treasure 25
picture 25
usually 26
quietly 26
truthful 27
cheerful 27

Group 28

/àn/ is sometimes spelled en as in *golden*.

kitten
sudden
open
chicken
golden
listened
broken
happen
kitchen
eaten
given
taken
eleven
listen
forgotten
oven
passenger
benefit
calendar
happened
intelligent

Group 29

/àl/ can be spelled le as in *little*, el as in *rebel*, al as in *total*, il as in *council*, ol as in *capitol*, ul as in *consul*, and ile as *futile*.

people
little
uncle
awhile
castle
animal
purple
turtle
nickel
middle
table
bicycle
lettuce
sprinkle
tale
devil
celery
elbow
medal
carnival

Group 30

Words are normally made plural by adding s.

minutes (R)
holidays (R)
trees (R)
horses (R)
wheels (R)
smells (R)
rocks (R)
says
ears
steps
eggs
brothers
doctors
monsters
games
places
planes
teachers
feels
wieners
streets
bees
holes
eats

Group 32

When adding a suffix to a word ending in y, change the y to i, unless a vowel proceeds the y, as in try to *tried* and baby to *babies*.

memories (R)
libraries (R)
bakeries (R)
easily (R)
easier (R)
groceries (R)
married
buried
worried
countries
cherries
worrying
hurrying
centuries
studied
carried
earlier
hurried
activities
colonies
studies
parties
berries
pennies
colonists

Group 35

Proper nouns must begin with a capital letter because they refer to a specific name or title of a person, place, time, thing, or idea such as Monday.

Arctic (R)
Germans (R)
Easter (R)
February (R)
November (R)
Michigan
Kansas
Tennessee
Maine
Arizona
Montana
Delaware
Kentucky
Oregon
Georgia
Utah
Nevada
Iowa
Alabama
Vermont
Connecticut
Oklahoma
Arkansas
Nebraska
Minnesota
Wisconsin
Ohio
Alaska
Texas
Louisiana
Hawaii
Colorado
Massachusetts
Missouri
Pennsylvania
Illinois
Wyoming
Washington
California
Virginia
Mississippi
Florida

Important Notes

- The "jump" in Group Numbers is intentional. See Page 122, "Grouping within Levels" for an explanation.
- Words followed by an (R) are Review words. Do not say the (R) when dictating them.
- Words in [brackets] are the British spelling. When correcting the test, use the proper spelling for your country.

Review Test 4

listened
eleven
calendar
kitchen
intelligent
little
awhile
medal
people
nickel
brothers
feels
wieners
ears
married
countries
centuries
activities
pennies
Connecticut
Minnesota
Massachusetts
Illinois
Florida

Group 36

New words are often made by putting two short words together into one word as in cowboy.

everybody (R)
without (R)
upon (R)
everything (R)
everyone (R)
outside (R)
airplane
footsteps
inside
mailman
became
grandmother
onto
tonight
upstairs
bedroom
tablecloth
Maryland
butterfly
midnight
forgot
downstairs
bulldog
classroom
strawberry

Level E

Group 37

An apostrophe is used to take the place of a letter when two words are joined. These words are called contractions.

that's (R)
it's (R)
you're (R)
don't (R)
o'clock (R)
they're (they are) (R)
she's (R)
she'd
shouldn't
you'd
he'd
he'll
you'll
you've

Group 38

Some words are joined by a hyphen, such as twenty-two.

good-bye
twenty-one
twenty-five
face-off
twenty-four
week-end
ninety-nine
x-ray
baby-sit
grown-ups
week-end
crash-landing
drive-in
jack-o'-lantern
ice-skating
brand-new
up-to-date
play-offs
one-way
well-known
runners-up
old-fashioned
thirty-five
twenty-two
sixty-four

Note: some compound English words are hyphenated if they are one part of speech and not hyphenated if they are another part of speech. As an example, *first class* is a noun while *first-class* is an adjective.

Group 39

Sometimes two words are used together but are spelled separately, such as home school.

all right (R)
dining room (R)
a lot (R)
United States (R)
high school (R)
contact lens
North Carolina
District of Columbia
Rhode Island
South Dakota
New Jersey
New Mexico
New Hampshire
West Virginia
vice president
leap year
first aid
question mark
science fiction
life preserver
parcel post
real estate
day care
fire escape
credit card

Group 41

A period is used after most abbreviations such as in Sun. for Sunday. Initials are also abbreviations and should be followed with a period. Two letter state and provincial postal are exceptions.

Jan.
Feb.
Mar.
Apr.
Aug.
Sept.
Oct.
Nov.
Dec.
U.S.A.
N.W. (northwest)
Rd.
P.S.
Hwy.
Blvd.
N.E. (northeast)
S.W. (southwest)
yrs. (years)
lbs. (pounds)
P.O. (post office)
Jr. (junior)
Ave.

Group 47

These words are unusual words and are exceptions to the most common generalizations.

friend (R)
again (R)
many (R)
truly (R)
against (R)
busy (R)
ninth (R)
ready (R)
weather (R)
young (R)
wolf
machine
built
piano
country (R)
restaurant
ache
mystery
cousins
touched
feather
death
ahead
bread

Review Test 5

The following words have been previously tested. (Student need not record this statement.)

grandmother
tablecloth
downstairs
Maryland
restaurant
shouldn't
you'd
you've
machine
he'll
baby-sit
up-to-date
old-fashioned
twenty-one
piano
North Carolina
question mark
real estate
credit card
mystery
U.S.A.
Blvd.
Sept.
Ave.
Apr.

Delayed Recall Test 2 Form A

Before administering this test, read pgs 45-46.

usually 26
accidentally 26
thankful 27
colorful [colourful 27]
eleven 28
benefit 28
uncle 29
animal 29
holes 30
monsters 30
countries 32
activities 32
Louisiana 35
Minnesota 35
tonight 36
strawberry 36
she'd 37
shouldn't 37
twenty-two 38
play-offs 38
Rhode Island 39
West Virginia 39
Hwy. 41
restaurant 47
country 47

Delayed Recall Test 2 Form B

friendly 26
finally 26
beautiful 27
healthful 27
calendar 28
broken 28
table 29
sprinkle 29
ears 30
teachers 30
centuries 32
studied 32
Pennsylvania 35
Kentucky 35
footsteps 36
midnight 36
he'd 37
you'll 37
thirty-five 38
crash-landing 38
New Hampshire 39
New Jersey 39
Blvd. 41
feather 47
mystery 47

End of Level E Test Form A

Before administering this test, read pgs 45-46.

path 1
fresh 2
million 3
straight 6
price 7
driver 8
goals 9
moisture 18
government 20
quiet 21
psalm 22
stuff 24
gesture 25
accidentally 26
beautiful 27
calendar 28
people 29
holes 30
studied 32
Louisiana 35
Maryland 36
shouldn't 37
sixty-four 38
high school 39
yrs. 41
piano 47

End of Level E Test Form B

bank 1
twenty 2
minute 3
eighty 6
reason 7
size 8
moment 9
disappointed 18
wondered 20
quest 21
signs 22
recess 24
figure 25
directly 26
dreadful 27
eleven 28
little 29
places 30
centuries 32
Wisconsin 35
onto 36
you've 37
ninety-nine 38
South Dakota 39
Sept. 41
restaurant 47

Important Notes

- The "jump" in Group Numbers is intentional. See Page 122, "Grouping within Levels" for an explanation.
- Words followed by an (R) are Review words. Do not say the (R) when dictating them.
- Words in [brackets] are the British spelling. When correcting the test, use the proper spelling for your country.

Level E

Level F

Group 1

Usually /a/ is spelled a as in *cat*.

blanket (R)
plants (R)
catch (R)
calf
crash
gang
plant
thank
bath
flat
rat
sand
sang
angry
band
crack
dance
thanks
blast
dragon
flash
trash
drank
cash
packed

Group 2

Usually /e/ is spelled e as in *nest*.

then (R)
twenty (R)
when (R)
every (R)
second (R)
tenth (R)
hen
medicine
send
fed
held
spent
bet
electric
net
cents (money)
parents
seconds
jet
president
dentist
telephone
yell
seventeen
twentieth

Group 3

Usually /i/ is spelled i as in *big*.

since (R)
which (R)
minute (R)
visit (R)
thing (R)
million (R)
inch (R)
picnic
thinking
filled
stick (R)
swing
village
fifty
missed
fifth
kicked
arithmetic
picking
finger
split
lip
twin
pit
kid

Group 4

Usually /o/ is spelled o as in *not*.

lot (R)
clock (R)
soft (R)
off (R)
contest (R)
closet
coffee
cottage
object
songs
strong
shop
donkey
locked
rod
crossed
trot
rocky
helicopter
fog
dolls
frogs
problems

Group 5

Usually /u/ is spelled u as in *run*.

bug (R)
mud (R)
bunch (R)
puppy (R)
dug (R)
dust (R)
gum (R)
sunny (R)
pups (R)
buffalo
bunny
club
bumped
trucks
drums
drunk
hundredth
trunk
hunt
shut
husband
bumpy
dusty

Review Test 1

The following words have been previously tested. (Student need not record this statement.)

calf
angry
thanks
dragon
drank
packed
medicine
electric
president
seventeen
twentieth
picnic
thinking
arithmetic
twin
fifty
coffee
strong
locked
helicopter
problems
buffalo
bumped
hundredth
husband

Group 6

/ā/ can be written ay, ai, ey, ei, eigh, ea, or a followed by a consonant and silent e.

neighbor [neighbour] (R)
break (apart) (R)
wait (stay) (R)
laid
laying
paid
paint
radio
station
raining
greatest
snakes
states
trains
lakes
save
chase
brain
daisy
age
ray
trailer
chased
wake
case

Group 7

/ē/ can be spelled ea, ee, y, ie, ei, ey, or e followed by a consonant and silent e.

received (R)
screamed (R)
piece (of meat) (R)
chief (R)
week (day of) (R)
between (R)
reading (R)
fifteen (R)
niece
alley
bee
keeper
speed
being
cleaned
needed
beaver
bean
beast

Group 8

/ī/ can be spelled ie, igh, y, or i followed by two consonants as in *wild* or as i followed by a consonant and silent e as in *kite*.

science (R)
die (not alive) (R)
lion (R)
mind (R)
pie (R)
alive (R)
surprise
frightened
child
cry
arrived
smile
pirates
pile
kites
higher
lighting
bite
fired
dinosaur
spy
hide
prize
wide
shine

Group 9

/ō/ can be spelled oe, ow, oa, or o followed by two consonants as in *told* or as o followed by a consonant and silent e as in *home*.

almost (R)
follow (R)
ocean (R)
soap (R)
coach (R)
poem (R)
clothes (R)
colt
awoke
alone
shadow
roll
thrown
blowing
grown
holy
opening
throat
supposed
willow
gopher (R)
rose
mow
close
zero

Important Notes

- The "jump" in Group Numbers is intentional. See Page 122, "Grouping within Levels" for an explanation.
- Words followed by an (R) are Review words. Do not say the (R) when dictating them.
- Words in [brackets] are the British spelling. When correcting the test, use the proper spelling for your country.

Level F

Group 12

/ûr/ can be spelled ir as in *bird*, er as in *her*, ur as in *survey*, er as in *eternity*, ear as in *pearl*, our as in *journal*, or or after w as in *work*.

were (R)
sure (R)
silver (R)
heard (R)
later (R)
world (R)
upper (R)
rather (R)
stubborn (R)
master
matter
butcher
number
thunder
player
motor
nurse
church
early
learned
dirty
hurry
circus
drinker
saucer

Review Test 2

radio
greatest
states
brain
trailer
alley
speed
butcher
cleaned
beaver
surprise
frightened
arrived
pirates
dinosaur
alone
thrown
grown
opening
supposed
number
thunder
learned
hurry
saucer

Group 13

/or/ can be spelled or as in *corn*, oar as in *boar*, oor as in *door*, our as *your*, and ar as *dwarf*.

morning (R)
fourth (R)
horror (R)
your (R)
before (R)
doctor (R)
course (R)
courtesy
score
towards
sport
important
forty
north
wore
board
forward
porridge
horn
mayor
reward
tractor
history

Group 14

/âr/ can be spelled are as *care*, air as in *hair*, ere as in *there*, ear as in *bear*, and eir as in *their*.

there (location) (R)
their (possessive pronoun) (R)
where (R)
care (R)
chair (R)
wear (R)
scare (R)
carry
fair (weather)
prairie
stairs
wearing
bare (empty)
fairy
carrot
baron
carrots
characteristic
carrying
pair (two of)
narrow
share
pairs
prepared
area
prepare

Group 15

/îr/ can be spelled ear as in *hear*, eer as in *deer*, ere as in *here*, ier as in *pier*, er as in *period*, or eir as in *weird*.

hear (R)
here (R)
near (R)
deer (R)
dear (R)
clear (R)
fear (R)
ear (R)
smear
spear
period
hearing
pier (dock)
peer (look closely)
beer
weird
appear
series
materials
disappeared
experience
beard

Group 16

Usually /ou/ is spelled ou before most consonants as in *cloud*. Sometimes /ou/ is spelled ow before final l or n as in *howl* or *clown* or at the end of a word or syllable as in *how* or *tower*.

our (R)
around (R)
found (R)
town (R)
house (R)
mouth (R)
about (R)
crowd
south
shouted
power
cloud
count
owl
pound
sounded
tower
announcer
cows
sour
trout
powers
clouds
thousands

Group 21

Q is always followed by u in English words such as in *quite*.

quilt (R)
quite (R)
quit (R)
queen (R)
quarter (R)
square (R)
liquid (R)
questioned
question
quick
frequently
quality
required
squares
equator
require
requires
unique
equation
quarters
quantities
qualities
queer
squad
squawk
equality
quieter
quote
requirement
quotation

Review Test 3

The following words have been previously tested.

important
forward
history
forty
prairie
characteristic
prepared
period
weird
appear
disappeared
experience
shouted
sounded
announcer
thousands
questioned
frequently
equation
qualities
requirement

Delayed Recall I Form A

Before administering this test, read pgs 45-46.

thank 1
dance 1
medicine 2
telephone 2
village 3
fifty 3
arithmetic 3
object 4
hundredth 5
daisy 6
cleaned 7
prize 8
surprise 8
opening 9
player 12
important 13
forty 13
narrow 14
prairie 14
characteristic 14
materials 15
weird 15
appear 15
announcer 16
quarters 21

Delayed Recall I Form B

crack 1
medicine 2
electric 2
fifty 3
fifth 3
arithmetic 3
closet 4
trunk 5
paint 6
niece 7
surprise 8
higher 8
thrown 9
shadow 9
nurse 12
mayor 13
forty 13
wearing 14
characteristic 14
weird 15
hearing 15
appear 15
crowd 16
question 21
equator 21

Group 22

Some words have silent letters such as with the <u>k</u> in *knew*, the <u>w</u> in *write*, and the <u>l</u> in *talk*.

answer (R)
island (R)
whole (R)
thumb (R)
often (R)
written (R)
signs (R)
knowing (R)
honor [honour] (R)
palm (R)
islands
column
knowledge
answers
unknown
salmon
walks
folks
autumn
signed
sword
wretched
wrought
answered

Group 24

Consonant letters are often doubled after a short vowel in short vowel words such as *egg*, *fluff*, *sniffle*, and *mess*.

guess (R)
across (R)
doll (R)
glass (R)
hall (R)
recess (R)
dull
addressed
annual
gallant
latter
marriage
mattress

Important Notes

- The "jump" in Group Numbers is intentional. See Page 122, "Grouping within Levels" for an explanation.
- Words followed by an (R) are Review words. Do not say the (R) when dictating them.
- Words in [brackets] are the British spelling. When correcting the test, use the proper spelling for your country.

Level F

Group 30

Words are normally made plural by adding s, but if the word ends with sh, zh, z, s, j, ch, or x sounds, the plural is generally formed by adding es, which is pronounced as a separate syllable.

cats (R)
holes (R)
planes (R)
teachers (R)
guns
kittens
mountains
names
neighbors [neighbours]
pounds
presents
rides
works
bicycles
blows
bugs
doors
guys
wings
stores
cans
hills
branches
mosquitoes
dishes

Group 31

Plurals of some nouns are formed irregularly. A few nouns form their plural by changing a single vowel, such as in man to men.

foot; feet
tooth; teeth
goose; geese
child; children
brother; brethren
ox; oxen

Group 32

When adding a suffix to a word ending in y, change the y to i, unless a vowel proceeds the y, as in try to *tried* and baby to *babies.*

earlier (R)
centuries (R)
studies (R)
studied (R)
parties (R)
earlier (R)
luckily
heavier
earliest
tiniest
happiest
discoveries
healthiest
hungrier
dirtier
crazier
busily
dries
angriest
scariest
handicrafts
occupied
satisfied
factories

Review Test 4

The following words have been previously tested. (Student need not record this statement.)

column
knowledge
answers
autumn
wrought
addressed
annual
gallant
latter
marriage
mattress
mountains
neighbors [neighbours]
bicycles
branches
mosquitoes
teeth
children
luckily
earliest
discoveries
healthiest
scariest
handicrafts
factories

Group 33

When adding a suffix that begins with a vowel, the final e is usually dropped, as in *chase* to *chasing.*

becoming (R)
simplest (R)
measuring (R)
using (R)
raising (R)
smiling (R)
shining (R)
dying (R)
encouraging
indispensable
striking
surprising
closing
producing
preparing
staring
losing
forcible
issuing
salable
sizable
suing
sensible
consensus

Group 34

In short vowel words, the final consonant is usually doubled before adding a suffix, such as when changing in stop to stopped.

planning (R)
grabbed (R)
whizzed (R)
rubbed (R)
winning (R)
biggest (R)
stopping (R)
happened (R)
putting (R)
dressed (R)
beginning
spinning
splitting
forgetting
shrugged
bragging
drummers
chopping
fatter
foggy
snapping
begged
winner
tipped
jogging

Group 35

Proper nouns must begin with a capital letter because they refer to a specific name or title of a person, place, time, thing, or idea such as Monday.

God (R)
Tuesday (R)
Wednesday (R)
Connecticut (R)
Massachusetts (R)
Pennsylvania (R)
Alberta
Indian
America
Saskatchewan
Chile
Canadians
France
German
Toronto
Vancouver
Jamaica
Haiti
Barbados
Bahamas
Peru
Columbia
Quebec
Ontario
Argentina
Panama
Caribbean

Note: The word "Columbia" in Group 35 refers to (British) Columbia, (District of) Columbia, or the Columbia (River). "Colombia" (The South American country) is not a high frequency word and does not appear in the Spelling Power Flow-Word-Lists.

Group 36

New words are often made by putting two short words together into one word as in cowboy.

outside (R)
without (R)
everything (R)
grandmother (R)
butterfly (R)
midnight (R)
forgot (R)
downstairs (R)
forget
cannot
anymore
bathroom
pancake
underdog
homework
snapdragon
passersby
everyday
driveway
underwater
underground
peanuts
airplanes
cowboys

Group 37

An apostrophe is used to take the place of a letter when two words are joined. These words are called contractions.

don't (R)
can't (R)
it's (R)
they're (they are) (R)
you're (R)
hadn't
haven't
weren't
we'd
here's
they'd
they'll
ain't
who's

Review Test 5

The following words have been previously tested. (Student need not record this statement.)

encouraging
indispensable
forcible
issuing
salable
sizable
suing
sensible
consensus
beginning
forgetting
America
Canadians
Vancouver
Columbia
cannot
bathroom
homework
everyday
underground
haven't
here's
they'll
who's

Group 38

Some words are joined by a hyphen, such as twenty-two.

good-bye (R)
twenty-one (R)
face-off (R)
week-end (R)
twenty-four (R)
grown-up (R)
ice-skating (R)
one-way (R)
ninety-nine (R)
crash-landing (R)
left-hand
baby-sitter
cross-country
great-grandfathers
happy-go-lucky
morning-glory (family of plants)
air-conditioned
first-class (adj.)
by-products
full-fledged
matter-of-fact
self-conscious
self-defense

Important Notes

- *The "jump" in Group Numbers is intentional. See Page 122, "Grouping within Levels" for an explanation.*
- *Words followed by an (R) are Review words. Do not say the (R) when dictating them.*
- *Words in [brackets] are the British spelling. When correcting the test, use the proper spelling for your country.*

Group 41

A period is used after most abbreviations such as in Sun. for Sunday. Initials are also abbreviations and should be followed with a period. Two letter state and provincial postal are exceptions.

U.S.A. (R)
Dr.
St.
etc.
AR (Arkansas)
KS (Kansas)
AZ (Arizona)
BC (British Columbia)
CA (California)
CO (Colorado)
MS (Mississippi)
DE (Delaware)
FL (Florida)
NF (Newfoundland)
GA (Georgia)
HI (Hawaii)
IA (Iowa)
ME (Maine)
IL (Illinois)
MI (Michigan)
PQ (Quebec)
IN (Indiana)
KY (Kentucky)
LA (Louisiana)
MD (Maryland)
MN (Minnesota)
AL (Alabama)
MO (Missouri)
AB (Alberta)
MT (Montana)
CT (Connecticut)
NC (North Carolina)
ND (North Dakota)
ID (Idaho)

Group 42

/shun/ can be spelled tion as in *vacation*, sion as in *division*, or cian as in *physician*.

vacation
information
invitation
repetition
description
exhibition
competition
preparation
direction
addition
edition
position
section
action
attention
nation
motion
solution
population
education
dictionary
nations
functions
situations
division
pollution

Group 46

The addition of a prefix does not usually change the spelling of the root word. Some prefixes signify quantity as in uni for one in *uniform* or bi for two in *bicycle*.

tricolor [tricolour]
tricycle
triple
triplicate
uniform
bi-weekly
bi-monthly
milligram
milliliter [millilitre]
millimeter [millimetre]
kilogram
kilometer [kilometre]
centimeter [centimetre]
centiliter [centilitre]
decameter [decametre]
kiloliter [kilolitre]
hectoliter [hectolitre]
triangular
bifocal
biannual
bicentennial
decimeter [decimetre]

Group 47

These words are unusual words and are exceptions to the most common generalizations.

fiend (R)
truly (R)
busy (R)
two (R)
weather (R)
of (R)
trouble (R)
machine (R)
piano (R)
feather (R)
cousins (R)
touch (R)
restaurant (R)
bureau
trophy
wolverine
sew (to stitch)
museum
headed
notice
gym
health
thread
steady
typical
syllable
heads
heavy
rhythm
leather

Review Test 6

The following words have been previously tested. (Student need not record this statement.)

left-hand
baby-sitter
air-conditioned
first-class (adj.)
self-conscious
MO (Missouri)
MD (Maryland)
CT (Connecticut)
IA (Iowa)
invitation
repetition
exhibition
competition
preparation
addition

Test continues on next column

direction
pollution
triplicate
bi-weekly
bi-monthly
centiliter
biannual
decimeter
museum
trouble
health
syllable
rhythm

Delayed Recall Test 2 Form A

Before administering this test, read pgs 45-46.

column 22
addressed 24
latter 24
marriage 24
neighbors 30 [neighbours] 30
bicycles 30
children 31
happiest 32
factories 32
encouraging 33
forcible 33
issuing 33
spinning 34
beginning 34
America 35
Canadians 35
everyday 36
anymore 36
weren't 37
here's 37
baby-sitter
U.S.A. 41
invitation 42
direction 42
triplicate 46

Delayed Recall Test 2 Form B

knowledge 22
annual 24
gallant 24
mattress 24
presents 30
mosquitoes 30
teeth 31
scariest 32
discoveries 32
indispensable 33
sizable 33
sensible 33
bragging 34
forgetting 34
Indian 35
Quebec 35
driveway 36
airplanes 36
hadn't 37
who's
matter-of-fact 38
etc. 41
repetition 42
addition 42
kilogram 46

End of Level F Test Form A

Before administering this test, read pgs 45-46.

thanks 1
medicine 2
fifty 3
helicopter 4
hundredth 5
station 6
being 7
surprise 8
awoke 9
church 12
forty 13
prairie 14
weird 15
south 16
squares 21
knowledge 22
addressed 24
branches 30
feet 31
happiest 32
consensus 33

Test continues on next column

beginning 34
America 35
pancake 36
hadn't 37
left-hand 38
Dr. 41
direction 42
uniform 46
trophy 47

End of Level F Test Form B

bath 1
medicine 2
arithmetic 3
strong 4
bunny 5
chased 6
beast 7
kites 8
throat 9
circus 12
forward 13
characteristic 14
appear 15
cloud 16
quieter 21
unknown 22
marriage 24
mountains 30
oxen 31
hungriest 32
indispensable 33
forgetting 34
Columbia 35
homework 36
who's 37
one-way 38
U.S.A. 41
population 42
bicentennial 46
museum 47

Important Notes

- The "jump" in Group Numbers is intentional. See Page 122, "Grouping within Levels" for an explanation.
- Words followed by an (R) are Review words. Do not say the (R) when dictating them.
- Words in [brackets] are the British spelling. When correcting the test, use the proper spelling for your country.

Level F

Level G

Group 1

Usually /a/ is spelled a as in *cat*.

than (R)
hang
plan
planted
salad
match
attacked
banana
bang
captain
danced
cast
chance
fan
package
pan
ranch
splash
track
trap
smashed
shaft
woman
pack
ham
hanging
grand
snack
swan
wand

Group 2

Usually /e/ is spelled e as in *nest*.

then (R)
except (R)
seventeen (R)
twentieth (R)
seconds (R)
electric (R)
president (R)
dentist (R)
pen
engine
spend
nest
west
belt
led
step
lesson
smelling
ballet
wrestler
comet
lemon
elf
checked
racket
render
letters
pens
scent
telling

Group 3

Usually /i/ is spelled i as in *big*.

its (own) (R)
arithmetic (R)
fifth (R)
which (R)
inch (R)
fifty (R)
fixed
thin
trick
wing
string
wished
drinking
mischief
mixed
silly
ticket
kitty
minister
clip
film
skit
injured
prim
stink
victim
whimper
lift

Group 5

Usually /u/ is spelled u as in *run.*

buffalo (R)
husband (R)
hundredth (R)
such (R)
funny (R)
just (R)
stump
jumps
buttons
hundreds
hunters
lungs
trumpets
tunnels
uncles
pumpkin
study
puppet
punch
numbers
thus
subject
public
hung
studying
subjects
results
product
industry
sum

Group 6

/ā/ can be written ay, ai, ey, ei, eigh, ea, or a followed by a consonant and silent e.

taste (R)
eighty (R)
daisy (R)
grey (R)
straight (R)
mail (this letter)
waited
painted
afraid
gay
gray
lazy
staying
weighed
mane (of a horse)
saved
base
changed
bake
hated
claimed
trainer
mistake
shaped
trained
stray
swaying
tame
stranger
waved

Review Test 1

The following words have been previously tested. (Student need not record this statement.)

banana
track
woman
chance
captain
smashed
smelling
wrestler
engine
lesson
ballet
lemon
mischief
minister
injured
whimper
victim
wished
hundreds
studying
industry
pumpkin
subject
public
weighed
stray
staying
hated
saved
afraid

Level G

Important Notes

- The "jump" in Group Numbers is intentional. See Page 122, "Grouping within Levels" for an explanation.
- Words followed by an (R) are Review words. Do not say the (R) when dictating them.
- Words in [brackets] are the British spelling. When correcting the test, use the proper spelling for your country.

Group 7

/ē/ can be spelled ea, ee, y, ie, ei, ey, or e followed by a consonant and silent e.

chief (R)
scream (R)
piece (of pie) (R)
niece (R)
relieve (R)
alley (R)
steel (metal)
valley
key
lead (take the)
least
region
seed
sheep
teach
agreed
breathe
easy
evening
seeing
sixteen
stream
screaming
sneak
speak
sneeze
seize

Group 8

/ī/ can be spelled ie, igh, y, or i followed by two consonants as in *wild* or as i followed by a consonant and silent e as in *kite*.

surprise (R)
science (R)
pile (R)
smile (R)
higher (R)
nineteen (R)
eye (R)
size (R)
idea
tie
blind
diamond
dry
lying
invited
pine
prime
ninety
strike
realized
shiny
gigantic
dive
scientist
wire
twice
pirate
private
tire
lie

Group 9

/ō/ can be spelled oe, ow, oa, or o followed by two consonants as in *told* or as o followed by a consonant and silent e as in *home*.

shadow (R)
holy (R)
supposed (R)
window (R)
yellow (R)
below (R)
toe (R)
goes (R)
robot
located
boating
goalie
although
closed
solo
stove
showing
slow
suppose
violet
spoke
toad
lower
growing
program
shown
shows
coast
growth
smoke

Group 10

/ū/ can be spelled ew as in *few*, ue as in *blue*, ui as in *suit*, o as in *to*, or as u followed by a consonant and silent e as in *mule*.

through (finished) (R)
together (R)
smooth (R)
to (R)
too (also) (R)
whose (R)
loose
shoe
united
human
noon
suit
chew
rooster
spooky
stupid
moose
fooling
boo
tour
tulip
prove
juice
pollute
spook
suited
super
community
movie
beauty

Group 11

/àr/ is usually spelled ar as in *jar*.

grammar (R)
started (R)
hard (R)
garage (R)
stars (R)
heart (R)
star
larger
largest
farmers
marks
army
market
chart
charge
harder
similar
particular
marked
familiar
variety
character
popular
particles
apparatus
cards
articles
artist
harvest
carbon

Review Test 2

The following words have been previously tested. (Student need not record this statement.)

seize
sneak
breathe
sixteen
valley
region
ninety
diamond
invited
realized
gigantic
scientist
located
suppose
violet
program
coast
although
untied
rooster
fooling
tulip
pollute
suited
similar
familiar
apparatus
largest
variety
harvest

Level G

Important Notes

- The "jump" in Group Numbers is intentional. See Page 122, "Grouping within Levels" for an explanation.
- Words followed by an (R) are Review words. Do not say the (R) when dictating them.
- Words in [brackets] are the British spelling. When correcting the test, use the proper spelling for your country.

Group 12

/ûr/ can be spelled ir as in *bird*, er as in *her*, ur as in *survey*, er as in *eternity*, ear as in *pearl*, our as in *journal*, or or after w as in *work*.

different (R)
later (R)
world (R)
first (R)
gather
shelter
whether
center [centre]
entered
remembered
interesting
longer
bother
rubber
danger
older
owner
shirt
worked
word
burning
worry
further
earn
fur
turning
furry
searched

Group 13

/or/ can be spelled or as in *corn*, oar as in *boar*, oor as in *door*, our as *your*, and ar as *dwarf*.

course (R)
before (R)
courtesy (R)
grammar (R)
forty (R)
tractor (R)
history (R)
record
ore
sore
sort
corn
fourth (R)
orbit
scored
explore
ordinary
yours
sports
colors [colours]
worms
court
according
tore
force
northern
source
foreign
chauffeur

Group 17

/ô/ can be spelled a, o, and au before most consonants as in *already*, *cost*, and *sauce* or as augh or ough before t as in *sought* and *caught* or as aw before final k, l, n as *hawk*, *crawl*, and *lawn* or at the end of a word or stressed syllable as in *awful* or *law*.

already (R)
awful (R)
wants (R)
always (R)
thought (R)
brought (R)
because (R)
straw (R)
watching
fought
cough
hawks
taught
draws
smaller
law
drawn
smallest
salt
lawn
author
caused
drawing
raw
causes
crawled
waters

Group 18

/oi/ can be spelled oy as in *toy* or oi as *boil*.

poison (R)
voices (R)
join (R)
choice (R)
point (R)
toy (R)
loyal (R)
joint (R)
noises (R)
avoid (R)
enjoyed (R)
disappointed (R)
destroyed
voyage
pointing
coins
rejoice
appoint
oyster
noisier
annoyance
ointment
void
noisy
moist
boiling
destroy

Group 20

Sometimes the letter o represents unexpected sounds as in *come*, *mother* and *one*.

probably (R)
among (R)
government (R)
cover (R)
colored [coloured] (R)
dozen (R)
governor (R)
other (R)
another (R)
brother (R)
once (R)
money (R)
blood (R)
month (R)
ones (R)
wondering
discovered
becomes
company
covers
monkeys
sons
onions
ton
smother
overcome
canoe
bothered
bishop

Review Test 3

The following words have been previously tested. (Student need not record this statement.)

interesting
remembered
searched
burning
danger
whether
chauffeur
according
foreign
fourth
explore
northern
watching
cough
smallest
causes
crawled
drawn
destroyed
rejoice
oyster
ointment
annoyance
boiling
discovered
company
smother
bothered
bishop
monkeys

Level G

Important Notes

- The "jump" in Group Numbers is intentional. See Page 122, "Grouping within Levels" for an explanation.
- Words followed by an (R) are Review words. Do not say the (R) when dictating them.
- Words in [brackets] are the British spelling. When correcting the test, use the proper spelling for your country.

Delayed Recall Test I Form A

Before administering this test, read pgs 45-46.

woman 1
track 1
lesson 2
scent 2
minister 3
injured 3
hundreds 5
industry 5
weighed 6
trained 6
seize 7
sneak 7
ninety 8
diamond 8
although 9
suppose 9
human 10
loose 10
similar 11
familiar 11
apparatus 11
searched 12
chauffeur 13
fourth 13
fought 17
causes 17
ointment 18
annoyance 18
becomes 20
monkeys 20

Delayed Recall Test I Form B

banana 1
smashed 1
smelling 2
west 2
mischief 3
whimper 3
pumpkin 5
trumpets 5
stranger 6
afraid 6
sneak 7
seize 7
ninety 8
gigantic 8
growing 9
although 9
pollute 10
beauty 10
similar 11
familiar 11
apparatus 11
interesting 12
chauffeur 13
scored 13
smallest 17
taught 17
rejoice 18
oyster 18
discovered 20
onions 20

Group 23

No English words end with the letter v.

twelve (R)
leave (R)
drive (R)
drove (R)
have (R)
five (R)
glove
observe
wave
shove
grave
swerve
groove
pave
strive
preserve
believe

Group 24

Consonant letters are often doubled after a short vowel in short vowel words such as *egg, fluff, sniffle,* and *mess.*

till (R)
across (R)
dress (R)
glass (R)
addressed (R)
gallant (R)
sell (R)
fill
troll
putt
sheriff
shall
princess
business
cross
unless
embarrass
exaggerate
spell
shell
add

Group 25

Sometimes /yûr/ can be spelled ure as in *pure.*

temperature (R)
measure (R)
nature (R)
pressure (R)
future (R)
pure (R)
pleasure (R)
mixture (R)
figures
structure
measures
creatures
furniture
pictured
features
temperatures
creature
captured
pasture
culture
literature
structures
figured
capture
measured
departure
ensure
secure
posture

Group 29

/àl/ can be spelled le as in *little*, el as in *rebel*, al as in *total*, il as in *council*, ol as in *capitol*, ul as in *consul*, and ile as *futile*.

nickel (R)
people (R)
little (R)
uncle (R)
awhile (R)
animal (R)
able
control
couple
jail
special
terrible
trail
cattle
horrible
cool
example
pencil
hotel
invisible
mammal
saddle
battle
bubble
circle
general
needle
maple
popsicle
possible

Group 30

Words are normally made plural by adding s, but if the word ends with sh, zh, z, s, j, ch, or x sounds, the plural is generally formed by adding es, which is pronounced as a separate syllable.

mountains (R)
bicycles (R)
neighbors [neighbours] (R)
elephants (R)
minutes (R)
cans (R)
hills (R)
wings (R)
guys (R)
fingers
kills
mines
needs
pants
pets
pieces
poles
rivers
sisters
sleeps
soldiers
nights
prices
roads
rooms
seems
twins
ways
wins
bats

Review Test 4

The following words have been previously tested. (Student need not record this statement.)

observe
believe
swerve
grave
strive
shove
embarrass
exaggerate
sheriff
business
princess
spell
temperatures
structure
departures
furniture
literature
culture
terrible
special
needle
hotel
bubble
possible
soldiers
fingers
pieces
sleeps
nights
prices

Level G

Important Notes

- The "jump" in Group Numbers is intentional. See Page 122, "Grouping within Levels" for an explanation.
- Words followed by an (R) are Review words. Do not say the (R) when dictating them.
- Words in [brackets] are the British spelling. When correcting the test, use the proper spelling for your country.

Group 32

When adding a suffix to a word ending in y, change the y to i, unless a vowel proceeds the y, as in try to *tried* and baby to *babies*.

worried (R)
studied (R)
activities (R)
satisfied (R)
ladies (R)
stories (R)
tries (R)
magnify
cloudiness
windiness
replied
supplies
heavily
busier
classifying
abilities
communities
companies
steadily
boundaries
memorize
funniest
dutiful
gloomiest
pastries
trophies
victories
liberties
supplied

Group 35

Proper nouns must begin with a capital letter because they refer to a specific name or title of a person, place, time, thing, or idea such as Monday.

August (R)
Saskatchewan (R)
Massachusetts (R)
Caribbean (R)
Argentina (R)
Thursday (R)
March (R)
Arctic (R)
July (R)
Norway
Mercury
Britain
Scotland
English
American
French
Europe
Africa
Spanish
Greek
Chinese
Pacific
Atlantic
Germany
Newfoundland
Italy
Latin
China
Japanese
Roman
Asia

Group 38

Some words are joined by a hyphen, such as twenty-two.

vice-president (R)
left-handed (R)
grown-up (R)
great-grandfathers (R)
air-conditioned (R)
full-fledged (R)
matter-of-fact (R)
by-products (R)
first-class (R)
baby-sitter (R)
twenty-one (R)
close-up
first-born (adj.)
all-around
brothers-in-law
sisters-in-law
daughter-in-law
sons-in-law
mother-in-law
brother-in-law
self-discipline
dead-end (adj. or adv.)
self-reliance
merry-go-round
worn-out
long-distance
make-believe
drive-ins
tune-ups
right-handed
loose-leaf
best-seller

Note: some compound English words are hyphenated if they are one part of speech and not hyphenated if they are another part of speech. As an example, *first class* is a noun while *first-class* is an adjective.

Group 39

Sometimes two words are used together but are spelled separately, such as home school.

all right (R)
dining room (R)
home school (R)
tape recorder (R)
a lot (R)
United States (R)
New Hampshire (R)
West Virginia (R)
Rhode Island (R)
Puerto Rico
Nova Scotia
British Columbia
dead end (noun)
bulletin board
credit card (R)
motion picture
first born (noun)
chop suey
chow mein
day care (R)
cold front
sea gull
contact lens
Morning Glory (specific plant)
field trip
vice president (R)
post office

Note: the term *home school* is relatively new and there are different opinions regarding its spelling. We have chosen the two word compound because it is consistent with other similar compound words, i.e. high school, grade school, private school, etc.

Group 40

An apostrophe is used to show ownership such as in the boy's ball except for the neuter pronoun it (its: possessive, it's: contraction of it is).

boy's
mother's
brother's
dog's
sister's
dad's
man's
earth's
father's
world's
today's
America's
Tom's
teacher's
boys'
else's
anybody's
brothers'
grandma's
nobody's
grandfather's
daughter's
neighbor's [neighbour's]
someone's
witnesses'
friends'
actress's
enemy's
community's

Review Test 5

The following words have been previously tested. (Student need not record this statement.)

boundaries
communities
companies
cloudiness
funniest
victories
Britain
American
Atlantic
Japanese
Mercury
Africa
close-up
mother-in-law
merry-go-round
make-believe
long-distance
all-around
Columbia
dead end
contact lens
child care
field trip
post office
credit card
mother's
nobody's
grandma's
community's
first-class (adj.)
America's
witnesses'

Level G

Important Notes

- The "jump" in Group Numbers is intentional. See Page 122, "Grouping within Levels" for an explanation.
- Words followed by an (R) are Review words. Do not say the (R) when dictating them.
- Words in [brackets] are the British spelling. When correcting the test, use the proper spelling for your country.

Group 41

A period is used after most abbreviations such as in Sun. for Sunday. Initials are also abbreviations and should be followed with a period. Two letter state and provincial postal are exceptions.

MB (Manitoba)
NH (New Hampshire)
WY (Wyoming)
AK (Alaska) (R)
DC (Washington DC) (R)
ME (Maine) (R)
ON (Ontario)
MI (Michigan) (R)
DE (Delaware) (R)
IN (Indiana) (R)
MA (Massachusetts)
IA (Iowa) (R)
SK (Saskatchewan)
NM (New Mexico)
SC (South Carolina)
NY (New York)
OH (Ohio)
TN (Tennessee)
OK (Oklahoma)
OR (Oregon)
PA (Pennsylvania)
RI (Rhode Island)
NJ (New Jersey)
SD (South Dakota)
NV (Nevada)
TX (Texas)
NE (Nebraska)
UT (Utah)
VA (Virginia)
NS (Nova Scotia)
VT (Vermont)
WA (Washington)
WI (Wisconsin)
WV (West Virginia)

Group 42

/shun/ can be spelled tion as in vacation, sion as in division, or cian as in physician.

invitation (R)
repetition (R)
exhibition (R)
preparation (R)
direction (R)
addition (R)
directions
sections
expression
television
condition
conservation
collection
construction
production
subtraction
punctuation
foundation
exclamation
investigation
attraction
consideration
concession
tuition
operation
combination
transportation
stationery
possession
definition

Group 46

The addition of a prefix does not usually change the spelling of the root word. The prefixes de can mean down or from such as in the words describes and delivery.

describes
deposits
delight
despite
demand
demanded
delivered
debate
detective
devoted
defeat
delivery
decrease
deposit
deceit
dehydrate
depose
decorator
debris
deprivation
deprive
destructive
deception
delinquent
demographic
demolish
deplorable
detain
detention
deport

Group 47

These words are unusual words and are exceptions to the most common generalizations.

friend (R)
many (R)
truly (R)
bureau (R)
restaurant (R)
against (R)
ninth (R)
ready (R)
weather (R)
meant
spread
healthy
breath
wee
aches
iron
imagine
shoulder
guide
height
broad
volume
empty
country (R)
trouble (R)
touching
tough
southern
flood

Review Test 6

The following words have been previously tested. (Student need not record this statement.)

OH (Ohio)
VA (Virginia)
VT (Vermont)
NV (Nevada)
NE (Nebraska)
WI (Wisconsin)
WA (Washington)
WY (Wyoming)
concession
tuition
possession
television
punctuation
investigation
transportation
debate
deception
deplorable
detention
delivery
deprivation
destructive
volume
healthy
imagine
country
touching
southern
flood
meant

Delayed Recall Test 2 Form A

Before administering this test, read pgs 45-46.

observe 23
believe 23
exaggerate 24
embarrass 24
temperatures 25
furniture 25
terrible 29
able 29
sisters 30
soldiers 30
communities 32
companies 32
boundaries 32
Britain 35
American 35
all-around 38
right-handed 38
field trip 39
Puerto Rico 39
teacher's 40
enemy's 40
NE (Nebraska) 41
WI (Wisconsin) 41
concession 42
tuition 42
possession 42
detective 46
destructive 46
volume 47
height 47

Important Notes

- The "jump" in Group Numbers is intentional. See Page 122, "Grouping within Levels" for an explanation.
- Words followed by an (R) are Review words. Do not say the (R) when dictating them.
- Words in [brackets] are the British spelling. When correcting the test, use the proper spelling for your country.

Level G

Delayed Recall Test 2 Form B

groove 23
believe 23
exaggerate 24
embarrass 24
literature 25
departure 25
terrible 29
horrible 29
prices 30
fingers 30
communities 32
boundaries 32
companies 32
Britain 35
Japanese 35
first-born 38
long-distance 38
sea gull 39
Newfoundland 39
boy's 40
America's 40
NV (Nevada) 41
WA (Washington) 41
concession 42
tuition 42
possession 42
delivery 46
decorator 46
volume 47
country 47

End of Level G Test Form A

Before administering this test, read pgs 45-46.

banana 1
racket 2
minister 3
hundreds 5
lazy 6
seize 7
lying 8
although 9
rooster 10
similar 11
remembered 12
chauffeur 13
author 17
voyage 18
smother 20
observe 23
embarrass 24
measures 25
terrible 29
soldiers 30
communities 32
Britain 35
close-up 38
Puerto Rico 39
neighbor's [neighbour's] 40
OH (Ohio) 41
concession 42
dehydrate 46
volume 47
aches 47

End of Level G Test Form B

woman 1
telling 2
injured 3
studying 5
saved 6
sixteen 7
ninety 8
suppose 9
stupid 10
familiar 11
interesting 12
chauffeur 13
drawing 17
noisier 18
becomes 20
believe 23
exaggerate 24
posture 25
terrible 29
pieces 30
companies 32
Britain 35
worn-out 38
British Columbia 39
actress's 40
NE (Nebraska) 41
possession 42
deprive 46
volume 47
flood 47

Level H

Group 1

Usually /a/ is spelled a as in *cat.*

track (R)
woman (R)
banana (R)
plastic
strap
accept
language
map
fact
added
faster
stands
lands
act
average
wagon
plans
dad
gathered
chapter
ants
flag
passing
dancing
adding
basic
paragraph
vast
manner
attack

Group 2

Usually /e/ is spelled e as in *nest.*

medicine (R)
then (R)
every (R)
seventh (R)
when (R)
telephone (R)
benefited
check
edge
necessary
sets
method
desert
separate
settled
regular
cent
protect
member
spelling
plenty
suggested
helping
enemy
invented
deck
message
strength
western
spelled

Group 3

Usually /i/ is spelled i as in *big.*

arithmetic (R)
since (R)
brilliant (R)
picnic (R)
village (R)
which (R)
discipline
list
begins
interest
missing
interested
insects
continued
millions
winds
lifted
chickens
lips
spirit
thick
difficult
begin
finish
consider
electricity
listed
printed
ability
strip

Important Notes

- The "jump" in Group Numbers is intentional. See Page 122, "Grouping within Levels" for an explanation.
- Words followed by an (R) are Review words. Do not say the (R) when dictating them.
- Words in [brackets] are the British spelling. When correcting the test, use the proper spelling for your country.

Group 4

Usually /o/ is spelled o as in *not.*

hockey (R)
helicopter (R)
strong (R)
coffee (R)
chocolate (R)
object (R)
following
committee
common
products
modern
copy
cloth
crops
proper
solid
belong
blocks
copper
pocket
property
log
drops
develop
discover
oxygen
objects
jobs
opposite
discovery

Group 6

/ā/ can be written ay, ai, ey, ei, eigh, ea, or a followed by a consonant and silent e.

afraid (R)
weighed (R)
wait (stay) (R)
neighbor [neighbour] (R)
laid (R)
paid (R)
weight (number of pounds)
raised
raise
plain (flat area)
grain
plains
remain
clay
sailed
papers
daily
players
page
state
placed
shape
greater
trade (R)
stage
phrase
range
rate
based
plate

Review Test I

The following words have been previously tested. (Student need not record this statement.)

accept
benefited
necessary
separate
committee
develop
opposite
property
chapter
paragraph
settled
millions
discovery
weight (number of pounds)
language
suggested
regular
discipline
interested
difficult
oxygen
average
plastic
continued
ability
phrase
raised
remain
soiled
daily

Group 7

/ē/ can be spelled ea, ee, y, ie, ei, ey, or e followed by a consonant and silent e.

received (R)
piece (of pie) (R)
relieve (R)
breathe (R)
steel (metal) (R)
week (day of) (R)
conceive
either
heat
seem
feeling
east
neither
speech
indeed
steam
keeping
reasons
meeting
wheat
leader
peace
keeps
leading
freedom
speaking
weak (faint)
eastern
beyond
meaning

Group 8

/ī/ can be spelled ie, igh, y, or i followed by two consonants as in *wild* or as i followed by a consonant and silent e as in *kite*.

surprise (R)
science (R)
lie (R)
twice (R)
realized (R)
scientist (R)
finding
supply
climate
lies
silent
library
highest
divided
alike
decide
type
rise
divide
smiled
flight
design
price
diagram
wise
slight
pipe
provided
nineteenth
ninetieth

Group 9

/ō/ can be spelled oe, ow, oa, or o followed by two consonants as in *told* or as o followed by a consonant and silent e as in *home*.

almost (R)
although (R)
shown (R)
shows (R)
lower (R)
growing (R)
cost (R)
program (R)
growth (R)
smoke (R)
row
boats
holding
noticed
notes
bowl
clothing
bow
post
holds
rows
stone
note
tone
flow
bone
chosen
follows
fellow
homes

Level H

Important Notes

- The "jump" in Group Numbers is intentional. See Page 122, "Grouping within Levels" for an explanation.
- Words followed by an (R) are Review words. Do not say the (R) when dictating them.
- Words in [brackets] are the British spelling. When correcting the test, use the proper spelling for your country.

Group 10

/ū/ can be spelled ew as in *few*, ue as in *blue*, ui as in *suit*, o as in *to*, or as u followed by a consonant and silent e as in *mule*.

to (R)
through (finished) (R)
too (also) (R)
whose (R)
two (R)
together (R)
loose (R)
beauty (R)
community (R)
prove (R)
value
tube
ruler
choose
unit
roots
news
schools
fruit
root
drew
whom
tools
foods
view
lose
produce
produced

Group 11

/àr/ is usually spelled ar as in *jar*.

familiar (R)
grammar (R)
apparatus (R)
cards (R)
articles (R)
harvest (R)
artist (R)
carbon (R)
similar (R)
partner (R)
harbor [harbour]
farming
cart
harm
marched
standard
stared
charged
martin
peculiar
cargo
carved
alarm
cellar
marsh
shark
jargon
spark
marbles
scarf
harsh
starve
carpet
parking

Review Test 2

The following words have been previously tested. (Student need not record this statement.)

speech
nineteenth
ninetieth
chosen
flight
standard
produced
stared
conceive
neither
wheat
reasons
climate
peculiar
noticed
bowl
library
holding
cellar
stone
diagram
follows
tools
starve
schools
choose
roots
fruit

Group 12

/ûr/ can be spelled ir as in *bird*, er as in *her*, ur as in *survey*, er as in *eternity*, ear as in *pearl*, our as in *journal*, or or after w as in *work*.

sure (R)
whether (R)
further (R)
later (R)
world (R)
worst
surveying
certain
return
returned
turns
verb
workers
learning
worth
current
service
persons
serve
burned
perfect
served
during
perhaps
per
pattern
silver (R)
purpose
determine
journey

Group 13

/or/ can be spelled or as in *corn*, oar as in *boar*, oor as in *door*, our as *your*, and ar as *dwarf*.

before (R)
doctor (R)
fourth (R)
your (R)
course (R)
forty (R)
tore (R)
northern (R)
court (R)
according (R)
source (R)
foreign (R)
stormy
order
forms
formed
nor
report
forth
forests
ordered
forced
major
support
factory
effort
correct
porch
torn
pour

Group 15

/îr/ can be spelled ear as in *hear*, eer as in *deer*, ere as in *here*, ier as in *pier*, er as in *period*, or eir as in *weird*.

experience (R)
weird (R)
materials (R)
appear (R)
here (R)
hear (R)
peer (look closely)(R)
pier (dock)(R)
dear (R)
deer (R)
period (R)
appeared
atmosphere
nearest
series (R)
appears
tears
nearer
engineer
engineers
theory
periods
rear
interior
cleared

Important Notes

- The "jump" in Group Numbers is intentional. See Page 122, "Grouping within Levels" for an explanation.
- Words followed by an (R) are Review words. Do not say the (R) when dictating them.
- Words in [brackets] are the British spelling. When correcting the test, use the proper spelling for your country.

Level H

Group 16

Usually /ou/ is spelled ou before most consonants as in *cloud*. Sometimes /ou/ is spelled ow before final l or n as in *howl* or *clown* or at the end of a word or syllable as in *how* or *tower*.

around (R)
thousand (R)
proud
showers
amount
allowed
towns
noun
outer
doubt
nouns
crowded
route
counting
bound
powder
counted
flour
grounds
surrounding
aloud
amounts
thou
rounded
mount
mounted
compounds
mouths
louder
shouting

Group 17

/ô/ can be spelled a, o, and au before most consonants as in *already*, *cost*, and *sauce* or as augh or ough before t as in *sought* and *caught* or as aw before final k, l, n as *hawk*, *crawl*, and *lawn* or at the end of a word or stressed syllable as in *awful* or *law*.

draw (R)
salt (R)
drawing (R)
caused (R)
waters (R)
drawn (R)
smallest (R)
causes (R)
author (R)
raw (R)
lawn (R)
crawled (R)
awful (R)
always (R)
author (R)
already (R)
thought (R)
taught (R)
false
guard
dawn
drawings
jaws
adults
sought
fault
exhaust
ought
watering
laws
papa
falling
thoughts
auditions
assault
authorize
astronaut
launch
auction
laundry
clause
applaud
aeronautical
automotive

Review Test 3

The following words have been previously tested. (Student need not record this statement.)

determine
current
surveying
returned
journey
correct
factory
ordered
stormy
forced
atmosphere
engineers
theory
interior
nearest
surrounding
allowed
counting
compounds
shouting
exhaust
thoughts
auditions
authorize
astronaut
aeronautical
learning
certain
forth (go)
laundry

Delayed Recall Test I Form A

Before administering this test, read pgs 45-46.

accept 1
average 1
benefited 2
necessary 2
discipline 3
interested 3
committee 4
develop 4
greater 6
phrase 6
speech 7
keeping 7
nineteenth 8
ninetieth 8
chosen 9
clothing 9
schools 10
root 10
marbles 11
standard 11
surveying 12
journey 12
support 13
effort 13
atmosphere 15
theory 15
surrounding 16
counting 16
exhaust 17
authorize 17

Delayed Recall Test I Form B

accept 1
paragraph 1
benefited 2
separate 2
continued 3
difficult 3
opposite 4
committee 4
plate 6
remain 6
speech 7
leading 7
nineteenth 8
ninetieth 8
chosen 9
noticed 9
fruit 10
produce 10
peculiar 11
partner 11
determine 12
purpose 12
ordered 13
correct 13
engineer 15
interior 15
mounted 16
allowed 16
astronaut 17
applaud 17

Important Notes

- The "jump" in Group Numbers is intentional. See Page 122, "Grouping within Levels" for an explanation.
- Words followed by an (R) are Review words. Do not say the (R) when dictating them.
- Words in [brackets] are the British spelling. When correcting the test, use the proper spelling for your country.

Group 22

Some words have silent letters such as with the k in *knew*, the w in *write*, and the l in *talk*.

answer (R)
column (R)
whole (R)
island (R)
knowledge (R)
written (R)
autumn (R)
salmon (R)
debtor
solemn
receipt
pseudonym
succumb
ecstatic
heir
knock
knob
wreath
wrist
gnawing
rescind
scissors

Group 23

No English words end with the letter v.

twelve (R)
observe (R)
swerve (R)
believe (R)
shove (R)
dissolve
involve
saliva
thrive
figurative
resolve
deserve
approve
dove
deceive
engrave
instinctive
attentive
appreciative
productive
imaginative
illustrative
progressive
conserve
imperative
oppressive
possessive

Level H

Group 24

Consonant letters are often doubled after a short vowel in short vowel words such as *egg, fluff, sniffle*, and *mess*.

guess (R)
business (R)
addressed (R)
annual (R)
gallant (R)
latter (R)
marriage (R)
mattress (R)
embarrass (R)
exaggerate (R)
goddess
mass
skill
cell
discuss
success
process
cotton
progress
press
odd
loss
passage
compass
ill
brass
stiff
recall
mill
staff
drill

Group 26

When adding the suffixes ness and ly to words not ending in y the spelling of the base word stays the same, as in *slowly*.

really (R)
finally (R)
accidentally (R)
lovely (R)
quietly (R)
surely (R)
directly (R)
likely (R)
clearly
carefully
especially
exactly
actually
certainly
completely
correctly
rapidly
closely
generally
immediately
softly
mostly
particularly
gradually
darkness
greatly
merely
entirely
purposely
incidentally

Group 28

/àn/ is sometimes spelled en as in *golden*.

benefit (R)
calendar (R)
intelligent (R)
listened (R)
forgotten (R)
passenger (R)
eleven (R)
oven (R)
recommend
apparent
expense
kindergarten
length
energy
ends
ancient
century
scientific
student
gently
recent
identify
engines
depends
ending
represents
students
wooden
hidden
messenger

Review Test 4

The following words have been previously tested. (Student need not record this statement.)

solemn
receipt
goddess
incidentally
immediately
deceive
saliva
figurative
instinctive
appreciative
illustrative
ecstatic
scissors
pseudonym
wrist
discuss
compass
success
especially
particularly
progress
cotton
gradually
purposely
apparent
ancient
scientific
messenger
represents
identify

Group 29

/àl/ can be spelled le as in *little*, el as in *rebel*, al as in *total*, il as in *council*, ol as in *capitol*, ul as in *consul*, and ile as *futile*.

nickel (R)
principal (R)
terrible (R)
control (R)
analyze [analyse]
simple
travel
rule
deal
capital
level
equal
scale
total
wheel
metal
vowel
final
usual
double
bottle
angle
sail
handle
model
alcohol
cancel
journal
signal
political
style

Group 30

Words are normally made plural by adding s, but if the word ends with sh, zh, z, s, j, ch, or x sounds, the plural is generally formed by adding es, which is pronounced as a separate syllable.

soldiers (R)
fingers (R)
twins (R)
teachers (R)
mines (R)
blankets
bones
brakes
buildings
falls
faces
fans
fields
hits
learns
oats
machines
swans
teams
thinks
tracks
weeds
planets
records
ships
sorts
springs
streams
tanks
waves
boxes
passes
reaches
goods
quizzes

Level H

Important Notes

- The "jump" in Group Numbers is intentional. See Page 122, "Grouping within Levels" for an explanation.
- Words followed by an (R) are Review words. Do not say the (R) when dictating them.
- Words in [brackets] are the British spelling. When correcting the test, use the proper spelling for your country.

Group 31

Plurals of some nouns are formed irregularly. Some words derived from foreign languages retain the plural of those languages such as datum to data.

datum; data
criterion; criteria
larva; larvae
crisis; crises
matria; matrices
focus; foci
monsieur; messieurs
fungus; fungi
cherub; cherubim
seraph; seraphim
cactus; cacti
die; dice
alumna; alumnae (women)
alumnus; alumni (men)
stimulus; stimuli

Group 36

New words are often made by putting two short words together into one word as in cowboy.

without (R)
nowadays (R)
everybody (R)
afternoon (R)
breakfast (R)
rainbow
throughout
watermelon
however
understand
itself
herself
railroad
whatever
whenever
within
nearby
understanding
sunlight
newspapers
fireplace
railroads
sunshine
outdoors
basketball
cardboard
underneath

Group 41

A period is used after most abbreviations such as in Sun. for Sunday. Initials are also abbreviations and should be followed with a period. Two letter state and provincial postal are exceptions.

etc. (R)
NB (New Brunswick)
IA (Iowa) (R)
DE (Delaware) (R)
TN (Tennessee) (R)
PE (Prince Edward Island)
WI (Wisconsin) (R)
VT (Vermont) (R)
YT (Yukon Territories)
NE (Nebraska) (R)
OH (Ohio) (R)
OR (Oregon) (R)
NT (Northwest Territories)
UT (Utah) (R)
Apt. (apartment)
Co. (company)
Inc. (incorporated)
NASA (National Aeronautics and Space Administration)
C.O.D. (Cash on Delivery)
Corp. (corporation)
I.O.U. (I owe you)
UFO (unidentified flying object)
PhD. (Doctor of Philosophy)
R.S.V.P. (from the French for "please respond")
R.D. (Rural Delivery)

Review Test 5

The following words have been previously tested. (Student need not record this statement.)

analyze [analyse]
alcohol
cancel
journal
capital
angle
quizzes
streams
planets
machines
buildings
reaches
criterion
data
crisis
focus
fungi
cactus
throughout
understanding
herself
underneath
cardboard
whatever
Inc. (incorporated)
etc. (et cetera)
NASA (National Aeronautics and Space Administrarion)
Apt. (apartment)
C.O.D. (cash on delivery)

Group 42

/shun/ can be spelled tion as in vacation, sion as in division, or cian as in physician.

concession (R)
tuition (R)
possession (R)
direction (R)
invitation (R)
preparation (R)
exhibition (R)
conservation (R)
punctuation (R)
organization
protection
location
relationship
selection
explanation
imagination
stations
descriptions
fraction
communication
combinations
action (R)
occasion
impression
examination
demonstration
adoration
exposition
satisfaction
association

Group 43

/às/ can be spelled ous as in nervous or ace as in menace.

famous
outrageous
humorous [humourous]
courteous
disastrous
jealous
mischievous
grievous
enormous
dangerous
delicious
mysterious
conscious
obnoxious
ingenious
infectious
ambitious
ridiculous
surface
various
serious
curious
religious
previous
nervous
place
precious
tremendous
numerous
continuous

Group 44

/ànse/ can be spelled ance as in substance or ence as in experience.

absence
sense
substance
sentence
difference
differences
instance
balance
appearance
importance
distance
sentences
distances
substances
glance
performance
advanced
advance
ancestors
glanced
endurance
violence
disturbance
reference
acceptance
nuisance
conscience
license
maintenance

Level H

Important Notes

- The "jump" in Group Numbers is intentional. See Page 122, "Grouping within Levels" for an explanation.
- Words followed by an (R) are Review words. Do not say the (R) when dictating them.
- Words in [brackets] are the British spelling. When correcting the test, use the proper spelling for your country.

Group 45

/ment/ is usually spelled ment as in elements.

elements
judgment
experiment
element
disappointment
basement
amusement
cement
enjoyment
experiments
instrument
statements
movement
statement
development
excitement
instruments
environment
apartment
arrangement
settlement
department
moments
movements
treatment
measurement
measurements
argument

Group 46

The addition of a prefix does not usually change the spelling of the root word. The prefix re can mean back or again as in the words remake or reduced.

resort
respectable
remake
rewrap
rewrite
reunion
relax
refill
replay
remark
reduced
receives
regarded
returning
remind
recover
recook
rearranged
refined
retain
reunite
reform
remainder
relieved
regretted
responded
reflect
recollect
recollection
recount
revision

Review Test 6

The following words have been previously tested. (Student need not record this statement.)

occasion
outrageous
humorous [humourous]
courteous
disastrous
jealous
mischievous
grievous
ridiculous
reference
acceptance
nuisance
conscience
license
maintenance
argument
disappointment
experiments
development
excitement
respectable
returning
rearranged
remainder
relieved
recollection
relationship
demonstration
satisfaction
communication
organization

Delayed Recall Test 2 Form A

Before administering this test, read pgs 45-46.

solemn 22
receipt 22
figurative 23
conserve 23
goddess 24
progress 24
immediately 26
incidentally 26
recommend 28
scientific 28
analyze 29 [analyse] 29
alcohol 29
cancel 29

Test continues on next column

buildings 30
fungi 31
stimuli 31
throughout 37
whatever 37
R.S.V.P. 41
etc. 41
occasion 42
descriptions 42
outrageous 43
courteous 43
reference 44
nuisance 44
conscience 44
argument 45
refined 46
remainder 46

Delayed Recall Test 2 Form B

solemn 22
receipt 22
thrive 23
instinctive 23
goddess 24
passage 24
immediately 26
incidentally 26
apparent 28
identify 28
analyze 29 [analyse] 29
alcohol 29
journal 29
machines 30
alumnae 31
larva 31
understand 37
newspapers 37
corp. w41
R.S.V.P. 41
occasion 42
location 42
humorous [humourous] 43
disastrous 43
acceptance 44
license 44
maintenance 44
argument 45
reform 46
regretted 46

End of Level Test Form A

Before administering this test, read pgs 45-46.

accept 1
necessary 2
discipline 3
committee 4
remain 6
speech 7
nineteenth 8
chosen 9
fruit 10
peculiar 11
learning 12
support 13
nearest 15
grounds 16
aeronautical 17
solemn 22
appreciative 23
goddess 24
immediately 26
kindergarten 28
alcohol 29
blankets 30
messieurs 31
throughout 37
R.S.V.P 41
occasion 42
outrageous 43
nuisance 44
argument 45
reunite 46

End of Level Test Form B

accept 1
benefited 2
interested 3
develop 4
placed 6
speech 7
ninetieth 8
noticed 9
view 10
jargon 11
determine 12
ordered 13
cleared 15
counting 16
auditions 17
receipt 22
imaginative 23
discuss 24
incidentally 26
scientific 28
political 29
reaches 30
cherubim 31
underneath 37
C.O.D. (cash on delivery) 41
impression 42
enormous 43
endurance 44
amusement 45
relieved 46

Important Notes

- The "jump" in Group Numbers is intentional. See Page 122, "Grouping within Levels" for an explanation.
- Words followed by an (R) are Review words. Do not say the (R) when dictating them.
- Words in [brackets] are the British spelling. When correcting the test, use the proper spelling for your country.

Level H

Level I

Group 1

Usually /a/ is spelled a as in *cat*.

average (R)
paragraph (R)
language (R)
plastic (R)
than (R)
accept (R)
branch
traffic
established
exact
cap
banks
lack
tax
lamp
gasoline
tank
acts
swam
wagons
hats
bags
asking
bands
ant
magazine
dam
lad
statue
baskets
tasks
blank
graph
handed
landing

Group 2

Usually /e/ is spelled e as in *nest*.

then (R)
separate (R)
desert (R)
benefited (R)
necessary (R)
led (R)
except (R)
specimen
chest
separated
tests
welcome
shelf
melted
memory
shed
stem
elected
beds
bent
bend
respect
stretch
select
poet
complex
pledge
envelope
veterinarian
stretched
fled
hedge
shred
crept
descendent

Group 3

Usually /i/ is spelled i as in *big*.

considered (R)
its (own) (R)
arithmetic (R)
which (R)
fifth (R)
electricity (R)
tin
silk
visitors
military
bringing
rings
gift
dish
trips
fix
brings
sink
slip
spin
wishes
brick
religion
printing
kings
privilege
pitcher
visited
whispered
strip (R)
distant
pitch
basis
considered
kick

Group 4

Usually /o/ is spelled o as in *not*.

develop (R)
property (R)
along (R)
oxygen (R)
modern (R)
discovery (R)
belongs
logs
crop
colony
pot
stock
belonged
stops
project
octagon
lock
promise
longest
combined
observed
composed
completed
atomic
topic
recognized
obtain
consonant
involved
possibly
billion
constant
accommodate
competent

Group 5

Usually /u/ is spelled u as in *run*.

studying (R)
hundredth (R)
trumpets (R)
public (R)
hungry (R)
begun
rushed
luck
brush
judge
nuts
hunter
rush
lumber
drum
cuts
hunted
jumping
bucket
pump
cups
multiply
plus
minimum
fully
suggests
subtract
struggled
swung
adult
thrust
published
crust
customs

Review Test I

The following words have been previously tested. (Student need not record this statement.)

magazine
statue
specimen
privilege
minimum
recognized
combined
established
traffic
consonant
veterinarian
gasoline
handed
bucket
whispered
welcome
jumping
observed
descendent
envelope
struggled
topic
accommodate
pitch
religion
considered
military
published
customs
multiply

Important Notes

- The "jump" in Group Numbers is intentional. See Page 122, "Grouping within Levels" for an explanation.
- Words followed by an (R) are Review words. Do not say the (R) when dictating them.
- Words in [brackets] are the British spelling. When correcting the test, use the proper spelling for your country.

Group 6

/ā/ can be written ay, ai, ey, ei, eigh, ea, or a followed by a consonant and silent e.

based (R)
straight (R)
daily (R)
phrase (R)
indicate
brave
escape
safety
frame
arranged
remained
indicated
replace
rays
native
training
sailors
chain
sailing
aid
failed
pain
gain
weigh
freight
ascertain
neighbor [neighbour] (R)
nails
neighborhood [neighbourhood]
acres
shade
date
exclaimed
waste
locate

Group 7

/ē/ can be spelled ea, ee, y, ie, ei, ey, or e followed by a consonant and silent e.

chief (R)
scream (R)
niece (R)
seize (R)
alley (R)
lead (take the) (R)
region (R)
speak (R)
scene (R)
sneak (R)
belief
succeed
describe
effect
represent
related
believed
beneath
agree
increase
increased
repeated
leaf
disease
cheese
receive
knees
tea
beans
sheet
sees
pleased
steep
reader
screen
created
feelings
breathing
degree
repeat

Group 8

/ī/ can be spelled ie, igh, y, or i followed by two consonants as in *wild* or as i followed by a consonant and silent e as in *kite*.

surprise (R)
science (R)
lying (R)
ninety (R)
nineteenth (R)
ninetieth (R)
nineteen (R)
library (R)
climate (R)
recognize
types
tight
pilot
lighted
finds
pioneers
lighting (R)
lions
pioneer
rice
slide
mighty
realize
aside
designed
spite
combine
diameter
writer
buying
siren
tribe
invite
shy
spiders

Group 9

/ō/ can be spelled oe, ow, oa, or o followed by two consonants as in *told* or as o followed by a consonant and silent e as in *home.*

clothes (R)
holy (R)
chosen (R)
follows (R)
fellow (R)
homes (R)
goes (R)
told (R)
although (R)
load
rolling
oldest
owned
loaded
toes
soldier
floating
float
goat
poems
oak
coats
soda
throwing
automobiles
globe
hoped
potato
poetry
role
vote
slope
chose
solar
borrowed

Group 10

/ū/ can be spelled ew as in *few,* ue as in *blue,* ui as in *suit,* o as in *to,* or as u followed by a consonant and silent e as in *mule.*

together (R)
lose (R)
choose (R)
loose (R)
huge (R)
prove (R)
smooth (R)
through (finished) (R)
to (R)
too (also) (R)
value (R)
including
proved
included
uses
rules
includes
units
moves
truth
fruits
boots
pupils
wound (hurt)
duty
goose
movies
due
removed
improve
review
youth
remove
molecules

Review Test 2

The following words have been previously tested. (Student need not record this statement.)

safety
freight
ascertain
belief
succeed
effect
disease
receive
lighted
breathing
fruits
molecules
includes
arranged
training
neighborhood
[neighbourhood]
recognize
realize
designed
diameter
combine
wound (hurt)
pupils
proved
automobiles
borrowed
floating
poetry
owned
soldiers

Important Notes

- The "jump" in Group Numbers is intentional. See Page 122, "Grouping within Levels" for an explanation.
- Words followed by an (R) are Review words. Do not say the (R) when dictating them.
- Words in [brackets] are the British spelling. When correcting the test, use the proper spelling for your country.

Group 12

/ûr/ can be spelled ir as in *bird*, er as in *her*, ur as in *survey*, er as in *eternity*, ear as in *pearl*, our as in *journal*, or or after w as in *work*.

whether (R)
certain (R)
different (R)
determine (R)
journey (R)
were (R)
first (R)
girl (R)
remember (R)
purpose (R)
worth (R)
members
exercise
enter
settlers
direct
search
term
burst
worse
herd
thirteen
clerk
determined
layer
research
concerned
refer
stronger
younger
spider
covering
machinery

Group 13

/or/ can be spelled or as in *corn*, oar as in *boar*, oor as in *door*, our as *your*, and ar as *dwarf*.

fourth (R)
before (R)
foreign (R)
courtesy (R)
course (R)
forth (R)
chauffeur (R)
forces
orders
horn (R)
pour (R)
corners
boards
orchestra
fourteen
oranges
fork
perform
origin
stored
poured
organized
courage
factor
shorter
worn
resources
laboratory
opportunity
warrant
afford
favor [favour]
port
sailor

Group 14

/âr/ can be spelled are as *care*, air as in *hair*, ere as in *there*, ear as in *bear*, and eir as in *their*.

where (R)
carrying (R)
wear (R)
their (possessive pronoun) (R)
there (location) (R)
prairie (R)
prepare (R)
characteristic (R)
characters
aware
declare
unaware
dairy
spare
vary
rare
primary
shared
charitable
fairness
beware
repair
affair
paralyzed [paralysed]
rarely
unbearable
transparent
flair
secretary
plagiarism
affairs
carriage
marry
declared

Group 15

/îr/ can be spelled ear as in *hear*, eer as in *deer*, ere as in *here*, ier as in *pier*, er as in *period*, or eir as in *weird*.

experience (R)
weird (R)
tears (R)
engineers (R)
theory (R)
materials (R)
interior (R)
beard (R)
hear (R)
deer (R)
clear (R)
series (R)
period (R)
disappeared (R)
appear (R)
atmosphere (R)
feared
bacteria
career
frontier
nuclear
clearing
sphere
weary
irresponsible
disappearing
sheer
inferior
eerie
pierce
spherical
premiere
chandelier
shears
irritable

Group 21

Q is always followed by u in English words such as in *quite*.

quiet (R)
quite (R)
quotation (R)
quarter (R)
equality (R)
turquoise (R)
quest (R)
squeeze (R)
quote (R)
acquainted
acquire
acquitted
conquer
conqueror
equipped
quantity
acquiesce
liquefy
liquefaction
questionnaire
acquaint
quench
antique
quarry
squash
picturesque
bouquet
plaque
quartet
quadruple
quilt
acquittal
croquet
etiquette
quadrangle
quiche
tranquil
equivalent

Review Test 3

The following words have been previously tested. (Student need not record this statement.)

laboratory
opportunity
secretary
premiere
acquiesce
liquefy
exercise
determined
research
machinery
concerned
thirteen
conquer
orchestra
fourteen
unbearable
transparent
chandelier
spherical
bacteria
clearing
disappearing
questionnaire
quadruple
tranquil
acquaint
organized
resources
charitable
unaware
carriage

Important Notes

- The "jump" in Group Numbers is intentional. See Page 122, "Grouping within Levels" for an explanation.
- Words followed by an (R) are Review words. Do not say the (R) when dictating them.
- Words in [brackets] are the British spelling. When correcting the test, use the proper spelling for your country.

Level I

Delayed Recall Test I Form A

Before administering this test, read pgs 45-46.

magazine 1
baskets 1
specimen 2
envelope 2
privilege 3
religion 3
combined 4
recognized 4
minimum 5
published 5
safety 6
ascertain 6
belief 7
succeed 7
disease 7
receive 7
lighting 8
types 8
throwing 9
poetry 9
removed 10
molecules 10
determined 12
covering 12
laboratory 13
opportunity 13
secretary 14
affairs 14
premiere 15
frontier 15
acquiesce 21
liquefy 21

Delayed Recall Test I Form B

baskets 1
magazine 1
memory 2
specimen 2
whispered 3
privilege 3
belonged 4
accommodate 4
struggled 5
minimum 5
ascertain 6
freight 6
disease 7
belief 7
succeed 7
effect 7
receive 7
pioneer 8
lighting 8
poem (9)
potato (9)
includes 10
fruits 10
thirteen 12
machinery 12
opportunity 13
laboratory 13
charitable 14
secretary 14
premiere 15
bacteria 15
acquiesce 21
liquefy 21

Group 24

Consonant letters are often doubled after a short vowel in short vowel words such as egg, *fluff*, *sniffle*, and *mess*.

business (R)
till (R)
compass (R)
addressed (R)
annual (R)
mattress (R)
progress (R)
goddess (R)
accomplish
across (R)
allow
butter
occur
offered
account
suggest
attached
college
balloon
differ
arrow
carries
mirror
collect
connected
offer
balls
willing
villages
valleys
affect
hollow
scattered
arrange

Group 25

Sometimes /yûr/ can be spelled <u>ure</u> as in *pure*.

leisure (R)
furniture (R)
creature (R)
culture (R)
structure (R)
features (R)
literature (R)
temperature (R)
amateur
manufacture
premature
signature
conjecture
brochure
connoisseur
manicure
torture
rupture
transfigure
procedure
pasteurize
carburetor [carburettor]
discouraging
discouraged
encourage
exposure
discourage
venture
encouragement
detour
impure
courageous
agriculture
immature
adventures

Group 26

When adding the suffixes <u>ness</u> and <u>ly</u> to words not ending in y the spelling of the base word stays the same, as in *slowly*.

finally (R)
really (R)
likely (R)
particularly (R)
deeply (R)
lightly (R)
badly (R)
accidentally (R)
incidentally (R)
intentionally
occasionally
recently
highly
partly
fairly
eventually
naturally
perfectly
tightly
mainly
firmly
widely
equally
properly
originally
constantly
extremely
lively
respectfully
unfortunately
practically
approximately
obviously

Group 27

When added to another syllable or used as a suffix, <u>till</u> and <u>full</u> are spelled with only one l as in *until* and *beautiful*.

careful (R)
until (R)
thankful (R)
delightful (R)
healthful (R)
successful
peaceful
useful
powerful
helpful
thoughtful
beautiful (R)
spoonful
flavorful [flavourful]
mouthfuls
delightful (R)
truthful (R)
boastful
unskillful [unskilful]
deceitful
grateful
meaningful
forceful
skillful [skilful]
doubtful
disgraceful
resourceful

Important Notes

- The "jump" in Group Numbers is intentional. See Page 122, "Grouping within Levels" for an explanation.
- Words followed by an (R) are Review words. Do not say the (R) when dictating them.
- Words in [brackets] are the British spelling. When correcting the test, use the proper spelling for your country.

Level I

Group 28

/àn/ is sometimes spelled <u>en</u> as in *golden*.

ancient (R)
benefit (R)
calendar (R)
intelligent (R)
messenger (R)
recommend (R)
apparent (R)
expense (R)
kindergarten (R)
permanent
prevalent
listening
represented
continent
prevent
spoken
depend
frozen
citizens
excellent
enemies
fastened
fallen
accident
driven
percent
event
happening
presented
mental
independent
passengers
currents
essential
centers [centres]

Review Test 4

The following words have been previously tested. (Student need not record this statement.)

college
arrange
manufacture
amateur
procedure
respectfully
intentionally
deceitful
fulfil
useful
grateful
permanent
prevalent
butter
account
connected
scattered
connoisseur
transfigure
procedure
pasteurize
occasionally
constantly
eventually
unfortunately
beautiful
meaningful
continent
independent
essential
excellent

Group 29

/àl/ can be spelled <u>le</u> as in *little*, <u>el</u> as in *rebel*, <u>al</u> as in *total*, <u>il</u> as in *council*, <u>ol</u> as in *capitol*, <u>ul</u> as in *consul*, and <u>ile</u> as *futile*.

capital (R)
angel (R)
nickel (R)
principal (R)
analyze [analyse] (R)
fundamental (R)
schedule (R)
control (R)
possible (R)
alcohol (R)
cancel (R)
journal (R)
signal (R)
political (R)
style (R)
title
individual
noticeable
parallel
social
local
central
article
personal
unusual
physical
chemical
original
natural
several
tickle
tunnel
national
automobile
coal
muscles
minerals
angles
fuel
meal
wool
musical
unable
valuable
impossible
available

Group 30

Words are normally made plural by adding s, but if the word ends with sh, zh, z, s, j, ch, or x sounds, the plural is generally formed by adding es, which is pronounced as a separate syllable.

paragraphs (R)
minutes (R)
seems (R)
machines (R)
planets (R)
buildings (R)
scientists (R)
homes (R)
degrees (R)
streams (R)
touches
patterns
facts
happens
seeds
terms
besides
cells
degrees
maps
cases
events
details
methods
stones
factors
sticks
shoulders
verbs
meanings
phrases
layers
remains
bits
oceans
atoms
produces
consists
numerals
rights
edges

Group 32

When adding a suffix to a word ending in y, change the y to i, unless a vowel proceeds the y, as in try to *tried* and baby to *babies*.

tries (R)
easily (R)
magnify (R)
abilities (R)
communities (R)
companies (R)
memorize (R)
ladies (R)
stories (R)
boundaries (R)
dormitories
occupied (R)
livelihood
loneliness
replies
windier
sunnier
mysteries
delaying
copies
preying
wealthier
plentiful
multiplied
assemblies
biographies
friendliness
allergies
dizziness
tardiness
obituaries
accessories
authorities
policies

Group 35

Proper nouns must begin with a capital letter because they refer to a specific name or title of a person, place, time, thing, or idea such as Monday.

Britain (R)
Tuesday (R)
Arctic (R)
Wyoming (R)
Washington (R)
California (R)
Texas (R)
Wednesday (R)
European
India
Lincoln
London
Paris
Italian
Spain
Dutch
African
Greeks
Columbus
Australia
Greece
Gulf
Russia
Rome
Russian
Philadelphia
Egypt
Mexican
Roosevelt
Mediterranean

Level I

Important Notes

- The "jump" in Group Numbers is intentional. See Page 122, "Grouping within Levels" for an explanation.
- Words followed by an (R) are Review words. Do not say the (R) when dictating them.
- Words in [brackets] are the British spelling. When correcting the test, use the proper spelling for your country.

Group 36

New words are often made by putting two short words together into one word as in cowboy.

nowadays (R)
wherever (R)
within (R)
without (R)
throughout (R)
everybody (R)
itself (R)
extraordinary
oneself
halfway
handsome
somehow
income
backward
background
otherwise
overrun
foresee
somewhat
therefore
meanwhile
nevertheless
ourselves
fisherman
gentleman
classmates
rainfall
underline
understood
upward
outline
online

Review Test 5

The following words have been previously tested. (Student need not record this statement.)

noticeable
parallel
occupied
dormitories
livelihood
loneliness
replies
overrun
foresee
methods
numerals
patterns
degrees
details
oceans
online
background
nevertheless
gentlemen
fundamental
original
biographies
European
Mediterranean
Australia
automobile
impossible
Italian
Philadelphia
Roosevelt

Group 42

/shun/ can be spelled tion as in vacation, sion as in division, or cian as in physician.

communication (R)
occasion (R)
explanation (R)
invitation (R)
repetition (R)
preparation (R)
direction (R)
imagination (R)
stationery (R)
civilization
suggestions
revolution
functions (R)
fractions
relation
observation
election
pronunciation
relations
constitution
additional
professional
discussion
mission
expressions
mentioned
invention
generation
mention
traditional
recognition
participation
infection
opposition

Group 43

/às/ can be spelled ous as in nervous or ace as in menace.

conscious (R)
courteous (R)
disastrous (R)
grievous (R)
humorous [humourous] (R)
jealous (R)
mischievous (R)
enormous (R)
mysterious (R)
delicious (R)
outrageous (R)
ridiculous (R)
religious (R)
mysterious (R)
continuous (R)
conscientious
sacrilegious
treacherous
momentous
analogous
barbarous
incredulous
mountainous
courageous
obvious
marvelous
cautious
anonymous
subconscious
monotonous

Group 44

/ànse/ can be spelled ance as in substance or ence as in experience.

absence (R)
appearance (R)
reference (R)
acceptance (R)
nuisance (R)
conscience (R)
license (R)
maintenance (R)
importance (R)
performance (R)
nonsense
patience
allowance
assistance
dependence
attendance
trance
admittance
dispense
innocence
preference
silence
audience
influence
evidence
experiences
presence
independence
entrance
convenience
existence
guidance
intelligence
occurrence

Group 45

/ment/ is usually spelled ment as in elements.

arrangement (R)
environment (R)
statement (R)
judgment (R)
argument (R)
development (R)
experiment (R)
excitement (R)
measurement (R)
amusement (R)
instruments (R)
disappointment (R)
department (R)
achievement
parliament
temperament
improvement
punishment
compartment
monument
replacement
refreshment
astonishment
assignment
comment
entertainment
torment
compliment
establishment
accomplishment
retirement
tournament
acknowledgement

Level I

Important Notes

- The "jump" in Group Numbers is intentional. See Page 122, "Grouping within Levels" for an explanation.
- Words followed by an (R) are Review words. Do not say the (R) when dictating them.
- Words in [brackets] are the British spelling. When correcting the test, use the proper spelling for your country.

Group 46

The addition of a prefix does not usually change the spelling of the root word. The prefixes con, com, cor, col, sym or syn all usually mean with or together.

conditions
congress
compound
compare
continue
complete
containing
contains
contain
composition
comparison
computer
sympathy
synonym
symphony
symptom
symbolic
system
synthesis
systematic
symbol
confuse
confined
consist
convince
compute
congratulations
coexist
contestant
conjunction
commit
concentrate
consume
coauthor

Review Test 6

The following words have been previously tested. (Student need not record this statement.)

pronunciation
conscientious
sacrilegious
treacherous
analogous
barbarous
incredulous
preference
existence
occurrence
conditions
congress
compound
continue
complete
containing
contain
composition
congratulations
civilization
professional
temperament
punishment
entertainment
accomplishment
acknowledgement
observation
constitution
attendance
convenience

Delayed Recall Test 2 Form A

Before administering this test, read pgs 45-46.

college 24
arrange 24
amateur 25
procedure 25
intentionally 26
eventually 26
useful 27
grateful 27
permanent 28
passengers 28
noticeable 29
musical 29
shoulders 30
produces 30
dormitories 32
livelihood 32
replies 32
Philadelphia 35
Mediterranean 35
foresee 36
classmates 36
conscientious 38
sacrilegious 38
barbarous 38
pronunciation 42
suggestions 42
preference 44
existence 44
parliament 45
acknowledgement 45
congratulations 46
conditions 46
complete 46

Delayed Recall Test 2 Form B

arrange 24
college 24
procedure 25
encouragement 25
respectfully 26
originally 26
deceitful 27
forceful 27
prevalent 28
citizens 28
parallel 29
available 29
degrees 30
happens 30
occupied 32
loneliness 32
authorities 32
European 35
African 35
overrun 36
handsome 36
treacherous 38
analogous 38
incredulous 38
expressions 42
participation 42
occurrence 44
independence 44
astonishment 45
compartment 45
composition 46
containing 46
continue 46

End of Level Test Form A

Before administering this test, read pgs 45-46.

magazine 1
specimen 2
privilege 3
accommodate 4
minimum 5
safety 6
belief 7
lighting 8
owned 9
molecules 10
research 12
orchestra 13
secretary 14
premiere 15
acquiesce 21
connected 24
connoisseur 25
approximately 26
grateful 27
represented 28
noticeable 29
numerals 30
livelihood 32
Dutch 35
halfway 36
observation 42
incredulous 43
occurrence 44
entertainment 45
comparison 46

End of Level Test Form B

statue 1
veterinarian 2
considered 3
belonged 4
published 5
ascertain 6
succeed 7
diameter 8
borrowed 9
included 10
exercise 12
laboratory 13
paralyzed [paralysed] 14
irresponsible 15
liquefy 21
attached 24
venture 25
eventually 26
deceitful 27
accident 28
available 29
shoulders 30
dormitories 32
Italian 35
understood 36
generation 42
courageous 43
admittance 44
accomplishment 45
concentrate 46

Important Notes

- The "jump" in Group Numbers is intentional. See Page 122, "Grouping within Levels" for an explanation.
- Words followed by an (R) are Review words. Do not say the (R) when dictating them.
- Words in [brackets] are the British spelling. When correcting the test, use the proper spelling for your country.

Level J

Group 1

Usually /a/ is spelled a as in *cat.*

accept (R)
statue (R)
track (R)
woman (R)
banana (R)
rats
stamps
catching
backs
patch
scratch
magazines
raft
gathering
accepted
accurate
appropriate
arrive
hammer
mammals
cabbage
attitude
apply
attracted
attract
matters
associated
magnet
atom
managed
gravity
habit
granted
tragedy

Group 2

Usually /e/ is spelled e as in *nest.*

necessary (R)
desert (R)
benefited (R)
specimen (R)
enemy (R)
medicine (R)
strength (R)
separate (R)
envelope (R)
melt
nests
vessels
attempt
affected
seldom
insect
swept
depth
exist
developing
estimate
reflected
jacket
protected
selected
rockets
electrons
wedge
attendant
drenched
jest
pedestrian
elementary

Group 3

Usually /i/ is spelled i as in *big.*

discipline (R)
privilege (R)
considered (R)
brilliant (R)
interest (R)
picnic (R)
since (R)
village (R)
which (R)
pin
sits
mix
rid
ink
swinging
visitor
print
timber
sixth
visiting
slid
bricks
whip
admitted
bitter
illustrate
officials
specific
introduced
activity
limited
definite
opinion
instant
chin

Group 4

Usually /o/ is spelled o as in *not*.

committee (R)
opposite (R)
competent (R)
possibly (R)
billion (R)
octagon (R)
constant (R)
accommodate (R)
develop (R)
stops (R)
shops
pockets
adopted
prophesy
rhapsody
concede
apostrophe
colossal
bottles
ribbon
obtained
dot
complicated
contrast
contained
properties
costs
columns
continues

Group 6

/ā/ can be written ay, ai, ey, ei, eigh, ea, or a followed by a consonant and silent e.

ascertain (R)
freight (R)
based (R)
neighbor [neighbour] (R)
laid (R)
paid (R)
tails
sails
bay
rainy
rains
navy
painting
pale
nail
sale
female
male
detail
stable
raced
remaining
tape
trace
flame
gained
replaced
slave
shake
exchange
image
damage
stated
faced
awake

Review Test I

The following words have been previously tested. (Student need not record this statement.)

appropriate
tragedy
definite
prophesy
rhapsody
concede
apostrophe
complicated
electrons
introduced
pedestrian
drenched
specific
magazines
associated
affected
opinion
seldom
illustrate
remaining
exchange
painting
gravity
accurate
elementary
stable
awake
female

Level J

Important Notes

- The "jump" in Group Numbers is intentional. See Page 122, "Grouping within Levels" for an explanation.
- Words followed by an (R) are Review words. Do not say the (R) when dictating them.
- Words in [brackets] are the British spelling. When correcting the test, use the proper spelling for your country.

Group 7

/ē/ can be spelled ea, ee, y, ie, ei, ey, or e followed by a consonant and silent e.

belief (R)
succeed (R)
conceive (R)
disease (R)
divide (R)
decide (R)
neither (R)
speech (R)
weak (faint) (R)
week (day of) (R)
create
seats
treated
fever
feeding
diseases
teaching
treat
beef
seek
meals
neat
heels
feast
dreamed
succeeded
eager
brief
deeper
reaching
heated
increasing
beam
ceiling
beating

Group 8

/ī/ can be spelled ie, igh, y, or i followed by two consonants as in *wild* or as i followed by a consonant and silent e as in *kite*.

surprise (R)
science (R)
library (R)
recognize (R)
diameter (R)
realize (R)
strikes
minds
pipes
item
mild
wine
empire
ripe
rider
reply
franchise
hygiene
divine
fiery
mileage
tide
advice
pride
lined
desire
device
sighed
rhyme
thy
sizes
writers
reptiles
drivers
devices

Group 9

/ō/ can be spelled oe, ow, oa, or o followed by two consonants as in *told* or as o followed by a consonant and silent e as in *home*.

almost (R)
although (R)
chosen (R)
shown (R)
borrowed (R)
potato (R)
poetry (R)
chose (R)
solar (R)
clothes (R)
holy (R)
swallowed
approached
approach
lowest
telescope
flowing
code
folded
noted
tones
slopes
shadows
purposes
hopes
ropes
fold
shone
joke
stroke
microscope
mold [mould]
meadow
glow
kimono
rotary

Group 10

/ū/ can be spelled ew as in *few*, ue as in *blue*, ui as in *suit*, o as in *to*, or as u followed by a consonant and silent e as in *mule*.

through (finished) (R)
whose (R)
two (R)
choose (R)
loose (R)
lose (R)
together (R)
altogether (R)
huge (R)
smooth (R)
tool
fool
assume
mood
universe
fewer
tune
refused
manufacturing
foolish
formula
values
tropes
tubes
maneuver
university
clues
ruled
clue
cooled
loop
pursue
parachute
deuce

Group 12

/ûr/ can be spelled ir as in *bird*, er as in *her*, ur as in *survey*, er as in *eternity*, ear as in *pearl*, our as in *journal*, or or after w as in *work*.

sure (R)
exercise (R)
foreign (R)
fourth (R)
later (R)
perhaps (R)
world (R)
journey (R)
curve
behavior [behaviour]
former
birth
performed
chamber
curved
firm
clever
laughter
camera
interests
deserts
warmer
directed
worker
prefer
thermometer
stir
numbered
searching
speaker
counter
earned
operate

Review Test 2

The following words have been previously tested. (Student need not record this statement.)

ceiling
rhyme
divine
fiery
mileage
franchise
hygiene
kimono
rotary
maneuver
pursue
parachute
deuce
journey
diseases
increasing
eager
dreamed
create
telescope
meadow
microscope
approach
universe
manufacturing
camera
behavior
searching
laughter
operate
thermometer

Important Notes

- The "jump" in Group Numbers is intentional. See Page 122, "Grouping within Levels" for an explanation.
- Words followed by an (R) are Review words. Do not say the (R) when dictating them.
- Words in [brackets] are the British spelling. When correcting the test, use the proper spelling for your country.

Group 13

/or/ can be spelled or as in *corn*, oar as in *boar*, oor as in *door*, our as *your*, and ar as *dwarf*.

before (R)
doctor (R)
fourth (R)
your (R)
opportunities (R)
warrant (R)
coarse (R)
chauffeur (R)
laboratory (R)
forty (R)
afford (R)
corresponding
territory
roar
aboard
victory
labor [labour]
warning
vapor [vapour]
reported
recorded
border
reports
sources
explorers
herds
authority
warmth
comfort
storms
coarse
dinosaurs
majority
cord
fortune

Group 18

/oi/ can be spelled oy as in *toy* or oi as *boil*.

destroy (R)
poison (R)
void (R)
oyster (R)
ointment (R)
disappointed (R)
loyal (R)
boys (R)
noise (R)
voice (R)
avoid (R)
moisture (R)
voyage (R)
moist (R)
buoyance (R)
annoyance (R)
adjoin
poisonous
decoy
toil
anoint
embroidery
broil
oily
rejoin
appointed
employed
employ
appointment
poise
loiter

Group 24

Consonant letters are often doubled after a short vowel in short vowel words such as *egg*, *fluff*, *sniffle*, and *mess*.

across (R)
arrange (R)
business (R)
guess (R)
addressed (R)
annual (R)
gallant (R)
latter (R)
marriage (R)
mattress (R)
embarrass (R)
exaggerate (R)
college (R)
accumulate
occurring
omission
omitted
professor
villain
collected
skills
effects
unhappy
messages
tossed
lessons
shallow
tobacco
ladder
pressed
button
pulls
selling
adds
mills
rolls
bills
filling
inflammable
allege
ballot
tariff
vaccinate
buzz
thrill
address

Important Notes

- The "jump" in Group Numbers is intentional. See Page 122, "Grouping within Levels" for an explanation.
- Words followed by an (R) are Review words. Do not say the (R) when dictating them.
- Words in [brackets] are the British spelling. When correcting the test, use the proper spelling for your country.

Group 26

When adding the suffixes <u>ness</u> and <u>ly</u> to words not ending in y the spelling of the base word stays the same, as in *slowly*.

especially (R)
generally (R)
immediately (R)
practically (R)
really (R)
respectfully (R)
accidentally (R)
lovely (R)
finally (R)
really (R)
likely (R)
approximately (R)
strictly
loudly
largely
apparently
scarcely
commonly
swiftly
relatively
sharply
chiefly
proudly
differently
brightly
obviously (R)
silently
seriously
eagerly
strongly
sadly
smoothly
regularly
comparatively
formally
formerly
hurriedly
undoubtedly
universally

Group 28

/ȧn/ is sometimes spelled <u>en</u> as in *golden*.

ancient (R)
excellent (R)
benefit (R)
calendar (R)
intelligent (R)
messenger (R)
recommend (R)
apparent (R)
expense (R)
kindergarten (R)
consistent (R)
prevalent (R)
strenuous (R)
tendency (R)
permanent (R)
ascend
descend
tendency
efficient
incidents
influential
consistent
extend
gardens
penny
hydrogen
expensive
blend
extended
pretend
enters
content
accent
continents
intended
attend
spending
bench
patient
tense
challenge
legend
citizen
tend
depending
entry
parentheses
extends

Review Test 3

The following words have been previously tested. (Student need not record this statement.)

coarse
accumulate
occurring
omission
omitted
professor
comparatively
formally
formerly
hurriedly
undoubtedly
universally
territory
majority
corresponding
authority
inflammable
annoyance
poisonous
embroidery
appointment
anoint
loiter
hydrogen
continents
parentheses
influential
expensive
tendency

Level J

Delayed Recall Test I Form A

Before administering this test, read pgs 45-46.

appropriate 1
tragedy 1
mammals 1
pedestrian 2
developing 2
attempt 2
admitted 3
definite 3
swinging 3
prophesy 4
apostrophe 4
rhapsody 4
remaining 6
female 6
painting 6
dreamed 7
ceiling 7
increasing 7
franchise 8
mileage 8
rhyme 8
kimono 9
approached 9
swallowed 9
maneuver 10
pursue 10
refused 10
thermometer 12
performed 12
camera 12
corresponding 13
dinosaurs 13
warning 13
reported 13
majority 13

Delayed Recall Test I Form B

tragedy 1
appropriate 1
accurate 1
drenched 2
electrons 2
seldom 2
introduced 3
opinion 3
timber 3
rhapsody 4
concede 4
prophesy 4
replaced 6
damage 6
rainy 6
increasing 7
succeeded 7
meals 7
divine 8
fiery 8
sighed 8
rotary 9
microscope 9
stroke 9
parachute 10
deuce 10
universe 10
counter 12
laughter 12
former 12
explorers 13
reported 13
sources 13

Group 29

/àl/ can be spelled le as in *little*, el as in *rebel*, al as in *total*, il as in *council*, ol as in *capitol*, ul as in *consul*, and ile as *futile*.

alcohol (R)
cancel (R)
journal (R)
fundamental (R)
noticeable (R)
article (R)
several (R)
unusual (R)
terrible (R)
triangle
normal
plural
industrial
numeral
struggle
principle
vertical
settle
actual
tropical
jungle
whistle
label
mineral
canal
official
practical
medical
candle
rifle
electrical
commercial
soul
muscle
counsel
manual
federal
mechanical
sample
royal
puzzle

Group 30

Words are normally made plural by adding s, but if the word ends with sh, zh, z, s, j, ch, or x sounds, the plural is generally formed by adding es, which is pronounced as a separate syllable.

vegetables (R)
paragraphs (R)
numerals (R)
meanings (R)
seems (R)
minutes (R)
spaces
languages
seas
fits
wires
flows
leaders
signals
dots
travels
tables
items
skins
gods
rises
tribes
principles
indicates
stems
tons
fires
lengths
dreams
mathematics
claws
slaves
circles
models
serves
hundredths
politics
succeeds

Group 35

Proper nouns must begin with a capital letter because they refer to a specific name or title of a person, place, time, thing, or idea such as Monday.

February (R)
Massachusetts (R)
November (R)
Missouri (R)
Pennsylvania (R)
Illinois (R)
January (R)
Virginia (R)
Arctic (R)
Britain (R)
Tuesday (R)
Michigan (R)
Delaware (R)
September (R)
Louisiana (R)
Romans
Irish
Switzerland
Soviet
Israel
Christian
Swiss
Senate
Jackson
Jefferson
Ireland
Venus
Egyptian
Apollo
Denmark
Homer
Wright
Antarctic
Pittsburgh

Group 37

An apostrophe is used to take the place of a letter when two words are joined. These words are called contractions.

who's (R)
don't (R)
o'clock (R)
they're (they are) (R)
you're (R)
can't (R)
it's (R)
shouldn't (R)
you'd (R)
you'll (R)
wouldn't (R)
doesn't (R)
she'll
needn't
who'd
what'll
it'll
we've
where's
would've
must've
they've
mustn't
could've
should've

Level J

Important Notes

- The "jump" in Group Numbers is intentional. See Page 122, "Grouping within Levels" for an explanation.
- Words followed by an (R) are Review words. Do not say the (R) when dictating them.
- Words in [brackets] are the British spelling. When correcting the test, use the proper spelling for your country.

Group 42

/shun/ can be spelled tion as in vacation, sion as in division, or cian as in physician.

pronunciation (R)
concession (R)
description (R)
tuition (R)
possession (R)
dictionary (R)
constitution (R)
revolution (R)
occasion (R)
stationery (R)
explanation (R)
decision (R)
divisions
conclusion
emotional
introduction
absorption
commission
distinction
immigration
perception
perspiration
prohibition
physician
recommendation
accommodation
cancellation
imitation
installation
abbreviation
permission
tradition
confession
instruction
reflection

Review Test 4

The following words have been previously tested. (Student need not record this statement.)

mathematics
serves
hundredths
politics
succeeds
absorption
physician
industrial
commercial
mechanical
whistle
medical
candle
mustn't
should've
would've
what'll
we've
needn't
Pittsburgh
Antarctic
Egyptian
Christian
Switzerland
Israel
recommendation
confession
immigration
emotional

Group 43

/às/ can be spelled ous as in nervous or ace as in menace.

conscious (R)
courteous (R)
disastrous (R)
grievous (R)
humorous [humourous] (R)
jealous (R)
mischievous (R)
enormous (R)
mysterious (R)
delicious (R)
outrageous (R)
ridiculous (R)
religious (R)
mysterious (R)
continuous (R)
conscientious (R)
sacrilegious (R)
treacherous (R)
precious (R)
barbarous (R)
analogous (R)
incredulous (R)
conspicuous
presumptuous
simultaneous
suspicious
synonymous
gracious
contagious
gaseous
malicious
rebellious
repetitious
intravenous
unanimous

Group 44

/ànse/ can be spelled ance as in substance or ence as in experience.

balance (R)
audience (R)
maintenance (R)
license (R)
reference (R)
absence (R)
acceptance (R)
nuisance (R)
conscience (R)
preference (R)
appearance (R)
difference (R)
independence (R)
instance (R)
sense (R)
sentence (R)
existence (R)
guidance (R)
intelligence (R)
occurrence (R)
alliance
defenseless
immense
elegance
precedence
resistance
vengeance
vigilance
dominance
hindrance
conference
allegiance
coincidence
brilliance

Group 45

/ment/ is usually spelled ment as in elements.

arrangement (R)
argument (R)
judgment (R)
development (R)
environment (R)
experiment (R)
statement (R)
achievement (R)
parliament (R)
temperament (R)
astonishment (R)
compliment (R)
establishment (R)
acknowledgement (R)
tournament (R)
adjournment
allotment
amendment
commitment
endorsement
envelopment
management
parliamentary
unemployment
supplement
investment
advertisement
documentary
complementary
complimentary
attachment
inducement
ligament
sentiment

Group 46

The addition of a prefix does not usually change the spelling of the root word. The prefix ex usually means out of, away, or from as in the words explore and extent.

express
expect
expected
extra
explain
explained
examples
export
exclaim
exterior
exile
extreme
explored
expanded
excite
explode
external
explorer
expedition
expand
exit
extent
exclude
exert
explanatory
expose
exhibit
expressive
extrasensory
exception
expert
excess
expectation
exponent

Important Notes

- The "jump" in Group Numbers is intentional. See Page 122, "Grouping within Levels" for an explanation.
- Words followed by an (R) are Review words. Do not say the (R) when dictating them.
- Words in [brackets] are the British spelling. When correcting the test, use the proper spelling for your country.

Level J

Group 47

These words are unusual words and are exceptions to the most common generalizations.

friend (R)
truly (R)
two (R)
volume (R)
meant (R)
ready (R)
wealth (R)
country (R)
trouble (R)
typical (R)
adjectives
services
positive
primitive
effective
negative
relative
wealth
breaks
wilderness
society
examine
adjective
active
feather (R)
sweat
submarine
provides
improved
cylinder

Review Test 5

The following words have been previously tested. (Student need not record this statement.)

analogous
incredulous
express
expect
expected
extra
explain
explained
examples
expert
cylinder
endorsement
parliamentary
documentary
inducement
sentiment
adjournment
defenseless
precedence
vigilance
dominance
allegiance
unanimous
malicious
presumptuous
primitive
wilderness
improved
society
synonymous

Delayed Recall Test 2 Form A

Before administering this test, read pgs 45-46.

annoyance 18
embroidery 18
appointment 18
accumulate 24
omitted 24
professor 24
comparatively 26
formerly 26
undoubtedly 26
parentheses 27
hydrogen 27
challenge 27
commercial 29
mechanical 29
industrial 29
principles 30
mathematics 30
hundredths 30
Switzerland 35
Christian 35
Denmark 35
needn't 37
what'll 37
they've 37
recommendation 42
immigration 42
perception 42
analogous 43
rebellious 43
intravenous 43
precedence 44
resistance 44
difference 44
management 45
advertisement 45
adjournment 45
explained 46
examples 46
expedition 46
negation 47
cylinder 47
adjectives 47

Delayed Recall Test 2 Form B

poisonous 18
embroidery 18
employed 18
occurring 24
omission 24
inflammable 24
formally 24
hurriedly 26
universally 26
continents 27
expensive 27
depending 27
tropical 29
whistle 29
mineral 29
politics 30
succeeds 30
indicates 30
Antarctic 35
Egyptian 35
Senate 35
could've 37
should've 37
needn't 37
accommodation 42
prohibition 42
conclusion 42
incredulous 43
repetitious 43
malicious 43
vigilance 44
dominance 44
hindrance 44
parliamentary 45
documentary 45
allotment 45
expert 46
explained 46
expose 46
wilderness 47
submarine 47
sweat 47

End of Level J Test Form A

Before administering this test, read pgs 45-46.

appropriate 1
developing 2
definite 3
prophesy 4
concede 4
painting 6
remaining 6
succeeded 7
teaching 7
franchise 8
mileage 8
microscope 9
manufacturing 10
maneuver 10
thermometer 12
prefer 12
corresponding 13
coarse 13
annoyance 18
accumulate 24
occurring 24
comparatively 26
formally 26
parentheses 28
industrial 29
politics 29
mathematics 30
Ireland 35
should've 37
analogous 43
presumptuous 43
coincidence 44
complementary 45
expanded 46
negative 47
documentary 47

End of Level J Test Form B

tragedy 1
pedestrian 2
admitted 3
apostrophe 4
rhapsody 4
exchange 6
replaced 6
increasing 7
diseases 7
rhyme 8
hygiene 8
purposes 9
parachute 10
pursue 10
performed 12
numbered 12
authority 13
comfort 13
poisonous 18
omission 24
professor 24
universally 26
hurriedly 26
influential 28
electrical 29
succeeds 29
hundredths 30
Egyptian 35
recommendation 37
incredulous 43
synonymous 43
precedence 44
inducement 45
expedition 46
submarine 47
complementary 47

Level J

Important Notes

- The "jump" in Group Numbers is intentional. See Page 122, "Grouping within Levels" for an explanation.
- Words followed by an (R) are Review words. Do not say the (R) when dictating them.
- Words in [brackets] are the British spelling. When correcting the test, use the proper spelling for your country.

Level K

Group 1

Usually /a/ is spelled a as in *cat*.

than (R)
accept (R)
tragedy (R)
appropriate (R)
magazine (R)
statue (R)
track (R)
language (R)
paragraph (R)
woman (R)
asks (R)
banana (R)
granted (R)
data
programs
advantage
adapted
sprang
acting
tap
damp
dramatic
lap
fancy
dashed
vocabulary
associated (R)
smash (R)
grasp
wasp
snag
catastrophe
battalion
bankruptcy
haphazard
pamphlet
pageant
panic
slant
draft
melancholy

Group 2

Usually /e/ is spelled e as in *nest*.

necessary (R)
desert (R)
separate (R)
benefited (R)
specimen (R)
except (R)
led (R)
strength (R)
enemy (R)
medicine (R)
stretch (R)
resting
estimated
escaped
web
magnetic
electronic
hemorrhage
legitimate
relevant
temporary
cemetery
ecstasy
accessory
accessible
vessel
necessity
descent
dependent
pledges
extension
experimentation
excessive
employee
embassy
embrace
emigrants
medication
chemist

Group 3

Usually /i/ is spelled i as in *big*.

its (own) (R)
arithmetic (R)
privilege (R)
brilliant (R)
considered (R)
since (R)
definite (R)
fifth (R)
religion (R)
village (R)
which (R)
discipline (R)
picnic (R)
instant (R)
interest (R)
eligible
eliminate
affiliate
diphtheria
discrepancy
indelible
inveigle
inhabitant
illegal
strings
bridges
ribs
swift
width
delicate
rapid
acid
twisted
aluminum [aluminium]
switch
limit
illustrated
industries

Group 5

Usually /u/ is spelled u as in *run*.

minimum (R)
studying (R)
subjects (R)
industry (R)
husband (R)
numbers (R)
lungs (R)
buffalo (R)
struck (R)
hundred (R)
product (R)
struggled (R)
customs (R)
published (R)
construct
budget
bulb
trust
custom
rushing
justifiable
subsidy
successor
buckets
clumsy
bulletin
shrunk
republic
triumph
album
knuckled
auditorium
insulate
insult
grumble
suffix
luggage

Review Test 1

catastrophe
battalion
bankruptcy
haphazard
pamphlet
pageant
hemorrhage
legitimate
relevant
temporary
cemetery
ecstasy
accessory
accessible
aluminum [aluminium]
eligible
eliminate
affiliate
diphtheria
discrepancy
indelible
inveigle
inhabitant
illegal
bulletin
justifiable
budget
auditorium
insulate
successor
melancholy

Group 6

/ā/ can be written ay, ai, ey, ei, eigh, ea, or a followed by a consonant and silent e.

ascertain (R)
freight (R)
based (R)
neighbor [neighbour] (R)
laid (R)
escape (R)
phrase (R)
wait (stay) (R)
eighty (R)
they (R)
awake (R)
gained (R)
plates
tales
grains
weighs
bases
cakes
blanks
whales
claim
faint
dates
frames
ages
mate
cane
parade
aim
pace
maintain
saint
frail
traits
prey
pray
campaign

Level K

Important Notes

- The "jump" in Group Numbers is intentional. See Page 122, "Grouping within Levels" for an explanation.
- Words followed by an (R) are Review words. Do not say the (R) when dictating them.
- Words in [brackets] are the British spelling. When correcting the test, use the proper spelling for your country.

Group 7

/ē/ can be spelled ea, ee, y, ie, ei, ey, or e followed by a consonant and silent e.

scream (R)
received (R)
receive (R)
niece (R)
describe (R)
region (R)
safety (R)
ceiling (R)
breathe (R)
opinion (R)
speak (R)
belief (R)
relief
sweeping
beats
seized
leaned
behave
leaped
released
leap
lean
ease
feasible
fiend
seasons
leads
reads
beads
peak
precede
proceed
decide
divide
siege
renown
preceding
preliminary
reveal

Group 12

/ûr/ can be spelled ir as in *bird*, er as in *her*, ur as in *survey*, er as in *eternity*, ear as in *pearl*, our as in *journal*, or or after w as in *work*.

world (R)
different (R)
sure (R)
whether (R)
certain (R)
directed (R)
prefer (R)
thermometer (R)
earned (R)
operate (R)
further (R)
later (R)
perhaps (R)
exercise (R)
journey (R)
lighter
lowered
slavery
owners
circuit
deferred
intercede
interfere
murmur
shepherd
persuade
accelerate
controversy
illiterate
inaugurate
interfered
preferable
surgeon
catcher
thirsty
drawer
nerve
curl
survive
hurricane

Group 13

/or/ can be spelled or as in *corn*, oar as in *boar*, oor as in *door*, our as *your*, and ar as *dwarf*.

before (R)
course (R)
doctor (R)
fourth (R)
your (R)
opportunity (R)
foreign (R)
laboratory (R)
warrant (R)
courtesy (R)
forth (R)
origin (R)
perform (R)
chauffeur (R)
dinosaurs (R)
authority (R)
coarse (R)
forty (R)
corrugated
notoriety
rhetoric
acorns
forgive
organ
inform
chore
flavor [flavour]
tornado
stroll
worm
humor [humour]
orchard
terror
actor
bore
armor [armour]
forming
minor
warned
roared

Group 26

When adding the suffixes ness and ly to words not ending in y the spelling of the base word stays the same, as in *slowly*.

really (R)
respectfully (R)
especially (R)
extremely (R)
finally (R)
generally (R)
immediately (R)
occasionally (R)
particularly (R)
practically (R)
usually (R)
comparatively (R)
formally (R)
formerly (R)
hurriedly (R)
strictly (R)
undoubtedly (R)
universally (R)
accidentally (R)
lovely (R)
incidentally (R)
consecutively
evidently
homely
personally
publicly
privately
securely
beautifully
peacefully
faithfully
thoroughly
supposedly
melancholy
uncertainly
unearthly

Review Test 2

campaign
weighs
whales
faint
feasible
fiend
relief
proceed
siege
renown
reveal
corrugated
notoriety
tornado
rhetoric
warmed
deferred
intercede
interfere
murmur
shepherd
persuade
undoubtedly
universally
most
consecutively
privately
beautifully

Delayed Recall Test 1 Form A

Before administering this test, read pgs 45-46.

catastrophe 1
battalion 1
bankruptcy 1
advantage 1
hemorrhage 2
relevant 2
cemetery 2
accessible 2
eligible 3
discrepancy 3
indelible 3
inhabitant 3
budget 4
justifiable 4
bulletin 4
album 4
campaign 6
saint 6
frames 6
whales 6
relief 7
feasible 7
siege 7
reveal 7
deferred 12
interfere 12
shepherd 12
controversy 12
corrugated 13
rhetoric 13
forming 13
orchard 13
undoubtedly 26
personally 26
homely 26
securely 26

Important Notes

- The "jump" in Group Numbers is intentional. See Page 122, "Grouping within Levels" for an explanation.
- Words followed by an (R) are Review words. Do not say the (R) when dictating them.
- Words in [brackets] are the British spelling. When correcting the test, use the proper spelling for your country.

Level K

Delayed Recall Test I Form B

haphazard 1
pamphlet 1
pageant 1
dramatic 1
legitimate 2
temporary 2
ecstasy 2
accessary 2
eliminate 3
diphtheria 3
inveigle 3
illegal 3
published 4
auditorium 4
grumble 4
successor 6
maintain 6
parade 6
traits 6
prey 7
weighs 7
fiend 7
proceed 7
renown 7
intercede 12
murmur 12
persuade 12
inaugurate 12
notoriety 13
tornado 13
warned 13
chore 13
universally 26
uncertainly 26
privately 26
beautifully 26

Group 28

/àn/ is sometimes spelled en as in *golden*.

independent (R)
ancient (R)
benefit (R)
calendar (R)
intelligent (R)
recommend (R)
apparent (R)
expense (R)
kindergarten (R)
consistent (R)
strenuous (R)
tendency (R)
ascend (R)
descend (R)
efficient (R)
incidents (R)
influential (R)
permanent (R)
excellent (R)
messenger (R)
representative
merchant
insisted
superintendent
skeleton
organs
harmony
economic
eminent
precedents
prevalent
beneficial
confident
defendant
enterprise
envelop
prominent
recipient
repellent
sufficient
tenant
souvenir
tentacles
delicatessen

Group 29

/àl/ can be spelled le as in *little*, el as in *rebel*, al as in *total*, il as in *council*, ol as in *capitol*, ul as in *consul*, and ile as *futile*.

capital (R)
schedule (R)
article (R)
principle (R)
column (R)
solemn (R)
personal (R)
physical (R)
control (R)
possible (R)
practical (R)
parallel (R)
counsel (R)
manual (R)
federal (R)
alcohol (R)
analyze [analyse] (R)
mechanical (R)
cycle
council
eagle
formal
cruel
vowels
travelers [travellers]
chemicals
controls
puzzled
crystals
singular
morale
obstacle
peaceable
permissible
psychology
simile
soliloquy
symmetrical
tranquillity
steal (to take)
flexible
serial
susceptible
tangible
scholastic

Group 32

When adding a suffix to a word ending in y, change the y to i, unless a vowel proceeds the y, as in try to *tried* and baby to *babies*.

theories (R)
mystifying (R)
easily (R)
stories (R)
tries (R)
occupied (R)
dormitories (R)
livelihood (R)
loneliness (R)
replies (R)
ladies (R)
boundaries (R)
obituaries (R)
authorities (R)
married (R)
countries (R)
harmonious
galleries
facilities
securities
sturdiest
wittiest
costliest
hastily
daintier
loneliest
untidiness
applying
emptiness
notified
dairies
impurities
pitied
creamier
livelier
steadier
priorities
amplifier
accompanied
personalities

Group 34

In short vowel words, the final consonant is usually doubled before adding a suffix, such as when changing in stop to stopped.

swimming (R)
happened (R)
running (R)
biggest (R)
putting (R)
grabbed (R)
shopping (R)
wrapped (R)
winning (R)
beginning (R)
forgetting (R)
upsetting
humming
submitting
benefitted
omitting
stunned
forbidding
outfitting
snobbish
conferring
forbidden
permitting
shredded
cunning
swapped
patrolling
occurred
expressed
discussed
controlled
referred
personnel
transferred

Group 36

New words are often made by putting two short words together into one word as in cowboy.

everybody (R)
itself (R)
without (R)
therefore (R)
nowadays (R)
overrun (R)
foresee (R)
nevertheless (R)
throughout (R)
gentleman (R)
underneath (R)
otherwise (R)
platform
someday
moreover
daylight
doorway
westward
upset
downward
forehead
moonlight
household
highways
extraordinary (R)
forthright
foursome
oneself (R)
playwright
shipment
heartrending
passageway
trustworthy
spacecraft
eyesight
leftovers
overdue
overdo
roommate
rosebushes
teammates
stockholder
hardware
paperback

Level K

Important Notes

- The "jump" in Group Numbers is intentional. See Page 122, "Grouping within Levels" for an explanation.
- Words followed by an (R) are Review words. Do not say the (R) when dictating them.
- Words in [brackets] are the British spelling. When correcting the test, use the proper spelling for your country.

Review Test 3

superintendent
eminent
delicatessen
souvenir
representative
defendant
tentacles
council
morale
obstacle
peaceable
permissible
harmonious
securities
untidiness
impurities
accompanied
personalities
referred
personnel
transferred
occurred
forbidding
passageway
trustworthy
spacecraft
extraordinary

Group 42

/shun/ can be spelled tion as in vacation, sion as in division, or cian as in physician.

description (R)
concession (R)
tuition (R)
possession (R)
decision (R)
dictionary (R)
explanation (R)
imagination (R)
occasion (R)
stationery (R)
invitation (R)
repetition (R)
preparation (R)
exhibition (R)
pronunciation (R)
absorption (R)
physician (R)
accommodation (R)
immigration (R)
cancellation (R)
abbreviation (R)
intersection
exploration
decoration
sensational
termination
celebration
correction
cooperation
declaration
graduation
navigation
destination
confusion
affection
explosion
digestion
suggestion
violation

Group 44

/ànse/ can be spelled ance as in substance or ence as in experience.

appearance (R)
preference (R)
reference (R)
absence (R)
acceptance (R)
nuisance (R)
conscience (R)
sentence (R)
maintenance (R)
convenience (R)
existence (R)
intelligence (R)
occurrence (R)
precedence (R)
resistance (R)
vengeance (R)
vigilance (R)
perseverance
acquaintance
significance
magnificence
circumference
interference
circumstance
suspense
residence
correspondence
insurance
abundance
resemblance
inheritance
persistence
repentance
subsistence

Important Notes

- *The "jump" in Group Numbers is intentional. See Page 122, "Grouping within Levels" for an explanation.*
- *Words followed by an (R) are Review words. Do not say the (R) when dictating them.*
- *Words in [brackets] are the British spelling. When correcting the test, use the proper spelling for your country.*

Group 46

The addition of a prefix does not usually change the spelling of the root word. The prefixes dis, mis, des, irr, non, de, in, un, im and ill usually mean not or incorrect as in the words disappear and mistake.

disappear
disappoint
mistakes
dissatisfied
despite (R)
disagree
disable
dismiss
misplace
disobey
disconnect
disloyal
irregular
nonviolent
discriminate
defective
uncertain
impatient
unnecessary
inexpensive
inexperienced
illiteracy
unpaid
nonfiction
incorrect
illogical
insane
unlucky
incompatible
unselfish
dissatisfy
disgrace
nonresident
inability
impractical
impolite
improper
nonprofit
unskilled
uneducated

Group 47

These words are unusual words and are exceptions to the most common generalizations.

friend (R)
many (R)
truly (R)
busy (R)
height (R)
bureau (R)
restaurant (R)
volume (R)
weather (R)
pleasant (R)
trouble (R)
typical (R)
rhythm (R)
syllable (R)
positive (R)
relative (R)
height (R)
genius (R)
against (R)
two (R)
ninth (R)
pleasant (R)
meant (R)
ready (R)
country (R)
primitive (R)
cylinder (R)
rheumatism
tyranny
bureaus
gauge
rhubarb
cynical
gymnasium
idiosyncrasy
symmetry
hypocrisy

Review Test 4

acquaintance
tyranny
bureaus
gauge
rhubarb
cynical
gymnasium
idiosyncrasy
subsistence
heartrending
perseverance

Test continues on next column

circumference
correspondence
resemblance
inheritance
discriminate
inexperienced
impractical
nonviolent
unnecessary
illiteracy
intersection
termination
destination
violation
sensational
celebration

Delayed Recall Test 2 Form A

Before administering this test, read pgs 45-46.

superintendent 28
beneficial 28
sufficient 28
merchant 28
morale 29
obstacle 29
permissible 29
symmetrical 29
harmonious 32
loneliest 32
creamier 32
accompanied 32
occurred 34
referred 34
personnel 34
transferred 34
extraordinary 36
spacecraft 36
teammates 36
paperback 36
exploration 42
sensational 42
cooperation 42
navigation 42
acquaintance 44
suspense 44
resemble 44
circumstance 44
unnecessary 46
unselfish 46
dissatisfy 46
illiteracy 46
tyranny 47
gauge 47
cynical 47

Level K

Delayed Recall Test 2
Form B

eminent
confident
souvenir
tentacles
council
peaceable
psychology
tranquillity
sturdiest
impurities
amplifier
personalities
submitting
forbidding
shredded
expressed
heartrending
eyesight
stockholder
westward
decoration
celebration
destination
confusion
magnificence
residence
abundance
interference
inexperienced
unlucky
illogical
defective
bureaus
rhubarb
gymnasium

End of Level K Test
Form A

Before administering this test, read pgs 45-46.

catastrophe 1
haphazard 1
hemorrhage 2
legitimate 2
diphtheria 3
inhabitant 3
budget 5
justifiable 5
campaign 6
faint 6
feasible 7
fiend 7
deferred 12
intercede 12
rhetoric 13
corrugated 13
undoubtedly 26
universally 26
superintendent 28
eminent 28
morale 29
peaceable 29
impurities 32
personalities 32
occurred 34
referred 34
forthright 36
overdo 36
celebration 42
suggestion 42
acquaintance 44
perseverance 44
nonviolent 46
disconnect 46
tyranny 47
bureaus 47

End of Level K Test
Form B

battalion 1
pamphlet 1
temporary 2
accessible 2
illegal 3
eliminate 3
bulletin 5
auditorium 5
parade 6
frames 6
siege 7
reveal 7
murmur 12
shepherd 12
orchard 13
forming 13
personally 26
melancholy 26
enterprise 28
tentacles 28
obstacle 29
permissible 29
creamier 32
amplifier 32
personnel 34
transferred 34
household 36
overdue 36
destination 42
violation 42
circumstance 44
magnificence 44
discriminate 46
inexperienced 46
cynical 47
gymnasium 47

The 12,000 Most Frequently Used and Misspelled Words

The base list in this section was compiled using a number of U.S. and Canadian word frequency studies. The author then modified the list by adding words which have recently come into use (mostly computer related) and deleting a few archaic words.

The resulting list was compared to lists used in five other commercial spelling series to help determine the grade level at which these words are taught in the average public or private grade schools. Once this list was compiled, an additional 258 frequently misspelled words by grade school, high school, and college students, and secretaries and business people were added. The list was then compared by computer to several lists of words with 'British spellings' to add those variations. Frequently misspelled (problem) words are identified by symbols following the words.

The key to the symbols following the words is as follows: Letter-## is Spelling Power level word is first taught at. A## is usage by adults; C## is usage by children; (#.##) is average grade level word is taught at. £ Means the word is also in the list with a 'British' spelling. Brackets ([]) around a word indicate it is a 'British spelling' variation. As an example:

answer D-22 C10 A3 (4.25) ¡

The word "answer" is first introduced in the *Spelling Power* program at Level D, in Group 22. It is in the 1000 frequency level in the Canadian (Children) List and the 300 frequency level in the American Heritage List. An average of the five other spelling programs shows this word is taught in the first quarter of the fourth grade. Finally, the word ``answer" causes problems for college students (¡) and elementary students (it is in **bold face type**). (A copy of this key appears on the bottom of each even numbered page.)

A

a A-47 A1 C1 1.50
a lot D-39 8.75
a.m. (morning) D-41 7.42
AB (Alberta) F-41
abacus A99
abandon A100 7.50
abandoned A48 7.75
abbreviate 8.50
abbreviated A95
abbreviation J-42 A80 6.75
abbreviations A75
abdomen A91 8.25
abduct 9.00
Abe A55
abilities G-32 A81 6.50
ability H-3 A18 6.75
able G-29 A4 C12 4.00
abnormal 8.67
aboard J-13 A28 5.25
abolish 8.25
abolition 8.25
about A-16 A1 C1 3.44
above C-20 A3 C12 4.08
abroad A51 9.00
abrupt 8.88
abruptly A79
abscess 8.50
absence H-44 A61 6.67 ¡
absent A75 6.25
absolute A46 8.63
absolutely A47 8.50
absorb A64 7.83
absorbed A46
absorption J-42 ¡¿
abstract 8.08
absurd 5.75 ¡
abundance K-44 A59 9.00
abundant A61 8.13
abuse 7.38
academic 7.50
academy A53 ¡
accelerate K-12 9.00 ¿
accent J-28 A33 7.00
accented A52
accept H-1 A26 6.38 ¡
acceptable A71 9.00
acceptance H-44 A79 9.00
accepted J-1 A26
accepting A95 9.00
access A84 8.50
accessible K-2 9.00 ¿
accessories I-32 8.25
accessory K-2 8.08 ¿
accident I-28 A25 7.25
accidentally E-26 A83 6.67 ¡¿
accidents A40 C14
accommodate I-4 8.08 ¡¿
accommodation J-42 ¿
accompanied K-32 A50 7.75
accompaniment A84
accompany A59 8.25
accomplice 7.88
accomplish I-24 A74 8.00 ¡
accomplished A46
accomplishment I-45 A101 7.50
accomplishments A93
accordance 8.50
according G-13 A12 6.13
accordingly A81 8.50
accordion 8.00
account I-24 A21 6.81
accountant 8.06
accounting 9.00
accounts A51 8.50
accumulate J-24 8.50 ¡¿
accuracy A58 8.67
accurate J-1 A28 7.38
accurately A45
accuse 6.25
accused A78 6.25
accustom ¡
accustomed A55 8.06
ache E-47 C20 5.56
aches G-47
achieve A47 6.50
achieved A42
achievement I-45 A72 8.25 ¡¿
achievements A68
aching A81
acid K-3 A35
acids A68
acknowledge 8.75
acknowledgement I-45 7.58
acknowledgment 9.00 ¿
acorn 7.50
acorns K-13 A88 4.25
acquaint I-21 7.25
acquaintance K-44 8.75 ¿
acquainted I-21 A67 6.25 ¡
acquiesce I-21 ¿
acquire I-21 A75 7.25 ¡
acquired A59
acquittal I-21 8.50
acquitted I-21 ¡
acre A54 5.00
acreage 8.25
acres I-6 A29 7.75
acrobat 9.00
acronym 8.00
across C-24 A3 C5 3.67 ¡
act H-1 A11 4.50
acted A41
acting K-1 A38
action F-42 A10 5.75
actions A32
active J-47 A25 5.00
actively 5.75
activities E-32 A19 7.25
activity J-3 A26 6.75
actor K-13 A65 5.58
actors A60
actress's G-40 7.50
acts I-1 A25
actual J-29 A27 9.00
actually H-26 A11 8.00
acute A76 7.25
Adam A85
Adams A43
adapt A100 7.67
adaptation 7.75
adapted K-1 A39 8.50
add G-24 A4 3.17
added H-1 A6
adding H-1 A11
addition F-42 A9 6.38
additional I-42 A25 6.75
address J-24 A40 4.33
addressed F-24 A68 8.75 ¡
addresses 6.17
adds J-24 A35
adequate A82 7.13
adhesive 8.67
adios 9.00
adjacent A71 8.75
adjective J-47 A25 6.00
adjectives J-47 A29
adjoin J-18 8.38
adjoining A101
adjourn 8.63
adjourned 9.00
adjournment J-45 ¿
adjust A64 6.63
adjusted A76 9.00
adjustment 7.88
administer 7.88
administration A74 8.50
admiral A55 6.50
admiration A69 7.50
admire A55 6.25
admired A60
admiring A93
admissible 8.50

Alphabetical List

admission A90 8.50
admit A54 7.13
admittance I-44 8.75
admitted J-3 A39 7.25
adobe A82 8.17
adolescent 7.83
adopt 7.25
adopted J-4 A38 8.50
adorable 6.50
adoration H-42 7.75
adore 6.42
adorn 8.25
adrift 8.25
adult I-5 A30 6.00
adults H-17 A37
advance H-44 A33 7.75
advanced H-44 A32 7.25
advancement 7.00
advances A60
advancing A82
advantage K-1 A33 7.50
advantages A45
adventure E-25 A27 C12 6.17
adventures I-25 A33
adventurous A99
adverb A47 6.88
adverbs A51 7.50
adverse 9.00
advertise A99 7.67
advertisement J-45 A99 8.38
advertisements A93
advertising A61 7.00
advice J-8 A29 6.94
advisable 8.38
advise A80 7.19
advised A71 8.50
adviser ¡
advises 9.00
advising 8.50
advisor 8.00
advisory 7.63
advocate 8.50
aerial 8.83
aeronautical H-17 7.00
aeronautics 8.75
affair I-14 A64 6.25
affairs I-14 A39
affect I-24 A25 7.38 ¿
affected J-2 A36
affection K-42 A78 6.75
affectionate 8.38
affectionately 9.00
affects A57 ¡
affiliate K-3 ¿
afford I-13 A39 6.38
afraid G-6 A9 C17 3.88
Africa G-35 A11
African I-35 A23
Africans A73
after A-12 A1 C1 3.13
afternoon C-36 A10 C6 3.5
afterward A48 7.00
afterwards A40 7.25
again B-47 A2 C2 3.00
against D-47 A3 C10 4.94 ¡
age F-6 A8 C14 3.50
aged A74
agencies A71
agency A84 8.50
agent A42 6.17
agents A71 9.00
ages K-6 A39
aggravate 8.67 ¡
aggressive 8.69
agility 7.75
Agnes A99
ago C-9 A4 C6 3.67
agony A100
agree I-7 A18 4.50
agreeable 7.75
agreed G-7 A15 C17 4.75
agreement A43 6.00
agrees A95
agricultural A51 7.75
agriculture I-25 A45 8.25
ahead E-47 A9 C14 4.08
aid I-6 A23 4.25
aided A95
aids A83
ailment 5.25
aim K-6 A38 4.75
aimed A64
aims A84
ain't F-37 A32
air A-14 A2 C4 3.75
air conditioner 8.75
air-conditioned F-38 7.75
aircraft A49
airline A84 5.63
airlines A99
airmail 6.50
airplane E-36 A16 C8 4.25 £
airplanes F-36 A26 C17 £
airport A34 C17 4.08
airports A84
aisle 7.56
aisles 7.00
AL (Alabama) F-41
Alabama E-35 A63 5.50
Aladdin A99
Alamo A86
Alan A94
alarm H-11 A37 4.33
alarmed A78
alas A69
Alaska E-35 A20 5.50
Alaskan A101
Albany A80
albatross 8.63
Albert A35
Alberta F-35 C12 7.00
album K-5 7.13
alcohol H-29 A48 8.75
Alec A78
alert A51 5.58
Alexander A51
alfalfa 8.83
Alfred A83
algae A73 7.25
algebra A100 8.25
Algeria A94
Ali A57
alias 8.00
alibi 8.25
Alice A26
alien 8.13
alike H-8 A11 4.08
alive E-8 A14 C11 4.00
all A-17 A1 C1 2.25
all right D-39 5.42 ¡¿
all-around G-38 8.25
Allan A69
allege J-24 ¿
allegiance J-44 7.50
Allen A48
allergies I-32 7.75
allergy 9.00
alley F-7 A74 C11 6.42 ¡
alliance J-44 7.75
allied A101 8.50
allies A94
alligator A78 7.50
alligators A87
alliteration 8.50
allotment J-45 ¿
allotted ¡
allow I-24 A21 5.00
allowable 8.00
allowance I-44 A71 7.08
allowed H-16 A16 7.50
allowing A77 9.00
allows A55
alloy A100
allude 8.63
ally 7.38 ¡
almanac 8.00
almost C-9 A3 C4 3.08 ¡
aloft A95 8.25
alone F-9 A6 C12 4.38
along A2 C4 2.63
alongside A44
aloud H-16 A24 5.42
alphabet A25 4.42
alphabetical A46 8.75
Alps A65
already C-17 A5 C7 4.19 ¡¿
also B-9 A2 C2 3.56
altar A100 7.63 ¡
alter A98 6.73 ¡
altered A73
alternate A75
alternating A94
although G-9 A6 C17 4.88 ¡
alto 6.25
altogether A36 6.50 ¡
[aluminium] K-3
aluminum K-3 A37 8.00 ¡£
alumna; alumnae (women) H-31
alumnae 8.25
alumni 8.25
alumnus; alumni (men) H-31 ¡
Alvin A98
always B-17 A2 C3 4.88 ¡
am B-1 A5 C2 2.08 ¢
amateur I-25 A71 8.88 ¡
amaze 5.38
amazed A62
amazement A70
amazing A40 8.00
Amazon A73
ambition A72 8.00
ambitious H-43 A77 8.75
ambulance C14 6.75
amendment J-45 5.75 ¿
amendments 7.50
America F-35 A5 C17 6.00
America's G-40 A35
American G-35 A4
Americans A11
Americas A98
amid A78
amino A100
ammonia 8.75
ammunition A76
amnesia 8.00
among E-20 A4 4.38 ¡
Amos A99
amount H-16 A9 5.00
amounting 8.50
amounts H-16 A24
amphibian 6.50
amphibians A72
ample 7.88
amplifier K-32 7.00
Amsterdam A82
Amtrak 8.25
amuse A97 6.13
amused A78
amusement H-45 A73 5.69
amusing A60
Amy A61
an A-1 A1 C1 2.25
analogous I-43 ¡
[analyse] H-29
analyses 8.25
analysis A59 9.00 ¡
analyze H-29 A71 7.56 ¡¿£
anatomy 8.75
ancestor A94 8.25
ancestors H-44 A35
anchor A44 6.25
anchored A65
ancient H-28 A10 6.25
and A-1 A1 C1 2.63 ¢
Anderson A69
Andes A70
Andre A93
Andrew A47
Andy A24
Andy's A100
angel A75 5.88 ¡
angels A91 7.25
anger A42 5.50
angle H-29 A16 6.13 ¡
angles I-29 A20 7.25
Anglo-Saxon A82
angriest F-32 6.50
angrily A42
angry F-1 A14 C14 3.88
animal E-29 A5 C7 4.88
animal's A78
animals B-30 A3 C3 4.88
ankle A72 5.63
ankles 7.25
Ann A15
Ann's A74
Anna A37
Anne A51 C11

Key: Letter-## is *Spelling Power* level word is first taught at. A## is usage by adults; C## is usage by children. (#.##) Average grade level word is taught at; ¢ High School Problem Word, ¡ College Problem Word. ¿ Business Problem Word. £ British spelling (alternate) is also in this list. [word] is British spelling. Elementary Problem words are set in **Boldface** type.

Annie A53
anniversary A91 7.94
announce A75 7.13
announced A26
announcement A80 7.00
announcer F-16 C17 7.75
annoy E-18 5.50
annoyance G-18 7.25
annoyed A88
annoying 5.75
annual F-24 A41 5.75 ¡
annually A77
anoint J-18 8.25
anonymous I-43 8.00
another A2 C2 3.75
answer D-22 A3 C10 4.25 ¡
answered F-22 A8
answering A42
answers F-22 A9
ant I-1 A33 3.63
Antarctic J-35 A74 ¿
Antarctica A65
antecedent 8.75
antenna A88 7.67
antennae A86
antennas 8.25
anthem 7.50
anthology 8.50
anthropology 8.50
antibiotic 8.75
anticipate 7.50
antidote 8.75
antifreeze 8.75
antipollution 6.75
antique I-21 7.38
antiseptic 8.67
antisocial 8.50
antitoxin 8.50
Antonio A80
antonym 8.25
ants H-1 A18
anxiety A85 8.25 ¡
anxious A41 8.13
anxiously A48
any B-47 A2 C3 2.56
anybody A26 C17 7.00
anybody's G-40 5.75
anyhow A75 4.38
anymore F-36 C14 5.75
anyone A9 C14 3.63
anything C-36 A5 C6 3.88
anyway A23 C12 5.08
anywhere A22 C17 5.25
apart D-11 A12 C14 5.38
apartment H-45 A27 6.33
apartments A86
apiece A94 7.50
Apollo J-35 A38
apologize 8.00
apology 7.00
apostrophe J-4 A63 7.25 ¿
Appalachian A65
Appalachians A84
apparatus G-11 A60 8.88 ¡¿
apparel 8.25
apparent H-28 A46 8.25 ¡¿
apparently J-26 A33
apparition 7.50
appeal A48 7.00
appealed A91 8.50
appealing A82
appeals A87
appear F-15 A12 6.25
appearance H-44 A20 7.75 ¡¿
appeared H-15 A14 6.50
appearing A72
appears H-15 A18
appendicitis 9.00
appendix 8.38
appendixes 7.75
appetite A73 7.38
applaud H-17 6.88
applause A79 8.25
apple C-1 A16 C5 3.33
apples D-30 A18 C7
applesauce 7.00
appliance 9.00
applicable 8.75
applicant 8.00
application A55 8.75
applications 9.00
applied A28 7.50
applies A72
apply J-1 A33 6.25
applying K-32 A70 7.00
appoint G-18 6.00
appointed J-18 A40 5.50
appointment J-18 A99 6.00
appreciate A64 6.88
appreciated A100 6.75
appreciation A70 8.33
appreciative H-23 9.00
apprentice A85 8.25
approach J-9 A34 6.58
approached J-9 A36
approaches A56
approaching A40
appropriate J-1 A28 8.50 ¡
approval A62 7.00
approve H-23 A100 6.63
approved A78 8.50
approximate A59 8.33
approximately I-26 A32 9.00
Apr. E-41 4.63
apricot 8.75
April B-35 A26 4.19
April Fools' Day 4.67
apron A46 5.42
apt A75
Apt. H-41 4.50
aquarium A53 7.00
AR (Arkansas) F-41
Arab A55
Arabia A66
Arabian A62
Arabic A75
Arabs A50
Arbor Day 5.00
arc A53
arch A89 5.50
archaeologists A89
archeology 7.00
archery 8.25
Archimedes A101
architect A94
architects A87
architecture A57 8.00
arcs A95
Arctic D-35 A81 6.42 ¡
are B-11 A1 C1 2.31
area F-14 A5 5.58
areas A9
aren't A19 C10 4.17
arena A99
Argentina F-35 A64 6.25
argue A62 5.56
argued A60
arguing A94 7.25 ¡
argument H-45 A41 7.31 ¡
arguments A66
arise A60 6.83
arisen 7.75
arising ¡
arithmetic F-3 A29 C14 6.13 ¡
Arizona E-35 A47 5.50
Arkansas E-35 A67 5.75
arm C-11 A11 C12 3.00
armada 8.00
armchair 6.25
armed A38
armies D-32 A42 4.50
armor K-13 A53 5.75 £
arms C-11 A9 C10 3.00
Armstrong A89
army G-11 A13 4.75
aroma 9.00
arose A46
around A-16 A2 C1 3.88 ¡
arouse A100 7.50 ¡
aroused A79
arrange I-24 A25 5.50 ¡
arranged I-6 A19
arrangement H-45 A29 7.33 ¡
arrangements A70 8.50
arranging A82
array A60
arrest A96 6.25
arrested A73 5.75
arrival A53 8.00 ¡
arrive J-1 A28 5.75
arrived F-8 A14 C11
arrives A64
arriving A60
arrow I-24 A23 4.25
arrows A25
art C-11 A15 C12 3.38
artery 8.25
arthritis 8.50
Arthur A35
article I-29 A19 7.63 ¡
articles G-11 A27
artificial A48 8.58
artillery A97
artist G-11 A39 6.75
artistic A71 6.00
artists A42
arts A42
as A-1 A1 C1 2.58
ascend J-28 ¡
ascent 7.75
ascertain I-6 9.00
ash A73
ashamed A66 6.63
ashes A43 7.00
ashore A44 8.25
Asia G-35 A18
Asian A86
aside I-8 A24
ask D-1 A7 C7 2.63
asked B-1 A2 C2 3.00
asking I-1 A31
asks A31 ¡
asleep E-7 A18 C9 4.19
aspect A64
aspects A62
aspiration 8.75
assassin 8.00
assault H-17 7.75
assemble A76 7.00
assembled A59
assemblies I-32 7.25
assembly A41 7.75
asset 7.75
assign 6.88
assigned A52 9.00
assignment I-45 A58 6.81
assignments A88
assist A77 7.00
assistance I-44 A67 7.63
assistant A61 8.42
assistants A98
assisted A98
associate A76 7.69
associated J-1 A38
association H-42 A62 7.50
associations A95
assorted 7.75
assortment 9.00
assume J-10 A37 7.63
assumed A45
assuming A95
assumption A96 8.75
assurance 9.00
assure E-25 A98 6.00
assured A54 8.50
assuring 8.50
asthma 7.50
astonish 8.25
astonished A63
astonishing A76
astonishment I-45 A83 6.75
astride 8.25
astrology 8.25
astronaut H-17 A44 7.58
astronauts A40
astronomer A69
astronomers A44
astronomy A68 8.50
at A-1 A1 C1 1.50
ate D-6 A12 C3 2.50
atheist 8.75
Athens A56
athlete A77 5.25 ¡
athletes A70
athletic A64 8.38 ¡
athletics 7.75
Atlanta A97
Atlantic G-35 A16 6.25
atlas 8.50
atmosphere H-15 A16 7.00
atmospheric A77
atom J-1 A27 8.25
atomic I-4 A24 8.50
atoms I-30 A22
attach A70 5.25
attached I-24 A21
attaching 8.50
attachment J-45 8.75
attack H-1 A18 5.25
attacked G-1 A38 C17 4.50

Alphabetical List

attacking A69
attacks A52
attain A98 7.25
attempt J-2 A29 8.08
attempted A50
attempting A81
attempts A43
attend J-28 A34 4.75
attendance I-44 8.08
attendant J-2 7.25
attended A42
attending A79 5.75
attention F-42 A11 5.58
attentive H-23 8.75
attic A68 4.25
attitude J-1 A33 7.83
attitudes A50
attorney 8.50
attorneys 8.25
attract J-1 A38 6.75
attracted J-1 A36
attraction G-42 A53 7.75
attractive A40 6.75
auction H-17 7.25
audible 8.13
audience I-44 A22 6.67 ¡
audiences A99
audition 7.50
auditions H-17
auditorium K-5 A86 6.75
Aug. E-41 4.63
August B-35 A29 C17 4.19
Augustus A89
aunt C-47 A38 C6 4.75
aunt's 5.00
aunts 6.00
aural 8.50
Australia I-35 A25
Austria A47
Austrian A84
authentic 8.38
author G-17 A23 5.69 ¡
author's A74
authorities I-32 A65 8.25
authority J-13 A37 7.25
authorize H-17 7.63
authorized 9.00
authors A63
auto A79 6.50
autobiography 8.13
autograph 7.56
automatic A44 7.33
automatically A52
automation 9.00
automobile I-29 A19 6.63
automobiles I-9 A26
automotive H-17 7.00
autos 6.25
autumn F-22 A30 6.56
auxiliary A59 8.63 ¡
available I-29 A21 8.75
Ave. E-41 6.17
avenue A52 4.92
average H-1 A14 6.13
averages A93
aviation A95
aviator 7.00
avocado 8.00
avoid E-18 A20 6.13
avoided A57
await 9.00
awaited A89
awaiting A96 5.75
awake J-6 A31 4.56
awakened A48 8.00
award A87 6.25
awarded A71
aware I-14 A25 5.50
awareness A73 7.50
away B-6 A2 C2 2.63
awe A80 7.25
awful C-17 A42 C17 5.25
awfully A65 6.50
awhile E-29 A62 C5 5.00
awkward A49 7.58 ¡
awoke F-9 A59 C14
ax A45 6.25
axe A98
axes A62 8.50
axis A43 8.50
axle A70 6.13
aye A71
AZ (Arizona) F-41

B

babble 7.25
babe A57
babies C-32 A23 C7 3.50
baby B-6 A7 C2 2.42
baby's A73 8.00
baby-sit E-38 5.50
baby-sitter F-38 7.50
Babylon A94
back A-1 A2 C1 3.00
backbone A99
backed A47
background I-36 A31 5.42
backing A85
backs J-1 A37
backward I-36 A31 7.00
backwards A64 5.50
backyard A71 5.00
bacon A47 5.50
bacteria I-15 A36 7.83
bacteriology 8.50
bad B-1 A9 C3 2.00
bade A98
badge 5.50
badly E-26 A26 6.25
badminton 9.00
baffle 7.50
baffling 7.75
bag D-1 A14 C7 2.25
baggage 5.25
bags I-1 A29
Bahamas F-35 6.25
bail 7.75
bait A68 6.50
bake G-6 A56 C17 2.75
baked A43 3.75
baker A63 5.00
bakeries D-32 5.25
bakery A84 7.50
baking A45 4.50
balance H-44 A18 6.83 ¡
balanced A51
balcony A70 9.00
bald A84 5.25
bale 7.75
ball A-17 A5 C3 2.63
ballerina 8.00
ballet G-2 A56 C17 8.25
balloon I-24 A22 3.63
balloons A43
ballot J-24 9.00 ¿
balls I-24 A24
Baltimore A56
bamboo A52 6.75
banana G-1 A54 C17 5.50 ¿
bananas A32
band F-1 A13 C14 3.25
bandage 4.75
bandaging 8.25
bands I-1 A31
bang G-1 A46 C17
banged A87
banging A84
banjo 6.63
bank E-1 A11 C8 2.63
banking 5.50
bankrupt 9.00
bankruptcy K-1 8.63 ¿
banks I-1 A22
banner 5.63
banquet 6.75
bar C-11 A16 C10
Barbados F-35 6.25
Barbara A68
barbarous I-43 ¡¿
barbecue 6.63
barbecued 7.75
barbed wire 6.50
barber A72 4.67
bare F-14 A22 C17 4.25
barefoot 6.25
barely A47 6.38
bargain A63 7.33
barge A85 5.38
barges A65
baring ¡
bark C-11 A21 C11 3.75
barked A62 6.00
barking A59 6.00
barks 5.00
barley A65 7.50
barn B-11 A15 C7 3.69
barns A64 7.50
barnyard 4.50
barometer 8.50
baron F-14 C17
barred A90
barrel A41 5.58
barrels A56
barren A52
barricade 7.75
barrier A64 6.75
barriers A73
barring ¡
bars D-11 A24 C17
Bart A46
Bartholomew A95
Barton A98
base G-6 A7 C17 5.75
baseball B-36 A15 C5 4.50
based H-6 A15 ¡
baseman A92
basement H-45 A69 5.75
bases K-6 A32
basic H-1 A11 5.63
basically A56
basin A58 6.00
basis I-3 A23 7.63
basket A20 C14 3.75
basketball H-37 A34 4.75
baskets I-1 A34 4.00
bass A41 7.25
baste 7.75
bat D-1 A18 C6 2.00
batch 8.25
batches 6.25
Bates A88
bath F-1 A40 C12 3.42
bathe A99 5.38
bathing A78 5.00
bathrobe 7.00
bathroom F-36 A69 C14 5.00
bathtub A86 5.00
batik 7.50
bats G-30 A41 C17
battalion K-1 8.25 ¿
batted 3.00
batter A57 6.00
battered A77
batteries A74 4.92
battery A44
batting A64 3.00
battle G-29 A18 C17 4.67
battles A48
bay J-6 A34
bays A100
bazaar 6.92
BC (British Columbia) F-41
be A-7 A1 C1 1.94
beach C-7 A16 C7 2.88
beaches A54 3.00
beacon 4.75
bead 6.25
beads K-7 A31
beak A67
beam J-7 A32
beams A56
bean F-7 A48 C14 3.38
beans I-7 A24
bear A-14 A10 C2 3.75
beard F-15 A43 C14 4.63
bearing A54 8.50 ¡
bearings A96
bears B-14 A23 C6
beast F-7 A36 C11 4.88
beasts A49
beat E-7 A11 C12 4.50
beaten A50
beating J-7 A32
beats K-7 A38
beautified 7.50
beautiful E-27 A5 C3 4.44
beautifully K-26 A53 6.75
beauty G-10 A15 C14 4.50

Key: Letter-## is *Spelling Power* level word is first taught at. A## is usage by adults; C## is usage by children. (#.##) Average grade level word is taught at; ¢ High School Problem Word, ¡ College Problem Word. ¿ Business Problem Word. £ British spelling (alternate) is also in this list. [word] is British spelling. Elementary Problem words are set in **Boldface** type.

Alphabetical List

beaver F-7 A39 C11
beavers A70
became E-36 A4 C9 5.25
because A-17 A2 C1 3.19 ¢
become E-20 A4 C11 5.17
becomes G-20 A11
becoming D-33 A24 ¡
bed B-2 A7 C2 1.58
bedding A98
bedroom E-36 A34 C10 4.50
beds I-2 A32
bedspread 5.00
bedtime A84 8.00
bee F-7 A35 C12 2.75
beef J-7 A34 6.25
been B-47 A1 C3 2.31
beer F-15 A99 C17
bees E-30 A26 C10
beet 4.42
beetle A69 6.00
beetles A73
beets A68 7.50
before A-13 A2 C3 3.31 ¡
befriend 8.25
beg A-2 A71 3.25
began C-7 A3 C7 4.25
beggar A79 5.58 ¡
begged F-34 A48 5.00
begging A74 ¡
begin H-3 A6 4.00
beginner's luck 5.75
beginning F-34 A5 5.58 ¡
beginnings A61
begins H-3 A9 6.75
begun I-5 A21
behalf 9.00
behave K-7 A36 5.00
behavior J-12 A27 9.00
behind D-7 A4 C7 3.94
behold A89
beige 7.63
being F-7 A3 C14 3.00
beings A32
Belgian A100
Belgium A60
belied A54
belief I-7 7.00
beliefs A57 6.75
believable 7.75
believe G-23 A11 C7 4.69 ¡
believed I-7 A15 8.25
believes A73
believing A83 ¡
Belinda A99
belittle 8.25
bell C-24 A15 C8 2.50
bellow 7.25
bells A25
belly A68
belong H-4 A15 4.08
belonged I-4 A28
belonging A50
belongings A94
belongs I-4 A22
beloved A75
below E-9 A2 C14 4.63
belt G-2 A25 C17 4.38
belts A41
Ben A18
bench J-28 A35 6.00
benches A76 4.25
bend I-2 A27 4.25
bending A56
bends A58
beneath I-7 A15 7.25
beneficial K-28 8.25 ¿
benefit E-28 A48 7.00 ¡
benefited H-2 7.75 ¡¿
benefits A59
benefitted K-34 7.75
Benjamin A33
Benny A93
bent I-2 A21 4.50
beret 8.00
Berlin A72
berries E-32 A39 4.00
berry 5.08
Bert A40
beside C-36 A8 C6 4.31
besides I-30 A13 5.25
Bess A100
Bessie A76
best B-2 A3 C2 2.92
best seller G-39 7.25
best-known A75
bet F-2 A28 C14 5.25
Beth A91
betray 7.25
betrays 8.50
Betsy A23
better A-12 A3 C3 3.67
Betty A37 C10
between E-7 A2 C11 4.08
beverage 8.25
beware I-14 6.00
bewilder 8.25
bewilderment 9.00
beyond H-7 A10 4.00
bi-monthly F-46
bi-weekly F-46
biannual F-46 7.50
Bible D-35 A39
bibliography 8.63
bicentennial F-46 7.50
biceps 8.25
bicycle E-29 A24 C10 5.06
bicycles F-30 A60 C12
bid A76 6.25
bifocal F-46 7.50
bifocals 7.88
big A-3 A2 C1 1.50
bigger B-34 A15 C11 3.00
biggest B-34 A22 C11 4.25
bike B-8 A40 C4 3.00
bikes D-30 C6 1.00
bilingual 8.17
bill A-24 A21 C3
Bill's A44
billboard 6.75
billed 8.50
billing 9.00
billion I-4 A34
billions A62
billow 9.00
bills J-24 A39
Billy A13 C7
Billy's A71
bimonthly 7.75
bin A90
bind A89
binding A72
binoculars 8.38
biographies I-32 7.25
biography A97 7.00
biologists A96
biology A84 8.44
bionic 7.50
birch A74 7.25
birchbark 5.25
bird C-12 A7 C4 3.25
bird's A55
birds B-30 A5 C2 3.75
birds' A83 4.75
birth J-12 A28 4.75
birthday B-36 A19 C3 3.50
birthplace 7.25
biscuit 7.75 ¡
biscuits A80
bisect 7.75
bishop G-20 A93 6.50
bit C-3 A9 C6 2.58
bite F-8 A25 C14 2.83
bites A67 6.50
biting C-33 A64 C17 4.00
bits I-30 A22
Bitsy A78
bitten A79 6.75
bitter J-3 A36 5.50
bitterly A68
bitterness 7.50
biweekly 7.75
bizarre 7.75
black B-1 A4 C2 2.13
blackboard A75 5.00
Blackie C12
blackness A97
blacksmith A79
blade A46 4.25
blades A58
Blake A82
blame A44 6.25
blaming 6.50
Blanche A81
blank I-1 A21 4.63
blanket E-1 A24 C10 4.81
blankets H-30 A33 C17
blanks K-6 A33
blast F-1 A45 C11 4.88
blaze A78 7.00
blazing A66
bleachers 7.25
bleeding A77 8.00
blend J-28 A32 5.88
blends A66
bless 9.00
blessed A91
blessing A94
blew C-10 A22 C10 3.25
blind G-8 A26 C17 3.67
blinded A100
blindfold 5.25
blinking A90
blip G-3 C17
blister 7.00
blizzard 7.25
block D-4 A17 C14 4.81
blockade 7.25
blocked A66
blocks H-4 A17
blood C-20 A9 C7 5.00
bloody A64
bloom A49 4.50
blooming 6.50
blossom A74 5.63
blossoms A47 6.50
blouse A88 6.50
blow E-9 A12 C9 3.00
blowing F-9 A24 C17
blown A40 6.25
blows F-30 A35 C12 2.75
blue B-10 A5 C3 2.19
blue jay D-39 6.50
blueberries 4.50
blueberry 4.50
bluebird 3.75
blues A98
bluff A90 7.75
blunder 5.25
blunt A87
blur 5.50
Blvd. E-41 4.50
board F-13 A10 C14 5.25
boarded A96
boarder A30 7.88
boards I-13 A32
boardwalk 7.25
boast 5.25
boasted A101
boastful I-27 7.75
boat B-9 A6 C3 2.63
boating G-9 C17
boats H-9 A13
Bob A10 C9
Bob's A63
bobbin 9.00
bobbing A99
Bobby A47 C7
bodies D-32 A14 4.50
body A4 C8 3.33
bodyguard 4.75
boil B-18 A51 4.00
boiled A49 7.50
boiler A81
boiling G-18 A36
boils A94
bok choy 8.75
bold A41 4.75
bolder 7.75
boldface A91
boldly A72
Bolivia 6.25
bologna 7.13
bolt A65 4.75
bolted A90
bomb E-22 A55 C14 6.06
bombard 7.25
bombs A74
bonanza 8.17
bond A74 8.50
bondage 8.50
bonds A78 8.50
bone H-9 A19 2.63
bones H-30 A11 C17 4.50
bonnet 8.00
bonus 8.13
bony A64
boo G-10 C17
book B-19 A4 C7 2.50
bookkeeper 8.50
bookkeeping 8.25

booklet 5.50
books D-19 A6 C14 4.50
bookstore 7.75
boom A54 5.25
boomerang 6.75
booming A77
Boone A71
boost 5.38
booster 8.25
boot A-10 A73 3.58
booth A84 5.17
boots I-10 A25
border J-13 7.00
borders A52
bore K-13 A42 5.63
bored A59 6.75
boredom 7.83
boring A87
born D-13 A9 C8 3.75
borne A95
borrow A44 5.75
borrowed I-9 A31 5.75
borrowing A97
boss C-24 A45 C8 3.75
bossy 6.50
Boston C-35 A19 C6
botanist 8.73
both D-9 A2 C7 2.94
bother G-12 A42 C17 5.75
bothered G-20 A78 6.50
bottle H-29 A15 4.13
bottles J-4 A34
bottom D-4 A6 C7 5.31
bough 6.42
bought B-17 A4 C4 4.19
bouillon 8.88
boulder 7.75
boulders A82
boulevard 8.50
bounce A62 4.50
bounced A72
bouncing A76 5.50
bound H-16 A25 6.50
boundaries G-32 A56 ¡
boundary A50 7.75
bounded A82
bouquet I-21 8.00
boutique 8.58
bow H-9 A18 3.75
bowed A55
bowl H-9 A16 3.67
bowling A-9 A73 3.75
bowls A55 8.00
bows A71 6.50
box B-4 A5 C4 1.83
box's 5.75
boxer A100
boxes H-30 A16 3.58
boxing A98 3.75
boy B-18 A3 C2 2.67
boy's G-40 A24 C12 5.25
boycott 7.13
boyhood A87
boys B-18 A3 C3
boys' G-40 A72 5.75
bracelet 7.50
braces A92

bracket 9.00
brackets 7.25
Bradford A78
bragging F-34 5.75
braid 6.25
braiding 7.75
Braille 9.00
brain F-6 A18 C12 6.50
brains A60
brainstorm 6.50
brake A52 5.42
brakes H-30 A50 C17
branch I-1 A19
branches F-30 A14 C11 3.58
brand A58 5.25
brand-new E-38 6.13
brass H-24 A28 6.75
brave I-6 A18 3.94
bravely A68 7.50
bravery A95
braves A100
bravest 8.00
Brazil A43 6.25
Brazilian A97
bread E-47 A11 C11 3.88
break E-6 A10 C9 4.17
breakable 9.00
breakfast C-36 A13 C7 3.88
breaking A28
breaks J-47 A33
breast A59
breath G-47 A14 4.31
breathe G-7 A27 C17 5.75 ¡
breathed A65
breathes A78
breathing I-7 A22 8.26
breathless A82 5.88
breathlessly A101
breed A68
breeding A81
breeze A30 C12 5.00
breezes A79
brevity 8.75
brew 5.25
Brewster A96
Brian A100
brick I-3 A30 4.25
bricks J-3 A39 5.00
bridal 8.50
bride A60
bridge E-3 A18 C10 4.75
bridges K-3 A36
bridle A79 6.50
brief J-7 A28 6.67
briefly A50
bright C-8 A7 C8 3.42
bright-colored A90 £
[bright-coloured]
brighten 5.75
brighter A59
brightest A95
brightly J-26 A37
brightness A73
brilliance J-44 7.75
brilliant A33 7.88 ¡
bring D-3 A5 C6 2.81
bringing I-3 A25

brings I-3 A28
brisk A89
briskly A92
bristle 6.25
Britain G-35 A33 C17 ¡
Britannica ¡
British D-35 A10 C14
British Columbia G-39 7.00
Brittany Ann 1.43
brittle A85
broad G-47 A16 5.88
broadcast A66 7.75
broadcasting A77
Broadway A75
broccoli 7.67
brochure I-25 8.42
broil J-18 4.58
broke C-9 A13 C5 4.25
broken E-28 A9 C11 4.50
bronco 7.50
broncos 8.38
bronze A53 6.75
brook D-19 A54 C17 4.08
Brooklyn A71
broom A-10 A46 4.17
broth 7.25
brother A-20 A9 C2 2.44
brother's G-40 A70 C14 5.75
brother-in-law G-38 6.75
brother; brethren F-31
brothers E-30 A14 C9
brothers' G-40 5.75
brothers-in-law G-38 8.25
brought B-17 C3 4.50
brow A76
brown C-16 A10 C4 2.13
brownie 8.00
brownish 6.00
browse 7.50
Bruce A66
bruise 5.25
bruised A94
brunch 5.38
brunette 9.00
brush I-5 A24 3.33
brushed A45
brushes A78 4.63
brushing A76
bubble G-29 A56 C17 4.75
bubbles A42
bubbling A88 7.75
buck A90
bucket I-5 A35 4.63
buckets K-5 A65 5.00
buckle 7.50
buckskin A98
Bucky A88
bud A41
buddies 3.75
budge 6.00
budget K-5 A92 6.50 ¿
buds A57 8.00
buffalo F-5 A24 C11
buffaloes A56 5.75
buffet 7.88
bug C-5 A65 C11 2.08
buggy A70 3.25

bugle A70 6.25
bugs F-30 A59 C12
build D-47 A6 C8 3.75
builder A93
builders A69
building D-47 A6 C10 4.50
buildings H-30 A12 C17
builds A55 7.50
built E-47 A5 C14 4.25
built-in A100
bulb K-5 A33 4.75
bulbs A77 7.00
bulk A88
bulky A100
bull C-24 A45 C7 4.75
bulldog E-36 C17
bulldozer 5.50
bullet A55 6.75
bulletin K-5 A71 5.50
bulletin board G-39 8.25
bullets A71
bump A71 3.92
bumped F-5 A65 C14
bumping A95
bumps A94
bumpy F-5 C17
bun A-5 2.25
bunch D-5 A38 C12 5.25
bunches A79 4.88
bundle A40 6.88
bundles A44
bunk C17 5.25
bunnies 8.00
bunny F-5 C11
Bunyan A96
buoy A86
buoyance ¿
buoyant 8.25 ¡
burden A69 5.92
bureau F-47 A55 6.88 ¡
bureaus K-47 ¿
burglar 6.58
buried E-32 A28 C17 5.25
burlap 9.00
burn A24 C11 3.75
burned H-12 A18 4.00
burning G-12 A17 C17
burns A41
burnt A68 5.75
burro A63 7.50
burrow A65
burst I-12 A23 4.67
bursting A76
bury A66 5.08
bus B-5 A14 C5 1.83
buses A55 3.58
bush D-19 A34 C14 3.38
bushel 6.50
bushels A85
bushes A23 C17 3.92
bushy A92
busier G-32 6.50
busily F-32 A92 6.75
business G-24 A8 C17 6.13 ¡¿
businesses A63 9.00
businessman A86
businessmen A66

Key: Letter-## is *Spelling Power* level word is first taught at. A## is usage by adults; C## is usage by children. (#.##) Average grade level word is taught at; ¢ High School Problem Word, ¡ College Problem Word. ¿ Business Problem Word. £ British spelling (alternate) is also in this list. [word] is British spelling. Elementary Problem words are set in **Boldface** type.

busy D-47 A10 C9 4.25 ¡
but A-5 A1 C1 1.75
butcher F-12 A80 C17 6.50
butter I-24 A21 3.63
butterflies A45 3.38
butterfly E-36 A46 C14
button J-24 A31 4.69
buttons G-5 A35 C17
buttress 8.00
buy D-8 A7 C6 2.94
buyer A88
buying I-8 A44 4.50
buys A67 7.50
buzz J-24 A83 3.75
buzzed A100
buzzing A61
by A-8 A1 C1 2.38
by-line 8.25
by-product 8.50
by-products F-38 8.25
bye D-8 C9
byte 6.25

C

C.O.D. H-41 8.25
CA (California) F-41
cab A59
cabbage J-1 A33 5.33
cabin E-1 A13 C9 5.08
cabinet A63 7.33
cabins A56 4.00
cable A65 4.25
cablegram 8.25
cables A60
cacti 5.75
cactus A48 9.00
cactus; cacti H-31
Caddie A82
Cadillac A72
Caesar A77
cafeteria 7.75
cage E-6 A20 C10 3.92
cages A67
Cairo A100
cake D-6 A19 C7 2.58
cakes K-6 A32
calcium A73
calculate A83
calculated A74
calculator 8.00
calendar E-28 A54 7.06 ¡¿
calf F-1 A32 C11 4.08
Calgary C-35 C5
calico A93
California E-35 A13 5.67
calisthenics 8.00
call A-17 A4 C4 2.94
called B-17 A1 C2 3.00
calling C-17 A21 C11
callous 8.50
calls A20
callus 8.50
calm C-17 A29 C17 6.13
calmly A67
calories A78 7.25
calves D-31 A62 C17 5.38
came A-6 A2 C1 1.88
camel A47 5.00
camels A52 5.00
cameo 8.00
cameos 9.00
camera J-12 A28 5.25
cameras A51
camouflage 8.00
camp C-1 A13 C4 3.38
campaign K-6 A45 7.58 ¿
camped A95 6.50
camper 5.38
campfire A66 3.75
camping E-1 A48 C8 3.75
camps A60 8.00
campsite 7.63
campus 7.17
can A-1 A1 C1 1.31
can't B-37 A5 C4 3.56 ¡
Canada C-35 A19 C7 6.25
Canadian A46
Canadians F-35 C17
canal J-29 A29
canals A50 7.00
canary A93 6.00
cancel H-29 8.50
canceled 8.50 £
canceling 7.25 £
cancellation J-42 7.50 ¿
[cancelled]
[cancelling]
cancer A85
candidate A56 8.00 ¡
candidates A80
Candita A70
candle J-29 A32 4.75
candles A43
candy D-1 A19 C7 3.42
cane K-6 A36 3.88
canned A59 8.00
canning 4.50
cannon A40 5.13
cannot F-36 A4 C11 3.25
canoe G-20 5.38
canoes A52
cans F-30 A33 C14
cantaloupe 9.00
canvas A48 8.08
canvass 8.50
canyon A46 6.38
canyons A75
cap I-1 A21 1.25
capable A41 6.75
capacity A53 6.75
cape A101 4.25
capillaries 8.75
capital H-29 A10 7.06
capitalized A93
capitals A95
capitol A82 6.25
caps A47 6.0
capsule A54 7.50
captain G-1 A14 C17 5.31
captains A99 7.00
captive 7.13
captivity 9.00
capture G-25 A39 5.08
captured G-25 A28
car B-11 A4 C2 2.69
caramel 5.25
caravan 9.00
caraway 6.50
carbohydrates A83
carbon G-11 A21 5.63
carburetor I-25 ¿£
[carburettor] I-25
card D-11 A21 C18 3.50
cardboard H-37 A31 4.50
Cardinal A83
cards G-11 A24 5.00
care B-14 A6 C8 3.83
cared A-14 A49 3.63
career I-15 A36 6.75
carefree 6.13
careful A12 4.81 ¡
carefully H-26 A5 6.13
careless A51 5.81
carelessly A92
carelessness 7.75
cares A73
cargo H-11 A39
cargoes A91 6.25
Caribbean F-35 A69 6.25
caribou A80 7.63
caring A90 4.50
Carl A47
carloads 7.50
Carlos A24
carnival E-29 A70 5.33
Carol A52
carols 7.00
carpenter A58 7.00
carpenters A98
carpentry 7.00
carpet H-11 A56 5.00
carriage I-14 A34 6.50
carriages A86
carried E-32 A6 5.08
carrier A67
carries I-24 A23 3.00
Carroll A94
carrot F-14 A66 C17 5.75
carrots F-14 A75 C18
carry F-14 A6 C12 3.19
carrying F-14 A12 4.00 ¡
cars B-30 A8 C3
cart H-11 A32 4.50
Carter A54
carton A55 6.63
cartons A92
cartoon 7.42
cartridge 7.50
carts A69
cartwheel 5.75
carve A90 5.50
carved H-11 A39
carving A91
case F-6 A8 C12 4.63
cases I-30 A16
Casey A30
cash F-1 A39 C14 5.00
cashier 7.83
cassette 7.00
cast G-1 A29 C18 6.25
casting A87
castle E-29 A25 C7 5.19
castles A74
casts A101
casual A86
casualty 6.00
cat B-1 A9 C2 1.83
cat's A88 5.75
catalog 7.25 £
catalogs 9.00 £
[catalogue]
[catalogues]
cataract 8.75
catastrophe K-1 8.83 ¿
catch C-1 A8 C5 2.88
catcher K-12 A69 4.25
catches A41
catching J-1 A36
categories A95
category A90 8.75
caterpillar A63 7.50
caterpillars A91
catfish A92
cathedral A86
Catholic A65
cats B-30 A21 C5
cattle G-29 A9 C14 5.00
caucus 8.75
caught B-17 A7 C2 3.00
cauliflower 8.50
cause A10 C18 4.19
caused G-17 A14
causes G-17 A20
causing A43
caution A70 6.33
cautious I-43 8.38
cautiously A63
cave A-23 A18 C3 4.25
cavern A94 7.75
caves A53 6.00
cavities D-32 4.75
cavity A89
cease A87 6.25
ceased A67
cedar A80 6.67
ceiling J-7 A32 6.00 ¡¿
celebrate A68 5.58
celebrated A65 7.00
celebration K-42 A54 5.88
celery E-29 A86 4.50
cell H-24 A20
cellar H-11 A45 5.13
cello 7.88
cells I-30 A13
cellulose A95
cement H-45 A43 5.50
cemetery K-2 8.25 ¡¿
censorship 8.50
census 7.25
cent H-2 A14 4.42
center G-12 A6 C17 4.17 £
centered A86 £
centers I-28 A30
centigrade 8.75
centigram 5.75
centiliter F-46 6.50 £
[centilitre] F-46
centimeter F-46 6.00 £
[centimetre] F-46
central I-29 A19 4.75
[centre] G-12
[centred]
[centres] I-28
cents (money) F-2 A17 C14
centuries E-32 A15
century H-28 A10 6.25
ceramics 7.75
cereal A67 6.19
ceremonies A82
ceremony A60 8.00

Alphabetical List

certain H-12 A4 4.25 ¡
certainly H-26 A13
certificate 7.00
certificates 9.00
chain I-6 A22 3.88
chains A51 6.50
chair B-14 A12 C9 2.75
chairman A59 8.50
chairs A29 C12
chalet 8.25
chalk A60 5.58
chalkboard A57 5.63
challenge J-28 A36 7.17
challenged A77
challenging A85
chamber J-12 A28
chambers A93
champion A44 6.42
championship 7.00
chance G-1 A9 C18 4.63
chances A42
chandelier I-15 7.42
change C-6 A3 C3 3.92
changeable 7.75 ¡
changed G-6 A7 C17
changes A7
changing D-33 A13 4.50 ¡
channel A51 6.06
channels A77
chant A97
chaos 7.83
chap 7.75
chapel A98 6.25
chaperon 8.25
chapter H-1 A16 6.38
chapters A58
character G-11 A20 7.44
characteristic F-14 A31 8.63 ¡
characteristics A25
characterize 9.00
characterized A84
characters I-14 A28
charcoal A68 7.38
charge G-11 A17 5.25
charged H-11 A29
charges A42
charging 9.00
chariot A89
charitable I-14 7.75
charity 7.17
Charles A20
Charley A77
Charlie A36 C12
Charlotte A71
charm A55 5.50
charming A51 8.00
chart G-11 A15 5.50
charter 8.25
charts A41
chase F-6 A41 C11 2.94
chased F-6 A49 C12 3.88
chases 6.75
chasing A54 4.50
chasm 7.25
chat 4.50
chatter A72
chattering A72

chauffeur G-13 7.25 ¡¿
cheap A53 5.00
cheaper A88 9.00
cheat 6.25
check H-2 A6
checkbook 7.00 £
checked G-2 A28 C18
checkers A101 5.50
checking A47 4.50
checkmate 6.50
checks A53 8.50
Cheddar 8.25
cheek A-7 A46 3.38
cheeks A40
cheer B-15 A42 4.63
cheered A70
cheerful E-27 A41 5.58
cheerfully A62
cheering A58
cheerleader 6.58
cheers A91
cheese I-7 A22 3.33
cheeseburger 6.50
cheetah 8.00
chef 7.25
chef's 6.50
chemical I-29 A17 5.88
chemicals K-29 A37
chemist K-2 A82 8.38
chemistry A55 7.25
chemists A80
[chequebook]
cherish 8.25
cherished A94
cherries E-32 A56 C18 4.06
cherry B-14 A44 C10 3.25
cherub; cherubim H-31
chess 7.25
chest I-2 A21 5.00
Chester A77
chests A88
Chet A83
chew G-10 A62 C18 3.50
chewed A75
chewing A48
chic 8.25
Chicago D-35 A21 C10
chicken E-28 A21 C6 4.81
chicken pox D-39 5.75
chicken's 8.00
chickens H-3 A20
chicks A93 6.50
chief D-7 A12 C17 4.69 ¡
chiefly J-26 A34
chiefs A70
child F-8 A8 C14 3.56
child's A47
child; children F-31
childhood A50 5.50
childish 6.38
children A3 C3 2.38
children's A42 6.50
Chile A58 6.25
chili F-35 A63
chili con carne 7.63
chill E-3 2.25
chilly A85

chimney A47 8.13
chimneys A86 6.13
chimpanzee 8.75
chin J-3 A35 2.33
China G-35 A17
Chinese G-35 A15
chip C-3 3.25
chipmunk 7.00
chips A69
chirp 6.75
chivalry 7.25
chlorine A91
chlorophyll A88 7.75
chocolate D-4 A31 C10 5.33
choice E-18 A22 4.33
choices A72
choicest 8.50
choir A89 6.38
choke 5.25
choked A99
choking A95
choose H-10 A8 4.50 ¡
chooses A98
choosing A48
chop A-4 A85 2.83
chop suey G-39 8.75
chopped A89 5.00
chopping F-34 4.00
chorale 8.50
chord A53 6.75
chords A53
chore K-13 4.83
choreography 8.88
chores A56 6.50
chorus A52 6.08
chose I-9 A30 4.58 ¡
chosen H-9 A20 5.42 ¡
chow mein G-39 8.00
chowder 7.00
Chris A73
Chris's 4.75
Christ A95
Christian J-35 A35
Christianity A67
Christians A69
Christmas C-35 A12 C4 4.67
Christopher A54
chrome 6.88
chromosome 8.75
chromosomes A79
chronic 8.88
chronology 9.00
chronometer 8.75
Chuck A77
chuckle 7.50
chuckled A70
chunks A59
church F-12 A12 C12 4.13
churches A43 3.63
churn 5.50
cider 6.63
cigar A83
cigarette A70
cigarettes A99
Cindy C7
cinema 8.63
cinnamon A101 5.50

circle G-29 A7 C18 4.00
circled A52
circles J-30 A28
circling A65
circuit K-12 A38 8.00
circular A46 7.13
circulate 8.25
circulation A75 8.75
circumference K-44 A64 7.75
circumnavigate 7.75
circumstance K-44 8.25
circumstances A47 8.5
circus F-12 A22 C11 3.75
circuses 3.25
cite 8.50
cities C-32 A7 C12 5.50
citizen J-28 A37 5.75
citizens I-28 A22
citrus A99 9.00
city C-3 A3 C4 3.75
city's A73
civil A48 6.25
civilian 7.75
civilization I-42 A35 7.88
civilizations A98
civilize 7.38
civilized A62
claim K-6 A33 5.75
claimed G-6 A42 C18
claims A62
clam A70
clamp 5.00
clams A63
clap B-1 A96 2.25
clapped A65
clapping A90
Clara A55
Clarence A74
clarify 8.00
clarity A92 8.75
Clark A41
class C-24 A5 C8 2.42
classes A26 3.25
classic A70 8.50
classical A75 7.00
classification A80
classified A45 8.25
classify A56
classifying G-32 8.50
classmate 6.63
classmates I-36 A34
classroom E-36 A22 C18 3.25
clatter A93
Claus A77
clause H-17 A62 6.88
clauses A79
claw A95 5.25
claws J-30 A30
clay H-6 A18 3.63
clean D-7 A10 C7 3.19
cleaned F-7 A35 C14
cleaner A81
cleaners A91
cleaning A40
cleanse 6.25
clear B-15 A7 C14 3.67
cleared H-15 A29

Alphabetical List

Key: Letter-## is *Spelling Power* level word is first taught at. A## is usage by adults; C## is usage by children. (#.##) Average grade level word is taught at; ¢ High School Problem Word, ¡ College Problem Word. ¿ Business Problem Word. £ British spelling (alternate) is also in this list. [word] is British spelling. Elementary Problem words are set in **Boldface** type.

clearer A72
clearing I-15 A37
clearly H-26 A15
clerk I-12 A37 5.69
Cleveland A71
clever J-12 A31 5.38
click A81 7.00
clicking A101
cliff E-24 A39 C9 5.25
cliffs A57
climate H-8 A16 5.13
climates A55
climax A87 8.25
climb E-22 A17 C8 3.50
climbed A12 C12 4.00
climbing A33 C14 4.25
climbs A71
cling A74
clinging A67
clinic 7.00
Clinton A89
clip A94 7.75
clipper A95
clipping A101
clips A99
clique 7.00
cloak A70
clock C-4 A15 C11 4.50
clocks A47
clockwise 8.00
close F-9 A4 C13 3.33
close-up G-38 7.88
closed G-9 A9 C17 4.50
closely H-26 A15
closeness 5.75
closer D-12 A13 C8 4.50
closes A67
closest A43 4.50
closet F-4 A48 C14 5.31
closing F-33 A35 4.00
cloth H-4 A12 3.67
clothes C-9 A9 C7 6.00 ¡
clothing H-9 A16 4.50
cloud F-16 A17 C14 3.88
cloudburst 5.00
cloudiness G-32 6.50
clouds F-16 A11 C17
cloudy A59 7.50
clout 8.50
clover A45 5.33
clown C-16 A57 C8 3.50
clowns A88 8.00
club F-5 A20 C12 3.92
clubs A50 5.50
clue J-10 A35 4.56
clues J-10 A34
clump A74
clumsy K-5 A58 5.38
clung A64
cluster A54
clusters A59
clutch A93 5.75
clutched A97
clutching A99
Clyde A73
CO (Colorado) F-41
Co. H-41 7.00
coach D-9 A29 C13 4.75
coaches A88 5.00
coal I-29 A14 4.75
coalition 6.75
coals A70
coarse J-13 A53 6.75 ¡
coast G-9 A10 4.75
coastal A50 7.75
coasting 6.00
coastline A87
coasts A70
coat D-9 A13 C7 2.56
coated A81
coating A65
coats I-9 A34
coauthor I-46 7.75
coaxed 7.00
cocked A101
cocoa A69 5.17
coconut A55 6.50
coconuts A81
cocoon A88 7.25
cod A98
code J-9 A31 5.25
coexist I-46 6.75
coffee F-4 A16 C14 5.13
coffin A100
coil E-18 A65 5.38
coiled A89
coin E-18 A35 C17 4.00
coincide 8.75
coincidence J-44 7.13
coins G-18 A32
cold B-9 A4 C4 2.56
cold front G-39 7.63
colder A42
coldest A89 6.00
colds 7.50
coliseum 7.00
collaborate 7.42
collage 7.00
collapse 6.25
collapsed 5.75
collapsible 9.00
collar A41 5.17
collect I-24 A24 5.17
collected J-24 A27
collectible 9.00
collecting A50 8.00
collection G-42 A22 5.75
collections A64
collective A92
collector A80
collects A63
college I-24 A22 7.25 ¿
colleges A73 8.00
collide 7.08
collie 8.00
collision 7.13
cologne 9.00
Colombia 6.00
colon 7.75
colonel A43 7.38
colonial A41
colonies E-32 A23
colonist 6.00
colonists E-32 A35
colony I-4 A26 5.75
color D-13 A8 C8 3.33 £
Colorado E-35 A38 5.63
colored E-20 A15
colorful E-27 A36 C18 5.33 £
coloring A59 7.50 £
colorless A97 £
colors G-13 A13 C17 £
colossal J-4 7.75 ¿
[colour] D-13
[colourful] E-27
[colouring]
[colourless]
[colours] G-13
colt F-9 A38 C11 4.58
colts A99
Columbia F-35 A47
Columbus I-35 A25
Columbus Day 4.50
column F-22 A12 6.69 ¡
columnist 8.38
columns J-4 A32
coma 8.00
comb C-22 A51 4.08
combat A81
combed A88
combination G-42 A24 6.75
combinations H-42 A32
combine I-8 A23 6.75
combined I-4 A22
combines A49
combining A50
combustion A101
come A-20 A2 C1 2.58
comedian 8.25
comedy A101 6.63
comes C-20 A4 C5 6.75
comet G-2 C18 6.00
comets A96
comfort J-13 A34 5.13
comfortable A24 6.38
comfortably A64
comic A69
comical 7.50
comics 5.00
coming B-33 A5 C3 3.00 ¢¡
comma A67
command A27 4.75
commanded A65
commander A44 7.75
commandment 7.00
commands A95
commas A59
commencement 9.00
comment I-45 A69 6.75
commentary 7.75
commented A97
commerce A54 7.00
commercial J-29 A33 7.88
commission J-42 A49 8.38 ¡
commit I-46 8.50
commitment J-45 8.00 ¿
committed A98 7.00 ¡
committee H-4 A34 7.06 ¡¿
committees A84
commodity 8.50
common H-4 A5 4.94
commonly J-26 A33
commonplace A82
commotion 7.42
communicate A42 7.88
communication H-42 A31
communications A54
Communist A48
Communists A64
communities G-32 A34 8.25
community G-10 A14 C14 7.0
community's G-40 8.25
commute 7.25
commuter 7.00
compact A63
companies G-32 A25 4.75
companion A45 6.50
companions A41
companionship 8.00
company G-20 A14 5.75
company's 9.00
comparable A91 8.00
comparative A81 ¡
comparatively J-26 A72 ¡
compare I-46 A11 6.63
compared D-33 A26
compares A90
comparing A47
comparison I-46 A33 9.00
comparisons A70
compartment I-45 A101 6.00
compass H-24 A26
compassion 8.38
compel 9.00 ¡
compelled 8.00 ¡
compensation 8.63
compete A78 7.00
competent I-4 8.75 ¡
competition F-42 A52 C18 7.88
competitive 8.00
competitor 8.25
complain A78 6.44
complained A58
complaint 8.50
complement A58 7.50
complementary J-45 8.50
complete I-46 A5 5.83
completed I-4 A24
completely H-26 A14 8.00
completes A72
completing A88
complex I-2 A23 5.50
complexion 8.25
compliance 9.00
complicate 7.75
complicated J-4 A29
complication 7.75
compliment I-45 7.50
complimentary J-45 8.50
comply 8.50
complying 9.00
compose A72 6.58
composed I-4 A24
composer A63 7.50
composers A67
composition I-46 A18 7.63
compositions A47
compound I-46 A14 6.38
compounds H-16 A30
comprehension 7.75
compress 9.00
compressed A63
compression 7.38
compromise A90 8.25
compulsory 9.00
compute I-46 A95 6.75
computer I-46 A53 5.75
computers A60
comrades A77
conceal 7.00

Alphabetical List

concealed A93
concede J-4 9.00 ¡¿
conceit 7.00
conceited 7.38
conceivable ¡
conceive H-7 8.50 ¡
conceived A86
concentrate I-46 A75 8.50
concentrated A56
concentration A71 6.83
concept 8.75
concepts A42
concern A37 6.42
concerned I-12 A23
concerning A44
concerns A85
concert A53 7.00
concession G-42
concise 8.25
conclude A69 6.75
concluded A71
conclusion J-42 A33 7.58
conclusions A59
Concord A81
concrete A42 7.25
condemn 7.25
condemnation 8.50
condition G-42 A22 6.33
conditions I-46 A14
condominium 6.75
conduct A46 8.75
conducted A55
conductor A44 8.25
conductors A87
cone C-9 A42 4.50
cones A54 7.50
confederate A75
confederation 7.50
confer 8.50
conference J-44 A77 7.63
conferred ¡
conferring K-34 7.25
confess 6.63
confessed 7.00
confession J-42 6.92
confetti 8.25
confidant 8.25
confide 7.25
confidence A44 7.75
confident K-28 A69 7.75 ¿
confidential 9.00
confined I-46 A76 6.25
confirm 7.00
confirmed A96
conflict A37 6.75
conflicts A100
conform A83 8.25
conformity 9.00
confront 6.75
confuse I-46 A89 6.08
confused A50
confusing A85
confusion K-42 A42 6.38
Congo A62
congratulate 9.00
congratulations I-46 8.25
congress I-46 A18 6.25
congruent A101
conjecture I-25 9.00
conjunction I-46 A94 9.00
conjunctive 8.75
connect A44 7.08
connected I-24 A24
Connecticut E-35 A48 6.00
connecting A43
connection A48 6.75
connections 9.00
connective A97
connects A84
connoisseur I-25 8.75
conquer I-21 A62 7.13 ¡
conquered A45
conqueror I-21 ¡
conquerors A98
conquest A74
conscience H-44 A71 7.58 ¡¿
conscientious I-43 8.75 ¡¿
conscious H-43 A57 7.63 ¡
consciousness A93 7.75
consecutively K-26 ¿
consensus F-33 ¿
consent A70 6.63
consequence A93 8.88
consequences A83
consequently A68 8.50
conservation G-42 A68 7.44
conservative 8.50
conserve H-23 8.75
consider H-3 A15 6.38
considerable A33 7.92
considerably A56 8.50
considerate 6.75
consideration G-42 A57 7.75
considered I-3 A14 ¡
considering A53 7.50
consist I-46 A50 6.38
consisted A66
consistent J-28 A100 ¡
consisting A52
consists I-30 A22
consolation 8.25
console 8.38
consonant I-4 A25 6.75
consonants A44
conspicuous J-43 9.00 ¿
conspiracy 8.92
constant I-4 A28 5.50
constantly I-26 A29
constituents A97
constitute A89
constitution I-42 A37 6.42
construct K-5 A34 6.75
constructed A42
construction G-42 A23 7.88
consuls general 8.25
consult A68 6.75
consume I-46 8.75
consumer 7.33
contact A34 6.75
contact lens G-39 7.00
contagious J-43 6.75
contain I-46 A11 6.50
contained J-4 A28
container A46
containers A85
containing I-46 A20
contains I-46 A11
contaminate 8.50
contemporary A56 8.25
contempt A94
content J-28 A33 6.00
contented A88
contents A49 9.00
contest D-4 A31 C14 6.50
contestant I-46 8.13
contests A79
context A63
continent I-28 A21 5.75
continental A62 8.50
continents J-28 A34
continual 7.88
continually A51
continue I-46 A16 6.00
continued H-3 A12
continues J-4 A34
continuing A53
continuous H-43 A39 8.25 ¡
continuously A90
contour A82
contract A41 6.58
contraction A55 8.75
contractions A79
contractor 8.75
contracts A91 9.00
contradict 8.75
contradiction 8.75
contrary A51 8.50
contrast J-4 A30
contrasting A81
contrasts A86
contribute A66 6.75
contributed A44
contribution A59 7.75
contributions A53
control G-29 A10 C12 6.58 ¡
controlled K-34 A36 8.50 ¡
controller 8.25
controlling A89
controls K-29 A38
controversial 9.00
controversy K-12 8.75 ¿
convenience I-44 A68 9.00 ¡
convenient A45
convention A68 8.00
conventional A69
conversation A22 6.83
conversations A78
converse 8.63
convert A71 8.88
converted A59
convertible 8.13
convey A75
conveyed 7.50
convict 6.00
conviction 5.88
convince I-46 A59 6.00
convinced A43
convincing A83
convoy 6.00
cook B-19 A20 C12 3.00
cooked A44
cookie A79 4.00
cookies C-32 A29 C11 3.88
cooking D-19 A27
cookout 5.00
cooks A73 8.00
cool G-29 A10 C12 2.75
cooled J-10 A37
cooler A46
cooling A62
cools A57
Cooper A94
cooperate A99 7.31 ¡
cooperation K-42 A73 6.75
cooperative A95 8.75
coordinate A89 8.50
coordination 7.38
cop A97
copied A98 8.00
copies I-32 A63 6.08
copper H-4 A17 4.50
copy H-4 A8 3.75
copying A98
copyright 8.00
coral A43 8.00
cord J-13 A35 6.08
cordial 7.67
cordially 9.00
cords A65
corduroy 7.33
core A52
cork A61 5.25
corn G-13 A10 C17 3.42
corner D-13 A9 C10 4.81
corners I-13 A28
cornet 7.38
cornfield A68
coronet 7.38
corp. H-41 8.25
corporal 7.75
corporation 8.13
Corps A84
corpuscle 8.25
corral A60 8.00
correct H-13 A7 6.00
corrected A64 8.50
correction K-42 6.00
correctly H-26 A14
correspond A93 8.25
correspondence K-44 A86 8.50
correspondent 9.00
corresponding J-13 A35
corresponds A97
corridor A93 7.63
corrode 7.25
corrugated K-13 ¿
corrupt 8.38
corruption 8.00
corsage 8.00
Cortez A98
[cosier]
cosmic 8.25
cost C-4 A11 C10 3.25
Costa Rica 6.25
costliest K-32 7.50
costly A62
costs J-4 A31
costume A44 5.58

Alphabetical List

Key: Letter-## is *Spelling Power* level word is first taught at. A## is usage by adults; C## is usage by children. (#.##) Average grade level word is taught at; ¢ High School Problem Word, ¡ College Problem Word. ¿ Business Problem Word. £ British spelling (alternate) is also in this list. [word] is British spelling. Elementary Problem words are set in **Boldface** type.

costumes A46
[cosy]
cottage F-4 A44 C14 4.75
cotton H-24 A11 4.50
couch A77 4.56
cougar 8.25
cough G-17 A79 C17 4.63
could B-19 A1 C1 2.75
could've J-37 4.50
couldn't B-37 A7 C3 4.42
council K-29 A38 6.94 ¿
[councillor]
councilor 7.00 £
counsel J-29 7.67 ¡¿
[counsellor]
counselor 7.63 £
count F-16 A12 C14 3.81
countdown 7.00
counted H-16 A28
counter J-12 A38 6.25
[counter-revolution]
counteract 8.50
counterattack 8.50
counterfeit 8.56
counterrevolution 8.50 £
counters A85
counting H-16 A24 4.25
countless A49 5.92
countries E-32 A8 C18 5.25
countries' 8.25
country C-47 A3 C7 5.00 ¡
country's A35
countrymen A91
countryside A42
counts A75 8.00
county A46 5.00
couple G-29 A23 C12 4.67
couplet 9.00
coupon 6.92
courage I-13 A21 6.50
courageous I-43 A77 7.63
course B-13 A4 C6 5.13 ¡
courses A53 9.00
court G-13 A19 7.08
courteous H-43 A98 8.25 ¡
courtesy F-13 A75 6.38 ¡
courthouse A97
courts A46
courtyard A58
cousin C-47 A38 C7 4.63
cousins E-47 A61 C12 ¢
cover E-20 A9 4.08
covered E-20 A6 C17 5.75
covering I-12 A25
covers G-20 A23 3.25
cow C-16 A18 C4 2.63
coward A83 6.44
cowboy A22 C17
cowboy's A100
cowboys F-36 A27 C18
cower 6.50
cows F-16 A16 C6
coyote A85 7.00
coyotes A67
cozier 7.50 £
cozy A86 5.25 £
crab A52
crabs A73
crack F-1 A28 C14 3.38
cracked A47 4.25
cracker A98 7.50
cracking A73
cracks A44
cradle A73 6.88
craft A40 6.25
craftsmen A75
crafty 7.75
crammed 8.50
cranberry 8.50
crane A74
cranes A92
crank A85 5.50
crash F-1 A35 C11 3.83
crash-land 5.75
crash-landing E-38
crashing A78
crater A90 7.75
craters A92
crawl A49 3.92
crawled G-17 A38
crawling A59
crayon 4.75
crayons A95 5.25
crazier F-32 6.00
crazy A47 3.75
creak 4.75
cream E-7 A19 C10 4.75
creamier K-32 6.75
create J-7 A23 5.75
created I-7 A21
creates A55
creating A49
creation A67
creative A58 6.58
creator 8.50
creature G-25 A26 6.42
creatures G-25 A21 7.50
credit A40 5.75
credit card E-39 8.25
credited 7.75
credits 9.00
creek D-7 A38 C7 4.00
creep A75 5.25
creeping A69
crepe 5.25
crept I-2 A43 6.50
crest A67
crests A101
crevice 9.00
crew D-10 A18 C14 5.17
crews A71
cricket A70
crickets A84
cried C-32 A7 C9 4.00
cries C-32 A41 3.00
crime A64 4.75
crimes A93
criminal A91 7.50
criminology 8.50
crimson A89 7.88
cringe 7.25
crippled A96 8.00
crises 7.75
crisis A101 6.50
crisis; crises H-31
crisp A78
criteria 8.25
criterion; criteria H-31
critical A62 8.25
criticism A92 7.00 ¡
criticize 7.19 ¡
critics A80
crochet 7.38
crocodile A54 5.50
crocodiles A57
crook 5.50
crooked D-19 A77 C14 6.00
crooks D-19 C17
crop I-4 A24 3.33
crops H-4 A13
croquet I-21 8.50
cross G-24 A10 C18 3.33
cross-country F-38 7.00
crossed F-4 A18 C18
crosses A49
crossing A28
crouch 6.75
crouched A77
crow A60 4.25
crowd F-16 A13 C11 4.19
crowded H-16 A21
crowding A79
crowds A43
crown A42 3.88
crowned A94
crows A70
crucial 9.00
crude A51 8.00
cruel K-29 A39 5.50
cruelest 6.75
cruelty 7.75 ¡
cruise 5.67
crumb 5.83
crumbs A92 7.50
crumpled A97 6.25
crunchy 5.50
crusade 7.25
Crusaders A82
crush A100 4.88
crushed A46
crushing A84
crust I-5 A32 6.00
crutches 6.25
cry F-8 A16 C14 2.63
crying E-8 A29 C10 4.25
crystal A44 5.56
crystals K-29 A39
CT (Connecticut) F-41
cub A67
Cuba A61
cube A-10 A54 2.88
cubes A60
cubic A57 7.25
cubs A84
cucumber 7.25
cue 7.00
cultivated A64
cultivation A97
cultural A72
culture G-25 A32 6.25
cultures A81
cunning K-34 A65 7.75
cup C-5 A17 C7 1.92
cupboard A77 C17 6.42
cupfuls 7.38
cups I-5 A36
curb A80 6.08
cure E-25 A61 5.63
curiosity A45 6.75 ¡
curious H-43 A23 6.00
curiously A63
curl K-12 4.67
curled A47
curls A79 6.50
curly A70 6.50
currant 8.13
current H-12 A14 7.00
currents I-28 A29
curry 8.50
curtain A44 5.42
curtains A62 7.00
curve J-12 A26 5.00
curved J-12 A28
curves A60
cushion 5.50
custodian 8.25
custody 8.25
custom K-5 A38 6.75
customary A94
customer A61 7.00
customers A47 8.50
customs I-5 A30
cut B-5 A4 C5 1.83
cute C-10 A90 C10 2.69
cutest 8.00
cuts I-5 A32
cutting C-34 A20 C17 4.50
cycle K-29 A37 6.33
cycles A86
cyclone 8.00
cylinder J-47 A38 8.00 ¡¿
cylinders A78
cymbal 7.25
cynical K-47 ¿
Cyrus A81
Czechoslovakia A69

D

dachshund 8.75
dad H-1 A16 2.38
dad's G-40 C17
daddy E-1 A48 C8 2.75
daddy's 6.50
daily H-6 A20 5.13
daintier K-32 7.50
dainty A101
dairies K-32 6.50
dairy I-14 A36 5.42
daisies C-32 4.00
daisy F-6 C14 4.58
dam I-1 A33
damage J-6 A30 4.92
damaged A52 5.75
Dame A98
damp K-1 A35 4.75
dams A49
Dan A10
Dan's A80
dance F-1 A12 C14 3.25
danced G-1 A36 C17
dancer A92
dancers A68
dances A40
dancing H-1 A20 3.67
dandelion A91
dandruff 8.75
dandy 7.50
danger G-12 A13 C17 4.56
dangerous H-43 A16 C17 6.31
dangers A49

dangling A85
Daniel A28
Danish A52
Danny A29
dare A43 4.56
dared A55
daring A48 5.00
dark B-11 A5 C4 2.25
darkened A91
darker A56
darkness H-26 A19 5.63
Darlene C12
darling A82 8.00
darted A72
dash A48
dashboard 8.25
dashed K-1 A38
data K-1 A32 7.42
date I-6 A21 3.50
dated 8.50
dates K-6 A35
dating A88
datum; data H-31
daughter C-17 A17 C12 5.13
daughter's G-40 6.50
daughter-in-law G-38 7.50
daughters A90
Dave A38
David A27 C12
David's A99
Davis A52
Davy A45
dawn H-17 A28 5.67
Dawson A82
day A-6 A2 C1 2.08
day care E-39 7.75
day's A40
daybreak A94
daydream 7.00
daylight K-36 A35 4.17
days B-30 A3 C3 3.38
daytime A59 5.25
daze 7.75
dazzle 7.75
dazzling A86
DE (Delaware) F-41
dead A-47 A9 C6 3.63
dead end G-39 8.25
deadly A55
deaf A60 4.92
deal H-29 A10 5.00
dealer A84 5.75
dealers 9.00
dealing A65
deals A68
dealt ¡
Dean A98
dear B-15 A13 C5 4.00
dearest 6.50
death E-47 A10 C14 4.13
deaths A82
debate G-46 A83 6.13
debater ¡
debris G-46 8.50
debt A67 7.08
debtor H-22 8.00
debts A82
Dec. E-41 4.63
decade A71 8.13
decades A68
decameter F-46 6.50
[decametre] F-46
decay A58 5.67
decayed 7.50
deceit G-46 8.25
deceitful I-27 ¡
deceive H-23 7.38
December B-35 A34 4.94
decent 7.31
deception G-46 8.75
decide K-7 A10 4.58 ¡
decided C-7 A7 C4 5.00
decides A62
deciding A62 4.00
decimal A41 6.75
decimeter F-46 5.50
[decimetre] F-46
decision A33 6.92 ¡
decisions A42
deck H-2 A20 5.25
decks A97
declaration K-42 A73 6.75
declare I-14 A84 5.00
declared I-14 A28
decline A97 7.00
decorate A93 6.25
decorated A51 C17
decorating 5.50
decoration K-42 6.75
decorations A68 7.00
decorator G-46 8.50
decoy J-18 7.75
decrease G-46 A96 6.50
dedicate 7.00
dedicated A72
deducted 8.50
deduction 8.83
deed A92 9.00
deeds A78
deep E-7 A5 C10 2.92
deep-sea A100
deeper J-7 A30
deepest A60
deeply E-26 A29
deer A16 C6 4.58
defeat G-46 A45 6.75
defeated A42
defective K-46 5.75
[defence] I-44
[defenceless]
defend A49 5.25
defendant K-28 8.50 ¿
defending A100
defense A37 7.58 £
defenseless 7.00 £
defer 8.75
deferred K-12 ¡¿
define A46
defined A40
definite J-3 A28 7.00 ¡¿
definitely A66 8.00
definition G-42 A26 7.42
definitions A65
deflect 9.00
deformity 8.00
degree I-7 A23 5.00
degrees I-30 A14
dehydrate G-46 8.50
dehydrated 8.00
Delaware E-35 A53 5.75
delay A67 5.50
delayed A80 8.50
delaying I-32 5.50
delegates A83
deliberate A99 8.75
deliberately A69
delicate K-3 A35 7.00
delicatessen K-28 8.92
delicious H-43 A44 C17 5.38
delight G-46 A34 4.50
delighted A40
delightful E-27 A88 5.75
delinquent G-46 8.75
deliver A48 6.25
delivered G-46 A40 6.13
delivering A94
delivery G-46 A83 6.75
demand G-46 A36 7.50
demanded G-46 A38
demanding A101
demands A53
democracy A56 8.25
democratic A72 7.00
Democrats A98
demographic G-46 8.75
demolish G-46 8.75
demolition 8.75
demonstrate A58 7.00
demonstrated A61
demonstration H-42 A78 7.75
den A60 7.50
denied A67 8.50
denim 7.75
Denmark J-35 A39
denominator A76 6.75
dense A46
density A45
dent D-2 5.50
dental A91
dentist F-2 A65 C17 6.25
Denver A86
deny A79 5.92
deodorant 8.00
departed A85
department H-45 A39 6.00
departments A78 8.50
departure G-25 A77 7.00
depend I-28 A22 5.00
dependable A78 8.63
depended A56
dependence I-44 7.63
dependent K-2 A50 7.69
depending J-28 A38
depends H-28 A20
deplorable G-46 8.75
deploy 7.25
deport G-46 8.88
depose G-46 8.50
deposit G-46 A75 6.00
deposited A85
depositing 7.75
deposits G-46 A36
depot 8.00
depress 8.00
depression A85 6.75
deprivation G-46 8.50
deprive G-46 8.50
dept. 9.00
depth J-2 A29 6.25
depths A45
derby 9.00
derived A42 ¡
dermatology 8.67
descend J-28 ¡
descendant 6.75
descendants A71
descended A71
descendent I-2 7.00
descending A88
descent K-2 A78 7.63
describe I-7 A11 6.88 ¡
described 6.75
describes G-46 A34
describing A41
description F-42 A31 7.81 ¡
descriptions H-42 A61
descriptive A63 8.25
desert H-2 A11 5.58
deserted A62 7.75
deserts J-12 A31
deserve H-23 A89 6.50
design H-8 A17 6.94
designated A94
designed I-8 A24
designing A88
designs A48 8.00
desirable A67 7.88 ¡
desire J-8 A31 6.33
desired A43
desires A76 9.00
desirous 9.00
desk A15 C18 3.92
desks A-2 A76 3.25
desolate A93 7.88
despair A62 6.75 ¡
desperate A55 6.88 ¡
desperately A60
despise 8.06
despite G-46 A35 5.25
dessert E-2 A81 6.19
destination K-42 A76 6.25
destroy G-18 A34 5.19 ¡
destroyed G-18 A27
destroying A73
destructible 8.75
destruction A65 9.00
destructive G-46 A78 8.75
detail J-6 A31 5.50
detailed A57 6.25
details I-30 A16 6.75
detain G-46 8.75
detect A87 7.88
detected A96
detection 7.25
detective G-46 A51 6.38
detention G-46 8.75
determination A62
determine H-12 A18 6.92

Key: Letter-## is *Spelling Power* level word is first taught at. A## is usage by adults; C## is usage by children. (#.##) Average grade level word is taught at; ¢ High School Problem Word, ¡ College Problem Word. ¿ Business Problem Word. £ British spelling (alternate) is also in this list. [word] is British spelling. Elementary Problem words are set in **Boldface** type.

determined I-12 A22
determining A56 7.25
detour I-25 7.50
detract 9.00
Detroit A61
deuce J-10 ¿
develop H-4 A13 7.50 ¡¿
developed A9
developing J-2 A30 7.25
development H-45 A15 6.88 ¡¿
developments A54
develops A66
device J-8 A31 7.75 ¡
devices J-8 A31
devil E-29 A62 4.50
devise 8.00 ¡
devised A52
devote 5.63
devoted G-46 A49 7.50
devotion A83
devour 7.67
dew A50 5.67
Dewey A97
diagnoses 8.25
diagnosis 8.75
diagonal A73 8.00
diagram H-8 A19 8.25
diagrams A44
dial A68 6.33
dialect 8.50
dialogue A75 8.38
diameter I-8 A27 7.13
diamond G-8 A36 C17
diamonds A56 7.50
diaphragm A94
diaries D-32 5.25
diary A59 6.75
dice 5.75
Dick A20 C10
dictate 8.75
dictation 7.50
dictator A83 8.63
dictionaries A80
dictionary F-42 A17 7.38 ¡
did A-3 A1 C1 1.38
didn't B-37 A4 C2 4.08 ¢
die E-8 A14 C11 3.50
die; dice H-31
died (not living) D-8 A11 C6 4.63
dies A63
diesel 7.92
diet A42 6.33
dietician 8.00
differ I-24 A22 8.50
differed 7.25
difference H-44 A7 7.63 ¡
differences H-44 A14
different C-12 A2 C4 5.38 ¡
differently J-26 A36
differs A60
difficult H-3 A9 5.50
difficulties A42
difficulty A27
dig E-3 A24 C12 2.00
digest 7.50
digested A92
digestible 8.38
digestion K-42 A84 6.13
digestive A91 8.75
digging D-34 A34 3.00 ¡
digit A89 8.50
digits A59
dignified A89
dignity A61 9.00
digs A94
dike A90
dikes A97 8.00
dilemma ¡
dilute 8.25
dim A45 6.25
dime A41
dimension 7.50
dimensions A54
dimes A63
dimly A80
dimmed 4.50
dimming 7.75
dine 6.25
diner 5.00
dining A42 8.25 ¡
dining room D-39 ¡
dinner C-12 A12 C6 3.75
dinosaur F-8 A39 C12 5.25
dinosaurs J-13 A38
dioxide A41
dip A53 5.50
diphtheria K-3 ¿
diplomacy 8.25
diplomat 8.25
dipped A54 7.50
dipper A99
direct I-12 A17 5.50
directed J-12 A33
directing 5.75
direction F-42 A8 6.00
directions G-42 A10
directly E-26 A14
director A49 6.75
directors 9.00
Dirk A91
dirt D-12 A23 C10 4.38
dirtier F-32 6.00
dirty F-12 A28 C14 7.13
disable K-46 6.00
disagree K-46 A83 5.88
disappear K-46 A45 5.31 ¡¿
disappeared F-15 A20 C11
disappearing I-15 A78 4.50
disappears A78
disappoint K-46 5.92 ¡¿
disappointed E-18 A38
disappointment H-45 A20 7.50
disapprove 5.38
disarmament 7.75
disassemble 8.00
disaster A69 7.25
disastrous H-43 6.75 ¡
disbelief 7.00
disc A100
discarded A88
discharge 4.75
discipline H-3 A84 8.25 ¡
disconnect K-46 6.38
discount 6.31
discourage I-25 7.38
discouraged I-25 A53 7.38
discouraging I-25 7.25
discover H-4 A14 7.06
discovered G-20 A8 4.00
discoveries F-32 A36
discovering A70
discovery H-4 A21 7.25
discrepancy K-3 ¿
discriminate K-46 6.00
discuss H-24 A18 6.00
discussed K-34 A34
discussion I-42 A29 6.17
discussions A78
disease I-7 A22 7.31 ¡
diseases J-7 A32
disgrace K-46 A93 7.25
disgraceful I-27 7.00
disguise A95 7.13
disguised 6.75
disgust 8.00
dish I-3 A26 2.42
dishes F-30 A18 C14 3.25
dishonest 5.67
dishonor 9.00 £
[dishonour]
disinfectant 7.75
disk A69
dislike A77 5.25
dislocate 9.00
disloyal K-46 6.50
dismal A101 9.00
dismay A86
dismayed 7.50
dismiss K-46 6.00
dismissal 8.58
dismissed 8.00
Disneyland D-35 C12
disobey K-46 6.38
dispatch 4.75
dispense I-44 9.00
display A43 4.75
displayed A63
displays 8.25
disposal A93 7.50
dispose 6.58
disposed 8.50
disposition 8.00
dispute A84 5.00
disrespectful 9.00
disrupt 8.50
dissatisfied K-46 ¡¿
dissatisfy K-46 6.88
dissimilar 7.75
dissipate ¡
dissolve H-23 A55 8.00
dissolved A53
dissolves A88
distance H-44 A6 6.19
distances H-44 A26
distant I-3 A23
[distil]
distill 8.25 £
distinct A49
distinction J-42 A71 ¡
distinctive A70
distinctly A75 8.50
distinguish A44
distinguished A47
distract 7.67
distraction 8.75
distress A89 7.00
distribute 8.25 ¡
distributed A59 6.75
distribution A62 8.25
district A48 5.50
District of Columbia E-39 7.
districts A93
disturb 6.83
disturbance H-44 6.75
disturbed A56
ditch E-3 A54 5.06
ditches A90 8.00
ditto 8.75
dive G-8 A42 C18 4.25
dived A61
diver A55
divers A47
diverse 8.88
diversion 7.50
divert 8.88
divide K-7 A13 4.63 ¡
divided H-8 A10 6.50
dividend 7.50
divides A57
dividing D-33 A31 5.00
divine J-8 A80 ¡¿
diving C-33 A42 C17
divisible 8.38
division F-42 A18 6.13
divisions J-42 A39
dizziness I-32 6.50
dizzy 5.67
do A-10 A1 C1 2.42
dock D-4 A42 C8 5.25
docks A66
doctor D-13 A12 C6 3.38 ¡
doctor's A89
doctors E-30 A29 C10
document A83 7.75
documentary J-45 8.38
dodge 5.50
does C-20 A2 C4 2.94
doesn't A9 C10 3.83
dog A-4 A4 C1 2.25
dog's G-40 A48 C14
dogs C-30 A8 C5
doing C-10 A6 C5 4.50
doll C-24 A29 C11 2.25
dollar C-11 A22 C12 3.50
dollars C-30 A11 C5
dollhouse 4.50
dolls F-4 A46 C17 2.75
dolly 7.50
dolphin A98 6.00
dolphins A90
dome A84 6.25
domestic A59 7.83
domesticate 6.00
dominance J-44 ¿
dominant A67 8.75
dominate 8.75
dominated A81
dominoes 6.33
Don A25
don't B-37 A2 C2 3.56 ¢¡
Donald A52
donating 7.25
donation 8.75
done C-20 A4 C10 3.06
donkey F-4 A29 C17
donkeys A76 5.25
donor 7.88
door A-13 A4 C2 3.06
doorbell A82 4.50

Alphabetical List

doors F-30 A20 C12
doorway K-36 A35
dormitories I-32 ¡
dormitory 8.25
dot J-4 A27 3.25
doth A99
dots J-30 A24
dotted D-34 A34 3.75
double H-29 A14 4.58
doubled A45 5.50
doubt H-16 A20 5.50
doubtful I-27 A78 6.63
doubtless 9.00
dough A63 5.50
doughnut A98 7.63
doughnuts A74
Douglas A58
dove H-23 A86 7.00
doves A99
down A-16 A1 C1 2.92
downhill A71
downstairs E-36 A44 C12 4.63
downstream A72
downtown A52 C14 5.00
downward K-36 A37
dozen C-20 A20 5.33
dozens A43
Dr. F-41 A13 6.17
draft K-1 A57 5.50
drag A41 4.75
dragged C-34 A38 C17
dragging A76 8.50
dragon F-1 A32 C11 5.42
dragons A95
drain A71 4.92
drained A64
dram 6.50
drama A48 6.75
dramatic K-1 A36 6.75
dramatics 9.00
drank F-1 A39 C14 3.25
draw A4 2.81
drawer K-12 A69 4.67
drawers A94
drawing G-17 A14 3.00
drawings H-17 A27
drawn G-17 A17 5.38
draws G-17 A62
dread A84
dreaded A97
dreadful E-27 A61 5.92
dream D-7 A20 C7 3.63
dreamed J-7 A38
dreaming A50 8.00
dreams J-30 A29
drenched J-2 7.25
dress C-24 A14 C6 2.31
dressed B-34 A16 C9
dresser A94 6.50
dresses A45 4.00
dressing A77 6.50
drew H-10 A16 4.06
dried D-32 A21 5.83
dries F-32 A96 6.75
drift A47 5.25
drifted A47
drifting A70
drill H-24 A36 4.13
drilled A75
drilling A93
drills A96
drink E-3 A14 C9 2.75
drinker F-12 C12
drinking G-3 A30 C17
drinks A61 5.00
drip A81
dripping A60
drive A-23 A10 C9 2.50
drive-in E-38 5.75
drive-ins G-38 7.50
driven I-28 A25
driver E-8 A16 C9 4.25
driver's A74
drivers J-8 A32
drives A47 7.5
driveway F-36 A79 C18 6.63
driving C-33 A19 C18 3.75
drizzle 6.50
droop 6.25
drop C-4 A12 C18 2.25
droplets A84
dropped B-34 A12 C9 4.67
dropping A48 4.00
drops H-4 A20
drought A98 7.63
drove A-23 A14 C7 2.38
drown A87 4.81
drowned A54 7.00
drowsy 5.33
drudgery ¡
drug A65 4.25
drugs A47
drugstore A61 5.00
drum I-5 A32 3.00
drummers F-34 4.25
drums F-5 A41 C14
drunk F-5 A87 C14
dry G-8 A6 C18 2.75
drying A61 8.00
dual 7.75
duck C-5 A21 C10 2.13
ducked A97
duckling A78
ducks D-5 A28 C10
due I-10 A21 5.33
duel 7.75
duet 7.88
duffel 8.25
dug C-5 A26 C12 2.25
dugout A95
Duke A45 5.25
dull F-24 A28 C14 4.67
duly 8.50
dumb C-22 A74 C8 4.58
dumfound 8.25
dump A81 4.75
dumped A68
Duncan A78
dune A99
dunes A62
dungeon 7.08
duplicate A100 8.00
duplication 7.33
duplicator 8.75
durable 7.00
during H-12 A3 4.83
dusk A66 5.25
dust D-5 A14 C12 3.75
dusted A99
dusty F-5 A46 C18
Dutch I-35 A21
duties A50 7.50
dutiful G-32 7.50
duty I-10 A27 5.06
dwarf 7.50
dwell A100 5.25
dwellers A87
dye A81 8.00
dyed 6.25
dyeing 7.92
dying D-33 A41 6.69 ¡
dynamite A96 6.25
dynamos 7.50
dynasty 8.75

E

E. (east) D-41 4.50
each A-7 2.50
eager J-7 A27 6.25
eagerly J-26 A39
eagerness A99
eagle K-29 A38 3.94
eagles A75
ear B-15 A16
earl A72 5.25
earlier E-32 A17 7.13
earliest F-32 A31 6.75
early F-12 A4 C12 3.75
earn G-12 A25 C18 4.08
earned J-12 A38
earnest A85 6.75
earnings A96
ears E-30 A11 C9 3.75
earth C-12 A3 C6 4.69
earth's G-40 A19
earthquake A48 5.58
earthquakes A87
ease K-7 A38
eased A100
easel 7.25
easier D-32 A14 5.25
easiest C-32 A58 4.50
easily D-32 A8 7.17 ¡
east H-7 A12 4.50
Easter D-35 A97 C7 5.00
eastern H-7 A19
eastward A50
easy G-7 A6 C17 3.44
eat A-7 A4 C2 2.25
eaten E-28 A18 C12 5.50
eaters A93
eating A13 C11 3.75
eats E-30 A32 C11
eavesdrop 7.13
echo A46
echoed A64
echoes A68 6.50
eclipse 7.17
ecology 7.58
economic K-28 A33
economics A94
economize 8.25
economy A40 8.38
ecstasy K-2 8.75 ¡¿
ecstatic H-22 8.75
Eddie A26
Eddie's A84
Edgar A93
edge H-2 A8 4.56
edges I-30 A23
edible 8.38
Edison A59
edit 7.50
edition F-42 7.81
editor A50 7.50
editorial 8.25
Edmonton C-35 C6
Edmund A89
educate E-2 6.00
educated A44
education F-42 A17 6.08
educational A75 8.75
Edward A24
Edwards A78
eel A101
eerie I-15 6.88
effect I-7 A13 7.58 ¡¿
effective J-47 A31 7.00
effectively A54
effects J-24 A27 ¡
efficiency A70
efficient J-28 A42 8.00 ¡
efficiently A94
effort H-13 A20 6.38
efforts A32
egg C-24 A16 C7 2.83
eggs E-30 A8 C8
ego 8.00
Egypt I-35 A30
Egyptian J-35 A38
Egyptians A45
eight C-6 A8 C6 2.42
eighteen A46 6.13
eighteenth A82
eighth A51 5.75 ¡
eighty E-6 A65 5.00
Einstein A59
Eisenhower A92
either H-7 A5 4.31
elaborate A56 8.50
elastic A84 8.25
elated 7.25
elbow E-29 A58 4.75
elbows A70
elder A92 7.00
elderly A96
elders A92
eldest A73
elect E-2 A80 6.00
elected I-2 A31
electing 5.25
election I-42 A38 5.88
Election day 4.50
elections A80
electric F-2 A11 C14 4.25
electrical J-29 A33
electrically A101
electrician 8.17

Key: Letter-## is *Spelling Power* level word is first taught at. A## is usage by adults; C## is usage by children. (#.##) Average grade level word is taught at; ¢ High School Problem Word. ¡ College Problem Word. ¿ Business Problem Word. £ British spelling (alternate) is also in this list. [word] is British spelling. Elementary Problem words are set in **Boldface** type.

electricity H-3 A14 6.75
electron A63
electronic K-2 A37 8.50
electronics A92
electrons J-2 A32
elegance J-44 7.75
elegant A78 8.25
element H-45 A19 6.00
elementary J-2 A77 7.33
elements H-45 A12
elephant D-2 A23 C6 5.50
elephants D-30 A28 C7
elevation A63
elevator A43 6.00
elevators A96
eleven E-28 A28 C14 6.00
elf G-2 C18
Elia A87
eligible K-3 8.38 ¡¿
eliminate K-3 A74 7.00 ¡¿
eliminated A77
Elizabeth A35
Ella's 7.50
Ellen A30
Elmer A73
else D-2 A6 C7 4.69
else's G-40 A93 5.75
elsewhere A49 9.00
elude 8.25
elves D-31 6.63
embargo 8.88
embarrass G-24 7.56 ¡¿
embarrassed A70
embassy K-2 8.25
emblem 7.38
embrace K-2 8.25
embroidery J-18 7.42
embryo A101
emcee 7.00
emerge A88 8.75
emerged A62
emergency A57 6.13
emigrants K-2 8.25
emigrate 8.38
Emily A52
eminent K-28 8.25 ¡¿
emission 8.75
Emma A86
emotion A73 7.50
emotional J-42 A41 6.75
emotions A56
emperor A50 7.25
emphasis A49
emphasize A76 8.06
emphasized A96
empire J-8 A36 6.92
employ J-18 A80 5.67
employed J-18 A42 5.50
employee K-2 8.25
employees A95 9.00
employer 6.50
employers A99
employs A101
emptied A100
emptiness K-32 6.50
empty G-47 A13 4.25
enable A45 7.63
enabled A64
enables A55
enamel A85
enchilada 7.00
enclose 6.67
enclosed A74 8.50
enclosing 8.50
enclosure 9.00
encore 6.50
encounter A76 8.13
encountered A67
encourage I-25 A64 7.38
encouraged A43 8.75
encouragement I-25 A92 7.50
encouraging F-33 A88 ¡
encyclopedia A52 6.13
encyclopedias A90
end C-2 A2 C4 2.42
endanger 7.63
endangered 7.13
endeavor 7.63 £
[endeavour]
ended A20
ending H-28 A15
endings A48
endless A47 5.67
endorse 8.25
endorsement J-45 ¿
endow 8.25
ends H-28 A9
endurance H-44 A92 6.25
endure A74
enemies I-28 A24 5.17
enemy H-2 A17 5.50 ¡
enemy's G-40 7.50
energetic A87 8.75
energy H-28 A7 5.75
enforce A98 7.08
engage A84 7.08
engaged A43
engagement 9.00
engine G-2 A10 C15 4.50
engineer H-15 A27 7.50
engineering A59
engineers H-15 A32
engines H-28 A20 5.00
England D-35 A7 C9
England's A80
English G-35 A4 5.88
Englishman A61
Englishmen A98
engrave H-23 7.50
enjoy E-18 A12 3.88
enjoyable A83 6.63
enjoyed E-18 A21
enjoying A51 6.50
enjoyment H-45 A59 5.63
enjoys A80
enlarged A73
enlargement 8.00
enormous H-43 A25 C15 6.25
enough C-47 A3 C6 4.44
enriched A91
ensemble 9.00
ensure G-25 7.00
entangle 8.25
enter I-12 A18 5.08
entered G-12 A19 C15
entering A45
enterprise K-28 A80 7.67 ¿
enters J-28 A33
entertain A80 9.00
entertained A95
entertainment I-45 A56 7.25
enthusiasm A52 8.25
enthusiastic A84 8.58
entice 8.25
entire A13 6.50
entirely H-26 A22 6.50
entitle 7.75
entitled A67 8.50
entrance I-44 A35 6.25
entries A79
entry J-28 A38 5.88
envelop K-28 ¿
envelope I-2 A53 6.67
envelopes 9.00
envelopment J-45 ¿
envied 5.50
environment H-45 A22 7.08 ¡
envy A91 9.00
enzyme 8.75
epic 9.00
epidemic 8.75
episode 8.75
equal H-29 A11 5.25
equaled 6.50 £
equality F-21 A76 6.75
[equalled]
equally I-26 A28
equals A52
equation F-21 A33 6.33
equations A42
equator F-21 A28 6.25
equipment E-21 A17 C17 6.13
equipped I-21 A50 7.25 ¡
equivalent I-21 A31
era A54
eraser A94 5.88
erasure 9.00
erect A71
erected A92
Eric A68
Erie A53
Ernest A92
erode 7.75
erosion A66
errand 8.25
errands 5.00
error A43 6.83
errors A40
eruption 8.50
escape I-6 A18 6.00
escaped K-2 A39 5.75
escapes A92 8.00
escaping A94
Eskimo A72
Eskimos A43
especially H-26 A8 6.88 ¡
essay A82 7.17
essays 8.25
essential I-28 A29 8.06
essentially A76
est A99
establish A41 6.75
established I-1 A20
establishment I-45 A76 7.50
estate A59 7.25
estimate J-2 A31
estimated K-2 A38 7.25
estimates A95
etc. F-41 A24 6.00 ¡
etching 8.25
eternal A101
Ethiopia A96
etiquette I-21 8.50
Europe G-35 A8 9.00
European I-35 A18
Europeans A43
evacuation 7.75
evaluate A89 8.50
evaporate 7.88
evaporates A93
evaporation A101
eve A60 4.50
even B-7 A2 C3 3.50
evening G-7 A10 C18 4.63
evenings A77
evenly A51
event I-28 A25 5.88
events I-30 A16
eventually I-26 A25
ever B-12 A3 C3 3.17
Everest A83
everlasting 6.25
every B-2 A2 C3 2.75
everybody C-36 A14 C8 4.19 ¢¡
everyday F-36 A33 C18 5.0
everyone C-36 A5 C5 3.50
everyone's A95 7.25
everything C-36 A5 C4 3.83
everywhere A15 C15 5.25
evidence I-44 A23 8.75
evident A64 7.75
evidently K-26 A60 8.50 ¿
evil A49 5.06
evoke 8.75
evolution A93
evolve 8.88
evolved A83
exact I-1 A20 5.92
exactly H-26 A8 7.50
exaggerate G-24 8.63 ¡
examination H-42 A49 7.58
examinations 7.00
examine J-47 A23 6.50
examined A32
examining A66
example G-29 A3 C15 6.50
examples J-46 A9
exams 7.50
exceed 9.00 ¡
exceedingly 8.50
excel 8.75
excellence 8.67
excellent I-28 A24 6.31 ¡
except C-2 A7 C5 4.88 ¡
exception J-46 A44 8.08
exceptional 7.75 ¡
exceptions A65
excess J-46 A67 8.50
excessive K-2 A96 8.00
exchange J-6 A30 6.38
exchanged A79
excite J-46 5.63
excited E-8 A18 C9 6.00
excitedly A50
excitement H-45 A19 6.63
exciting A14 C11 4.67
exclaim J-46 7.25
exclaimed I-6 A22
exclamation G-42 A101 7.75
exclude J-46 7.50

Alphabetical List

exclusive 8.88
excusable 8.00
excuse A45 6.56
executed A96 9.00
execution A100
executive A69 7.38
exercise I-12 A11 6.17 ¡
exercises A22 7.25
exert J-46 7.63
exhaust H-17 A80 6.67 ¡¿
exhausted A59 9.00
exhibit J-46 A64 7.83
exhibition F-42 C18 7.92 ¿
exhilarate ¡
exile J-46 7.25
exist J-2 A30 7.50
existed A50
existence I-44 A41 8.75 ¡¿
existing A68
exists A48
exit J-46 A90 6.92
exotic A99
expand J-46 A41 5.38
expanded J-46 A33
expanding A79
expands A68
expanse A89
expansion A51 6.00
expect J-46 A13 5.25
expectation J-46 8.50
expected J-46 A16 5.25
expecting A87 7.00
expects A81
expedition J-46 A40 7.75
expeditions A76
expense H-28 A75 8.25 ¡
expenses A67 8.50
expensive J-28 A32 7.67
experience F-15 A14 C14 6.94 ¡
experienced A44
experiences I-44 A28
experiment H-45 A12 6.81 ¡
experimental A72
experimentation K-2 A89 8.00
experimenting A68
experiments H-45 A20
expert J-46 A38 5.92
experts A47
expire 8.75
explain J-46 A7 5.38
explained J-46 A15
explaining A57 9.00
explains A45
explanation H-42 A30 8.00 ¡
explanations A71
explanatory J-46 7.75
explode J-46 5.83
exploded A77
exploit 7.25
exploration K-42 A46 6.75
explore G-13 A25 C18 6.00
explored J-46 A39
explorer J-46 A57 7.67
explorers J-13 A31
exploring C-33 A41 C13
explosion K-42 A47 6.00
explosive A86 8.25
explosives A88
exponent J-46 8.50
export J-46 A83 7.06
exports A70 7.50
expose J-46 7.75
exposed A47
exposition H-42 7.75
exposure I-25 A93 7.38
express J-46 A14 6.38
expressed K-34 A24
expresses A51
expressing A49
expression G-42 A18 6.13
expressions I-42 A37
expressive J-46 8.00
exquisite 8.88
extend J-28 A31 6.00
extended J-28 A33 5.25
extending A55 9.00
extends J-28 A39
extension K-2 A82 8.00
extensive A59
extent J-46 A40 7.00
exterior J-46 A100 6.75
external J-46 A93 7.50
extinct A88 7.38
extra J-46 A17 5.25
extract A95 8.63
extraordinary I-36 A53 7.94 ¿
extrasensory J-46 8.00
extravagant 9.00
extreme J-46 A39 7.00
extremely I-26 A31 ¡
extremes A91
extrovert 8.88
eye E-8 A8 C9 2.75
eyebrow 5.25
eyebrows A99
eyed A95 7.50
eyeing 7.88
eyelashes 4.50
eyelids A92
eyes B-47 A3 C4 3.13
eyesight K-36 7.50

F

fable A95 5.63
fabric A67 8.00
face C-6 A4 C5 3.75
face-off E-38 C18
faced J-6 A31
faces H-30 A13 C18
facial 8.50
facilities K-32 A65 7.63
facing D-33 A30
fact H-1 A6
factor I-13 A22 7.25
factories F-32 A18 C17 5.00
factors I-30 A18
factory H-13 A20 5.00
facts I-30 A10
faculty 7.25
fade A68 4.25
faded A54
fading A78
Fahrenheit A56 8.50
fail A41 4.25
failed I-6 A23
fails A90
failure A46 6.33
faint K-6 A33
fainted 4.63
faintly A93
fair F-14 A13 C14 5.19
fairies A-14 A75 3.75
fairly I-26 A25
fairness I-14 6.00
fairy F-14 A46 C18
fairyland 7.50
faith A60 5.25
faithful A92
faithfully K-26 A100 6.75
fall B-17 A6 C5 3.08
fallen I-28 A24
falling H-17 A19 3.00
falls H-30 A15 C17
false H-17 A26 4.75
falsehood 8.25
fame A43
famed A100
familiar G-11 A12 7.88 ¡¿
families C-32 A13 C18 4.50
family B-1 A4 C3 3.63
family's A83
famine 7.00
famous H-43 A8 C14 4.75
fan G-1 A49 C18 5.00
fancy K-1 A37 5.63
fans H-30 A47 C18
fantastic A53 7.58
fantasy 8.50
far B-11 A3 C6 3.00
far-away A101
far-off A62
faraway A48 5.00
fare A61 6.17
farewell A63 6.25
farm B-11 A7 C2 3.19
farmer D-11 A12 C18 4.06
farmer's A49
farmers G-11 A9
farmhouse A61
farming H-11 A28
farmland A86
farms D-11 A16 C12
farther C-11 A11 C12 6.17
farthest A54
fascinate 8.00 ¡
fascinated A62
fascinating A46 7.50
fascination 8.25
fashion A32 6.13
fashionable 6.00
fast C-1 A5 C4 2.33
fasten A41 6.17
fastened I-28 A24
faster H-1 A10
fastest A45
fat D-1 A16 C6 2.25
fatal A72 7.42
fatality 8.50
fate A54 9.00
father A-17 A2 C2 2.67
father's G-40 A20
fathers A45
fatigue A80 7.25
fats A84 7.50
fatter F-34 6.75
faucet 6.67
fault H-17 A37 5.50
faults A88
favor I-13 A34 4.75 £
favorable A58 8.50 £
favored A66 6.50 £
favorite B-13 A16 C8 5.63 £
favorites A92 £
favors 8.50 £
[favour] I-13
[favourable]
[favoured]
[favourite] B-13
[favourites]
[favours]
fawn 5.25
fear B-15 A11 4.13
feared I-15 A36
fearful A46 5.50
fears A72
feasible K-7 ¿
feast J-7 A37 4.50
feather E-47 A36 4.58
feathers A17 C13 7.00
feature E-25 A46 6.83
features G-25 A24
Feb. E-41 4.63 ¢
February B-35 A34 4.19 ¡¿
fed F-2 A23 C12 2.25
federal J-29 A35
fee A100 8.50
feed C-7 A13 C6 2.75
feeder A98
feeding J-7 A32 3.75
feeds A60 7.00
feel C-7 A4 C4 2.83
feelers A84
feeling H-7 A10 3.00
feelings I-7 A21
feels E-30 A24 C8
feet B-7 A3 C3 2.25
fell A-24 A7 C3 2.75
fellow H-9 A17 5.44
fellows A45
felt D-2 A5 C6 4.25
female J-6 A31 4.50
fence D-2 A15 C6 4.25
fences A54
fern 4.83
ferns A79
ferry A74 7.25
fertile A43 6.50
fertilize 7.75
fertilizer A67
festival A55 5.38
festivals A77
fetch A58
feud 8.25
fever J-7 A31 5.67
few B-10 A2 C5 4.92
fewer J-10 A26
fiance 8.00
fiber A74 8.00 £

Key: Letter-## is *Spelling Power* level word is first taught at. A## is usage by adults; C## is usage by children. (#.##) Average grade level word is taught at; ¢ High School Problem Word, ¡ College Problem Word. ¿ Business Problem Word. £ British spelling (alternate) is also in this list. [word] is British spelling. Elementary Problem words are set in **Boldface** type.

fiberglass 8.75 £
fibers A49 £
[fibre]
[fibreglass]
[fibres]
fiction A54 6.38
fictional 8.75
fictitious 8.67
fiddle A58 8.00
fidgeting 9.00
field C-7 A6 C5 4.58
field trip G-39 6.00
fields H-30 A9 C18
fiend K-7 ¿
fierce A28 6.44
fiercely A52
fiery J-8 A56 7.25 ¡¿
fiesta 7.17
fifteen E-7 A19 C13 6.00
fifteenth A95 8.00
fifth F-3 A25 C14 4.88 ¡
fifths A98
fifty F-3 A16 C13 3.75
fig A47
fight C-8 A10 C5 3.50
fighter A68
fighters A82
fighting E-8 A17 C8
fights A71 6.00
figurative H-23 9.00
figure E-25 A7 C9 4.92
figured G-25 A38
figures G-25 A14
filament A95
file A46 6.13
files 8.50
filing 9.00
fill G-24 A10 C15 2.50
filled F-3 A8 C12
fillet 9.00
filling J-24 A37
fills A57
film G-3 A29 C18 4.25
films A89
filter A91 8.25
filtered 6.50
fin A88
final H-29 A13 5.08
finale 7.75
finalist 9.00
finally E-26 A5 C3 5.63 ¡
financial A59 8.25
financier ¡
find B-8 A1 C3 2.75
finding H-8 A13
findings A64
finds I-8 A29
fine C-8 A5 C5 3.00
finer A74
finest D-33 A30 6.50
finger F-3 A13 C13 5.13
fingerprints A86
fingers G-30 A10 C15 3.25
finish H-3 A14 3.58
finished C-3 A9 C5 5.50
finishes A100
finishing A66 6.50
Finland A78
fins A69
fir A71 6.25
fire C-8 A4 C5 2.75
fire escape E-39 8.25
firecracker 5.50
firecrackers 6.50
fired F-8 A30 C14
fireman A73 8.00
firemen A61 7.00
fireplace H-37 A30 4.83
fireproof 6.25
fires J-30 A29
firewood A76
fireworks A72 7.50
firing A69
firm J-12 A28 4.67
firmly I-26 A27
firms A101
first A-12 A1 C2 3.31
first aid E-39 7.00
first-born G-38 8.25
first-class F-38 7.75
fish B-3 A4 C2 2.00
fished A74 6.50
fisherman I-36 A50 7.50
fishermen A31
fishes A46
fishing C-3 A14 C4 3.00
fist D-3 A49 4.25
fists A77
fit A11 C17 2.58
fits J-30 A24
fitted D-34 A38
fitting A61 6.50
five A-23 A3 C3 1.69
fix I-3 A27 2.25
fixed G-3 A22 C15 4.00
fixing A78 7.00
fixture 5.75
FL (Florida) F-41
flag H-1 A19 2.31
Flag Day 4.50
flags A50
flair I-14 6.88
flakes A94 8.00
flame J-6 A27 5.42
flames A46
flaming A78
flammable 7.75
flap A75
flapping A72 4.25
flaps A78
flare 6.67
flash F-1 A35 C13 3.25
flashed A51
flashes A84 4.25
flashing A55
flashlight A44 C14 5.67
flask A80
flat F-1 A8 C12 2.25
flats A98
flattened A65
flattery 7.83
flavor K-13 A64 5.00 £
flavorful I-27 8.00 £
[flavour] K-13
[flavourful] K-13
flaw 6.25
flax 7.50
flea A95 5.38
fled I-2 A43 6.50
fledgling 6.50
flee A88 5.50
fleet A41 5.25
flesh A41
flew D-10 A13 C13 3.81
flexible K-29 A70 8.25 ¿
flies D-32 A20 3.00
flight H-8 A15 4.75
flights A48
flimsiest 7.50
flint A94
flipped 4.50
flippers A100
flirt 5.75
float I-9 A32 3.25
floated A41
floating I-9 A29 7.75
floats A78
flock A49 4.75
flocks A60
flood G-47 A32
flooded A63 7.50
floods A58 7.50
floor B-13 A6 C6 4.25
floors A43
Florence A65
florescent 8.25 £
Florida E-35 A26 5.67
flounder 7.25
flour H-16 A32 4.67
flourish A90 7.33
flourished A69
flow H-9 A15 4.75
flowed A50
flower C-16 A16 C5 3.92
flowering A74
flowers B-30 A8 C3 2.75
flowing J-9 A31
flown A55
flows J-30 A24
flu 5.88
fluent 8.75
fluffy A71 8.00
fluid A66 7.00
fluke 7.75
flung A57
[fluorescent]
flurries 6.50
flushed A83
flute A93 4.75
flutes A96
fluttered A81
fluttering A92
fly C-8 A7 C4 1.88
flying D-8 A10 C4 1.00
foam A73 5.75
focus A55 8.08
focus; foci H-31
focused A85
foe A89 7.00
fog F-4 A22 C18 2.75
foggy F-34 A73 4.13
foil B-18 A68 3.75
fold J-9 A34 4.31
folded J-9 A31
folding A64
folds A59
foliage 7.25
folk E-22 A33 4.25
folks F-22 A30 4.50
follow D-9 A5 C14 4.17
followed E-9 A6 C10 4.50
followers A65
following H-4 A3 6.25
follows H-9 A14
fond A42 4.92
food B-10 A3 C3 2.50
foods H-10 A16
fool J-10 A36 4.08
fooled A84
fooling G-10 C18
foolish J-10 A31 6.42
foolproof 7.00
foot B-19 A6 C9 2.83
foot; feet F-31
football C-36 A20 C7 3.50
footprint 4.75
footprints A72
footsteps E-36 A42 C8
for A-13 A1 C1 2.88 ¢
forbid 5.75
forbidden K-34 A68 8.13
forbidding K-34 7.50
force G-13 A9 5.00
forced H-13 A19
forceful I-27 6.25
forces I-13 A16
forcible F-33 ¿
forcing A95
Ford A44
forecast A83 6.25
forehead K-36 A39 6.25
foreign G-13 A20 6.44 ¡
foreigners A91
foreman A99
forenoon 8.25
foresee I-36 ¡
forest D-13 A8 C6 4.75
forestry 6.50
forests H-13 A15
forever A36 C17 4.50
forfeit 7.92 ¡
forgave 5.25
forge 7.00
forgery 7.63
forget F-36 A15 C12 3.92
forgetful E-27 5.75
forgetting F-34 6.08
forgive K-13 4.50
forgiveness 6.50
forgot E-36 A22 C14 3.50
forgotten E-28 A22 C18 7.13
fork I-13 A39 4.13
forks 7.00
form A3 4.08
formal K-29 A39 7.50
formally J-26 8.50 ¡
formation A50
formed H-13 A8
former J-12 A27 7.00
formerly J-26 A52 8.25 ¡
formidable A94
forming K-13 A33
forms H-13 A6
formula J-10 A31 8.00
formulas 8.25
forsake 7.25
fort B-13 A29 C6 4.25
forth H-13 A12 6.75 ¡
forthright K-36 ¿
fortress A100 7.00

Alphabetical List

forts A92
fortunate A61 7.50
fortunately A44
fortune J-13 A39 5.88
fortunes A91
forty F-13 A27 C13 4.42 ¡¿
forward F-13 A9 C14 6.13
forwarded 8.50
forwarding 8.50
fossil A67 6.25
fossils A43
foster A61 7.25
fought G-17 A18 C17 5.75
foul A78 5.92
found A-16 A2 C2 3.33
foundation G-42 A58 7.63
foundations A94
founded A40
founder 8.50
founding A101
fountain A51 5.33
four A-13 A3 C3 2.38
fours A84
foursome K-36 ¿
fourteen I-13 A37 6.00
fourth B-13 A15 C17 4.06 ¡
Fourth of July 5.00
fourths A71
fowl A99 6.42
fox C-4 A27 C9 1.50
foxes A55 5.00
foyer 7.25
fraction H-42 A31 6.75
fractional A65
fractions I-42 A37
fracture 8.67
fragile A100 8.19
fragment 8.88
fragments A60
fragrance A90 9.00
fragrant A95 6.75
frail K-6 A80 8.75
frame I-6 A19 5.25
frames K-6 A36
framework A56
France F-35 A10 C17
France's A98
franchise J-8 ¿
Francis A48
Frank A17
Frankie A95
Franklin A32
frankly 9.00
frantic A93 9.00
frantically A78 ¡
Franz A95
fraternity 9.00 ¡
freckles 5.50
Fred A27 C11
Freddy A80
Frederick A60
free D-7 A7 C8 2.38
freed A82
freedom H-7 A17 6.50
freely A40
freeway 4.00
freeze A-7 A53 5.75
freezer 3.00
freezes A69
freezing A40 5.75
freight I-6 A41 6.25
French G-35 A7
Frenchman A67
Frenchmen A72
frequency A46
frequent A58 7.92
frequently F-21 A19 7.75
fresh E-2 A10 C9 4.25
freshly A92
freshman A91 ¡
fret 8.50
Fri. D-41 4.13
friction A52 6.25
Friday A-35 A31 C7 4.08
fried A55 6.50
friend A-47 A6 C2 2.50 ¢¡
friend's 8.00
friendlier 8.00
friendliness I-32 7.50
friendly E-26 A15 C14 5.63
friends B-30 A5 C2 4.00
friends' G-40 7.38
friendship A63 6.25
fright A-8 A52 4.25
frighten A56 5.83
frightened F-8 A19 C11
frightening A50 8.25
fringe 6.25
friskier 7.50
fro A82
frog C-4 A27 C10 1.75
frogs F-4 A33 C17
frolicking 6.50
from A-20 A1 C1 1.75 ¢
front C-20 A4 C6 3.25
frontier I-15 A37 6.50
frost A43 4.75
frostbite 7.50
frosty A71
frown A71 4.25
frowned A65
froze 6.25
frozen I-28 A22 5.63
fruit H-10 A13 4.58
fruits I-10 A23
frustrated 7.25
fry A73 4.38
frying A77 4.50
ft. (foot) D-41 A52 5.50
fudge 5.00
fuel I-29 A21 6.88
fuels A77
fulcrum A93
[fulfil]
fulfill 8.50 £
full A-24 A5 C5 3.00
full-fledged F-38 8.25
full-grown A64
fully I-5 A28 6.50
fume 5.25
fumes A92
fun B-5 A8 C2 1.44
function A19
functions F-42 A37
fund A95 5.25
fundamental I-29 A68 8.50 ¡
funds A62 6.25
funeral A82 7.50
fungi A81 5.75
fungus A96 8.00
fungus; fungi H-31
funnel A62 6.75
funnier 6.50
funniest G-32 8.50
funny A17 C4 3.19
fur G-12 A18 C18 4.33
furious A72 6.00
furiously A79
furlong 6.50
furlough 8.25
furnace A42 5.67
furnaces A90
furnish A57 6.17
furnished A64 8.00
furnishing 8.50
furniture G-25 A22 5.75 ¡
furry G-12 A83 C17
furs A47 6.5
further G-12 A14 C17 6.00 ¡
furthermore A48 5.50
fury A83 5.50
fuse 6.50
fuss A94
future E-25 A14 5.58
fuzzy 5.50

G

GA (Georgia) F-41
Gabby A77
Gabriel A82
gadget 6.50
gaily A76
gain I-6 A24 4.88
gained J-6 A27
gaining A68
gains A69
galaxies A99
galaxy A84 6.00
gale A87
Galileo A76
gallant F-24 6.75 ¡
galleries K-32 7.75
gallery 8.33
gallon A59 5.88
gallons A42
gallop A79
galloped A72
galloping A82
galvanize 9.00
gambling ¡
game D-6 A5 C3 1.88
games E-30 A14 C8
gang F-1 A51 C11
gap A63
garage D-11 A29 C18 5.50
garbage D-11 A51 C12 5.19
garden B-11 A9 C5 4.75
gardener 9.00
gardens J-28 A31
garlic 6.25
garment 6.75
garters 7.50
Gary A72
gas D-1 A11 C7 3.50
gaseous J-43 9.00
gases A33 7.50
gasoline I-1 A25 5.94
gasped A58
gate E-6 A19 C8 2.63
gates A49
gather G-12 A21 C18 4.75
gathered H-1 A16
gathering J-1 A39 5.75
gathers A84
gauge K-47 A61 8.88 ¿
gauze 8.75
gave A-23 A4 C2 1.75
gay G-6 A32 C17
gaze A76 6.25
gazed A53
gazelle 8.75
gear A46 4.63
gee A71
geese A45 5.67
gelatin 7.25
gem D-2 5.13
genealogy 8.50
general G-29 A9 C18 5.31
generally H-26 A16 ¡
generate 7.75
generation I-42 A36 7.88
generations A42
generator A86
generators A96
generous A56 7.50
genes 6.25
genetics 8.75
Geneva A91
genius A50 8.00
gentle A22 4.25
gentleman I-36 A33
gentlemen A42 6.75
gently H-28 A19 6.50
genuine A89 7.00
geographic A101
geography A42 8.31
geologists A83
geology A98 8.44
geometric A62 8.50
geometry A53 8.25
George A7
George's A90
Georgia E-35 A47 5.67
Georgie A75
geranium 6.50
gerbil 5.25
germ 4.92
German F-35 A15 C17
Germanic A90
Germans D-35 A46 C14
Germany G-35 A16
germs A52 6.25
gesture E-25 A82 6.75
gestures A71
get A-2 A2 C1 1.58
gets C-30 A10 C5
getting B-34 A6 C3 3.00 ¢
geyser 8.75

Key: Letter-## is *Spelling Power* level word is first taught at. A## is usage by adults; C## is usage by children. (#.##) Average grade level word is taught at; ¢ High School Problem Word, ¡ College Problem Word. ¿ Business Problem Word. £ British spelling (alternate) is also in this list. [word] is British spelling. Elementary Problem words are set in **Boldface** type.

ghastly 6.25
ghetto 7.75
ghost C-22 A31 C5 3.25
ghosts E-22 A66 C13
giant D-8 A15 C9 4.13
giants A54
giblet 9.00
gift I-3 A26 3.58
gifts A33
gigantic G-8 A73 C18 6.00
giggled A101
Gilbert A90
gills A73
gilt 8.50
gin A95
ginger A77 5.50
gingerbread A84
gingham 7.75
giraffe A-12 A78 3.67
girl A-12 A5 C2 2.67
girl's A60 5.00
girls C-30 A5 C4
girls' A93 4.75
git A97
give A-23 A2 C3 2.94
given E-28 A4 C13 5.50
gives E-3 A8 C10
giving B-33 A12 C11 3.00
glacier A87 7.63
glaciers A46
glad D-1 A10 C6 2.56
gladly 8.50
glance H-44 A31 4.63
glanced H-44 A39
glancing A89
glands A57
glare A77 4.63
glaring A96
glass A6 C11 3.00
glasses A29 3.63
glaze 8.25
gleam A87
gleamed A96
gleaming A70
Glen A93
Glenn A91
glide A88
glider A76
glimpse A57 6.25
glisten 6.17
glistening A92
glittering A64
global 8.13
globe I-9 A22 4.00
globular 8.50
gloom A89
gloomiest G-32 7.50
gloomy A86 5.50
Gloria A46
glorious A64 8.50
glory A-13 A60 4.00
glossary 7.50
glove G-23 A68 3.38
gloves A57 3.50
glow J-9 A39 4.25
glowed A80
glowing A50
glue A40 4.19
gnarled 8.25
gnat 5.00
gnaw 5.58
gnawing H-22 ¿
gnome 8.25
go A-9 A2 C1 1.50
goal D-9 A30 C8 5.00
goalie G-9 C17
goals E-9 A62 C9
goat I-9 A33 3.08
goats A46
gobble 8.00
God A-35 A33 C11
goddess H-24 A64 ¡
goddesses A95
gods J-30 A25
goes A-9 A6 C6 3.88
goin' A61
going A-9 A2 C1 1.00 ¢
gold B-9 A6 C3 2.50
golden E-28 A16 C9
goldfish A67 6.00
golf A59 8.00
gone B-47 A5 C5 2.50
gong 6.50
gonna A61
good B-19 A2 C2 2.38
good-bye E-38 A31 C6 4.0 ¢
good-natured A85
goodness A44 4.83
goods H-30 A16
goose I-10 A28
goose; geese F-31
gopher E-9 C15 6.50
gophers C13
Gordon A98
gorilla 8.33
gossiping 7.25
got A-4 A3 C1 1.38
gotten A62 5.00
gourmet 8.58
govern A79 7.00
governed A78 8.00
government E-20 A7 5.83 ¡¿
governments A44
governor E-20 A39 6.75 ¡¿
gown A91 4.50
grab C-1 A49 3.25
grabbed B-34 A29 C11 3.75
grabbing 5.25
grace A64
graceful E-27 A63 5.75
gracious J-43 A90 6.25
grade B-6 A26 C5 2.25
grades C-30 A55 3.75
gradual A87 7.25
gradually H-26 A19 9.00
graduate A73 7.67
graduated A68 7.50
graduation K-42 A86 6.75
graffiti 7.38
graham A66 7.50
grain H-6 A16 7.50
grains K-6 A30
gram 6.00
grammar C-11 A66 7.19 ¡¿
grand G-1 A35 C18 3.25
grandchildren 6.25
granddaughter 8.25
grandeur ¡
grandfather A24 C11 4.17
grandfather's G-40 A95 6.50
grandma C-36 A51 C7
grandma's G-40 5.75
grandmother E-36 A30 C9 4.13
grandmothers 7.00
grandpa A60 C11
grandparent 5.25
grandparents A76
granite A56 8.00
grant A87 5.25
granted J-1 A32
granular 8.75
granulated 7.25
grape A-6 3.88
grapefruit 5.88
grapes A44
graph I-1 A23 5.50
graphic 8.75
graphite 8.50
graphs A70
grasp K-1 A48 5.25
grasped A85
grass A-24 A7 C3 2.50
grasses A42
grasshopper A68 8.00
grasshoppers A66
grasslands A58
grassy A61
grate 8.50
grateful I-27 A53 6.33 ¡
gratitude 7.75
grave G-23 A46 5.75
gravel A43 7.63
gravely A99
gravest 6.75
graveyard 7.75
gravitation 7.50
gravitational A92
gravity J-1 A28 7.08
gravy C-33 C15 5.25
gray G-6 A11 C18 2.69
graze A64 5.92
grazing A40
grease A54 5.75
greasy A90
great B-6 A2 C4 2.81
Great Britain A48
great-grandfathers F-38 7.25
greater H-6 A9
greatest F-6 A10 C13
greatly H-26 A21
greatness A80
Greece I-35 A27
greedy A97 5.42
Greek G-35 A13
Greeks I-35 A24
green B-7 A4 C2 1.69
Greenland A80
greens A81
greet A68 5.25
greeted A49
greeting A48
greetings 5.25
Gregory A83
Gretel A77
grew D-10 A7 C11 3.44
grey E-6 A89 C10
greyhound 9.00
grief A68 6.25
grieves D-31
grievous H-43 ¡¿
grill 6.25
grim A63 6.25
grimace 7.25
grin A51
grind A67 4.58
grinding A55
grinned A42 3.75
grinning A67
grip C-3 A66 4.75
gripped A79
grizzly A82
groan A99 4.42
groaned A68
groceries D-32 A97 4.94
grocery A61 6.00
groove G-23 A76 6.25
grooves A87
gross A100 9.00
grouchy 7.50
ground C-16 A4 C4 4.00
Groundhog Day 4.75
grounds H-16 A38
group H-10 A4 3.94
grouped A45
grouping A45
groups H-10 A7
grove A71 5.25
groves A86
grow C-9 A4 C6 2.25
growers A96
growing G-9 A8 4.00
growl A95 5.00
growled A60
grown F-9 A11 C18 4.75
grown-up A49 7.00
grown-ups E-38 A87 5.75
grows E-9 A15 C13
growth G-9 A17 5.75
grudge 7.25
gruesome 8.25
grumble K-5 6.00
grumbled A101
grumpy 3.50
grunted A80
guacamole 8.00
guarantee A88 7.94 ¡
guaranteed A93
guard H-17 A27 5.94 ¡
guarded A85
guardian 8.25
guarding A92
guards A50 8.00
guerilla 8.50
guess C-24 A9 C5 3.92 ¢¡
guessed A56 9.00
guesses A97 3.25
guest A43 5.00
guests A28
guidance I-44 A85 ¡
guide G-47 A14 5.67
guided A72
guides A55
guilt A74 6.75
guilty A67 8.50
guitar A50 7.00
Gulf I-35 A27
gull A100
gulls A57
gum C-5 A46 C12 3.25
gumbo 7.25

Alphabetical List

gun B-5 A13 C4
Gunn A79
guns F-30 A26 C11
guppies A84 3.75
gust 5.50
guy D-47 A58 C8
guys F-30 A61 C12
gym F-47 A79 C18 3.67
gymnasium K-47 A97 7.50 ¿
gymnastics 7.13
Gypsies D-32 4.00
Gypsy A75 3.75

H

ha 5.00
habit J-1 A30 4.67
habits A29
hacienda 9.00
had A-1 A1 C1 1.67
hadn't F-37 A19 5.75
[haemorrhage]
haiku A101 6.50
hail A65
hair B-14 A7 C5 4.31
haircut 5.13
hairs A58
hairy A89 4.50
Haiti F-35 6.25
Hal A101
half C-1 A4 C4 3.19
halfway I-36 A26 6.25
hall E-24 A17 C11 3.83
Halloween C-35 A59 C6 4.75 ¢
halls A69 6.50
halt A67
halves D-31 A51 6.38
ham G-1 A53 C17
hamburger A89 6.06
hamburgers A99
Hamilton A64
hammer J-1 A32 3.83
hammered A84
hammering A80
hammers A101
hammock 7.50
hamper 7.00
hand C-1 A3 C4 2.50
handed I-1 A23
handful E-27 A49 4.75
handfuls 7.50
handicraft 6.00
handicrafts F-32
handing A89
handkerchief A50 6.17
handkerchiefs 5.50
handle H-29 A16 5.06
handled A53 7.50
handles A56
handling A40
hands D-30 A4 C7 2.50
handsome I-36 A27 6.33
handwriting A60
handy A63 6.00
hang G-1 A25 C15 3.83
hangar 6.50
hanging G-1 A22 C17 5.00
hangs A53
Hank A47
Hans A44
Hansel A86
Hanukkah 4.75
haphazard K-1 ¿
happen E-28 A11 C11 3.67
happened E-28 A6 C3 3.50
happening I-28 A26
happenings A75
happens I-30 A10
happier A58 8.00
happiest F-32 A85 6.00
happily A29 C12 5.63
happiness C-32 A44 6.08
happy B-1 A7 C3 3.06
happy-go-lucky F-38 7.25
harass ¡
harbor H-11 A27 5.25 £
harbors A74 £
[harbour] H-11
[harbours]
hard B-11 A3 C4 3.00
harden 5.00
hardened A97
harder G-11 A20
hardest A61 6.50
hardly C-11 A12 C10 4.63
hardship A84 7.00
hardships A79 8.00
hardware K-36 A84 7.75
hardy A96 8.00
hare 5.00
harm H-11 A34 4.17
harmful E-27 A45 5.67
harmless A84 6.00
harmonious K-32 7.75
harmony K-28 A36
harness A45 5.50
Harold A58
harp 8.00
harpoon A72
Harriet A91
Harris A78
Harry A29
harsh H-11 A52 4.88
Harvard A79
harvest G-11 A37 5.25
harvested A77
harvesting A100
Harvey A83
has A-1 A1 C1 2.00
hasn't A40 5.17
hast A78
haste A82
hasten 7.50
hastily K-32 A60 7.50
Hastings A69
hat C-1 A11 C4 1.38
hatch A43 5.13
hatched A64 7.50
hatchery 8.25
hate C-6 A36 C7 3.50
hated G-6 A41 C18
hath A60
hatred A89 7.50
hats I-1 A29
haughty 7.25
haul A54 5.17 ¡
hauled A54 8.50
hauling A98
haunt 5.88
haunted C-17 A67 C9 5.00
have A-23 A1 C1 2.25 ¢
haven't F-37 A21 5.06
having B-33 A6 C7 3.00 ¡
Hawaii E-35 A40 6.50
Hawaiian A72
hawk A67 5.42
hawks G-17 A67 C18
hay D-6 A27 C7 4.00
hazard A94 8.25
haze A90
hazel 5.50
hazier 7.50
he A-7 A1 C1 1.56
he'd E-37 A17 C18 5.75
he'll E-37 A25 C18 4.75
he's B-37 A8 C5 4.06
head A-47 A3 C3 2.25
headache 6.44
headed F-47 A26 C15
heading A30
headings A51
headline 8.25
headlines A84
headphone 7.00
headquarters A58 7.13
heads F-47 A14
heal 5.38
health F-47 A18 4.75
healthful E-27 6.00
healthier 8.50
healthiest F-32
healthy G-47 A33 5.50
heap A61 6.25
heaped A101
heaps 9.00
hear B-15 A3 C2 3.83
heard B-12 A3 C2 3.50
hearing F-15 A23 C16
hears A51
heart D-11 A6 C14 3.67
[heart-rending]
heartbroken 7.25
hearth A90
heartily 9.00
heartrending K-36 ¿£
hearts A67 6.50
hearty A72 8.00
heat H-7 A7 4.25
heated J-7 A30
heating A51
heats A83
heaved 9.00
heaven A73 5.13
heavens A47
heavier F-32 A31
heaviest A74 7.50
heavily G-32 A35 7.50
heavy F-47 A5 3.75
heavyweight 6.25
Hebrew A100
hectoliter F-46 6.50
[hectolitre] F-46
Hector A74
hedge I-2 A99 6.25
heel A78 5.38
heels J-7 A36
height G-47 A15 5.50 ¡
heights A44
heir H-22 8.75
held F-2 A5 C13 4.88
Helen A31
Helen's A92
helicopter F-4 A49 C18 8.00
helicopters A70
helium A84
hell A61
hello E-2 A28 C10 3.94
helmet A46 5.58
helmets A91
help B-2 A2 C3 2.75
helped E-2 A8 C10
helper A70 4.00
helpers A69
helpful I-27 A22 2.63
helping H-2 A17 3.75
helpless A54 6.00
helplessly A87
helps A9
hemisphere A51 8.63
hemorrhage K-2 ¿£
hen F-2 A45 C13 1.58
hence A53 8.50
Henry A9 C8
Henry's A80
hens A61 6.00
her A-12 A1 C1 2.17
herb 5.75
Herbert A69
herbicide 6.50
herbs A96
herd I-12 A26 5.00
herds J-13 A34
here B-15 A2 C2 3.67 ¢
here's F-37 A34 6.13
hereditary 8.25
heredity 9.00
hereto 9.00
heretofore 9.00
herewith 8.50
heritage A71 6.50
Herman A68
hero 5.75
heroes A48 6.50 ¡
heroic A84 7.25
heroine ¡
herring A94
hers A57 4.75
herself H-37 A13 4.17
hesitancy ¡
hesitant 7.75
hesitate A80 7.25
hesitated A59 7.50
hey D-6 A33 C9
hi D-8 A48 C6
HI (Hawaii) F-41
hibernate 7.88
hibernation 7.00
hiccup 8.25
hickory 8.00

Key: Letter-## is *Spelling Power* level word is first taught at. A## is usage by adults; C## is usage by children. (#.##) Average grade level word is taught at; ¢ High School Problem Word, ¡ College Problem Word. ¿ Business Problem Word. £ British spelling (alternate) is also in this list. [word] is British spelling. Elementary Problem words are set in **Boldface** type.

hid A36 C18 2.58
hidden H-28 A21 5.63
hide F-8 A19 C12 2.25
hides A42
hiding C-33 A31 3.00
high C-8 A3 C4 3.13
high jump 8.25
high school D-39 7.67
high-pitched A97
high-school A91
high-speed A89
higher F-8 A10 C15 5.67
highest H-8 A17 4.50
highlands A79
highly I-26 A22
highway A23 C18 5.00
highways K-36 A36 5.25
hike E-8 A73 C10
hiked 3.50
hiking A85 4.75
hill A-24 A12 C5 2.17
hills F-30 A12 C14
hillside A66
hillsides A85
hilly A83
him A-3 A1 C1 1.63
himself C-36 A3 C6 3.83
hind A42
hinder 7.25
hindrance J-44 8.75 ¿
Hindu A94
hinge 5.63
hint A54 4.25
hints A95
hip A87
hippopotamus A66 9.00
hips A76
hire A73 6.25
hired A48 6.75
his A-3 A1 C1 2.17
historian 7.75
historians A90
historic A53 7.63
historical A41 7.25
history F-13 A8 C18 6.83
hit B-3 A9 C3 1.92
hitch 8.25
hitched A80 8.00
Hitler A73 C18
hits H-30 A47 C18
hitting C-34 A50 C18 4.88
hive A66
ho 7.00
hoard 7.75
hoarse A96 5.88
hoaxes 7.75
hobbies C-32 4.81
hobby A48 4.50
hockey C-4 C5 4.38
hoe A85 6.25
hog C-4 A78 C9
hogs A58 6.00
hoist 5.75
hold E-9 A5 C9 3.06
holder A101
holding H-9 A14
holds H-9 A19
hole C-9 A10 C5 3.06
holes E-30 A18 C11
holiday D-4 A36 C7 5.25
holidays B-30 A57 C4 4.50
Holland A46
hollow I-24 A25 5.08
holly 7.50
Holmes A72
holy F-9 A68 C18 ¡
home A-9 A2 C1 2.08
home school D-39
[home-made]
homeland A79
homely K-26 ¿
homemade A85 5.13 £
Homer J-35 A39
homes H-9 A9
homesick 5.42
homeward A98
homework F-36 A53 C15 5.38
hominy 7.25
homograph 8.75
homonym 8.00
homonyms A90
homophone 7.38
honest A43 5.42
honestly 9.00
honesty 9.00
honey C-20 A35 C11 4.00
honor E-22 A21 5.44 £
honorable 6.00 £
honorary 8.25
honored A64 £
honors A74 £
[honour] E-22
[honourable]
[honoured]
[honours]
hood B-19 A75 C17 4.75
hoofs A53
hook D-19 A35 C13 4.25
hooked A58
hooks A63 7.50
hoop A68 6.25
hop A-4 A49 1.56
hope C-9 A10 C4 2.67
hoped I-9 A23 5.75
hopeful E-27 A101 4.00
hopefully A84 8.00
hopeless A82 5.50
hopes J-9 A34
hoping D-33 A39 4.42 ¡
hopped D-34 A52 C16 5.75
hopping A91 3.75
hops A97
Horace A92
horde 7.75
horizon A44 6.75
horizontal A41 8.50
horn F-13 A27 3.75
horns A28 C13
horrible G-29 A75 C14 6.42
horrified 7.50
horror D-13 A71 6.50
horse B-13 A5 C2 3.75
horse's A52
horseback A40 5.25
horsemen A91
horsepower 7.75
horses B-30 A7 C3 5.25
horseshoe A96
hose E-9 A49 C11 5.44
hosiery 8.25
hospital D-4 A28 C7 4.94
hospitals A66
host A43 4.25
hostage 8.75
hostile A75 7.50
hot B-4 A5 C3 1.50
hotel G-29 A37 C16 5.63
hotels A78 7.00
hotter A65
hottest A90 6.75
hound A70
hounds A80
hour C-22 A6 C5 4.25
hours C-22 A6 C5 4.00
house A-16 A2 C1 3.50
household K-36 A39 6.75
houses C-16 A8 C5 5.50
housewife A85
housework 5.63
housing A56
Houston A60
how A-16 A1 C2 3.25
how's 6.00
Howard A53
however H-37 A3 4.75
howl A84 5.69
howled A81
howling A71 8.00
Huck A95
huddled A69
Hudson A40
hue 5.25
hug 1.50
huge C-10 A9 C9 3.19 ¡
hugged A81
hugging 3.00
Hugh A82
hull E-24 A80 C9
hum A55
human G-10 A8 C16 5.69
humanity 8.25
humanoid 7.50
humans A62
humble A69 7.00
humid A74 6.00
humidity 4.75
humming K-34 A68 7.75
humor K-13 A47 5.33 £
humorless 7.25 £
humorous H-43 A65 6.88 ¡£
[humour] K-13
[humourless]
[humourous] H-43
hundred B-5 A5 C5 5.08
hundreds G-5 A10 C18
hundredth F-5 6.00
hundredths J-30 ¡
hung G-5 A16 4.25
Hungarian A82
Hungary A88
hunger A42 6.63
hungrier F-32 8.50
hungry C-5 A13 C9 4.00
hunt F-5 A18 C16 3.08
hunted I-5 A33
hunter I-5 A30 4.75
hunters G-5 A21 C18
hunting D-5 A15 C9 3.75
hunts A90
hurdle 6.67
hurl 5.88
hurled A81
hurricane K-12 A50 4.75
hurried E-32 A19 5.63
hurriedly J-26 A83 ¡
hurry F-12 A16 C14 4.33
hurrying E-32 A52 5.63
hurt C-12 A12 C5 3.31
hurtle 8.00
hurts A95 7.50
husband F-5 A22 C18 4.63
hush A59
husky A96 7.00
hustle 7.50
hut A-5 A43 3.25
huts A57 6.00
Hwy. (highway) E-41 4.50
hydrant 7.92
hydroelectric 8.50
hydrogen J-28 A31 5.25
hygiene J-8 7.92 ¿
hygienic ¡
hymn D-22 A95 6.50
hyphen 6.75
hypnosis 8.00
hypnotize 8.50
hypocrisy K-47 ¿
hypothesis A79
hysteria 8.75
hysterical 8.50

I

I A-8 A1 C1 1.44
I'd B-37 A11 C7 4.56
I'll B-37 A4 C2 3.56
I'm B-37 A4 C2 3.81 ¢
I've A8 C6 3.81
I.O.U. H-41 8.25
IA (Iowa) F-41
ice D-8 A6 C5 3.50
ice cream D-39 A80 C14 4.75
ice-skating E-38 5.88
iceberg A76 6.25
icebergs A92 8.00
Iceland A76
icicle 6.38
icicles 7.50
icy A41
ID (Idaho) F-41
Idaho A84 6.08
idea G-8 A4 C15 5.00
ideal A54 7.25
ideals A100
ideas A7 5.00
identical A63
identification A89
identified A43
identify H-28 A20 6.75
identifying 7.50
identity A57
idiosyncrasy K-47 ¿
idle A83 6.50
idol 7.50
if A-3 A1 C1 2.25
igloo 7.00
ignite 7.25
ignition 8.00
ignorance A97
ignorant A79 7.33
ignore A86 6.67

ignored A67
IL (Illinois) F-41
ill H-24 A27 3.25
illegal K-3 7.75 ¿
illegible 7.88
Illinois E-35 A30 6.00
illiteracy K-46 7.50
illiterate K-12 8.00 ¿
illness A49 5.00
illogical K-46 7.75
illusion 8.00
illustrate J-3 A35
illustrated K-3 A36
illustrates A58
illustration A41 8.50
illustrations A62 8.50
illustrative H-23 8.75
illustrator 8.38
image J-6 A30 6.38
imagery 9.00
images A54
imaginable 8.38
imaginary A46 7.88 ¡
imagination H-42 A31 6.88 ¡
imaginative H-23 A81 9.00
imagine G-47 A12 5.38
imagined A50
imitate A65 7.25
imitation J-42 A85 7.25 ¿
imitative ¡
immature I-25 7.75
immediate A52 7.00
immediately H-26 A16 7.50 ¡¿
immense J-44 A68 7.63
immigrant 6.75
immigrants A60 8.25
immigrate 8.38
immigration J-42 ¡
imminent 8.25 ¡
immobile 9.00
immodest 9.00
immortal 7.83
immortality 8.50
immovable 8.00
immunity 8.25
immunize 8.50
impact A48
impart 7.00
impartial 8.75
impatient K-46 A73 6.75
impatiently A78
imperative H-23 8.75
imperfect 7.88
implication 8.75
implore 8.75
imply 8.25
impolite K-46 6.83
import A85 6.50
importance H-44 A20 6.75
important F-13 A3 C12 4.92
imported A68
imports A92
impose 7.75
imposed A100
imposition 7.75
impossible I-29 A19 6.33
imposter 8.50
impractical K-46 6.75
impress 7.38
impressed A52
impression H-42 A36 7.38
impressions A60
impressive A61 8.50
imprisoned A88
imprisonment 7.00
impromptu ¡
improper K-46 7.42
improve I-10 A23 6.42
improved J-47 A33
improvement I-45 A61 6.00
improvements A63
improving A58
improvise 8.17
impulse A66
impulses A86
impure I-25 7.50
impurities K-32 9.00
in A-3 A1 C1 1.69
IN (Indiana) F-41
in. (inch) D-41 5.50
inability K-46 7.63
inaccurate 7.63
inactive 6.75
inasmuch as 8.50
inaugurate K-12 ¿
Inc. H-41 7.63
Inca A72
incapable 7.67
incense 7.00
inch D-3 A11 C14
inches A7 C15 3.63
incident A56 8.50
incidental 8.25
incidentally H-26 8.50 ¡¿
incidents J-28 A81 ¡
inclination 8.50
incline 8.50
inclined A62 7.00
include A11 5.75
included I-10 A20
includes I-10 A18
including I-10 A17 6.75
inclusive 9.00
income I-36 A26 8.25
incomes A100
incompatible K-46
incomplete A63 6.50
inconsiderate 8.00
inconvenience 8.50
inconvenienced 9.00
inconvenient 8.00
incorporate 8.50
incorrect K-46 A83 6.38
increase I-7 A18 5.42
increased I-7 A20
increases A40
increasing J-7 A30
increasingly A45
incredible A74 7.83
incredulous I-43 ¡
indeed H-7 A12 5.25
indefinite A87 7.88
indelible K-3 ¿
indent 4.75
independence I-44 A32 6.88 ¡¿
Independence Day 4.50
independent I-28 A29 6.67 ¡
indestructible 9.00
index A43 7.50
indexes 8.25
India I-35 A19
Indian F-35 A5 C12 5.50
Indiana A64 5.63
Indians D-35 A5 C7
indicate I-6 A17 5.25
indicated I-6 A20
indicates J-30 A27
indicating A64
indication A82
indicator 7.50
indictment 8.63
Indies A53
indifferent A98 8.75
indirect A71 6.25
indirectly A94
indispensable F-33 ¡
indisputable 7.75
individual I-29 A17 7.00
individuals A43
Indonesia A95
indoors A53 5.00
induce 9.00 ¡
induced A90
inducement J-45 8.75
industrial J-29 A25 7.75
industrialize 7.75
industries K-3 A26
industrious 8.00
industry G-5 A15 6.50
inevitable A81 8.75
inexact 8.75
inexpensive K-46 A96 7.50
inexperienced K-46 7.50
infant A88 7.13
infection I-42 A85 7.38
infectious H-43 8.75
infer 8.38
inference 8.50
inferior I-15 8.00
infield 5.00
infinite A80 ¡
inflammable J-24 8.38 ¿
inflammation 8.50
inflate 7.25
inflation 7.75
inflection 9.00
influence I-44 A23 6.75 ¡
influenced A41
influences A73
influential J-28 ¡
influenza 6.38
inform K-13 4.75
informal A79 7.06
information F-42 A7 C13 6.50
informed A63 8.50
informing 9.00
ingenious H-43 8.75
ingredient 6.25
ingredients A74
inhabitant K-3 ¿
inhabitants A46
inhabited A90
inherit 7.00
inheritance K-44 8.75
inherited A78
initial A62 6.75
inject 8.00
injection 9.00
injunction 8.75
injured G-3 A50 C18 4.75
injuries A77
injury A62 6.67
ink J-3 A39 3.25
inland A41
inn A49 6.50
inner A31 6.75
inner tube D-39 5.75
inning A73 4.00
innocence I-44 9.00
innocent A67 7.08
inoculate 8.25
inquire 6.58
inquired A83
inquiries 9.00
inquiring 9.00
inquiry 8.50
insane K-46 7.75
insanity 7.75
inscribe 8.50
inscription 8.38
insect J-2 A26 4.83
insects H-3 A12 4.75
insecure 6.75
insensitive 8.75
insert A59 4.75
inserted A91
inside E-36 A4 C8 3.69
insight A91
insignificant 9.00
insist A75 4.75
insisted K-28 A36
insistent 8.88
insomnia 7.75
inspect 6.38
inspection A81 6.00
inspector 8.58
inspiration A81 7.88
inspire 7.75
inspired A61
install 6.17
installation J-42 ¿
installed A61
instance H-44 A16 6.25 ¡
instances A69
instant J-3 A30 6.50 ¡
instantly A47
instead C-47 A5 C7 6.08
instinct A61
instinctive H-23 9.00
instinctively A97
institute A64 9.00
institution A92 8.00
institutions A79
instruct 6.75
instructed 8.50
instruction J-42 A59 6.83
instructions A43
instructor 7.75

Key: Letter-## is *Spelling Power* level word is first taught at. A## is usage by adults; C## is usage by children. (#.##) Average grade level word is taught at; ¢ High School Problem Word, ¡ College Problem Word. ¿ Business Problem Word. £ British spelling (alternate) is also in this list. [word] is British spelling. Elementary Problem words are set in **Boldface** type.

instrument H-45 A20 6.75
instruments H-45 A14
insulate K-5 7.00
insulation A81 8.00
insult K-5 5.75
insurance K-44 A57 8.75
insure A86 5.88
insured 9.00
intake A88
intellectual A83 ¡
intelligence I-44 A48 8.31 ¡
intelligent E-28 A47 7.38 ¡
intend A83 4.75
intended J-28 A34
intense A57
intensity A56
intent A82
intention A94 5.00
intentionally I-26 ¡
intently 8.75
intercede K-12 8.75 ¡¿
intercept 8.33
interchange 8.50
interest H-3 A9 7.00 ¡
interested H-3 A11 4.50
interesting G-12 A8 C16 6.38
interests J-12 A31
interfere K-12 A77 7.00 ¡¿
interfered K-12 8.25 ¿
interference K-44 7.88
interior H-15 A28 6.75
interject 9.00
interjection 8.00
intermediate A100 8.25
intermission 8.42
internal A46 8.50
international A40 7.25
interpret A58 8.50
interpretation A59
interpreted A79
interrupt 7.42
interrupted A43
interruption 9.00
intersect A89 8.50
intersection K-42 A49 6.75
interstate 7.25
interval A84 7.00
intervals A49
interview A101 6.67
intestine 8.75
intimate 8.50
into B-36 A1 C1 2.42
intramural 8.13
intrastate 8.13
intravenous J-43 8.50
intricate A85
intrigue 8.00
introduce A52 8.00
introduced J-3 A26
introduction J-42 A47 7.38
introductory 8.75
intrude 8.00
intruder 8.25
invaded A51
invaders A71
invalid 8.13
invariably A91
invasion A65
inveigle K-3 ¿
invent D-2 A47 5.58
invented H-2 A19
invention I-42 A27 6.38
inventions A46
inventive 9.00
inventor A60 5.75
inventory 9.00
inverted 8.75
investigate A47 8.33
investigation G-42 A43 7.75
investigations A96
investment J-45 8.25
invisible G-29 A35 C16 6.83
invitation F-42 A58 6.38 ¡
invitations 7.50
invite I-8 A41 4.50
invited G-8 A28 C15 4.50
inviting A101 4.00
invoice 8.25
invoices 8.50
invoke 8.75
involve H-23 A72 8.00
involved I-4 A22 8.75
involvement 7.00
involves A51
involving A57
inward A100
iodine A91 9.00
Iowa E-35 A64 5.67
Iraq A96
Ireland J-35 A38
Irish J-35 A34
iron G-47 A8 4.50
ironing 7.50
irons 7.50
irregular K-46 A51 7.50
irrelevant 8.00 ¡¿
irreplaceable 9.00
irresistible 7.63 ¡¿
irresponsible I-15 8.31
irrigation A54 7.75
irritable I-15 7.75
irritate 8.31
is A-3 A1 C1 1.56
island E-22 A9 C9 4.08 ¡
islands F-22 A15
isle 7.50
isles A61
isn't A9 C9 3.81
isolated A62
isolation A77
Israel J-35 A35
Israeli A91
issue A43 5.88
issued A59 8.50
issues A68
issuing F-33 ¿
it A-3 A1 C1 1.38
it'll J-37 A58 6.13
it's B-37 A3 C2 3.75 ¢¡¿
Italian I-35 A20
Italians A66
italicized A51
italics A94
Italy G-35 A16
itch 8.00
item J-8 A34 7.25
itemize 8.38
itemized 9.00
items J-30 A25
itinerary 8.75
its C-3 A1 C4 5.13 ¡¿
itself H-37 A6 5.50 ¡
Ivan A80
ivory A86

J

Jack C-35 A10 C4
Jack's A85
jack-o'-lantern E-38 5.75
jacket J-2 A31 4.33
jackets A81
jacks 6.50
Jackson J-35 A36
Jacob A44
Jacques A85
jagged A68
jaguar 6.75
jai alai 6.50
jail G-29 A60 C12 4.25
Jake A81
jam A65 3.50
Jamaica F-35 6.25
James A16 C12
James's 7.38
Jamestown A66
jammed A71 5.25
Jan. E-41 A43 4.63 ¢
Jane A13 C16
Jane's A71
Janet A81 C12
Janey A65
Janie A89
janitor 6.13
January B-35 A29 4.19
Japan D-35 A21 C13
Japanese G-35 A17
jar C-11 A19 C13 2.88
jargon H-11 3.75
jars A44
Jason A82
Jasper C10
jaw A67 4.25
jaws H-17 A34
Jay A65
jazz A87 6.25
jealous H-43 6.08 ¡
Jean A32
jeans A99 4.13
jeep A77
Jeff A28
Jefferson J-35 A37
jelly C-2 A43 4.25
Jenkins A55
Jenny A76
jerk D-2 A99 5.25
jerked A59
Jerome A90
Jerry A35
Jerusalem A83
jest J-2 7.25
Jesus D-35 C13
jet F-2 A21 C12 2.00
jets A85
jewel 5.38
[jewellery]
jewelry A49 8.33 £
jewels A49 5.50
Jewish A58
Jews A60
Jill A60
Jim C-35 A8 C5
Jim's A50
Jimmy A22
Joan A60
job C-4 A6 C8 2.63
jobs H-4 A19 4.75
Jody A52
Joe C-35 A8 C5
Joe's A53
Joey A57
jogger 5.75
jogging F-34 4.50
Johann A52
John A-35 A4 C3
John's A44
Johnny A11 C14
Johnny's A65
Johnson A26
join B-18 A13 4.19
joined E-18 A12 C16
joining A50
joins A58
joint B-18 A45 4.92
joints A64
joke J-9 A36 3.75
jokes A46
joking A98 4.75
jolly A70 3.50
Jon A99
Jonas A86
Jonathan A62
Jones A25
Joneses' 7.50
Jordan A76
Joseph A36
journal H-29 7.38
journalism 8.50
journalist 8.25
journey H-12 A20 5.63 ¿
jovial 9.00
joy B-18 A20 C16 3.81
joyful E-27 A97 4.75
Jr. (junior) F-41 A77 6.17
Juan A50
jubilant 7.50
jubilee 9.00
judge I-5 A25 4.25
judged A82
judges A44
judging A74
judgment H-45 A52 7.75 ¡
Judy C-35 A42 C5
jug A68 3.50
juggle 5.75
juice G-10 A31 C20 4.13
juices A84
juicy C-33 A68 C15
jukebox 7.25
Julie A65
Juliet A89
July B-35 A23 C16 4.19
jumble 6.25
jump D-5 A13 C6 3.08
jumped C-5 A12 C4
jumper 7.00
jumping I-5 A33 3.00
jumps G-5 A46 C16
junction 8.08
June B-35 A23 C8 4.13
jungle J-29 A28 5.56

jungles A54
junior A44 6.69
junior high school D-39
junk A70 5.25
Jupiter A41
jury A70 7.00
just A-5 A1 C1 2.75
justice A44 6.42
justifiable K-5 ¿
justified 7.50
justify 8.50
juvenile 8.00

K

kangaroo A66
Kansas E-35 A40 5.50
karate 6.13
Karen A100 C13
Karl A64
Kate A52
Kathy A59 C12
Katie A56
Kay A99
kayak 8.13
keen A53 6.25
keep B-7 A3 C5 1.88
keeper F-7 A66 C12
keeping H-7 A14
keeps H-7 A17
Keller A94
Kelly A60
Ken C12
Kennedy A52
kennel 5.63
Kentucky E-35 A41 5.75
Kenya A87
kept D-2 A5 C6 3.88
kernel A75 7.00
kerosene A95
kettle A41 5.13
key G-7 A11 C15 3.31
keys A40 4.50
khaki 8.17
Khan A94
kick I-3 A39 3.06
kickball 4.75
kicked F-3 A46 C14
kicking A66
kicks A96
kid F-3 A46 C16 2.25
kids C-30 A29 C5
kill A-24 A17 C4
killed C-3 A12 C4
killer A84
killing E-3 A42 C10
kills G-30 A72 C15
kilogram F-46 6.00
kiloliter F-46 6.50 £
[kilolitre] F-46
kilometer F-46 6.00 £
[kilometre] F-46
Kim A98
kimono J-9 8.50 ¿
kind C-8 A3 C5 2.75
kindergarten H-28 A93 8.50 ¡
kindest 8.50
kindly A43
kindness A52 4.25
kinds D-30 A4 C6 4.25
king B-3 A10 C3 2.92
king's A50
kingdom A61 7.50
kings I-3 A33
Kirby A79
kiss C-24 A68 C18 3.38
kissed A57 7.50
kisses 5.00
kit A70
kitchen E-28 A11 C11 4.63
kite A-8 A45 2.25
kites F-8 C14
kitten E-28 A40 C4 3.17
kittens F-30 A70 C11
kitty G-3 A81 C18
knapsack 7.00
knead 5.63
knee A40 C18 3.63
kneel 5.83
knees I-7 A23 4.25
knelt A57
knew C-22 A3 C4 3.31
knife C-22 A15 C10 3.92
knight A49 5.13
knights A54
knit C-22 A91 4.13
knitting D-22 A93 6.50
knives D-31 A51 5.13
knob H-22 A63 4.81
knobs A98
knock H-22 A43 C17 3.31
knocked E-22 A33 C9 4.25
knocking A80 8.00
knot A-22 A44 3.75
knots A52
knotty 5.50
know C-22 A1 C1 3.13 ¢
knowing E-22 A18
knowledge F-22 A12 6.00 ¡¿
known A4 C18 4.58
knows E-22 A10 C18
knuckle 7.25
knuckled K-5
Korea A89
KS (Kansas) F-41
KY (Kentucky) F-41

L

LA (Louisiana) F-41
label J-29 A29 4.81
labeled A43 7.88 £
[labelled]
labels A74
labor J-13 A28 5.92 £
Labor Day 4.83
laboratories A72
laboratory I-13 A32 8.06 ¡¿
laborer 9.00 £
[labour] J-13
[labourer]
Labrador A85
labs 8.00
lace A59 8.25
lack I-1 A23 5.50
lacked A64
lacking A81
lacks A96
lad I-1 A34
ladder J-24 A31 4.00
ladders A92
ladies C-32 A33 C18 6.38 ¡
lading 8.50
lady A10 C4 3.88
lagoon A100 7.75
laid F-6 A13 C11 4.92 ¡
lair 5.25
lake D-6 A15 C2 2.75
lakes F-6 A20 C14
lamb C-22 3.13
lambs A69
lame A85 7.50
lamp I-1 A24 4.50
lamps A50 7.00
land D-1 A3 C6 2.50
landed C-1 A24 C5 4.50
landing I-1 A24
landmarks A100
landowners A91
lands H-1 A11 3.75
landscape A46 7.88
landslide A56 8.25
lane A56
lanes A95
language H-1 A6 6.25
languages J-30 A24
lantern A48 6.17
lap K-1 A36 6.25
lard 6.50
large B-11 A2 C5 3.33
largely J-26 A31
larger G-11 A8 4.50
largest G-11 A9 4.50
lariat 8.50
Larry A66
larva; larvae H-31
larvae A81 5.75
larynx ¡
lasagna 8.00
lasagne 7.50
laser 7.50
lashed A85
lasso 7.50
last B-1 A2 C2 2.58
lasted A42
lasting A80
lasts A67
latch 7.25
late D-6 A8 C7 2.25
lately A69 5.83
later B-12 A4 C3 6.25 ¡
latest A40
lather 7.25
Latin G-35 A16
latitude A47
latitudes A74
latter F-24 A40 8.00 ¡
laugh D-47 A17 C9 3.63
laughable 6.00
laughed D-47 A10 C8 4.00
laughing D-47 A20 C9 5.25
laughs A73
laughter J-12 A32 5.50
launch H-17 A73 8.00
launched A54
launching A83
laundry H-17 A73 6.42
Laura A44
Laurie A91
lava A46
law G-17 A12 3.63
lawn G-17 A32 5.06
lawns A75
Lawrence A53
laws H-17 A15
lawyer A65 6.38
lawyers A72
lay E-6 A6 C9 3.42
layer I-12 A22
layers I-30 A21
laying F-6 A59 C11 8.50
lays A50 6.50
lazy G-6 A38 C18 4.75
lbs. (pounds) E-41 7.00
lead G-7 A10 C15 5.33 ¡
leader H-7 A16 4.75
leaders J-30 A24
leadership A51 6.50
leading H-7 A17
leads K-7 A33
leaf I-7 A21 5.25
leaflet 7.25
leafy A87
league A42 C18 7.38
leak A86 8.00
lean K-7 A38 4.25
leaned K-7 A35
leaning A47
leap K-7 A37
leap year E-39 7.00
leaped K-7 A37
leaping A74
leaps A75
learn D-12 C8 4.00
learned F-12 A4 C12
learning H-12 A13
learns H-30 A55 C18
lease 5.25
least G-7 A6 C15 4.75
leather F-47 A22 5.42
leave A-23 A5 C9 3.13
leaves D-31 A6 C7 5.38
leaving B-33 A15 C14 4.00
Lebanon A82
lecture E-25 6.13
lecturer 8.50
led G-2 A9 C18 5.67 ¡¿
ledge A55 5.13
Lee A29
left B-2 A2 C2 3.25
left-hand F-38 A67 7.75
leftovers K-36 7.50
leg E-2 A15 C8 1.75
legal A56 6.08
legality 8.50
legend J-28 A37 8.00
legendary A100
legends A50
legible 7.88
legion 8.25

Key: Letter-## is *Spelling Power* level word is first taught at. A## is usage by adults; C## is usage by children. (#.##) Average grade level word is taught at; ¢ High School Problem Word, ¡ College Problem Word. ¿ Business Problem Word. £ British spelling (alternate) is also in this list. [word] is British spelling. Elementary Problem words are set in **Boldface** type.

legislative A80 7.75
legislature A72 8.00
legitimate K-2 ¿
legs D-30 A7 C6 2.50
leisure A68 7.00 ¡
lemon G-2 A75 C18 4.75
lemonade A69 5.63
lend D-2 A64 5.25
length H-28 A7 5.38
lengths J-30 A29
lengthwise A92 8.25
lens A40
lenses A81 6.25
leopard A82 9.00
leotard 9.00
leprechaun 5.50
less A4 3.38
less harmful 8.50
lesser A89
lesson G-2 A20 C18 3.63
lessons J-24 A29
lest A83
let B-2 A3 C3 1.94
let's B-37 A6 C6 4.06
lets E-2 A46 C8
letter C-2 A4 C5 3.88
letters G-2 A4 C18
letting A48 4.00
lettuce E-29 A70 4.00
level H-29 A10 4.42
leveled 8.50 £
[levelled]
levels A42
lever A41
levers A74
Lewis A37
Lexington A80
liability 9.00
liable ¡
liar 6.88
liberal A92 8.50
liberties G-32 6.00
liberty A46 6.25
librarian 8.50
libraries C-32 A60 4.00
library H-8 A17 5.63 ¡
license H-44 A81 6.50 ¡
lick A82 6.25
licked A57
lid A39 3.25
lie G-8 A12 3.75
lied 5.50
lies H-8 A16
lieutenant A75 8.00
life C-8 A3 C4 3.44
life preserver E-39 7.25
lifeguard 5.75
lifeless 6.50
lifetime A43
lift G-3 A17 3.75
lifted H-3 A16
lifting A46
lifts A70
ligament J-45 8.75
light C-8 A3 C5 2.75
lighted I-8 A28
lighter K-12 A39
lighthouse A71
lighting F-8 C11
lightly E-26 A31
lightning A32 7.83 ¡
lights D-30 A13 C7
lightweight A85
likable 9.00
like A-8 A1 C1 1.58
liked C-8 A9 C5 3.00
likelihood 6.88 ¡
likely E-26 A15 5.88 ¡
likeness 6.00
likes C-30 A20 C4
likewise A67 7.88
liking B-33 A83 3.75
lilies A96 6.50
lily A82
limb A81 5.13
limbs A50 8.00
lime A65 7.00
limerick 9.00
limestone A58
limit K-3 A38 5.38
limited J-3 A27 7.13
limits A46
limousine 8.00
limp A81 6.25
Lincoln I-35 A19
Lincoln's A71
Lincoln's Birthday 4.50
Linda A45 C8
Lindy A94
line D-8 A2 C6 3.50
linear 6.50
lined J-8 A31
linen A68 6.92
lines A4
lining A50
link A47
linked A60
linking A70
links A60
linoleum 7.50
lion E-8 A18 C11 4.81
lions I-8 A35
lip F-3 A66
lips H-3 A20
liquefaction I-21 ¿
liquefy I-21 ¿
liquid E-21 A14 6.88
liquids A51
list H-3 A5 3.58
listed H-3 A17
listen E-28 A7 C14 4.38
listened E-28 A19
listener A65
listeners A62
listening I-28 A21 6.50
listens A76
listing A81
lists A41 3.25
lit A41
liter 6.00 £
literacy 8.50
literal 9.00
literally A60
literary A76 8.75
literature G-25 A35 8.17 ¡
[litre]
litter A93 6.25
little E-29 A1 C1 3.00
live A-23 A3 C3 2.31
lived B-3 A4 C3 3.00
livelier K-32 6.75
livelihood I-32 8.25 ¡¿
lively I-26 A31
liver A62
lives D-31 A7 C6
livestock A68
living B-33 A4 C7 3.25
living room 6.75
lizard A65 5.75
lizards A55
load I-9 A21 3.00
loaded I-9 A25 4.25
loading A71
loads A49 6.00
loaf A52 5.25
loan A85 5.50
loaves A86 6.56
lobster A91 7.25
lobsters A82
local I-29 A18 6.83
locality 8.50
locate I-6 A24 6.13
located G-9 A15 C16
locating A88
location H-42 A28 6.50
locations A69
Loch Ness 7.75
lock I-4 A33 5.25
locked F-4 A36 C18
locks A69
locomotive A57
lodge A74 5.58
loft A87
lofty A77 7.25
log H-4 A19 2.88
logging A86
logic 8.00
logical A53 8.75
logs I-4 A23
loiter J-18 6.88
London I-35 A19
lone A63 5.50
loneliest K-32 7.08
loneliness I-32 A85 ¡¿
lonely E-26 A22 C15 5.63
lonesome A64 5.25
long B-4 A1 C2 2.63
long-distance G-38 7.00
long-lived 8.25
long-range 8.25
longed A68
longer G-12 A5 C16
longest I-4 A35
longing A93
longitude A69
look B-19 A2 C2 2.56
looked B-19 A2 C2 4.63
looking B-19 A4 C4 3.00
lookout A65
looks D-19 A7 C6
loom A73 7.00
loop J-10 A38
loops A77
loose G-10 A20 C15 4.44 ¡¿
loose-leaf G-38 9.00
loosely A78
loosen A90 6.63
loosened A87
lord A43 5.25
lords A67
Los Angeles A45
lose H-10 A17 3.83 ¡¿
loses A47
losing F-33 A39 4.00 ¡
loss H-24 A25 6.25
losses A69 4.25
lost B-4 A7 C5 2.42
lot B-4 A8 C3 2.81
lots B-30 A20 C3 5.25
Lou A78
loud C-16 A13 C8 3.69
louder H-16 A35
loudly J-26 A31
loudspeaker 8.25
Louis A21
Louisa A98
Louise A85 C12
Louisiana E-35 A54 6.50
lounge 7.25
lovable 7.25
love A-20 A10 C3 3.00
loved E-20 A17 C11 3.50
lovely E-26 A18 C15 5.00 ¿
lover A74 9.00
lovers A78
loves A61 4.50
loving B-33 A83 3.00
lovingly 6.00
low E-9 A6 C10 2.88
lower G-9 A8 3.50
lowered K-12 A38
lowering A95
lowest J-9 A29
lowland A67
lowlands A57
loyal B-18 A72 4.92
loyalty A87 5.58
luck I-5 A24 2.83
luckily F-32 A70 6.00
lucky C-5 A26 C10 3.88
Lucy A47
luggage K-5 6.33
Luke A90
lumber I-5 A31 5.42
lump A44 6.25
lumps A69
lunar A65 6.25
lunch C-5 A16 C8 3.38
luncheon 7.00
luncheons 9.00
lung A93
lungs G-5 A30 C18 8.75
lure 5.50
luster 8.25
[lustre]
luxury A86 7.88
Lydia A98
lying G-8 A17 C18 4.50 ¡
lyric 8.75
lyrics 7.50

M

m.p.h. A83 7.00
Ma A32
MA (Massachusetts) G-41
ma'am A74 7.50
macaroni A81 7.25
machine E-47 A7 C13 4.58
machinery I-12 A25 7.88
machines H-30 A12 C19

Mack A88
macrame' 6.50
mad C-1 A26 C4 3.25
madam A92 9.00
madame A66
made B-6 A1 C2 2.44
Madison A69
magazine I-1 A33 6.83 ¡
magazines J-1 A38
Magellan A78
magic D-1 A17 C7 4.33
magician A76 7.50
magnesium A98
magnet J-1 A26 6.00
magnetic K-2 A35 8.63
magnetism A79
magnets A46
magnificence K-44 7.75
magnificent A48 7.81
magnifies 9.00
magnify G-32 7.25
magnifying A72 8.50
magnitude A81
maid A60 5.25
maiden A65
mail G-6 A23 C16 4.44
mailbox 4.38
mailed 5.25
mailing 8.50
mailman E-36 C8
main E-6 A6 C9 5.50
Maine E-35 A46 5.50
mainland A49 7.00
mainly I-26 A27
maintain K-6 A38 7.00 ¡
maintained A61
maintaining A100
maintenance H-44 A92 8.25 ¡¿
maize 8.50
majestic A92
majesty A70
major H-13 A11 6.00
majority J-13 A35 7.25
make B-6 A1 C2 1.56
make-believe G-38 A62 7.50
[make-up]
maker A73
makers A64
makes C-30 A4 C5
makeup 7.00
making B-33 A4 C8 3.00
malaria A91 7.25
male J-6 A32 5.67
males A82
malfunction 8.75
malicious J-43 9.00
malnutrition 8.75
Mama A17 5.50
Mama's A75
mammal G-29 A94 C16 5.75
mammals J-1 A32
mammoth 8.00
man A-1 A2 C1 1.50
man's G-40 A10 C18
man-made A45
man; men F-31
manage A43 5.33
manageable 9.00
managed J-1 A27
management J-45 A77 7.63 ¿
manager A43 6.00
managers A101
mane G-6 A56 C16 5.50
maneuver J-10 7.25 ¡¿£
maneuverable 9.00 £
manger 7.00
Manhattan A73
manicure I-25 8.75
manila 7.00
manipulate 8.75
Manitoba 7.00
mankind A44
manned A84
manner H-1 A17 7.08
manners A45
[manoeuvrable]
manor 7.75
mansion 8.00
mantle A62
manual J-29 8.63 ¡¿
Manuel A85
manufacture I-25 A40 5.13
manufactured A43
manufacturer A70 ¡
manufacturers A64 7.50
manufacturing J-10 A30 7.75
manuscript A88 8.88
many A-47 A1 C2 2.69 ¡
map H-1 A6
maple G-29 A38 C19
mapped 6.50
maps I-30 A15
mar 9.00
Mar. E-41 4.63
marathon 8.88
marble A59 5.00
marbles H-11 A40 4.25
Marc A49
March B-35 A21 C15 4.19
march 6.50
marched H-11 A34
marching A43
Marco A68
mare A61 6.25
Margaret A59
margarine 6.75
margin A54 7.00
margins A76
Maria A28
Marie A48
marine A59 7.00
mark C-11 A7 C10 3.75
marked G-11 A13
marker A78
market G-11 A13 4.42
markets A47
marking A60
markings A67
marks G-11 A12
maroon 7.42
marooned 7.75
marriage F-24 A46 6.83 ¡
married E-32 A24 C13 5.33
marry I-14 A33 4.00
Mars C-35 A26 C6
marsh H-11 A62 5.25
marshal 6.50
Marshall A99
marshes A81
marshmallow 6.50
Martha A48
Martian C14
martin H-11 A29
Martin Luther King D 5.00
marvel A95
[marvellous]
marvelous I-43 A55 8.00 £
Mary A9 C14
Mary's A56
Maryland E-36 A64 5.67
mascot 8.25
mask A58 5.25
masks A83
mass H-24 A15
Massachusetts E-35 A34 6.00 ¡
massacre 8.25
massage 8.00
masses A31 6.25
massive A50
mast A66
master F-12 A15 C13 5.00
master's A97
masterpiece 7.25
masters A59
masthead 8.25
masts A70
mat A74 4.75
matador 9.00
match G-1 A14 C16 3.00
matched A48
matches A37 5.00
matching A59
mate K-6 A35
material A9 6.75 ¡
materials F-15 A10
math C-1 3.25
mathematical A47
mathematician A91 8.25
mathematics J-30 A30 8.50 ¡¿
matria; matrices H-31
mats A82
Matt A89
matter F-12 A5 C14 4.25
matter-of-fact F-38 8.25
matters J-1 A39
Matthew A82
mattress F-24 7.25 ¡
mature E-25 A71 6.25
maturity A96
maverick 7.25
Max A63 C7
maximum A53
may C-6 A1 C4 2.63
May Day B-35 5.00
maybe C-36 A8 C6 3.69
Mayflower A100
mayonnaise 7.88
mayor F-13 A41 C14 5.58
maze 8.50
MB (Manitoba) G-41
MD (Maryland) F-41
me A-7 A2 C1 1.50
ME (Maine) F-41
meadow J-9 A38 5.50
meadows A56
meal I-29 A21 3.50
meals J-7 A35
mean C-7 A4 C5 2.81
meaner 4.50
meanest 4.50
meaning H-7 A5
meaningful I-27 A67 6.00
meaningless A95
meanings I-30 A19
means E-7 A3 C10
meant G-47 A9 4.75 ¡
meantime A70 8.50
meanwhile I-36 A31 5.25
measles A89 5.25
measure E-25 A7 6.00
measured G-25 A22
measurement H-45 A34 7.13
measurements H-45 A36
measures G-25 A18
measuring D-33 A26
meat E-7 A10 C8 3.50
meats A73
mechanic 6.92
mechanical J-29 A35 6.75
mechanics A63
mechanism A89
mechanize 7.75
medal E-29 A89 5.25
meddle 8.00
media 6.38
median 8.50
medical J-29 A32 6.75
medication K-2 8.25
medicine F-2 A22 C11 6.25 ¡
medicines A77
medieval A75
meditation 8.25
Mediterranean I-35 A33
medium A41 7.67
meet E-7 A8 C9 3.94
meeting H-7 A16
meetings A49 7.00
meets A45
Mel A95
melancholy K-26 A91 8.25
mellow 7.25
melodies A85
melody A46 6.13
melon 6.75
melt J-2 A37 4.92
melted I-2 A29 4.25
melting A34
melts A54
member H-2 A14 4.75
members I-12 A7
membership A89 9.00
membrane A61
memo 9.00
memoir 8.88
memorable 8.63
memorandum 8.50
memorial A95
Memorial Day 4.83

Key: Letter-## is *Spelling Power* level word is first taught at. A## is usage by adults; C## is usage by children. (#.##) Average grade level word is taught at; ¢ High School Problem Word, ¡ College Problem Word. ¿ Business Problem Word. £ British spelling (alternate) is also in this list. [word] is British spelling. Elementary Problem words are set in **Boldface** type.

memories D-32 A68 5.38
memorize G-32 A73 7.63
memory I-2 A29 7.00
memos 8.25
Memphis A93
men B-2 A2 C2 1.75
men's A56 5.25
menace 7.25
mend A82 5.75
mended A98
mental I-28 A27 6.25
mentally A64
mention I-42 A39 6.33
mentioned I-42 A27
menu 7.63
merchandise 7.83
merchant K-28 A36 5.38
merchants A52
merciful 7.50
Mercury G-35 A41 7.50
mercy A87 7.25
mere A43 6.25
merely H-26 A21 7.25
merge 9.00
meridian A75
meridians A99
merit 7.00
mermaid 5.25
merrily A89 7.50
merry A41 3.75
merry-go-round G-38 A101 6.0
mesa 7.75
mess E-24 A81 C18 3.88
message H-2 A20 5.50
messages J-24 A27
messenger H-28 A57 7.00 ¡
met C-2 A12 C5 2.42
metal H-29 A12 4.31
metallic A67
metals A29
metaphor 8.88
meteorite 6.25
meteorology 8.50
meteors A93
meter A41 6.00
meters A74
method H-2 A10 6.88
methods I-30 A16
metric A88 7.25
metropolitan 9.00
mew 4.50
Mexican I-35 A31
Mexicans A80
Mexico D-35 A14 C12 6.25
mg. A99
MI (Michigan) F-41
Miami A86
mice A22 C9 4.58
Michael A45 C16
Michigan E-35 A42 5.67
microbes A82
microfilm 8.00
microphone 7.88
microscope J-9 A37 7.56
microscopic 7.75
mid 9.00
midday A94
middle E-29 A8 C8 4.13
midget 6.50
midnight E-36 A32 C13 6.25
midst A48
Midwest A85
might B-8 A2 C3 3.69
mighty I-8 A23 6.25
migrate A88 7.25
migrating A98
migration A74
Mike A14
mild J-8 A35 4.67
Mildred A94
mile E-8 A15 C9 4.00
mileage J-8 7.63 ¿
miles C-30 A3 C5 4.50
military I-3 A25
militia A101
milk C-3 A8 C5 3.33
milked 7.50
milking A81 7.00
milkman 8.00
milky A70
mill H-24 A30
Miller A59
milligram F-46 6.00
milliliter F-46 6.00 £
[millilitre] F-46
millimeter F-46 6.00 £
[millimetre] F-46
million E-3 A9 C9 5.50
millions H-3 A13
mills J-24 A35
mimic 7.25
mimicking 6.50
mind E-8 A5 C11 3.13
minds J-8 A38
mine D-8 A14 C7 4.00
mined A66
miner 7.00
mineral J-29 A29 7.00
mineralogy 8.50
minerals I-29 A19
miners A68
mines G-30 A33 C15
miniature A72 7.81 ¡
minimum I-5 A61 9.00
mining C-33 A41 C16
minister G-3 A44 C16 6.75
Minnesota E-35 A69 5.75
minor K-13 A34 7.75
minority 8.25
minus A67 6.25
minute E-3 A8 C10 6.00
minutes B-30 A7 C5 6.25 ¡
miracle A56
mirage 8.00
mirror I-24 A23 4.81
mirrors A52
misbehave 7.75
misc. 7.00
miscellaneous 8.50
mischief G-3 A87 C19 7.00
mischievous H-43 7.81 ¡
misdemeanor 8.63 £
[misdemeanour]
misdirect 9.00
miserable A64 8.00
misery A81 8.25
misfortune A100 6.75
misled 5.00
misplace K-46 5.92
miss C-24 A23 C6 2.50
missed F-3 A24 C13
missile A66 7.58
missiles A97
missing H-3 A10 3.00
mission I-42 A30 6.25
missionaries A70
missionary A95 9.00
missions A81
Mississippi E-35 A23 5.67 ¡
Missouri E-35 A32 6.00
misspell 6.83
misspelled A67 ¡
mist A55 5.88
mistake G-6 A25 C19 5.00
mistaken A62 6.50
mistakes K-46 A35
mister A75
mistletoe 5.50
mistress A89 7.50
mistrust 8.75
mists A93
misunderstand 6.75
misunderstanding 9.00
misuse 5.00
mitten 5.08
mittens A83 7.50
mix J-3 A38 2.25
mixed G-3 A15 C19 5.75
mixes 5.00
mixing A57
mixture E-25 A28 6.00
MN (Minnesota) F-41
MO (Missouri) F-41
mo. 5.00
moan A89
moaned A97
mobile 8.13
moccasin 7.63
moccasins A72
mock 7.25
mode A79
model H-29 A16 5.44
modeling 7.50 £
[modelling]
models J-30 A34
moderate A63 8.25
moderation 8.25
moderator 8.00
modern H-4 A8 6.00
modernize 6.50
modest A73 7.38
modified A57
modifiers A83
modifies A89
modify A73 8.50
moist G-18 A36 5.06
moisture E-18 A32 7.75
molar 8.00
molasses A67
mold J-9 A39 7.00 £
molds A65 £
mole A78
molecule A42 8.75
molecules I-10 A21
Molly A98
molten A73
mom B-4 A35 C2 3.25
mom's C10 5.75
moment E-9 A7 C14 4.88
momentous I-43 ¡
moments H-45 A39
Mommy D-35 C12
Mon. D-41 4.13
monarch 7.25
monarchy 8.00
Monday A-35 A36 C8 3.94
money C-20 A4 C3 3.00
monitor 7.13
monkey D-4 A29 C6 4.50
monkeys G-20 A32 6.63
monks A99
monogram 8.17
monologue 8.75
monopoly 8.13
monorail 8.00
monotone 8.00
monotonous I-43 8.13
monsieur A90
monsieur; messieurs H-31
monsoon 9.00
monster C-12 A37 C4 4.38
monsters E-30 C10 6.25
Montana E-35 A65 6.00
month C-20 A12 C7 4.63
monthly A90 8.50
months E-20 A8 C9 5.75
Montreal C-35 C4
monument I-45 A80 6.08
monuments A96
mood J-10 A26 6.50
moods A97
moon B-10 A5 C4 4.00
moon's A72
moonlight K-36 A39 5.75
moons A57
Moore A93
moose G-10 A64 C16 7.33
mop 1.75
moral A60 7.42
morale K-29 7.75 ¡
morality 8.25
more A-13 A1 C2 3.06
moreover K-36 A34
Morgan A37
mormor 1.43
morning A-13 A4 C2 3.25
morning-glory F-38 7.25
mornings A76 7.50
Morocco A75
morpheme A77
Morse A81
mortal A94
mortar A88 7.00
mortgage 8.25
Moscow A78
Moses A92
Moslem A99
mosquito E-21 A52 C13 7.50
mosquitoes F-30 A37 C11 7.0
moss A45 4.50
mosses A89
most B-9 A1 C3 3.50
mostly H-26 A18 4.50
motel A85 4.75
moth A61 7.50
mother A-20 A3 C1 2.25
mother's G-40 A23 C13 5.75
mother-in-law G-38 8.25
mothers E-20 A31 C9
moths A66 4.25

Alphabetical List

motion F-42 A13 6.33
motion picture G-39 8.25
motionless A67
motions A52
motor F-12 A23 C11 4.42
motorcade 8.25
motorcycle 7.50
motors A49
motto 8.00
mottoes 7.75
[mould] J-9
[moulds]
mound A59 6.25
mounds A87
mount H-16 A29 4.75
mountain C-16 A7 C5 5.25
mountainous I-43 A53 8.38
mountains F-30 A5 C11
mountainside A85
mounted H-16 A31
mounting A70
mourn 6.33
mournful A94
mouse C-16 A23 C6 3.88
mousse 7.25
[moustache]
mouth C-16 A8 C8 3.69
mouthfuls I-27 7.50
mouths H-16 A39
movable 9.00
move C-10 A4 C8 3.08
moveable A80 6.00
moved D-10 A5 C9 3.50
movement H-45 A11 5.67
movements H-45 A24
mover 6.00
moves I-10 A11
movie G-10 A27 C14 4.75
movies I-10 A37 4.88
moving B-33 A6 C10 3.00
mow F-9 C16
Mr. D-41 A2 C2 6.17
Mrs. D-41 A4 C3 6.17 ¢
MS (Mississippi) F-41
Ms. D-41 6.69
MT (Montana) F-41
Mt. A62
much B-5 A2 C2 2.38
mud C-5 A16 C11 2.00
muddy A41 5.00
muffin 6.50
muffle 7.50
muffled A81
mule A45 2.88
mules A63
multiple A51 6.75
multiples A66
multiplication A44 8.75
multiplied I-32 A63 7.25
multiply I-5 A37
multiplying A75
mumble 7.25
mumps 6.50
mural 7.42
murder A72
murmur K-12 6.94 ¡¿
murmured A70
Murphy A79
Murray A91
muscle J-29 A34 6.38 ¡
muscles I-29 A16
muscular A65 7.38
museum F-47 A41 C19 6.00
museums A69
mushroom A81
mushrooms A75
music C-10 A6 C8 4.58
musical I-29 A22 6.00
musician A67 7.42
musicians A53
musket A86
muskrat 7.58
must B-5 A2 C5 2.67
must've J-37 6.63
mustache A98 8.25 £
mustang 8.17
mustard A98 4.00
mustn't J-37 A92 6.63
mute 5.25
muttered A54
mutton 7.50
mutual A97 9.00
mutually 8.50
muzzle A96
my A-8 A1 C1 2.13
myself C-36 A13 C7 2.92
mysteries I-32 A85 6.58
mysterious H-43 A30 C19 7.13 ¡
mystery E-47 A37 C11 7.38
mystic 8.00
mystify 8.50
mystifying 6.75
myth A88 6.50
mythology 8.67
myths A75

N

N. (north) D-41 4.50
N.E. (north east) E-41
N.W. (north west) E-41 4.50
nail J-6 A31 2.75
nailed A86
nails I-6 A26
naked A60
name C-6 A2 C2 1.56 ¢
named D-6 A6 C2 3.00
namely 9.00
names F-30 A6 C11
naming A49 5.00
Nancy A38
nap A77 3.25
napkin A96 6.50
Napoleon A47
narration 8.25
narrative 8.50
narrator A94 7.50
narrow F-14 A12 5.75
NASA H-41 7.63
Nat A101
Nathan A70
Nathaniel A98
nation F-42 A12 5.75
nation's A49
national I-29 A17 7.13
nationality 6.50
nations F-42 A18
native I-6 A21 6.63
natives A50 5.00
natural I-29 A7 6.50
naturally I-26 A26 7.63
nature E-25 A12 5.08
nature's A82
naughty C-17 C14 6.00
Nautilus A95
naval A64 7.25
navel 7.25
navigation K-42 A79 6.75
navy J-6 A36 4.92
nay A90
NB (New Brunswick) H-41
NC (North Carolina) F-41
ND (North Dakota) F-41
NE (Nebraska) G-41
near B-15 A3 C7 3.75
nearby H-37 A15 5.33
nearer H-15 A27
nearest H-15 A16
nearly E-26 A7 C18 6.38
neat J-7 A36 4.25
neatly A44
Nebraska E-35 A64 6.08
necessarily A50
necessary H-2 A8 7.08 ¡¿
necessity K-2 A66 7.63
neck E-2 A14 C10 3.50
necklace A61 4.75
necks A75 7.50
necktie 6.25
nectar A61
Ned A39
need E-7 A3 C8 2.94
needed F-7 A5 C14
needle G-29 A24 C18 4.94
needles A40
needless 8.00
needn't J-37 A94 6.00
needs G-30 A9 C15
negative J-47 A26 6.75
neglect D-2 5.75
neglected A80 8.50
neighbor C-6 A25 4.19 ¡£
neighbor's G-40 A65 6.50 £
neighborhood I-6 A29 6.25 £
neighboring A53 £
neighbors F-30 A18 C11 £
neighbors' 6.50 £
[neighbour] C-6
[neighbour's] G-40
[neighbourhood] I-6
[neighbouring]
[neighbours] F-30
[neighbours']
neither H-7 A12 5.88 ¡
Nelly A79
Nelson A99
neon 7.00
nephew 5.75
Neptune A87
nerve K-12 A42 5.17
nerves A40
nervous H-43 A28 7.83
nervously A75
nest G-2 A15 C16
nesting A85
nests J-2 A38 4.25
net F-2 A34 C14 2.88
Netherlands A47
nets A47
network A49 7.92
neutral A61 8.42
neutrality 8.50
neutrons 8.75
Nevada E-35 A63 6.08
never B-12 A2 C2 3.83
nevertheless I-36 A36 6.67
new B-10 A2 C3 3.31
New Hampshire E-39 A83 5.63
New Jersey E-39 A49 6.08
New Mexico E-39 A67 6.00
New Orleans A43
New Year 5.50
New Year's 6.50
New Year's Day D-39 5.58
New York D-39 A8 C19 5.50
New York City D-39 A29
New Zealand A61
newborn 7.00
newcomers A89
newer A79
newest A74
Newfoundland G-35 A93 7.0
newly A40
news H-10 A13 5.75
newscast 6.50
newspaper A16 C20 5.00
newspapers H-37 A22 3.75
newsroom 7.00
newsstand 8.25
Newton A75
next B-2 A2 C2 2.75
NF (Newfoundland) F-41
NH (New Hampshire) G-41
nice A-8 A13 C2 2.83
nicely A72 5.00
nicer 4.50
nicest 8.00
Nick A68
nickel E-29 A39 C10 4.67 ¡¿
nickels A72 8.00
nickname A76
niece F-7 6.50 ¡
Nigeria A98
night B-8 A3 C2 2.75
[night-time]
nightfall A97
nightgown 6.00
nights G-30 A26 C16
nighttime 6.67 £
Nile A50
nine B-8 A12 C5 2.08
nineteen E-8 A65 6.00
nineteenth H-8 A64 ¡¿
ninetieth H-8 ¡
ninety G-8 A73 C16 6.63 ¡¿
ninety-nine E-38 4.50
ninth B-47 A68 4.88 ¡¿
nitrogen A45
Nixon A83

Key: Letter-## is *Spelling Power* level word is first taught at. A## is usage by adults; C## is usage by children. (#.##) Average grade level word is taught at; ¢ High School Problem Word, ¡ College Problem Word. ¿ Business Problem Word. £ British spelling (alternate) is also in this list. [word] is British spelling. Elementary Problem words are set in **Boldface** type.

NJ (New Jersey) G-41
NM (New Mexico) G-41
no A-9 A1 C2 1.56
no one 4.88
no. 7.00
nobility 9.00
noble A58 9.00
nobles A55
nobody B-36 A16 C7 4.19
nobody's G-40 5.75
nod A95
nodded D-34 A24
noise B-18 A13 C6 3.81
noises E-18 A39 C18
noisier G-18 6.00
noisy G-18 A38 6.17
nomad 9.00
nominate 8.50
nomination 9.00
[non-profit]
none C-20 A12 C18 3.25
nonessential 7.75
nonexistent 7.75
nonfiction K-46 6.88
nonflammable 8.00
nonpartisan 8.75
nonproductive 8.75
nonprofit K-46 7.67 £
nonresident K-46 7.50
nonsense I-44 A52 7.50
nonstop 7.75
nonviolent K-46 6.38
noodle 8.00
noon G-10 A22 C16 3.58
nor H-13 A9 6.25
normal J-29 A25 5.83
normally A47
Norman A89
north F-13 A8 C13 4.88
North Carolina E-39 A63 5.50
North Dakota 6.08
northeast A49 6.00
northeastern A81
northern G-13 A13
northward A61
northwest A47 6.25
northwestern A86
Norway G-35 A29 C16
Norwegian A69
nose D-9 A10 C7 2.13
noses A57
nostril 6.50
nostrils A71
not A-4 A1 C1 1.38
notation A40
notch A91 7.25
notches A98
note H-9 A9 3.42
notebook A41 5.00
notebooks A99 6.50
noted J-9 A28
notes H-9 A15
nothing D-4 A4 C6 4.75
notice F-47 A5 C18 5.25
noticeable I-29 A86 8.50 ¡¿
noticed H-9 A15 5.25
noticing 7.25
notified K-32 7.50
notify 8.50
noting A101
notion A69 6.75
notoriety K-13 ¿
noun H-16 A13 5.44
nouns H-16 A18
nourish 6.25
Nov. E-41 5.42
Nova Scotia G-39 7.00
novel A52 6.58
novelette 9.00
novels A75
novelty 8.38
November B-35 A32 4.19
now A-16 A1 C1 3.00 ¢
nowadays A66 ¡¿
nowhere A47 6.25
nozzle 6.25
NS (Nova Scotia) G-41
NT (Northwest Territories) H-41
nuclear I-15 A37 7.38
nuclei A96
nucleus A54 8.75
nuisance H-44 A86 8.25
numb C-22 6.50
number F-12 A2 C13 4.25
numbered J-12 A37
numbers G-5 A5
numeral J-29 A26 6.75
numerals I-30 A23
numerator 6.75
numerous H-43 A34 7.38
nurse F-12 A41 C11 4.56
nursery A69 7.00
nurses A62 8.00
nut A-5 A71 1.63
nutrients A75
nutrition 7.50
nutritious 9.00
nuts I-5 A29
NV (Nevada) G-41
NY (New York) G-41
nylon A67 7.25
nymphs A88

O

o'clock B-37 A19 C18 4.50 ¡
o'er A67
oak I-9 A33 3.94
oar A80
oars A55
oases 6.75
oasis 6.50
oath A72 7.75
oatmeal 6.17
oats H-30 A50 C18 7.00
obedient 7.58
obey A58 5.94
obeyed A75 4.50
obituaries I-32 8.25
object F-4 A8 C14 4.83
objected A99
objection 7.75
objective A52 7.25
objects H-4 A11
obligate 6.00
obligation 9.00
oblige 7.00 ¡
obliged 8.50
obnoxious H-43 8.75
observant 8.63
observation I-42 A38
observe G-23 A15 6.75
observed I-4 A24
observer A67
observers A99
observing A52
obstacle K-29 8.92 ¡
obstinate 8.75
obstruction 8.75
obtain I-4 A25 7.00
obtainable 9.00
obtained J-4 A26
obtaining A82 9.00
obvious I-43 A44 7.88
obviously I-26 A38
occasion H-42 A34 7.38 ¡¿
occasional A56 8.75
occasionally I-26 A29 8.63 ¡¿
occasions A45
occult 8.00
occupant 8.75
occupation A51 7.50
occupational 7.75
occupations A92
occupied F-32 A39 5.50
occupy A60 7.00
occur I-24 A21 7.13 ¡
occurred K-34 A30 7.00 ¡¿
occurrence I-44 8.13 ¡¿
occurring J-24 A96 ¡
occurs A28
ocean E-9 A7 C11 4.67
oceanographer 8.00
oceans I-30 A22
Oct. E-41 4.63
octagon I-4 8.75
octave 8.75
October B-35 A28 4.19
octopuses 8.25
odd H-24 A23 3.58
oddly A87
odds A66
odor A46 6.13 £
odors A75 £
[odour]
[odours]
Odysseus A82
of A-47 A1 C1 1.58
off A-4 A2 C1 2.31
offensive A92
offer I-24 A24 4.58
offered I-24 A21 6.13 ¡
offering A50 8.50
offers A47 9.0
office D-4 A11 C10 5.67
officer C-33 A27 C15 6.25
officers A30 ¡
offices A43
official J-29 A30 6.63 ¡
officially A78
officials J-3 A35
offshore 6.50
offspring A98
often D-22 A2 4.33
ogre 6.50
oh B-9 A5 C2 1.75
OH (Ohio) G-41
Ohio E-35 A27 5.50
oil B-18 A8 C9 3.81
oils A74
oily J-18 4.75
ointment G-18 7.25
OK A86 C8
OK (Oklahoma) G-41
okay C-6 A53 C5
Oklahoma E-35 A65 5.75
okra 7.25
old B-9 A2 C2 2.67
old-fashioned E-38 A57 7.67
old-time A95
olden 5.50
older G-12 A12 C15
oldest I-9 A23
olive A50
Oliver A88
olives A69 8.00
Olympic A62 9.00
omelet 8.00 £
[omelette]
omen 8.00
omission J-24 ¡¿
omit A76 ¡
omitted J-24 A68 7.25 ¡
omitting K-34 7.75
on A-4 A1 C1 1.88
ON (Ontario) G-41
once A-20 A3 C1 3.00
one A-20 A1 C1 1.94
one's A43
one-fourth A75
one-half A40
one-third A71
one-way E-38 7.00
ones C-20 A6 C7
oneself I-36 ¿
onion A97
onions G-20 A75 3.75
online I-36
only B-9 A1 C2 2.81
Ontario F-35 7.00
onto E-36 A12 C9 3.00
open E-28 A4 C4 3.50
opened C-9 A8 C4 5.00
opening F-9 A13 C18
openings A52
opens A42
opera A51 7.92
operate J-12 A39 6.38
operated A53 9.00
operates A84
operating A54 9.00
operation G-42 A23 7.25
operations A32
operator A57 8.25
operators A100
operetta 8.50
opinion J-3 A28 7.58 ¡
opinions A49 9.00
opossum 7.50
opponent A97 7.75
opportunities A52 9.00
opportunity I-13 A28 8.25 ¡
oppose 7.08
opposed A63
opposing A94
opposite H-4 A9 6.75 ¿
opposition I-42 A75 7.38
oppressive H-23 9.00
oppressor 8.00
optimism ¡
optimistic ¡

option 8.25
optional 8.75
or A-13 A1 C1 2.75
OR (Oregon) G-41
oral A72 7.88
[orang-utan]
orange B-13 A21 C6 2.69
oranges I-13 A38
orangutan 8.00 £
orbit G-13 A24 C18 6.13
orbits A66
orchard K-13 A64 5.33
orchards A67
orchestra I-13 A36 6.50
order H-13 A4 4.25
ordered H-13 A17 5.75
ordering 8.50
orderly A59
orders I-13 A26
ordinarily A56
ordinary G-13 A17 C18 7.50
ore G-13 A28 C15 6.38
Oregon E-35 A44 5.75
ores A83
organ K-13 A49 4.75
organic A76 6.50
organism A91 8.75
organisms A57
organization H-42 A27 8.00
organizations A52
organize A50 7.19
organized I-13 A23
organizing A75
organs K-28 A39
Orient A90
Oriental A88
origin I-13 A25 ¡
original I-29 A12 6.88 ¡
originality 7.25
originally I-26 A29
originated A65 8.00
origins A74
ornament 8.50
ornaments 7.00
orphan 5.50
orphanage 8.50
Orville A79
Oscar A51
ostrich A79
other A-20 A1 C2 3.67
other's A56
others E-20 A3 C8 4.00
otherwise I-36 A31 8.00
otter A94
Otto A68
ought H-17 A21 5.83
ounce A69 5.75
ounces A50
our A-16 A2 C1 3.44 ¢
ours A38
ourselves I-36 A30 6.00
out A-16 A1 C1 3.00
out-of-doors A84
outcome A76
outdoor A70
outdoors H-37 A33 4.83
outer H-16 A19
outfield 7.25
outfit A57 5.25
outfitting K-34 7.75
outlaw 6.50
outline I-36 A24 6.63
outlined A77 9.00
outlines A74
outlook 8.25
output A50
outrageous H-43 8.33 ¡
outside B-36 A5 C3 3.88
outstanding A42
outward A50
outwit 8.38
oval A68
oven E-28 A38 C18 5.25
over A-12 A1 C1 2.50
over-all A87
overall A96
overalls A86 5.00
overboard A96
overcharge 9.00
overcoat 7.00
overcome G-20 A40 4.50
overdo K-36 7.50
overdue K-36 7.50
overhead A32
overlook A95 4.75
overlooked A98 8.50
overlooking A85
overnight A54
overrate 8.25
overrun I-36 ¡
overseas A97 7.50
overshoes 7.50
oversight 9.00
overwhelming A79
owe A82 4.50
owes A100
owing 8.50
owl F-16 A31 C14 4.25
owls A67
own D-9 A2 C7 3.13
owned I-9 A23
owner G-12 A26 C15 4.33
owners K-12 A37
ownership A72 7.00
owns A53 8.00
ox A61
ox; oxen F-31
oxen A50 5.83
oxide A82
oxygen H-4 A14 4.50
oyster G-18 A67 6.19
oysters A80

P

p.m. (afternoon) D-41 C20 7.42
P.O. (post office) E-41 4.50
P.S. E-41 6.00
Pa A24
PA (Pennsylvania) G-41
Pablo A79
pace K-6 A38 5.92
Pacific G-35 A15 6.25
pack G-1 A22 C16 4.00
package G-1 A27 C18 4.81
packages A44
packed F-1 A27 C13
packing A55 6.00
packs A91
pad A43
paddle A51 4.75
paddled A84
paddles A73
paddling A91
pads A89
page H-6 A3 3.94
pageant K-1 8.75 ¿
pages A8
paid F-6 A13 C11 5.13 ¡
pail A45 4.33
pain I-6 A24 4.25
painful E-27 A78 5.50
painfully A101
painless 6.00
pains A76
paint F-6 A20 C11 3.19
painted G-6 A23 C16
painter A76
painting J-6 A37 5.13
paintings A50
paints A70 6.00
pair F-14 A9 4.08
pairs F-14 A16
pajamas A71 6.38 £
pal A92 6.50
palace A29 5.00
palaces A87
palate 7.75
pale J-6 A27 4.38
paleness 5.75
paler 6.75
Palestine A76
palette 7.75
palm A34 5.94
palms A59
palominos 5.75
pamphlet K-1 8.38 ¿
pan G-1 A23 C19 1.75
Panama F-35 A66 6.25
pancake F-36 C14
pancakes 3.75
pane A98 5.13
panel A67 6.75
panic K-1 A73 5.38
panicked 7.33
pans A48 5.50
panther 7.00
panting A91
pantomime 8.58 ¡
pants G-30 C15 4.75
papa H-17 A19 5.50
Papa's A77
papaya 9.00
paper D-12 A3 C9 4.13
paperback K-36 7.67
papers H-6 A19
parachute J-10 A89 6.42 ¿
parade K-6 A37 4.67
parades A90
paradise 6.13
paradox 8.75
paraffin 8.13
paragraph H-1 A12 6.75
paragraphs A33
parallel I-29 A18 7.67 ¡¿
parallelogram 8.50
parallels A81
[paralyse]
[paralysed] I-14
paralyze 7.56 £
paralyzed I-14 £
paramedic 7.75
paraprofessional 7.75
parasite 7.75
parcel A81 7.50
parcel post E-39 7.75
pardon A87 5.58
pardoned 6.50
pare 8.50
parent A57 4.63
parentheses J-28 A39
parenthesis 8.13
parents F-2 A12 C12 4.63
parfait 7.25
Paris I-35 A19
park B-11 A18 C6 3.92
parka 8.88
parked A47
Parker A70
parking H-11 A61 5.00
parks A42
parliament I-45 A59 5.75 ¡
parliamentary J-45 ¿
parlor A64 7.50 £
[parlour]
parrot A42
part B-11 A2 C6 3.00
part-time 8.75
parted A92
partial A58 6.75
partially A86
participant 8.75
participate 7.38
participation I-42 A87 7.88
particle A67
particles G-11 A20
particular G-11 A12 7.38
particularly H-26 A18 8.13 ¡
parties E-32 A34 4.00
partition 8.50
partly I-26 A22
partner H-11 A37 6.13 ¡
partners A53
partnership A97
parts D-11 A3 C19
parts of speech D-39 5.50
party B-11 A9 C7 3.33
pass E-24 A10 C9 3.00
passable 6.75
passage H-24 A26 6.67
passages A57
passageway K-36 7.25
passed E-1 A7 C9 4.25
passenger E-28 A35 C16 6.83
passengers I-28 A29
passers-by F-38 7.63
passes H-30 A21
passing H-1 A19 5.25
passion A83 8.25

Key: Letter-## is *Spelling Power* level word is first taught at. A## is usage by adults; C## is usage by children. (#.##) Average grade level word is taught at; ¢ High School Problem Word, ¡ College Problem Word. ¿ Business Problem Word. £ British spelling (alternate) is also in this list. [word] is British spelling. Elementary Problem words are set in **Boldface** type.

Passover 5.00
past E-1 A5 C10 3.75
pasta 7.25
paste A48 4.38
pasted 8.00
Pasteur A76
pasteurize I-25 7.81 ¿
pastime ¡
pastrami 6.50
pastries G-32 8.25
pasture G-25 A28 5.13
pastures A58 8.00
pat A62 2.25
patch J-1 A37 4.17
patches A57 5.00
patent A75 7.75
path E-1 A12 C10 4.50
pathology 8.50
paths C-1 A46 3.25
patience I-44 A54 7.50
patient J-28 A35 6.50
patiently A63
patients A60 7.50
patio 6.58
Patrick A57
patriot 6.25
patriotic 6.88
patrol A63
patrolled 7.25
patrolling K-34 8.38
patrols C19
patronage 8.50
Patsy A73
patted A54 3.75
pattern H-12 A6 6.75
patterns I-30 A10
Patty A76
Paul A11
Paul's A69
pause A40 5.83
paused A54
pave G-23 6.25
paved A70
pavement A83 5.00
paw A52 3.38
paws A49 5.50
pay E-6 A8 C10 3.13
payable 8.50
paying A40
payment A66 5.00
payments A96 8.50
pays A53 8.00
PE (Prince Edward Island) H-41
pea A73
peace (quiet) H-7 A16 5.08
peaceable K-29 ¡¿
peaceful I-27 A35 C20 5.38
peacefully K-26 A89 6.75
peach A48 4.88
peaches A35 3.75
peacock A96
peak K-7 A41 4.25
peaks A42
peanut A66 3.00
peanut butter D-39 5.88
peanuts F-36 A43 C16
pear B-14 A83 4.25
pearl A71 5.81
pearls A58
pears A84 6.50
peas A61 6.50
peasant A67
peasants A58 8.00
pebble A72
pebbles A55
pecan 8.00
peck 8.00
Pecos A98
peculiar H-11 A41 8.25 ¡¿
pedal A71 6.08
peddle 5.75
peddler A99
pedestrian J-2 7.25
Pedro A47
peek 4.25
peel A92
peep 6.50
peer F-15 6.42
peered A49
peering A76
peg A101
Peggy A73
Peking A100
Pekingese 8.75
pelican 6.50
pen G-2 A24 C15 4.50
penalize 7.63
penalty E-2 6.00
pencil G-29 A17 C15 4.44
pencils A43
pendulum A100 8.13
penetrate A91
penguin 6.75
penguins A80
penicillin 8.25
peninsula A57
penmanship 7.00
Penn A79
pennant 8.25
pennies E-32 A38 4.00
Pennsylvania E-35 A30 6.00
penny J-28 A31 3.38
pens G-2 A83 C18
pension 8.63
pentagon 8.63
people E-29 A1 C1 2.94
people's A48 7.50
peoples A29
pepper A65 5.50
per H-12 A7
perceive A90 7.88 ¡
percent I-28 A25 6.75
percentage A66 7.63
perception J-42 8.38 ¡
perch A73 6.50
perched A58
percussion A94
peremptory ¡
perfect H-12 A18 4.81
perfection A78 6.00
perfectly I-26 A26
perform I-13 A25 7.00 ¡
performance H-44 A32 6.63
performances A97
performed J-12 A28
performers A95
performing A56
perfume A55 6.25
perhaps H-12 A4 4.92 ¡
peril 7.50
perimeter A93 8.50
period F-15 A9 C8 5.25
periodical 7.25
periods H-15 A23
peripheral 8.75
periscope 8.75
perish 7.63
perjury 8.38
permanent I-28 A35 7.58 ¡¿
permanently A88
permissible K-29 8.58 ¡¿
permission J-42 A40 7.19
permit A45 5.88
permits A96
permitted A45
permitting K-34 7.13
perpendicular A50 8.50
perpetual 8.75
persecute 8.08
perseverance K-44 ¡
Persia A88
Persian A58
persist 7.00
persistence K-44 8.88
persistent A83 8.00
person C-12 A5 C7 4.56
person's A43
personal I-29 A19 6.58 ¡
personalities K-32 8.25
personality A41 8.38
personally K-26 A86 8.75 ¿
personification 9.00
personnel K-34 A89 7.58 ¡
persons H-12 A16
perspective 8.75
perspiration J-42 A74 8.75 ¡
perspire 7.25
persuade K-12 A69 7.00 ¡¿
persuaded A65
persuasion 7.58
persuasive 9.00
pertain 7.25 ¡
pertinent 8.75
Peru F-35 A59 6.25
pervade ¡
pesticide 6.50
pet B-2 A22 C3 1.56
pet's 5.75
petal 6.50
petals A76
Pete A37
Peter A12
Peter's A88
Peters A77
petite 9.00
petition A82 8.50
petrify 8.50
petroleum A48 7.38
pets G-30 A42 C15 1.00
petty cash 8.25
petunia 1.43
Ph.D. H-41
phantom 7.50
pharmacist 8.00
pharmacy 8.92
phase A76 7.25
pheasant 6.00
phenomena 8.25
phenomenon A79 8.63
Phil A88
Philadelphia I-35 A30
Philip A43
Philippine A87
Philippines A66
philosopher A86
philosophers A100
philosophy A67 9.00
Phoebe A90
phone D-9 A47 C8 5.75
phoned E-9 C9
phoning 4.50
phonograph A72 8.38
photo A69 5.50
photocopy 8.50
photogenic 8.50
photograph A47 5.25
photographed A99
photographer 8.25
photographic A80
photographs A46 8.25
photography A94 8.42
photosynthesis A93 8.75
phrase H-6 A14 6.50
phrases I-30 A19
Phyllis's 8.25
physical I-29 A20 6.17 ¡
physically A74
physician J-42 A78 9.00 ¿
physicist A81
physics A49 6.75
physiology 8.75
physique 9.00
pianist 8.00
piano E-47 A23 C14 6.67
pianos 6.63
piccolo 8.00
pick C-3 A11 C5 2.56
picked C-3 A10 C5 3.00
picking F-3 A36 C12
pickle 5.88
pickles 6.50
picks A48
picnic F-3 A33 C11 3.08 ¡
picnicking 6.00 ¡
picture E-25 A3 C9 4.58
pictured G-25 A24
pictures E-25 A6 C12 3.25
picturesque I-21 A87 8.00
pie E-8 A20 C12 2.75
piece E-7 A5 C7 3.56 ¡
pieces G-30 A7 C15 6.50
pier F-15 A73 6.42
pierce I-15 6.58
piercing A97 7.25
Pierre A36 C13
pies A49 6.00
pig C-3 A31 C7 1.67
pigeon A70 6.63
pigeons A45
pigs E-3 A24 C9
pile F-8 A23 C15 4.50
piled A41
piles A51
pilgrim 5.75
Pilgrims A45
pillar 5.63
pillow A48 4.67
pillows 5.00
pilot I-8 A26 4.50
piloting 6.50

Alphabetical List

pilots A44
pimento 8.50
pin J-3 A35 2.25
pinch A85 4.25
pine G-8 A22 C15 4.25
pineapple A84
pines A70
pink D-3 A21 C8 3.42
pinned A85
pins A49 7.00
pint A78 4.25
pints A83
pioneer I-8 A38 6.00
pioneers I-8 A32
pipe H-8 A20 3.25
pipes J-8 A34
Pippi A100
pirate G-8 A60 C20 5.67
pirates F-8 A50 C13
pistol A68 6.50
piston A79
pit F-3 A51 C19
pitch I-3 A21 4.00
pitched A59
pitcher I-3 A34 4.08
pitchers A91
pitches A83
pitching A65
pitied K-32 7.00
pits A80
Pittsburgh J-35 A57 ¿
pity A59 9.00
pivot A96 9.00
pizza 6.50
Pl. 4.50
place H-43 A2 C2 2.63
placed H-6 A8
places E-30 A4 C8
placing A44
plagiarism I-14 ¿
plague A84 8.00
plaid 7.00
plain H-6 A14 2.81
plainly A62
plains H-6 A17
plan G-1 A7 C15 2.58
plane C-6 A7 C4 2.63
planes E-30 A15 C10 1.00
planet D-1 A18 C6 4.92
planetarium 9.00
planets H-30 A17 C20
plank E-1 A78 4.25
plankton A73
planned C-34 A18 C16 3.00 ¡
planning D-34 A24 C20 3.13
plans H-1 A15
plant F-1 A6 C11 3.00
plantation A58 7.00
plantations A63 7.50
planted G-1 A21 C15
planters A98
planting A52 7.00
plants E-1 A4 C9
plaque I-21 8.00
plaques 5.50
plasma 8.75
plaster A62
plastic H-1 A28 C20 4.88
plastics A77
plate H-6 A16 2.50
plateau A44 7.17
plates K-6 A30
platform K-36 A33
play A-6 A3 C1 1.81
play-offs E-38 6.75
played C-6 A9 C4 1.00
player F-12 A20 C11 3.00
players H-6 A20
playful E-27 A83 4.75
playground A42 4.25
playhouse 6.50
playing C-32 A10 C3 3.75
playmate 6.50
playmates 6.50
plays E-6 A17 C9
playwright K-36 7.42 ¿
plaza 8.50
plea 8.50
pleaded A75
pleasant A17 5.83 ¡
pleasantly A88
please C-7 A10 C6 2.42
pleased I-7 A24
pleasing A65 4.50
pleasure E-25 A25 5.92
pleasures A81
pledge I-2 A101 6.75
pledges K-2 7.75
plentiful I-32 A55 7.50
plenty H-2 A15 5.38
pliable 8.75
pliers 7.75
plot A43 6.25
plow A47 4.50
plowed A61
plowing A75
plows A86
pluck A79
plucked A87
plug A66
plum A78 5.75
plumber 6.75
plump A78 6.25
plums A87
plunge A80 6.75
plunged A55
plunger 9.00
plunging A94
plural J-29 A25 5.75
plurals A77
plus I-5 A25 3.25
Pluto A68
Plymouth A68
plywood A96 5.25
pneumonia 8.58
poach 7.00
pocket H-4 A18 4.75
pocketbook 6.00
pockets J-4 A39 4.00
poem E-9 A14 C13 6.42
poems I-9 A33
poet I-2 A25 6.63
poetic A74
poetry I-9 A29 8.25
poets A47
poinsettia 8.63
point E-18 A3 C16 3.81
pointed E-18 A13 C19 5.00
pointing G-18 A28
pointless 8.50
points E-18 A6
poise J-18 6.50
poised 8.25
poison B-18 A47 C13 4.94 ¡
poisonous J-18 A51 7.92
poked A73
Poland A66
polar A48 5.58
polar bear 8.63
pole A20 C15 5.13
poles G-30 A18 C15 8.50
police B-47 A18 C3 4.44
policeman A29 C13
policemen A63
policies I-32 A78 7.75
policy A45 6.75
polio A83
polish A68 6.00
polished A41
polite A51 4.63
politely A52
political H-29 A17 7.13
politician 8.50 ¡
politicians A85
politics J-30 A54 7.50 ¡
polka 7.50
poll 5.50
pollen A52 7.25
polls 8.50
pollute G-10 C20 6.00
polluted 6.50
pollution F-42 C5 6.88
Polly A55
polo 6.50
polygon 8.50
poncho 8.88
ponchos 5.75
pond D-4 A19 C14 2.50
pondered 7.25
ponds A52
ponies A53 7.00
pony C-9 A23 C5 4.58
Pooh A90
pool C-10 A22 C7 3.38
pools A56 8.00
poor B-13 A6 C6 5.00
pop C-4 A33 C10 3.00
popcorn A64 5.50
Pope A98
popped D-34 A64 C20 4.25
popper A80
popping A95 3.75
popsicle G-29 C19
popular G-11 A15 6.81
popularity A82 7.25
populate 6.00
populated A71
population F-42 A14 6.56
populations A71
porcelain 8.00
porch H-13 A26 4.00
porcupine A90
pore 6.75
pork A66 6.25
porpoise 6.88
porridge F-13 C14
port I-13 A27 5.25
portable 7.50
porter A91 8.00
portfolio 9.00
portion A34 6.83
portions A56
portrait A95 7.88
portray 7.25
ports A54 7.50
Portugal A72
Portuguese A60
position F-42 A10 5.75
positions 9.00
positive J-47 A29 6.92
positively A77 9.00
possess A74 7.25 ¡
possessed A69
possession G-42 A42 7.88 ¡¿
possessions A58
possessive H-23 A60 9.00
possibilities A54
possibility A56 8.50
possible G-29 A6 C19 5.92 ¡
possibly I-4 A30 4.50
post H-9 A18 4.13
post office G-39 5.44
postage 5.67
postal 9.00
posters A76 7.50
postman 5.00
postpone 7.83
postponed 8.25
posts A45
postscript 8.63
posture G-25 A87 8.38
postwar 8.50
pot I-4 A26 1.75
potato I-9 A32 6.00 ¿
potatoes D-31 A18 C10 6.00
potential A57 8.75
Potomac A85
pots A43
pottery A52 7.88
pouch A80 7.38
poultry A80 9.00
pound F-16 A22 C15 4.81
pounded A51
pounding A43
pounds F-30 A10 C11
pour H-13 A28 5.94
poured I-13 A23
pouring A54
pours A94
poverty A61
powder H-16 A26 5.25
powdered A75
power F-16 A5 C13 3.75
powered A98
powerful I-27 A16 5.42
powers F-16 A29 C15
PQ (Quebec) F-41
practical J-29 A30 7.38 ¡

Alphabetical List

Key: Letter-## is *Spelling Power* level word is first taught at. A## is usage by adults; C## is usage by children. (#.##) Average grade level word is taught at; ¢ High School Problem Word, ¡ College Problem Word. ¿ Business Problem Word. £ British spelling (alternate) is also in this list. [word] is British spelling. Elementary Problem words are set in **Boldface** type.

practicality 8.25
practically I-26 A33 C20 7.38 ¡
practice A9 C13 5.00 £
practiced A43 £
practices A60
practicing A43 £
[practise]
[practised]
[practising]
prairie F-14 A31 C13 6.83 ¡¿
prairies A65
praise A63 5.50
praised A89
praiseworthy 8.25
pray K-6 A56 6.00
prayed A68
prayer A54 8.00
prayers A63
preach 6.25
preamble 7.88
prearrange 8.13
prearranged 5.75
precaution 7.25
precede K-7 7.88 ¡¿
preceded A61
precedence J-44 ¡
precedents K-28 ¡
preceding K-7 A43 8.25 ¿
precious H-43 A30 8.25 ¿
precipitation 9.00
precise A49 8.25
precisely A52
precision A59 7.00
preclude 9.00
preconceive 8.75
preconception 8.75
precook 5.75
predatory 8.75
predicament 8.63
predicate A37 6.00
predict A53 6.88
predictable 9.00
predicted A90
prediction 8.56
predominant 8.75
prefer J-12 A34 6.42 ¡
preferable K-12 8.50 ¿
preference I-44 8.50 ¡
preferred A44 7.08 ¡
prefix A50 5.94
prefixes A88
prehistoric A59 6.17
prejudge 7.67
prejudice A97 8.00 ¡
prejudiced 5.75
preliminary K-7 A88 8.75 ¿
prelude 8.75
premature I-25 8.75
premier 7.25
premiere I-15 9.00
premise 6.25
premium 7.50
premonition 8.00
preoccupied 8.75
prepaid 6.17
preparation F-42 A52 7.58 ¡
preparations A81
prepare F-14 A22 5.56 ¡
prepared F-14 A17
preparing F-33 A37 5.50
preposition A85 8.00
prepositional A71
preschool 5.75
prescribe 9.00
prescription 8.75
presence I-44 A32 7.25
present E-2 A7 C8 4.75
present-day A69
presentable 8.50
presentation 8.50
presented I-28 A27
presenting A86
presently A47
presents F-30 A30 C11
preserve G-23 A59 6.33
preserved A58
preside 8.50
president F-2 A24 C16 5.88
President's A81
presidential A91
Presidents' Day 5.00
press H-24 A22 3.75
pressed J-24 A31 5.00
presses A59
pressing A48
pressure E-25 A12 7.08
pressures A86
pressurize 9.00
presto 8.00
presume 7.63
presumption 8.75
presumptuous J-43 ¿
[pretence]
pretend J-28 A33 6.33
pretended A54
pretending A67
pretense 9.00 £
pretest 5.75
prettier C-32 4.00
prettiest C-32 A90 5.63
pretty B-47 A9 C3 2.81 ¢
pretzel 7.38
prevail 8.75
prevalent K-28 8.75 ¡¿
prevent I-28 A21 6.13
prevented A86
preventing A101
prevention 7.00
prevents A78
preview 6.25
previous H-43 A26 7.17
previously A58 9.00
prey K-6 A47 8.25
preying I-32 5.50
price H-8 A18 3.58
priced 9.00
prices G-30 A40 C16
prickly A98
pride J-8 A29 5.25
pried 8.00
priest A53 7.25
priests A54
prim G-3 C19
primarily A49
primary I-14 A34 8.50
prime G-8 A28 C16
primer 8.50
primitive J-47 A26 7.50 ¡
prince D-3 A38 C7 4.75
princes A89
princess G-24 A36 C15 3.50
princesses 4.50
Princeton A99
principal A23 C19 6.38 ¡¿
principle J-29 A26 7.06 ¡¿
principles J-30 A26
print J-3 A37 3.25
printed H-3 A18
printer A91
printing I-3 A33 6.50
prints A78 8.00
prior 7.50
priorities K-32 9.00
priority 8.25
prism A63
prison A42 6.92
prisoner A62 7.08 ¡
prisoners A68
private G-8 A28 C20 6.25
privately K-26 A96 6.50
privilege I-3 8.63 ¡¿
privileges A89
prize F-8 A26 C12 3.50
prized A82
prizes A61
probability A72 8.00
probable A83 8.50
probably E-20 A5 C8 6.75 ¡
probe A94
problem D-4 A5 C10 6.17
problems F-4 A6 C15
procedure I-25 A42 8.08 ¡¿
procedures A90
proceed K-7 A56 7.13 ¡¿
proceeded A86
proceeding 8.25
process H-24 A12 7.00
processed A87
processes A38
processing A75
procession A57 8.50
proclaim 6.83
proclaimed A85
prodigy ¡
produce H-10 A9 6.17
produced H-10 A10 5.75
producer A92 8.75
produces I-30 A22
producing F-33 A37
product G-5 A11 5.38
production G-42 A23 6.88
productive H-23 A75 9.00
productivity 8.75
products H-4 A7
profession A81 7.25 ¡
professional I-42 A33 8.75
professor J-24 A58 8.50 ¡¿
profit A56 7.25
profitable 6.50
profited 7.25
profits A82
profound A87 7.25
program G-9 A17 5.00
programmer 8.75
programs K-1 A32
progress H-24 A20 7.67
progressive H-23 A81 9.00
prohibit 7.00
prohibition J-42 7.00 ¡
project I-4 A31 6.83
projection A85
projector 8.13
projects A44
prolong 7.13
promenade 8.88
prominent K-28 A55 8.75 ¿
promise I-4 A34 5.63
promised D-33 A29 C20 5.50
promises A93 9.00
promising A76
promissory ¡
promote 6.63
promotion 5.75
prompt 5.88
promptly A55 8.50
pronoun A45 6.94
pronounce A40 7.13
pronounced A40
pronouns A66
pronto 9.00
pronunciation I-42 A39 7.42 ¿
proof A43 5.67
proofread A86 7.00
prop 4.25
propaganda 8.25
propel 8.75
propellant 9.00
propelled 8.50
propeller A75 6.00
propelling 7.25
proper H-4 A13 6.69
properly I-26 A28
properties J-4 A27 7.50
property H-4 A18 6.50
prophecy 8.00 ¿
prophesy J-4 ¿
prophet 8.75
proportion A44 8.50
proportions A57
proposal 8.00
propose A101 5.83
proposed A53 7.50
proposition 7.75
pros 5.75
proscribe 9.00
prose A90 9.00
prosecute 8.08
prosecution 8.50
prospect A87 7.58
prospector 8.00
prospects 8.50
prosperity A87
prosperous A79 8.50
protect H-2 A14 5.92
protected J-2 A32
protecting A70
protection H-42 A28 5.50
protective A54 6.88
protects A65
protein A54 5.63
proteins A74
protest A67 5.25
protested A69
protoplasm 8.75
protractor A87
protrude 8.75
proud H-16 A14 C20 4.00
proudly J-26 A35
prove G-10 A18 C19 5.00 ¡
proved I-10 A19

proves A89
provide A14 6.63
provided H-8 A20
Providence A90
provides J-47 A35
providing A59 5.75
province A52
provinces A62
provision 7.38
provisions A76
provoke 8.63
prowl 5.25
prowling 8.50
psalm E-22 8.88
pseudonym H-22 8.00
psychic 7.75
psychological A96
psychologist 8.00
psychology K-29 8.83 ¡
public G-5 A12 4.67
publication 8.50
publicly K-26 A100 ¿
publish A96 6.33
published I-5 A31
publisher 8.25
puck D-5 C10
pudding A88 4.50
puddle 4.50
pueblo 8.17
Puerto Rico G-39 A62 6.63
puff A65
puffed A81
puffing A85
puffs A84
pull B-19 A9 C10 3.13
pulled E-24 A7 C5
pulley A79 4.75
pulling D-19 A20 C16
pulls J-24 A32
pulp A65 8.00
pulse A58 6.25
pump I-5 A36 4.92
pumped A56
pumping A85
pumpkin G-5 A53 C20 4.25
pumpkins A92 6.50
pumps A65
punch G-5 A72 C20 5.00
punched A94
punctual 9.00
punctuate 7.75
punctuation G-42 A40 7.63
punish A84 5.67
punishable 7.75
punished A77 8.00
punishment I-45 A64 6.00
pup A92 6.50
pupil A43 5.17
pupils I-10 A27 5.50
puppet G-5 A70 C20
puppies C-32 A78 C13 3.94
puppy D-5 A45 C11 2.50
pups D-5 C13
purchase A46 6.58 ¡
purchased A66 8.00
purchases 9.00
purchasing 9.00
pure E-25 A22 5.63
purely A97
purify 6.50
purple E-29 A26 C7 2.92
purpose H-12 A13 5.50
purposely H-26 5.75
purposes J-9 A33
purse A56 5.50
pursue J-10 A99 8.25 ¡¿
pursued A89
pursuing 7.50
pursuit A70 ¡
push D-19 A15 3.58
pushed D-19 A13 C11 4.38
pushes A38
pushing D-19 A25
put B-19 A2 C2 3.31
puts D-19 A27
putt G-24 C19
putting B-34 A13 C15 4.00 ¡
puzzle J-29 A37 5.31
puzzled K-29 A36
puzzles A86
puzzling A95
[pyjamas]
pyramid A53 8.50
pyramids A83 5.25
python 6.25

Q

quack 7.50
quadrangle I-21 8.75
quadruple I-21 8.38
quail 8.00
quake 6.25
qualified 8.25
qualify 8.50
qualifying 8.25
qualities F-21 A38 7.50
quality F-21 A20 7.00
quantities F-21 A35
quantity I-21 A47 7.31 ¡
quarantined 9.00
quarrel A57 6.17
quarry I-21 7.75
quart E-21 A56 4.00
quarter E-21 A19 C16 5.50
quarterback A91 4.00
quarters F-21 A34
quartet I-21 8.00
quarts A64
quartz A86
Quebec F-35 A99 7.00
queen E-21 A21 C9 3.92
queer F-21 A39 4.50
quench I-21 7.25
question F-21 A6 5.25
question mark E-39 7.00
questioned F-21 A91 C20
questionnaire I-21 8.13 ¿
questions E-21 A5 C16
quiche I-21 8.75
quick F-21 A12 3.38
quicker A79
quickly E-21 A5 C7 4.50
quiet E-21 A10 C13 5.38 ¡
quieter F-21 6.75
quietest 8.50
quietly E-26 A14 C20 5.75
quills A96
quilt I-21 4.50
quit E-21 A51 C15 4.56
quite E-21 A6 C6 4.81 ¡
quiz E-21 5.33
quizzed 7.75
quizzes H-30 ¡
quotation F-21 A54 7.25
quotations 9.00
quote F-21 6.75
quoted 8.50
quotient A76
quotients A96
quoting 8.50

R

R.D. (rural delivery) H-41 4.50
R.S.V.P. H-41 7.00
rabbit C-1 A22 C4 3.50
rabbits E-1 A26 C8
raccoon A52 4.42
race D-6 A9 C6 3.13
raced J-6 A26
races E-6 A36 C9
racial A97 9.00
racing B-33 A27 C11 3.00
rack D-1 A64 3.50
racket G-2 A97 C19 7.00
radar A56 7.00
radiant A88
radiation A57
radiator A101 7.50
radical A93
radio F-6 A10 C11 4.75
radioactive A69 8.75
radios A56 6.75
radishes 6.25
radius A57 6.75
raft J-1 A38 4.25
rag A77 6.50
rage A-6 A49 3.50
raged A98
ragged A54 8.00
raging A79
rags A94 4.00
raid A81
rail A42 4.25
railing A85
railroad H-37 A15 4.81
railroads H-37 A31
rails A54
railway A68 8.50
rain B-6 A6 C5 2.44
rainbow H-37 A48 C20 4.50
raindrops A88
rained A62 4.00
rainfall I-36 A36 6.50
raining F-6 A58 C12
rains J-6 A36
rainy J-6 A35 5.00
raise H-6 A14 5.25
raised H-6 A10 3.88
raises A51
raisin 6.25
raising D-33 A30
raisins 8.00
rake A-6 A78 3.50
rally A59
Ralph A36
ram A76
ramble 9.00
Ramon A81
ramp E-1 4.25
ran B-1 A5 C2 1.75
ranch G-1 A21 C19 4.50
rancher A101
ranchers A73
ranches A51 4.25
random A79
Randy A93
rang D-1 A32 C6 3.25
range H-6 A14 5.75
ranges A40
ranging A75
rank A45 4.75
ranks A60
rapid K-3 A35 6.00 ¡
rapidly H-26 A15
rapids A74
rapport 8.75
rare I-14 A33 5.13
rarely I-14 A40 5.75
rascal 9.00
raspberries 8.25
raspberry 7.88
rat F-1 A44 C13
rate H-6 A14
rates A48 8.50
rather A7 C12 4.75
ratio A64 6.75
rational A57
ratios 8.25
rats J-1 A35
rattle A67 6.25
rattles A84
rattlesnake A94
rattlesnakes A94
rattling A96
raven 8.25
ravine A96
ravioli 7.33
raw G-17 A25 4.38
ray F-6 A44 C12
rayon A84
rays I-6 A20
razor 6.50
Rd. (road) E-41 4.50
reach D-7 A8 C10 4.00
reached D-7 A6 C7 5.25
reaches H-30 A23
reaching J-7 A30
react A70 5.00
reaction A32
reactions A65
read B-7 A2 C5 2.94
reader I-7 A25 6.25
readers A49 6.50
readily A51 8.50
reading E-7 A6 C12 4.00
reads K-7 A37
ready B-47 A4 C4 4.50 ¡
real C-7 A6 C4 4.17

Key: Letter-## is *Spelling Power* level word is first taught at. A## is usage by adults; C## is usage by children. (#.##) Average grade level word is taught at; ¢ High School Problem Word, ¡ College Problem Word. ¿ Business Problem Word. £ British spelling (alternate) is also in this list. [word] is British spelling. Elementary Problem words are set in **Boldface** type.

real estate E-39 7.75
realistic 8.25
reality A55
realize I-8 A23 6.67 ¡
realized G-8 A21 C16
realizing A97
really E-26 A4 C4 3.75 ¡
realm A98
reappoint 5.75
rear H-15 A28 5.00
reared A81
rearranged H-46 5.75
reason E-7 A7 C10 4.81
reasonable A50 7.00
reasonably A92
reasoning A74 6.50
reasons H-7 A14
rebel A101 6.50
rebelled 8.38
rebellion A95 8.75
rebellious J-43 9.00
rebound 4.75
rebuild 5.08
rebuilt A101
recall H-24 A30 5.38
recalled A72
recalls A100
recede 9.00 ¡
receipt H-22 7.06 ¡¿
receipts 9.00
receive I-7 A22 5.56 ¡¿
received D-7 A13 C20 7.50 ¢
receiver A52 7.25
receives H-46 A34 6.75
receiving A51 8.50
recent H-28 A19 6.50
recently I-26 A22 6.75
reception 8.75
recess E-24 A72 C12 4.58
recessive 8.75
recipe A76 7.00
recipient K-28 ¿
recital 7.92
recite 6.42
reckless 7.50
reckon A61
reclaim 8.75
reclamation 8.75
recognition I-42 A54 8.00
recognize I-8 A19 7.75 ¡
recognized I-4 A25
recognizes A97 7.25
recognizing A89
recoil 8.25
recollect H-46 7.75
recollection H-46 7.75
recommend H-28 7.56 ¡¿
recommendation J-42 8.50 ¿
recommended A76 9.00
reconstruct 8.75
recook H-46 5.75
record G-13 A8 C16 7.13
recorded J-13 A30
recording A48
records H-30 A20 C20
recount H-46 7.75
recover H-46 A73 5.75
recovered A59 9.00
recovery A87
recreation A60 7.50
rectangle A51 7.38
rectangular A50
recuperation 9.00
recycle 6.00
red B-2 A4 C2 1.63
redeem 8.75
redemption 8.75
reduce A44 6.38
reduced H-46 A35
reducible 8.38
reduction A90 7.92
reed A93 4.00
reeds A51
reef A66
reel 7.00
refer I-12 A23 7.50
referee 7.75
reference H-44 A33 8.63 ¡¿
referred K-34 A36 6.50 ¡¿
referring A61 8.50
refers A40
refill H-46 5.38
refined H-46 A72 6.75
refinery 8.25
reflect H-46 A44 7.75
reflected J-2 A31
reflecting A92
reflection J-42 A74 7.25
reflects A59
reform H-46 A77 6.83
reformation 8.75
reformatory 8.75
reformer 8.00
reforms A99
refrain 8.00
refreshment I-45 6.58
refreshments 8.00
refrigerate 8.50
refrigerator A48 7.00
refrigerators A87
refuel 6.00
refuge A70 8.00
refugee 8.00
refund 8.50
refuse A55 5.75
refused J-10 A27
regard A46 5.92 ¡
regarded H-46 A39
regarding 8.50
regardless A58 6.50
regards 7.50
region G-7 A9 C15 7.00 ¡
regions A17
register A60 7.25
registered A93 9.00
regret A73 8.00
regretted H-46 7.50
regretting 9.00
regular H-2 A13 6.67
regularity 8.50
regularly J-26 A39
regulate A94 6.00
regulation 6.75
regulations A84
rehearsal 8.25
rehearse 6.25
reheat 6.00
reign A87 7.44
rein 8.50
reindeer A65 4.88
reins A62
reject 8.38
rejected A97
rejection 6.75
rejoice G-18 5.88
rejoin J-18 3.75
relate A73 5.00
related I-7 A14
relation I-42 A37 6.63
relations I-42 A39
relationship H-42 A29 7.00
relationships A42
relative J-47 A32 7.31
relatively J-26 A34
relatives A51 7.00
relax H-46 A69 5.38
relaxed A64
relay A70
relayed 5.50
release A40 7.00
released K-7 A37
relevant K-2 ¿
reliable A80 8.31
reliance 8.50
relief K-7 A36 7.13 ¿
relies 6.00
relieve A93 7.00 ¡
relieved H-46 A72 7.25
religion I-3 A33 7.00 ¡
religions A82
religious H-43 A24 ¡
reload 5.00
reluctantly A89
rely A67 5.75
remain H-6 A17 5.25
remainder H-46 A48 7.00
remained I-6 A19
remaining J-6 A26
remains I-30 A22
remake H-46 3.75
remark H-46 A62 5.50
remarkable A29 6.50
remarked A55
remarks A62 9.00
remedial 8.50
remedy 8.50
remember C-12 A4 C6 4.63
remembered G-12 A15 C15
remembering A50
remembers A88
remind H-46 A37 6.08
reminded A41
reminds A72
remit 8.50
remittance 8.50
remnant 8.75
remote A51 6.00
removal A84
remove I-10 A25 5.00
removed I-10 A21
removing A66
renaissance A82
rename 5.00
render G-2 C19
rendered 8.50
rendezvous 7.50
renew 5.50
renewal 9.00
renown K-7 7.25 ¿
rent A48 4.75
rented A80
repaint 6.00
repair I-14 A45 5.50
repaired A66 9.00
repairs A79 8.50
repay 5.50
repeat I-7 A24 5.58
repeated I-7 A20
repeating A42
repeats A82
repel 9.00
repelled 8.50
repellent K-28 ¿
repentance K-44 9.00
repetition F-42 A56 8.17 ¡
repetitious J-43 9.00
replace I-6 A20 5.00
replaced J-6 A28
replacement I-45 A74 6.50
replaces A95
replacing A71
replay H-46 5.38
replica 8.50
replied G-32 A13 C10 6.38
replies I-32 ¡¿
reply J-8 A39 4.75
replying 8.25
report H-13 A12 5.42
reported J-13 A30
reporter A55 7.69
reporters A84
reporting A101 9.00
reports J-13 A27
represent I-7 A13 5.75
representation 7.75
representative K-28 A56 8.50 ¡
representatives A58 8.00
represented I-28 A21
representing A47
represents H-28 A18
reproduce A65 8.75
reproduction A80
reptile A87 6.00
reptiles J-8 A31
republic K-5 A48 5.75
Republican A69
Republicans A89
reputation A52 9.00
request A62 6.38
requested 8.50
requesting 8.50
requests 9.00
require F-21 A29 6.50
required F-21 A21
requirement F-21 6.88
requirements A51 8.50
requires F-21 A29
requiring A99
reread A76
rerun 5.00
rescind H-22 ¿
rescue A46 6.00
rescued A89 5.00
rescuing 7.25
research I-12 A23 7.75
resemblance K-44 A97 8.75
resemble A54
resembled A92
resembles A72

resent 8.17
resentment 8.50
reservation A65 7.38
reserve A90 7.25
reserved A92
reservoir A88 C20 9.00
reside 8.38
residence K-44 A91 8.25
resident 6.00
residential 9.00
resign 7.00
resist A64 8.75
resistance J-44 A50 8.38 ¡
resolved H-23 A74
resort H-46 A93 7.63
resource A97
resourceful I-27 8.00
resources I-13 A24 6.50
respect I-2 A23 5.75
respectable H-46 A96 7.75
respected A73
respectful 6.88
respectfully I-26 8.50
respectively 8.50
respects A82
respelling A93
respiration A89 8.33
respond A57 5.75
responded H-46 A73 7.75
response A45
responsibilities A91
responsibility A34 8.00
responsible A31 7.56
rest C-2 A4 C5 3.25
restaurant E-47 A44 7.06 ¡¿
restaurants A71
rested A41
resting K-2 A38
restless A49 6.50
restore A77 6.50
restored A71
restricted A100
restrictive 9.00
rests A67
result A9
resulted A60 5.75
resulting A59
results G-5 A15
retail 8.25
retain H-46 A81 6.75
retained A88
retired A79
retirement I-45 7.50
retract 8.75
retreat A59 6.75
return H-12 A10 4.33
returned H-12 A11 4.25
returning H-46 A34
returns A47 9.0
reunion H-46 5.25
reunite H-46 6.75
reveal K-7 A54 5.25 ¿
revealed A47 8.50
reveals A76
revenge A99 6.25
reverse A57 8.75
reversed A91
reversible 8.69
revert 8.75
review I-10 A24 6.25
revise 8.25
revised 9.00
revision H-46 7.75
revoke 8.13
revolt A89 8.88
revolution I-42 A37 8.58
revolutionary A73 8.25
revolutions A94
revolve A95 8.75
reward F-13 A58 C12 5.38
rewind 6.00
rewrap H-46 3.75
rewrite H-46 A48 4.92
rhapsody J-4 8.25 ¿
rhetoric K-13 ¿
rheumatism K-47 8.00 ¡
Rhine A97
rhinoceros 8.63
Rhode Island E-39 A81 6.50
rhubarb K-47 ¿
rhyme J-8 A30 7.19 ¿
rhymes A56
rhythm F-47 A20 7.50 ¡¿
rhythmic A72 7.75
rhythms A77
RI (Rhode Island) G-41
rib A88
ribbon J-4 A34 5.00
ribbons A47
ribs K-3 A38
rice I-8 A21 4.25
rich E-3 A9 C8 2.50
Richard A20
richer A77
riches A61 6.75
richest A72 7.50
Ricky A42
rid J-3 A38 4.25
ridden A69 5.50
riddle E-3 A66 5.00
riddles A95
ride B-8 A9 C2 1.58
rider J-8 A37
riders A44
rides F-30 A41 C11
ridge A45 5.50
ridges A44
ridiculous H-43 A75 7.58 ¡¿
riding B-33 A17 C4 3.00
rifle J-29 A32 5.50
rifles A81
right¢ B-8 A2 C2 2.88
right-handed G-38 A66
rights I-30 A23
rigid A61 7.13
rim A47
ring E-3 A10 C11 2.83
ringing A50 6.00
rings I-3 A26
Rio Grande A55
riot 6.88
rip A98 9.00
ripe J-8 A36 4.08
ripped C-34 A65 C19
ripping 3.75
rise H-8 A13 5.25
rises J-30 A25
rising D-33 A21 5.75
risk A49 5.63
rival A79 7.25
rivaled 8.50 £
[rivalled]
river C-12 A5 C4 3.81
rivers G-30 A12 C15
road C-9 A5 C4 2.75
roads G-30 A14 C16
roadside A82
roam A64 5.75
roamed A83
roar J-13 A27 3.88
roared K-13 A34
roaring A47
roast E-9 A56 C13 4.38
roasted A88 6.50
roasting 5.25
rob A-4 2.25
robbed A95 8.00
robber A73 3.00
robbers A53 6.50
robe A77
Robert A19
robes A78
robin C-4 A38 C9 4.75
robins A61 3.25
Robinson A65
robot G-9 A60 C16 5.58
rock B-4 A6 C6 2.67
rocked A70
rocket C-4 A21 C5 5.13
rockets J-2 A32 4.50
Rockies A67
rocking A62
rocks C-30 A8 C5 4.25
rocky F-4 A29 C15
rod F-4 A20 C19 5.25
rode D-9 A13 C7 3.25
rodeo A80 6.67
rodeos 4.50
rods A46
Roger A42
Rogers A59
rogue 8.00
role I-9 A33
roles A98
roll F-9 A17 C16 3.58
rolled E-9 A15 C13
roller A77 7.00
roller skates 5.00
rollers A88
rolling I-9 A21 3.00
rolls J-24 A37
Roman G-35 A17
Romans J-35 A33
romantic A57 6.00
Rome I-35 A27
Romeo A73
roof D-10 A17 C13 4.17
roofs A55 7.25
rookie 7.25
room A-10 A3 C3 2.81
roommate K-36 7.50
rooms G-30 A20 C16
Roosevelt I-35 A32
roost 6.25
rooster G-10 A61 C19 5.25
root H-10 A15 4.25
rooted A84
roots H-10 A12
rope D-9 A11 C8 3.08
ropes J-9 A36
Rosa A85
rose F-9 A11 C15 4.17
rosebushes K-36 7.50
roses A47 C13 5.50
Ross A61
rotary J-9 ¿
rotate A87 8.13
rotates A92
rotation A86
rotten 6.50
rouge 8.00
rough D-47 A17 C10 4.38
roughly A57
round C-16 A5 C6 4.00
rounded H-16 A26
rounding A87
rounds A56
route H-16 A23 7.63
routes A45
routine A57
Rover A96
row H-9 A11 3.33
rowboat A85 3.75
rowdy 6.50
rowed A73 8.00
rowing A91
rows H-9 A19
Roy A75
royal J-29 A36 4.38
royalty 6.88
rub A-5 A44 2.88
rubbed D-34 A30
rubber G-12 A15 C16 3.75
rubbing A43 4.13
rubbish A87
rudder A97
rude A75 5.75
Rufus A67
rug A-5 A42 1.88
rugged A49
rugs A71 6.00
ruin A64 5.83
ruined A58 7.50
ruins A61 7.75
rule H-29 A9 3.25
ruled J-10 A33
ruler H-10 A20 4.25
rulers A45
rules I-10 A11
ruling A87
rum 7.50
rumor 6.75 £
[rumour]
run B-5 A4 C2 1.44
runaway A70
rung A92
runner A64 7.50
runners A60

Key: Letter-## is *Spelling Power* level word is first taught at. A## is usage by adults; C## is usage by children. (#.##) Average grade level word is taught at; ¢ High School Problem Word, ¡ College Problem Word. ¿ Business Problem Word. £ British spelling (alternate) is also in this list. [word] is British spelling. Elementary Problem words are set in **Boldface** type.

runners-up E-38 7.50
running B-34 A7 C5 3.38
runs D-5 A15 C9
runway A83
rupture I-25 8.00
rural A58 6.50
rush I-5 A30 3.50
rushed I-5 A23
rushes A65
rushing K-5 A39
Russell A99
Russia I-35 A27
Russian I-35 A28
Russians A56
rust A74 4.25
rustle 6.63
rustling A78
rusty A58
Ruth A60
rye A84 8.00

S

S. (south) D-41 4.50
S.E. (south east) 4.50
S.W. (south west) E-41
sabotage 8.00
sac A100
sack D-1 A41 3.50
sacks A77 6.50
Sacramento A95
sacred A51 7.25
sacrifice 7.75
sacrilegious I-43 ¡¿
sad D-1 A16 C6 2.50
saddest 6.75
saddle G-29 A27 C16 5.63
sadly J-26 A39 4.00
sadness A76 5.75
safari 8.75
safe E-6 A11 C10 3.88
safely E-26 A22 C15 6.25
safer A58 4.50
safety I-6 A19 6.00 ¡¿
Sahara A63
said A-47 A1 C1 2.06
sail H-29 A16 3.38
sailboat A86 4.75
sailed H-6 A18 3.75
sailing I-6 A22 4.25
sailor I-13 A38 6.08
sailors I-6 A22
sails J-6 A34
saint K-6 A63 4.25
sake A51 5.25
salable F-33 ¿
salad G-1 A95 C15 5.42
salami 8.00
salary A78 7.42
sale J-6 A29 3.94
sales A43 5.00
salesman A65 8.50
salesmen 9.00
salesmen's 8.25
salesperson 5.25
saliva H-23 8.00
Sally C-35 A19 C4
Sally's 4.75
salmon F-22 A25 7.00
salt G-17 A12 4.00
salty A58
salute A88 6.38
salvage A76 7.25
Sam C-35 A11 C4
Sam's A63
same B-6 A2 C5 3.38
Sammy A76
sample J-29 A36 6.25
samples A41
sampling A99
Samuel A55
San A55
San Francisco D-39 A31
sand F-1 C13 4.25
sandal 5.58
Sandra A61
sands A67
sandstone A94
sandwich A52 4.08 ¡
sandwiches A40 4.25
sandy D-1 A33 C6
sang F-1 A19 C13 3.25
sank A44
Santa A36
Santa Claus 2.00
sap A64 8.00
Sara A77
Sarah A40
Saskatchewan F-35 C16 7.00
sat C-1 A6 C4 2.00
Sat. D-41 4.13
satellite A33 6.88
satellites A29 7.50
satisfaction H-42 A40 7.58
satisfactorily 8.50
satisfactory A61 8.25
satisfied F-32 A29 8.25
satisfy A51 6.75
satisfying A69 7.50
Saturday A-35 A21 C5 3.94 ¢
Saturn A52
sauce A80 4.38
saucer F-12 A60 C13 5.33
saucers 7.50
sauerkraut 8.13
sausage 6.50
savage A56 5.75
savages A101
save F-6 A15 C11 3.25
saved G-6 A22 C16 3.50
saves 8.00
saving A46
savings A65
saw A-17 A2 C1 2.83
sawed 8.00
say D-6 A2 C3 2.38
saying E-6 A10 C8
says E-30 A5 C8 5.25
SC (South Carolina) G-41
scald 5.88
scale H-29 A11 5.25
scales A28
scalp A81
scamp C5
scampered A94
Scandinavia A100
Scandinavian A66
scar A92 5.38
scarce A50 4.63
scarcely J-26 A33 6.50
scare B-14 A61 C10 4.25
scarecrow A96
scared A-14 A30 C3 3.75
scarf H-11 A62 4.75
scariest F-32 6.00
scarlet A57 6.25
scarves D-31 6.33
scary C-33 A98 C12 5.25
scatter A89 6.50
scattered I-24 A25
scattering A92
scene A18 C19 4.75 ¡
scenery A58 6.08
scenes A54
scent G-2 A53 C20 5.42
schedule A62 5.92 ¡
scheduled A94
scheme A50 6.38
scholar A92 7.75
scholars A58
scholarship 6.25
scholastic K-29 ¿
school A-10 A3 C2 3.56
school's 8.25
schoolhouse A72 5.00
schooling A90
schoolmate 6.25
schoolroom A76 7.50
schools H-10 A13
schooner A85
science C-8 A9 C16 5.06 ¡
science fiction E-39 7.00
sciences A98
scientific H-28 A14 6.25
scientist G-8 A17 C19 6.25
scientists A6
scissors H-22 A52 6.67 ¿
scoff 7.25
scolded A66
scoop 5.38
scooped A97
scooter 4.75
scope A101
scorch 6.50
score F-13 A16 C10 4.50
scored G-13 A51 C15
scores D-30 A44 C6
scoring A90
scorn 6.25
Scotland G-35 A48 C20
Scott A41
Scottish A73
Scotty A59
scoundrel 7.25
scour 8.50
scout A57 5.50
scouts A59 6.50
scowl 6.00
scowled A86
scramble A101 5.75
scrambled A47
scrambling A98
scrap A76 4.00
scrapbook A90 5.50
scrape A64 5.42
scraped A66
scrapped 8.50
scraps A76
scratch J-1 A38 3.75
scratched A40
scratching A69
scream C-7 A62 3.33 ¡
screamed E-7 A42 C8 4.25
screaming G-7 A71 C15 6.25
screams A92
screech 6.50 ¡
screeching A99
screen I-7 A25 4.50
screens A89
screw A60
screwdriver 8.50
screws A84
scribble 7.25
scribbling 4.00
script 5.75
scrooge A73 6.25
scrub A77 4.33
scrubbed A97
scrubbing 5.25
scuba 7.42
sculptor A91 7.50
sculpture A97 7.92
SD (South Dakota) G-41
sea C-7 A3 C4 3.08
sea gull G-39 7.25
sea gulls 5.75
seal A40 5.38
sealed A52
seals A58 4.25
seam A68
seamen A79
seams A84
seaport A91 6.50
seaports 8.00
search I-12 A18 5.00
searched G-12 A45 C16 5.25
searching J-12 A37
seas J-30 A24
seashore A57
season D-7 A13 C10 4.92
seasonal A95
seasons K-7 A34
seat E-7 A14 C9 2.63
seat belt 4.50
seated A44
seats J-7 A28
Seattle A66
seaweed A69 5.25
secede 9.00
secluded 7.25
second C-2 A3 C4 3.42
secondary A57 8.25
seconded 8.50
seconds F-2 A20 C13
secret A17 C19 4.50
secretary I-14 A61 7.63 ¿
secretly A68
secrets A70
section F-42 A10 5.88
sections G-42 A20
secure G-25 A46 7.06
secured A80 8.50
securely K-26 A96 6.50
securing 8.50
securities K-32 7.50
security A59 7.25
see A-7 A1 C1 1.88
seed G-7 A26 C15 2.25
seeds I-30 A10
seeing G-7 A15 C19
seek J-7 A35 5.88

seeking A40 5.75
seeks A95
seem H-7 A7 3.38
seemed E-7 A5 C9 4.25
seemingly A86
seems G-30 A8 C16 5.25 ¡
seen C-7 A4 C4 4.88
sees I-7 A24
segment A52 8.50
segments A59
segregation 9.00
seize G-7 A69 7.00 ¡¿
seized K-7 A35
seizure 8.50
seldom J-2 A26 5.42
select I-2 A25
selected J-2 A32
selecting A63
selection H-42 A29 6.00
selections A80
selective 9.00
self C-2 A66 4.25
self-conscious F-38 8.25
self-defense F-38 8.25
self-discipline G-38 9.00
self-reliance G-38 8.25
selfish A87 6.08
sell A11 C16 4.13
seller 5.75
selling J-24 A32
sells A51
selves D-31
semester 8.00
semiannual 8.25
semicircle 8.00
semifinal 7.50
semifinalist 9.00
semisweet 7.75
Senate J-35 A36 8.00
senator A57 7.42
senators A72
send F-2 A10 C11 3.92
sending 3.00
sends A66 6.50
senior A97 6.94
sensation A67
sensational K-42 6.75
sense H-44 A9 5.25 ¡
sensed A93
senses A41
sensible F-33 A53 8.58 ¿
sensitive A44 7.50
sensory 9.00
sent E-2 A7 C8 3.94
sentence H-44 A3 6.00 ¡
sentences H-44 A4
sentiment J-45 8.75
sentry 8.75
separate H-2 A12 7.31 ¡¿
separated I-2 A21
separately A53 6.00
separates A51
separating A78 7.25
Sept. E-41 5.42
September B-35 A26 5.44
sequence A45
sequoia 9.00
seraph; seraphim H-31
sergeant A87 6.25 ¡
serial K-29 7.38 ¿
series F-15 A17 7.25
serious H-43 A16 6.67
seriously J-26 A38
seriousness 7.63
sermon 9.00
servant A55 6.58
servants A45
serve H-12 A17 3.75
served H-12 A20 5.50
serves J-30 A35
service H-12 A16 5.38
services J-47 A28
serving A69 3.00
sesame 6.50
session A60 6.75
set D-2 A2 C6 2.00
Seth A95
sets H-2 A10
setting A20 C19
settle J-29 A27 5.25
settled H-2 A13
settlement H-45 A33 5.92
settlements A50 8.00
settlers I-12 A17 5.75
settles A83
seven C-2 A8 C5 1.88
seventeen F-2 A54 6.00
seventeenth A68
seventh A-2 A56 3.75
seventy A62 7.00
seventy-five A75
several I-29 A3 C20 4.81 ¡
severe A42 7.00
severely A97
severest 7.50
severity 8.50
sew F-47 A67 C19 3.50
sewage A89
sewed A87 7.00
sewing A48 5.13
sex A56
shack A74 5.50
shade I-6 A21 4.33
shaded A42
shades A58
shading A99
shadow F-9 A21 C16 4.83
shadows J-9 A32 5.00
shadowy A84
shady A82
shaft G-1 A51 C16
shafts A87
shaggy A80 4.25
shake J-6 A29 5.75
shaken A68
shakes A69
Shakespeare A78
shaking A30 4.00
shall G-24 A6 C19 3.06
shallow J-24 A30 7.00
shame A57 4.25
shampoo 6.33
shan't 6.00
shape H-6 A8 3.38
shaped G-6 A22 C19
shapes A23 C19 3.25
share F-14 A13 4.50
shared I-14 A33
shares A87
sharing A67
shark H-11 A42 4.25
sharks A49 4.75
Sharon A95
sharp C-11 A10 C11 4.25
sharpen A96 5.75
sharpener 8.25
sharpest 6.75
sharply J-26 A34
shatter 7.25
shattered A70
shawl A76
she A-7 A1 C1 1.63
she'd E-37 A37 C15 6.25
she'll J-37 A54 4.75
she's A23 C13 4.06
shear 5.50
shears I-15 A101 7.50
sheaves 8.25
shed I-2 A30 5.00
sheep G-7 A11 C16 2.25
sheepish 6.75
sheer I-15 A63 7.25
sheet I-7 A24 5.63
sheets 6.00
sheik 8.75
shelf I-2 A28 3.25
shell G-24 A19 3.25
shells A19 4.00
shelter G-12 A28 C16 5.44
sheltered A74 5.75
shelves D-31 A40 6.44
shepherd K-12 A46 6.50 ¡¿
shepherds 6.00
sherbet 7.75
sheriff G-24 A56 C19 7.58
shield A65 7.17
shift A50 4.75
shifted A63
shifting A62
shiftless ¡
shillings A98
shine F-8 A28 C13 4.42
shines A51 7.50
shingle 7.25
shingles A98
shining C-33 A18 C13 4.00 ¡
shiny G-8 A33 C16 3.92
ship D-3 A6 C6 1.50
ship's A60
shipment K-36 8.50 ¿
shipments 8.50
shipped A41 5.13
shipping A49 8.50
ships H-30 A8 C20
shipwreck 7.75
shipyard 5.25
Shirley A76
shirt G-12 A21 C15 3.63
shirts A70 7.50
shish kebab 6.50
shiver A82
shivered A62
shivering A74
shock A40 4.25
shocked A69
shocks A96
shoe G-10 A27 C15 5.25
shoes D-30 A11 C7 5.50
shone J-9 A35 4.88 ¡
shook D-19 A14 C19 4.00
shoot D-10 A22 C10 4.58
shooting D-10 A30 C10
shoots C-10 A56 C8
shop F-4 A16 C16 2.19
shopping C-34 A44 C13 3.42
shops J-4 A35
shore D-13 A11 C9 4.38
shores A42
short D-13 A4 C7 3.00
shortage A93 5.75
shorten A93 6.00
shortened A95
shorter I-13 A22
shortest A61
shortly E-26 A36 C19
shorts 7.50
Shorty A84
shot B-4 A14 C4 2.75
shots A49
should B-19 A2 C3 3.00
should've J-37 5.25
shoulder G-47 A13 6.56 ¡
shoulders I-30 A18
shouldn't E-37 A43 C15 5.75
shout C-16 A30 C10 4.06
shouted F-16 A11 C12
shouting H-16 A34 5.25
shouts A64
shove G-23 5.50
shoved A86
shovel A54 5.38
shoveling 6.50 £
[shovelling]
shovels A97
show D-9 A2 C7 1.50
showed E-9 A11 C9
shower A65 5.19
showers H-16 A95 C20
showing G-9 A14 C20
shown G-9 A4 5.08 ¡
shows G-9 A5
shred I-2 6.25
shredded K-34 7.25
shriek 7.25 ¡
shrieked A95
shrill A48
shrimp A90
shrine A98
shrub A99 5.50
shrubbery 8.17
shrubs A63
shrugged F-34 A63 5.75
shrunk K-5 5.50
shudder 7.50
shut F-5 A18 C16 4.17
shuttle 8.75
shy I-8 A42 4.50
shyest 8.50

Key: Letter-## is *Spelling Power* level word is first taught at. A## is usage by adults; C## is usage by children. (#.##) Average grade level word is taught at; ¢ High School Problem Word, ¡ College Problem Word. ¿ Business Problem Word. £ British spelling (alternate) is also in this list. [word] is British spelling. Elementary Problem words are set in **Boldface** type.

Siberia A97
Sicily A95
sick D-3 A19 C8 2.75
sickness A54 5.67
side C-8 A3 C5 2.75
sideburns 9.00
sides A7
sidewalk A35 C15 4.17
sidewalks A78
sideways A63
siege K-7 6.88 ¡¿
sierra A85 8.50
siesta 8.50
sigh A61 4.67
sighed J-8 A32
sighing A93
sight E-8 A9 C9 3.50
sighted A59
sights A47 8.0
sign A9 C13 4.94
signal H-29 A17 5.63
signaled A64 8.50 £
[signalled]
signals J-30 A24
signature I-25 A66 7.08
signed F-22 A37
significance K-44 A62 7.75
significant A40 7.75 ¡
signified 8.50
signs E-22 A13
silence I-44 A22 7.50
silent H-8 A16 6.75
silently J-26 A38
silhouette 8.50
silk I-3 A23 5.25
silken A99
silky A81
sill A91
silly G-3 A30 C19 2.75
silos 5.75
silver D-12 A10 4.92
silvery A64
similar G-11 A10 7.50 ¡¿
similarities A71
similarity A97 8.13
similarly A59
simile K-29 9.00 ¡
Simon A46
simple H-29 A6 4.63
simpler A52 4.50
simplest D-33 A30 5.63
simplicity A91 8.75
simplified A70
simplify A93 8.75
simply A12 6.13
simultaneous J-43 ¿
simultaneously A97
since D-3 A3 C6 4.00 ¡¿
sincere 7.38
sincerely 5.33
sincerity 7.88
sing C-3 A12 C7 2.63
singer A56 3.88
singers A86
singing E-3 A16 C9 4.50
single A7 C19 5.67
sings A49 5.00
singular K-29 A37 6.00
sinister 7.50
sink I-3 A28 4.50
sinking A71
sinks A87
Sioux A72
siphon 8.63
sir D-12 A18 C9 4.25
siren I-8 4.75
sister B-12 A12 C3 2.67
sister's G-40 C16 6.50
sisters G-30 A25 C15
sisters' 6.50
sisters-in-law G-38 7.00
sit C-3 A10 C7 1.50
site A40 6.88
sits J-3 A37
sitting B-34 A11 C8 3.00
situate 6.75
situation A20 7.13
situations F-42 A46
six B-3 A4 C4 2.17
sixteen G-7 A38 C19 6.00
sixteenth A76
sixth J-3 A38 4.08
sixty A34 C20
sixty-four E-38
sizable F-33 ¿
size E-8 A6 C10 3.50
sizes J-8 A26
SK (Saskatchewan) G-41
skate A-6 A89 3.63
skated 6.00
skater 4.50
skates A49 4.50
skating B-33 A57 C9 4.00
skeleton K-28 A39 4.75
skeletons A73
sketch D-2 A45 6.00
sketches A72
ski A86 4.75
skied 4.50
skier D-47 4.00
skies A46 8.25
skiing D-47 4.00
[skilful] I-27
skill H-24 A17 4.25
skilled A40
skillful I-27 A45 6.50 £
skills J-24 A27
skim A55
skimming A69
skin E-3 A8 C16 3.75
skinned 3.25
skinny A91
skins J-30 A25
skip D-3 A58 3.25
skipped 4.50
skipper A101
skipping A70 4.25
skirt A50 4.92
skirts A53
skis 6.92
skit G-3 C19
skull A51
skunk C-5 A55 C7 6.92
skunks A101
sky C-8 A6 C5 3.17
skyscraper A88 6.50
skyscrapers A87
slab A86
slacks 7.50
slain A92
slalom 8.75
slam B-1 2.75
slammed C-34 A82 C16 5.13
slang A101
slant K-1 A49 5.50
slanted A92
slanting A73
slap A81
slapped A80
slash A88
slaughtered 9.00
slave J-6 A28
slavery K-12 A36 8.75
slaves J-30 A27
sled A-2 A40 2.08
sledding 3.00
sledge 8.50
sleds A85 3.50
sleek A74
sleep B-7 A8 C3 1.81
sleepier C-32 4.00
sleeping D-7 A18 C7 1.00
sleeping bag D-39 6.75
sleepless 6.00
sleeps G-30 A63 C15
sleepy A40 5.75
sleeve A67 4.75
sleeves A62 C20
sleigh 7.50
slender A41
slept E-2 A24 C10 3.83
sleuth 8.75
slice A-8 A43 3.25
slices A59
slick A86 8.00
slid J-3 A39 3.38
slide I-8 A23 2.13
slides A65 8.00
sliding B-33 A46 3.00
slight H-8 A19 6.25
slightest A71
slightly E-26 4.50
slim A73
sling 4.50
slingshot 5.25
slip I-3 A29 2.50
slipped D-34 A22 C20 4.92
slipper C-34 C13 5.25
slippers A73 5.75
slippery A57 5.08
slipping A54 6.75
slips A78
slit A84
sliver 9.00
slogan 7.38
slope I-9 A29 5.25
slopes J-9 A34
sloping A78 5.75
slot A83
slouch 7.75
slouched 8.50
slow G-9 A13 C20 1.88
slowed A-9 A48 1.00
slower A57
slowing A88
slowly E-26 A5 C9 4.25
slumber 7.00
slung A101
small A-17 A2 C4 3.31
smaller G-17 A8
smallest G-17 A17
smallpox 6.25
smart C-11 A35 C8 3.83
smash E-1 4.50
smashed G-1 A51 C15
smear F-15 5.38
smell A-24 A15 C3 3.33
smelled A51 4.25
smelling G-2 A81 C19 4.50
smells C-30 A46 C5
smile F-8 A18 C16 3.50
smiled H-8 A14
smiles A54
smiling D-33 A32 3.58
smirk 7.25
Smith D-35 A22 C7
Smith's A90
smog 7.38
smoke G-9 A15 3.81
smoked A80
smoking A61 7.50
smoky A90 6.00
smooth D-10 A16 C8 4.63 ¡
smoothed A70
smoothly J-26 A39
smorgasbord 8.00
smother G-20 6.25
smudge 7.25
snack G-1 C19 5.25
snag K-1 5.25
snagged 5.75
snail C-6 A66 4.00
snails A71
snake D-6 A22 C7 2.58
snakes F-6 A27 C13
snap A51 4.25
snapdragon F-36 C15
snapped A41
snapping F-34 A77 4.75
snare 5.25
snarl 7.08
snarled A72
snatched A90
sneak G-7 A93 C19 3.25 ¿
sneakier 8.50
sneer 7.25 ¿
sneeze G-7 A80 C20 4.25
snicker 7.25
sniffed A58
sniffing A93
snobbish K-34 6.75
snoopy D-10 C9
snorkel 8.50
snorted A85
snout A100
snow B-9 A6 C4 2.94
snowball 5.00
snowballs 4.00
snowed A-9 1.00
snowflakes A97 4.75
snowing 4.00
snowman
snowmobile 7.50
snows A89 6.50
snowy A59 7.50
snug A89
so A-9 A1 C1 1.56
so-called A57
soak A96 5.31
soaked A66

Alphabetical List

soap D-9 A30 C11 3.25
soap opera 6.50
soar 5.75
soared A87
soaring A86
sobbing A100
soccer D-4 C10 6.88
social I-29 A18 7.25
societies A67
society J-47 A25 8.08
sociology 8.50
sock C-4 C19 3.25
socks A49 5.00
sod A88
soda I-9 A37 4.00
sodium A62
sofa A72
soft C-4 A8 C13 3.33
soften A101
softened A97
softer A56
softly H-26 A17
softness 5.50
soil E-18 A8 4.25
soils A76
solar I-9 A30 6.38
sold E-9 A11 C13 4.00
soldier I-9 A28 7.33
soldiers G-30 A11 C15 4.75
sole A76 6.25
solemn H-22 A58 7.56
solemnly A82
solid H-4 A13 5.75
solids A69
soliloquy K-29 ¡
solitary A93
solo G-9 A69 C19 7.25
Solomon A88
solution F-42 A14 6.75
solutions A46
solve A12 6.25
solved A40
solving A59
sombrero 8.00
some A-20 A1 C1 2.44 ¢
somebody A26 C15 5.69
someday K-36 A34
somehow I-36 A27 7.25
someone C-36 A6 C5 3.31
someone's G-40 A90 7.25
something B-36 A2 C2 3.38
sometime A55 3.75
sometimes B-36 A3 C3 3.25 ¢
somewhat I-36 A19
somewhere A21 C13 4.88
son C-20 A9 C13 3.94
son's A93
sonar 8.25
sonata 8.75
song B-4 A10 C8 3.17
songs F-4 A19 C13
sons G-20 A37
sons-in-law G-38 7.75
soon B-10 A3 C3 2.94
sooner A41
soothe 8.75
sophisticated A100 9.00
sophomore 7.75 ¡
soprano 8.38
sopranos 8.00
sore G-13 A68 C15 4.50
Sorrell A94
sorrow A63 5.83
sorry B-47 A20 C7 3.83
sort G-13 A13 C15 5.25
sorts H-30 A43 C20
sought H-17 A39 6.83
soul J-29 A34 5.50
souls A93
sound C-16 A2 C6 3.42
sounded F-16 A21 C19
sounding A63 5.25
soundly A86
sounds C-16 A5 C8
soup D-10 A31 C11 4.69
sour F-16 A91 C15 5.38
source G-13 A16 5.94
sources J-13 A28
south F-16 A8 C11 5.42
South Carolina A59 5.50
South Dakota E-39 A82 6.08
southeast A56 6.00
southeastern A62 8.00
southern G-47 A14 7.25
southward A50
southwest A55 5.50
southwestern A85
souvenir K-28 8.88 ¿
sovereign 9.00
Soviet J-35 A35
sow 4.63
soybean 5.63
soybeans A94
space C-6 A4 C4 4.33
spacecraft K-36 A47 7.50
spaced A78
spaces J-30 A24
spaceship A83 5.25
spacious 8.63
spade 5.25
spaghetti A97 6.92
Spain I-35 A19
span A60
Spaniards A47
Spanish G-35 A12
spare I-14 A39 4.63
spared A91
spark H-11 A46 4.00
sparkle 6.50
sparkled A92 7.50
sparkling A49
sparks A68
sparrow 6.50
sparrows 8.00
speak G-7 A8 C20 3.75 ¡
speaker J-12 A37 5.75
speakers A87
speaking H-7 A17
speaks A67
spear F-15 A42 4.63
spears A58 6.50
special G-29 A5 C13 4.75
[speciality]
specialize A90 8.50
specialized A53
specially A71
specialty 7.75 £
species A29 7.63
specific J-3 A26 7.75
specifications 9.00
specified 7.50
specify 8.50
specimen I-2 A71 ¡
specimens A66
speck A101
spectacle 9.00
spectacles 8.00
spectacular A60 8.38
spectator 8.58
spectators A65
spectrum A61
speculate 9.00
sped A75
speech H-7 A12 5.50 ¡¿
speeches A58 4.25
speechless 5.88
speed F-7 A7 C12 4.75
speeding A66 8.00
speedometer 9.00
speeds A42
spell G-24 A16 C20 3.08
spellbound 9.00
spelled H-2 A20
spelling H-2 A15 4.50
spellings A70
spells A57
spend G-2 A12 C15 4.25
spending J-28 A35
spends A52
spent F-2 A10 C13 4.33
sperm A72
sphere I-15 A37 8.50
spheres A82
spherical I-15 8.75
spices A61 7.50
spider I-12 A25 5.08
spiders I-8 A42 4.50
spied A88 6.00
spies 4.13
spikes A100
spill D-3 A99 3.75
spilled A56 8.00
spin I-3 A30 6.25
spinach 6.17
spinal A82 8.75
spine A74
spines A101
spinning F-34 A33 5.75
spins A66
spiral A76 8.00
spirit H-3 A20 6.44
spirits A41
spiritual A71
spit A93
spite I-8 A24
splash G-1 A45 C19 4.75
splashdown 8.25
splashed A68
splashing A70
splendid A41 7.00
splendor A81 £
[splendour]
splint 5.50
splinter 6.25
split F-3 A27 C13 5.00
splits A85
splitting F-34 ¿
splotch 8.25
spoil B-18 A52 3.75
spoiled A55 5.25
spoke G-9 A11 C20 3.75
spoken I-28 A22 5.00
sponge A55 7.25
sponges A72
sponsor 7.67
spook G-10 C20
spooky G-10 C15
spool 4.75
spoon A60 4.58
spoonfuls I-27 7.50
spoons A98 6.50
sport F-13 A33 C10 3.33
sports G-13 A26 C16 5.88
spot C-4 A12 C9 2.08
spotless 5.75
spots A28 C20
spotted B-34 A39 C11 5.75
spout A97
sprain A-6 3.50
sprained 8.00
sprang K-1 A38 5.75
sprawling 8.50
spray A55 4.25
spread G-47 A10 3.56
spreading A45
spreads A65
spring B-3 A7 C2 3.31
springs H-30 A39 C20
springtime A91
sprinkle E-29 A74 4.42
sprinkled A94
sprint 5.75
sprout 4.88
spruce A70 8.50
spun A52
spurs A100
spy F-8 A67 C12 4.50
squad F-21 6.25
squall 7.25
square E-21 A7 C20 5.06
square root 8.75
squared A98
squares F-21 A28
squash I-21 A60 8.00
squawk F-21 6.25
squeak A79 6.25
squeeze E-21 A60 4.83
squeezed E-21 A53 5.50
squeezing A90 4.88
squirm E-21 5.75
squirrel E-21 A41 C15 4.42
squirrels E-21 A43 C13 8.75
squirt E-21 5.75
squirting 6.50
St. F-41 A18 6.17
stability 7.75
stable J-6 A36 6.00
stack A65 6.25

Key: Letter-## is *Spelling Power* level word is first taught at. A## is usage by adults; C## is usage by children. (#.##) Average grade level word is taught at; ¢ High School Problem Word, ¡ College Problem Word. ¿ Business Problem Word. £ British spelling (alternate) is also in this list. [word] is British spelling. Elementary Problem words are set in **Boldface** type.

stacked A77
stadium A101 7.50
staff H-24 A32 5.25
stage H-6 A14 4.58
stagecoach A96
staged 5.75
stages A49
staggered A90
stain 5.25
stair A-14 3.75
stairs F-14 A25 C10 3.88
stairway A88
stake A76 6.13
stalk A51 5.75
stalks A60
stall A49 7.75
stallion A77
stammer 7.25
stamp A45 3.94
stamped A54 8.50
stampede 7.75
stamping A82
stamps J-1 A35
Stan A67
stand E-1 A5 C8 3.42
[stand-by] 8.42
standard H-11 A22 6.50
standardize 6.00
standards A42
standby (n) 7.50 £
standing E-1 A9 C9
stands H-1 A10
Stanley A75 C13
stanza A62 7.88
stanzas A101
staple 8.50
star G-11 A13 C20 3.33
starboard A98
starch A64 6.38
starches 6.25
stare B-14 A51 4.25
stared H-11 A25 5.13
starfish A69
staring F-33 A37
starred 5.75
starry 8.25
stars C-11 A8 C10
start B-11 A5 C6 3.00
started B-11 A4 C2 3.00
starting C-11 A14 C12
startle 7.25
startled D-11 C16
startling A74
starts D-11 A18 C16
starvation A99 8.00
starve H-11 A85 4.92
starved A93
starving A99 5.00
state H-6 A5 2.83
state's A84
stated J-6 A30 2.34
statehood 5.75
stately A85
statement H-45 A13 5.67 ¡
statements H-45 A20
states F-6 A9 C13
static A67 8.25
stating A94 8.50
station F-6 A14 C11 5.50
stationary A90 7.50 ¡
stationed A89
stationery G-42 7.50 ¡
stations H-42 A31
statistics A65
statue I-1 A34 7.63 ¡
statues A95
stature ¡
status A66
statute 8.50 ¡
stay C-6 A6 C3 2.88
stayed D-6 A15 C6 4.88
staying G-6 A53 C19
stays 6.50
steadier K-32 6.75
steadily G-32 A32
steady F-47 A19 4.25
steak A85 5.92
steal K-29 A45 5.31 ¡
stealing A69
steam H-7 A14 5.17
steamboat A77 7.75
steamer A83
steaming A61
steel G-7 A12 C19 5.56 ¡
steep I-7 A25 5.25
steeple 7.25
steer A50 5.25
steering A50 6.50
stem I-2 A31
stems J-30 A27
stenographer 8.50
stenography 8.75
step G-2 A8 C19 2.75
Stephen A77
stepped C-34 A20 C16 4.38
stepping A66 3.75
steps E-30 A8 C9
stereo 4.50
stereos 6.33
sterilize 8.75
stern A47 5.67
sternly A82
stethoscope 9.00
Steve A35
Stevenson A93
stew A56 4.00
stewardess 6.25
stick E-3 A10 C12 3.13
sticking A50 7.50
sticks I-30 A18
sticky A47 C20
stiff H-24 A30 3.25
stiffly A83
still A-24 A2 C3 2.75
stillness A70 6.00
stimuli 8.25
stimulus; stimuli H-31
sting D-3 A79 3.67
stingy 7.13
stink G-3 C20
stir J-12 A38 5.13
stirred A41
stirring A49
stirrup A95
stitch A88 5.25
stitches 5.50
stock I-4 A27 5.17
stockade A97
stockholder K-36 7.75
stocking A82 5.50
stockings A72 7.00
stocks A72
stole A61 5.75
stolen A61 4.75
stomach E-20 A25 C16 5.50
stomachs 4.25
stone H-9 A9 3.17
stones I-30 A17
stony A94
stood D-19 A5 C8 4.06
stool A-10 A58 4.25
stoop A89 7.50
stooped A72
stop B-4 A5 C3 1.33
stopped B-34 A6 C5 3.42 ¡
stopping B-34 A31 5.75 ¡
stops I-4 A30 ¡
storage A64 6.00
store B-13 A8 C4 2.67
stored I-13 A25
storekeeper A86
stores F-30 A23 C13
stories C-32 A8 C13 4.25 ¡
storm D-13 A15 C8 4.69
storms J-13 A34
stormy H-13 A68 C20
story A-13 A3 C3 2.06
storyteller A91
stout A62 5.08
stove G-9 A25 C19 4.67
stoves A88 7.50
stow 6.25
straight E-6 A7 C9 3.81 ¡
straighten 5.75
straightened A57
straightest 8.50
strain A51 6.00
strained A62
straining A100
strands A64
strange E-6 A8 C9 4.31
strangely A58
stranger G-6 A25 C20 4.25
strangers A42
strap H-1 A70 C20 4.25
strapped A84
straps A92
strategies 8.25
strategy 6.75
straw A-17 A21 C16 3.88
strawberries A66 7.50
strawberry E-36 A91 C19 5.63
straws A100
stray G-6 A73 C20 5.50
strays A40
streak A58
streaked A95
streaks A90
stream G-7 A14 C19 3.81
streamed A101
streaming A97
streamline 7.00
streamlined 6.50
streams H-30 A19 C20
street C-7 A7 C4 3.88
streetcar 7.00
streets E-30 A11 C10
strength H-2 A14 6.13 ¡
strengthen A66 9.00
strengthened A93
strenuous 8.25 ¡
stress A41 6.13
stressed A88
stretch I-2 A24 3.88 ¡
stretched I-2 A18
stretches A42
stretching A49
strict A65 6.25
stricter 8.50
strictly J-26 A70 9.00 ¡¿
stride A99 5.25
strike G-8 A19 C16 5.00
strikes J-8 A39
striking F-33 A34
string G-3 A12 C16 3.31
string beans D-39 6.88
strings K-3 A35
strip H-3 A22
stripe 4.50
striped A53 5.13
stripes A65 6.50
stripped 5.13
strips A28
strive G-23 6.25
strode A94
stroke J-9 A36 4.33
stroked A76
strokes A47
stroll K-13 A83 5.25
strong F-4 A5 C15 3.06
stronger I-12 A23 4.50
strongest A55 4.50
strongly J-26 A39
struck D-5 A17 C10 4.19
structural A79
structure G-25 A15 8.50
structures G-25 A37
struggle J-29 A26 6.25
struggled I-5 A39
struggles A96
struggling A63 7.50
strung A83
Stuart A75
stubborn D-12 A75 5.50
stubbornness 8.75
stuck D-5 A24 C9 4.50
student H-28 A17 6.42
students H-28 A11
studied E-32 A11 C20 4.75
studies E-32 A23 6.75
studio A73 8.25
studios 8.25
studious 8.50
study G-5 A3 C20 4.13
studying G-5 A17 4.75 ¡
stuff E-24 A34 C8 2.81
stuffed A66 7.50
stumble 6.25
stumbled A63 7.00
stump G-5 A75 C19 5.25
stung A94 6.25
stunned K-34 6.75
stunt A82 5.67
stunts 8.00
stupid G-10 A54 C15 6.38
sturdiest K-32 7.50
sturdy A56 6.50
style H-29 A17 5.19
styles A54
sub A83

Alphabetical List

subconscious I-43 8.00
subdivide 8.25
subdivision 6.75
subject G-5 A8 6.00
subjects G-5 A19
submarine J-47 A33 8.00
submarines A86
submerge 8.58
submerged A90
submit 8.38
submitted 8.50
submitting K-34 7.75
subscribe 8.00
subscription 8.33
subsequent 8.75
subsidy K-5 ¿
subsistence K-44 9.00
substance H-44 A22 C19 8.50
substances H-44 A26
substantial A87 8.63
substitute A42 7.94
substituted A78
subtle A82 8.08
subtract I-5 A36 6.75
subtraction G-42 A74 7.75
suburb 8.75
suburban 8.42
subway A72
succeed I-7 A60 8.50
succeeded J-7 A38 7.75
succeeds J-30 ¡
success H-24 A18 6.88
successful I-27 A19 6.88 ¡
successfully A46
succession A59 8.50
successive A74
successor K-5 ¿
succotash 7.25
succumb H-22 8.25
such C-5 A2 C8 2.75
suck A86
sucking A71
sudden E-28 A20 C4 4.31
suddenly E-26 A6 C3 4.75
Sue A36 C15
suede 9.00
suffer A54 5.88
suffered A40
suffering A51 7.38
suffice 8.25
sufficient K-28 A42 8.00 ¿
sufficiently A79 9.00
suffix K-5 A45 6.25
suffixes A70
suffrage 8.75
sugar D-19 A11 C16 4.25
suggest I-24 A21 5.58
suggested H-2 A15
suggesting A99
suggestion K-42 A71 6.17
suggestions I-42 A35
suggests I-5 A31
suing F-33 ¿
suit G-10 A17 C16 3.81
suitable A31 6.00
suitcase A76 5.38
suite 8.00
suited G-10 A46 C20
suits A40
sulfur A92 6.00 £
sullen 8.25
Sullivan A68
[sulphur] 8.42
Sultan A90
sum G-5 A19 6.75
summarize ¡
summary A83 7.81
summer B-12 A5 C2 3.81
summers A49
summertime A97
summit A79 7.75
summon 7.50
summoned A97
sums A52
sun B-5 A3 C4 2.75
sun's A48
Sun. D-41 4.13
sunburn 5.00
Sunday A-35 A22 C5 3.75 ¢
sundown A94 4.75
sung A50
sunglasses 7.88
sunk A62 6.25
sunlight H-37 A18
sunnier I-32 6.50
sunny D-5 A32 C12 3.25
sunrise A58
sunset A45 5.00
sunshine H-37 A31 4.33
super G-10 C20
superabundant 8.50
superb 7.25
supercharger 8.50
superficial 8.75
superintendent K-28 7.75 ¡¿
superior A55 7.38
superlative 8.50
supermarket A89 8.00
supernatural 7.25
supersede 8.75 ¡
supersonic 7.63
superstars 7.25
superstition 8.25
superstitious 9.00
supervise 8.38
supervision 7.75
supervisor 9.00
supper B-12 A16 C3 4.63
supplement J-45 A101 8.25
supplemented 9.00
supplied G-32 A43 6.00
supplies G-32 A20 4.50
supply H-8 A13 5.67
supplying A93
support H-13 A15 6.88
supported A44 5.75
supporting A57
supports A61
suppose G-9 A7 C20 4.75
supposed F-9 A22 C16 5.25
supposedly K-26 8.25
suppress 8.63 ¡
supreme A58 5.13
sure C-12 A3 C4 5.08 ¡
surely E-26 A20 C20 5.75
surf A86
surface H-43 A5 6.58
surfaces A44
surgeon K-12 7.58 ¿
surgery A80 7.00
surplus 7.33
surprise F-8 A13 C12 5.31 ¡¿
surprised E-8 A15 C10
surprises A73
surprising F-33 A34 8.25
surprisingly A70
surrender A63 7.13
surrendered A85
surrey 9.00
surround A71 5.83
surrounded A26 6.75
surrounding H-16 A34
surroundings A47 8.50
surrounds A82
survey A53 7.25
surveying H-12 C20
surveyor 9.00
surveys 8.00
survival A74 7.63
survive K-12 A41 4.75
survived A66
Susan A31
susceptible K-29 ¿
suspect A65 8.88
suspected A70
suspended A64
suspense K-44 A84 8.00
suspension 7.75
suspicion A98 8.00
suspicious J-43 A74 9.00 ¿
sustain 7.25
sustained A86
swain A97
swallow A50 6.58
swallowed J-9 A34
swallowing A98
swallows A76
swam I-1 A26
swamp A52 7.75
swamps A53
swampy A94
swan G-1 C19
swans H-30 C19
swapped K-34 5.25
swarm D-13 A94 C11 5.75
swarming A91
sway E-6 A1 C3 5.00
swayed A98
swaying G-6 A101 C20
swear A88
sweat J-47 A37 5.25
sweater A59 5.17
sweaters A101
Sweden A41
Swedish A81
sweep A44 5.25
sweeping K-7 A39
sweeps A74
sweet E-7 A16 C8 4.58
sweetest 6.75
sweetheart 5.50
swell A60 4.50
swept J-2 A27 4.92
swerve G-23 5.75
swift K-3 A33 5.25
swiftly J-26 A34
swim D-3 A16 C6 2.00
swimmer A84 5.75
swimmers A100
swimming B-34 A17 C3 4.38
swims A72
swing F-3 A23 C12 1.75
swinging J-3 A35
swings A66 6.50
swirl 5.75
swirling A96 5.25
swish A95
Swiss J-35 A36
switch K-3 A37 4.88
switched A72
switches A90
Switzerland J-35 A35
swollen A77 5.75
sword F-22 A39 5.67
swords A75
swore A86
swung I-5 A30
syllable F-47 A26 5.75 ¡
syllables A26
symbol I-46 A15 7.50
symbolic I-46 8.88
symbolism 8.75
symbolize 8.38
symbols A13
symmetrical K-29 ¡
symmetry K-47 ¿
sympathetic 8.25
sympathize 8.25
sympathy I-46 A65 7.38
symphony I-46 A84 7.75
symptom I-46 8.25
synagogue 7.63
synchronize 7.00
synonym I-46 A90 8.25
synonymous J-43 ¿
synonyms A73
synthesis I-46 8.75
synthetic A74 8.63
Syria A96
syrup A64 5.75
system I-46 A5 6.38
systematic I-46 8.75
systematize 8.75
systems A24

T

T.V. D-41 A25 7.00
table E-29 A4 C9 4.31
tablecloth E-36 C10
tables J-30 A25
tablet 5.00
tablets 7.00
tack A86
tackle A61
tackling 9.00
tacks 6.25
taco 6.50
tacos 7.25

Key: Letter-## is *Spelling Power* level word is first taught at. A## is usage by adults; C## is usage by children. (#.##) Average grade level word is taught at; ¢ High School Problem Word, ¡ College Problem Word. ¿ Business Problem Word. £ British spelling (alternate) is also in this list. [word] is British spelling. Elementary Problem words are set in **Boldface** type.

tadpoles A87 8.00
tag A55 2.25
tagged A95
tagging 3.25
tail D-6 A9 C6 3.19
tailor A76 5.75
tails J-6 A32
take D-6 A2 C2 2.25
taken E-28 A5 C13
takes D-30 A6 C7
taking B-33 A7 C8 4.00
tale E-29 A40 4.50
talent A67 5.88
talented A92
tales K-6 A30
talk D-22 A5 C6 3.25
talked A13 C11
talking C-22 A9 C5 5.00
talks A44
tall B-17 A6 C7 4.25
taller A43
tallest A51
tame G-6 A54 C20 4.75
tamed A84
tan A57 5.50
tangent 8.50
tangible K-29 8.50 ¿
tangle A90 6.00
tangled A62
tango 9.00
tank I-1 A25
tanks H-30 A36 C20
tanning 4.50
tantalize 9.00
tantrum 7.50
tap K-1 A39
tape J-6 A26 3.50
tape recorder D-39 6.75
tapped A70
tapping A100 3.58
tar A86 6.25
tardiness I-32 6.00
tardy 5.63
target A41 6.33
tariff J-24 7.67 ¿
task A23 4.25
tasks I-1 A50
taste C-6 A18 C5 3.50
tasted E-6 A46 C10
tastes D-30 A57 C7
tasting A99 4.00
tasty A83 5.00
taught G-17 A17 C20 4.25
taunt 7.25
tavern A87
tax I-1 A24 6.25
taxation 7.75
taxes A43 4.88
taxi A74 6.25
taxiing 8.50
taxis 6.00
Taylor A80
tea I-7 A23 4.25
teach G-7 A22 C16 2.63
teacher A-12 A7 C5 3.31 ¢
teacher's G-40 A59 5.75 ¢
teachers E-30 A27 C8
teaches 7.00
teaching J-7 A33
team D-7 A9 C8 3.17
[team-mate] 8.42
[team-mates] 8.42
teammate 6.63 £
teammates K-36 7.50 £
teams H-30 A27 C19 2.75
tear B-15 A31 4.25
tearing A49
tears H-15 A21
tease A89 5.17
teased A101 8.00
teasing A78 6.50
teaspoon A100 5.50
technical A43 8.50
technician 8.50
technique A63 8.00
techniques A40
technology A58 8.42
Ted A39
Teddy A61 C20
teenager 8.00
teenagers A87
teens A82
teepee 7.25
teeth E-7 A10 C11 2.81
telecast 7.75
telegram 7.50
telegraph A43 6.38
telephone F-2 A16 6.17
telephones A80
telescope J-9 A31 6.63
telescopes A74
televise 7.00
television G-42 A12 6.58
tell A-24 A2 C4 2.33
telling G-2 A14 C20
tells A7
temper A55 4.50
temperament I-45 7.88 ¡
temperate A98
temperature E-25 A9 C20 7.33 ¡
temperatures G-25 A26
temple A53 5.50
temples A57
tempo A77 7.75
temporary K-2 A54 7.38 ¿
ten C-2 A5 C4 1.58
tenant K-28 7.50 ¿
tend J-28 A37
tended A70
tendency J-28 A67 8.75 ¡
tender A41 6.08
tending A101
tends A55
Tennessee E-35 A45 5.50
tennis A45 4.88
tenor 7.00
tens A43
tense J-28 A35 6.50
tension A64
tent E-2 A24 C8 3.63
tentacles K-28 9.00
tenth A-2 A50 3.75
tents A42 4.25
tepee 7.50
teriyaki 7.25
term I-12 A21 5.17
terminal A77 6.50
termination K-42 6.75
termites A99
terms I-30 A12
terrain A85
terrestrial 7.50
terrible G-29 A19 C13 5.94 ¿
terribly A55 8.50
terrific A92 8.00
terrified A69
terrify 6.88
territories A97
territory J-13 A32 7.75
terror K-13 A46 5.50
Terry A50 C8
test E-2 A9 C10 4.75
test tube 5.25
tested A44
testified 7.50
testify 8.50
testimony 8.50
testing A51
tests I-2 A26
Texans A90
Texas E-35 A15 5.67
text A54
textbook A80 5.50
textbooks A91
textile A84 8.00
textiles A75
texture E-25 A67 8.38
Thames A99
than C-1 A1 C4 2.88 ¡
thank F-1 A18 C11 2.75
thanked A75 7.00
thankful E-27 A96 4.19
thanking 8.00
thanks F-1 A25 C13
Thanksgiving D-35 A42 C12 5.19 ¢
that A-1 A1 C1 2.33
that's B-37 A5 C4 3.75 ¢
the A-47 A1 C1 1.81
the Smiths' 8.25
theater A45 7.50 £
theaters A86 7.50 £
[theatre] 8.42
[theatres] 8.42
thee A23
theft 5.50
their A-14 A1 C1 2.81 ¢¡¿
theirs A53 4.75
them A-2 A1 C1 2.33
theme A44 6.83
themes A63
themselves D-31 A6 C19 6.25
then A-2 A1 C1 2.42 ¡
Theodore A56
theology 8.75
theories A50 8.25
theory H-15 A23 8.13
therapist 8.00
there A-14 A1 C1 2.88 ¢¡
there'll A93
there's D-37 A9 C7 4.08
thereafter A80
thereby A70 9.00
therefore I-36 A10 6.25 ¡
thermal 8.50
thermometer J-12 A34 8.75
thermometers A81
thermos 8.50
thermostat 8.63
thesaurus 9.00
these C-7 A1 C3 3.06
they A-6 A1 C1 2.75 ¢
they'd F-37 A37 5.75
they'll F-37 A35 5.50
they're D-37 A17 C7 5.50 ¡
they've J-37 A66 5.50
thick H-3 A9 3.44
thicken 6.00
thicker A73
thicket A79
thickly A96
thickness A50
thief A48 7.13
thief's 7.50
thieves D-31 A77 5.88
thigh A98 5.25
thimble A98
thin G-3 A9 C15 3.42
thing B-3 A3 C3 2.42
things B-30 A2 C2 2.75
think B-3 A2 C2 2.63
thinking F-3 A8 C11 5.00
thinks H-30 A20 C19
thinner A58 6.75
third D-12 A6 C8 3.69
thirds A58
thirst A80
thirsty K-12 A55 4.56
thirteen I-12 A34 5.25
thirty D-12 A21 C9 4.88
thirty-five E-38 A64 7.75
this A-3 A1 C1 2.19
Thomas A21
Thompson A94
thorn A88 7.25
thorns A85
Thornton A90
thorough A86 7.00 ¡
thoroughly K-26 A43 7.25
those C-9 A2 C6 2.69
thou H-16 A26
though D-9 A4 C9 4.25
thought B-17 A2 C2 4.13 ¡
thoughtful I-27 A53 5.00
thoughtfully A61
thoughtless 7.13
thoughts H-17 A20
thousand C-16 A9 C7 6.25
thousands F-16 A8 C19
thousandths ¡
thread F-47 A21 5.00
threads A40
threat A65 6.00
threaten 5.88
threatened A45
threatening A100
threats A93
three B-7 A2 C2 1.92
threw C-10 A16 C8 3.75
thrift 5.50
thrifty 7.50
thrill J-24 A93 3.75
thrilling A75 7.50
thrive H-23 A99 8.50
thriving A92
throat F-9 A22 C19 4.25
throats A86
throbbing 8.50
throne A48 6.00
through B-10 A2 C2 4.67 ¢¡

throughout H-37 A11 C20 5.92
throw D-9 A16 C10 3.58
throwing I-9 A35 6.5
thrown F-9 A24 C16 5.25
throws A54 7.50
thrust I-5 A31
thud A90
thumb E-22 A29 C20 4.13
thump A63
thunder F-12 A37 C13 5.38
thundered A101
Thurs. D-41 4.13
Thursday A-35 A48 C15 3.94
thus G-5 A7 8.25
thy J-8 A28
tick A91
ticket G-3 A38 C19 5.08
tickets E-3 A35 C10 7.00
tickle I-29 C19 5.25
tickled A100
ticklish 6.00
tidal A72
tide J-8 A27
tides A44
tidy A85
tie G-8 A19 C15 2.92
tied E-8 A13 C8 4.25
ties A45
tiger E-8 A36 C10 4.17
tigers A83 6.50
tight I-8 A21 3.69
tighten A97
tighter A98
tightly I-26 A26
tile A95
tiles A80
till E-24 A14 C8 2.75 ¡
tilt A95
tilted A69
Tim A26 C13
timber J-3 A38 4.75
time A-8 A1 C1 1.75 ¢
times D-30 A3 C7
timid A96 5.25
timing 5.75
Timothy A67
tin I-3 A21
tiniest F-32 6.00
tinsel 8.00
tiny D-8 A6 C7 3.92
tip A18 C20 6.25
tipped F-34 A87 8.00
tips A41
tire G-8 A40 C20 3.88
tired D-8 A11 C6
tires A42
tissue A40 5.50
tissues A61
title I-29 A17 4.50
titles A42
TN (Tennessee) G-41
to A-10 A1 C1 2.63 ¢¡
toad G-9 A47 C20 4.50
toads A55
toast A61 4.44
tobacco J-24 A30
toboggan 6.38
Toby A83
today B-36 A3 C4 3.69 ¢
today's G-40 A26
toe A-9 A40 2.88
toes I-9 A26
together B-10 A2 C4 3.81 ¡
toil J-18 A90 8.25
token 9.00
Tokyo A60
told B-9 A3 C2 3.63
toll A83
Tom A-35 A7 C3
Tom's G-40 A39
tomato A86 7.50
tomatoes A62 6.38
tomb E-22 A90 6.50
Tommy A20 C10
Tommy's A99
tomorrow B-10 A14 C7 4.25 ¢
ton G-20 A71 4.25
tone H-9 A15
tones J-9 A32
tongue A17 7.00
tongues A63
tonight E-36 A23 C9 4.13
tons J-30 A28
tonsils 5.00
Tony A31
too A-10 A2 C1 3.13 ¢¡¿
took B-19 A3 C2 2.81
tool J-10 A37 5.08
tools H-10 A16
tooth D-10 A41 C13 3.69
tooth; teeth F-31
toothache 7.25
toothbrush 6.25
top B-4 A3 C4 1.75
topic I-4 A24 5.88
topics A47
tops A25 C20
topsoil 4.75
torch A96
tore G-13 A47 C20 5.00
toreador 9.00
torment I-45 7.25
torn H-13 A27 3.75
tornado K-13 A70 5.25
tornadoes 6.25
Toronto F-35 C19
torpedoes 5.75
tortilla 7.63
tortoise 7.92
torture I-25 7.88
toss A55 5.50
tossed J-24 A29
tosses 4.25
tossing A62
total H-29 A11 4.94
totally A85
totem 7.25
touch D-47 A12 C9 3.25
touchdown 5.67
touched E-47 A23 C13
touches I-30 A37
touching G-47 A39 C20 6.50
tough G-47 A25 C20 4.81
tougher 8.50
tour G-10 A66 C19 5.00
tourist A69 4.88
tourists A53
tournament I-45 7.50
tourniquet 8.50
tow A82
toward D-13 A3 C10 5.08
towards A43 C16
towel A60 5.17
towels A63
tower F-16 A24 C19 4.25
towering A57
towers A67
town A-16 A5 C3 3.25
towns H-16 A17 5.00
townspeople A96
toy B-18 A29 C6 3.17
toys B-18 A38 C10 3.75
trace J-6 A26
traceable 8.75
traced A60 4.50
tracer 9.00
traces A70
track G-1 A15 C19 3.81 ¡
tracked A100
tracks H-30 A22 C19
tract ¡
tractor F-13 A60 C15 4.83
tractors A91
Tracy C13
trade A-6 A12 3.25
traded A54 3.00
trader A68 6.75
traders A51 6.50
trading C-33 A33
tradition J-42 A53 7.13
traditional I-42 A44 8.00
traditions A84
traffic I-1 A19 5.92
tragedy J-1 A84 7.69 ¡¿
tragic A87 6.13
trail G-29 A16 C13 5.67
trailer F-6 A77 C12 4.75
trailing A75
trails A48 8.00
train E-6 A10 C8 2.67
trained G-6 A24 C20
trainer G-6 C19 4.75
training I-6 A21
trains F-6 A25 C13
trait A95 6.25
traitor 7.00
traits K-6 A87 8.75
tramp A77 5.88
trample 7.50
trance I-44 8.00
tranquil I-21 9.00
tranquillity K-29 ¡
transaction 8.63
transcontinental 6.75
transcript 8.25
transfer A59 8.25
transferal 8.25 £
[transferral] 8.42
transferred K-34 A56 7.00 ¡¿
transfigure I-25 8.25
transform A91 8.25
transformation A94
transformed A69
transfuse 8.25
transfusion 7.63
transistor 6.00
transit 8.25
translate A80 8.00 ¡
translated A73
translation A82
transmission 7.75
transmit A97 8.13
transmitted 7.50
transmitter A84 8.75
transparent I-14 A59 7.69
transplant 8.00
transport A69 7.38
transportation G-42 A24 7.50
transported A82
transpose 8.50
trap G-1 A30 C19 2.13
trapped D-34 A48 C19 4.00
trapper A96
trappers A68
trapping A64
traps A61
trash F-1 C13 3.25
travel H-29 A7 4.00
traveled A16 8.25 £
traveler A44 5.00 £
travelers K-29 A36 £
traveling I-29 A18 3.75 £
[travelled] 8.42
[traveller] 8.42
[travellers] K-29 8.42
[travelling] I-29 8.42
travels J-30 A25
tray E-6 A53 4.25
trays 5.25
treacherous I-43 A90 8.50 ¡
treasure E-25 A35 C16 5.92
treasurer 8.50 ¡
treasures A75
treasury 7.50
treat J-7 A34 4.08
treated J-7 A30
treatment H-45 A32 5.50
treaty A51 5.75
tree B-7 A4 C2 1.75
trees B-30 A4 C3 2.50
treetops A91
trek 8.38
tremble A99 6.88
trembled A78
trembling A63
tremendous H-43 A30 8.58
trend A91
trespass 8.00
trial 6.38
trials A91
triangle J-29 A22 7.75
triangles A40
triangular F-46 A64 7.50
tribal A82
tribe I-8 A26
tribes J-30 A25
trick G-3 A24 C15 2.58
tricks E-3 A29 C10

Key: Letter-## is *Spelling Power* level word is first taught at. A## is usage by adults; C## is usage by children. (#.##) Average grade level word is taught at; ¢ High School Problem Word, ¡ College Problem Word. ¿ Business Problem Word. £ British spelling (alternate) is also in this list. [word] is British spelling. Elementary Problem words are set in **Boldface** type.

tricky A87
tricolor F-46 7.50 £
[tricolour] F-46
tricycle F-46 7.50
tried C-32 A5 C3 4.17
tries C-32 A31 C19 3.00 ¡
trillion 8.00
trim A54 5.25
trimmed A78 4.25
trimming 5.75
Trinidad 6.25
trinket 7.25
trio 7.75
trip C-3 A8 C4 1.75
triple F-46 7.50
triplets 8.13
triplicate F-46 7.50
tripod 8.75
tripped C-34 A82 C16 3.13
tripping 3.88
trips I-3 A27
triumph K-5 A54 7.00
triumphant A96 8.00
trivia 6.75
troll G-24 C15
troop A93 5.75
troops A28
trophies G-32 6.13
trophy F-47 C15 5.88
tropical J-29 A27 7.00
tropics A71
trot F-4 A96 C15
trotted A68
trotting C-34 C16 5.50
trouble C-47 A8 C7 3.75 ¡
troubled A53
troubles A52 9.00
troublesome A69 5.75
trousers A54 5.25
trout F-16 A63 C15 5.25
Troy A84
truck C-5 A12 C5 2.50
trucks F-5 A22 C12
trudged A89
true C-10 A4 C8 3.25
truer 8.50
truly D-47 A34 4.92 ¡
trumpet A74 7.00
trumpets G-5 A97 C19
trunk F-5 A25 C15 3.17
trunks A45
trust K-5 A37 3.92
trusted A83
trusting 8.50
trustworthy K-36 7.25
truth I-10 A21 4.83
truthful E-27 5.50
try D-8 A3 C6 2.17
trying D-8 A7 C6
tub A-5 A50 2.25
tube H-10 A13 2.63
tuberculosis 7.50
tubes J-10 A29
tubing A83
tucked A57
Tues. D-41 4.13
Tuesday A-35 A48 C13 3.81 ¡
tug A80
tugged A80
tugging 6.75
tugs A99
tuition G-42
tulip G-10 C19 5.67
tulips 7.50
tumble A92
tumbled A75
tumbling A71
tuna A92 6.17
tundra A82
tune J-10 A30 4.25
tune-ups G-38 7.50
tuned A84
tunes A90
tuning A82
tunnel I-29 A37 C19 5.42
tunnels G-5 A51 C19
turbine A86
turkey D-12 A32 C9 5.00
turkeys A56 7.25
Turkish A57
Turks A85
turmoil 7.25
turn C-12 A4 C5 3.25
turned B-12 A3 C3 5.00
Turner A60
turning G-12 A12 C19
turnips A65 6.50
turnpike 5.88
turns H-12 A11 5.25
turquoise E-21 5.38
turtle E-29 A36 C7 4.50
turtles A46
tusks A72
tutor 6.63
tuxedo 9.00
Twain A97
twelfth A90 7.13
twelve A-23 A14 C9 6.00
twentieth F-2 A56 6.00
twenty E-2 A13 C9 4.17
twenty-eight A99
twenty-five E-38 A33 C16 6.00
twenty-four E-38 A47 C20
twenty-one E-38 A68 6.75
twenty-six A77
twenty-three A99
twenty-two E-38 A84
twice G-8 A12 C20 5.08
twig A83
twigs A49
twilight A74
twin F-3 A49 C16 4.75
twine 5.25
twinkle A74
twinkling A84
twins G-30 A49 C16
twirl 5.75
twist E-3 A46 5.25
twisted K-3 A36
twisting A55
two A-47 A1 C1 2.19 ¢¡
two-thirds A74
TX (Texas) G-41
tycoon 8.50
tying 7.00
type H-8 A11 5.44
types I-8 A17
typewriter A65 6.00
typhoid 8.00
typhoon 5.25
typical F-47 A27 7.75 ¡
tyranny K-47 ¡¿
tyrant 7.25

U

U.S.A. E-41 7.00
UFO H-41 8.25
UFO's 6.75
ugliest 8.50
ugly C-5 A32 C8 5.17
ukelele 7.75
ultimate A92
ultraviolet A92
Ulysses A62
umbrella A63 7.42
umbrellas A88
umpire A97 7.63
unable I-29 A33 6.17
unanimous J-43 8.38
unattainable 5.50
unaware I-14 A97 4.75
unbearable I-14 7.50
unbeaten 5.00
unbelievable A85
unbound 9.00
unbroken A89
unbutton 6.00
uncertain K-46 A70 7.13
uncertainly K-26 7.75
unchanged A89
uncle E-29 A11 C4 4.00
uncle's 7.25
uncles G-5 C19 3.25
uncles' 7.25
uncomfortable A62 8.75
uncommon 6.50
unconscious A94 8.75
uncover 6.00
uncovered A72
undecided 8.00
under B-5 A2 C5 3.13
underdog F-36 C13
undergo A92
underground F-36 A36 C19 6.08
underline I-36 A23
underlined A43
underlying A90
underneath H-37 A33 C19 6.25
undersea A94
underside A91
understand H-37 A5 4.50
understanding H-37 A16 5.50
understands A87
understood I-36 A23 5.50
underwater F-36 A38 C19 5.75
undone E-20 C19
undoubtedly J-26 A54 8.50 ¡¿
unearthly K-26 7.75
uneasy A78
uneducated K-46 8.00
unemployment J-45 8.00
unequal A98
uneven A81 5.75
unexpected A44 7.63
unfair 4.25
unfamiliar A61 8.75
unfortunate A83 7.50
unfortunately I-26 A49 5.00
unfriendly A93
unhappy J-24 A27 4.25
unicycle 7.75
uniform F-46 A35 7.00
uniforms A77
unify 8.25
uninhabited 7.00
uninterrupted 8.00
union A40 7.00
unions A57
unique F-21 A31 8.08
unison 8.00
unit H-10 A8 6.50
unite A86 6.50
united G-10 A51 C15 5.00
United States D-39 A4 6.13
units I-10 A13
unity A58 7.50
universal A57 7.50
universally J-26 ¡
universe J-10 A26 7.38
universities A63
university J-10 A29 8.00
unkind 4.38
unkindness 7.00
unknown F-22 A24 5.13
unless G-24 A12 C19 5.58
unlike A25 5.17
unlikely A79
unload A96 6.00
unloading A101
unlock 6.00
unlucky K-46 5.83
unmade 5.00
unnecessary K-46 A78 7.50
unpack 4.75
unpaid K-46 4.88
unpleasant A58 6.50
unpleasantness 7.00
unsafe 5.38
unseen A71
unselfish K-46 6.00
unskilled K-46 5.75
unskillful I-27 7.00
unsuccessful A92
untidiness K-32 7.00
untie 5.00
untied A92
until E-27 A3 C3 3.38 ¡
unto A52
untruthful E-27 5.75
unusual I-29 A19 5.17 ¡
unusually A53 9.00
unwanted 3.75
up A-5 A1 C1 1.56
up-to-date E-38 6.50
upon B-36 A4 C3 3.00
upper D-34 A15
upright A48 8.25
uproar 6.25
upset K-36 A36 5.25
upsetting K-34 7.75
upside A42
upstairs E-36 A37 C9 4.83
upstream A78
uptown 6.00
upward I-36 A24
uranium A35
Uranus A81
urban A79 7.13
urge A85 7.08
urged A49 8.75

urgent 7.50
urging A87
us A-5 A2 C1 1.58
usable 6.50
usage A85 7.63
use C-10 A1 C10 2.13
used B-10 A2 C5 3.63
useful I-27 A12 4.58 ¿
useless A40 5.38
uses I-10 A9
using C-33 A3 4.63 ¡
usual H-29 A14 5.42
usually E-26 A3 C9 6.17 ¡
UT (Utah) G-41
Utah E-35 A63 5.75
utensils A100
utmost A91
utter A90
utterly A85

VA (Virginia) G-41
vacancy ¡
vacant A82 6.81
vacation F-42 A31 C13 5.25
vaccinate J-24 7.13 ¿
vaccine A88
vacuum A40 6.50 ¡
vague A81 8.00
vain A56 6.63
vale 7.75
valentine 4.50
Valentine's Day 4.67
valentines 4.00
validate 6.00
valley G-7 A14 C15 4.38
valleys I-24 A25 5.25
valuable I-29 A18 7.17
value H-10 A11 5.88
valued A91 8.50
values J-10 A26
valve A86
valves A67
vampire C19
van A56
Vancouver F-35 C19
vandalism 9.00
vane A92 7.00
vanilla 7.69
vanish 5.25
vanished A50
vapor J-13 A29 6.13 £
[vapor] J-13
variable A62
variation A58
variations A43
varied A36 7.50
varies A44
varieties A49
variety G-11 A13 6.88
various H-43 A9 7.50
varnish 7.25
vary I-14 A37 6.25
varying A55
vase A81 6.50
vast H-1 A17 5.75
vault 5.92
vegetable A45 6.58 ¡¿
vegetables A17 7.00
vegetarian 8.00
vegetation A60
vehicle A56 8.58
vehicles A50
veil 6.42
vein A100 6.67
veins A50
velocity A59
velvet D-2 A58 5.50
vengeance J-44 8.25 ¡
Venice A96
venom 7.50
venture I-25 A62 7.50
ventured A83
Venus J-35 A38
verb H-12 A12 6.63
verbs I-30 A18
verdict 8.50
Vermont E-35 A98 5.63
versatile 8.50
verse A50 5.63
verses A99 7.50
version A53 7.92
versions A91
versus 8.00
vertical J-29 A27 8.58
very A-14 A1 C1 3.08 ¢
vessel K-2 A43 7.50
vessels J-2 A30
veteran 7.75
Veterans Day 4.50
veterinarian I-2 C20 7.63
veto 8.00
vetoes 6.25
viaduct 8.75
vibrate A50 7.50
vibrating A66
vibration A65
vibrations A43
Vic A79
vice 8.50
vice-president E-38 5.88
vicinity A86 9.00
vicious 8.75
victim G-3 A54 C20
victims A78
Victor A97
Victoria A94
victories G-32 A89 6.00
victory J-13 A28 6.50
[video-tape]
videotape 7.00 £
Vietnam A69
view H-10 A16 5.88
viewed A73
viewpoint 8.25
views A55 9.00
vigilance J-44 ¡
vigor A83 £
vigorous A61 8.75 £
vigorously A92 £
[vigour]
[vigourous]
[vigourously]
Vikings A81
village F-3 A8 C12 4.50 ¡
villagers A56
villages I-24 A24
villain J-24 A76 8.25 ¡¿
vine A81 6.25
vinegar A71 6.63
vines A50 6.50
vineyards A95
violate 7.75
violation K-42 7.25
violence H-44 A53 6.75
violent A44
violently A79
violet G-9 A68 C20 6.50
violets A92 7.50
violin A55 7.50
Virginia E-35 A23 5.63
virtually A66
virus A82 7.75
viruses A83
visible A38 7.00
vision A43 6.50
visit E-3 A11 C8 5.33
visited I-3 A21 4.25
visiting J-3 A39 5.75
visitor J-3 A36 4.75
visitors I-3 A25
visits A55
visual A67
visualize 7.75
vital A52 7.83
vitality 8.50
vitamin A69 7.88
vitamins A53 7.50
vivid A55 9.00
vocabulary K-1 A39 7.38
vocal A52 8.63
vocalize 8.75
vocation 8.75
vocational 8.88
voice B-18 A5 C6 3.81
voiced A93
voices E-18 A18
void G-18 6.50
volcanic A59 7.25
volcano A39 C13 7.75
volcanoes A49 6.25
volleyball 7.75
volume G-47 A19 ¿
volumes A93 9.00
voluntary A101 8.00
volunteers A77
vote I-9 A26 5.00
voted A58 7.50
voters A63
votes A63
voting A85
vow 6.50
vowel H-29 A13 7.50
vowels K-29 A35
voyage G-18 A28 5.38
voyages A74
VT (Vermont) G-41
vulgar 9.00

W

W. (west) D-41 4.50
WA (Washington) G-41
wade 8.00
waded A84
wading 8.00
wafer 8.00
waffle 8.00
wage A89 6.25
wages A48 9.00
wagged A98
wagging 3.25
wagon H-1 A15 5.25
wagons I-1 A29
wail 7.25
waist A45 5.81
wait B-6 A9 C6 4.13
waited G-6 A17 C15
waiter A91
waiting E-6 A11 C8
waits A93
wake F-6 A34 C13 2.75
wakes A94
waking A89
Wales A80
walk C-22 A6 C3 3.00
walked C-22 A6 C3
Walker A100
walking A11 C2 3.00
walks F-22 A29
wall C-17 A8 C8 3.42
Wallace A100
wallpaper 6.00
walls A11 4.50
walnut A62 6.50
walrus 6.25
Walter A38
waltz 7.58
wampum 7.25
wand G-1 C19
wander A51 8.00
wandered A49 6.38
wandering A45
want B-17 A2 C2 2.42
wanted B-17 A4 C2 4.00
wanting A53 3.00
wants A-17 A13 C12
war B-13 A7 C6
Ward A91
ware 5.50
warehouse A93 6.88
warfare A77
warm D-13 A5 C6 3.00
warmed A66
warmer J-12 A33
warming A96
warmly A81
warms A98
warmth J-13 A35 5.75
warn A54 5.25
warned K-13 A39
warning J-13 A29 6.50
warnings A79
warp 7.25
warrant I-13 8.25
warranty 8.25
Warren A67
warrior A54
warriors A45

Key: Letter-## is *Spelling Power* level word is first taught at. A## is usage by adults; C## is usage by children. (#.##) Average grade level word is taught at; ¢ High School Problem Word, ¡ College Problem Word. ¿ Business Problem Word. £ British spelling (alternate) is also in this list. [word] is British spelling. Elementary Problem words are set in **Boldface** type.

wars D-13 A44 C15
was A-47 A1 C1 2.38
wash C-17 A18 C15 3.00
washable 6.75
washed C-17 A19 C12
washes A101
washing A28 C19
Washington E-35 A10 5.67
Washington's A80
Washington's Birth** 4.50
wasn't B-37 A8 C4 4.31
wasp K-1 A94 5.25
waste I-6 A24 6.38
wasted A55 5.00
wasteful 8.00
wastes A59
wasting A89 4.50
watch A-17 A5 C4 2.50
watched C-17 A8 C12
watches A45 4.00
watchful E-27 5.75
watching G-17 A12 C16 3.63
watchman A88
water A-12 A1 C2 3.00
water's A80
watered A76 6.50
waterfall A92
waterfalls A96
watering H-17 A100 C20
watermelon H-37 A86 C20 5.50
waterproof 5.75
waters G-17 A16
waterway A90
watery A70
Watson A82
wave G-23 A16 2.75
waved G-6 A26 C20
waver 8.00
waves H-30 A9 C20
waving A40 3.75
wavy A92
wax A42
waxed A96
way B-6 A1 C2 2.81
ways G-30 A3 C16
we A-7 A1 C1 1.56
we'd F-37 A32 6.25
we'll A9 C10 3.81
we're D-37 A13 C6 4.06
we've J-37 4.17
weak H-7 A18 4.75 ¡
weakened A77
weaker A84
weakness A71 6.00
wealth J-47 A30 4.63
wealthier I-32 6.75
wealthy A52 7.00
weaning 7.50
weapon A53 7.42
weapons A35
wear B-14 A11 C10 5.25 ¡
wearily A99
wearing F-14 A19 C16
wears A44
weary I-15 A38 4.75
weather C-47 A6 C10 4.25 ¡
weathered A100
weatherman A101
weave A63 6.50
weaver 7.25
weaving A53
web K-2 A37
webs A91
Webster A63
wed 9.00
Wed. D-41 4.13
wedding A38 C20 7.25
wedge J-2 A80 7.25
Wednesday A-35 A62 C16 3.94 ¡¿
wee G-47 C20
weed A66
weeds H-30 A45 C19
week B-7 A7 C5 5.06 ¡
week's A88
week-end E-38 C20
weekend C-36 A69 C7 5.25
weekly A71 9.00
weeks C-30 A10 C4
weep A79
weeping A81
weigh I-6 A25 5.13
weighed G-6 A33 C19
weighing A58
weighs K-6 A31 5.00
weight H-6 A9 6.08
weights A64
weird F-15 A82 C20 5.38 ¡¿
weirdest 8.50
welcome I-2 A27 5.33
welcomed A75
welder 9.00
welfare A52 5.50 ¡
well A-24 A2 C2 2.00
well-known E-38 A41 7.50
Wellington A89
wells A62 5.00
Welsh A82
Wendy A92 C13
went A-2 A2 C1 2.00 ¢
wept A64
were A-12 A1 C1 3.08
weren't F-37 A28 4.50
werewolves 5.75
west G-2 A10 C16 4.50
West Virginia E-39 5.63
western H-2 A16 4.25
westward K-36 A36
wet E-2 A13 C8 1.83
whale A19 C19 4.00
whales K-6 A33
whaling A80
wharf A75 5.75
wharves D-31 7.50
what A-47 A1 C1 1.94
what'll J-37 6.00
what's A12 C12 4.75
whatever H-37 A15 6.13
wheat H-7 A16 4.25
wheel H-29 A12 2.38
wheelbarrow 7.75
wheelchair 5.50
wheeled A93
wheels B-30 A16 C20 4.25
when A-2 A1 C1 1.81
whenever H-37 A16 4.17
where A-14 A1 C2 3.00 ¡
where's J-37 A55 6.13
whereabouts 5.50
whereas A56 6.25
whereby 8.25
wherein 9.00
wherever A24 5.67 ¡
whether G-12 A5 C16 4.33 ¡
which B-3 A1 C3 2.63 ¡
whichever 8.75
while B-8 A2 C3 3.17
whim 7.25
whimper G-3 C20 7.08
whine 5.75
whining 5.75
whip J-3 A39 3.25
whipped A63 6.25
whipping 6.50
whirl A87 5.50
whirled A57
whirling A62
whiskers A55
whisper A49 5.44
whispered I-3 A21
whispering A74
whistle J-29 A28 4.75
whistled A64
whistles A73
whistling A57
white B-8 A3 C2 1.75
whites A48
Whitney A76
whittle 4.50
whizzed D-34 C20
who B-10 A1 C2 2.42
who'd J-37 6.00
who's F-37 A47 C20 6.17 ¡
whoever A69 5.25
whole C-22 A3 C4 3.50 ¡
wholesale 7.75
wholly A71 7.50 ¡
whom H-10 A16 5.25
whooping A100
whose C-10 A7 C19 5.13 ¡
why B-8 A2 C2 2.44
WI (Wisconsin) G-41
wicked A52 8.00
wicker 8.75
wide F-8 A6 C13 2.75
widely I-26 A27
widened A97
wider A44
widespread A69
widest A86
widow A58 5.38
width K-3 A34 4.50
wiener C20 6.50
wieners E-30 C9
wife D-8 A9 C7 3.25
wife's A97
wigwam 7.25
Wilbur A57
wild C-8 A1 C5 3.42
wilderness J-47 A32 5.67
wildlife A69 5.88
wildly A64
will A-3 A79 C1 1.92
William A12
Williams A49
Williamsburg A98
willing I-24 A24
willow F-9 A63 C19
Wilson A25
win D-3 A15 C8 1.75
wince 7.25
wind C-3 A4 C5 3.75
windier I-32 6.50
windiness G-32
winding A47
windmill A78 6.38
windmills A89 7.00
window C-9 A7 C4 3.75
windows A15 C13
winds H-3 A14
windshield 8.25
windy A57 5.00
wine J-8 A37
wing G-3 A27 C15 3.25
winged A80
wings F-30 A11 C12 4.50
wink A75
winked A84
winner F-34 A51 5.00
winners A74
winning D-34 A37 C15 5.13
wins G-30 A58 C16
winter C-12 A5 C6 3.31
winter's A97
winters A53
wintry ¡
wipe A-8 A79 3.63
wiped A46
wiping A101
wire G-8 A11 C19
wired 8.50
wires J-30 A24
wiry A101 ¡
Wisconsin E-35 A63 6.08
wisdom A42 7.25
wise H-8 A19 4.88
wisely A72
wish B-3 A8 C4 2.69
wished G-3 A19 C16
wishes I-3 A30 4.17
wishing A62 5.00
wit A81
witch D-3 A38 C6 6.25
witch's 5.75
witches D-31 A94 C10
with B-3 A1 C1 2.38
withdraw A101
withdrew A91 8.25
withhold 8.25
within H-37 A6 5.00 ¡
without B-36 A3 C8 3.50 ¡
withstand 8.25
witness A71 7.42
witness's 7.25
witnesses 7.50
witnesses' G-40 7.25
wits A79
wittiest K-32 7.50
witty 8.00
wives D-31 A54 5.13
woke C-9 A34 C4 3.42
wolf E-47 A30 C11 4.00
wolverine F-47 C15
wolves D-31 A38 C9 6.17
woman G-1 A8 C16 3.63 ¡
woman's A55
women A9 C19 5.50 ¡
women's A87 6.83
won C-20 A11 C4 4.50
won't B-37 A8 C6 3.81
wonder C-20 A11 C13 3.88

wondered E-20 A19 C13 6.75
wonderful E-27 A15 C7 5.13
wonderfully A94
wondering G-20 A39 C20 6.5
wonders A40
wonton 7.25
wood B-19 A7 C10 3.50
woodchuck A81 7.25
woodcut 7.50
wooded A90
wooden H-28 A13 5.92
woodland A76 5.25
woodpecker 8.00
woods B-19 A9 C4
wool I-29 A21 3.75
woolen A69 5.13 £
[woollen]
word G-12 A2 C16 3.50
words D-30 A1 C10 4.00
wore F-13 A15 C13 3.38
work B-12 A2 C3 3.06
[work-out]
workable 6.75
worked G-12 A6 C15
worker J-12 A34
workers H-12 A12
working D-12 A7 C9
workmen A46
workout 6.88 £
works F-30 A10 C11
workshop 6.50
world B-12 A2 C2 4.31 ¡
world's G-40 A20 8.25
worlds A82 7.00
worm K-13 A48 5.33
worms G-13 A37 C19
worn I-13 A22 4.88
worn-out G-38 6.50
worried E-32 A27 C15 5.08
worries A97
worrisome 8.25
worry G-12 A23 C16 4.25
worrying E-32 A76 4.50
worse I-12 A24 4.33
worship A54 5.75
worshipped 6.75
worst H-12 A35 C20 5.00
worth H-12 A14 4.63
worthless A101 6.25
worthwhile A98 7.17
worthy A68 6.25
would B-19 A1 C1 3.17
would've J-37 6.63
wouldn't D-37 A10 C6 4.50
wound I-10 A27 5.63
wounded A46 5.50
wounds A73
wove A83
woven A48
wow A94
wrap E-1 A48 3.58
wrapped C-34 A27 C16 5.50
wrapper 7.63
wrapping A81
wrath 7.25
wreath H-22 4.75
wreaths 8.00
wreck A48 5.31
wreckage 8.50
wrecked C-22 A85 4.25
wren 4.17
wrench E-22 6.00
wrenches 5.75
wrestle E-22 6.75
wrestled 6.25
wrestler G-2 C16
wrestling 5.50
wretched F-22 7.88
wriggle E-22 7.50
wriggled A80
Wright J-35 A39
wring 5.63
wrinkle C-22 6.38
wrinkled A56
wrist H-22 A51 5.00
wristwatches 6.25
write C-22 A2 C5 3.00 ¢
writer I-8 A27 4.25
writers J-8 A30
writes A52 7.50
writing B-33 A6 C11 4.63 ¢¡
writings A65
written E-22 A6 4.63 ¡
wrong A9 C11 3.50
wrote A7 C13 3.50
wrought F-22 A85 8.25
WV (West Virginia) G-41
WY (Wyoming) G-41
Wyoming E-35 A60 C20 6.0

X

x-ray E-38 5.25
xylophone 8.25

yacht 8.50
Yale A101
Yankee A53
Yankees A69
yard B-11 A11 C7 3.25
yardage 5.75
yards A14 C20
yarn A53 5.38
yawned A93
yd. (yard) D-41 5.50
yeah A51
year B-15 A3 C3 3.75
year's A58 9.00
yearly A71
years B-30 A2 C3 2.50
yeast A97
yell F-2 A62 6.25
yelled D-2 A27 C6
yelling E-2 A59 C10
yellow C-9 A8 C5 1.69
Yellowstone A79
yells A90
yes B-2 A4 C3 1.42
yesterday D-12 A20 C9 5.38
yet E-2 A4 C9 3.25
yield A60 6.92
yields A96
yodel 8.50
yogurt 7.25
yoke 7.25
yolk 7.42
yonder A93
York A87
you A-10 A1 C1 2.67 ¢
you'd E-37 A21 C16 6.25
you'll E-37 A10 C19 4.50
you're D-37 A7 C7 4.83 ¡
you've E-37 A17 C19 6.63
young D-47 A3 C8 3.08
younger I-12 A25 4.50
youngest A49 4.50
youngster A94 6.75
youngsters A77
your A-13 A1 C1 3.19 ¢¡
your're 3.00
yours G-13 A25 C15 5.13
yourself A7 C13 4.25
yourselves A89 7.25
youth I-10 A24 5.25
yr. (year) 5.00
yrs. (years) E-41 7.00
YT (Yukon Territories) H-41

Z

zebra C13 4.25
zebras A89
zenith 8.25
zero F-9 A25 C13 4.50
zeros 7.75
Zeus A86
zinc A64
zipper C-34 C19 4.88
zone A49 5.00
zones A76
zoo C-10 A30 C6 4.75
zoology 8.67
zooming 5.50
zoos A79
zucchini 8.42

Key: Letter-## is *Spelling Power* level word is first taught at. A## is usage by adults; C## is usage by children. (#.##) Average grade level word is taught at; ¢ High School Problem Word, ¡ College Problem Word. ¿ Business Problem Word. £ British spelling (alternate) is also in this list. [word] is British spelling. Elementary Problem words are set in **Boldface** type.

Discovery Activities

Selecting and Assigning Discovery Activities

This section of your manual is designed as a resource for Skill-Building Activities. Skill-Building Activities are usually conducted during the final five minutes of each spelling session. The resources in this section fall into seven categories as described below.

Activity Task Cards provide you with directions for 85 activities plus ideas for basic frameworks you can use to create Activity Task Cards for your student. The categories of Activity Task Cards presented in your *Spelling Power* manual include: Drill Activities, Skill Builders, Writing Prompters, Dictionary Skills, Homonyms, and Proofreading Exercises. Samples for each category are provided.

Once created, Activity Task Cards are the easiest format for assigning Skill-Building Activities to your student. You may also purchase a ready-to-use Activity Task Card box featuring additional activities.

Word Card Activities are generally inductive games that allow your student to manipulate the words or spelling principles they are learning. Some word card activities focus on individual drill of your student's spelling words. Most word card activities require only 2"x3½" (business card size) cards on which are written the student's spelling words.

Worksheet-type Activities provide you with ideas for creating worksheets personalized to your student's needs. Many of the ideas can actually be created on Activity Task Cards. Other activities include masters (See Teaching Aids and Masters section) which make it easy for you to create your own versions. In addition to the resources provided in this section, you can use worksheet activities from other sources to provide variety to your spelling program.

Teacher-Made Games give you a number of ideas for creating board and card games which your students can play to build specific spelling skills or provide fun drill of spelling words.

Teacher-Directed Activities include 29 ideas for game- type activities. Most can be played anytime and anywhere. Some of the activities require groups or a whole classroom of students, but many can be played by an individual or a family. Particularly interesting are the "games" which are designed to replace the traditional Spelling Bee.

Dictation Exercises provide you with directions for conducting effective dictation exercises and a number of suggestions on selecting dictation exercises for use with your students.

Commercial Games and Software Reviews are provided to aid you in selecting material which is commercially available. A section of product reviews is provided.

Indexes To Discovery Activities

The easiest way for you to select activities appropriate for your student is to determine which group number he is currently working at and use the Group Number Index for suggestions of activities which target that skill.

Not every card, game, or activity is listed on this index. Those activities which are non-group related are not listed. In most case, Drill Activities, Writing Prompters, Dictionary Activities, Proofreading, and Dictation Activities can be used with **any** Group Number. Non-group related activities are perfect for the second day (or any additional days) your student works with a particular group or on days he is working with Review Groups, Delayed Recall, or End-of-Level Tests.

In addition to activities which are described in this manual, we have listed those activities included in the optional Activity Task Card box. If you own this box, you only need to look at this one index to select activities, rather than having also to refer to the Teacher's Guide that accompanies the box.

Group Number Index

Group #1: atc: 100, 101; WCG: 1; TDA: 1, 2, 3, 6,; ATC: 81, 82, 83, 141, 315, 330, 355
Group # 2: atc: 100, 101; WCG: 1; TDA: 1 2, 3, 6,; ATC: 81, 82, 83, 102, 141, 315, 330, 342, 355
Group # 3: atc: 100, 101; WCG: 1; TDA: 1, 2, 3, 6; ATC: 81, 82, 83, 102, 219, 315, 330, 355
Group # 4: atc: 100, 101; WCG: 1; TDA: 1, 2, 3, 6; ATC: 81, 82, 83, 141, 315, 330, 355
Group # 5: atc: 100, 101; WCG: 1; TDA: 1, 2, 3, 6; ATC: 81, 82, 83, 315, 330, 355,
Group # 6: atc: 100, 101; WCG: 1; TDA: 1, 2, 3, 6; ATC: 81, 82, 83, 121, 122, 142, 316, 332, 345, 357
Group # 7: atc: 100, 101; WCG: 1; TDA: 1, 2, 3, 6; ATC: 81, 82, 83, 121, 122, 142, 317, 335, 346, 358
Group # 8: atc: 100, 101; WCG: 1; TDA: 1, 2, 3, 6; ATC: 81, 82, 83, 121, 122, 142, 318, 336, 347
Group # 9: atc: 100, 101; WCG: 1; TDA: 1, 2, 3, 6; ATC: 81, 82, 83, 121, 122, 142, 319
Group # 10: atc: 100, 101, WCG: 1; TDA: 1, 2, 3, 6; ATC: 81, 82, 83, 121, 122, 142, 320, 349
Group # 11: atc: 100, 101, WCG: 1; TDA: 1, 2, 3, 6; ATC: 81, 82, 83, 143,
Group # 12: atc: 100, 101, D-901, WCG: 1; TDA: 1, 2, 3, 6; ATC: 81, 82, 83, 143, 359
Group # 13: atc: 100, 101, WCG: 1; TDA: 1, 2, 3, 6; ATC: 81, 82, 83, 143, 321, 351, 360
Group # 14: atc: 100, 101, WCG: 1; TDA: 1, 2, 3, 6; ATC: 81, 82, 83, 143, 321, 338
Group # 15: atc: 100, 101, WCG: 1; TDA: 1, 2, 3, 6; ATC: 81, 82, 83, 143, 323
Group # 16: atc: 100, 101, WCG: 1; TDA: 1, 2, 3, 6; ATC: 81, 82, 83, 143, 145, 324
Group # 17: atc: 100, 101, WCG: 1; TDA: 1, 2, 3, 6; ATC: 81, 82, 83, 143, 145
Group # 18: atc: 100, 101, WCG: 1; TDA: 1, 2, 3, 6; ATC: 81, 82, 83, 144, 145, 361
Group # 19: atc: 100, 101, WCG: 1; TDA: 1, 2, 3, 6; ATC: 81, 82, 83, 144, 145, 324
Group # 20: atc: 100, 101, WCG: 1; TDA: 1, 2, 3, 6; ATC: 81, 82, 83
Group # 21: TDA: 3; ATC: 83, 123
Group # 22: atc: Any Drill Card or Writing Prompter WCG: 2, 6, 7, 8, 9, 11; TMG: 2, 3, 4; ATC: 83, 86, 124, 325, 362
Group # 23: TDA: 3; ATC: 83;
Group # 24: atc: Any Drill Card or Writing Prompter WCG: 2, 6, 7, 8, 9, 11; TMG: 2, 3, 4: ATC: 83, 105, 125
Group # 25; TDA: 1, 2, 3, 6; ATC: 83;

Key to Group Number Index

atc:= Activity Task Cards in this manual (starts page 273)

WCG: = Word Card Games (starts on page 284)

TDA= Teacher-Directed Activities (starts on page 291)

ATC= Optional Activity Task Card box

TMG: Teacher-Made Game (starts on page 289)

WS: Worksheet (starts on page 287)

DE: Dictation Exercises (starts on page 298)

Group # 26: TDA: 3; ATC: 126
Group # 27: TDA: 3; ATC:
Group # 28: atc: 100, 101, WCG: 1; TDA: 1, 2, 3, 6,
Group # 29: atc: 100, 101, G-902; WCG: 1; TDA: 1, 2, 3, 6,; ATC: 106, 146
Group # 30: WCG: 5; TMG: 6; TDA: 3; ATC: 87, 88, 127, 128, 147, 168, 291
Group # 31: atc: 102 WCG: 5; TMG: 6; TDA: 3; ATC: 107, 127, 129, 148, 168, 291
Group # 32: TMG: 6; TDA: 3; ATC: 89, 108, 130, 149
Group # 33: TMG: 6: TDA: 3; ATC: 90, 91, 109, 130
Group # 34: TMG: 6; TDA: 3: ATC: 92, 93, 110, 130
Group # 35: atc: 408, 409, Any Drill Card or WCG: 2, 6, 7, 8, 9, 11; ATC: 94, 95, 96, 111, 112, 113, 131, 132, 150, 169, 173, 190, 191, 352
Group # 36: 103, WCG: 3, 4 TMG: 7: TDA: 3, 4, 9; ATC: 97, 113, 133, 135, 150
Group # 37: atc: 104; TDA: 29; ATC: 98, 114, 135, 174, 179, 326
Group # 38: WCG: 3; TMG: 7; TDA: 9; ATC: 115, 116, 134, 152, 327
Group # 39: WCG: 3; TMG: 7; TDA: 9; ATC: 116, 134, 152
Group # 40: DA: 53; ATC: 56, 64, 128, 136, 137
Group # 41: atc: 609, TMG: 5; ATC: 117, 118, 138, 139, 140, 153; Any Drill Card or WCG: 2, 6, 7, 8, 9, 11,; TDA: 3
Group # 42: atc: 106, WCG: 1: TDA: 3; ATC: 119, 130, 154, 294, 363
Group # 43: WCG: 1: TDA: 3; ATC: 130, 155, 294
Group # 44: WCG: 1: TDA: 3; ATC: 130, 294, 365
Group # 45: WCG: 1: TDA: 3; ATC: 130, 294
Group # 46: WCG: 3; TMG: 1: TDA: 3, 16; ATC: 120, 156, 157
Group # 47: atc: Any Drill Card or Writing Prompter WCG: 2, 6, 7, 8, 9, 11; TMG: 2, 3, 4, TDA: 10, 12, 13; ATC: 328, 340

Modality Index

This index is provided to help you select activities which are best suited to the learning style of your student. Activity suggestions provided in this manual and the optional Activity Task Card box which focus on one of the four predominant modalities or learning styles include visual, auditory, kinesthetic, and tactile. To use this index, first look up suggested activities for the group number your student is working on. Now, cross-reference to the modality index to fine-tune the best activity choice for your student.

You should note that many activities which emphasize visual learning styles are not only excellent choices for visual learners, they may be selected to help a student who lacks visualization skills to develop this skill. Visual imagery appears to be widely used by good spellers. Likewise, many of the activities labeled "auditory" may aid in building auditory discrimination skills, as well as aid learning and retention for auditory learners.

Kinesthetic methods add an additional sensory experience and form of imagery frequently valuable to the student who is a tactile learner, younger students, or those who have extreme difficulty with spelling. While many of the tactile activities are also excellent kinesthetic activities, you should be aware of the difference between the tactile and kinesthetic learning styles. Tactile learners need to touch and feel, but the kinesthetic learner needs movement and involvement. Almost all tactile activities will benefit kinesthetic learners, whereas kinesthetic activities will not always be beneficial to tactile learners.

Auditory

atc: 2, 17, 31, 102, 603, 605; WCG: 1; TMG: 2, 3, 4; ATC: 1, 6, 7, 27, 34, 37, 43, 50, 54, 58, 72, 74, 78, 83, 84, 85, 102, 103, 105, 106, 121, 122, 123, 124, 125, 142, 144, 145, 146, 255, 278

Kinesthetic

atc: 1, 3-6, 8-11, 14-16, 18-21, 31, 39, 51
All Word Card Games and Teacher-Made Games.
ATC: 2, 4, 5, 6, 8, 9, 10, 12, 13, 14, 20, 23, 25, 26, 27, 30, 33, 34, 37, 38, 40, 43, 52, 57, 59, 60, 61, 66, 68, 80, 81, 104, 106, 112, 140, 143, 144, 145, 241, 247, 255, 256, 257, 260, 261, 262, 263, 264, 266, 267, 268, 281, 282, 297, 298

Tactile

atc: 3, 4, 5, 7, 10, 9, 11, 12, 16, 19; ATC: 3, 5, 9, 12, 13, 23, 37

Visual

atc: 3-9, 12-24, 26-30, 32-40, 51-56, 75-76, 78

Almost all Writing Prompters, Dictionary Activities, Homonym Matches, Proofreading Activities, Word Card Games, Teacher-Made Games, Worksheet-type activities, and commercial games.

ATC: 4, 7, 8, 10, 11, 14-15, 16, 17, 18, 19, 20, 21, 22, 24, 28, 29, 31, 32, 33, 34, 35, 36, 37, 38, 39, 40, 42, 43, 44, 45, 46, 47, 48, 51, 53, 54, 55, 57, 58, 59, 60, 61, 62, 63, 65, 66, 67, 68, 69, 70, 71, 73, 75, 76, 77, 79, 80, 81, 82, 84, 85, 93, 98, 103, 104, 105, 106, 107, 114, 121, 122, 124, 125, 126, 127, 128, 129, 130, 140, 141, 142, 143, 144, 145, 146, 147, 148, 149, 150, 151, 241, 247, 248, 257, 261, 262, 263, 264, 265, 266, 281, 297, 298

Number of Participants Required

Discovery Activities fall into four groups in regards to number of participants required: **Individual** (I) for the learner working independently, **Partners** (P) for the student and the teacher or another student to work together, **Group** (G) of three to six students working together; and **Class** (C) for large groups of six or more students. The number of participants indicated for "group" and "class" are determined by the minimum number of participants. Many of the "group" activities can be used by whole classrooms, but any activity labeled "class" requires more than six students to be used effectively.

Most of the activities are for individual students working alone with the exception of the following:

Partners

atc: 10, 11, 13, 17, 33, 36, 38, 40, 603; ATC: 3, 4, 7, 21, 23, 28, 31, 36, 38, 40, 59, 60, 72, 139, 140, 247, 255, 256, 260, 273, 285; WCG: 6, 8, 11; TMG: 2, 3, 5, 6; TDA: 3, 5, 6, 10, 11, 14, 15, 16, 21, 22, 23, 24, 25, 26, 27, 28, 29

Partners optional

atc: 39, 102, 103; WCG: 2, 7; ATC: 101, 143, 144, 278

Group

WCG: 11; TMG: 2, 5, 6; TDA: 1, 2, 3, 5, 6, 7, 8, 9, 10, 11, 13, 14, 17, 18, 21, 22, 23, 24, 25, 26, 27, 28, 29

Class

atc: 12; TDA: 1, 2, 3, 4, 5, 7, 8, 9, 10, 11, 12, 13, 14, 17, 18, 19, 20, 21, 22, 23, 24, 25, 27, 28, 29

Key to Group Number Index

atc:= Activity Task Cards in this manual (starts page 273)

WCG: = Word Card Games (starts on page 284)

TDA= Teacher-Directed Activities (starts on page 291)

ATC= Optional Activity Task Card box

TMG: Teacher-Made Game (starts on page 289)

WS: Worksheet (starts on page 287)

DE: Dictation Exercises (starts on page 298)

Activity Task Cards

Activity Task Cards provide your student with specific tasks to complete. They may be created using the ideas presented in this section as well as by adapting ideas in other chapters or sections or from other resources.

Each activity is written, in language appropriate for your student, on a separate 4"x6" index card. Remember, your younger student may not only need simpler language but also may need larger print. The card examples included here have notes to teachers written in parentheses; these notes should not be copied onto cards used by your students.

Activity Task Cards can be copied onto the index cards as they are assigned and stored in an index box in an accessible location for future use by your student. For ease of use, the cards should be organized by type of activity and separated by index dividers. Convenient categories (for which samples are provided) are: Drill Activities, Skill-Building Activities, Writing Prompters, Dictionary Activities, Homonyms, and Proofreading. You may establish different or additional categories if you wish.

While it may not always be possible, try to arrange the activities within each category from easiest to hardest. We have done this as much as possible in the samples provided for you. You may also wish to color-code the cards to indicate the level of difficulty. (In the optional Activity Task Card box, the color codes are: pink (or red) for primary; blue for elementary; green for intermediate; and yellow for advanced.)

For ease in indexing and assigning, you should give each task card a separate number. To make it easier to add additional cards, assign a sequence of numbers to each category of cards, e.g. 1-99 Drill Activities. The examples provided have begun this system for you, making it easy for you to get started. This numbering system will also make it easier for your student to record his work and replace the card upon completion of the assignment.

The optional (pre-prepared) Activity Task Card box is basically designed and organized in the manner described here. Only a small number of the actual examples presented in this section are duplicated in the prepared set to provide you with more activity choices. The Activity Task Card box's numbering system is consecutive from 1-365. Cards from this box are included in the Discovery Activity Index preceded by "ATC:".

Time Needed to Use Activities

Normally, Activity Task Cards require between five and ten minutes for the average student to complete. However, some activities may be played over and over again which will require adjustment of time allowed for the activity. Likewise, many students like to spend more time with the arts and crafts type activities which are presented through the many drill activities, taking the ideas and applying them in a variety of ways. You should make clear your policy regarding time spent on Discovery Activities before beginning to assign the activities.

Once the Activity Task Cards have been introduced, students should be encouraged to use them during free time outside of the spelling period. Activity Task Cards, teacher-directed activities, and commercial spelling games can all be used as rainy day activities when outdoor "recess" must be cancelled or by individual students who have finished other schoolwork early.

Drill Activities (Numbers 1-99)

Drill activities are generally multisensory, inductive activities that require the repetitive use of a word. They are highly effective for students who tend not to be "visual learners." These students also tend to be the students who have the most difficulty with spelling.

Because they are not "Group" specific, Drill Activities can be used anytime and with any group, making them perfect for those days you do not have time to be selective. (You can say, "Just do any card from the drill section today.") Drill Activities are also excellent choices for those days students are working with Group 47, Review Groups, Delayed Recall, or End-of-Level tests.

Ability Levels

Although it is not always possible to ascribe a precise age level to each activity, the drill activities have been separated into four ability levels as follows:

Cards 1-25 = Primary: Kindergarten to third grade or ages 5 to 7 years old.

Cards 26-50 = Elementary: third to sixth grades or ages 8 to 12 years old.

Cards 51-75 = Intermediate: sixth to ninth grades or 13 to 15 years old.

Cards 76-100 = Advanced: ninth grade to adult or 16 to 100 years old.

These levels are flexible. Many of the activities can be adapted to fit the needs of the students. In many cases, if the game is too difficult, simpler words can be used, or the rules may be relaxed. Likewise, if the game or activity seems too easy, more difficult words can be used. Many activities include "Variations and Extensions" for escalating or simplifying the activity.

Primary and above

1. Dial-A-Word

Dial your words on a telephone. If you use a real telephone, make sure that the receiver is down. Say each letter as you dial it.

2. Tape Your Words

Tape record the spelling of your study words. Say each word and then spell it. Play the tape back and check the spelling of each word.

3. Word Scrape

Write each word with a thick crayon. Go back over each word and gently scrape each letter with your fingernail or some other semi-sharp object.

4. Paint Your Words

Paint your words. Make them fancy.

5. Word Trace

Trace your words with your finger on the table or on the chalkboard. Repeat each word twice. Say the letters softly to yourself as you trace them.

6. Cut-Out Letters

Cut letters out of the newspaper or a magazine to spell your study words. Paste them on a piece of paper.

7. Yarn Words

Glue yarn on pieces of heavy paper so that it spells each of your words. Close your eyes and have a friend hand you the cards one at a time. Feel the yarn spelling on each card. Say the word and spell it.

8. String Beads

String letter beads on a string to spell each word.

9. Sand Words

Write your words in sand. After you have written each word, check to see that you have spelled it correctly. Erase each word and write another one.

10. Exchange List

Exchange study word lists with a friend. Take turns doing the following steps: Close your eyes. Have a friend print each word with his finger on your forehead. Try to guess each word.

11. Blackboard Writing

Stand facing a blackboard and have a friend stand in back of you. Give your friend your study word list. Your friend will draw the letters to spell each word on your back. As he traces the letters on your back, you will write them on the blackboard. When you have finished writing each word, say the word and spell it orally to your friend, who will check the list to make sure that you spelled it correctly.

12. Tile Scramble

Select enough letter tiles to spell all of the spelling words on your list and then add ten other letter tiles. Turn the tiles over so that you cannot see the letters and mix them up. Play spelling solitaire. Turn over the tiles one at a time until you come to a letter which will begin a word or be the next letter in a word which has already been started. The tile should be turned back over if you cannot use it. Lay down the tiles in a vertical line. Continue until you have spelled out all of your words. (Directions for making letter tiles are provided at the end of this chapter.)

13. Select-A-Tile

Select enough letter tiles to spell out all of the spelling words on your list. Place the letters on the floor or tabletop so that the letter side is up. Mix up the letters. Have a friend call out your spelling words one at a time. As each word is called, pick up the letters to spell that word in correct order. Time yourself to see how long it takes you to reorganize the letters of all your spelling words. Make sure you spell each word correctly. Try it again some other day and compare your times. (Directions for making letter tiles are provided at the end of this chapter.)

14. Label Maker

Punch out your study words using a label maker (plastic, self-adhesive strips that affix to paper, etc.).

15. Toothpick Words

Use toothpicks to spell your words. If you wish to have a permanent record of your words, glue the toothpick letters on paper.

16. Eraser Words

Use the eraser on the end of your pencil to erase each of your spelling words onto pictures from old magazines.

17. Test a Friend

Ask one of your parents or an older friend to spell each word on your list. Check each word as they spell it to make sure that they have done it correctly. Give them a hug if they do well.

18. Sidewalk List

Write your study words with chalk on the sidewalk. Make the words big.

19. Finger Paint Words

Cover a piece of paper with finger paints. Roll up your sleeves and begin finger painting your spelling words.

20. Letter Tiles

Use the letter tiles to spell out your spelling words. After you have arranged the letters, check to see that you have spelled them correctly. Cover up each word and try to spell it from memory. (Directions for making letter tiles are provided at the end of this chapter.)

21. Cut Up Words

Write each word with a thick crayon. Cut out the letters and mix them up. Rearrange them in the correct order to spell each word. Paste them on a piece of paper.

22. Mark a Vowel

Mark the vowels in your words. Mark short vowels and long vowels and cross out any silent letters.

23. Picture Words

Look at your words one at a time. Close your eyes and see if you can picture your word in your mind. If you could not picture the word, open your eyes and look at the word again. Say each letter softly to yourself as you look at it.

24. Configuration Words

Print each of your spelling words. Then draw around each word. Study the shape of each word.

Not all numbers have been used at each level. This allows you to insert additional activities for each approximate level.

Elementary and Above

A master for creating crossword puzzles and word find puzzles is found in the Teaching Aids and Masters section.

26. Look at Words

Look at each word and see if you can do one of the following things:

Can you find smaller words within the word?

Does the word spell anything backwards?

Using the letters of the word, can you make any other words?

live — evil   who — how

27. Draw Words

Draw your words in interesting ways that indicate their meaning.

28. Graphic Design

Create a graphic design with your words. With a pencil, lightly outline a design or picture. Outline the perimeter of your design with your spelling words or fill in the interior of your design by writing each spelling word several times. Display your masterpiece.

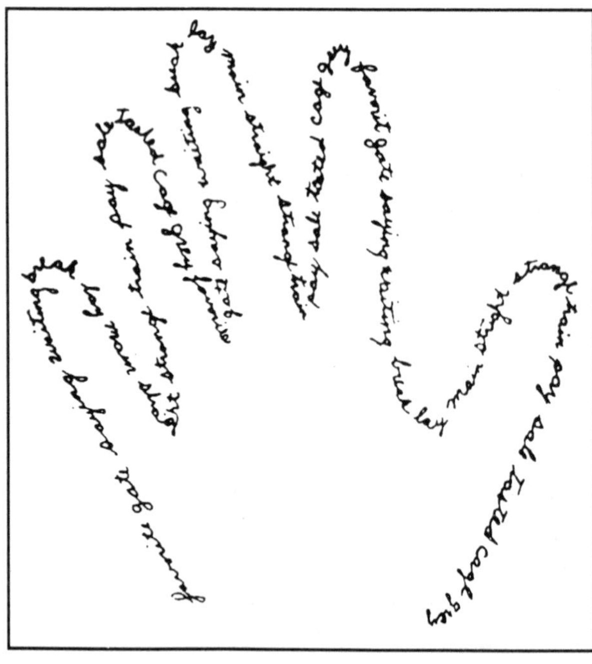

Word cards can be made using backs of old business cards or index cards cut to size.

29. Shuffled Word Cards

Write each of your study words on a word card. Cut each card in half or into syllables, using a different cutting pattern or design for each card. Shuffle the pieces and then match each half. Store your Word Card Puzzle pieces in an envelope so you can use them again.

30. Synonym Hunt

Words that mean the same or almost the same thing are called synonyms. Look up each of your study words in the thesaurus. What synonyms can you find for each word? Make a list of two similar words for each word on your list.

31. Cheer Words

Develop a cheer for each of your study words. Make it snappy, make it catchy, but make sure you spell out the letters of each word.

32. Crossword Puzzle

Make a crossword puzzle using your study words. Find someone else who is also making a crossword puzzle. Trade and work out each other's puzzle.

33. Word-Find Puzzle

Make a word-find puzzle with a friend. Trade lists of spelling words and use the list to make a word-find puzzle. First write all of the words on graph paper and then fill in around the words with other letters. Trade puzzles, and go to work trying to find the words.

34. Type Words

Type your study words on your typewriter or computer. After typing each word, check to make sure that you have spelled it correctly.

35. Packaged Words

Find as many of your study words on the outside packaging of a product (candy bar wrapper, box of cereal, carton of milk, etc.) as you can. Then do at least one of the following:

a) Keep the packaging on your desk during the week, so you can periodically review your words.

b) Use these words to design a new package for your product.

c) Use these words in a letter you write to the manufacturer of this product.

d) Cut out the words and paste them on a piece of paper.

36. Secret Word Lists

Trade spelling lists with a friend. Write each other's words in a secret code. (You can make up your own code.) Trade papers and decode the words. Check to make sure your friend spelled the words correctly.

37. Gibberish

Write your study words in "gibberish." Leave them in your desk or folder for a day or two. Then take out your list and try to separate them into the correct spelling.

How to write your words in "gibberish":

First, write all of the words together as if they were one big word. If you have a lot of words you may wish to divide them into two or three lines.

Then divide the letters into new words which may or may not make sense.

fish fire eight plant eye

fishfireeightplanteye

fis hfi ree igh tpl ant eye

38. Connect-A-Word

Write one of your study words on the chalkboard or on graph paper. Now have a friend connect one of his study words, crossword puzzle fashion, to your word. Continue until no more words can be added.

```
   fresh
      i
      delay
      e
 follow
      a
      laugh
      k
```

39. Concentration

Play concentration with a friend. Make duplicate cards of each of your spelling words. Place your cards and your friend's word cards face down on the table or on the floor. Take turns turning over two cards. If the words on the two cards match, you keep the pair. If the words do not match, they are turned face down again and it is your partner's turn to choose two cards. Continue until all of the cards have been removed. The person with the greatest number of paired cards wins the game.

39. Palindrome

A palindrome is a word that is spelled the same backward or forward. *Radar*, *eye*, and *deed* are all palindromes. Spend five minutes trying to come up with as many palindromes as you can. You may keep adding to this list throughout the day (or week). Then share your list with your teacher and friends.

40. Tile Scrabble™

Find one or two friends to play this game with. Separate the Letter Tiles into vowels and consonants. Turn all of the tile letters face down (keeping the groups of Vowels and Consonants separate). The first player draws ten tiles from the consonant group and five from the vowel group. He tries to form a word from his word card stack. One point is scored for each letter used. If the word is misspelled, the player receives no points. After he has attempted his word list, all letters are returned to the separate piles and it is the next player's turn.

Not all numbers have been used at each level. This allows you to insert additional activities for each approximate level.

Intermediate and above

51. Parts of Speech

Decide what part of speech each of your study words is. Then do one of the following for each word:

Adjective or adverb — what would you describe with this word? Find at least three things you can describe. What is the comparative and superlative of each word?

Verb — Find a describing word. What are the other tenses of the word? Add a suffix or prefix. How does it change the meaning?

Noun or pronoun — Is it a person, place, or thing? Is it singular or plural? What would its other form (singular or plural) be?

52. Classify Words

Classify your study words according to syllables.

one	two	three
cat	brother	optical
pet	ego	elastic

53. Possessive Nouns

Make each noun on your list possessive.

dog dog's

54. Root Words

Look for the root words within your spelling words. Circle the root words.

55. In the News

Make a list of the words used in your last testing session (the Group List). Find each of these words in today's newspaper. Circle or highlight each of them, every time they are used. Put a tally mark next to the word each time you locate it. Now make a graph, showing the frequency of use of each of the words.

56. Adjectives

Write an adjective with as many of your study words as possible. Try to use the less commonly used adjectives.

Advanced

76. Acrostic

Make up acrostics using as many of your study words as possible. You may use a word more than once, but only once in each acrostic.

Laughter	**F**orever
Imagination	**A**live
Fun	**I**n
Energy	**T**hy
	Heart

77. Anagrams

An anagram is formed when the letters in a word are transposed to form a new word.

large:	regal, glare
eat:	ate, tea
late:	tale, teal
list:	slit, silt
lead:	deal, dale, lade

See how many anagrams you can make using your study words.

78. Suffixes

Add as many different suffixes to each of your study words as you can think of. When finished, check your work in the dictionary.

Skill Builders (Numbers 100-399)

Skill Builders are cards designed to teach and/or reinforce the application of phonetic principles and spelling rules. The samples listed here are mainly inductive activities. Most of those activities focusing on phoneme-grapheme relationships can easily be adapted for use with any letter/sound combination.

Additional skill builders can be made using the suggestions listed under Worksheet-type activities. Task cards make a perfect medium for presenting questions or workbook-type problems. Often, especially for younger students, a few problems written directly on an Activity Task Card is sufficient. These can be made to meet the specific needs of the student or use words which the student is currently studying.

100. Circle the Vowels

Look at all of your spelling words and find all the cases where two letters come together and make one sound. Circle the two letters.

101. Rhyme List

Make a list of words that rhyme with each of your study words, then write rhyming verses for each pair.

102 Irregular Plurals

Find as many irregular plurals as you can in the Sunday paper or a favorite magazine. Make a master list of the irregular plurals you have found. You may work with a friend and continue building your irregular plurals list all week.

103. Compound Antonyms

Working alone or with a partner, make lists of compound words that are antonyms, such as: within-without.

104. Contraction Rewrite

Select any story from your daily newspaper or a favorite magazine. Rewrite the story using contractions wherever possible. (Note: The teacher may wish to select the story so that an answer key may be created.)

105. Newspaper Titles

Cut out a newspaper or magazine article that contains titles used before names. Underline the capital letters and circle periods in title. (Note: The teacher may wish to select the story so that an answer key may be created.)

106. Suffix-a-tion

List all the words you can think of in five minutes that end in the suffixes "ion" or "tion." (This can be done with any suffix or prefix.)

Writing Prompters (Numbers 400-599)

Activities which promote the use of new words in meaningful writing provide the most logical intrinsic motivation for practicing spelling. Here, a genuine need for spelling is evident. According to numerous studies, when your student participates in writing activities which require him to use his spelling words, he will transfer up to five times more of his spelling words into his daily writing than do students who do not participate in such activities. If moving words into daily writing is the purpose of the spelling program, as it should be, then your students should participate in a variety of writing activities to maximum transfer. In the *Spelling Power* program, these transfer activities are provided for through the sentence writing required on the 10-Step-Study Sheets. However, additional materials can also be made which encourage writing. Such activities are referred to in this program as Writing Prompters.

Not all numbers have been used at each level. This allows you to insert additional activities for each approximate level.

Writing Prompters provide stimulus material e.g., pictures, famous paintings, story beginnings, and skeletal plots which lend themselves to eliciting words and concepts recently studied. We have provided some samples below. They provide enjoyable and effective means for practicing newly-learned words and writing concepts.

Writing Prompters, like other Activity Task Cards, can be made on 4"x6" index cards and stored in index card file boxes. However, they may be made larger to suit the teacher's needs.

400. Silly Sentences

Using the beginning letter of each word, write same-letter sentences.

"Susan sent seashells to sailors swiftly."

401. Sentence Writing

Write sentences using your study words. Use as many of the words as possible in each sentence. Try to keep the number of sentences as low as possible.

402. Story Writing

Write a story using your study words. Be sure the story has a good plot, but select one which makes use of all the words.

403. Write A Story

Write a story using your study words. After you have written a story, go back to proofread the story and try to find each word. Be sure that you have spelled each one correctly.

404. 10-Word Story

Write a story using at least ten words you have studied since the last review test. Here's the catch: You must select the words before you begin writing.

405. Word Rhyme

Make a short rhyme for each of your study words. Do you see any similarities between your spelling words and each of the rhyming words?

406. Poetry

Write a poem using your spelling words. Play with the sounds in the words in order to make an almost musical or artistic quality to your poem.

407. Riddles

Write riddles using the words from your spelling list. Words may be in either the riddle or its solution.

408. Months and Holidays

Write the names of the months and list the holidays or holy days which occur during each month. Now choose your favorite month and holiday and describe it, as well as tell why you like it.

409. Capitals

Choose any subject you wish to write a paragraph about. When you write your paragraph, use as many capitalized words as possible.

410. Sudden, Plus

Write as many phrases as you can think of in five minutes using sudden, such as sudden noise. (May be played with any adjective.)

411. Simile

Write a simile (using the word **like** to compare two things) that contains alliteration (repetitions of the same sounds) for each of your spelling words. You may find the dictionary or thesaurus helpful.

Here are two samples of alliterative similes:

Melba's mediocre metaphor is **like** mustard minus its tang.

Sol's scintillating simile cut **like** a sickle.

412. *TV Guide* Story

Write a story based on a movie synopsis found in a movie or TV guide. Try to include at least your last ten study words in your story. After you have written the story, go back and look for your study words. Underline each word. Double-check that you spelled them correctly.

Dictionary Activities (Numbers 600-699)

Activity Task Cards which focus on use of the dictionary make excellent supplementary activities or follow-up activities to the sequential presentation of skills presented in Chapter Five. They are not intended to replace direct teaching of the skills. The Dictionary Activities presented here are in the general sequence they are presented in Chapter Five for your convenience.

600. Alphabetical

Put your words in alphabetical order. (Student must be able to alphabetize beyond third letter to complete this activity.)

601. Word Meaning

Find the meaning of each of your study words. If there is more than one meaning, write the most common meaning.

602. Word Definition

Write your own definition for each word. Then look up the word in the dictionary to see if you are right.

603. Phonetic Spelling Codes

Each dictionary entry word is followed by a respelling, in parentheses, which shows how to pronounce the entry word. It is made up of phonetic symbols. Each of these represents one sound in the word. The pronunciation key at the beginning of the dictionary tells what sound each symbol represents. Trade study lists with a friend. Write each other's study words in dictionary respelling form. When you trade back lists, try to decode each word into its regular spelling.

604. Entry Word Search

Words defined in a dictionary are entry words; listed in alphabetical order. Guide words are the two words found at the top of a dictionary page that tell the first and last word on that page. Find the entry words for each of your study words in the dictionary. Make a list of the guide words that are found on the dictionary page for each of your study words.

605. Phonetic Spelling Codes

Each dictionary entry word is followed by a respelling, in parentheses, which shows how to pronounce the entry word. It is made up of phonetic symbols. Each of these represents one sound in the word. The pronunciation key at the beginning of the dictionary tells what sound each symbol represents. Write your study words in dictionary respelling form. Set them aside for an hour or day, then try to decode them into the regular spelling.

607. Dictionary Origins

Look in the dictionary for the origin of your words. Either write the origin for each word or categorize the words according to origin.

608. Etymology

A dictionary entry may include a word history or etymology. Etymologies appear in brackets. Write the etymologies for each of your study words.

Example: Sandwich [John Montagu, Earl of Sandwich, 1718-1792, supposedly the inventor]

609. Acronyms

The word BASIC is an acronym. It is formed from the first letters of the words "Beginner's All-purpose Symbolic Instruction Code."

a. Try to figure out the acronym for each word group below. Check your answer in an unabridged dictionary.

1. Women's Army Corps

2. Zone Improvement Plan (-code)

3. Radio detecting and ranging

4. Self-contained, underwater breathing apparatus

b. Try to make as many acronyms as you can using your study words.

610. Antonym Hunt

Antonyms are words that mean the opposite of each other. Write an antonym for each of your study words. Check your words in the dictionary or thesaurus.

Not all numbers have been used at each level. This allows you to insert additional activities for each approximate level.

Homonyms (800-899)

Homonyms (both homophones and homographs) comprise about 13 percent of the high frequency words the average person uses. These words cause the greatest difficulty for spellers and represent a much higher percentage of those words which are frequently misspelled. They simply must be memorized by your students. But not only must your student memorize his spelling, he must memorize which spelling goes with which meaning. Therefore, in addition to the work the student does with homonyms in the regular course of Flow-Word-List testing, he needs to complete activities which focus on the differences between the homonym mates in context.

The sample activities below give you several formats for creating Activity Task Cards and/or worksheet problems. For a list of homonyms and other easily confused words, consult the Miscellaneous section.

800 Fill a Blank (After Level A)

1. Mary was _____ pleased with her ability to _______. (so, sew, sow)
2. Would you _____ like a ride ______ school, _____? (two, to, too)
3. I would like ______ pancakes ____ my brothers. (four, for)
4. John went ______ to get _______ car. (there, their)

801. Arrow Match Up (After Level B, Group 10)

Draw a line to connect the homophone pairs. The first one is done for you.

blue	night
right	read
week	blew
maid	write
red	weak
knight	made

Not all numbers have been used in sequence to allow you to insert additional activities of your own in each activity category.

802. Pick One (After Level C, Group 10)

For each of the following sentences, underline the homophone that makes the most sense in the sentence.

1. The tugboat blew (its, it's) whistle.
2. We will go by (plane, plain) to Denver.
3. He (eight, ate) pancakes for breakfast.
4. The cowboy (road, rode) his horse to town.
5. John (through, threw) the ball to Mary.

803. Mix and Match (After Level D)

The six word pairs below are homophones. These are words that sound the same, but are spelled differently and have different meanings.

wait, weight hay, hey bye, buy, by plain, plane

Choose the correct homophone to complete each of the sentences from this list.

1. I could not _____ to go to the store.
2. My sheep love new _____.
3. Will you ______ a new book ____ Tuesday.
4. Please, put it in a _______ wrapper.

804. Mixed Up Story (After Level E)

Find each of the homophones in the following story. Write each homophone on a sheet of paper. Next to it write what it means.

Angie moved at a fast gait. She had to hurry to meet her friend. If she was late there would be no peace. The thought brought a tear to her eye. She would rather die than fight with her friend.

805. Circle and Write (After Level F)

Circle the homophone in each sentence. On a sheet of paper write a sentence using its homophone mate.

1. Suzy yelled, "Hit the brake!"
2. The cupboards were bare.
3. Please pay your fare quickly.
4. I would like a new pair of shoes.
5. Someone your age is considered your peer.

806. Meaning Mates (After Level G)

Match each of the words to the phrase that tells what it means.

mane	a metal material
mail	contraction for it is
lead	horse's hair
steel	letter
it's	take charge

The sample homonym activities on this page give you ideas for several formats which can be used when you create activity task cards or worksheets of your own.

Proofreading (Numbers 900-999)

As has already been discussed, the most effective way to teach proofreading skills is with the student's own writing. However, preplanned, systematic exercises in proofreading may be desirable in special circumstances. In this category are two types of planned exercises that have consistently proven valuable: story correction and standardized test format exercises. Inclusion of these activities offers variety and novelty to the spelling program.

Not all numbers have been used in sequence to allow you to insert additional activities of your own in each activity category.

Most standardized achievement tests in spelling and grammar skills are really nothing more than proofreading and visual discrimination exercises. It is by nature impossible to determine a student's ability to use grammar correctly and spell accurately with multiple-choice-type questions. This is especially true in the area of spelling. A good reader, who is a poor speller, can often locate misspelled words that he is unable to spell when the word is dictated to him or when he needs it in his own writing. However, occasionally a student lacks the visual discrimination necessary to locate the correct spelling of a word when a number of very similar options are offered. Such students may be aided with Activity Task Cards (or worksheets) that are designed to replicate achievement test items. These are quite easy to make using words from the Flow-Word-Lists. The following examples illustrate the three basic formats found on standardized achievement tests.

901. Pick an Error (D-12)

Directions: Decide which underlined word is spelled wrong. If all words are spelled correctly, fill in the space that goes with the word "None."

These samples illustrate three basic formats for proofreading exercises.

1. <u>Yesturday</u> we <u>visited</u> the new building. None
   A B C
2. What in the <u>werld</u> were you <u>thinking</u>? None
3. My <u>silvor</u> necklace is <u>broken</u>. None
4. I'd like a <u>differant</u> kind of <u>cake</u>. None
5. My <u>brother</u> is in <u>furst</u> grade. None

902. Choose an Answer (G-29)

Directions: Choose the word that is spelled correctly and best completes the sentence.

1. The food at summer camp was ___________________.
   A. horribal B. horrible
   C. horribul D. horribel
2. I earned twelve _____________ cleaning the car.
   A. nickles B. nickuls
   C. nickels D. nickals
3. My favorite ____________ will visit next week.
   A. uncal B. uncul
   C. uncol C. uncle

903. Messed-Up Story

Directions: The paragraphs below contain many errors. Rewrite them on your own paper. As you rewrite, correct the errors.

The president of the united states is William Jefferson Clinton. President Clinton is the 46th presadent of our country. He was alected presedent the furst time in 1992. He is now serveing his secound term as our president.

Mr. Clinton was boren in Arkansas. He lived their all his life. His hometown is Hope, AR. Well, he is president he lives in the White Horse in our nations capital.

Word Card Activities

Word Card Activities are, for the most part, games which require your student to manipulate the words to learn or discover particular spelling principles. Some Word Card Activities focus on individual drill of your student's spelling words. They lend a particular game-like atmosphere to the spelling lessons which is particularly appealing to some students.

Word Card Activities and games are usually workable with any list of words the student needs to drill. However, some activities require that specific word family cards be created for them.

Most Word Card Activities use only business-card-sized cards on which are written the student's spelling words. However, some also require other props and materials. Blank and prepared Word Cards, used in the activities in this section, do not need to be large or expensive to make. The cards themselves can be made by cutting index cards or tagboard into 2"x3½" rectangles. For Word Cards requiring use of only one side of the card, a free alternative is to ask a local printer to save any misprinted business cards. Making the Word Cards this size allows them to be neatly stored, for easy access, in a business card file box available at most office supply stores.

Prepared Word Cards should have the words written neatly in black ink and in as large a print as possible. It is important to remember that your handwriting serves as a model for your student. Likewise, your student should be reminded to use his best handwriting when creating his own Word Cards.

Word cards can be made using backs of old business cards or index cards cut to size.

1. Linguists

Using a list of words containing a common phoneme (sound) represented by a variety of graphemes (letters), let the student regroup the words so that phoneme represented by the same grapheme are grouped together. Students may then work as "linguists" to unlock the rules which govern phoneme-grapheme relationships. Instructions which could be used to guide exploration, if the guidance is desired, might include:

1. List all the graphemes you can find for /a/ and record the number of times each is used.

2. Arrange the graphemes for /a/ in order of frequency.

3. List the graphemes for /a/ which you find used at the beginning of a syllable and record the number of times each is used. Arrange these in order of frequency.

4. List the graphemes for /a/ which you find used at the end of a syllable and record the number of times each is used. Arrange these in order of frequency.

5. List the graphemes for /a/ which you find used in the middle of a syllable and record the number of times each is used. Arrange these in order of frequency.

6. List graphemes for /a/ which you find used in only one position.

Variations:

1. Individual words may be written on Word Cards, shuffled and sorted according to the grapheme representing the phoneme.

2. A variation that works especially well with good readers who are poor spellers is to utilize written material within the reading capacity of the student **instead** of providing a list of words. The material should be selected because it frequently uses the phoneme being explored and its respective grapheme correspondences in proportion which approximate that of American English.

2. Parts of Speech

Use heavy cardboard. Divide the board into five parts. Label the top of each column with a part of speech—noun or pronoun, verb, adjective, or adverb, and article or conjunction. Students will place their Word Cards under the correct heading and then ask to have their work corrected before removing their cards. You may need to remind your student that the part of speech to which a word belongs is determined by how it is used in a sentence. Have him base his decision according to how he used it in the sentence which he wrote on his 10-Step-Study Sheet.

A blackline master of the Parts of Speech Chart is included in the "Teaching Aids and Masters" section. You can make copies for your students to write this information for each study sheet word.

3. Concentration

This versatile game can be used to teach synonyms, antonyms, homonyms, compound words, prefixes and suffixes, or any desired combination of them. As its name indicates, it promotes concentration and requires a good visual memory.

Preparation:

1. A deck of cards arranged in matched pairs is prepared by the teacher (or the student). The pairs of words selected for the cards will depend on what is to be taught and the level of difficulty desired. Thus, if antonyms are to be matched, cards may include at the elementary level pairs like *fat* and *skinny*, *stop* and *go*, *night* and *day*, *short* and *tall*. Correspondingly more difficult pairs can be added as students progress to a more advanced level.

Concentration games can be made to teach prefixes, suffixes, homonyms, compound words, as well as other skills.

2. The number of cards in the deck will depend on the players' powers of concentration. A great strain is placed on their memory if more than 40 cards, (i.e., 20) pairs, are used at one time, but extra sets with different pairs of words can be kept in reserve for successive rounds.

How to Play.

All the cards, after being thoroughly shuffled, are spread out, helter-skelter, face down on the table. The first player then picks up two cards at random and shows them to his opponent. If the cards match, i.e., if they make an appropriate pair, the first player places them face up on his side of the table and scores one point. He may then have another try at finding a matching pair. If he cannot do so, he must return one of them—after showing both to his opponent—face down to its former place.

The second player now picks one card at random from those lying face down on the table. He tries to remember the position and the wording of the card that was put down by his opponent in order to determine whether it will match the card in his hand. If (either through luck in picking up his second card or through correctly remembering the location of the card he needs) he succeeds in getting a matched pair, he lays both cards down, face up, on his side of the table, scores one point, and draws again. He continues trying to make matches until he selects two unmatched cards. Then the other play is allowed to draw. The player with the most matched sets is declared the winner.

4. Word Combinations

In this game, simple words are composed from still simpler ones. It is an ideal game for a student to play by himself or with a classmate.

Preparation: Prepare a set of cards by writing on each a word that could form a part of a longer word, e.g., stick, tar, be, off, ball, am, ice, get, sea, house, store, horse, etc. Such words can easily be found in many words of three or more syllables, like together, incapable, gasoline, lieutenant, diploma, cockatoo, origin, and even in some words of two syllables, like fortune, message, current, grammar, brandish, hermit, mayor, and season. For each word on a card there must be another card with a word that can combine with it.

How to Play: The player or players try to form as many new, longer words as possible by combining the cards in various ways. Thus, words that might be built with the elements listed here are beam, target, office, etc.

Creating a word box for each student will facilitate playing many of the Teacher-Directed Games.

5. Plural Patterns

An understanding of the patterns that exist within English words can be an aid to the writer attempting to record his ideas. Give the students these four sets of words:

Pattern A	Pattern B	Pattern C	Pattern D
days	wives	churches	tries

They must determine in which of the two patterns other related words belong: *journeys, blueberries, plays, armies, ladies, monkeys, valleys, alleys, assemblies*. Then they must add s or change the y to i and add -es to the following words: *dry, lay, boy, joy, alloy, injury, jury*, and *strawberry*. The word puzzle to be solved is "In what cases do we change the y to i and add -es?" The student can apply this understanding as he checks words about which he is uncertain. (Words to be used for these activities will be found in Groups 30 and 31.)

6. Word Box

This activity is best carried out by pairs of students with similar spelling needs. Appropriate words for the pair are placed in a box (or two different boxes). One student draws a word from his box (or stack) and hands it to his partner who pronounces the word and uses it in a sentence (in the same manner as the Flow-Word-Lists are tested.). The student who drew the word then spells it (or writes it on paper). If he spells it correctly, it is returned to the box; if incorrectly, he keeps the word for study in his Student Record Book for this study period. The students alternate the selection and spelling of words. The activity provides an interesting variation for pretesting words and for reviewing words previously studied.

7. Word Card Testing

Word Cards can be used in place of or in addition to the regular self-corrected test procedure. Such use has proven excellent for remedial students and useful for independent study. Word Cards are prepared for each word the student needs to learn. Only one word is placed on each card. A study record is also prepared containing the list of the words to be practiced. The study words are at the head of the columns of squares in which check marks indicating successes or errors are to be placed.

The card is exposed for one, two, or three seconds, depending upon the age and ability of the student. The word is pronounced by the teacher and repeated by the student. If the student is working alone, he reads the word orally. After the brief exposure, the card is turned over and the student is asked to write the word on a regular test sheet in his Student Record Book or on a separate test sheet. He corrects his work by turning the card back over. After two successfully correct daily spellings, the word drops to the "once-a-week" list and a new word is added in its place for daily practice. After the student has correctly spelled a word for several weekly tests, it can then be moved to a monthly list and so on. The flexible nature of the cards allows these cards to be arranged to easily facilitate this testing and review method. Storing the cards in a business card file box, with dividers for the daily, weekly, monthly, and occasional test categories, makes self-testing easy. The tangible picture of progress afforded by the check sheet provides the student with a picture of his continued progress.

8. Word Cards as Flash Cards

Gilbert[1] reported the results of using rapid exposure flash-card exercises in teaching spelling. He concluded that teaching by flash cards had a definite value in focusing attention and sharpening perception. Presenting study words on flash cards and pronouncing them clearly as they are flashed aids visualization. The flash-card method is also extremely popular with students. The attractive features are the surprise and suspense elements; the quick movement captures attention, and the separate cards help the student concentrate on one particular word at a time.

9. Missing Letters

A variation of the flash-card method is to place on one side of the card an incomplete word (e.g., pl __ __ se), to pronounce the word, and ask the student to write it. If he cannot, he is shown the reverse side of the card containing the whole word. Flash cards made in this manner can also be used individually. In this case, the student will look at the complete word and then turn the card over and try and write the whole word. He checks his work by turning the card back over.

10. Homonym Word Cards

An especially valuable Word Card Activity for studying homonyms is to write a meaningful sentence, with the study word indicated with blanks, on one side of the card and the study word by itself written on the other side of the card. To use these cards, the student first looks carefully at the study word, then he turns the card over and attempts to write the entire sentence, writing the complete study word in place of the blanks. He can then turn the card back over to check his work.

11. Independent Study

Each word is shown quickly to the student studying it with the instructions, "Take a mental picture of it." The student then writes the word and checks its spelling. A word may be presented several times if it appears to be difficult. This activity is most appropriately used with pairs or small groups with one of the students flashing the words.

12. Syllabification

This activity can be conducted using Word Cards with which a student is currently working. The student should be provided with a box of toothpicks with which to divide the words into syllables. His results should then be checked in the dictionary.

Worksheet-type Activities

Worksheet-type activities can be a blessing or a curse. It isn't the worksheets which cause the problem. It is the method of assignment. If you carefully tailor them or select them to meet the current needs of your student, they can provide excellent, efficient learning. If, on the other hand, you assign them day after day, without much thought as to how they contribute to your student's needs, they are a waste of your student's time. Unfortunately, most worksheet-type exercises in traditional spelling programs are prescribed in just this indiscriminate manner. *Spelling Power's* design allows you and encourages you to take a different approach by providing you with resources to totally individualize your instruction. In this section, you are given a number of ideas for creating your own worksheets. These ideas can be used to create personalized worksheets that meet the specific needs of your student or use words which he is currently studying. Often, especially for younger students, a few problems as suggested under Worksheet-type activities, written directly on an Activity Task Card, is sufficient.

By creating masters for each worksheet, you will be able to gradually develop quite an inventory of worksheets. You can expand your inventory further by trading with a friend who is also using the program. Worksheet masters from grammar programs or other spelling programs or books may also prove to be valuable resources. (An excellent source for additional worksheet-type activities which can be completed with any spelling list is *Spelling Works* published by Learning Works Co.)

These suggestions are designed to give you several basic formats which can be used to create your own worksheets and additional task cards.

1. Dictionary Skills

When students have access to identical dictionaries, practice in locating words may use coded messages. The code for a given word may be a series of three numerals designating the page, column, and position of the word in that column. For example, 36-1-5, would indicate that the coded word is the fifth word in the first column on page 36. Maximum benefit is derived from the encoding process when students must locate their words in the dictionary in order to solve a coded message. Students seem to really enjoy it when the words are organized into meaningful messages.

Variations and Extensions:

1. Coding of letters in words by indicating a page number on which words beginning with that letter can be located.

2. Coding of letters by using the number representing the ordinal number associated with the letter in the alphabet.

3. Coding of letters to symbols for which a key is provided.

2. Alphabetizing Dots

A fun version of dot-to-dots that reinforces Alphabetizing Skills can be made using letters instead of numbers. To make dot-to-dot puzzles, use large, simple drawings such as are found in young children's coloring books. Make dots along the main outlines onto plain paper laid over the original drawing. This is easy to do if the original is taped to a brightly lit window and the plain paper taped over it. It will be easy to see the outline of the original. Make sure you save your master so that the dot-to-dot can be used by more than one student.

3. Crossword Puzzles

Crossword puzzles may be constructed which use current and review spelling words. If necessary, everyday words and words from other academic areas—reading, language, social studies, science, and mathematics—may be added. An excellent collection of crossword puzzles may be built up over a period of time keyed with respect to spelling difficulty and filed for convenient, independent use by students. You may use the crossword puzzle master provided in the "Teachers Aids and Masters" section as a base for your crossword puzzles. You will also find that there are a number of excellent computer shareware (often free) crossword puzzle generator programs. If you visit our web site at www.castlemoyle.com you will be able to find up-to-date information regarding how to access these and similar programs.

Variations and Extensions:

1. Provide students with graph paper so that they can create crossword puzzles of their own. They can then have their friends or teacher try to solve them.

2. Many crossword puzzle books are on the market for various ages.

Collect crossword puzzles from every possible source: student's magazines, newspapers, crossword puzzle books, etc., and make them available to your students for free-time use.

If you can create some crossword puzzle addicts, you have given these students not only a pleasant and mentally challenging recreation, but also a lifetime source of vocabulary and spelling enrichment.

4. Building Words

Building Word puzzles can be teacher-made or the students can make them to challenge other students. All the words in this puzzle must end with the same letter. Each word must be one letter longer than the one before, until the fifth word, then each succeeding word becomes one letter shorter. Clues are provided for students to help them fill in the boxes created for the game.

e _
he __
she ___
shoe ____
house _____
hose ____
bee ___
we __
e _

1. A word for him. 2. A word for her. 3. You wear it on your foot. 4. A place to live in. 5. Something to use to water the garden. 6. A stinging insect. 7. A word for us.

5. Configuration Exercises

1. Write words which fit given configurations. The words may be drawn from the week's spelling list or may be left to the choice of the students.

2. Draw an outline of the configuration of words on a given spelling list. This is especially appropriate when silent letters or unusual phoneme-grapheme correspondences are present.

6. Proverb Scrabble™ (I & A)

Prepare a worksheet with the words to proverbs scrambled for the student to unscramble. Five to ten proverbs to a worksheet is sufficient. In the examples below, the first example is more easily discernible than the second.

AN EWB ROOMS WEEP SCLE AN.

(A new broom sweeps clean.)

RETNIEH A RWORORBE ORN A EDNERL EB

(Neither a borrower nor a lender be.)

Teacher-Made Games

Board games and card games really appeal to many students. They can especially be helpful in reaching and teaching students with little or no academic motivation. The six basic game formats presented here can be adapted to create many additional games. Adaptations and variations are suggested following each game.

You can easily and inexpensively make these games for repeated use by your student. Follow the directions to create and decorate the game boards. If you create a master of the game board on 11"x17" paper and use only black lines, they can be copied to provide multiple games, to provide students copies for home use, or to trade with other teachers. After the games are decorated, they can be pasted onto the inside of a manila file folder. (If you buy the folders just for this use, you may want to spend a few cents more and get the pretty, colored folders. The colors can also be used to color code for ability levels.) The game's directions and objectives can be typed up and pasted to the front of the file folder. For extra durability, the folders can be laminated with clear contact paper. Old wire record stands make an excellent storage and display device. Be sure to number each game and any pieces that go with them so that they can be easily put away after use.

1. Suffixes

Make a game board on the inside of a file folder. Draw this frame on the board. Fill in with words to which suffixes can be added. The first player throws the die to find out how many squares to advance. The player reads the word on the square reached and adds as many suffixes as possible. When he is finished, if the other players doubt his spelling, they may challenge him to prove his word (with the dictionary). He is awarded one point for each correct word and has deducted two points for each incorrect word. The winner is the player with the highest score, when all players have reached the finish line.

Variations and Extensions:

1. Other topics may be used, e.g., synonyms, homophones, antonyms, or prefixes.

2. Instead of using a game board, this game can be played using 15 to 20 word cards spread out on the floor or tabletop in a configuration of the game. You may wish to add *start* and *finish* cards as well. Game is then played as above.

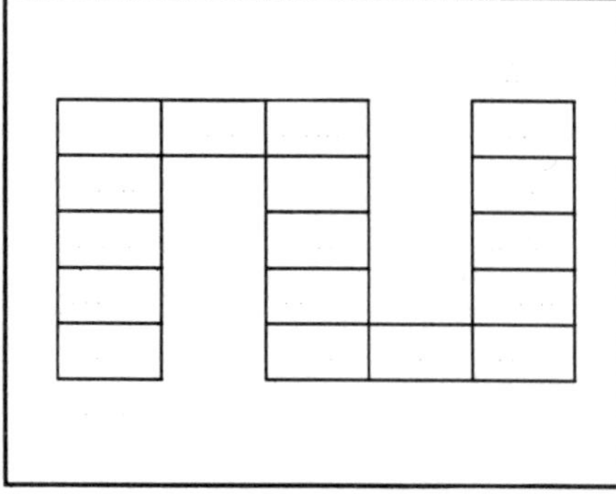

2. Spelling Golf

Spelling Golf can be played singly, in pairs, or in small groups. The principal objective is to keep the score as low as possible. In one variation, nine or 18 holes may be played with a par established for each hole. A different set of Word Cards is assigned to each hole. If par is three for a particular hole, three letters are omitted from each word assigned to that hole, and the student attempts to fill in the missing letters until he correctly completes the word. (The correct spelling is found on the back.) Each attempt at spelling the word counts as a stroke. When one word for the hole has been correctly completed, the player has "hit the ball into the hole" and moves on to the next hole.

If played singly, the "course" may be played several times during a week with the student keeping a record of his scores to determine progress; if played in pairs or small homogeneous groups, the players may compare scores with each other.

3. Spelling Football

The paper or toy football is placed on the 50-yard line of a scale football field drawn on the inside of a file folder. Each player has a stack of Word Cards which can include frequently misspelled words or words from the student's study sheet (see Word Box below). His opponent draws cards from his stack to dictate to the player who "has the ball." He is given six plays, or straight words, to advance the ball. With each correct word, the ball advances ten yards toward the opponent's goal line. For each word missed, the player loses ten yards. A score of six points is given for each "touchdown" (crossing the opponent's goal line).

Variations and Extensions: May be played as a group impromptu game. Draw the football field on the blackboard and use "frequently misspelled words" that all students in the group should know. Team players take turns and teams should be evenly divided.

4. Advanced Football

A. Play is begun on the 20-yard line of the football field. The offensive team (player) is given four downs to advance the ball.

Advanced Football uses the same game board as described in 3. Spelling Football.

B. Before a word is given to the team member, he must choose to run, punt, or pass. If he chooses to run, and spells the word correctly, the ball advances five yards. If he chooses to pass or punt, he may state the number of yards he wishes to go. If he spells the word correctly, the ball advances that distance. If he misspells the word, the opposing team may intercept the pass merely by spelling the word correctly.

In the case of a punt, usually on the fourth down, a correct word will give the opposing team the ball at the point first chosen by the player in his yardage choice. If both teams misspell the word, the ball is returned to the line of scrimmage or to the point where the play began.

C. Ten yards must be gained by the offensive teams in each group of four plays, or the ball is given to the opposing team.

Mother

~~oness~~ once

twelVe

leave

Still

~~grase~~ grass

tuesday

wednesday

~~sead~~ said

friend

Mother

Once

twelve

leave

Still

Grass

Tuesday

wednesday

Said

friend

D. One point, the "conversion," is given for one word spelled correctly after each goal is made.

5. Abbreviation Crossroads

This is a great game for long car rides. Can be played by one or more students. Appropriate for students ages ten and up.

Preparation: Make a copy of the game board master found in the "Teaching Aids and Masters" section. You may want to laminate the "playing board" and paste it inside a file folder. This will make it a wipe-off game board.

How to Play: The first player closes his eyes and puts his pen point on the board. If the pen touches a line, the player misses his chance, and it is the next player's turn to try. If the pen touches a box, the player shades it in. Then he must try to make as many meaningful abbreviations as he can with the eight letters with which that box is aligned vertically, horizontally, and diagonally. He is given a time limit for making his abbreviations list. For each letter in his abbreviations he scores one point.

Succeeding players follow the same procedure. If a player touches a box that has already been marked, he gets two additional chances to "hit" an empty box. The game ends either within a set time or when all the boxes have been marked. (Or when the players are exhausted and agree to quit.) A dictionary should be readily available to settle disputed points.

Variations and Extensions: Have students try to make words using the letters. You can experiment with different shaped grids: circle, triangle, octagon, and so on.

6. Word Authors

Word Authors is a variation of the familiar game, Authors. The cards for playing can be made by either the teacher or the students. A book is four variations of a word, i.e., play, plays, playing, played. The student having the most books is the winner.

7. Compound Word Rummy

Write one word part that may be used in a compound word on each card that you plan to use for this activity. The number of words used depends upon the number of players. (You will need a minimum of ten sets of cards for each player.) Each student receives five cards and draws one from the remaining cards. As soon as a player can make a compound word from two cards, he places them on the table and receives one point. If he cannot make a word after drawing a card, he must discard one card.

Teacher-Directed Activities

Many of the Teacher-Directed Activities listed in this section are "impromptu" activities, that is, games that take little or no preparation and materials. They can be played anywhere, at any time. Most are great for occupying time while riding in cars, waiting for appointments, or standing in line.

1. Phonics Square

Draw three squares on the board. Label them "initial, middle, and final."

Prepare a list of sounds to be stressed, and a list of words containing those sounds in initial, middle, and final positions. See example below:

St	Stoop	restore	feast
	store	castaway	guest
	sting	poster	lost
	staff	justice	greatest
	stone	canister	pest

"Our stressed sound today is 'st.' Listen for the 'st' sound in each word I pronounce. Is it at the beginning, in the middle, or at the end of the word?

"One person will come to the board. He will point to the square which tells the position of st in each word as I pronounce it." Pronounce about five words for each student if the group is large. This activity is best used, however, for one student or a small group that needs added drill.

This game can be played with simple phonics, such as shown above, or present more advanced phonemes as in the example below:

Er-IR-UR

urgent	dirigible	bother
ermine	sturdy	stir
irk	blurred	occur

2. Phonetical Chairs

This game requires phonic sound cards (flash cards showing consonant blends, single consonants, long and short vowel sounds, digraphs, etc.) You will need one card for each student playing, minus one.

All of the players except the person who is "It" will be seated in a circle, holding a sound card. "It" has no card and no chair. He will stand in the middle of the circle and everyone will hold up his card so "It" can see the cards.

"It" will call two sounds. The people holding cards with those sounds must quickly change seats. "It" will try to get one of those two seats first. Whichever of the three people is left without a seat becomes the next "It."

3. Find the Pattern

Distribute old newspapers or magazines to each student. Review one of the phonetic principles or spelling rules. Have students in teams of four, pairs, or individually (must be fairly homogeneously grouped) search for the words that fit the rule. The one with the most words wins.

4. Compound Confusion

This game requires a lot of movement and would be best played in the gymnasium or on the playground. Make large Word Cards (at least one for each student). Each card should have written on it a word which must be part of a compound word and has a mate. Mix up the cards by shuffling them and give each student one. Have the students stand in a large circle holding their cards so that the other students can see them. When you say go (or blow the whistle) they must find their "mate." As they find their partner (make up a complete word), they line up in order so that the whole word can be read.

The game can be further complicated if a long word, like penmanship, is broken up into three parts, each of which is a word in itself: pen, man, and ship.

5. Question Box Game

With the dictionary at your elbow, write ten to 15 questions and put them in a box. Let each member of the group pick out a question, read it silently, and find the answer in the dictionary. Don't make the questions too easy, or the game won't be interesting. Hard questions won't discourage the younger students because they have to look up the answer anyway.

This is excellent training in spelling, a vocabulary builder, and good practice in finding words in the dictionary.

Sample questions: 1) Is a "blatherskite" a fish, an Australian sportsman, or a talkative person? 2) What does the abbreviation Au mean?

Variations and Extensions:

1. Students enjoy a turn at coming up with questions for others to answer as well.
2. The same type of questions can be provided in a worksheet format.

6. Common Sound

I Am In...

A. I am in fed, fat, and fox. What sound am I?

B. I am in fish, calf, and cafe. What sound am I?

C. I am in fish, telephone, and rough. What sound am I?

Answers to all three = /f/

The above examples illustrate the adaptability of this activity to various levels of difficulty. In the first example, both the grapheme representing the phoneme and the position of the phoneme have been held constant. The second example varies the position of the phoneme but holds the grapheme constant. The third example varies both the grapheme and the position. Activities such as these may be constructed with all phonemes, arranged in an appropriate order of difficulty, and used with individuals as the need arises. This is a great game to play anywhere and really builds auditory skills.

7. Alphabetizing

Alphabetize a common spelling list. (Since most lists require that the student have experience alphabetizing beyond the second letter, you must check the list before making this assignment to an individual student.) A good source for such lists are lists of commonly misspelled words.

Divide the class or small group into two teams. Have a student from the first team write any spelling word on the chalkboard, and then let him choose a student from the other team to come to the chalkboard. The first student must tell the other student to write the spelling word that comes alphabetically before or after the word given. The second student's team may call out words they think are correct, but the student at the chalkboard must spell the word correctly to receive points. Then the student may write a word on the chalkboard and choose a student from the other team to continue the game.

8. Teakettle

This old favorite is an excellent game for teaching the difference in meaning between homonyms. One player, the victim, goes out of the room, while the rest of the players agree on a pair of homonyms. When the victim returns, he asks each player a question in an effort to determine what the homonyms are. The responses must be so phrased as to require the use of either one of the homonyms, but the word "teakettle" must be substituted for them. From these clues the victim must discover the words that "teakettle" stands for.

Victim: Is it something you buy?

Player 1: You can buy a false teakettle, but not the real teakettle.

Victim: Is it something you wear?

Player 2: Everyone teakettles he has a teakettle, but you can't wear a real teakettle.

Victim: Is it something you do?

Player 3: It's something you can do. Everyone here now teakettles but you!

Victim: Is it something in this room?

Player 4: It's as plain as the teakettle on your face. (After that clue, let us hope the victim *knows* his *nose*!)

Good sets of homonyms for this game can be found in the "Miscellaneous" section of this manual.

Variations and Extensions: A variation of this game can be played by using "teakettle" to represent two entirely different meanings of the same word (homophones), such as hind (a deer and rear), left, beam, part, fare, game, rose, safe, soil, stole, etc.

9. Compounds

Have two teams ready. A student on one team says a word that is part of a compound word. A member of the other team must spell a compound word which has that word as a part. Give a point for each correctly spelled word. A point is deducted if the word given is not part of a compound word. Have dictionaries available in case disputes arise about words.

Variations and Extensions: The game can also be played with prefixes and suffixes.

10. Word Chains

This game may be played by any number of students from one to the entire class. If the emphasis is on the individual, the student would write as many words as possible in a given length of time with each succeeding word beginning with the letter at the end of the preceding word. If more than one student is involved, the spelling is rotated systematically among the participants. A brief sample of a word chain follows: chain, net, tent, table, end.

An interesting variation of this game substitutes phonemes for the letters. If points are given for the words spelled correctly, bonus points can be given when different letters are used to represent the same phoneme, e.g., laugh, philosophy.

11. The NYM GAME

A word is pronounced by a caller who indicates whether it is a synonym, antonym, or homonym (homophone). The group then writes both the word and the "nym" which goes with it.

12. Checkers

The problem with the old-fashioned "Spelling Bee" is the one who needs the most practice with spelling participates the shortest amount of time. Here is a version that is just the opposite. The students line up in a single line (of ten or more students). The teacher then dictates a word from the frequently misspelled word list (located in the "Miscellaneous" section of this manual) to the first person in line. If the word is spelled correctly, the student "jumps" two persons in the direction of the end of the line. When he reaches the end, he goes to his seat to watch or do other school work. If he misspells the word, the next person has an opportunity to try the word. When the teacher comes to the end of the line, she begins at the front of the line again.

13. Spelling Baseball

Divide the class into two teams. Establish definite rules patterned after the rules of baseball. At a simple level, a word given by the "pitcher" and spelled correctly by the "batter" would count as a run. At an advanced level, word lists of increasing difficulty could be used for singles, doubles, etc. (Each student asks the pitcher for the hit of his choice.) Any word misspelled should be spelled correctly. It could be given to the next batter or given to a player on the opposing team to see if he can "put out" the batter.

Lists used should be selected from the frequently misspelled words or use the review test lists for a level which all the students have completed. The pitcher can also "pitch words" from the opponent's word cards.

14. Pantomime Word Cards

One student "acts out" a spelling word selected from his opponent's word cards or off a Flow-Word-List he has studied since the last review or Delayed- Recall Test. If the person "up" correctly guesses the word and spells it correctly, he becomes the pantomimist. If the word is spelled correctly, give a point to the speller; give a point to the pantomimist if incorrectly spelled.

15. Grid Game

The object of the game is to make as many words horizontally and vertically as possible. The players alternately choose a letter which each must place somewhere on his grid. When all the spaces are filled, each player counts the scores: each word made counts as many points as there are letters in it—five points for five-letter words, four points for four-letter words, and so on.

Variation and Extensions: Each player may choose two or three squares to be blocked in as in a crossword puzzle.

16. Prefix Tic-Tac-Toe

Draw a standard tic-tac-toe board large enough that a word can be written in each square. Each player must a select a different prefix (instead of Xs or Os). A player must, taking turns, write three words beginning with "his prefix" in a horizontal, diagonal, or vertical line.

Variations and Extensions: In addition to a prefix, the common element might end with the same suffix, or contain the same phoneme (e.g., long a sound).

17. Flying Words

To play this game, which builds strong visualization skills, divide the group or class into two teams with equal numbers of "players." Write a list of words on the board. Ask the students to look closely as one word is going to "fly" away. Quickly erase a word and have them write the erased word. If the students are on teams, a team could score a point for each student who spells the word correctly. Begin with a short list, but increase it as adeptness is shown.

18. Big Words

Choose a word of at least seven to ten letters and write it on the board. Each student is to make and write as many new words as he can from the letters in your word. Letters may be used in any order and each new word must contain at least three or four letters. A letter may be used in a new word as many times as it appears in the word you have written. The student with the longest list of new words wins.

19. Silly Sentences

Divide the class into two or more teams of at least five players each. One student from each team writes the first word of a sentence on the board. The next student writes a second word, and so on. The team finishing first receives five points if its sentence makes "sense." One point is deducted for any spelling mistake made by either team.

20. Pass a Note

Allow students to pass notes silently for ten minutes, keeping track of the number of spelling words they write. The winner is the student with the highest total. You might declare as second-place winner the student who collects the most spelling words in the notes he receives.

21. Homonym Match

In this game, the players learn to distinguish among homonyms by matching them in complete sentences in which they are used correctly.

How to play: The first player writes a sentence in which he uses a word that he knows has a homonym. For example, he may begin by saying, "She will sew a dress."

The second player has to decide, within a given time, which word in that sentence is a homonym and then use the homonym correctly in a matching sentence of his own. He would be wrong, for example, if he wrote, "Is she still at the same address?" But he would be right and score a point if he wrote, "So, what?" If he cannot think of a homonym to match his opponent's, he may challenge his opponent to supply a sentence with its appropriate matching homonym. Since there is a penalty of two points for failure to do so, the formation of sentences with words that have no homonyms is discouraged.

Let us follow this particular dialogue for a while:

I know it.

No, you don't. Didn't you see it?

Yes, it's floating on the sea. It's a flea.

Perhaps it's trying to flee. I'll see you later.

On a desert isle, I suppose.

See the Homonym Dictionary (located in the "Miscellaneous" section of this manual) for some suggested homonyms.

22. Visualization

Write each word on the blackboard, magic slate, or white board. After the students have looked at the word, the difficult part (usually vowel combinations or suffixes) is erased and the students are directed to visualize or write the whole word.

23. Hangman

Hangman is an old favorite, but still worth mentioning. Draw a "gallows" on the chalkboard or on paper. The students may take turns choosing a word from a group list that the other student is working with. Draw a blank line below the drawing for each letter in the word. One by one, the students guess a letter that the word may contain. If the guess is correct, write the letter on the blank line where it would appear in the word. If it is incorrect, draw the head, body, arm, or leg of the man to be hung. If a student completes the word or guesses it before the "hangman" is completely drawn, he receives a point. Then he selects a word from his partner's list.

You may also use words that you have decided should be learned from "unit study," such as state names.

24. Word Salad

Write a word such as multiplication or America on the board (or slip of paper) and have the student make as many words as possible by using only the letters that appear in the word you choose (be sure that the word contains several different vowels).

25. Stringing Along

This game teaches spelling and vocabulary and trains the student's visual memory.

To play, the first player starts by naming any letter of the alphabet. Each player in turn must "string along" by adding one letter, either before or after those already called out, to form a word. The ever-growing necklace of words, formed by adding one letter at a time to either end, constitutes a challenge to keep building longer words by the same process.

Thus, a game might proceed from *i* to *it* to *pit* to *spit* and *spite*. Or *rip*, *trip*, *tripe*. Another might begin with *o* and go on to *on*, *one*, *tone*, and *stone*. Still another might start with *a* and string along from *at* to *ate* to *late* to *plate*.

Variations and Extensions: The game can be made more difficult by permitting a letter to be inserted also anywhere in the middle of a word to form a new word. Thus, pit might be transformed into pint, then to print, and finally to sprint. Since this places a greater strain on the memory, more time should be allowed for each answer.

26. Spell and Check

This activity can be used with a group to introduce, reinforce, or review words, spelling patterns, and generalizations. It features proofreading and allows a great deal of flexibility in what is taught. The teacher uses a word list selected from a group list, list of frequently misspelled words, or a list of words made up by the teacher. Each individual student's list can be used if students take turns.

Each student in the group writes either on paper or at the chalkboard. The teacher dictates a word and the students write it. The students proofread and correct misspellings from a student or teacher's model. The teacher then requests the students to do various things with the word, depending on what needs reinforcing. Some examples are:

Underline the silent letter.

Circle the blend.

Circle the long vowel.

Use the word orally in a sentence.

Add a prefix to the word.

Add a suffix to the word.

Change the vowel in the word to make a new word.

Change the beginning of the word to make a rhyming word.

27. Pronunciation

Prepare a set of Word Cards, each card showing one word. The words should be ones frequently mispronounced, or ones very difficult to pronounce. Some sample words are (others may be obtained by listening to your students):

library (not lie-barry)

pumpkin (not pun-kin)

our (not are)

just (not jest)

mirror (not mere)

February (not Feb-u-ary)

pin (not pen)

picture (not pitcher)

Divide the group into two teams, in lines facing each other. Show the first person on Team 1 a word and have him pronounce the word. If his pronunciation is correct, he stays where he is. If he mispronounces the word, he must go to the end of the opposite team's line. Then show the first person on Team 2, and so on. At the end of the playing time, the team with the most players wins.

After the student attempt, the teacher should pronounce the word correctly and all students repeat it.

28. Listening Lab

To develop auditory awareness of the schwa sound, read the following word pairs slowly and have students raise their hands each time they hear a word containing the schwa. This game can be used with any sound.

opera	again	open	spring	root
eight	only	pupil	fought	soda

29. Contraction Race

Have the students write as many contractions as possible within a given period of time. It may be helpful to point out that two or more words have the same contractions, for example: I would, I should, or I had; what is, and what has; and we will and we shall. Also explain that a spelling change is sometimes made when a verb is combined with not, such as when changing will not to won't.

Dictation Exercises

Writing from dictation is good supplemental practice to direct word study because the words are written in context and the vocabulary is controlled. Dictation exercises simulate the feeling of continuous, meaningful writing without the complication of needing to compose (as in original writing). They are also useful for lengthening your student's auditory memory span and provide an excellent opportunity for handwriting practice.

How to Conduct a Dictation Session

Prior to the dictation, exercise you should read the entire selection to your student. Read the piece with feeling and proper intonation.

Actual dictation begins by having your student date his paper. Next have him record the title of the piece if it is longer than a single sentence. This gives the work "character."

You may now begin dictating. Sentences too long to be remembered are divided, but always into meaningful units, the length of the units differing with the ability of your student.

Read the first unit, then your student will repeat it, and write it from memory without prompting. (You should not omit this step, as it helps lengthen your student's auditory memory. After several weeks of dictation, you may sometimes allow your student to omit repeating the unit orally, but simply pause long enough for him to say it silently to himself, thus placing more responsibility upon him.)

Some students must be told when to begin a new sentence and when to indent for a new paragraph. Others will need very little assistance in recognizing these transitions. Other than these cues, no other talking should be done by either you or your student after the sentence is read. Otherwise, you will disrupt the feeling of continuous writing.

Your student should be responsible for the spelling of any word in a dictation exercise because you have taken the care to give him only words which he should know: phonetic words, rule words (rules already studied), any generalization mastered, and learned words. If the selection includes a word for which your student is not yet prepared, it should be written on a piece of paper and placed beside him to copy.

The continuity of thought should not be allowed to be broken by your student asking for the spelling of words after the dictation exercise has begun. If one word after another is asked for and repeated, the exercise becomes merely horizontal spelling. Also, the realization that no help will be given stimulates more careful listening to the passage in advance.

Proofreading skills can be reinforced upon the completion of dictation activities as part of the grading process. When the last group of words has been written, encourage your student to discover and correct as many of his own errors as he can. Then provide him with an original (perfect) copy against which he can check his work. After your student has corrected all the errors he can discover, you should indicate any errors he missed using standard proofreading marks as described in the section on "proxy-coaching" in Chapter Three.

Selection of Material for Dictation Exercises

Sources for dictation material abound. Carefully selected material may be chosen to reinforce unit studies and aid in vocabulary building. Almost any worthy piece of writing, from one sentence in length to a page or more, may be used depending on the ability of your student. Famous quotations or proverbs, poetry, Bible verses, and excerpts of famous speeches all make excellent choices for memory building and to reinforce studies in other areas of the curriculum.

It is not always possible to find a really suitable exercise short enough to be dictated at one sitting. This should cause no anxiety. In these situations, you may need to adapt those taken from a book so that they have a definite beginning and end. You may also need to break up a larger work into several reasonable sections, spreading the work over several days or weeks. If your student's past dictation work has consisted of a few short sentences, he will be delighted when he finds his work lengthening to several paragraphs or pages.

Generally, a new selection is chosen each week or for each unit of study. Many teachers, especially in multi-level classrooms, use these selections in varying ways with each level of student. The youngest may be required to memorize the selection. Those who are mastering or have acquired some facility with handwriting are required to memorize and to copy it in their best handwriting. Finally, the oldest students, who should know how to spell all the words, are required to reproduce the same piece from dictation.

Since the chief value of exercises in dictation is to give a feeling of continuous, meaningful writing, it is important that each selection should be interesting to the student. For students ages eight to 12, many suitable poems will be found in Stevenson's *Child's Garden of Verses*. Selections from Shel Silverstein's books of zany poems and rhymes are also sure to be popular. Other poems which have proven popular with students of this age group include:

Firefly by Elizabeth Maddox Roberts

The Mist and All by Dixie Willson

Taxis by Rachel Field

Indian Children by Annette Wynne

Sea Shell by Amy Lowell

Chickadee by Hilda Conkling

Experience with teens has shown that they enjoy taking dictation and then memorizing the larger composition from which many smaller famous quotations are derived. An all-time favorite poem of this category has been *The New Colossus* by Emma Lazarus (of Statue of Liberty fame). Patrick Henry's *Speech in the Virginia Convention* (which ends with "Give me liberty or give me death") is another favorite piece that teens seem to enjoy learning. With junior and senior high students and other students old enough to appreciate more mature thought, *The Fountain* by Lowell, *The Eagle* by Tennyson, *A Nation's Builders* by Emerson, and *Under the Greenwood Tree* from *As You Like It* have also been used successfully.

Using Dictation Exercises as Skill Builders

While usually you will choose selections because they are interesting, it is also possible and desirable for them not only to appeal to the student in content, but at the same time to reinforce formal drill. They may motivate the introduction of a new spelling rule or test its mastery or stress a new word or combination of sounds (phonemes) in words. Arbitrary associations, with a large element of fun, found in many nonsense verses and jingles, often serve to fix the spelling of a troublesome word and homonyms. A few examples follow. (A list of homonyms can be found in the Miscellaneous section.)

Does he need a *dose* of medicine?

You wouldn't believe a lie for a minute,
But the word *believe* has a *lie* right in it.

Whether the weather be cold
Or whether the weather be hot,
Whether the weather be dry
Or whether the weather be not,
We must weather the weather
Whatever the weather,
Whether we like it
Or not.

Spelling Rules or Generalizations

The function of the final e is often clearer if the form without the final e is a real word. Here are some sample dictation sentences that can help clarify this rule as well as a few that clarify other sounds and rules.
He *ate* lunch *at* noon.
We *can* see a *cane* in the man's hand.
The cat was sleeping with his *mate* on the *mat*.
I saw a *dime* in the *dim* light.
The *tube* of toothpaste has fallen into the *tub*.
How could he *hope* to *hop* so far?
He *cut* his hand on the *cute* little saw.
It was her *fate* to be *fat*.
"I *hate* that *hat*," she said.
Please b*ake* a c*ake* for me to t*ake* when we m*ake* the trip to the l*ake*.
Mrs. Cat c*augh*t her n*augh*ty d*augh*ter and t*augh*t her to clean her face.

Intermediate Double Dictation

Another way to reinforce spelling generalizations and rules is to have students compose their own sentences, paragraphs, and stories using the words from the "Flow-Word-List" that they are currently studying. This enables the student, through intermediate double dictation (student to teacher, teacher to student) to translate his own thoughts into written material.

Commercial Games

Rummy Roots

This is a great game for ages eight to adult. It teaches 42 Greek and Latin roots through four different game formats as vocabulary enhancement and spelling aid. Highly recommended!

More Roots

This game has the same playing format as *Rummy Roots*, but teaches 42 additional Greek and Latin roots plus 10 additional review roots. *Rummy Roots* primarily consists of Greek roots, science exposure, and technological devices. *More Roots* has been designed to emphasize prefixes, Latin roots, and more commonly used English words such as "concur," "infect," and "protract."

Both *Rummy Roots* and *More Roots* are produced by **Eternal Hearts**. They are available for purchase from most educational dealers.

Scrabble™

A classic, fun way to practice spelling and dictionary skills. Every family and classroom should have at least one version of the game. It is now available in four editions including Deluxe for the serious player ages eight and up; Regular also for ages eight and up, Junior for ages five and up, and the Sesame Street edition for ages three to five. Two or more players. Produced by Milton Bradley and available at most toy stores.

Scrabble™ is now also available as a computer game through Virgin Mastertronic International at many computer outlets.

Up Words

Scrabble™ fans and experts love this game, which is a 3-D version of *Scrabble*™ . Designed for ages ten and up, it is more appropriate for teens and adults. Created by Milton Bradley. Available at most toy stores.

Hangman

Milton Bradley has brought the classic chalkboard game up to the twentieth century with this game. Two or more players, aged eight and up, play this game exactly like the classic version, only a little machine draws the various stages of "hanging." May be a little expensive ($10 range) for what it is, but does add novelty. Available at most toy stores.

The Word 2 (Adult Version)

The Word 2 is a vocabulary game which expands and builds the players' knowledge of thousands of vocabulary words. Also builds dictionary skills. The object of the game is for players to race around the board, answering questions whenever they land on "The Word" spaces or "At a Loss for Words" spaces. Two to six players, ages 13 to adult, can play the game. Created by Intelligames, it is available only at some toy stores.

Letter Dice with Timer Spelling Games

The following games are letter dice games in which the players attempt to make the longest and/or most words from the assortment of letters which show up on the dice after they have been mixed up in a shaker of one kind or another. They usually come with a timer, so each player has a limit to each of his efforts. Can be played with any number of players ages eight and up. Also can be adapted for individual activity. Prices vary greatly; at time of publication the games ranged in price from $4.99 to $14.99. Available at most toy stores.

Spell Way (Get Away Games)
Spill and Spell (Parker Brother Toys)
Perquackey (Hollingsworth Brothers)
Word Maker (Got A Minute Games)
Boggle (8+) & Boggle Jr. (3-6) (Parker Brothers)

Computer Software

SuperSolvers — Spellbound

(Ages Seven to 12; limited to 3,000 words; talks)

One excellent feature of this program is that it makes kids practice words before they can test themselves with a Spelling Bee. Mostly visualization activities. The Learning Co.

Spell It, Plus!

(Ages six to adult; voice; includes 1,000 most frequently used words; teacher support materials available; IBM/Mac) Davidson & Associates, Inc.

Spelling Adventures

(Ages five to 12; voice; IBM Only) ZugWare

Super Speak 'n Spell

This is not a software program, but a complete machine marketed by Texas Instruments. This teaching machine has eight different games which can be played independently. It is marketed for ages six to 12, but adults and teens really enjoy it, too! Uses an excellent quality voice simulation. Extra cartridges are available to expand word list and to offer variety. Not inexpensive, but highly recommended. Available at most toy stores.

Creating Letter Tiles

Letter Tiles (or moveable alphabets) are used in many of the Activity Task Card activities presented in this section. Letter Tiles are small squares (1"x1" or 2"x2") with a letter of the alphabet centered on each square. These can be simple squares of paper or tagboard or real ceramic or plastic tiles. Real tiles are suggested for classroom use because they are more durable. For home use, however, simple squares of paper are suitable. Masters for making paper Letter Tiles, in a style which coordinates with the *Italic Handwriting Series*, are provided in the "Teacher Aids and Masters" section.

When making Letter Tiles, print all the vowels on blue paper or tiles or write them in blue ink. Consonants should be in red. You will need—on separate tiles—both capital and lowercase letters. Generally you will need about six copies of each consonant tile and nine-ten copies of vowels.

To make paper or tagboard tiles, simply make three photocopies of each of the masters onto the appropriate color of paper (separate masters are provided for vowels and consonants) and cut them along the outline separating the tiles. You may wish to laminate the tiles. The tiles should be laminated after they are cut or the edges of the laminating material will separate. Many teachers like to provide each student with his own set of Letter Tiles for home use.

To make real Letter Tiles the teacher will need to purchase tiles from a local hardware store. Tiles can be a neutral color such as white or beige with the letter printed in the appropriate color or letters can be printed in black on red and blue tiles. The easiest way to create neat letters is to trace over each letter master, using carbon paper between the tile and the master. Then, using indelible ink, trace over the carbon marks.

At this point, the teacher might be wondering about the importance of the color scheme. This color scheme comes from the Montessori method. It provides, especially for younger students, a valuable visual clue and self-checking device which can be used when composing words and sentences with the Letter Tiles or moveable alphabet. Students are instructed that no word can be written without at least one vowel (or blue) letter in each syllable. This color coding is less important for students using the *Spelling Power* program, but if the teacher is using an introductory phonics program that precedes this program with her younger students, she can eliminate the need for two sets of Letter Tiles by creating them using the color codes. If she is only teaching older students, she can simply make her Letter Tiles any color she wishes.

Both types of tiles can easily be stored in a hardware storage box which has at least 26 drawers. These boxes usually have dividers in each drawer so you can easily separate the capitals from the lowercase letters.

References For This Section

1 L. C. Gilbert, L.C., "Experimental Investigation of a Flash-Card Method of Teaching Spelling," *Elementary School Journal*, XXXII (1932), pp. 337-51.

Teaching Aids & Masters
(Blackline Masters)

Table of Contents

Forms Masters

Teaching Aids

Blackline Masters

______________ Test

Name: ____________________ Date: ______________ Form: ________

1 ____________________

2 ____________________

3 ____________________

4 ____________________

5 ____________________

6 ____________________

7 ____________________

8 ____________________

9 ____________________

10 ____________________

11 ____________________

12 ____________________

13 ____________________

14 ____________________

15 ____________________

16 ____________________

17 ____________________

18 ____________________

19 ____________________

20 ____________________

21 ____________________

22 ____________________

23 ____________________

24 ____________________

25 ____________________

26 ____________________

27 ____________________

28 ____________________

29 ____________________

30 ____________________

31 ____________________

32 ____________________

33 ____________________

34 ____________________

35 ____________________

36 ____________________

37 ____________________

38 ____________________

39 ____________________

40 ____________________

41 ____________________

42 ____________________

43 ____________________

44 ____________________

45 ____________________

46 ____________________

47 ____________________

48 ____________________

49 ____________________

50 ____________________

10-Step Study Sheet

Date: __________ Level: _____ Group: _____

Spelling Study Tips:

Words to learn	Say	Look	Say	Close Eyes	Check	Trace & Say	Check	Write	Check	Repeat
________	☐	☐	☐	☐	☐	☐	☐	________	☐	☐
________	☐	☐	☐	☐	☐	☐	☐	________	☐	☐
________	☐	☐	☐	☐	☐	☐	☐	________	☐	☐
________	☐	☐	☐	☐	☐	☐	☐	________	☐	☐
________	☐	☐	☐	☐	☐	☐	☐	________	☐	☐
________	☐	☐	☐	☐	☐	☐	☐	________	☐	☐
________	☐	☐	☐	☐	☐	☐	☐	________	☐	☐
________	☐	☐	☐	☐	☐	☐	☐	________	☐	☐
________	☐	☐	☐	☐	☐	☐	☐	________	☐	☐
________	☐	☐	☐	☐	☐	☐	☐	________	☐	☐
________	☐	☐	☐	☐	☐	☐	☐	________	☐	☐
________	☐	☐	☐	☐	☐	☐	☐	________	☐	☐

Use each study word in a sentence.

Daily Test

Date: ____________________ Level: __________

____

____

____

Test Words	Words to Learn

______________ *Test*

Name: ______________ Date: ______________ Form: ______________

1 ______________
2 ______________
3 ______________
4 ______________
5 ______________
6 ______________
7 ______________
8 ______________
9 ______________
10 ______________
11 ______________
12 ______________
13 ______________
14 ______________
15 ______________
16 ______________
17 ______________
18 ______________
19 ______________
20 ______________
21 ______________
22 ______________
23 ______________
24 ______________
25 ______________
26 ______________
27 ______________
28 ______________
29 ______________
30 ______________
31 ______________
32 ______________
33 ______________
34 ______________
35 ______________
36 ______________
37 ______________
38 ______________
39 ______________
40 ______________
41 ______________
42 ______________
43 ______________
44 ______________
45 ______________
46 ______________
47 ______________
48 ______________
49 ______________
50 ______________

10-Step Study Sheet

Date: ________ Level: _____ Group: _____

Spelling Study Tips:

Words to learn	Say	Look	Say	Close Eyes	Check	Trace &Say	Check	Write	Check	Repeat
	☐	☐	☐	☐	☐	☐	☐		☐	☐
	☐	☐	☐	☐	☐	☐	☐		☐	☐
	☐	☐	☐	☐	☐	☐	☐		☐	☐
	☐	☐	☐	☐	☐	☐	☐		☐	☐
	☐	☐	☐	☐	☐	☐	☐		☐	☐
	☐	☐	☐	☐	☐	☐	☐		☐	☐
	☐	☐	☐	☐	☐	☐	☐		☐	☐
	☐	☐	☐	☐	☐	☐	☐		☐	☐
	☐	☐	☐	☐	☐	☐	☐		☐	☐
	☐	☐	☐	☐	☐	☐	☐		☐	☐
	☐	☐	☐	☐	☐	☐	☐		☐	☐
	☐	☐	☐	☐	☐	☐	☐		☐	☐

Use each study word in a sentence.

Daily Test

Date: ________________ Level: __________

Test Words	Words to Learn

_______________ Test

Name: ____________________ Date: ______________ Form: _________

1		19	
2		20	
3		21	
4		22	
5		23	
6		24	
7		25	
8		26	
9		27	
10		28	
11		29	
12		30	
13		31	
14		32	
15		33	
16		34	
17		35	
18		36	

10-Step Study Sheet

Spelling Study Tips:

Date: __________ Level: _____ Group: _____

Words to learn	Say	*Look*	Say	Close Eyes	Check	Trace &Say	Check	Write	Check	Repeat
______	☐	☐	☐	☐	☐	☐	☐	______	☐	☐
______	☐	☐	☐	☐	☐	☐	☐	______	☐	☐
______	☐	☐	☐	☐	☐	☐	☐	______	☐	☐
______	☐	☐	☐	☐	☐	☐	☐	______	☐	☐
______	☐	☐	☐	☐	☐	☐	☐	______	☐	☐
______	☐	☐	☐	☐	☐	☐	☐	______	☐	☐
______	☐	☐	☐	☐	☐	☐	☐	______	☐	☐
______	☐	☐	☐	☐	☐	☐	☐	______	☐	☐

Use each study word in a sentence.

Daily Test

Date: ________________ Level: __________

Test Words

Words to Learn

______________ *Test*

Name: ______________________ Date: ________________ Form: ________

1 ______________________

2 ______________________

3 ______________________

4 ______________________

5 ______________________

6 ______________________

7 ______________________

8 ______________________

9 ______________________

10 ______________________

11 ______________________

12 ______________________

13 ______________________

14 ______________________

15 ______________________

16 ______________________

17 ______________________

18 ______________________

Daily Test

Date: ____________________ Level: __________

Test Words

Words to Learn

Test Words

Words to Learn

10-Step Study Sheet

Date: ________ *Level:* _____ *Group:* _____

Spelling Study Tips:

Words to learn	Say	Look	Say	Close Eyes	Check	Trace &Say	Check	Write	Check	Repeat
	☐	☐	☐	☐	☐	☐	☐		☐	☐
	☐	☐	☐	☐	☐	☐	☐		☐	☐
	☐	☐	☐	☐	☐	☐	☐		☐	☐
	☐	☐	☐	☐	☐	☐	☐		☐	☐
	☐	☐	☐	☐	☐	☐	☐		☐	☐

Use each study word in a sentence.

"My Dictionary" Page for Letter _____

Check, C.A.T.C.H.

C. = Does it clearly communicate?

A. = Have I analyzed the structure?

T. = Have I checked all the technicalities?

C. = Are all the words correctly spelled?

H. = Have I used my best handwriting and used the proper headings?

and Correct

Symbols for Proofreading

Instruction	*Margin Mark*	*Mark In Text*	*Corrected Version*
Insert	*black*	*the^purse*	*the black purse*
Delete		*the black purse*	*the purse*
Let it Stand	*stet*	*the black purse*	*the black purse*
Capitalize	*Cap*	*the purse*	*the Purse*
Make lower case	*lc*	*the Purse*	*the purse*
close space		*the pur se*	*the purse*
transpose	*tr*	*the pruse*	*the purse*
spell out	*sp*	*40 purses*	*forty purses*
Insert space	#	*thepurse*	*the purse*
Insert period		*Carry the purse^*	*Carry the purse.*
Insert Comma		*purses^belts, and wallets*	*purses, belts, and wallets*
Start new paragraph	¶	*Mary bought a new purse. She went to a gala ball.*	*Mary bought a new purse. She went to a gala ball.*
Run in	*runin*	*Mary bought a new purse. She went to a gala ball.*	*Mary bought a new purse. She went to a gala ball.*

Error Analysis

❑ Mechanics (Technicalities)

Student's Name: ____________________

❑ Usage and Grammar

Date begun: ____________________

Skill																				

	Level A	Level B	Level C	Level D	Level E	Level F	Level G	Level H	Level I	Level J	Level K
Group 1											
Group 2											
Group 3											
Group 4											
Group 5											
Group 6											
Group 7											
Group 8											
Group 9											
Group 10											
Group 11											
Group 12											
Group 13											
Group 14											
Group 15											
Group 16											
Group 17											
Group 18											
Group 19											
Group 20											
Delayed Recall 1 Form A											
Delayed Recall1 Form B											
Group 21											
Group 22											
Group 23											
Group 24											
Group 25											
Group 26											
Group 27											
Group 28											
Group 29											
Group 30											
Group 31											
Group 32											
Group 33											
Group 34											
Group 35											
Group 36											
Group 37											
Group 38											
Group 39											
Group 40											
Group 41											
Group 42											
Group 43											
Group 44											
Group 45											
Group 46											
Group 47											
Delayed Recall 2 Form A											
Delayed Recall 2 Form B											
End of Level Form A											
End of Level Form B											

Weekly Spelling Contract

Name: ______________________________ Date: ______________

My words for this week are:

1.	______________	11.	______________
2.	______________	12.	______________
3.	______________	13.	______________
4.	______________	14.	______________
5.	______________	15.	______________
6.	______________	16.	______________
7.	______________	17.	______________
8.	______________	18.	______________
9.	______________	19.	______________
10.	______________	20.	______________

Activities which I plan to do:	Completed

Pretest score __________ Final test score: ______________

I could do better next week if I ______________________________

____

Name	Level	1	2	3	4	5	6	7	8	9	10	11	12	13	14	15	16	17	18	19	20	21	22	23	24	25	26

27	28	29	30	31	32	33	34	35	36	37	38	39	40	41	42	43	44	45	46	47	EOL A	EOL B	Level	Name

Spelling Prescription

For: ______________________________

Date: ______________________________

Assignment: ______________________________

____

____

____

____

____

____

______________ ______________
Teacher Signature Student Signature

Spelling Prescription

For: ______________________________

Date: ______________________________

Assignment: ______________________________

____

____

____

____

____

____

______________ ______________
Teacher Signature Student Signature

Spelling Prescription

For: ______________________________

Date: ______________________________

Assignment: ______________________________

____

____

____

____

____

____

______________ ______________
Teacher Signature Student Signature

Spelling Prescription

For: ______________________________

Date: ______________________________

Assignment: ______________________________

____

____

____

____

____

____

______________ ______________
Teacher Signature Student Signature

Prescription Record

Name: ______________________________ Class: ________________

Level: ______________________________ Date of Pretest: __________

Activity Type	Number	Description	Date Completed

A	E	I	O	U	a	e	i
o	u	A	E	I	O	U	a
e	i	o	u	A	E	I	O
U	a	e	i	o	u	A	E
I	O	U	a	e	i	o	u
A	E	I	O	U	a	e	i
o	u	A	E	I	O	U	a
e	i	o	u	A	E	I	O
U	a	e	i	o	u	E	e

B	C	D	F	G	H	J	K
L	M	N	P	Q	R	S	T
V	W	X	Y	Z	b	c	d
f	g	h	j	k	l	m	n
p	q	r	s	t	v	w	x
y	z	b	c	d	f	g	h
j	k	l	m	n	p	q	r
s	t	v	w	x	y	z	b
c	d	f	g	h	j	k	l

Build a Crossword

Instructions: Make the words join. Darken the squares where there are no letters. Use all your spelling words!

Name: ____ Date: __________________

Group: _________________________ Level: ___________________

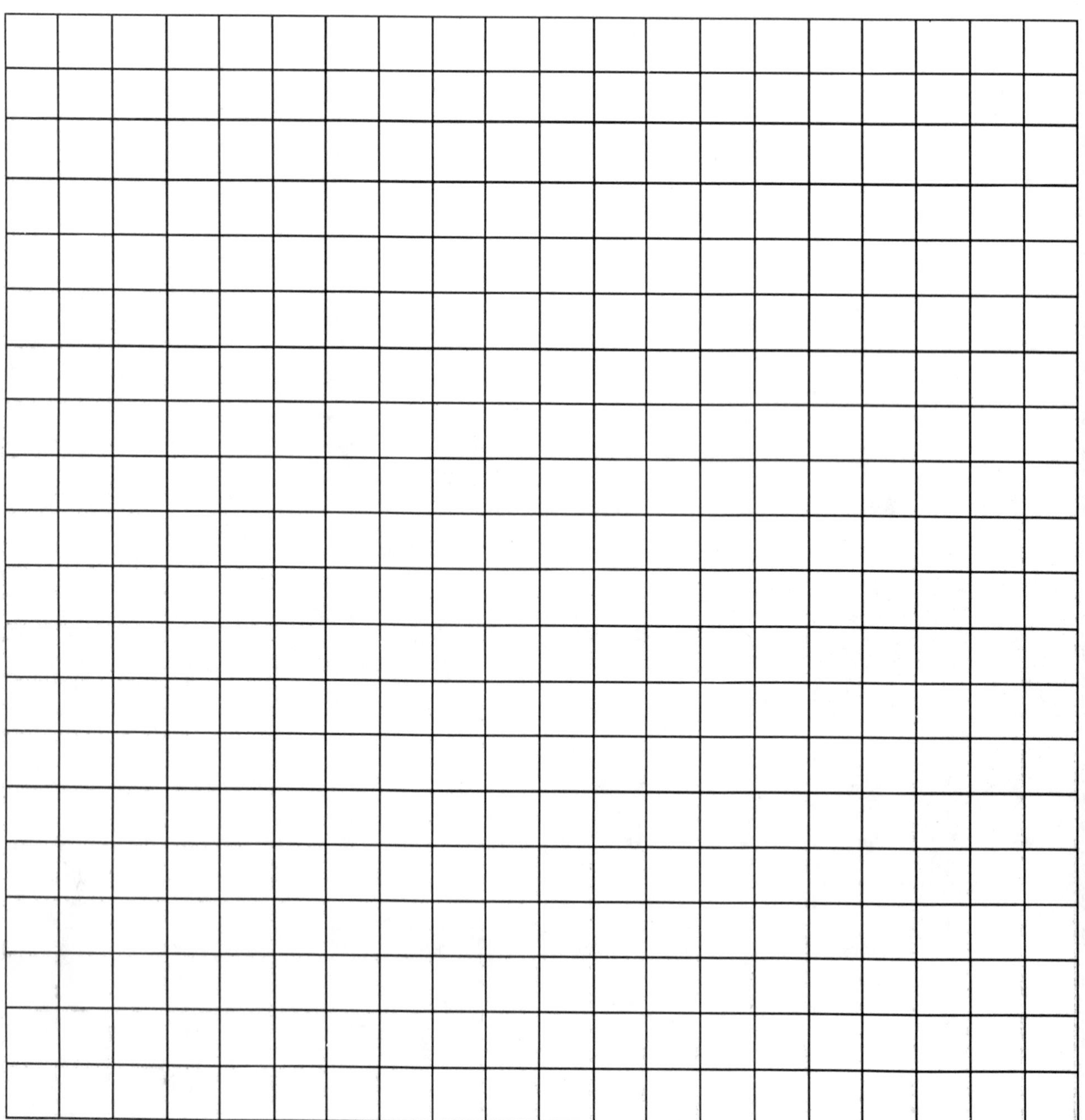

Build a Hidden Word Puzzle

Instructions: Write your spelling words in the squares from left to right or top to bottom. (Leave one or more blank squares between your words.) Scatter the words around. Use all of your spelling words. Then fill in the blanks with randomly selected letters.

Name: ____ Date: ________________

Group: _________________________ Level: ________________

Crossroads

Basic Instructions: The first player closes his eyes and puts his pen point on the board. If the pen touches a line, the player misses his chance, and it is the next player's turn to try. If the pen touches a box, the player shades it in. He then makes as many words as he can with the eight letters with which that box is aligned vertically, horizontally, and diagonally. He is given a time limit for making his abbreviations list. For each letter in his abbreviations he scores one point.
Variations and Extensions: Have students make words using the letters. You can experiment with different shaped grids: circle, triangle, octagon, and so on.

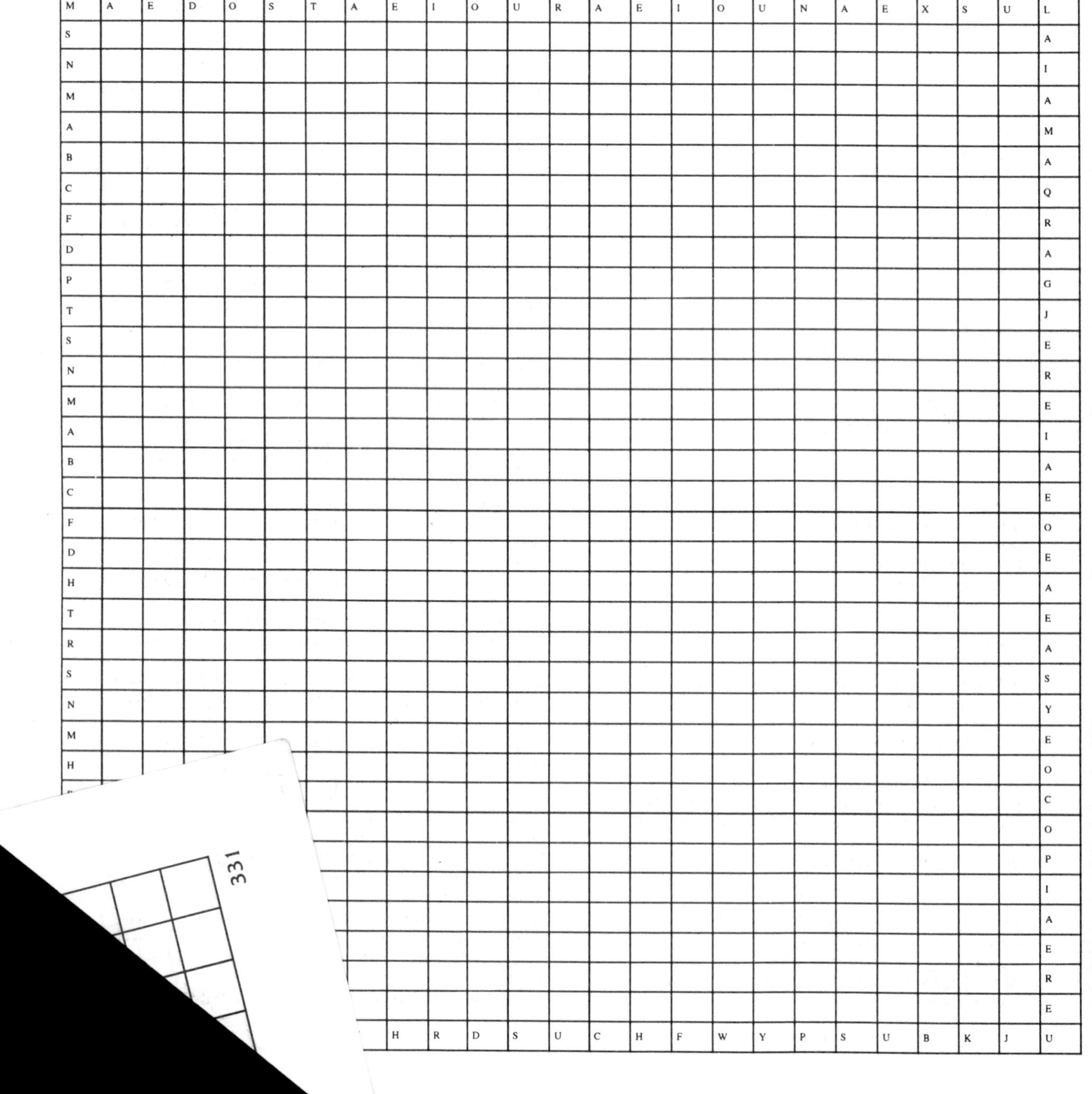

Homonyms and Other Often Confused Words

A

accept (to receive), except (to exclude)
advice (noun), advise (verb)
affect (influence), effect (bring to pass)
aid (to help); aide (an assistant)
air; heir (one who inherits)
aisle (passageway); isle (island); I'll (contraction for I will)
all (entirety); awl (tool)
all ready (all are ready), already (previously)
all right (there is no such word as alright)
all together (everyone together), altogether (entirely)
alley (back street), ally (to confederate)
allusion (a reference), illusion (deceiving appearance)
aloud; allowed (permitted)
alter (to change), altar (for worship)
angel, angle
arc (part of a circle); ark (Noah's boat)
ascent (act of rising); assent (agreement)
ate, eight

B

bail; bale (large, closely pressed package)
bald (lacking hair); bawled (past tense of bawl)
ball (round toy); bawl (to cry loudly)
baring (making bare), barring (obstructing), bearing (carrying)
bare (endure, empty), bear (animal)
bares, bears (animal)
baron (nobleman); barren (incapable of producing offspring; lacking vegetation)
base (foundation); bass (deep sound or tone)
beach (shore of ocean); beech (kind of tree)
beat (to hit repeatedly); beet (a vegetable)
berry (fruit); bury (to place under earth)
berth (job or position); birth (act of being born)
billed (past tense of bill); build (to make, establish)
blew (past tense of blow); blue (color)
bloc (a group); block (rectangular solid; a city square; to obstruct; to shape)
boar (male pig); bore (to drill a hole)
board (piece of wood, meals provided with rent, persons managing a firm, being on ship or train); bored (uninterested)
boarder (one who rents a room); border (dividing line, an edge)
bolder (more forward, more courageous); boulder (a large rock)
born (given birth), borne (carried)
bough (branch of tree); bow (to bend at waist, front part of ship)
brake (device for stopping a machine), break (shatter, fracture, rest)
breath (noun), breathe (verb)
bred (past tense of breed); bread (food made from flour)
bridal (pertaining to a bride or wedding): bridle (part of a horse's harness)
by (next to); buy (to purchase); bye (leaving)

C

cannon (large weapon); canon (church law)
canvas (a cloth), canvass (to solicit)
capital (a city), capitol (a building)
carrot (vegetable); caret (proofreading symbol); carat (weight of precious stones)
ceiling (top of a room); sealing (fastening or closing tightly)
cell (small, bare room); sell (to exchange for money)
cellar (underground room); seller (one who transfers property)
censer (an incense burner); censor (a person who examines material for portions deemed objectionable or harmful)
cent (penny coin); scent (an odor); sent (past tense of send)
cents (plural of cent); sense (functions of hearing sight, smell, taste, and touch, point or meaning, ability to think soundly)
cereal (grain used as food); serial (story published or broadcast one part at a time)
chased (paste tense of chase); chaste (virtuous, modest)
cheap (not expensive); cheep (bird sound)
choir (group of singers); quire (set of twenty-four or twenty-five sheets of paper the same size and stock)
choose, chose
chute (an inclined passage to slide things down), shoot (to let fly, to photograph, a young outgrowth of a shrub, an exclamation)
clause (separate section of a formal document, a group of words containing a subject and verb); claws (sharp curved nails on an animal)
clothes (garments), cloths (pieces of cloth)
coarse (rough, crude), course (route, part of a meal, series of studies)
coin; quion
colonel (a high army officer); kernel (a grain or seed)
complement (something that completes); compliment (remark that is kind)
confidant (one to whom secrets are entrusted); confident (assured, certain)
conscious (aware); conscience (an inner moral sense)
consul (country's representative); council (a group); counsel (advise, giving of advice)
cord (thick string); chord (musical note)
core (central or most important part); corps (a group of people having common activity)
correspondence (communication by letters); correspondents (plural of correspondent, one who communicates by letter)
cot ; caught
councilor (council member); counselor (gives advice)
creak (to move with a harsh, squeaky, grating noise); creek (small stream)
cue (a stick used in playing pool or billiards); queue (a waiting line)
currant (berry); current (now in progress, flowing in a definite direction, electric force)
cymbals (musical instrument); symbols (graphic signs/marks)
Czech; check

D

dairy (place for milk cows), diary (a book)
days (plural of day); daze (to dazzle or stupefy)
dear (beloved, costly, polite form of address); deer (an animal)
decent (adjective), descent (downward slope or motion), dissent (a disagreement)
dependence (the quality or state of being supported, reliance and trust); dependents (those who rely on another for support)
desert (a barren country or to leave), dessert (food)
device (noun); devise (verb)
die (to stop living, tool or device for stamping, singular of dice);

dye (to change the color through saturation)
discreet (showing good judgment); discrete (separate and distinct)
do (to carry out, perform); due (owed as a debt, owing to)
does (past tense of do), dose (a portion of medicine)
dual (having or composed of two parts), duel (a contest between two persons)

F

fain; fane
faint (not clear, feeble, without strength, to lose consciousness temporarily); feint (a movement intended to deceive)
fair (impartial, reasonable, light, clear, beautiful, festival); fare (sum of money paid for travel, range of food, to dine, to get along)
fate (destiny); fete (a festival)
feat (an act or accomplishment showing great daring skill or ingenuity); feet (plural of foot)
find (to discover); fined (past tense of fine)
fir (type of tree); fur (skin and hair of an animal)
first born (used as noun), first-born (used as an adjective)
fisher (a fisherman); fissure (crack in a wall or rock)
flair (a natural talent); flare (to burn unsteadily, to express strongly)
flee (to run away); flea (a small parasitic insect)
flew (past tense of fly, pass through the air); flue (a pipe for conveying smoke); flu (short for influenza, a virus disease)
flower (the bloom of a plant); flour (ground grain)
for (preposition); four (the number 4); fore (the front, toward the beginning)
forbear (to hold back, refrain); forebear (ancestor)
foreword (an introduction or preface); forward (at or near the front)
formally (in a formal way), formerly (in time past)
fort (a fortified building); forte (that in which one excels)
forth (forward, onward); fourth (preceded by three others)
foul (disgusting, unfair, out of bounds in ball games); fowl (bird used for food)

G

gait (manner of walking or running), gate (a movable structure across an entrance or exit)
gamble (to bet, wager); gambol (to skip about in play)
gorilla; guerilla
grate; great

H

hay (dried grass), hey (expression of surprise)
here, hear
hoarse, horse
hole, whole
holy, wholly
hour, our
Hungary; hungry

I

instance (an example), instants (periods of time)
isle (an island); aisle (a narrow passage)
its (possessive pronoun); it's (contraction of it is)

J

Job (Bible character); job (work)

K

knew, new
know, no

L

later (more late); latter (the second of two)
lead (to go first; or a heavy metal), led (past tense of lead)
lessen, lesson
loose (free), lose (loss)

M

maid; made
mail (letters or parcels, armor), male (man)
main (principal, chief part), mane (hair on back of a horse's neck)
meat, meet
miner (worker in a mine), minor (under legal age; less important)
moral (good, a lesson in conduct); morale (mental condition, spirit)

N

need, knead
nice (kind); Nice (city)
Nice (city); niece (relative)

P

pair (two), pare (cut or prune), pear (fruit)
past, passed
patience; patients
peace, piece
peaked; piqued; peek
peer (to look closely), pier (dock)
personal, personnel
Pilate (biblical character); pilot (flies airplanes)
plain (clear), plain (flat region), plane (flat), plane (geometrical term), and plane (airplane)
planed (past tense of plane); planned (past tense of plan)
plum; plumb
populous (lots of people); populace (the people)
pore; pour; poor
praise; prays; preys
pray; prey
precedence (act or right of preceding), precedents (things said or done before, now used as authority or model)
presence (state of being); presents (gifts)
pries; prize
principle, principal
proceed, precede
prophesy; prophecy

Q

quay; key
quit (stop), quite (completely, wholly, to great extent or degree), and quiet (still, silent)

R

rain, reign, rein
read; red
real; reel
right, write, rite (ceremony)
ring, wring
road, rode, rowed

S

sail; sale
seam; seem
see, sea
seen, scene
sense, cents, since
sew (combine fabrics with thread), so, sow (plant seed)
sheer; shear
shone, shown
sight (one of the five senses, something worth seeing); site (the

seat or scene of any specific thing, location of a building); cite (to quote as an authority)
stare, stair
stationary (in a fixed position), stationery (writing paper)
statue, stature, statute
steal (to take), steel (metal)
surplus (extra), surplice (religious garment)

T

tail; tale
than, then
there, their, they're
therefor (to that end); therefore (for that reason)
threw (pitch, cast through the air), through (finished), thru
to, too, two
toe; tow
tract (of land), tract (a treatise on religion), track (imprint or road)

V

very; vary

W

waist, waste
wait; weight
way, weigh
weak (faint, feeble, helpless), week (seven days)
weather, whether
which, witch
whole, hole
whose, who's
wood; would

Y

yews; ewes
yoke; yolk
you're, your

Words Commonly Misspelled by Elementary Students

about
address
afraid
after
afternoon
again
all
all right
along
already
always
am
an
and
animals
another
answer
anything
anyway
April
are
arithmetic
around
at
aunt
away
awhile
baby
back
balloon
baseball
basketball
bear
beautiful
beauty
because
been
before
began
behind
believe
better
bird
birthday
bought
boy
boys
break
broke
brother
brought
built
buys
bye
came
can
can't
cannot
catch
caught
chases
chief
children
Christmas
climbed
close
clothes
come
coming
could
couldn't
course
cousins
cute
daddy
day
dead
Dec.
decided
didn't
different
doctor
does
doesn't
don't
down
downstairs
Easter
eat
engines
especially
ever
every
everybody
everyday
everyone
everything
exciting
experience
family
father
favorite
Feb.
fell
few
field
finally
fine
finished
fired
first
flowers
football
for
found
fourth
Friday
friend
friends
frogs
from
fun
funny
getting
ghost
girls
goalie
goes
going
good
good-bye
got
grabbed
grade
grandma
ground
guess
had
Halloween
handkerchiefs
happened
happily
has
haunted
have
haven't
having
hear
heard
hello
her
here
him
his
hockey
hole
holiday
home
hope
horror
horses
hospital
house
how
how's
I
I'll
I'm
I've
in
Indians
inside
into
isn't
it
it's
its
Jan.
just
knew
know
lessons
let's
letter
like
likes
listened
little
lived
looked
lot
lots
loving
made
make
many
Mar.
maybe
me
met
might
miss
months
morning
mother
mountains
Mr.
Mrs.
much
my
name
names
neighbor
next
nice
no
nobody
nothing
Nov.
now
nowadays
o'clock
Oct.
of
off
once
one
others
our
out
outside
parents
party
people
picked
pictures
place
play
played
plays
please
pollution
practicing
pretty
probably
quiet

quit
quite
really
receive
received
recess
remember
right
said
Saturday
saw
scared
school
scream
screamed
second
shoot
shot
silver
sincerely
slept
snow
snowman
so
some
something
sometime
sometimes
soon
spotted
started
stationery
stepped
stopped
store
strange
straw
stubborn
studying
summer
Sunday
supper
suppose
sure
surely
surprise
swimming
take
teacher
teacher's
than
Thanksgiving
that's
the
their
them
then
there
there's
they
they're
things
think
thought
threw
through
throw
time
to
today
together
told
tomorrow
tonight
too
toys
trailer
train
tried
truly
turned
two
until
upon
vacation
very
wait
wants
was
wasn't
water
we're
weather
well
went
were
weren't
what
wheels
when
where
white
who
whose
will
with
without
wolf
won't
work
would
wouldn't
write
writing
years
you
you're
your
yours

Words Commonly Misspelled by High School Students

am
and
because
coming
cousins
didn't
don't
everybody
Feb.
for
friend
from
getting
going
good-bye
guess
Halloween
have
here
I'm
it's
Jan.
know
Mrs.
name
now
our
pretty
received
Saturday
some
sometimes
Sunday
teacher
teacher's
Thanksgiving
that's
their
there
they
through
time
to
today
tomorrow
too
two
very
went
write
writing
you
your

Words Commonly Misspelled by College Students

absence
absorption
absurd
academy
accept
accidentally
accommodate
accomplish
accumulate
accustom
achievement
acquainted
acquire
acquitted
across
addressed
adviser
affects
against
aggravate
all right
alley
allotted
ally
almost
already
altar
alter
although
altogether
alumnus; alumni
always
amateur
among
analogous
analysis
analyze
angel
angle
annual
answer
anxiety
apparatus
apparent
appearance
appropriate
Arctic
arguing
argument
arising
arithmetic
around
arouse
arrange
arrangement
arrival
article
ascend
asks
athlete
athletic
audience
author
auxiliary
awkward
balance
barbarous
baring
barring
based
bearing
becoming
before
beggar
begging
beginning
believe
believing
benefit
benefited
biscuit
boundaries
breathe
brilliant
Britain
Britannica
buoyant
bureau
business
busy
calendar
can't
candidate
careful
carrying
ceiling
cemetery
certain
changeable
changing
characteristic
chauffeur
chief
choose
chose
chosen
clothes
coarse
column
coming
commission
committed
committee
comparative
comparatively
compel
compelled
competent
concede
conceivable
conceive
conferred
conquer
conqueror
conscience
conscientious
conscious
considered
consistent
continuous
control
controlled
convenience
cooperate
counsel
country
course
courteous
courtesy
criticism
criticize
cruelty
curiosity
cylinder
dealt
debater
deceitful
decide
decision
deferred
definite
derived
descend
describe
description
desirable
despair
desperate
destroy
develop
development
device

devise
dictionary
difference
different
digging
dilemma
dining
dining room
disappear
disappoint
disastrous
discipline
disease
dissatisfied
dissipate
distinction
distribute
divide
divine
doctor
don't
dormitories
drudgery
dying
easily
ecstasy
effect
effects
efficient
eighth
eligible
eliminate
embarrass
eminent
encouraging
enemy
environment
equipped
especially
etc.
everybody
exaggerate
exceed
excellent
except
exceptional
exercise
exhaust
exhilarate
existence
expense
experience
experiment
explanation
extremely
familiar
fascinate
February
fiery
fifth
finally
financier
foreign
foresee
forfeit
formally
formerly
forth
forty
fourth
frantically
fraternity
freshman
friend
fulfil
fundamental
furniture
further
gallant
gambling
generally
goddess
government
governor
grammar
grandeur
grateful
grievous
guarantee
guard
guess
guidance
harass
haul
having
height
heroes
heroine
hesitancy
holy
hoping
huge
humorous
hundredths
hurriedly
hygienic
imaginary
imagination
imitative
immediately
immigration
imminent
impromptu
incidentally
incidents
incredulous
independence
independent
indispensable
induce
infinite
influence
influential
instance
instant
intellectual
intelligence
intelligent
intentionally
intercede
interest
interfere
invitation
irrelevant
irresistible
island
it's
its
itself
jealous
judgment
kindergarten
knowledge
laboratory
ladies
laid
larynx
later
latter
lead
led
leisure
liable
library
license
lightning
likelihood
likely
literature
livelihood
loneliness
loose
lose
losing
lying
magazine
maintain
maintenance
maneuver
manual
manufacturer
many
marriage
Massachusetts
material
mathematics
mattress
meant
medicine
messenger
miniature
minutes
mischievous
Mississippi
misspelled
momentous
morale
murmur
muscle
mysterious
necessary
neighbor
neither
nickel
niece
nineteenth
ninetieth
ninety
ninth
noticeable
nowadays
o'clock
oblige
obstacle
occasion
occasionally
occur
occurred
occurrence
occurring
offered
officers
official
omission
omit
omitted
opinion
opportunity
optimism
optimistic
origin
original
outrageous
overrun
paid
pantomime
parallel
parliament
particularly
partner
pastime
peaceable
peculiar
perceive
perception
peremptory
perform
perhaps
permanent
permissible
perseverance
personal
personnel
perspiration
persuade
pertain
pervade
physical
picnic
picnicking
piece
planned
pleasant
poison
politician
politics
possess
possession
possible
practical
practically
prairie
precede
precedence
precedents
prefer
preference
preferred
prejudice
preparation
prepare
prevalent
primitive
principal
principle
prisoner
privilege
probably
procedure
proceed
prodigy
profession
professor
prohibition
promissory
prove
psychology
purchase
pursue
pursuit
putting
quantity
quiet
quite
quizzes
rapid
ready
realize
really
recede
receipt
receive
recognize
recommend
reference
referred
regard
region
relieve
religion
religious
repetition
replies
representative
resistance
restaurant
rheumatism
rhythm
ridiculous
sacrilegious
safety
sandwich
scene
schedule
science
scream
screech
seems
seize
sense
sentence
separate
sergeant
several
shepherd
shiftless
shining
shone
shoulder
shown
shriek
siege
significant
similar
simile
since
smooth
soliloquy
sophomore
speak
specimen
speech
statement
stationary
stationery
statue
stature
statute
steal
steel
stopped
stopping
stops
stories
straight
strength
strenuous
stretch
strictly
studying
succeeds
successful
summarize
superintendent
supersede
suppress
sure
surprise
syllable
symmetrical
temperament
temperature
tendency
than
their
then
there
therefore
they're
thorough

thought
thousandths
through
till
to
together
too
track
tract
tragedy
tranquillity
transferred
translate
treacherous
treasurer
tries
trouble
truly
Tuesday
two
typical
tyranny
undoubtedly
universally
until
unusual
using
usually
vacancy
vacuum
vegetable
vengeance
vigilance
village
villain
weak
wear
weather
Wednesday
week
weird
welfare
where
wherever
whether
which
who's
whole
wholly
whose
wintry
wiry
within
without
woman
women
world
writing
written
you're
your

Words Commonly Misspelled by Secretaries and Other Business People

absorption
accelerate
accessible
accessory
accidentally
accommodate
accommodation
accumulate
achievement
acknowledgment
acquaintance
acquiesce
adjournment
affect
affiliate
all right
allege
allotment
already
aluminum
amendment
analyze
Antarctic
apostrophe
apparatus
apparent
appearance
ballot
banana
bankruptcy
barbarous
battalion
beneficial
benefited
budget
buoyance
bureaus
business
calendar
campaign
cancellation
carburetor
catastrophe
ceiling
cemetery
chauffeur
college
colossal
commitment
committee
concede
confident
conscience
conscientious
consecutively
consensus
conspicuous
controversy
corrugated
council
counsel
cylinder
cynical
defendant
deferred
definite
deuce
develop
development
diphtheria
disappear
disappoint
discrepancy
dissatisfied
divine
dominance
ecstasy
effect
eligible
eliminate
embarrass
eminent
endorsement
enterprise
envelop
envelopment
evidently
exhaust
exhibition
existence
extraordinary
familiar
feasible
February
fiend
fiery
flexible
forcible
forthright
forty
foursome
franchise
gauge
gnawing
government
governor
grammar
grievous
gymnasium
haphazard
heartrending
hemorrhage
hindrance
homely
hygiene
hypocrisy
idiosyncrasy
illegal
illiterate
imitation
immediately
inaugurate
incidentally
indelible
independence
inflammable
inhabitant
installation
intercede
interfere
interfered
inveigle
irrelevant
irresistible
issuing
it's
its
journey
justifiable
kimono
knowledge
laboratory
led
legitimate
liquefaction
liquefy
livelihood
loneliness
loose
lose
lovely
maintenance
management
maneuver
manual
mathematics
mileage
murmur
necessary
nickel
nineteenth
ninety
ninth
noticeable
notoriety
nowadays
occasion
occasionally
occurred
occurrence
omission
oneself
opposite
pageant
pamphlet
parachute
parallel
parliamentary
pasteurize
peaceable
peculiar
permanent
permissible
personally
persuade
physician
Pittsburgh
plagiarism
playwright
possession
potato
prairie
precede
preceding
precious
preferable
preliminary
presumptuous
prevalent
principal
principle
privilege
procedure
proceed
professor
prominent
pronunciation
prophecy
prophesy
publicly
pursue
questionnaire
receipt
receive
recipient
recommend
recommendation
reference
referred
relevant
relief
renown
repellent
replies
rescind
restaurant
reveal
rhapsody
rhetoric
rhubarb
rhyme
rhythm
ridiculous
rotary
sacrilegious
safety
salable
scholastic
scissors
secretary
seize
sensible
separate
serial
shepherd
shipment
siege
similar
simultaneous
since
sizable
sneak
sneer
souvenir
speech
splitting
strictly
subsidy
successor
sufficient
suing
superintendent
surgeon
surprise
susceptible
suspicious
symmetry
synonymous
tangible
tariff
temporary
tenant
terrible
their
too
tragedy
transferred
tyranny
undoubtedly
useful
vaccinate
vegetable
villain
volume
Wednesday
weird

Glossary

A

10-Step-Study: Use of research proven multisensory study steps as prescribed in the *Spelling Power* program.
Accent: The vocal prominence given to a particular syllable of a word by greater intensity (stress accent), or by variation of pitch or tone (pitch accent). In dictionaries, marks show the kind of emphasis required
Affix: [verb, transitive] to fasten or attach (something to something else).
adjective: a word that modifies or describes a noun or noun equivalent: one house, beautiful eyes.
Adverb: a word that modifies a verb, an adjective, or another adverb; answers the questions how, when, or where
Affix: something that is attached or joined to something else; esp., a word part, consisting of one or more syllables, that is attached to a root word or word stem in order to modify or change the meaning.
Alphabetical Word List: List of the 12,000 most frequently used words in alphabetical order. The list is found in the fourth section of the *Spelling Power* manual. Each word is followed by a series of codes which help parents access student writing or prioritize personal spelling words.
Analytical phonics: Method of teaching phonics to students which begins with individual letter sounds.
Antonyms: A pair of words which have opposite meanings, e.g. big, small.
Article: Words which are used with nouns to limit or give definiteness to the application of the noun, they include a, an, and the.
Auditory discrimination: The ability to discriminate between sounds.

B

Base word: *see root word*
Blackline Masters: Originals of forms or worksheets which are designed for teacher's to copy on a photocopy machine.

C

Closed syllables: a syllable which has one and only one vowel and ends in a consonant. The number of consonants before or after the single vowel does not matter (e.g., sock, tan, twelfth).
Code: a system of symbols or signals used to transmit messages.
Consonant: [noun; form the Latin verb consonare, to sound along with, to harmonize] (1) a speech sound made by partially or completely blocking the vocal air stream; or (2) a letter that represents such a sound.
Compound word: a word made up of two or more words that are spelled normally and, for the most part, retain their usual meanings. Compound words can be joined as in campfire, hyphenated as in mother-in-law, or two separate words which mean something distinct when used together, e.g. high school.
Configuration: The shape or outline of a word.
Consonant: a letter which has a "hard" sound or is produced by partial or complete obstruction of the breath stream.
Consonant blend: when two or more consonants appear together and you hear each sound that each consonant would normally make, the consonant team is called a consonant blend.
Consonant cluster: a group of consonants that combine a single-sound consonant team with a single consonant (e.g., shr and thr).
Core vocabulary: consists of those high frequency words, of which there are approximately 5,000, that comprise 80-90% the average person's spoken and written vocabulary.
Curriculum: the entire educational plan for a school, class, or academic year.

D

Deductive learning: educational process which focuses on direct statements of fact and lectures.
Delayed-Recall-Test: Test used to determine the student's long-term retention of material taught.
Derivation: a linguistic and morphological process of forming new words from existing words by adding one or more affixes to roots, stems, or words.
Diacritical marks: a mark or sign affixed to a letter to specify the sound it represents in a particular situation.
Dialect: regional or cultural variation of how words of a language are pronounced.
Digraph: a grouping of two or three letters that produces a single vowel sound, such as ee in see.
Diphthong: a complex sound made by gliding from one vowel sound to another within the same syllable (e.g., boy, out).
Discovery Activities: games, activities, and exercises which teach specific spelling and language arts skills as presented in the *Spelling Power* and *Writing Power* programs.
Dyslexia: See Strephosymbolism and/or Specific Language Disability.

E

Etymology: the study of the history of a word: the origin and analysis of the development of the word from its earliest form, through various changes, to its present form and meaning.
Experiential approach: a teaching approach which focuses on teaching skills as they are needed or experienced. This approach emphasizes the importance of using skills shortly after their introduction.

F

Fixed word list: word list for a "grade" which must be studied and mastered by all students of a particular grade regardless of readiness or past mastery.
Flow-Word-List: word list which uses the add-a-word approach. New words are added to the list as words are mastered.
Functional approach: approach which emphasizes teaching skills which have immediate application or function to the student.
Functional test: Test designed to replicate "real-life" applications of skills. In *Spelling Power* and *Writing Power* programs, it refers to actual student writing samples which are used to evaluate student skill level.

G

Generalizations: Spelling patterns or principles or phonetic principles which are generally true. More accurate term than rules, since most patterns have exceptions.

Grapheme: a letter or grouping of letters that represents a single phoneme.

H

Hands-on materials: educational materials which are manipulated by students as part of the learning process.
High frequency words: see CORE VOCABULARY.
Homographs: A word spelled the same as another but with a different meaning and origin, sometimes with different pronunciation: *bow* of a ship; bend a *bow*, having *wound* a bandage around a *wound*.
Homogeneous Group: Group of students at the same age or ability level.
Homonyms: a homophone or homograph.
Homophones: a word pronounced like another but different in spelling, origin, and meaning: *to, two, too.*

I

Immediate self-correction: The process of providing the student with a correct answer to a question immediately after his attempt so that he can check his own work.
Individualized instruction: lessons which are tailored to the needs of each individual student.
Individually Prescribed Instruction: the process used in *Spelling Power* to assign skill-building lessons and activities. See Chapter Four.
Inductive learning: process of helping the student to discover the underlying principle for himself.
Instructional Objectives: goals for educational outcomes, skills which students are to learn.
Integrated Functional Writing: process used in *Spelling Power* and *Writing Power* programs to integrate spelling instruction with the rest of the curriculum and especially with the language arts curriculum. See Chapter Three.
Intermediate Double Dictation: is used to help students with limited spelling ability record their own sentences. The student dictates the sentence for the teacher, she writes it out for the student to copy onto his own paper.
Intensive phonics: approach to phonics which systematically teaches each sound-letter correspondence along with other linguistic principles of English.
Invented spellings: spellings guessed at based on the student's current level of understanding of phonology and spelling system.
Irregular words: words which do not follow orthographic generalizations or break the "rules." Also known as outlaw words or sight words.

L

Learning Objectives: see INSTRUCTIONAL OBJECTIVES.
Learning style: characteristic cognitive, affective, and physiological behaviors that serve as relatively stable indicators of how learners perceive, interact with, and respond to the learning environment.
Letter-to-sound relationship (see PHONEME-GRAPHEME CORRESPONDENCES)
Lexicography: a branch of the discipline of linguistics concerned with the writing or compiling of a dictionary or dictionaries.
Linguistic approach: reading and phonics approach which includes the study of letter-sound correspondences, syllabication and morphography.
Linguistic principles: key aspects of a language's phonology, syntax, and semantics used as rules for spelling and writing.
Linguistics: the systematic study of language, and, more particularly, of the aspects of individual language, including phonology, syntax, and semantics. The discipline is sub-divided into descriptive linguistics, historical linguistics, psycholinguistics, comparative linguistics, geographical linguistics, dialectology, and lexicography.

M

Macron: A short, straight mark (-) placed horizontally above a vowel to indicate a long sound in pronunciations: as in the word trade.
Mnemonics: a technique or system using abbreviations, mottoes, formulas, or rhymes as an aid to memorization of material.
Modality: one of the five sensory modes of instruction which are generally selected to meet students' individual learning styles.
Monosyllabic words: words with only one syllable (e.g. mat).
Morpheme: the smallest meaningful unit in the language. A simple word like *Cat* is a morpheme as is the prefix *de-* in the word *deject*.
Morphology: the scientific study of language which concentrates on the smallest meaningful units or internal structure of words. In instructional settings, it usually refers to teaching the use and arrangement of affixes as related to reading and spelling.
Multi-Level materials: instructional materials which are used simultaneously by students at several ability, grade, or age levels.
Multisensory instruction: instruction which is designed to present material in ways that students of all learning styles will benefit from or which are specifically designed to use many sensorial activities to teach a single skill to a single student.
Multisyllable words: words with two or more syllables (e.g., tandem, caterpillar).

N

Noun: a type of word that names a person, place, thing, or idea.

O

Open syllable: has one and only one vowel or the vowel is the last letter in the syllable (e.g. no, she, mu*sic).
Orthography: the study or systematic use of standard, proper, or correct spelling of the words in a language. (The study of orthography means the study of the standard, proper, or correct sequences of letters in a written language system.)

P

Parts of speech: are nouns, pronouns, verbs, adverbs, adjectives, prepositions, conjunctions, determiners (a, an, the,) expletives (it, there), or exclamations (ouch!). Sometimes the part of speech can be told only by seeing how the word is used — whether it names, whether it describes, or whether it joins.
Phoneme: any one of the smallest, most basic units of sound in a spoken language.
Phoneme-Grapheme correspondences: shows the relationship of the sound and the letter or group of letters used to record that sound in written language.
Phonetic generalizations: a phonetic principle which is accurate for the majority of words the majority of the time. Also referred to as phonetic rule, but because there are exceptions to most, the term generalization is preferred.
Phonetic spelling: used in dictionaries, phonetic spellings use a single symbol or diacritical marking for each distinctive sound.

Phonetics: The study of how phonemes behave

Phonics: (noun; plural form, but takes singular verb] 1) the study of sound; (2) the method of using the sounds of a language when teaching people to read; or (3) (more recently) the letter-sound correspondences themselves. Generally a simplified version of phonetic knowledge.

Placement Test: Test to determine at what level at student begins instruction.

Positive reinforcement: providing immediate reward or confirmation of accuracy as a motivating factor.

Post-test: test following instruction used to determine student's retention of material taught.

Prefix: an affix attached to the beginning of a word or word stem.

Pretest: an examination which is designed to determine what material the student already knows and what material needs to be learned.

Prepositions: words that combine with a noun, pronoun, or noun equivalent (as a phrase or clause to form a phrase that usually acts as an adverb, adjective, or noun.

Pronoun: is a word that is used as a substitute for a noun or noun equivalent, takes noun constructions, and refers to person or things named or understood in the context. The noun or noun equivalent for which the pronoun substitutes is called the antecedent.

Pronunciation: the act or manner of enunciating words with reference to the production of sounds, the placement of accents, the accuracy of pitch or intonation.

Proofreading: careful, purposeful reading of a composition prior to public release or publication to discover and correct any possible errors.

R

R-influenced vowel (R-controlled vowel): when a vowel or vowel team is followed by an r, the sound is often distorted. (e.g., warm, skirt, horse)

Root word: also called a base word, is a linguistic form to which an affix (prefix or suffix) can be added.

S

Schwa: an obscure vowel sound found in more than 5,000 polysyllabic words in the 10,000 most common English words. It can be heard in the initial syllable of aside, in the second syllable of derivation, and in the final syllable of dyslexia.

Scope and Sequence: List, in order normally taught, of skills within a particular subject area; e.g. Spelling.

Self-corrected test: is a test which is corrected by the testee as part of the process of testing.

Self-paced materials: Educational materials which allow the student to work independently at his own speed.

Silent letters: are letters included in words when written which are not pronounced when speaking.

Specific Language Disability: is a learning disability which only affects the student's ability to learn material related to some aspect of language (such as spelling) or through language (such as reading).

Spelling conscience: is the writer's awareness of the importance of accurate spelling to his reader.

Spelling rules: statements which are used to explain the way in which words can be manipulated when adding affixes or that explain why a word is spelled the way it is spelled. The more accepted term is spelling generalization because the rule is generally true, but may have exceptions.

Spiral Curriculum: Educational programs which have built-in reviews with ever broadening ramifications.

Strephosymbolism: (literally twisted symbols). A term used to designate the tendency that certain students have to reverse letters, parts of words, or even whole words, especially in reading and spelling (saw for was, anaylze for analyze; 710 for oil.) Also referred to as dyslexia and Specific Language Disability.

Study-test plan: spelling instructional approach which begins with study of a predetermined list of words followed by a test to determine student's retention of its correct spelling.

Suffix: an affix attached to the end of a word or word stem.

Survey Test: Initial placement examination which helps determine where placement testing begins.

Syllable: (1) in a spoken language, any one of the basic units of uninterrupted sound that can be used to make up words; or (2) in a written language, any letter or symbol grouping that represents a spoken syllable

Synonym: a word that has a meaning similar or nearly similar to that of another word in the same language.

Systematic Spelling Study: process or session which focuses on the systematic learning of the core high frequency words. In the *Spelling Power* program, this refers to the 15 minute daily sessions.

Student Record Books: Workbook of forms used in the Spelling Power program. Available in four sizes of lines from your educational dealer.

T

Teaching Test: Daily pretest of Flow-Word-Lists.

Ten-step-study sheet: is a special form which guides the student through the ten research-proven steps to learning a word and also allows room for students to use the word in a sentence of their own creation.

Test-study-test plan: is an instructional approach which consists of a pretest prior to instruction, students then study material they need to master. A post-test is administered following study to determine retention of the material.

V

Verb: is a word expressing action or a condition. (Brittany learns something everyday. I am happy.

Visual discrimination: the ability to see the differences in objects, letters, and words.

Visualization: the ability to see (imagine) a word or object that is not actually present.

Vocabulary words: words for which the student must learn the definition.

Vowel: (1) a speech sound made by the relatively free movement of air through the mouth, usually forming the main sound of a syllable; or (2) a letter that represents such a sound.

Note: The vowels are a, e, i, o, and u. The letter y sometimes substitutes for i and is a vowel when it does so. Likewise, the letter w sometimes substitutes for u and is considered to be a vowel when it does so; in fact some people teach that the vowels include w. The difference between y and w, however is that y appears as the only vowel in many syllables (e.g., syll, gym, why), whereas w never appears as a vowel all by itself. When w is used as a vowel it always follows a, e, or o (e.g., paw, new, grow).

W

Word classes: see PARTS OF SPEECH.

Word configuration: see CONFIGURATION.

Selected Bibliography

Adler, Mortimer, J. *The Paideia Principles*. New York: Macmillan Publishing Co., Collier Books, 1984.

Adler, Mortimer, J. *The Paideia Program: An Educational Syllabus (Essays by the Paideia Group)*. New York: Macmillan Publishing Co., Collier Books, 1984.

Adler, Mortimer, J. *The Paideia Proposal: An Educational Manifesto*. New York: Macmillan Publishing Co., Collier Books, 1982.

Alexander, William M. and Saylor, J. Galen. *Modern Secondary Education: Basic Principles and Practices*. New York: Holt, Rinehart, and Winston, 1965.

Allred, Ruel A. *What Research Says to the Teacher: Spelling Trends, Content, and Methods*. Washington, D.C.: National Education Association, 1984.

Applegate, Mauree. *Easy In English: An Imaginative Approach to the Teaching of the Language Arts*. Evanston, Ill.: Harper & Row, 1960.

Ayer, Fred C. "An Evaluation of High School Spelling." *School Review 59*, April 1951, p. 236.

Ayres, Leonard. *A Measuring Scale for Ability in Spelling*. New York: Russell Sage Foundation, 1915.

Baker, Zelma W. *The Language Arts, The Child, and The Teacher*. San Francisco: Butler University, Fearon Publishers, 1955.

Bassett, T. Robert. *Education for the Individual*. New York: Harper & Row, Publishers, 1978.

Baugh, Albert C., and Cable, Thomas, *A History of the English Language*, 3rd ed., Englewood Cliffs, NJ: Prentice-Hall, 1984.

Bechtol, William M. *Individualizing Instruction and Keeping Your Sanity*, Chicago: Follet Publishing Company, 1973.

Beers, James, W., Beers, Carol S., and Grant, Karen, *The Logic Behind Children's Spelling, The Elementary School Journal*, Jan. 77, pp. 238-42.

Beers, James W. and Henderson, Edmund H. "A Study Developing Orthographic Concepts among First Graders," *Research In The Teaching of English II* (Fall 1977, pp. 133-48.

________. Developmental and Cognitive Aspects of Learning to Spell: A Reflection of Word Knowledge, Newark, DE: International Reading Association, 1980.

Bernstein, Abraham. *Teaching English in High School*. New York: Random House, 1961.

Bissex, Glenda L. *GNYS At Work: A Child Learns to Write and Read*, Cambridge: Harvard University Press, 1980.

Boyd, Gertrude A. and Talbert, E. Gene. *Spelling in the Elementary School*. (Arizona State University), Columbus, OH: Charles E. Merrill Publishing Co., 1971.

Breed, Frederick S. *How to Teach Spelling*. E.A. Owen Publishing Co., 1930.

Bryant, Peter and Bradley, Lynette. *The Rhyme and Reason in Reading and Spelling*. Ann Arbor: University of Michigan Press, 1985.

Bruner, Jerome S. *Toward a Theory of Instruction*, Cambridge: Harvard University Press, 1966. (1st: pp. 113-138 and 2nd p. 114)

Buckingham, B.R. and Dolch, E.W. *A Combined Word List*. New York: Ginn and Co., 1936.

Bugelski, B. R. *The Psychology of Learning Applied to Teaching*. Second Edition, Indianapolis: The Bobbs-Merrill Company, Inc., 1964.

Carmody, Harriett. *Let's All Teach Spelling*. Tacoma, WA: Tacoma Public Schools, 1952.

Carroll, John, Davies, Peter and Richman, Barry. *The American Heritage Word Frequency Book*, Boston: Houghton Mifflin Co. 1971.

Chomsky, Carol. "Reading, Writing and Phonology." *Harvard Educational Review*, Vol. 40, pp. 287-309, 1970.

Chomsky, Noam and Halle, Morris. *The Sound Pattern of English*. New York: Harper and Row, 1968.

Clarke, Louise. *Can't Read, Can't Write, Can't Talk Too Good Either: How to Recognize and Overcome Dyslexia in Your Child*. New York: Penguin Books, 1973.

Cohen, Leo A. *Evaluating Structural Analysis Methods Used in Spelling Books*, Ed. D. Thesis, Boston University, 1969.

Cole, Luella. *Psychology of the Elementary School Subjects*. New York: Farrar and Rinehart, Inc., 1934.

Cummings, D.W. *American English Spelling: An Informal Description*. Baltimore: The Johns Hopkins University Press, 1988.

Dale, Edgar and O'Rourke, Joseph, *The Living Word Vocabulary*, Field Enterprises Education Corporation, 1976.

Dallmann, Martha, *Teaching the Language Arts in the Elementary School*, Second Edition, Dubuque, IA: Wm. C. Brown Company, Publishers, 1966.

Dolch, Edward, *The 2,000 Commonest Words for Spelling*, Champaign, IL, Garrand Press, 1942.

________. Better Spelling, Champaign, Il., Garrand Press, 1942.

Doyle, Andrew M. A Study of Spelling Achievement, *Catholic Educational Review*, No. 48, 1950. (p. 171)

Duckworth, E. Language and Thought, In *Piaget in the Classroom*, ed. M. Schwebel and J. Ralph, New York: Basic Books, 1973.

Eaton, Marie D., Hansen, Cheryl L., Haring, Norris, G., Lovitt, Thomas, C. *The Fourth R: Research in the Classroom*, Columbus, OH: Charles E. Merrill Publishing Co., 1978.

Edwards, Sharon A. and Maloy, Robert W. *Kids Have All the Write Stuff: Inspiring Your Children to put Pencil to Paper*, New York: Penquin Group, 1992.

Ferreiro, Emilia, and Ana Teberosky, *Literacy Before Schooling*, Exeter, NH: Heineman Educational Books, 1982.

Fitzsimmons, Robert J., and Loomer, Bradley M. *Spelling: The Research Basis*, Iowa City, University of IA, 1980.

Flanagan, John C., Shanner, William, M., and Mager, Robert F. *Language Arts Behavioral Objectives: A Guide to Individualizing Learning - Primary - Intermediate - Secondary*, Palo Alto, CA: Westinghouse Learning Press, 1971.

Flesch, Rudolf, *Why Johnny Can't Read - and What You Can Do About It*, New York: Harper & Brothers, Publishers, 1955.

Foran, Thomas G. *The Psychology and Teaching of Spelling*, Washington, DC: The Catholic Education Press, 1934.

Frith, Uta, Editor, *Cognitive Processes in Spelling*, New York: Academic Press, 1980.

Gates, Arthur. *A List of Spelling Difficulties in 3,876 Words*. New York: Bureau of Publication, Teachers College, Columbia University, 1937.

________. *Generalization and Transfer in Spelling*, New York: Columbia University, 1935.

________. "An Experimental Comparison in the Study-Test and the Test-Study Method in Spelling." *Journal of Educational Psychology*, Vol. 22, Jan. 1931, pp. 1-19.

Gates, Arthur I., and Russell, D. H. *Diagnostic and Remedial Spelling Manual*, New York: Bureau of Publications, Teacher's College,

Columbia University, 1940.
Gentry, Richard J. *Spel is a Four-Letter Word.* Exeter, NH: Heinemanm Educational Books, 1987.
________. "Developmental Aspects of Learning to Spell." *Academic Therapy* 20 (September): pp. 11-19, 1984.
Gilbert, L.C. "Experimental Investigation of a Flash-Card Method of Teaching Spelling." *Elementary School Journal*, XXXII (1932), pp. 337-51.
Gillingham, Anna and Stillman, Bessie W. *Remedial Training for Children with Specific Disability in Reading, Spelling, and Penmanship.* 5th ed., Cambridge, Mass.: Educators Publishing Service, Inc., 1964.
Graham, Steve and Miller, Lamoine. "Spelling Research and Practice: A Unified Approach." *Focus on Exceptional Children* 12 (October): pp. 1-16, 1979.
Graves, Donald H. "An Examiniation of the Writing Processes of Seven Year Old Children." *Research in Teaching English* 9, 1975, pp. 227-241.
________. *Balance the Basics: Let Them Write*, New York: Ford Foundation, 1978.
________. Reseach Update: Spelling Text and Structural Analysis Methods." *Language Arts* 54 (January) 1977, pp. 86-90.
________. *Writing: Teachers and Children at Work.* Exeter, NH: Heinemann Educational Books, 1983.
Green, Harry A. The New Iowa Spelling Scale, Iowa City, State University of Iowa, 1954.
Groff, Patrick, Phonics: Why & How, Morristown, NJ., General Learning Press, 1977.
Haber, Ralph N. and Haber, Lyn R. The Shape of a Word can Specify Its Meaning, *Reading Research Quarterly*, Vo. XVI, No. 3, New York International Reading Association, Inc., 1981.
Haber, Ralph N. and Hershenson, Maurice, The Psychology of Visual Perception, New York: Holt Rinehart and Winston, 1973.
Hanna, Paul R., Hodges, Richard E., and Hanna, Jean S. Phoneme-Grapheme Correspondences as Cues to Spelling Improvement, Washington, DC: Government Printing Office, U.S. Office of Education, 1966.
________. *Spelling: Structure and Strategies*, Boston, Houghton Mifflin Co., 1971.
Haring, Norris G., Lovitt, Thomas C., Eaton, Marie D., and Hansen, Cheryl L. *The Fourth R: Research in the Classroom*, Columbus, OH: Charles E. Merrill Publishing Company, 1978.
Harris, Alber and Jacobson, Milton J. *Basic Elementary Reading Vocabularies.* New York: The Macmillan Co. 1972.
Henderson, Edmund H. *Learning to Read and Spell: The Child's Knowledge of Words.* DeKalb: Northern Illinois University Press, 1981.
________. *Teaching Spelling.* Boston: Houghton Mifflin Co., 1985.
Henderson, Edmund H. and Templeton, Shane. "A Developmental Perspective of Formal Spelling Instruction Through Alphabet, Pattern, and Meaning." *Elementary School Journal* 86 (January), pp. 304-316, 1986.
Hennings, Dorothy Grant and Grant, Barbara M. *Content and Craft: Written Expression in the Elementary School.* Englewood Cliffs, N.J.: Prentice-Hall, Inc., 1973.
Hildreth, Gertrude. *Teaching Spelling: A Guide to Basic Principles and Practices* New York: Henry Holt & Co., 1955.
________. *Learning the 3 R's.* Minneapolis: Cumberland Education Series, Educational Publishers, Inc., 1947.
________. *Teaching Reading: A Guide to Basic Principles and Modern Practices*, New York: Henry Holt & Co., 1958.
Hilgard, Earnest R., and Sers, Pauline S. "The Teacher's Role in the Motivation of the Learning, in Theories of Learning and Instruction." in *Sixty-third Yearbook of the National Society for the Study of Education*, pt I, Chicago: University of Chicago Press, 1964, pp. 184-187.
Hillerich, Robert L. *Spelling: An Element in Written Expression.* 2nd ed., Columbus, OH: Charles E. Merrill Publishing Company, 1981.
Hodges, Richard E. *Learning to Spell.* Urbana, Il.: National Council of Teachers of English and the ERIC Clearinghouse on Reading Communication, 1981.
Hodges, Richard E. and Rudof, E. Hugh. *Searching Linguistics for Cues for the Teaching of Spelling.*
Hook, J. N. *The Teaching of High School English.* Second Edition, New York: The Ronald Press Co., 1959.
Horn, Ernest. *A Basic Writing Vocabulary: 10,000 Frequently Used Words in Writing.* Iowa City: The University of Iowa, 1926.
________. *Teaching Spelling.* Department of Classroom Teachers, American Education Research Association of the National Education Association, p. 16, January 1954.
________. "Spelling." in *Encyclopedia of Educational Research*, New York: Macmillan and Company, 1960. (p. 1346)
________. *Spelling: What Research Says to the Teacher.* Washington D.C.: National Education Association, 1954.
Horn, Thomas D. "Spelling." in *Encyclopedia of Educational Research*, 4th ed, edited by R.C. Ebel, London: MacMillan Co. 1969, pp 1285-1299.
________. "The Effect of the Corrected Test on Learning to Spell." *Elementary School Journal 47*, pp 277-285, 1947.
Ingersoll, Gary and Smith, Carl. *Children's Writing Vocabulary.* 1982.
________. *Written Vocabulary of Elmentary School Pupils, Ages 6-14.* Indiana University, 1984.
Jones, Daisy M. *Curriculum Target in the Elementary School.* Englewood Cliffs, NJ: Prentice-Hall, Inc., 1972.
Kucera, Henry and Nelson, Francis. *Computational Analysis of Present-Day American English.* Providence, RI: Brown University Press, 1967.
Lee, Doris May and Lee, J. Murry. "Spelling Needs a Teacher." *Elementary English Review*, 1946, vol. 23, p. 203-206.
Lewis, Norman. *Correct Spelling Made Easy.* New York: Random House, 1963.
Loomer, Bradley M. *The New Iowa Spelling Scale.* Iowa City: Useful Curriculum Corporation, 1987.
Love, Pauline, ed. *Spelling Resource Book.* Seattle, WA: Shoreline Public Schools, no date given.
Lyman, Donald, E. *Making the Words Stand Still: A Master Teacher Tells How to Overcome Specific Learning Disability, Dyslexia, and Old-Fashioned Word Blindness.* Boston: Houghton Mifflin Co., 1986.
Marckwardt, Albert H., ed. "Linguistics in School Programs." in *Sixty-ninth Yearbook of the National Society of the Study of Education*, pt 2. Chicago: The University of Chicago Press, 1970.
Martin. *Stages of Progress in Language, In Talking and Writing.* ed. J. Brelton, London: Metheun, 1967.
Mazurkieewicz, Albert J. *Teaching About Phonics.* New York: St. Martin's Press, 1976.
McGuigan, C.A. "The Effects of a Flowing Word List and the Implementation of Procedures in the Add-a-word Spelling Paper." *Working Paper No. 52*, Experimental Education Unit, University of Washington, Seattle, WA: 1975.
McIntire, Alta. "Spelling Can Be Fun." *Elementary English Review*, 1945, Vol. 22, 271-272.

Nelson, Mary Ann. *Spelling Guide for Grades 1 to 6*. Tacoma, WA: Tacoma Public Schools, 1964.
Parker, Donald H. *Schooling for Individual Excellence*. New York: Thomas Nelson & Sons, 1963.
Peters, Robert A. *A Linguistic History of English*, Boston: Houghton Mifflin Co., 1968.
Platts, Mary E., Sr. Rose Marguerite, s.g.c., and Shumaker, Esther. *Spice: Suggested Activities to Motivate the Teaching of the Language Arts*. Stevensville, MI: Educational Service, Inc., 1960.
Platts, Mary E. *Anchor: A Handbook of Vocabulary Discovery Techniques for the Classroom Teacher*. Stevensville, MI: Educational Service, Inc., 1970.
Read, Charles and Hodges, Richard. *Spelling in Encyclopedia of Educational Research*. 5th ed. New York: The Free Press, 1982.
Read, Charles. *Children's Categorization of Speech Sounds in English*. Urbana, IL: NCTE, 1975.
________. "Pre-school Children's Knowledge of English Phonology." *Harvard Education Review* 41, pp. 1-34, 1971.
Rinsland, Henry. *A Basic Vocabulary of Elementary School Children* New York: Macmillan Co., 1945.
Sakiey, Elizabeth and Fry, Edward *3,000 Instant Words: Revised Edition*. Providence, RI: Jamestown Publishers, 1984.
Sayers, Dorothy L. *The Lost Tools of Learning*. London: Methuen, (pamphlet), 1948.
Schonell, Fred J. *The Essential Spelling List: 3200 Everyday Words Selected, Graded and Grouped According to Common Difficulty*. London: Macmillan Co., Ltd. 1932.
Scott, Louise Binder and Thompson, J. J. *Phonics: In Listening, In Speaking, In Reading, In Writing*. Webster Publishing Company, 1962.
Scragg, D. G. *A History of English Spelling*. Manchester: Manchester University Press, 1974.
Shane, Harold G., Walden, James, and Green, Ronald. *Interpreting Language Arts Research For the Teacher*. Washington DC: Association for Supervision and Curriculum Development, NEA, 1971.
Sherwin, Joseph S. *Four Problems in Teaching English: A Critique of Research*. Scranton, Penn.: International Textbook Co., 1969, p. 104.
Smith, Lee L. *A Practical Approach to the Nongraded Elementary School*. West Nyack, NY: Parker Publishing Company, Inc., 1968.
Spalding, Romalda Bishop with Spalding, Walter T. *The Writing Road to Reading*. New York: Quill/William Morrow, 1957.
Stetson, Eldon, Taylor, Wendy, and Bautin, Frances J. *Eight Years of Theory and Practice in Spelling and Those Who Wrote the Programs Forgot to Read the Literature*. Clearwater, FL: National Reading Conference, 1982.
Stevenson, Nancy. *The Natural Way to Reading: A How to Method for Parents of Slow Learners, Dyslexic, and Learning Disabled Children* Boston: Little Brown and Co., 1974.
Temple, Charles, and Wallace-Gillet, Jean. *Language Arts: Learning Processes and Teaching Practices*. Boston: Little, Brown and Co., 1984.
________. *Understanding Reading Problems: Assessement and Instruction*. 2nd ed., Boston: Little, Brown and Co., 1986.
________. *The Beginnings of Writing*. 2nd ed., Boston: Allyn and Bacon, 1988.
Templeton, Shane. :Spelling, First, Sound Later: The Relationship Between Orthography and Higher Order Phonological Knowledge in Older Students.: *Research in the Teaching of English* 13, October 1979, pp. 255-64.
Tiedt, Iris McClellan and Tiedt, Sidney Willis. *Elementary Teacher's New Complete Ideas Handbook*. Englewood Cliffs, NJ: Prentice-Hall, Inc., 1983.
Thomas, Ves. *Teaching Spelling: Canadian Word Lists and Instructional Techniques*. Calgary, Alberta: Gage Educational Publishing Limited, 1974.
________. "The Basic Writing Vocabulary of Elementary School Children." *The Alberta Journal of Educational Research* XVIII, No. 4, (December) 1972, pp 243-248.
________. "A Spelling Errors Analysis and an Appraisal of its Usefulness in Improving the Spelling of Selected Alberta Students." Doctoral dissertation, University of Oregon, 1966.
Trowbridge, C.R. *Constructive Spelling*. New York: Macmillan Co., 1928.
Vallins, G. H. *Spelling: With a Chapter on American Spelling by Professor John W. Clark*. Fair Lawn, NJ: Essential Books, Inc., 1954.
Venezky, Richard L. "English Orthography: Its Graphical Structure and Its Relation to Sound." *Reading Research Quarterly* 2, pp. 75-105, Spring 1967.
________. *The Structure of English Orthography*. The Hague: Mouton and Company, 1970.
Wagner, Hosier, Blackman. *Language Games* Darien, CN: Teacher's Publishing Corporation, 1963.
Wallace, Gerald and Larsen, Stephen C. *Educational Assessment of Learning Problems: Testing for Teaching*. Boston: Allyn and Bacon, Inc., 1978.
Washburne, Carleton W. and Marland, Sidney P., Jr. *Winnetka: The History and Significance of an Educational Experiment*, Englewood Cliffs, NJ: Prentice-Hall, Inc., 1963.
Warren, Virginia Burgess. *Tested Ways to Help Your Child Learn*. Englewood Cliffs, NJ: Prentice-Hall, Inc., 1961.
Wheat, Leonard B. "Four Spelling Rules." *Elementary School Journal*, May, 1952.
Williams, Ralph M. "The Teaching of Spelling" in *Encyclopedia of Education* (Vol. 8, pp. 387-391), New York: Crowell-Collier Educational Corporation, The Macmillan Co., 1971.
Wisconsin Cooperative Educational Planning Program. *Spelling in the Language Arts*. Madison: Wisconsin State Superintendent of Schools, 1949.
Wolfe, Donald M. *Creative Ways to Teach English: Grades 7 to 12*, New York: The Odyssey Press, 1958.
Zutell, Jerry, "Spelling Strategies of Primary School Children and Their Relationship to Piaget's Concept of Decentration." *Research in the Teaching of English* 13 (February) 1979, pp. 69-80.

Spelling Power Group Rules

Group 1 — Usually /a/ is spelled a as in *cat*.
Group 2 — Usually /e/ is spelled e as in *nest*.
Group 3 — Usually /i/ is spelled i as in *big*.
Group 4 — Usually /o/ is spelled o as in *not*.
Group 5 — Usually /u/ is spelled u as in *run*.
Group 6 — /ā/ can be written ay, ai, ey, ei, eigh, ea, or a followed by a consonant and silent e as in *day*, *came*, or *sprain*.
Group 7 — /ē/ can be spelled ea, ee, y, ie, ei, ey, io, or e followed by a consonant and silent e as in *freeze*, *field*, or *mean*.
Group 8 — /ī/ can be spelled ie, igh, y, or i followed by two consonants as in *wild* or as i followed by a consonant and silent e as in *kite*.
Group 9 — /ō/ can be spelled oe, ow, oa, or o followed by two consonants as in *told* or as o followed by a consonant and silent e as in *home*.
Group 10 — /ū/ can be spelled ew as in *few*, ue as in *blue*, ui as in *suit*, o as in *to*, or as u followed by a consonant and silent e as in *mule*.
Group 11 — /àr/ is usually spelled ar as in *jar*.
Group 12 — /ûr/ can be spelled ir as in *bird*, er as in *her*, ur as in *survey*, er as in *eternity*, ear as in *pearl*, our as in *journal*, or or after w as in *work*.
Group 13 — /or/ can be spelled or as in *corn*, oar as in *boar*, oor as in *door*, our as *your*, and ar as *dwarf*.
Group 14 — /âr/ can be spelled are as *care*, air as in *hair*, ere as in *there*, ear as in *bear*, and eir as in *their*.
Group 15 — /îr/ can be spelled ear as in *hear*, eer as in *deer*, ere as in *here*, ier as in *pier*, er as in *period*, or eir as in *weird*.
Group 16 — Usually /ou/ is spelled ou before most consonants as in *cloud*. Sometimes /ou/ is spelled ow before final l or n as in *howl* or *clown* or at the end of a word or syllable as in *how* or *tower*.
Group 17 — /ô/ can be spelled a, o, and au before most consonants as in *already*, *cost*, and *sauce* or as augh or ough before t as in *sought* and *caught* or as aw before final k, l, n as *hawk*, *crawl*, and *lawn* or at the end of a word or stressed syllable as in *awful* or *law*.
Group 18 — /oi/ can be spelled oy as in *toy* or oi as *boil*.
Group 19 — /u/ can be spelled u as in *put*, ou as in *would* or as oo as in *took*.
Group 20 — Sometimes the letter o represents unexpected sounds as in *come*, *mother* and *one*.
Group 21 — Q is always followed by u in English words such as in *quite*.
Group 22 — Some words have silent letters such as with the k in *knew*, the w in *write*, and the l in *talk*.
Group 23 — No English words end with the letter v.
Group 24 — Consonant letters are often doubled after a short vowel in short vowel words such as *egg*, *fluff*, *sniffle*, and *mess*.
Group 25 — Sometimes /yûr/ can be spelled ure as in *pure*.
Group 26 — When adding the suffixes ness and ly to words not ending in y the spelling of the base word stays the same, as in *slowly*.
Group 27 — When added to another syllable or used as a suffix, *till* and *full* are spelled with only one l as in *until* and *beautiful*.
Group 28 — /àn/ is sometimes spelled en as in *golden*.
Group 29 — /àl/ can be spelled le as in *little*, el as in *rebel*, al as in *total*, il as in *council*, ol as in *capitol*, ul as in *consul*, and ile as *futile*.
Group 30 — Words are regularly made plural by adding s, but if the word ends with sh, zh, z, s, j, ch, or x sounds, the plural is generally formed by adding es, which is pronounced as a separate syllable.
Group 31 — Plurals of some nouns are formed irregularly. **Level D:** Some nouns ending in f or fe change those terminations to ve in the plural form as in *leaf* to *leaves*. **Level E:** A few nouns form their plural by changing a single vowel, such as in *man* to *men*. **Level H:** Some words derived from foreign languages retain the plural of those languages such as *datum* to *data*.
Group 32 — When adding a suffix to a word ending in y, change the y to i, unless a vowel proceeds the y, as in *try* to *tried* and *baby* to *babies*.
Group 33 — When adding a suffix that begins with a vowel, the final e is usually dropped, as in *chase* to *chasing*.
Group 34 — In short vowel words, the final consonant is usually doubled before adding a suffix, such as when changing in *stop* to *stopped*.
Group 35 — Proper nouns must begin with a capital letter because they refer to a specific name or title of a person, place, time, thing, or idea such as *Monday*.
Group 36 — New words are often made by putting two short words together into one word as in *cowboy*.
Group 37 — An apostrophe is used to take the place of a letter when two words are joined. These words are called contractions.
Group 38 — Some words are joined by a hyphen, such as *twenty-two*.
Group 39 — Sometimes two words are used together but are spelled separately, such as *home school*.
Group 40 — An apostrophe is used to show ownership such as in *the boy's ball* except with the neuter pronoun it (its: possessive, it's: contraction of it is).
Group 41 — Words are sometimes shortened into abbreviations. A period is used after most abbreviations such as in *Sun.* for *Sunday*. Initials are also abbreviations and should be followed with a period. Two letter state and provincial postal are exceptions to this rule.
Group 42 — /shun/ can be spelled tion as in *vacation*, sion as in *division*, or cian as in *physician*.
Group 43 — /às/ can be spelled ous as in *nervous* or ace as in *menace*.
Group 44 — /ànse/ can be spelled ance as in *substance* or ence as in *experience*.
Group 45 — /ment/ is usually spelled ment as in *elements*.
Group 46 — The addition of a prefix does not usually change the spelling of the root word. **Level F:** Some prefixes signify quantity as in uni for one in *uniform* or bi for two in *bicycle*. **Level G:** The prefixes de can mean *down* or *from* such as in the words *describes* and *delivery*. **Level H:** The prefix re can mean *back* or *again* as in the words *remake* or *reduced*. **Level I:** The prefixes *con*, *com*, *cor*, *col*, *sym* or *syn* all usually mean *with* or *together*. **Level J:** The prefix ex usually means *out of*, *away*, or *from* as in the words *explore* and *extent*. **Level K:** The prefixes dis, mis, des, irr, non, de, in, un, im and ill usually mean *not* or *incorrect* as in the words *disappear* and *mistake*.
Group 47 — These words are unusual words and are exceptions to the most common generalizations.

American—British Spelling Comparison in the *Spelling Power* Program

airplane — aeroplane E-36
airplanes — aeroplanes F-36
aluminum — aluminium K-3
analyze — analyse H-29
armor — armour K-13
bright-colored — bright-coloured
canceled — cancelled
canceling — cancelling
carburetor — carburettor I-25
catalog — catalogue
catalogs — catalogues
center — centre G-12
centered — centred
centers — centres I-28
centiliter — centilitre F-46
centimeter — centimetre F-46
checkbook — chequebook
color — colour D-13
colorful — colourful E-27
coloring — colouring
colorless — colourless
colors — colours G-13
councilor — councillor
counselor — counsellor
counterrevolution — counter-revolution
cozier — cosier
cozy — cosy
defense — defence
defenseless — defenceless
dishonor — dishonour
distill — distil
endeavor — endeavour
equaled — equalled
favor — favour I-13
favorable — favourable
favored — favoured
favorite — favourite B-13
favorites — favourites
favors — favours
fiber — fibre
fiberglass — fibreglass
fibers — fibres
flavor — flavour K-13
flavorful — flavourful I-27
florescent — fluorescent
fulfill — fulfil
harbor — harbour H-11
harbors — harbours
heartrending — heart-rending K-36
hemorrhage — haemorrhage K-2
homemade — home-made
honor — honour E-22
honorable — honourable
honored — honoured
honors — honours
humor — humour K-13
humorless — humourless
humorous — humourous H-43
jewelry — jewellery
kiloliter — kilolitre F-46
kilometer — kilometre F-46
labeled — labelled
labor — labour J-13
laborer — labourer
leveled — levelled
liter — litre
maneuver — manoeuvre J-10
maneuverable — manoeuvrable
marvelous — marvellous I-43
milliliter — millilitre F-46
millimeter — millimetre F-46
misdemeanor — misdemeanour
modeling — modelling
mold — mould J-9
molds — moulds
mustache — moustache
neighbor — neighbour C-6
neighbor's — neighbour's G-40
neighborhood — neighbourhood I-6
neighboring — neighbouring
neighbors — neighbours F-30
neighbors' — neighbours'
nighttime — night-time
nonprofit — non-profit K-46
odor — odour
odors — odours
omelet — omelette
orangutan — orang-utan
pajamas — pyjamas
paralyze — paralyse
paralyzed — paralysed I-14
parlor — parlour
practice — practise
practiced — practised
practicing — practising
pretense — pretence
rivaled — rivalled
rumor — rumour
shoveling — shovelling
signaled — signalled
skillful — skilful I-27
specialty — speciality
splendor — splendour
standby — stand-by
sulfur — sulphur
teammate — team-mate
teammates — team-mates K-36
theater — theatre
theaters — theatres
transferal — transferral
traveled — travelled
traveler — traveller
travelers — travellers K-29
traveling — travelling I-29
tricolor — tricolour F-46
vapor — vapor J-13
videotape — video-tape
vigor — vigour
vigorous — vigourous
vigorously — vigourously
woolen — woollen
workout — work-out

Index

Now You Can Give Your Students

Writing Power Too!

Writing Power is a comprehensive curriculum guide for teaching compositions, grammar, usage, and punctuation to your preschool through high school level students. Written by *Spelling Power* author **Beverly L. Adams-Gordon**, *Writing Power* shows you how you can teach your children effective writing skills through multi-sensory, multi-level, and individualized approaches.

Writing Power uses a realistic, natural "family learning approach." No more will you be required to purchase a separate English program for each of your children, each year. *Writing Power* eliminates your having to juggle several completely different English lesson plans each day. Instead, everyone in your family is working together! Yet *Writing Power*'s approach allows you to focus on each individual family member's instructional needs. It is truly a program designed for and by home educators.

Writing Power gives you the background information you need to make writing an integral part of your entire home school day. It provides you with a systematic approach to teaching the necessary grammar and punctuation skills in an innovative way. You will also find important tools you can use to conduct exciting and effective composition instruction for your kindergarten to grade 12 students. The format is designed to allow you to review key concepts or learn them right along with your students. At the same time, those with more confidence can use the extensive resources found in *Writing Power* as they choose.

You will find that *Writing Power* fits in beautifully with many home school approaches, in particular unit study and literature-based approaches, Charlotte Mason, Montessori, and principle approaches, as well as traditional and classical home education models. Even if you are an "unschooler," you will find *Writing Power* an excellent resource for helping your student improve his writing.

You won't find boring "drill and kill" worksheets in *Writing Power*. Instead, you will find well-planned composition assignments and projects, concrete grading and scoring procedures, and fun, relevant activities and exercises. And most importantly, you will find each activity, exercise, and resource in *Writing Power* consistent with your Christian values.

Order: 238 ..... $49.95

Sound & Articulation Activities for children with Speech-Language Problems

While primarily a speech resource, this practical resource gives teachers a store of stimulating, easy-to-use activities to help students practice difficult sounds and words. The activities also help teach the sound/symbol associations. Beverly L. Adams-Gordon, author of the *Spelling Power* program, sees the book as a great value to most phonics programs and is currently using the activities in combination with other readiness materials and The Basic Phonics System with Brittany Ann.

"The sense of hearing must reach a certain level of development before phonics instruction can be effective. This book provides lots of fun ways to build auditory discrimination skills while providing other valuable language arts activities," says Adams-Gordon.

The activities are organized into 44 sections focusing on initial single consonant beginning sounds, final single consonant sounds, initial digraphs and blends, and final combined sounds.

Each section follows the same format and offers a variety of opportunities for children to practice a sound in context. It includes:

- ➔ flannel board story with four-color figures
- ➔ Vocabulary/Intensive Listening Practice Lists
- ➔ suggestions for extra practice activities
- ➔ reproducible activity pages.
- ➔ poem, emphasizing the sound, sung to familiar tunes
- ➔ puppet character to make with students
- ➔ song titles and literature to enhance the lessons

In *Spelling Power* author Beverly L. Adams-Gordon recommends *Sound & Articulation Activities for children with Speech-Language Problems* as an excellent resource for students in preschool through grade three who have difficulties in articulation and auditory discrimination (hearing the differences between sounds). Such difficulties can hinder your student's ability to learn to read and spell. According to research, mispronunciations cause approximately 33% of all spelling errors.

Order 128-5 .... $37.95

Spelling Power

A Comprehensive Multi-age, Multi-sensory Spelling Program

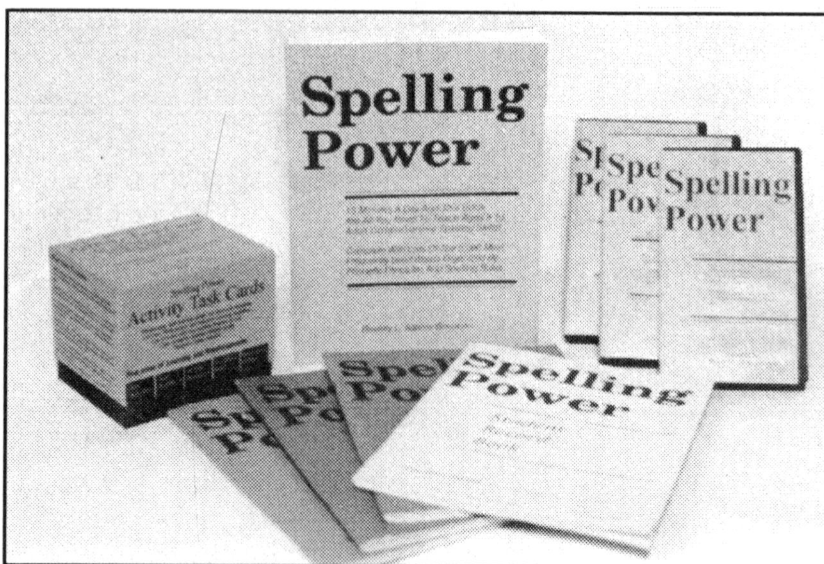

The Spelling Power *manual is described on this page. Optional materials are sold separately and described on the next page.*

Requiring just fifteen minutes a day, *Spelling Power* is totally individualized. This individualization allows each of your students to begin, progress and succeed at his own pace to master the 5,000 words children and adults use and misspell most frequently.

Your students will use the research proven test-study-test method, along with immediate self-correction, to master word lists which are organized by phonetic principles and spelling rules.

Additional words which your students need to master are discovered from your students' own writing errors and added to your *Spelling Power* program using the resources provided. Your students will continue to study each of these words until they have spelled them correctly at least once. Then *Spelling Power's* spiral curriculum approach of repeated, spaced review will ensure your students master every word they study. And your students **will** master them! The six levels of built-in review ensure that every word taught will be mastered.

Multi-sensory study steps, inductive learning activities, interesting games, and the incorporation of spelling into the rest of your curriculum are integral aspects of the *Spelling Power* program.

Everything you need to teach each of your students spelling skills to the college level is contained in this one easy-to-use, step-by-step curriculum manual. Even if you are new to teaching, you'll find that *Spelling Power's* easy to understand instructions will help you give each of your students **spelling power in only 15 minutes a day**.

19X **$49.95**

"You can successfully use this one book to teach all of your children throughout their school years."

Cathy Duffy
Christian Curriculum Manuals

"The work is a great contribution to spelling methodology."

Ted Wade
The Home School Manual

"Picks up where phonics leaves off."

Sarah Rose
Author, KONOS H. S. Program

"Independent home schoolers will appreciate the self-correction that is integral to the program."

Mary Ehrmin
The Drinking Gourd

"Spelling Power offers your child the academic equivalence of a daily trip to the gym: a well-balanced workout that pumps up those spelling muscles"

Mary Pride
Practical Homeschooling

For more information, visit our web page at: www.castlemoyle.com

Fonts for Teachers

Now you can create your own penmanship exercises and worksheets of all types. Fonts4Teachers is a CD-ROM containing the popular handwriting styles: Manuscript, D'Nealian, and Cursive. Letters available in any size with handwriting lines, dotted lines and arrows. Many options included. You'll also find handwriting preparation exercises, math, clocks, American Sign Language, clip-art, and decorative fonts. You'll find this a easy-to-use indispensable tool for creating your own materials for unit studies and more! PC/Mac compatible.

Order F4T03-0 .... **$39.95**

Here's a sampling of some of the fonts you get!

Abc Abc Abc Abc Abc

Activity Task Cards Ease Parents' Lesson Planning

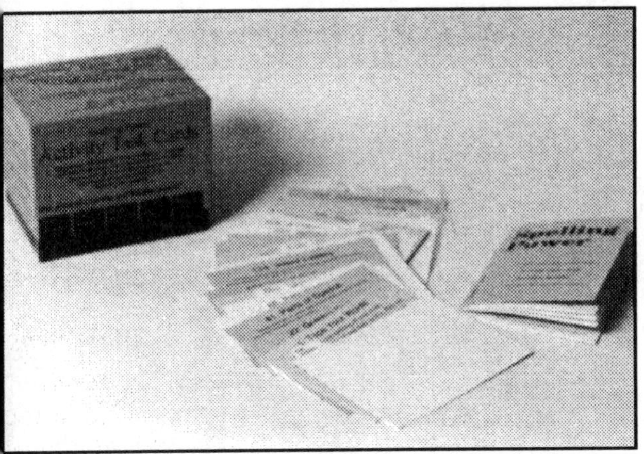

The 365 Activity Task Cards come in a sturdy box.

Spelling Power Activity Task Cards give you hundreds of ways to make spelling easy-to-teach and easy-to-learn. They help your student to master spelling words and strengthen language arts skills.

Just like *Spelling Power*, the *Activity Task Cards* box covers interest and ability levels ranging from eight years old to adult level. You will find the Activity Task Card box easy to use, since every card is color-coded by ability-interest level. Each instructional activity requires just five to ten minutes for students to complete on their own. The *Spelling Power Activity Task Cards* deliver FUNdamental learning with little or no teacher involvement.

Use these cards during *Spelling Power's* five minute "activity time." The handy *Teacher's Guide* included in the *Spelling Power Activity Task Cards* box can help you virtually eliminate lesson planning.

1-888827-10-6 .... **29.95**

Quick Start Video

Basic Approach To Daily Spelling Lessons

This all new video-seminar, presented by author Beverly L. Adams-Gordon, focuses on the basic approach to daily spelling sessions using *Spelling Power*. You'll be guided step-by-step through the key aspects of the *Spelling Power* program. After watching this 60-minute video-seminar you will be able to start using the *Spelling Power* program with little or no advanced preparation.

New Version!

Order: 246 .... **$24.95**

The Harp and Laurel Wreath

Poetry and Dictation for the Classical Curriculum

Convinced that a critical part of education is to foster in our children a love of the beautiful and true, teacher and writer Laura Berquist presents this wide selection of poetry for every age level from grades one to twelve. Language development is significantly enriched by exposure to good poetry. This book is an important resource because it provides in one volume many poems that concern noble actions or ideas presented in beautiful patterns of sound.

The Harp and Laurel Wreath contains all the poems recommended in Berquist's best-selling *Designing Your Classical Curriculum* and includes poems by Robert Louis Stevenson, Henry Wadsworth Longfellow, Robert Browning, William Shakespeare, G.K. Chesterton, William Butler Yeats, Robert Frost, and many others. There are three indices to help locate specific poems. This book also includes dictation selections that are useful tools in the development of the child's writing ability, as well as study questions and answers for each poem.

Order **HLW-037** $19.95

Spelling Power Blank Word Cards

These business-card sized blank cards are used for many of the games and activities described in the *Spelling Power* Manual and the Activity Task Card Boxes.

1-888827-bwc **3.95**

Students enjoy working in their own record books.

Student Record Books Save Time and Money

Each *Spelling Power* Student Record Book provides enough forms for one student to master the words on one level of the *Spelling Power* program. Conveniently bound, with all forms printed in light blue (so the student's own handwriting stands out), these pre-printed books cost less per page than photocopying the masters provided in the *Spelling Power* manual. **See back of Order Form for size recommendations.**

Available in four sizes of lines:

- Red (06-8)- 5/8" with broken mid-line for K-3rd
- Blue (07-6) - 1/2" with broken mid-line for 2-4th
- Green (08-4) - 3/8" with broken mid-line for 4th-6th
- Yellow (09-2)- No broken mid-line for 6th and up.

27-(specify color #) **$5.95**

Dictionaries and Reference Materia

The following dictionaries are recommended in the *Spelling Power* manual by author Beverly L. Adams-Gordon. The four volumes are graded for age appropriateness by the number of words listed, yet they all maintain the same diacritical marking system.

There are other advantages to Merriam-Webster dictionaries over other dictionaries. The most important of these is because the company only produces dictionaries and thesauri (and a few other select reference materials), you can high quality. Also, they are the original "Webster's" ing company, now known as Merriam-Webster. Not "Webster" dictionary is printed by the original comp Since the name is not trademarked or copyrighted, ar use it. Make sure you buy a "Merriam-Webster" whe look for dictionaries.

Merriam-Webster's Elementary Dictionary

For Grades 2 through 4, this beginning level dictionary contains over 32,000 entries and hundreds of full color illustrations. Easy-to-read type.

MWD575-4 $15.95

Merriam Webster's Intermediate Dictionary

For grades four through six, this dictionary contains over 58,000 entries. It includes a fifty page special section on "Using Your Dictionary."

MWD479-0 $15.95

Merriam-Webster's School Dictionary

For middle school and/or junior high students, this dictionary contains over 80,000 entries. Also includes biographical and geographical sections. Excellent resource.

MWD380-8 $15.95

Merriam Webste Collegiate Dictio

For high school stud adults, this dictionary 160,000 entries which over 23,875 verbal tions. Also includes 7 onym lists.

MWD708-0 19

Merriam Webster's School Thesaurus

Perfect for the intermediate age child (grades 4 through 8) with over 43,000 entries. Working with a thesaurus will help improve your student's vocabulary and writing.

MWD178-3 $15.95

Merriam Webster's Collegiate Thesaurus

For authoritative reference, this totally new thesaurus has more than 100,000 synonyms, antonyms, and related entries. Excellent choice for teens and adults. Indexed.

MWD169-4 $17.95

Elementary Grammar

Help your beginning writers acquire a firm foundation in the proper use of their language. Covers: sentence structure; nouns and pronouns, verbs, adjectives and adverbs; punctuation; word study, and includes exercises for practice after each topic. (1st-4th)

GB26 . . . . $13.95

Intermediate Gramr

Building on the ski taught in *Elementary Grammar*, you can use book to maximize you child's educational exp ence by putting the ans at his fingertips. Includ practice exercises for e topic covered. (5th-8tl

GB34 . . . . $1

Language Arts Materials

Rummy Roots and More Roots

Rummy Roots and *More Roots* are two card games designed to help increase English vocabulary in a fun and challenging way. Vocabulary is increased by learning the 42 Greek and Latin roots through playing each game (42 roots per deck). Greek and Latin roots form many of our English words. Knowing these roots adds a deeper level of comprehension to reading, aids understanding of how to spell words, and will help increase SAT scores.

These games can be played by the entire family (at least those over eight) or just mom and child together. The games incorporate all learning styles, so that everyone will benefit from participation. Each deck offers four levels of play and simple rules based on popular card games. Most importantly *Rummy Roots* and *More Roots* don't take a lot of "mom involvement" to keep the learning on track. The cards can even be used as a "concentration game" when your student is looking for something fun to do on his own.

Rummy Roots .... (ETH001) $14.95
More Roots .... (ETH002) $14.95

(New price effective 2/14/03)

Commas Are Our Friends

Here is the fun and easy way to introduce or review Grammar without grief and Punctuation without pain. Author Joe Devine uses the devices of fiction to explain the fine and essential elements of English grammar, punctuation and usage.

The book (really three separate stories spanning a total of 29 short chapters) presents all these mundane details in humorous and unforgettable style. The first story: *Aloysius Muldoon and the Parts of Speech* explains the use of each part of speech. The second story: *Commas Are Our Friends* describes the function and use of each of the punctuation marks. The final story: *Mudhill's Monument* discusses some of key usage and style elements needed for effective communication.

This book can be used by moms and dads as a fun refresher, a course for teens, or a family learn and read together. Highly recommended!

GSP1078 .... $14.95

How To Read A Book

This classic text, originally written in the 1940s, teaches teens (definitely high school level) and adults how to get more out of their reading and research. Gives an outline of a Great Books Reading Program. It explains various levels of reading and "interacting" with the author. Highly recommended. Parents will find it helpful for teaching their intermediate and above readers. Assigned reading for many Advance Placement courses because it really increases reading and study skills as well as discrimination skills.

SSPC97-2 --- $15.00

High School Materials

Home School, High School, and Beyond ...

This text is a nine-week (one-quarter credit), high school course designed to help your Christian home schooled teen take a more active, thoughtful role in his education. Beginning with goal setting, your teen will learn the importance of using their time and talents for God's glory!

You and your teen will learn the recommended high school course of study. You will learn how to create your own courses, including how to translate life experience into credits. You will be shown four approaches to high school: traditional, modified, unit study, and an independent.

Teens and their parents are guided in collecting, organizing, and maintaining high school home schooling records in preparation for college or other post-high school education and career. The reproducible forms provided will be used throughout the high school years.

Here's What You'll Do:

5th Edition with CD-ROM!

Learn Goal Setting
Master Time Management
Explore Career Options
Organize High School Records
Prepare For College

1-888827-15-7 .... $19.95

New products added weekly at www.castlemoyle.com

Italic Handwriting Series: A Complete Learning Program

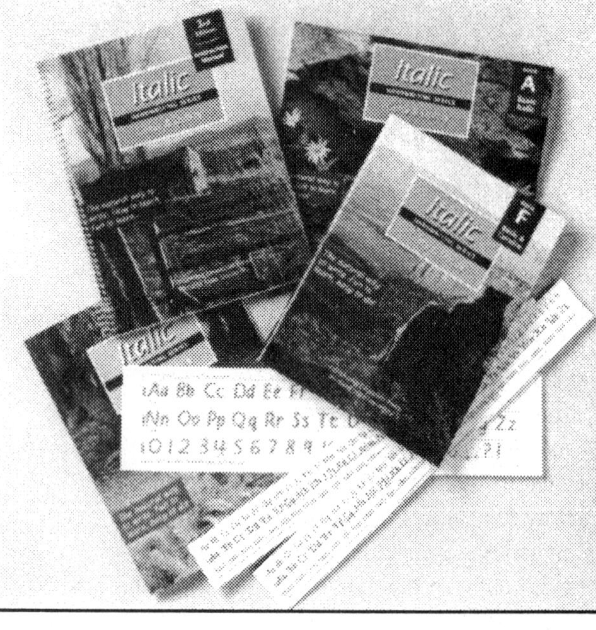

The *Italic Handwriting Series* by Barbara Getty and Inga Dubay is a comprehensive, self-directed handwriting program. The series contains everything you need to teach the italic hand to any age group and any kind of student — including right- or left-handed and gifted or learning disabled.

Italic is a simple, legible, logical way to write that smooths the troublesome printing-to-cursive transition and gives students a distinctive, readable hand that lasts a lifetime.

"The Italic Handwriting Series ... is the program recommended by this author for both beginning writers and those who have been unsuccessful in acquiring abilities in handwriting by other methods."

Beverly L. Adams-Gordon
Spelling Power

Since students develop at different rates, the determination of which book is appropriate for a student should be decided by the teacher in each case. For children who have already been introduced to another style, we suggest starting out with the book appropriate for their current grade level. Each book in the series reintroduces the basic italic alphabet, making it unnecessary for older students to start from the very beginning.

Book A - Kindergarten

With clever illustrations and plenty of space for writing and drawing, this book introduces basic italic lowercase and capital letters, one letter per page. Includes Numerals. Letter height - 14 mm.

PSU 108(A) $6.75

Book B - 1st Grade

For the beginning reader, this book covers the entire alphabet and numerals. With its short words and lively sentences, this book is a lot of fun. Letter height 11 & 9 mm.

PSU 108(B) $6.75

Book C - 2nd grade

This book is considered the transition book. Writing practice is devoted primarily to the acquisition of basic italic using days of the week, months of the year, and more. The entrance and exit strokes, which are added to form cursive italic, and the first five joins are introduced. Includes numerals. Letter height - 9 & 6 mm.

PSU 108(C) $6.75

Book D - 3rd grade

Who wouldn't enjoy writing that included tongue twisters and limericks? This book introduces all of the joins, vowel and consonant sounds, prefixes and suffixes, and twelve rules of capitalization. In addition, the introduction of cursive capitals. Letter height - 6 & 5 mm.

PSU 108(D) $6.75

Book E - 4th grade

With writing practice on topics ranging from the solar system to plants and animals, Book E is a welcome complement to your entire school curriculum. While practicing cursive italic joins, students explore the many facets of the world of science. As a special treat, upon completion of the book, students are shown how to make their own booklet and envelope! Letter height - 6, 5, & 4 mm.

PSU 108(E) $6.75

Book F - 5th grade

As they discover figures of speech, older students learn how our English language works. Writing practice includes: synonyms and antonyms, compound words, acronyms, analogies, metaphors, similes, idioms, euphemisms, vowel and consonant sounds, prefixes, suffixes, and abbreviations. Pop-Up Card is final project of book. Letter height - 6, 5, & 4 mm.

PSU 108(F) $6.75

Book G - 6th - 8th grade

This final book in the series contains writing practice paragraphs acquainting the student with a brief history of the origins of our letters, from cave paintings to copperplate. Rich in meaningful instruction, the last few pages of the book are reserved for experimentation with edged pens. Letter height - 6, 5, & 4 mm.

PSU 108(G) $6.75

Italic Handwriting Instruction Manual

An invaluable resource. This guid contains detailed instructions fo teaching each letter and join; nume ous assessment strategies; creativ student activities; techniques for in creasing speed, and developing a pe sonal style; and complete informatio needed to effectively teach italic hand writing. 108 pages.

PSU 108(I) $6.75

Write Now! Italic Handwriting Vide

This video is designed to suppo users of the italic program and can b used by parents or students. Each le ter is introduced showing accurate le ter formation. After introduction to ba sic italic, the viewer is shown the flui movements needed to form cursiv italic. The transition from printing t cursive is easy and fun.

0-9649215-02 .... $29.9

Write Now

A complete self-teaching prograr for better handwriting intended fo teens and adults, *Write Now* provide everything needed to enable student to develop a clean, elegant, and leg ible italic hand. You'll find it simpl to follow and full of step-by-step guid ance and tips. Changing your hand writing is surprisingly easy with regu lar practice. Makes a great gift.

PSU 125 .... $13.9

A Landscape with Dragons

The Battle for Your Child's Mind

In this study of the pagan invasion of children's culture, O'Brien, the father of six, describes his own coming to terms with the effect it has had on his family and on most families in Western society. His analysis of the degeneration of books, films, and videos for the young is incisive and detailed. Yet his approach is not simply critical, for he suggests a number of remedies, including several tools of discernment for parents and teachers in assessing the moral content and spiritual impact of this insidious revolution. In doing so, he points the way to rediscovery of time-tested sources, and to new developments in Christian culture.

If you have ever wondered why a certain children's book or film made you feel uneasy, but you couldn't figure out why, this book is just what you need. This completely revised, much expanded second edition also includes a very substantial recommended reading list of over 1,000 books for kindergarten through high school.

Order LWD-037 . . . . $12.95

Spelling Works

Spelling Works is filled with creative, challenging puzzles and activities that can be used with any spelling list (including those in the *Spelling Power* program). The flexibility of the activities makes *Spelling Works* ideal for use in your home school, with an entire class, or for individual and homework assignments. This 48 page consumable workbook is recommended by Beverly L. Adams-Gordon author of *Spelling Power.*

Order **SP-0307** $7.95

Dictionary Dig

Here are Creative Activities Designed for grades 4 to 6 to get kids into the dictionary. You can strengthen dictionary skills with this handy collection of activities. Covers guide words, pronunciations, derivations, parts of speech, and multiple meanings. Great supplement to activities presented in Chapter 5 of *Spelling Power.* (48 pages.) Recommended by Beverly L. Adams-Gordon author of *Spelling Power.*

Order DD-037 . . . . $7.95

Lear, Limericks & Literature

This literature unit study, created by Beverly L. Adams-Gordon, introduces your students to the zany rhymes made famous by Edward Lear in the late 1800s. The lessons use limericks to introduce a number of basic poetic devices. Understanding and using these devices can improve the student's general and creative writing. They also serve as models for teaching the disciplined, systematic art of limerick and poetry writing. Adaptable for students in kindergarten through college levels, highly recommended for grades 5 through 8th.

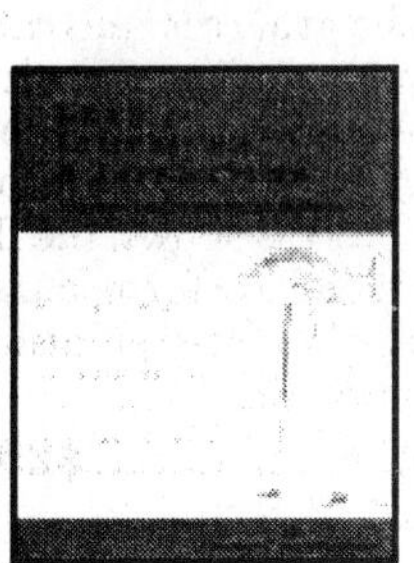

Order No. 21-1 . . . . $6.95

Complete Book of Nonsense

Access to a collection of Edward Lear's work is integral to completing the Lear, Limericks & Literature unit study. Beverly Adams-Gordon, the author of the literature study recommends the 1992 edition of *A Book of Nonsense,* published as part of the Everyman's Library: Children's Classics Collection. A beautifully printed hardbound edition your family will cherish for generations.

While the "read alone" level of *A Book of Nonsense* is junior high age, the wonderful words and limericks of Lear are of interest to pre-schoolers and above.

Order NON-21211 . . . . 13.95

Buy the Complete Book of Nonsense and Lear, Limericks, and Literature set for only $19.95

Order LearSet 19.95

Order Form

SP3Pom-7

Please complete the following information. Print clearly in ink. Orders normally shipped within 48 hours. Please allow seven to ten days for your package to arrive. Thank you.

Name: ____________________

Street Address: ____________________

City: ____________ State: ______ Zip: ________

Phone Number: ____________________

E-mail: ____________________

Free E-mail newsletter

Receive our free irregularly published newsletter directly in your electronic mailbox! Hints, tips, product evaluations, and more. Just provide your e-mail address on the line to the left. **We do not share your information with anyone.**

See back for information on selecting the proper Student Record Books and Student Daily Journals for your students.

Qty.	Item #	Title/Description	Price Each	Total

Credit Card Payments:
☐ VISA ☐ Mastercard ☐ Discover ☐ American Express

Card #: ____________________

Expires: ____________

Signature: ____________________

Total Value of Order	
WA. Residents Add 7.5% Tax	
Shipping & Handling (see below for costs) $5 minimum standard/$6.50 minimum Priority	
Total Order	

All payments should be in US funds.

All prices quoted are retail. Prices subject to change without notice after 6/31/03.

Shipping & Handling

U.S. Standard Shipping:

10% of Order with a $5 minimum. (U.S. Standard Shipping is U.S.P.S. "Media Mail" and requires 10-14 days delivery.)

Canadian and other Foreign Orders

Since foreign shipping charges vary according to country, weight, and speed of shipment, please call or e-mail for shipping charges.

U.S. Priority Shipping:

Priority Shipping via U.S.P.S. averages 3-4 days for delivery. **If you are East of the Mississippi**, your shipping is 20% of your order with a $7.50 minimum. **If you are West of the Mississippi**, your shipping is 17% of your order with a $6.50 minimum.

Please note that the shipping times above depend on when your order has been received, processed, and shipped. We normally ship within 24 to 48 hours upon receipt of your order.

Castlemoyle Books

PO Box 520 ● Pomeroy WA 99347 ● 509-843-5009 ● Fax 509-843-3183
orders@castlemoyle.com ● New products added weekly at: www.castlemoyle.com

Order Form

SP3Pom-7

'lease complete the following information. Print clearly in ink.
ders normally shipped within 48 hours. Please allow seven to ten days
your package to arrive. Thank you.

ame: ______________________________

eet Address: ______________________________

ty: ______________ State: ______ Zip: ______

one Number: ______________________________

mail: ______________________________

Free E-mail newsletter

Receive our free irregularly published newsletter directly in your electronic mailbox! Hints, tips, product evaluations, and more. Just provide your e-mail address on the line to the left. **We do not share your information with anyone.**

See back for information on selecting the proper Student Record Books and Student Daily Journals for your students.

Qty.	Item #	Title/Description	Price Each	Total

edit Card Payments:
VISA ☐ Mastercard ☐ Discover ☐ American Express

rd #: ______________________

pires: ______________

nature: ______________________

Total Value of Order	
WA. Residents Add 7.5% Tax	
Shipping & Handling (see below for costs) $5 minimum standard/$6.50 minimum Priority	
Total Order	

All payments should be in US funds.

All prices quoted are retail. Prices subject to change without notice after 6/31/03.

Shipping & Handling

U.S. Standard Shipping:

% of Order with a $5 minimum. (U.S. Standard Shipping is
.P.S. "Media Mail" and requires 10-14 days delivery.)

Canadian and other Foreign Orders

ce foreign shipping charges vary according to country, weight, and
ed of shipment, please call or e-mail for shipping charges.

U.S. Priority Shipping:

Priority Shipping via U.S.P.S. averages 3-4 days for delivery. **If you are East of the Mississippi**, your shipping is 20% of your order with a $7.50 minimum. **If you are West of the Mississippi**, your shipping is 17% of your order with a $6.50 minimum.

ase note that the shipping times above depend on when your order has been received, processed, and shipped. We normally ship
hin 24 to 48 hours upon receipt of your order.

Castlemoyle Books

PO Box 520 ● Pomeroy WA 99347 ● 509-843-5009 ● Fax 509-843-3183
orders@castlemoyle.com ● New products added weekly at: www.castlemoyle.com

Spelling Power Student Record Books Will Save You Time and Money

The *Spelling Power* program calls for the use of two different forms daily, as well as a number of other forms on a level-by-level basis. These forms are integral to the program. Each *Spelling Power Student Record Book* provides enough forms for one student to master the words on at least one level of the *Spelling Power*. You are also provided with forms for placement and delayed recall testing and a student progress chart. Conveniently bound, with all forms printed in light blue so the student's own handwriting stands out, the *Student Record Books* provide you a valuable record of your student's work. These pre-printed books cost less per page — about four cents a page — than it costs to photocopy the masters provided in the *Spelling Power* manual.

How To Select Student Record Books

Spelling Power Student Record books are un-graded, preprinted, blank testing forms. They are available in four sizes of lines. Below you will find a sample of the line size for each of the color-coded Student Record Books:

Red Student Book 5/8" for K-3rd

abj

Blue Student Book 1/2" for 2-4th

abj

Green Student Book 3/8" for 4-6th

abj

Yellow Student Book -- No mid line 6th & up

abj